STUDIES IN THE

LEGAL HISTORY OF THE SOUTH

Edited by Paul Finkelman and Kermit L. Hall

This series explores the ways in which law has affected the
development of the southern United States and in turn
the ways the history of the South has affected the development
of American law. Volumes in the series focus on a specific
aspect of the law, such as slave law or civil rights
legislation, or on a broader topic of historical significance
to the development of the legal system in the region,
such as issues of constitutional history and of law and society,
comparative analyses with other legal systems, and
biographical studies of influential southern
jurists and lawyers.

THE TRIAL OF DEMOCRACY

THE UNIVERSITY OF GEORGIA PRESS   ATHENS & LONDON

The Trial of Democracy

BLACK SUFFRAGE AND NORTHERN REPUBLICANS, 1860–1910

XI WANG

Paperback edition, 2012
© 1997 by the University of Georgia Press
Athens, Georgia 30602
All rights reserved
Designed by Sandra Strother Hudson
Set in 10.5 on 14 Bodoni by G & S Typesetters

Most University of Georgia Press titles are
available from popular e-book vendors.

Printed digitally

The Library of Congress has cataloged the
hardcover edition of this book as follows:

Wang, Xi.
The trial of democracy : black suffrage and northern Republicans,
1860-1910 / Xi Wang.
xxv, 411 p. : ill. ; 25 cm. – (Studies in the legal history of the South)
Includes bibliographical references (p. 375-395) and index.
ISBN 0-8203-1837-X (alk. paper)
1. Republican Party (U.S. : 1854–)–History.
2. African Americans–Suffrage–History.
3. United States–Politics and government–1861–1865.
4. United States–Politics and government–1865–1933.
I. Title. II. Series.
JK1781.W36   1997
324.6'2'08996073–dc20   95-046628
British Library Cataloging in Publication Data available

Paperback ISBN-13: 978-0-8203-4084-5

Title page: "Electioneering at the South," *Harper's Weekly*,
July 25, 1868.

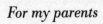

For my parents

CONTENTS

TABLES

PREFACE

This book originated from my intellectual curiosity about the meaning of American democracy. It is a revised and expanded version of my doctoral dissertation at Columbia University. The primary goal of this book is to provide a lucid, coherent, and analytical narrative of how African American voting rights, as part of the American ideological, political, and constitutional fabric, evolved from the Civil War until the Progressive Era; despite the extensive literature on the politics of Reconstruction, accounts such as the present one are still in short supply. The second goal of the book is, through documenting the history of the subject, to establish an understanding of the workings of American democracy, a subject that has never ceased to enchant scholars in America, as well as in other places, since the publication of Alexis de Tocqueville's *Democracy in America* in the 1830s and yet has still remained a myth to many. Such understanding may help to reveal certain historical details about changes and continuities of the meaning and practice of American democracy. More important, it might be useful to those (here I am thinking of some Chinese intellectuals of my generation) who like to engage themselves in an abstract debate about the merits or demerits of democracy as a system of government but have not had a chance to study it historically. I believe that, before one evaluates democracy, it is fairly important to understand what democracy is, how it works under certain historical circumstances, and how, given all its strengths and weaknesses, it evolves and transforms.

The book owes its birth to the generous support of several institutions. An Albert J. Beveridge Research Grant from the American Historical Association (1990) and two President's Fellowships from Columbia University (1987–89) helped start the initial research. A two-year predoctoral fellowship from the Frederick Douglass Institute for African and African-American Studies at the University of Rochester (1991–93) was crucial to later research and the completion of my dissertation. A research grant from the Huntington Library in San Marino, California (1993–94), and a postdoctoral fellowship from the W. E. B. Du Bois Institute for Afro-American Research at Harvard University (1993–94) allowed me to expand research beyond the dissertation. Finally, a faculty professional development award from the State System of Higher Education of

Pennsylvania (1995 – 96) provided needed release time and research assistance to complete the revision of the manuscript.

I am grateful to many libraries and archives where I received enormous assistance as I searched for materials. I would like to mention particularly the librarians at Columbia University's Rare Books and Manuscripts Library, the Rush Rhees Library of the University of Rochester, the Manuscripts Division of the Library of Congress, the Houghton Library of Harvard University, Massachusetts Historical Society, New Hampshire Historical Society, the Hayes Presidential Center, and the Huntington Library.

I am deeply in debt to my teachers, colleagues, and friends for their unfailing support and encouragement. Eric Foner, my adviser, provided crucial guidance throughout the entire process. His sharp but not intimidating comments on the earlier drafts not only guided me out of the labyrinth of writing but also compelled me to write with a judicious and analytical mind. I was fortunate to have Elizabeth Blackmar as the second reader of my dissertation, who effectively and efficiently challenged many doubtful parts of the dissertation and directed my attention to the relevant issues. I owe James P. Shenton a special debt for his inspiring graduate seminar, where the original idea of this manuscript was conceived and formulated. Two other members of the dissertation committee, Charles V. Hamilton and Patricia Williams, offered insightful suggestions for improving the original thesis. Members of the Frederick Douglass Institute at the University of Rochester, where I was a predoctoral fellow for two years, never failed to encourage me to talk about my subject and crucially called my attention to the role of African Americans in the whole process. I want to thank particularly Karen E. Fields for constantly reminding me about placing my research in a broader historical context and Stanley L. Engerman for continuously pushing me to be solid and perceptive.

Several people who read the dissertation provided critical assistance for revision. Michael Les Benedict offered a valuable and an unusually substantive critique that essentially helped to define the revision. Paul Finkelman, the co-editor of the series, worked with me closely during the entire revision process. His critical reading helped to improve the manuscript in terms of the use of sources, the formulation of arguments, and the style of writing. Kermit Hall, another coeditor, also offered encouragement and guidance. Stanley Hirshson, a pioneer in the study of the Republican party and black rights in the post-Reconstruction period, scrutinized the dissertation and gave detailed suggestions for improvement. Michael Vorenberg shared with me his thoughts and sources on the issue of Republican politics and black emancipation. Michael S. Green, a fellow student at Columbia, was not only generous in sharing his own research with me but also always ready to give a witty and constructive response to my questions despite his tight schedule to complete his own dissertation. His careful reading of the manuscript and very thoughtful questioning made it a much better work. Irwin Marcus, my colleague at the Indiana University of Pennsylvania (IUP), made perceptive comments on both the dissertation and the manuscript and directed my attention to a more elaborate literature relevant to the subject. I also thank Steven F. Miller of the Freedmen and Southern Society Project at the University of Maryland for assisting my review of some of their valuable collections. An anonymous reader also deserves my gratitude, for his or her comments helped me to clarify my thoughts and correct errors.

My thanks also go to Donald G. Nieman, Richard M. Valelly, Lea VanderVelde, Akhil Reed Amar, and Earl M. Maltz, who commented on part of the manuscript and offered good suggestions for revision. Members of the W. E. B. Du Bois Institute at Harvard (1993 – 94), especially George M. Fredrickson, Jean Fegan Yellin, Thadious M. Davis, Manisha Sinha, and Richard Newman (who also read part of the dissertation), provided helpful comments and suggestions. While the perceptive comments on the project made by Henry Louis Gates Jr., the director of the Institute, were especially memorable and warm, the direction to some important rare sources by Randall Burkett was very timely. My colleagues in the History Department at IUP assisted me with a warm and cheerful collegiality that enabled me to deal with first-year teaching and the completion of the manuscript with calmness. A group of undergraduate and graduate students from different institutions – Annisa Knox and Clarence Chan of Harvard; Tom Hetrick, Mark Evans, and Todd Stanford of IUP; and Liu Li of Seton Hill College – helped me to trace some obscure sources and, most important, set up an extensive Procite database from which were generated the voting records of nearly twenty-one hundred congressmen on major black suffrage and federal enforcement legislation from 1867 to 1894. I also want to thank Grace Buonocore, my copy editor, whose extraordinary and painstaking work has enormously strengthened the manuscript. I treasure the working relationship with the editorial staff of the University of Georgia Press, especially Kristine Blakeslee and Malcolm Call, whose courtesy and efficiency made the process a genuine joy.

My friends at the Forum of Chinese Students and Scholars at Columbia contributed invaluably to the writing of the original dissertation. Many of our debates and discussions – especially those with Ren Yue, Xie Wen, Tang Yiming, Shi Tianjian, Yang Lixin, Li Dong, Zhou Xijuan, Wang Xiaoping, Ruan Danching, and Harold Tanner – on the political cultures of the United States and China allowed me to absorb ideas from other disciplines and compelled me to write more solidly. I also benefited from the exchanges with a number of scholars from other fields, including George Jochnowitz, Osumaka Likaka, Chen Jian, Yue Mei, and Weng Naiqun, whose responses proved to be very insightful.

My family has been a constant source of support and understanding. My wife, Pang Jin, helped to type part of the manuscript and organize the statistical data. She and Dan, our son, deserve my deepest gratitude for their faith and patience as they have accompanied me along this mostly lonesome but eventually enjoyable process.

Finally, I want to thank Elizabeth Richardson, Pat Gilmore, and the late Jack Gilmore for their very special care and support. For Dr. Robert D. Richardson Jr. I can never express enough of my respect and gratitude. It was his profoundly intellectual yet deeply humane guidance and influence that gave me the initial courage to take the road "less traveled by."

INTRODUCTION

→ great for context in introduction

One of the most important results of the Civil War was the establishment of a new constitutional order in the United States. Under this new order, not only was slavery abolished, but African Americans were recognized as American citizens and received the immunities and privileges that white Americans had automatically assumed, and black men received the right to vote. Of the three Civil War constitutional amendments, the Fifteenth Amendment stood as the most revolutionary, for it put into the hands of millions of former slaves the right of suffrage, an essential right enabling a citizen to be politically accountable in a democracy. With the enactment of the Reconstruction Act of 1867, the passage of the Fifteenth Amendment in 1869, and its subsequent ratification in 1870, the Republican Congress secured the constitutionality of black suffrage and made protection of black voting rights a national obligation. As a result, black men participated in the process of reconstructing the postwar political and economic order at every level of government, national, state, and local. From 1869 until 1901 African Americans served in every session of Congress but one. Two sat in the United States Senate and fourteen in the House of Representatives. Meanwhile, more than fourteen hundred blacks occupied positions of political importance in the South.[1] Black participation in the workings of both national and state governments represented the beginning of a new American democracy, one that was radically different from that perceived by the framers of the original Constitution.

This new interracial democracy, however, could not be sustained without the support of the federal government, given the political circumstances under which blacks were enfranchised. From 1870 to 1891, the Republican party, which controlled the national government for most of this period, made serious efforts to enforce black male suffrage, hoping to maintain both the party's proclaimed principles of equal rights before the law and its political advantages over the opposing Democrats.[2] Between 1870 and 1872, the Republican-controlled Congress passed three enforcement acts
to enforcement, which empowered the federal gov
lenge southern political violence to resist black enfr

mention Republicans vs Democrats in context essay

xvii

federal enforcement declined after 1874, when the Democrats won control of the House. But even then the enforcement continued on a limited scale.

By 1877, much of the South was politically controlled by a Democratic party dedicated to white supremacy and determined to disable blacks in southern politics. Southern blacks were intimidated by Klansmen, who also tortured those blacks who dared to vote. Despite the intimidation and violence, blacks continued to vote throughout the 1870s and 1880s. Between 1877 and 1901, at least twelve blacks were elected to Congress.[3]

Throughout this period, the Republican party did not abandon the principle of federal enforcement of black suffrage, but the party was plagued by factional disputes over its southern policy and did oscillate between different approaches toward maintaining black suffrage in the South. In 1890, after they regained control of both the legislative and executive branches, the Republicans launched another battle to enact a new federal election bill, but it was defeated as a result of the desertion of the Republicans from the western states. Republicans stood together in 1893 and 1894 to resist the Democratic repeal of the 1870–72 enforcement acts, but by then the Democrats controlled every branch of the federal government and their will prevailed. Consequently, at the turn of the century, southern states, one after another, implemented new state constitutions that contained such restrictive devices as literacy tests, poll taxes, grandfather clauses, property requirements, and white primaries to disfranchise black voters. As a result, a substantial portion of blacks were disfranchised. The black voting population in Louisiana dropped from 130,000 in 1896 to 5,320 in 1900. In Georgia, registration of blacks was as low as 4.3 percent in 1910. By the beginning of World War I, African Americans composed only 2 percent of the voters in some states and only 15 percent in others. Four decades after the Fifteenth Amendment became law, black men were once again stripped of political rights, and the new southern interracial democracy projected by the reform-minded Republicans in the early Reconstruction was transformed into what J. Morgan Kousser terms a virtually oligarchical democracy in the South.[4]

Undoubtedly, the decline of the Republican commitment to black suffrage accounted in part for the eventual disfranchisement of blacks in the South. The federal enforcement of black suffrage during this period was neither permanently effective nor effectively permanent. After 1872, the course of enforcement was curtailed by the strong opposition of the liberal Republicans and the growing indifference of the Grant administration. In 1875, the party failed to mobilize its members in Congress to pass another enforcement act. In 1876, the

Republican-dominated Supreme Court found two sections of the first enforcement act "inappropriate." Federal troops guarding the Republican governments in the statehouses of South Carolina and Louisiana were ordered to withdraw by President Hayes in 1877. In the 1880s, the party shifted between different policies and really had no chance to enact new enforcement laws. In 1890, the party failed to pass a new federal election bill to revitalize enforcement of black suffrage, hence allowing black disfranchisement to become an accepted practice in the South.

Why did enforcement of black suffrage fail? Why was the Republican party unable to maintain the vitality of the Fifteenth Amendment? Historians have been debating these questions for generations. The Dunning school historians attributed the failure of enforcement to the radical and conspiratorial nature of Reconstruction, from which the enforcement acts were derived. They held that black suffrage was a device employed by radical Republicans to subordinate an "old political people" in the South to "a new political people created by Congress." Arguing from a racist point of view, John W. Burgess asserted that subordination of African Americans to whites was "something natural" but that there was "nothing natural in the opposite" because blacks were inferior to whites. Claude G. Bowers's *The Tragic Era*, which was termed by the historian Bernard A. Weisberger as a popular "operatic version" of Reconstruction, justified the Ku Klux Klan as proper to combat the "lustful assaults" of "the scum of Northern society, politicians, soldiers of fortune, and not a few degenerates." Walter L. Fleming, a student of Dunning, believed that the Republican party failed to implement its Reconstruction policies because the party's "serious divisions over the spoils" in the southern states caused the desertion of the party "by a large proportion of its white membership."[5] Black suffrage was part of the radical Republicans' scheme for "party aggrandizement," one of the earliest students of black suffrage enforcement writes; the South "had neither requested nor desired suffrage" for blacks.[6] Some others, admitting that the Republican enactment of the Fifteenth Amendment was motivated by mixed concerns, argued that the enforcement, in William Watson Davis's words, was doomed to fail because of the "arbitrary" nature of the enforcement acts, which "did not square with public consciousness either North or South" and suggested "an autocracy rather than a democracy."[7]

Some modern historians accepted the political expediency interpretation. William Gillette, in his modern account of the passage of the Fifteenth Amendment, examined the political development of the North and believed that black suffrage was in part pushed by Republicans to mobilize northern blacks to vote for the party. He concluded that "political expedience as a force in the framing of the Fifteenth Amendment was essential."[8] Others challenged this notion and argued, as John H. and LaWanda Cox did, that the Republicans pushed forward black suffrage on the grounds of principle even though they knew that black suffrage "constituted a clear and present danger" to the party's cause in the North.[9] Still, some others believed that Republican motivations for enacting the Fifteenth Amendment were mixed. Eric McKitrick argued that black suffrage was promoted both by the Republicans who truly believed in equal rights and by those who saw black suffrage as "a possible device for establishing some sort of Republican foothold in the South." Michael Les Benedict, in his detailed study of the division of the Republican party, argued that black suffrage conformed to the party's principles but the issue was shaped by intraparty debates among the party's radical, centralist, and conservative wings.[10]

Although the Republican motivations for black enfranchisement have been a classic topic, the enforcement of the Fifteenth Amendment has only recently begun to draw attention from scholars. Everette Swinney, in his pioneering account of federal enforcement history, defends the enforcement acts as having had "political overtones" and "reflecting genuine humanitarian idealism and sound democratic principle." He believes that southern resentment and the waning of northern support of enforcement in the mid-1870s caused the decline of enforcement.[11] Echoing Swinney's support for enforcement, Stephen Cresswell examines in detail the implementation of the enforcement acts in northern Mississippi and argues that adequate federal assistance and the loyalty of federal officials accounted for the brief success of enforcement in that region.[12] James E. Sefton's study demonstrates the difficulties of actual implementation of military enforcement in the South.[13] The most solid and perceptive account of enforcement between 1869 and 1879 is given by William Gillette, who discusses a number of factors that contributed to the fall of enforcement, including political corruption, the disappearance of the party's radical leadership, insufficient funds, and the low caliber of the enforcement officers.[14] In his recent general account of Reconstruction, Eric Foner further points out that political and economic changes in the North, the shift of the Republican political focus, the rise of the liberal Republicans, and the lack of modern bureaucratic machinery to enforce the Civil War amendments in any permanent manner contributed to the decline of enforcement.[15] In addition, several historians note that the lack of support from northern Republicans directly injured the party's cause of enforcing black suffrage. Northern Republican support of enforcement, Roger A. Cohen argues, was "conditioned by the political repercussions of the measure anticipated in their states, and not in the South."[16] John Sproat's *"The Best Men": Liberal Reformers in the Gilded Age* reveals the fundamental differences in ideology between the liberal and the stalwart Republicans and shows that the liberals' distrust of black political capacity contributed heavily to their opposition to enforcing black suffrage.[17] In his brief study on the Republican abandonment of black rights, Patrick Riddleberger concludes that the abandonment of blacks was the result of the ideological change from "the era of romantic reform" to "the era of nationalistic thought with its emphasis on slow evolutionary change under laws held to be immutable by human endeavor."[18]

The judicial inertia against enforcing civil and political equality for African Americans has been studied by several legal historians. Writing in the early 1970s, Harold M. Hyman recognized the revolutionary breakthrough brought by the postwar amendments in ending "the custom that States determined national citizenship," but Hyman believed that, given the constraining nature of the interactions between party politics and the Constitution, the Republicans could only initiate a "moderate revolution" to enforce black suffrage in 1871.[19] Later, Hyman and William M. Wiecek argued that Republican decision makers were forced to choose between "ideas about liberty" and "concerns about equality" in the 1870s. The Republicans chose the former because the changes in northern society gave the Republicans no alternative but to "dedicate [themselves] to preserving liberty and the federal system more than individuals' rights by means of government's interventions."[20] Focusing on the judicial role in federal enforcement in the 1870s, Robert Kaczorowski contended that the withdrawal from enforcing black suffrage was a "conscious choice made by the President and the Supreme Court . . . at the very moment when federal officers believed they were winning their struggle against Southern terrorism."[21]

The most important studies on the Republican party and the enforcement of the postwar amendments during the post-1877 years are Vincent P. De Santis's *Republicans Face the Southern Question* and Stanley Hirshson's *Farewell to the Bloody Shirt*. De Santis and Hirshson have respectively made important contributions to the understanding of post–Civil War Republican politics by offering comprehensive accounts of the Republican policies toward the South in the post-1877 years. While showing how the Republicans pragmatically responded to the post-Hayes political development in the South, both studies share the

notion that Republican leaders were no longer sincerely interested in issues regarding black rights but only chose to reward a few black leaders with federal
appointments as a means to keep blacks on the Republican side. However, neither of these two studies discusses the relations between the post-1877 Republican policies toward the South and the party's earlier policies regarding black
suffrage.[22] A brief but substantive discussion on the 1890 federal election bill
from Richard E. Welch Jr. helps to connect the Republican attempt to reenforce
the Fifteenth Amendment in 1890 with the party's earlier history.[23] Robert
Goldman's *"A Free Ballot and a Fair Count"* is special in the sense that it fo-
cuses on the Department of Justice's role in enforcing the enforcement acts in
the years after 1877, a subject that is generally neglected and still needs to be
studied. Goldman argues that enforcement was not discontinued in 1877, but
he admits that the post-1877 enforcement was not as effective.[24]

All of the above-mentioned studies have contributed to the understanding of
different facets of federal enforcement of the Fifteenth Amendment, but several
crucial questions remain unanswered. What were the political and constitutional resources and mechanisms for enfranchising blacks after the Civil War?
How did the Republicans use those resources and mechanisms? If we recognize
the mixture of Republican motivations for enfranchising blacks, how was black
suffrage as a principle of the party reconciled with black suffrage as a political
instrument for the party's ascendancy? How were Republican policies regarding
black suffrage and its enforcement formulated at different periods? Were these
policies different in principle or in tactics? How did different factors — intra-
and interparty politics, socioeconomic developments, and judicial tempers —
contribute either to sustain or to dismantle the party's cause of enforcement?
What role did African Americans play in gaining their political rights, and what
influence did they exert on the Republican lawmakers in the process of establishing and enforcing black suffrage?

This book is an effort to address these issues. Its primary objective is to present a clear account of how Republican perceptions of and policies toward
black suffrage and its enforcement evolved and transformed from the eve of the
Civil War to the period of black disfranchisement. In doing so, I demonstrate
the ideological, political, and constitutional connections between the black suffrage policies formulated by different Republican administrations and Congresses during this period. I do not dispute the traditional view that federal
enforcement declined after 1875, but I do argue that the official "ending" of
Reconstruction in 1877 did not mean the ending of Republican commitment

to black political rights, nor did it mean the ending of the vitality of the principles of federal protection of black rights as established by the Civil War amendments.

The reason I place the subject in such a time span (longer than the traditional time lines) is to generate a more nuanced discussion of the process by which the principle of black suffrage was conceived, constitutionalized, implemented, defended, and eventually curtailed. Black enfranchisement represented a radical change in the conventional beliefs and practices of American politics. Preceding or accompanying it was the process of redefining such fundamental concepts as citizenship, the republican form of government, federalism, and democracy. These concepts determined the essence of black suffrage and the extent of its applicability in the American polity. But these political concepts per se and their applications were in turn defined by other, even more fundamental changes that the nation was experiencing during this period: the nationwide economic transformation that would give rise to the comprehensive industrialization in the United States by the end of the century and would economically prepare the nation to be a real world power in the next century; the resurgence of new sectional alliance on the basis of local economic and social interests; the professionalization of party politics with political parties adjusting to the changed situations with a much greater adaptability and flexibility than the prewar time; the increasing conflicts of interest between various social segments of American society that would lead to the rise of the organized labor, populist, and socialist movements; the new interracial relations characterized by a black economic impoverishment in general and a growing economic dependency of southern blacks on the former planter class (both resulting from the absence of an economic reconstruction after the war) and the appearance of racial segregation in the South. All these ongoing changes circumscribed the political outlook of the Republican party and the space in which the party formulated its policies regarding black rights. In a way, I hope this study will be able to answer and explain such questions as: What changes did the Republican lawmakers make regarding African American male voting rights in the postwar years? What changes that the Republicans had made earlier were changed after Reconstruction? And what were the earlier changes that were maintained and continued throughout the period?

The second major concern of the study is to locate and describe the workings of the Republican establishment and enforcement of black suffrage. Despite the Union's victory and the Republican dominance of the national government in the postwar years, enfranchising former slaves still required a [constitutional justification and recognition] both had to be achieved through a political process affected by and operating under the party system. How did the party achieve this justification and recognition? After black suffrage was established, the party managed to keep black suffrage an inspiring political question and maintained the constitutionality of federal enforcement of the Fifteenth Amendment for more than two decades. How was it possible for the party to do that especially in a time when intra- and interparty politics were so intense, conflicts of interest were so intricate, racism was so prevalent, and judicial interpretations of the new constitutional order were so inconsistent?

To be sure, throughout the period between the 1860s and 1890s, the Republican party maintained a majority in the postwar Congresses and dominated the presidency (with two intervals of Cleveland, from 1885 to 1889 and from 1893 to 1897), but the party was not always a firm unit in dealing with the issue of black political rights. Even when they agreed to support black male suffrage, Republicans backed by different political interests had different policies regarding such issues as whether the ultimate control of suffrage should be removed from the states or how far the federal government should go to enforce black suffrage. Although the party enjoyed a major boost from the triumph of its antislavery cause, few Republicans had been prepared for a fundamental change of race relations in American society and certainly not a completely new democracy. But, despite all the differences and reservations, the Republican party had to maintain a working unity in order to obtain the passage of the policies (such as black enfranchisement and, later, federal enforcement of black suffrage) that would secure the outcomes of the Civil War, as well as enable the party to stay in power. The very symbiotic nature of black suffrage as a political principle of postwar American freedom and as a political instrument to realize and maintain that principle determined the foundation of the Republican party's working unity throughout this period.

From the beginning of black suffrage legislation, the Republicans linked principle and expedience together when they discussed issues of black suffrage and federal enforcement. Such linkage determined the party's standing on black suffrage, which was a result of the party's internal compromise. This compromise, however, did not eliminate the party's factional differences on black suffrage, nor did it prevent the reappearance of differences, especially when the circumstances changed. But the dual nature of black suffrage (and the enforcement of black suffrage) did create a working basis for different groups of Republicans who might differ from one another on many other issues. Although the Republicans might have failed to achieve unity on other issues (such as civil service reform, finance, immigration, or foreign policy), they were able to reach a temporary consensus on the issue of enforcing black voting rights, as in the presidential elections of 1872, 1876, 1880, and 1888.

For all its fragility, such a faction-unity complex was important in the sense that it kept black voting rights a living issue throughout all the years; more important, however, it consolidated the constitutionality of the issue by perpetuating its life. The faction-unity complex also provided an outlet for the party's African American supporters, who remained loyal Republicans throughout these years. As a political norm, the Republican faction-unity complex was instrumental in getting the party united, especially in election years or in dealing with partisan issues in Congress. But the unity was weak and usually short-lived, as it was founded upon the compromise of factional interests. As the political environments changed, factions brought into the party new demands and interests, and, once again, new negotiation started and new unity had to be formed in order to maintain a valid working basis of the party functions.

In a way, the conventional charge that Republicans waved the "bloody shirt" is true, but it was not merely rhetoric or only for campaign purposes. It was a working basis for the Republican coalition after 1868. This idea of a new birth of the nation and the promise of political equality between whites and blacks, both of which the party believed in, served as a powerful political identifier for many Republicans, including black Republicans. This political identity helped the party to reorganize and revitalize itself. The connotations of the "bloody shirt" went beyond South bashing. It contained the party's commitment to the national protection of citizens' equal rights and to the maintenance of the new freedom established by the Civil War. Such commitment was not permanently genuine, but neither was it consistently hypocritical.

THE TRIAL OF DEMOCRACY

CHAPTER ONE

The Road to the Fifteenth Amendment, 1860–1870

The Republican Party and Black Suffrage in 1860

Born during the political realignment of the mid-1850s, the Republican party was the first major political party in American history that directly challenged the legitimacy and legality of American slavery. Despite their diverse political origins, all Republicans shared the party's fundamental belief that the expansion of slavery had to be stopped and the southern "slave power" driven from national influence. Within six years of its formation, the party would unite various antislavery forces in the North and form a powerful coalition that eventually took control of the national government.[1] But, despite its determination to stop the spread of slavery, the Republican party had, from its beginnings, confronted a deep-seated disagreement over the political status of black Americans. While Republicans could, with a united voice, denounce slavery and articulate the political ideal of a free labor civilization, they were unable to develop a clear and firm political outlook on how, if slavery ended, the former slaves would fit into the framework of the American polity. Instead, before the Civil War, Republicans revealed mixed attitudes concerning how the rights of black Americans should be defined and whether they should be allowed to exercise the same political rights as whites.

Occupying the radical end of the spectrum of the party's attitudes toward black political rights were those Republicans who had originally been affiliated with the abolition and Free Soil movements at the beginning of the war. Having supported blacks' civil rights, and having worked at the state level to repudiate legal discrimination against blacks long before the birth of the Republican party, the radical Republicans advocated immediate emancipation, coupled with a full recognition of the equality of African Americans before the law.[2]

1

Grounding their arguments on the principle of equality inscribed in the Declaration of Independence, these radical Republicans argued that the existence of slavery and legal discrimination against blacks contradicted the republican principle that government was founded on the consent of the governed. The goal of the Republican party, claimed one of Charles Sumner's Philadelphia correspondents, was to mobilize political forces in the North "to present a united front for the perfect freedom of . . . Northern soil, & while reassuring the Decl. of Independence." To extinguish slavery was a historical mission that the Founding Fathers had failed to accomplish. Such a mission, in Sumner's words, was a noble cause: "nobler even than that of our Fathers, inasmuch as it is more exalted to struggle for the freedom of others, than for our own." James M. Ashley, a radical Republican from Ohio who would play a leading role in advocating black suffrage later, argued that the Republican party was a "party of freedom" and recognized "the natural right of every human being."[3] Lydia Maria Child, an antislavery activist and woman suffragist, complained to Sumner that Republicans showed cowardice to southern slaveholders, and she urged them to stand "*firmly* in one *united* phalanx . . . against the monster that [was] sucking [the nation's] life-blood." Writing before the election of 1860, a New Hampshire Republican opposed the idea that the party should be "a *white men's* party only" and "*evade* the great issue of freedom for *all men.*" He warned that if the party ignored the interests of the slaves in the South, it would be defeated in the coming election. But even white radicals such as Sumner predicted that the imminent Civil War would bring to the country an emancipation of slaves "as in St. Domingo"; they talked little about how the political status of blacks should be redefined if they were freed. Nor did the radicals discuss extensively how to use the Republican party as a political vehicle to push for black suffrage.[4]

The more conservative Republicans viewed the party's historical mission differently. More concerned with preventing the Union from falling apart over sectional disputes than with defending individual rights denied because of color and race, conservative Republicans suggested that the party avoid taking any firm position advocating civil and political equality for blacks, which would be too controversial for the party to handle. They warned that any imprudent action to change the civil or political status of blacks would endanger the party's internal unity and accelerate the Union's disintegration. To avoid Democratic accusations that the Republican party threatened the Union's existence and that its policy would disturb the race relations, conservatives preferred to disavow black rights or any other activities that might bring blacks into American political life. Writing in September 1860, Edward Bates, the Missourian who would soon become Lincoln's attorney general, ridiculed the Democratic charge "that the great principle of the Republicans [was] *negro equality*" as a "downright falsehood." The state constitution of Kansas in 1859 excluded both free blacks and slaves from voting. Soon after Lincoln won the 1860 presidential election, Gideon Welles, a Connecticut Republican leader and later Lincoln's secretary of the navy, urged Lincoln to pledge publicly to the South that the existing federal policy regarding slavery in the territories would not be changed in his administration. Such a pledge, reasoned Welles, would dismiss southern apprehensions that Republicans were "to be abolitionists" and "prepare[d] to interfere with slavery in the states."[5] Others who spoke about redressing the wrongs done by slavery were actually concerned about the rights of white laborers in the North. The Republican party, declared Republican senator Lyman Trumbull of Illinois in 1858, was "a white man's party" established "for free white men, and for making white labor respectable and honorable." Such remarks disappointed abolitionists such as Lewis Tappan and William Lloyd Garrison, who described the party as "a complexional party, exclusively for white men, not for all men."[6]

Other Republicans, whom we may conveniently call moderates, held a rather ambivalent attitude toward the issue of black rights. They strongly condemned the inhumanity of slavery and called for its ultimate extinction. Believing that slavery could only be eliminated through gradual plans of colonization and emigration, they opposed immediate emancipation of the slaves. For moderate Republicans, antislavery meant no drastic change in the status quo of racial hierarchy. They argued that blacks as human beings should be given what radical Ben Wade called "a full assurance of their manhood," but they refused to contemplate the possibility of racial equality between blacks and whites. The ambiguity of moderate Republican thought on black rights was articulated by Abraham Lincoln in his first debate with Stephen Douglas in August 1858. Lincoln denied an Ohio newspaper's assertion that he favored black suffrage, and he stressed that he had no intention of introducing "political and social equality" between the white and the black races. But Lincoln insisted that even with "a physical difference between the two [races]" that would "probably forever forbid their living together upon the footing of perfect equality," blacks were as entitled as whites to "all the natural rights enumerated in the Declaration of Independence, the right to life, liberty, and the pursuit of happiness."[7]

Echoing Lincoln's sentiments, the Republican platform of 1860 identified the party's ideological line with the principles promulgated in the Declaration of Independence. The platform claimed that government protection of the inalienable rights of all Americans was "essential to the preservation of . . . Republican institutions." It attacked Democratic claims that the Constitution allowed the expansion of slavery as "a dangerous political heresy." Although sharp and straightforward in denouncing slavery and Democratic threats of disunion, the platform avoided a clear statement on black political rights. It urged "full and efficient protection" of "the rights of all classes of citizens," but it was unclear whether blacks were included as citizens or whether such inalienable rights included political rights.[8]

The Republican use of the "inalienable rights" argument and its origins was a powerful weapon to challenge the legitimacy of slavery, but Republicans failed to spell out the sociological and political substance of the "inalienable" natural rights. In other words, they did not address how the "natural rights" were related to civil and political rights and how the slaves, if emancipated, would fit into the existing constitutional order of American society. Few Republicans projected the possibility of establishing a legal and political apparatus to help turn former slaves into citizens. Many of them either avoided considering or refused to consider how a civilly and politically disabled man could enjoy his "natural rights" in a highly political society.

Several factors contributed to the Republican party's reservations about black political rights. First, the idea of free labor, a major component of the party's prewar ideology, substantially influenced the Republican vision of black rights in the future.[9] An ideological expression of Lockean liberalism and economic individualism, the idea behind free labor was that every man had a right to rise economically and socially to the limit of his ability. Although recognizing equality in natural rights between white and black persons to compete for advancement in the economic marketplace, the free labor argument did not propel the party toward the establishment of equal civil and political rights, which were not only the concrete carriers of equality in natural rights but also indispensable to the protection and practice of the so-called inalienable natural rights. Meanwhile, many Republicans distinguished political rights from natural rights because they believed that exclusion from suffrage was not a violation of civil equality, given that women, children, and unnaturalized foreigners did not surrender their natural and civil rights because they could not vote.[10]

Correlated was the prevailing notion that the right to vote was not a birthright or part of civil rights but a privilege reserved only for those capable of understanding and appreciating the meaning of voting. Many Republicans, including some party leaders who were firm in dealing with the issue of abolishing slavery, shared the contemporary popular racism. William H. Seward of New York looked down on blacks as incapable of assimilation. Henry Wilson, a Republican senator from Massachusetts, endorsed the cause of black education and even full black citizenship because he saw no danger from blacks, who, he believed, never could join "in the mental or intellectual equality . . . with this proud and domineering white race."[11] Convinced that society was not ready for racial equality in every respect, Lincoln considered it impractical to promote black suffrage. The universal feeling among whites against racial equality might not accord "with justice and sound judgment," Lincoln told his audience in 1854, but this attitude, "whether well or ill-founded, [could] not be safely disregarded."[12] The *New York Tribune* campaigned for equal suffrage in the 1850s, but at the same time it admitted that blacks were hardly an attractive or "a favorite class" and possessed many faults, as did "all degraded, downtrodden tribes or races." It called on blacks to turn their efforts from "the sterile path of political agitation" to economic improvement. In their present "indolent, improvident, servile and licentious" condition, they could hardly convince the public of their ability to become useful members of society.[13]

Antebellum voting discrimination in the North also affected the party's attitudes toward black suffrage. Most of the original states did not have a racial qualification for suffrage during the revolutionary era. But as the property and religious qualifications declined and disappeared in many postrevolutionary state constitutions, race was added as a major qualification for voters. In 1821, New York removed property requirements for white voters but allowed a black man to vote only after he had been the owner of a freehold worth $250 and had been a citizen of the state for three years. In 1818 Connecticut allowed only those blacks to vote who had been freemen prior to 1804. Pennsylvania took suffrage away from blacks in 1838, New Jersey in 1807. Several northern and western states that joined the Union after the ratification of the Constitution, including Illinois, Iowa, Ohio, Michigan, Minnesota, Oregon, Nevada, and California, limited suffrage to white males. On the eve of the Civil War, except in five of the New England states, where less than 7 percent of the northern black population lived, every northern state barred blacks from voting in one way or another.[14]

On several occasions before 1860, white citizens and free blacks pushed for black enfranchisement in various states; but except in Rhode Island, where equal voting rights for blacks were secured in 1841, all such efforts ended fruitlessly. Republicans in Iowa who dominated the state constitutional convention

in 1857 submitted a referendum on black suffrage to the voters as a separate issue; the Republican-made state constitution was approved, but black suffrage
managed to win support from only 10.4 percent of the voters. Similarly, in other
northern states, Republicans won political control but proved unable to secure the passage of measures promoting black suffrage. Some Republicans denounced racism openly, but advocating black suffrage was regarded as "political
suicide."[15] In 1860, New York Republicans took a risk by placing a constitutional amendment to enfranchise blacks on the ballot in their state. It received
only lukewarm support from the party's newspapers, and although Republican
voters helped elect Abraham Lincoln to the presidency, nearly one-third of
them joined the Democrats in voting against the impartial suffrage amendment.
Frederick Douglass commented that the suffrage measure had been destroyed
by "the supineness of our friends" rather than "by the strength and activity of
our enemies." The leading black abolitionist observed that in the eyes of many
Republicans, "the black baby of Negro Suffrage was thought too ugly to exhibit
on so grand an occasion" and had to be "stowed away like some people put out
of sight their deformed children when company comes."[16]

   Nothing contributed more to Republican disagreement on black political
rights, however, than the nature of the Republican party and the politics of the
day. The party was a coalition of different political interests in the North, united
only by the "paramount common danger" of the expansion of the slave power
from the South. The pressing matter for the Republican party in 1860 was neither the emancipation of the slaves nor the establishment of their civil and political rights. Rather, saving the Union and stopping the expansion of slavery
were the overwhelming issues. In fact, instead of committing themselves to
black rights, many Republicans wanted as much as possible to disassociate the
question of race from the course of maintaining national unity. Realizing the
party's diversity, Russell Evrett warned New Jersey's Thomas Haines Dudley
that the Republican convention of 1860 had to be "such as to satisfy . . . varied
elements" of the party.[17] When the Civil War occurred, many Republicans perceived the conflict as a war to put down the rebellion of the slave power and to
halt the expansion of slavery into the North and West. "The South was fighting
to take slavery out of the Union," as Frederick Douglass later pointed out, with
"the North fighting to keep it in the Union; the South fighting to get it beyond
the limits of the United States Constitution, and the North fighting to retain it
within those limits."[18] Few Republicans expected that the Union cause would
have to be tied to the unconditional abolition of slavery. Few expected that the

former slaves' participation in the war would prove crucial to the Union's survival. Fewer still expected that the freedmen's political rights would become the core issue of postwar Reconstruction politics.

Emancipation and Black Suffrage during the Civil War

The attack by the South Carolina militia on Fort Sumter on April 12, 1861, marked not only the beginning of the Civil War but also the end of the old constitutional order, which had finally exhausted all its resources to compromise the sectional differences over slavery and the comprehension of American political values. The direct, bloody confrontations obviously had intensified the animosity between the North and South and, consequently, radicalized the political sentiments of the former abolitionists—who were now turning fast into radical Republicans—regarding black rights. Soon after the war started, Susan B. Anthony, the leader of the women's suffrage movement and an abolitionist, declared that the war's objective was to extend to blacks not only the rights to go to school, work, pray, sit in the theater, and share "in all the accommodations" but also to "let him vote and be voted for."[19]

However, what really started the serious talk about redefining blacks' legal status were the actions taken by the former slaves themselves. As the war developed and the Union army advanced into the South, slaves began to flee from their masters and run into Union army lines. The voluntary runaway of the slaves presented the Union generals and Lincoln's administration with an unexpected question: Should the fugitives be returned, confiscated as enemy property, or simply freed as human beings? Francis Lieber, the German-born legalist whom the historian Harold Hyman regards as "one of the major theoreticians of the Radical Republicans," immediately grasped the meaning of slaves' runaways and interpreted them as actions of self-liberation. Writing to his radical friend Charles Sumner in December 1861, Lieber stated that slavery existed only "by the municipal law or constitutional law," but, by warring against the Union, the South had virtually lost the claim of slavery as a legitimate institution. For the same reason, it also lost the right to claim the slaves as personal property. Lieber interpreted the Civil War as a war being carried on "by the Law of Nature," which "does not acknowledge the difference of skin." "[When] a negro presents himself to our troops, as coming from the enemy and claims our protection," Lieber reasoned, "he presents himself in the

same character with which a white man leaving the enemy's territory and coming into our ranks would be clothed"; thus the fugitives, Lieber later wrote to
Edward Bates, were to be thought free men and could not "be otherwise than
free."[20] Despite all his zeal for the freedom of fugitives, however, Lieber believed that the best protection that a freed slave could have was to "be sent
away, either abroad or out of the way," to avoid reenslavement "the moment
[Union] forces [left] his state."[21] John Bigelow, a New York Republican publicist who originally supported black colonization, sensed the important role that
blacks could play during the war. He felt that the Union should "emancipate
the negroes as a military necessity" and even, "by legislation," grant them some
rights that whites enjoyed, but, Bigelow wrote from Paris, "the first thing to do
[was] to make the negroes fight for their freedom."[22]

Other Republican legal minds were more careful in drawing the line between
freedom, citizenship, and suffrage. In his opinion concerning the citizenship of
a black captain of the schooner *Elizabeth and Margaret* in September 1862,
Bates ruled that American citizenship did not coexist with one's color, but he
mindfully separated suffrage from citizenship by emphasizing that the latter did
not necessarily depend upon nor coexist with the former. The contemporary
media interpreted Bates's opinion as an encouraging signal from the federal
government to offer free blacks unprecedented rights, including those to command vessels, sue in federal courts, and receive passports. Although Bates's
opinion contained nothing new to the radicals, Massachusetts Republican
Samuel E. Sewall wrote to Sumner, "Yet it is important as an authority coming
from the Atty Gen."[23] Theoretically, Lieber may not have exaggerated in calling
Bates's reasoning "one of the distinct milestones on the high road of jural
progress and legal science," considering that it challenged Roger Taney's *Dred
Scott* decision in 1857 and laid groundwork for the Civil Rights Act of 1866,
which established national and state citizenship for blacks. But Bates obviously
did not want his opinion to be misread as a support for black rights, particularly
the right of suffrage. In a stream of long letters between him and Lieber from
October to December 1862, Bates repeatedly stated that suffrage in the United
States was always exercised only by "a *minority*, selected by law" and "designated by certain adjunct facts & qualifications — such as social status (bond or
free), color, sex, ages," and residence, and that it was "a great error . . . to con-
found political *rights & powers*."[24] Bates's reservations may have arisen partly
from his concern about changing the original constitutional framework. As the
war unfolded and emancipation was inevitable, he was forced to deal with "hard
questions" presented to him by Lincoln and the various departments; wrote

Bates, "Some of those questions touch the organization of our system and the ground principles of our institutions."[25] Even the radical abolitionist George W. Julian, who began to talk about converting the rebellious states into "conquered provinces" as early as January 1862, believed that all the federal government could offer to blacks after the war was nothing but freedom.[26]

The Republican Congress and the Lincoln administration had known from the beginning of the war that slavery was a central issue, but they acted cautiously, sometimes even passively, in dealing with issues of slavery and black freedom. In the early stages of the war, Lincoln sought to interfere with slavery in the South by fostering a policy of gradual, compensated emancipation and colonization. Congress approved a series of antislavery acts, including barring the military from returning fugitive slaves, prohibiting slavery in territories, and abolishing slavery in the District of Columbia.[27] But it needs to be remembered that by the middle of 1862, the dynamics for a constitutional reconstruction were far from being consolidated. In addition, it was not entirely clear whether Congress or the president should have the ultimate authority to handle the issues regarding the slaves, who had been gradually emancipated as the Union army advanced. Although Congress often took the lead, the Lincoln administration intended to keep the slavery question under its control, fearing that congressional legislation, as Bates put it, "would damage the American social structure even more drastically."[28]

Not until September 1862, after General George McClellan's long-awaited spring offensive sputtered, when demands for military personnel and supply laborers increased and Washington's desire for European support grew urgent, did Lincoln and the party leaders realize that a bolder and more radical policy on the issue of slavery had become unavoidable. This concern was fully revealed by a letter from General George McClellan to Lincoln in July 1862. McClellan advised Lincoln that the time had come when the government had to "determine upon a civil and military policy, covering the whole ground" of the nation's trouble. Although he warned that "confiscation of property, political execution of persons, territorial organization of States, or forcible abolition of slavery" should not be considered for the moment, he suggested that "slaves, contraband under the act of Congress, seeking military protection, should receive it." He also suggested that working manumission might be extended "upon the ground of military necessity and security." McClellan stressed that "the future conduct of [their] struggle" should be governed by "[a] system of policy thus constitutional, and pervaded by the influences of Christianity and freedom" that "would receive the support of almost all truly loyal men, would deeply impress the rebel masses and all foreign nations, and . . . would commend itself to the favor of the Almighty."[29] By then, historian David Donald observed, "abolition of slavery became not merely a humanitarian striving but a desperately needed political requirement."[30]

Lincoln's Emancipation Proclamation — issued in preliminary form on September 22, 1862, and finally on January 1, 1863 — conditioned Union success to abolition. By issuing the proclamation, Lincoln virtually abolished slavery in the unoccupied Confederate states and, in terms of constitutional theory, transferred the ultimate authority over slavery from the states to the federal government, at least during wartime. The proclamation changed the nature of the Civil War, transforming it from a war to save the Union into a war to initiate an ideological, constitutional, and social reconstruction of the nation.

The proclamation also profoundly shaped the nature of the war in another sense: it created an opportunity for blacks to participate in the war. True, many slaves began to run to the Union armies before the proclamation was issued, but they were formally invited to join the Union armies when the proclamation authorized the enlistment and arming of the former slaves. This act, probably more than anything else, laid the legal foundation for blacks' claim to political rights in the years to come.[31] Large numbers of former slaves enlisted in Union armies as troops and served as a transportation and construction labor force for the other troops. The presence of so many black soldiers in the national military forces — nearly two hundred thousand servicemen and another three hundred thousand laborers[32] — created a precedent of unusual historical significance: black and white soldiers fought shoulder to shoulder for a common cause under the command of the federal government. This new type of racial relationship, together with the bravery and commitment demonstrated by black soldiers, exerted a tremendous impact on the Republican vision of postwar American society. For the first time, Republicans had not only become fully aware of black Americans' desire for freedom, but they also realized that blacks possessed a political ability and potential that could lend the party a valuable hand in outlining a new national political order in the postwar period. The war had united much of the southern white population against the Union, and Salmon P. Chase, the most radical member of Lincoln's cabinet, privately concluded before the proclamation took effect that "the black[s] were really the only loyal population worth counting" in the Gulf states and that black emancipation "might be made the basis of the necessary measures for their ultimate enfranchisement."[33]

Lincoln's Emancipation Proclamation and black participation in the war ensured the Union's victory and, at the same time, made the political and civil rights of blacks central to Reconstruction politics. As the war approached its end, Republicans were compelled to consider a series of difficult questions: What would the civil and political status of freed people be after they stopped being slaves? Would they automatically become citizens of the United States of America? If so, would they have all the civil and political rights that had been conferred on whites? Should they be allowed to participate in the process of political reorganization in the southern states? Should the reorganization involve granting the freedmen citizenship and suffrage, or should these matters be left to the states after they were readmitted into the Union?

Blacks themselves were among those who had first responded to these questions. Foreseeing the possibility of redefining their civil and political status in the postwar period, free blacks began to work strenuously to make that happen even before presidential or congressional reconstruction began. In February 1863, Frederick Douglass enthusiastically responded to Lincoln's issuance of the Emancipation Proclamation, which, he believed, had liberated both blacks and whites. He praised Lincoln's action as an event "mightier" than merely freeing slaves when it was viewed "in its relation to the cause of truth and justice throughout the world."[34] In the following months, together with other black and white leaders, Douglass helped raise a black regiment in Massachusetts. He urged blacks to adopt "the great national family of America," but he insisted that the Union for which black soldiers were to shed their blood must, in return, reward blacks with "all the rights, privileges and immunities enjoyed by any other members of the body politic." This, stressed Douglass, was the *"only solid,* and *final solution* of the problem."[35] About three weeks after Lincoln delivered his immortal Gettysburg Address on November 19, 1863, in which he announced to the world that the United States would have "a new birth of freedom" after the bloody war, Douglass spelled out what he believed should be the substance of the new American freedom:

> We are fighting for something incomparably better than the old Union. We are fighting for unity; unity of objects, unity of institutions, in which there shall be no North, no South, no East, no West, no black, no white, but a solidarity of the nation, making every slave free, and every freeman a voter.[36]

Black suffrage was the most important issue at the National Convention of Colored Men held in Syracuse, New York, in October 1864. Douglass and other black leaders welcomed the proposed Thirteenth Amendment but warned that without suffrage, black freedom could not be permanently maintained. The convention's resolution urged the Republican government to grant the elective franchise to blacks in all the states then in the Union and all states that would join the Union thereafter.[37]

In the meantime, free blacks in the South had also begun to agitate for suffrage. A black convention in Kansas in December 1863 issued an address declaring that blacks' right to vote was "natural and inherent." The address stated that "the restoration of the Union and the elevation of the black man [would] go hand in hand" and that "the nation [would] need the black man to vote for her."[38] Attempting to lobby for voting rights, New Orleans free blacks sent their representatives to Washington, D.C., to meet with important Republican leaders including Lincoln, Sumner, and Representative William D. Kelley. On March 10, 1864, two days before they were received by Lincoln in the White House, the two New Orleans black leaders, Jean-Baptiste Roudanez and Arnold Bertonneau, sent to Lincoln and Congress a letter challenging the notion that the federal government had no authority to interfere with state regulations of suffrage. The Louisiana state constitution had excluded men in military service from voting, reasoned the black leaders, but General Nathaniel P. Banks had ordered that those who had "volunteered for the defence of the country in the army or navy and who were otherwise qualified voters" should be "allowed to vote in the election precincts"; such order, argued Roudanez and Bertonneau, had enfranchised "those who were [disfranchised] by the Constitution and laws of Louisiana" and had therefore established a precedent that the federal government could have the authority to correct state regulations over voters' qualifications. The black representatives stressed that, although they were at this time only demanding suffrage for free blacks in New Orleans, the Republican party had to extend equal suffrage to whites, blacks, and even the former slaves if it wished to "secure the permanence of the free institutions and loyal governments now organized" in the South. Their reasoning undoubtedly influenced Republican lawmakers, some of whom were invited to attend the meetings at which black leaders spoke for black suffrage.[39] Black reasoning for suffrage demonstrates not only that they understood the relation between voting, freedom, citizenship, and American ideals at a profound ideological and constitutional level but also that they knew politically how to push Republicans toward a more radical direction in Reconstruction by linking black suffrage with the future of the nation and the party itself. Douglass's address delivered at the American Anti-Slavery Society in Philadelphia on December 4, 1863 best illustrated black leaders' skills of political engineering. In the address, Douglass told the Republican leaders that

> When this rebellion shall have been put down, when the arms shall have fallen from the guilty hand of traitors, you will need the friendship of the slaves of the South, of those millions there. Four or five million men are not of inconsiderable importance at anytime; but they will be doubly important when you come to reorganize and reestablish republican institutions in the South. Will you mock those bondmen by breaking their chains with one hand, and with the other giving their rebel masters the elective franchise and robbing them of theirs? I tell you the negro is your friend. But you will make him not only your friend in sentiment and heart by enfranchising him, you will thus make him your best defender, your best protector against the traitors and the descendants of those traitors who will inherit the hate, the bitter revenge which shall crystalize all over the South, and seek to circumvent the government that they could not throw off. You will need the black man there as a watchman and patrol; and you may need him as a soldier. You may need him to uphold in peace, as he is now upholding in war, the star-spangled banner.[40]

Undoubtedly, black agitation for suffrage contributed enormously to the ideological and political strength of the radical Republicans, who fought the same battle on the legislative front.

Indeed, radical Republicans shared much of black leaders' expectations. By 1864, radicals had ideologically advanced to the point of envisioning the postwar Union as a genuinely free and just society. The Union's impending victory had convinced them that such a society could be achieved by a political reconstruction of the South. The Civil War, Sumner declared, as a "sublime Revolution," had purified America.[41] The Union's victory, in the words of Daniel Morris of New York, gave Congress a "moment of greater responsibility than ha[d] devolved upon a like body since the year 1776." He believed that its action would give "perpetuity to a nation of freemen or of slaves"; echoing the call of Puritan John Winthrop, he stated, "The eyes of a world are upon us."[42] The new United States, Illinois Republican Isaac N. Arnold declared, would "be wholly free," with liberty and "equality before the law" being "the great corner-stone."[43]

But enfranchising blacks was no easy task, at least in 1864. The first complication was derived from the Constitution, which empowered the federal government to guarantee each state a "republican form of government" but left the states to prescribe voting qualifications.[44] Could the control of suffrage, which traditionally had been a state power, be transferred to the federal government? If so, how could the transfer be justified in constitutional theory and practice? Second, suffrage had been a right exercised by a selected group of citizens; if the federal government had the power to grant suffrage, what qualifications should be applied to voters? Could any citizen vote, especially blacks and women, who had been excluded from voting before the war? Third, the reorganization of the southern states would be a political process involving grassroots voters in different local and state elections. Should blacks be allowed to participate in the process of reconstruction? If so, how? If not, why not? Thus, enfranchising blacks defined not only their political status but also the new federal-state relations, the substance of American citizenship, and the nature of the "republican form of government."

For radical Republicans, emancipation and black participation in the war had legitimated the freedmen's status as citizens and entitled them to the civil and political rights enjoyed by whites. But there would be no permanent guarantee for the nation's safety and black rights until both were secured in the nation's Constitution. Discussion about how to amend the Constitution started as early as 1863 among the Republicans. Believing that the South had used the original Constitution to develop the states' rights doctrine that eventually led to rebellion, Francis Lieber began to prepare constitutional amendments on his own initiative in early 1864. Although he noted the danger in using a dictatorial power to remove slavery either through a constitutional amendment or a presidential proclamation, "the life of the nation [was] the first substantive thing, and far above the formulas which very properly had been adopted." For Francis Lieber, the ultimate goal of eliminating slavery was not to punish the South but to establish the "integrity" of the country and the "nationality" of its people.[45] While agreeing to Lieber's argument that the South had forfeited its legitimate rights and privileges by rebellion, Gideon Welles doubted how far the federal government could go in imposing conditions on the South in reorganization.[46] Resenting the radicals' "new heresy" that the rebellious South should be treated as conquered territories, Edward Bates insisted that the federal government could not exist without the "active cooperations of the States." He did not share Lieber's call for a strong national sovereignty.[47]

Radical Republicans were surely aware of the impending reality that the South could become politically more powerful when it returned to Congress after the war. Since emancipation had virtually voided the three-fifths clause of the Constitution, blacks in the South would be counted for national representation, and even if they remained disfranchised, the southern states would have an increase in their representation. Such a situation would subject the northern states once again to the rule of their former enemy. The radicals believed that without a permanent check on the former rebels, the old slave power could quickly return. For them, the most effective way to guard the results of the war was to turn black soldiers' military power during the war into political muscle after the war.[48] The radicals' logic was simple: since the survival of the Union was tied to the emancipation of slaves, the reconstruction of the Union must tie to the genuine freedom of blacks, whose votes were indispensable for the success and security of the Union. Therefore, southern freedmen must be allowed to participate in reorganizing the South and thus in redefining the future of the nation. In the eyes of the radical Republicans, the right to vote became the first and most important right that should be conferred upon blacks.

However, the radical vision of black suffrage lacked support from other Republican leaders, at least before the passage of the Thirteenth Amendment. The party was united to push for abolition but reluctant to connect black emancipation with black enfranchisement. In December 1863, James M. Ashley of Ohio, a radical Republican in the House, made the first effort to include black suffrage in the agenda of Reconstruction. In a reconstruction bill presented in December 1863, Ashley proposed that all male citizens over twenty-one, regardless of color, be allowed to vote at the election for a constitutional convention in the course of restoring the southern states.[49] Republicans in both houses, however, replaced the Ashley bill with the Wade-Davis bill, jointly proposed by Representative Henry Winter Davis of Maryland and Senator Ben Wade of Ohio. The Wade-Davis bill was not much different from Ashley's in terms of rejecting slavery and providing mechanisms for restoration, but it limited the ballot only to white men in the process of reorganizing the southern states. This was a clear effort to accommodate Lincoln's whites-only ballot policy, as indicated in his 10 Percent Plan in December 1863. But Lincoln, doubting the authority of Congress to pass such an act of coercive nature and refusing to alter his restoration plan, which was already under way in Louisiana and Arkansas, still killed the bill by a pocket veto in July 1864.[50]

Before the Wade-Davis bill, the radicals made another effort to establish black suffrage. When the bill to organize the Montana Territory was debated in Congress in March 1864, Senate Republicans managed to remove color as a qualification for voting in organizing new states, but the House insisted that control over suffrage was one of the rights reserved to the states. When some Senate Democrats called the bill "the merest abstraction," since no black person lived in Montana, Sumner responded that it made no difference whether there was or ever would be any black person living in Montana; what mattered was that black suffrage as "a principle" was not to be postponed. Meanwhile, Sumner worked hard to put black suffrage in the new city charter of the District of Columbia so that black male residents of the city could become electors. But none of his efforts was successful. Sumner's real objective was to set up a precedent of black suffrage in a federal jurisdiction. In January 1867, the same tactic would be employed again by the radicals when the admissions of Nebraska and Colorado were debated.[51]

Undaunted, Sumner tried again to tie black equality to the Thirteenth Amendment when it was introduced into the Senate in April 1864. The amendment, based on the bill of Missouri Senator John B. Henderson, intended to give Lincoln's proclamation – a wartime measure – permanence in peace and to make it effective throughout the country, but it said nothing specific about black rights.[52] Believing that the amendment should move beyond a mere constitutional declaration of the death of slavery, Sumner wanted it to "give completeness and permanence to emancipation, and bring the Constitution into avowed harmony with the Declaration of Independence."[53] But when he proposed to insert a provision into the amendment –"that all persons are equal before the law, so that no person can hold another as a slave; and the Congress may make all laws necessary and proper to carry this article into effect everywhere within the United States and the jurisdiction thereof"– his colleagues responded coldly and asked him to withdraw his proposal. Sumner later regretted succumbing to the pressure, but he must have realized how unprepared his colleagues were even to think about black rights when some of them were totally lost upon hearing the phrase "equality before the law."[54]

In the House, radical Republicans employed an argument that black leader Frederick Douglass and Republican theoretician Francis Lieber had used earlier: that is, the war had created a new nation, which required new responsibility from the federal government. Ashley argued that the supreme power of the national government had always been placed in the Constitution, which "secures nationality of citizenship" and "guarantees that the citizens of each State shall enjoy all the rights and privileges of citizens of the several States." Ashley identified national citizenship with national suffrage, declaring that "a universal franchise . . . [could not] be confined to States, but belong[ed] to the citizens of the Republic." By formulating such reasoning, Ashley helped translate the political ideals of radical Republicans and black leaders into constitutional language.[55] This new national citizenship and national rights argument would become an important principle of the Fourteenth Amendment two years later, but for the moment, the House refused to follow Ashley's argument.

While the Thirteenth Amendment was under debate in December 1864, the House asked Ashley to prepare a bill for the readmission of Louisiana, Arkansas, and Tennessee. In this new reconstruction bill (H.R. 602), Ashley agreed to facilitate quick reorganizations of the South, as Lincoln desired, but he conditioned the readmission of the southern states to their recognition of black suffrage. Seeing that the majority of the party and the Lincoln administration would not support his radical plan, Ashley amended the bill by supporting the initial registration of the whites in Louisiana (and, theoretically, in all other southern states), but he insisted on granting black soldiers the voting rights when a new state constitution and government were to be formed. In late 1864, after federal effort made by Union general Nathaniel P. Banks to persuade the white Louisianans to accept qualified black suffrage failed, radical Republicans began to take a firmer stance. In his revised reconstruction bill presented in January 1865, Ashley made it clear that southern reconstruction must be preconditioned with abolition of slavery, guarantee of freedom and civil rights to all persons, exclusion of high-ranking rebel officers from politics, and a registration of all citizens including blacks. Ashley again insisted that "universal suffrage to the liberated black men of the South," which he called of "paramount importance," should be a condition for the readmission of southern states. He told his colleagues, "We cannot obtain indemnity for the past, but it is the duty of statesmen . . . to demand security of the future."[56] Speaking in support of the bill, William D. Kelley, the Republican from Pennsylvania who had personally listened to southern black leaders' plea for suffrage in April 1864, lamented congressional inaction on black suffrage: "While we have professed to believe that their right to life, liberty, and the pursuit of happiness was inalienable — could not be alienated or relinquished by them, nor taken away by others — we have ignored their humanity, and denied them the enjoyment of any single political right." Kelley asked that blacks be "immediately clothed with all the rights of citizenship," including suffrage, which he believed would help blacks to be "improved, enriched and enlightened."[57]

Their colleagues were unconvinced. Henry L. Dawes, a moderate Republican congressman from Massachusetts, responded that Congress should fix "no unbending iron rule," nor should it prescribe "the method in which they [would] make their organic law." The South, Dawes felt, would "work out that problem for itself and in its own way."[58] But when asked to strike out the provision for universal suffrage, Ashley replied, "If there is to be any limitation of the right of suffrage in the reorganization of the rebel State governments, for one I am determined that it shall not be one of caste, of color, of nationality." Despite their efforts, the radicals failed to prevail. The majority of the House Republicans voted to postpone the discussion of the Ashley reconstruction bill on January 17, 1865. Later the House rejected the bill, fearing that if blacks were unprepared for the ballot, imposed suffrage would even hurt them and consequently injure the cause of black freedom. In the Senate radical Republicans had to prevent a vote on the readmission of Louisiana after the majority had rejected black suffrage.[59]

Thus, when the Thirteenth Amendment passed Congress in January 1865, it had one clearly defined objective: abolishing slavery forever.[60] It was silent on black political rights. Radical Republicans such as Chief Justice Salmon P. Chase extolled the amendment, for good reason; it had nationalized freedom. But they saw the potential to go still further. Its second section, which empowered Congress to enforce the abolition of slavery, might, in Chase's view, serve as a constitutional springboard for Congress to deal with black rights — including suffrage.[61]

Black Suffrage and the Making of the Fourteenth Amendment

Although radical Republicans such as Governor Michael Hahn of Louisiana believed that the passage of the Thirteenth Amendment had committed the nation to a moral reform of black rights, the prospect that the national government would or could impose black suffrage was still far from likely.[62] In addition to disagreements among congressional Republicans over national power to impose suffrage, the difficulty also resulted because Reconstruction before 1865 had essentially been conducted under Lincoln's leadership. Despite all of his prewar reservations about black political rights, Lincoln's attitude toward black suffrage was evolving at the end of the war. Like many other Republicans, Lincoln had been deeply touched by the bravery of black soldiers and come to realize the potential importance of black political power after the war. On March 12, 1864, Lincoln met with two free black leaders from New Orleans who asked his assistance in enfranchising southern blacks. The day after, in his famous letter to Hahn, Lincoln privately suggested granting suffrage to some intelligent blacks, especially those who had "fought gallantly" with the Union armies. These people, Lincoln noted, "would probably help, in some trying time to come, to keep the jewel of liberty within the family of freedom."[63]

Even so, Lincoln remained cautious about initiating any national action on black suffrage. Starting from his issuance of the Emancipation Proclamation, Lincoln maintained a positive sense of paradox, which featured his pragmatism in action and idealism in vision. Lincoln wanted a reconstruction of the Union without slavery and a recognition of black rights without much change in the original structure of American federalism. He noted that blacks' natural rights as free men had to be turned into civil and political rights, but he hoped that state governments would take the initiative. In his last public speech, on April 11, 1865, Lincoln told a crowd at the White House that he would be pleased if Louisiana enfranchised at least its literate black citizens and those who had borne arms for the Union, but he refused to make this a condition for Louisiana's readmission.[64] Despite radical complaints about his slowness in accepting "the truth," Lincoln was still very much their only hope for black suffrage.[65] And there were signs that, as both Charles Sumner and Salmon P. Chase optimistically indicated, Lincoln's mind was "undergoing change" and might eventually agree to a more radical step regarding black suffrage than the president had previously suggested.[66]

Such optimism soon died with Lincoln's assassination on April 14, 1865. Lincoln's death heightened the uncertainty over the issue of black suffrage, but it also, as Democrats feared, lent added muscle to the radical fight for a thorough reconstruction. While the normally scholarly Lieber reacted to Lincoln's assassination with an emotional cry, "Let the draft go on again, or call for volunteers to sweep — literally to sweep the South," Henry Winter Davis, who had expressed reservations on black suffrage a few months earlier, now asked to enfranchise blacks, the only people in the South who had "a deep interest in the continued supremacy of the United States."[67]

For a short while, radical Republicans hoped that Andrew Johnson, Lincoln's successor, would advance their cause. Johnson listened attentively to radical pleas and showed no sign of opposition.[68] This made radical Republicans believe that, in Sumner's words, *"on the question of colored suffrage the President is with us."*[69] Chase, who went to the South to study the political situation there, repeatedly urged Johnson to take action on black suffrage in making his reconstruction policy. North Carolina blacks also directly appealed to the president for suffrage.[70] But, in his first two reconstruction proclamations issued on May 29, 1865, Johnson laid out for the southern states the minimum conditions they had to meet for readmission: the abolition of slavery, the nullification of secession, and the repudiation of all state debts incurred during the period of the Confederacy. He did not endorse black suffrage. In his proclamation regarding the reorganization of North Carolina, Johnson directed the state's provisional governor to call a whites-only election of delegates to frame a new state constitution. In his annual message to Congress in December 1865, Johnson told Congress that he had no right to impose black suffrage on the South, although he held out the prospect of future state action to expand the suffrage.[71] Why did Johnson act as he did? It might be because he shared some of Lincoln's early doubts about federal authority to grant suffrage to blacks; as one of his confidants suggested to him, "If as President you can settle that question [of the right of suffrage] for the State of Tennessee or Louisiana, why may you not also settle it for Ohio and Pennsylvania[?] . . . *Let this question alone. Leave it where it has always been—with the States.*" Lincoln had later begun to realize that without blacks' political participation freedom could be endangered; Johnson, however, believed that black freedom did mean a dependence on federal government. Freedom, Johnson wrote to a group of black ministers in May 1865, "simply means liberty to work and enjoy the product of your own hands."[72]

Johnson's reconstruction policy intensified the debate among Republicans over black suffrage and exacerbated growing tensions between him and the radical Republicans. Professing "painful astonishment," Sumner vowed to "fight this battle" against Johnson's plan and not to let "this great and glorious Republic . . . sink to such an imbecile and shameful policy."[73] Chase branded Johnson's policy "a moral, political and financial mistake" because black laborers without suffrage could be neither respected nor productive.[74] John M. Forbes, a Republican financier, hoped that Johnson's plan was only "experimental," for returning blacks to the mercy of the planters was "mean and stupid."[75] Reacting angrily, Senator Jacob M. Howard of Michigan argued that black suffrage was the nation's "*only security* and the only means of making emancipation effectual." He called for the use of power by Congress to guarantee "a republican form of Government" in the states "at the *earliest possible* day so as to put an end to this executive reconstruction."[76] Sumner agreed, arguing that "a question of such transcendent magnitude should be referred to Congress."[77] Henry Winter Davis went even further, demanding a new constitutional amendment prescribing universal suffrage as the basis for state representation in Congress.[78]

Radical resentment over Johnson's policy derived from a rationale that Sumner had articulated in a letter to George Bancroft on Louisiana reconstruction:

> We shall insist upon the Decltn of Indp. as the foundation of the new State govts; & the argt. will be presented, *not merely on the grounds of human Rights, but of self-interest*. It will be shown that we shall need the votes of the negroes to sustain the Union, to preserve tranquility & to prevent the repudiation of the national debt. You are right in calling it a stupendous question.[79]

A month later, Sumner reiterated his rationale in a letter to the British reformer John Bright:

> The question [of black suffrage] has become immensely practical in this respect. Without their votes, we cannot establish stable govts. in the rebel states. Their votes are as necessary as their muskets. Of this I am satisfied. Without them, the old enemy will reappear &, under the forms of law, take possession of the govt.— choose magistrates & officers —&, in alliance with the Northern democracy, put us all in peril assailing the national debt. To my mind, the nation is now bound by self-interest — aye, *self-defence*— to be thoroughly just.
>
> The Declaration of Indep. has pledges which have never been redeemed. We must redeem them, at least as regards the rebel states which have fallen under our jurisdiction.[80]

The term "self-interest" included not only the interests of the North and the Union but also that of the Republican party. All these interests were interrelated and, to Republicans, shared the same goal: to reconstruct American society on the basis of the northern ideology of freedom. The radicals predicted a prolonged struggle, both ideological and political, between the Union and former Confederacy after the war. Political parties would be the main vehicles at the local and national levels to build up a force strong enough to resist the restoration of former enemies to political power. Black suffrage, in this circumstance, would be the most vital and effective weapon to sustain the Union and maintain Republican control of the national government.

For all its elegance, the radical argument for black suffrage was unpopular with other, less reform-oriented Republicans in the North in 1865. Northern Republican opposition to immediate black suffrage focused on the following points. First, black suffrage was not a "Federal question" and was, as Gideon Welles argued, "never intended by the founders of the Union" to be one.[81] Suffrage was purely a state business; Edward Bates cried, "What right has Ohio and R[hode] Island to meddle with suffrage in Va. and Florida?" Both Welles and Bates regarded the radical push for black suffrage either as "a species of fanaticism" or as motivated by hunger for power.[82] Second, enfranchising blacks in the South would inevitably challenge voting discrimination in the North and stir up other radical movements such as women's suffrage. In that case, Ohio's Jacob D. Cox announced, the party would be beaten in the North and West.[83] Although Republicans such as Secretary of the Interior James Harlan sympathized with the radicals' sense "of the duty of a statesman to *create* rather than to be controlled by circumstances," he advised them, "We must look at things as they are, and not as they should be in estimating the probabilities of success."[84] Third, blacks were not intelligent enough to vote. Downtrodden in slavery for a long time, blacks had not been able to acquire the "sturdy, patient self-asserting spirit by which the people of England and most of Europe ha[d] wrung freedom from feudalism."[85] Warned former general J. W. Phelps in January 1865, "The vote in the hands of ignorance is like a loaded revolver in the hands of a child, dangerous to itself and to others."[86] Before the blacks were ready in knowledge, experience, and economy, letting them vote, Indiana Republican governor Oliver P. Morton feared, could subject them "to a merciless persecution" rather than confer on them "any substantial benefit."[87] Even Lieber, a supporter of limited black suffrage by then, told Sumner, "Universal suffrage is no panacea for all wrongs."[88]

Despite all the opposition, radical Republicans tried to bring black suffrage into northern politics at the state and national levels. In 1865, Republicans in three states — Connecticut (where about two thousand blacks lived), Wisconsin, and Minnesota — and the Territory of Colorado struggled to put black suffrage on the state agenda for constitutional amendment, but voters in all the places turned down the radical proposal.[89] The results of these referenda could be interpreted as a defeat for black suffrage in the North and particularly in those states, but a careful analysis of the voting records would show that in all three states, the forces supporting black suffrage were nearly as strong as those opposing it.[90]

At the national level, in December 1865 and January 1866, radical Republicans introduced a bill intending to enfranchise male blacks living in the District of Columbia. The bill, known as the Wade-Kelley proposal, provided that the word *white* be struck from the suffrage laws of the District of Columbia and that no person should be disqualified from voting in the District of Columbia because of color.[91] House Republicans engaged in infighting at the caucus meeting of January 10, when moderates challenged Kelley's bill and asked for qualified suffrage in the District of Columbia. While radicals such as Thaddeus Stevens (R-Pa.) insisted on universal suffrage, other Republicans such as Rutherford B. Hayes, who reported the meeting to his wife, preferred to postpone the bill for "other and far more important business."[92] Although the bill passed the House, with fifteen Republicans – all from western or border states – joining Democrats to vote against the bill,[93] it died in the Senate, where Republicans such as William Stewart (R-Nev.) insisted that southern restoration precede black suffrage in the District of Columbia.[94] The first District of Columbia suffrage bill debate demonstrated perfectly that despite the unpopularity of black suffrage, radical Republicans did not give up their efforts to find a way to establish national authority for granting suffrage.[95]

The Republican force that held the balance between the president and radical Republicans at the end of 1865 was the moderate Republicans. Probably because the moderates saw Reconstruction as a process of repairing the flawed framework of American constitutionalism rather than an opportunity to usher in an open-ended social revolution, they were cautious about making laws relating to black rights. They did not desire to break with Johnson, even though they considered the president's policy unwise. It was foolish to "make a rupture with Johnson," Garfield reasoned, before he made "the breach with the party." Henry Wilson (R-Mass.) himself was a supporter of black suffrage, but he considered it more important to keep the party united. Johnson was the party's leader, and this could not be changed; thus Wilson told Sumner, "We had better stand by the administration and endeavor to bring it right. [But if Johnson] turns against our course[,] then we must follow where our principles lead whether to victory or to temporary defeat."[96] Thus, for a short while, the president and moderates maintained a tangible unity rooted in the faith that Republicans found themselves forced to repose in Johnson.

Their faith was soon to be betrayed when Johnson vetoed both the Freedmen's Bureau bill and the civil rights bill respectively on February 19 and March 27, 1866. The Freedmen's Bureau bill extended the tenure of the Freedmen's Bureau and enlarged its legal power to establish and protect blacks' civil rights in the South. The civil rights bill conferred national and state citizenship on all blacks and guaranteed them a number of crucial civil and economic rights, including the right to own property, make contracts, and sue. The purpose of these two bills was to invalidate the southern "Black Codes," the many restrictions on black freedom introduced in the restored southern states at the end of 1865 under the pretext of maintaining social order.[97] Neither of the two bills touched on black voting rights, yet, constitutionally speaking, they represented a bold and vigorous effort by the Republican Congress to expand the federal responsibility in protecting the rights of American citizens.[98] Lyman Trumbull (R-Ill.), author of the two bills and a leader of the Senate moderates, conferred with Johnson several times about this legislation and believed that he had the president's approval. Moderate Republicans such as Rutherford B. Hayes privately wished that Johnson would get back "into the bosom of the [Republican] family again" by approving these bills.[99] But Johnson branded both bills unconstitutional and unnecessary.[100]

Together with the southern Black Codes, Johnson's vetoes broke the previous political balance and created the opportunity for moderate and radical Republicans to work together in leading a congressional reconstruction.[101] By overturning Johnson's vetoes, this new radical-moderate coalition seemed to reach a consensus that the reorganization of the South must go beyond the previous presidential framework and create a new federal-state relationship. But radicals and moderates seemed unable to agree on how far Congress should go, to what extent Congress could set conditions for the return of the South, and what rights could be conferred on the freedmen by the federal government.

Moderates clearly understood the seriousness and urgency of the situation. When Sumner called Johnson's policy and the Black Codes "a terrible calamity" to southern blacks, James G. Blaine (R-Maine) well knew that former rebels were "not yet fitted to be entrusted with the administration of a State Government."[102] Moderates did consider black votes as an important check on the quick return of the former enemies: with "twenty-two Senators added to the twelve or fifteen [Democrats]" then in office, Hayes surmised that the political power of four million emancipated blacks in the House and the Electoral College was "a serious thing."[103]

However, using national authority directly to confer suffrage on blacks would be hard. When drafting the Civil Rights Act of 1866, Republicans detailed a number of civil rights attached to American citizenship, but they conspicuously left out political rights. That most of the northern states still withheld suffrage from blacks was certainly on the minds of many Republicans. The recent defeat of black suffrage in several northern states seemed to heighten northern conservatism on black political equality. Unlike the federal abolition of slavery, which the free North was more than willing to accept, federal enfranchisement of blacks would be regarded as a violation of states' rights in the North.[104]

Under such circumstances, the most expedient way to prevent the readmission of the South with a solid Democratic majority was to require the southern states to franchise their black citizens (who would then provide a political check against southern Democrats) or reduce their representation in the House. The rationale behind this was seemingly like that of presidential reconstruction: let the southern states handle the issue of black suffrage. But the difference was crucial. The president did not require state action on black suffrage as a precondition for readmission, but the Republican Congress did make it "a condition precedent" for the South's return. Moderate Republicans would apply a similar rationale in framing the Fourteenth Amendment.

The Fourteenth Amendment started as an attempt to deal with the issue of black suffrage, or more directly, representation in the House. On January 9, 1866, Thaddeus Stevens, the co-chair of the Joint Committee on Reconstruction, presented a resolution to the committee proposing that representation be apportioned "according to the number of [the states'] respective legal voters" and stating that the only persons not considered legal voters were those who were "not either natural born or naturalized citizens of the United States of the age of twenty-one years."[105] In submitting the much amended resolution to the House on January 31, Stevens made it clear that the resolution intended to impose "a penalty" on states that denied blacks the right to vote and that the penalty would continue until the states had "corrected [their] actions." Stevens confessed that he would very much like to withhold suffrage from the former rebels until Congress finished Reconstruction, but he realized that Congress had no power to enfranchise blacks directly or disfranchise rebellious whites.[106] In the meantime, the joint committee accepted a proposal drafted by John Bingham (R-Ohio), which empowered Congress to make laws to secure "to all citizens of the United States, in every State, the same *political rights and privileges*; and to all persons in every State equal protection in the enjoyment of life, liberty and property." Thus, these two proposals became what William E. Nelson calls "an embryonic form of the Fourteenth Amendment."[107] Both proposals explicitly expressed the committee's intention to enfranchise southern blacks and to include the right to vote as a right attached to federal citizenship.

During the later discussions, however, the committee's expressions on black suffrage became vague and elusive. On February 3, Bingham replaced his original proposal with a new one, which was almost identical except that the phrase "political rights and privileges" was replaced by "privileges and immunities." The committee accepted this new proposal by a very tight vote (7 yeas, 6 nays, and 2 not voting).[108] What did this substitution mean? What was the difference between these two phrases? No immediate explanation was given or recorded. But when the Fourteenth Amendment was being formally debated, Bingham, in a speech on May 10, defined the rights to elect "a Federal elective office" and choose representatives in Congress as "privileges of a citizen of the United States"; the joint committee agreed, however, that "the exercise of the elective franchise, though it [was] one of the privileges of a citizen of the Republic, [was] exclusively under the control of the States." The change of wording may have been a rhetorical tactic to avoid the sensitive issue of black suffrage, but it does demonstrate a crucial difference between moderates and radicals in understanding the legal connotations of the right to vote.[109] A year later, Sumner would be able to clear the confusion and reveal the difference: when suffrage was a privilege, it "was subject to such limitations as the policy or good will of the legislature chose to impose"; when it was "an essential right," government could only "regulate & guard, but [could not] abridge."[110]

Moderate Republicans remained wedded to their conservative stand on black suffrage even after they broke with Johnson in the fight for the civil rights bill and the Freedmen's Bureau bill in early 1866. On April 28, 1866, when the joint committee moved to revive the earlier proposals that the Senate had neglected, Robert Dale Owen proposed a new plan for the new constitutional amendment that prohibited racial discrimination in suffrage nationwide after 1876 and reduced state representation in the House before 1876 if racial qualifications were imposed by any state on its electorate.[111] But the joint committee, under pressure from the Republicans of both Illinois and Indiana (Owen's own state), decided to reject Owen's black suffrage proposal.[112] On April 30, Stevens presented the Fourteenth Amendment bill to the House in behalf of the joint committee. The first section of the amendment was modeled on Bingham's earlier proposal. The second section contained the essence of Stevens's original proposal but added a sex qualification and deleted the specific date for black enfranchisement, as Owen had proposed.[113] The handling of black suffrage was very much suited to the taste of moderate Republicans. The committee, as Jacob M. Howard (R-Mich.) later confirmed, shrank "from attempting to incorporate into the amendment of the Constitution of the United States" the right of blacks to vote.[114]

With these arrangements, the debates in both houses were relatively smooth. The Senate modified the first section by adding the citizenship clause. Republicans universally approved the section as a necessary measure, as James A. Garfield (R-Ohio) said, to lift the Civil Rights Act of 1866 "above the reach of political strife, [and] beyond the reach of the plots and machinations of any party."[115] But different concerns surrounded the second section in the House debates. Unsatisfied, Stevens regarded the second section as "most important," for it would "compel the States to grant universal suffrage" or "keep them forever in a hopeless minority in the national Government."[116] Garfield, normally a moderate, was disappointed to see that suffrage was not imbedded in the Constitution.[117] Although Nathaniel Banks (R-Mass.) held that a radical change "in the basis of political society" of the South was absolutely necessary, public opinion would not allow the federal government to impose black suffrage and comprehensive white disfranchisement. "It was therefore most wise on the part of the committee to waive this matter in deference to public opinion."[118] Moderates such as Henry J. Raymond (R-N.Y.), who disliked Owen's proposal, were pleased with the new second section.[119] George F. Miller (R-Pa.) hoped that by "conceding" the power to regulate suffrage to the states, the second section would settle "the complication in regard to suffrage and representation."[120] Hayes recorded that the nine members present at the Ohio Republican caucus in Congress overwhelmingly supported the proposed amendment and opposed "negro suffrage as a condition of restoration."[121] Both houses approved the bill with strong partisan support.[122]

The final version of the amendment accomplished much of the moderate agenda. It protected the North against an increase in southern white political power and punished the South for withholding suffrage from blacks but allowed northern states to do so with impunity, since their black population was too small to make a difference in representation. More important, the amendment avoided directly conferring on blacks the right to vote.[123]

Radicals felt disappointed, but the determination of the majority not "to yield their opinion" forced them to compromise. "I live among men and not among angels," Stevens said as he persuaded his radical colleagues to accept the amendment; "mutual concession, therefore, is our only resort, or mutual hostilities."[124] James Ashley felt that the final version was the best he could get: "As a practical man, I voted for [the clauses of the Fourteenth Amendment], and would do so again under the same circumstance if I could obtain nothing better."[125] Sumner resented "the imbecility of Congress, which shrank from a contest on principle." Although the radicals failed to "bring Congress to this duty" of enfranchising blacks, he did not "give it up."[126]

Enfranchising Blacks in the District of Columbia and Federal Territories

Although the Fourteenth Amendment disappointed the radicals, its passage represented a significant achievement of the congressional reconstruction and generated an enormous impact in several ways. First, the amendment creatively reconstructed American constitutionalism by defining national citizenship and establishing, in a fundamental and permanent form, national responsibility for protecting civil rights. Second, the amendment transformed the concepts of equal natural rights for blacks, as articulated by many Republicans before the Civil War, into positive legal rights. Third, the amendment justified the federal government's authority to regulate the rights attached to national citizenship, including the right to vote. Such justification allowed radicals to assume a stronger position and push black suffrage into federally controlled territories.[127]

Meanwhile, according to Hayes, during the discussion of the Fourteenth Amendment, Republicans reached a consensus that Congress would "leave to the States the question of suffrage" but "in the District and the Territories it [was] for Congress to lay down the rule."[128] This consensus, for Sumner, Chase, and "all the best Anti-Slavery lawyers of the country," was a road open for further actions shortly after the passage of the Fourteenth Amendment.[129]

In the meantime, the deteriorating situation in the South under Johnson's policy further alarmed the radicals. The North was shocked by the violent attacks of local whites against the unionists and blacks at the Mechanics' Institute in New Orleans in July 1866, in which 34 blacks and 4 whites died and 119 blacks and 27 whites were injured.[130] In the campaign of that year, northern newspapers blamed Johnson's policy for the rioting. But "federal bayonets [could] only give temporary & a precarious relief" in the South, Attorney General James Speed confided; "[until we] have our government founded upon impartial civil and political justice . . . we can not hope for permanent peace & assumed progress."[131] Black leaders also kept pressure on the Republicans. At a meeting with several ranking Republicans including Zachariah Chandler (R-Mich.) and Richard Yates (R-Ill.), Frederick Douglass cited the recent prosuffrage demonstration at Hyde Park in London as an indication of global awareness of the importance of manhood suffrage. "We want it not only because we are men, [but] because of what we are here in this country especially."[132] But the development that revitalized the radicals to fight for black suffrage was the Republican victory of 1866, which, in no small way, signified a national referendum approving congressional reconstruction. As a result, in the Fortieth Congress, Republicans would maintain a decisive majority over the Democrats and Johnson conservatives.[133]

Encouraged and prepared, radicals brought the issue of black suffrage back to Capitol Hill immediately after the 1866 elections. In the brief period between December 1866 and February 1867, Republicans succeeded in enacting black suffrage in the District of Columbia, removing the color qualification for suffrage from unorganized federal territories, and requiring impartial suffrage as a condition for admitting Nebraska and Colorado. During the intensive debates of this period, the radical Republicans substantially advanced their theories for the legitimacy of enacting black suffrage at the national level. Partially because of the federal nature of the cases, the radicals were able to obtain support for these measures from moderate Republicans who had opposed explicit federal action on black suffrage in the last session. These measures not only established the precedent of federal regulation of suffrage but also *constitutionally* paved the way for Congress to enact the first Reconstruction Act in March 1867, which required all of the southern states to enfranchise their black citizens in the process of reorganization.

The House had passed the District of Columbia suffrage bill (S. No. 1) at the last session, but the Senate decided to postpone the discussion of the bill, mainly because of the sickness of Lot M. Morrill (R-Maine), who was supposed to lead the debate.[134] Under pressure from Sumner, the Senate started to debate the bill again on December 10, 1866. Much of the debate focused on three issues: (1) whether the federal government had the power to grant suffrage to blacks in the District of Columbia; (2) to what extent voting rights should be extended (should women be granted the right to vote?); (3) what the relation was between suffrage, citizenship, and the republican form of government; and (4) how much black enfranchisement in the District of Columbia should affect the rest of the nation. These questions, both ideologically and constitutionally important, had yet to receive the full attention of the Republicans.

With Henry Wilson defining suffrage as "the right to protect his life, his liberty, his property, and the rights of his wife and children," Republicans seemed to sweep away the early elusiveness that surrounded the nature of suffrage.[135]

The party had freed blacks but was "perplexed to know how to define" them, Morrill admitted. As citizens, he reasoned, black men must be given the right to vote, because blacks constituted one-eighth of the national population. Fur- thermore, the unity of the American nation was no longer bound by states' rights or sovereignty but by "unity of faith in human rights . . . [and in] the de- velopment and protection of individual rights."[136] Blacks had earned the right to vote by fighting for the Union, Frederick Frelinghuysen of New Jersey stated in his moving speech, and enough white soldiers had seen "colored men lying in columns on the field of battle with the faces upturned to Heaven mutely pleading . . . for their rights of their race"; insisting that it was the white man's government would demonstrate nothing but "very little confidence in the en- ergy and courage and ability of the Anglo-Saxon race."[137]

Seeing the issue from an ideological viewpoint, both Ben Wade and William Sprague believed that the contest over black suffrage was actually over demo- cratic principles. "As you limit suffrage [in proportion]," Wade argued, "you create in the same degree an aristocracy, an irresponsible Government." Wade went further to charge that those who opposed black suffrage did not believe in the republican government.[138] When Democrats argued that unrestricted suf- frage would "corrupt and degrade elections" as ignorant votes poured into the ballot boxes, Frelinghuysen responded that the ballot was "a great education" by which black people's political consciousness and dignity would be elevated. Why in the world of nations did Americans rise "immensely higher" in "intel- lect and every quality?" Wade asked; he answered that it was because ordinary Americans "were compelled" to participate in both local and national affairs. This participation "elevate[d] a man."[139] Republicans clearly had gone well beyond their earlier attitudes – and were adopting much the same elegant rhet- oric that had long been uttered by black leaders and antislavery radicals in the middle of the war.

However, Republican unity proved short-lived. Edgar Cowan (R-Pa.) pro- posed to strike the word *male* from the Republican bill. His amendment, a de- vice to block the enactment of black suffrage, split the Republicans. While sev- eral Republicans, including Ben Wade, spoke in favor of women's suffrage, the majority of Republican senators vehemently opposed connecting the two dis- franchised groups. For Henry Wilson, black suffrage was "an imperative neces- sity" on which the nation depended for preserving its power, strength, and unity. To couple women's suffrage with the bill would only "endanger its imme- diate triumph."[140] Sumner agreed, arguing further that "the controlling necessity" would not allow Republicans to enfranchise both blacks and women simultaneously and that, for the sake of the Union's perpetuity, black men must have the right to vote first. He urged his colleagues to act "with little reference to theory": "You are bound by the necessity of the case."[141] Richard Yates and Henry Anthony endorsed women's suffrage in principle, but they believed that the timing was not yet ripe for it.[142] For other opponents, women's suffrage was simply political heresy. The idea of universal suffrage, argued Morrill, the bill's floor leader, would "contravene" all notions of the family: "'put asunder' husband and wife, and subvert the fundamental principles of family government, in which the husband is, by all usage and law, human and divine, the representative head."[143] Both Morrill and Frelinghuysen believed that by nature women were unfit for any political duties. God had stamped upon women "a milder, gentler nature, which not only makes them shrink from, but disqualifies them for the turmoil and battle of public life," in Frelinghuysen's words. Women's mission was "at home, by their blandishments and their love to assuage the passions of men as they [came] in from the battle of life."[144] As a result, Cowan's amendment was rejected.[145]

The Senate passed the District of Columbia suffrage bill (S. No. 1) on December 13, 1866, with a strict partisan vote. As table 1.1 shows, a substantial majority of Republicans voted for the bill, whereas more than half of the Democrats voted against it.[146] The next day, the House passed the bill again by a strict party vote of 118 to 46.

President Johnson vetoed the bill, reasoning that suffrage required "elevated character and patriotism of the elector" and that indiscriminate congressional enfranchisement of "a new class, wholly unprepared by previous habits and opportunities," would only degrade the "highest attribute of an American citizen."[147] But both houses overturned Johnson's veto and the District of Columbia suffrage bill became law.[148] Johnson was right when he described the District of Columbia suffrage bill as a danger to the states' rights to regulate suffrage. Some Republicans such as Frelinghuysen had hinted that the District of Columbia bill could be an experiment "in view of possible necessity of resorting to measures of this nature to secure a loyal constituency elsewhere."[149]

However, when the Senate began to debate the bills regarding the admission of Nebraska and Colorado on December 14, 1866, one day after it passed the District of Columbia suffrage bill, the previous array of Republican support of black suffrage changed.[150] Radical Republicans, led by Charles Sumner and George F. Edmunds (R-Vt.), asked to make impartial suffrage a condition for

Table 1.1

Senate Passage of District of Columbia Suffrage Bill

Party	Vote Distribution			
	Yeas	Nays	Not Voting	Total Votes
Republican	31	4	4[a]	39
	(80%)	(10%)	(10%)	(100%)
Democrat	1	7	3	11
	(9%)	(64%)	(27%)	(100%)
Others[b]	0	2	0	2
		(100%)		(100%)
Summary	32	13	7	

Source: CG, 39 Cong. 2 sess., 109.

[a] This includes Aaron H. Craig (R-N.H.), who was absent when the vote was taking place but later asked to have his vote recorded as *yea*.

[b] This category, which also appears in some of the subsequent tables throughout the study, includes those congressmen who were identified as "Whigs," "Conservatives," "Independents," or "Populists" by United States Congress, *Biographical Directory of the United States, 1774–1989 . . .* (Washington, D.C.: Government Printing Office, 1989).

the admission of the new states.[151] Others, lining up behind Wade, opposed such a move. The moderates' opposition rested on the rationale that the District of Columbia was a federal territory over which Congress wielded "plenary and supreme" power, but in Nebraska, a would-be state, Congress had no power to pass "a law to fix the qualifications of voters in a State that ha[d] not been in rebellion."[152] Both Philip Johnson (R-Pa.) and Jacob M. Howard (R-Mich.) reminded their radical colleagues that at the last session, the joint committee purposefully retreated from attempting to incorporate suffrage into the Fourteenth Amendment.[153]

The radicals' rationale was different: Congress had the power to set up conditions for new states, and, to guarantee a republican form of government, Congress had to be able to exercise its "legislative functions." Congress no longer functioned as "a mere machine" passively accepting new states but, in Edmunds's words, had "a right to create States" on certain conditions that Congress saw as proper and necessary.[154] When James Doolittle (R-Wis.) accused Edmunds of "a fundamental error" in defining congressional functions, Edmunds

Table 1.2

House Passage of District of Columbia Suffrage Bill

Party	Vote Distribution			
	Yeas	Nays	Not Voting	Total Votes
Republican	111	11	16	138
	(80%)	(8%)	(12%)	(100%)
Democrat	4	31	8	43
	(9%)	(72%)	(19%)	(100%)
Others	3	4	4	11
	(28%)	(36%)	(36%)	(100%)
Summary	118	46	28	

Source: *CG*, 39 Cong. 2 sess., 138.

offered a powerful yet highly creative rebuttal: "It is the act of admission that creates the political corporation which is a State. . . . If it is our will that creates it and brings it into life, we may modify and limit the exercise of its will according to our notions of justice and propriety." He explained the difference between his opponents (Doolittle, Wade, and Howard) and himself: "[The former] suppose that the State is a State in spite of us, and that we merely make a bargain and a treaty with her by which we came into an alliance"; his position was that the "law of Congress" created the state.[155] Sumner chimed in that if blacks were denied suffrage, the state government of Nebraska could not be republican. "It may be 'republican' according to the imperfect notions of an earlier period, or even according to the standard of Montesquieu, but it cannot be 'republican' in a country which began its national life in disregard of received notions and the standards of the past."[156] The radical arguments reflected not only a spirit of rational reform but also a profound understanding of the meanings of the nation's recent historical changes. Upon both, they constructed a novel relation between the federal and state government and a new definition of American constitutionalism. Finally, on January 9, 1867, with a plurality of two, the Senate accepted Edmunds's proposal that impartial suffrage be made a precondition for Nebraska's admission. On the same day, the Senate passed the bill.[157]

The House debate on the Nebraska bill focused on the same question, with James Ashley, Thaddeus Stevens, and George Boutwell heading the radical

Table 1.3

Senate Acceptance of Edmunds Amendment to the Nebraska Admission Bill

| | Vote Distribution | | | |
Party	Yeas	Nays	Not Voting	Total Votes
Republican	19	10	10	39
	(50%)	(25%)	(25%)	(100%)
Democrat	0	7	4	11
		(64%)	(36%)	(100%)
Others	1	1	0	2
	(50%)	(50%)		(100%)
Summary	20	18	14	

Source: CG, 39 Cong. 2 sess., 360.

force and John Bingham and James G. Blaine the moderates. The House modified the Senate bill essentially by replacing the Edmunds amendment with the "Boutwell amendment," which requested the impartial suffrage condition for Nebraska but asked the state legislature to accept the condition by a public proclamation.[158] Joined by five Democrats and five independents, the House Republicans carried the Boutwell amendment with a weak majority. The House then accepted the Nebraska bill on January 15, 1867.[159] The next day the Senate concurred in the House amendment to the bill.[160]

The discussion of the Nebraska admission bill cleared the way for the Colorado measure (S. No. 462). Both houses quickly passed the Colorado admission bill with impartial suffrage as a requirement for its admission. A few days before, both houses passed a bill prohibiting the denial of suffrage "in any of the Territories of the United States," or any territory to be organized thereafter, "to any citizen thereof, on account of race, color, or Previous condition of servitude." The bill became law on January 31, 1867, without the president's signature.[161] When Johnson vetoed the Nebraska and Colorado admission bills,[162] both houses overturned his veto on the Nebraska bill.[163] The Senate, however, failed to override Johnson's veto on the Colorado bill, falling short of two-thirds majority.[164]

Thus, by early February 1867, by pushing the four laws through Congress, Republicans enfranchised blacks in the District of Columbia and unorganized

Table 1.4

House Acceptance of Boutwell Amendment to the Nebraska Admission Bill

| Party | Vote Distribution | | | |
	Yeas	Nays	Not Voting	Total Votes
Republican	77	35	25	137
	(56%)	(26%)	(18%)	(100%)
Democrat	5	32	6	43
	(12%)	(74%)	(14%)	(100%)
Others	5	3	3	11
	(46%)	(27%)	(27%)	(100%)
Summary	87	70	34	

Source: CG, 39 Cong. 2 sess., 481.

federal territories and, most important, established a precedent for national enactment of black suffrage, at least in the federal territories. The radicals had no
intention of hiding their thoughts on how this precedent could be applied to the
South, as Boutwell stated during the debate of the Nebraska bill:

> I think the jurisdiction of Congress over a Territory applying for admission into
> the Union as a State is clear and exclusive. . . . My own opinion is that when, by an
> arbitrary rule, a State deprives a particular class of men and their posterity for all
> time of participation in the government under which they live, just to that extent
> the government fails to be republican in form. . . . [Congress] can hold the Terri-
> tory as a Territory until its people frame a government which we are willing to ac-
> cept as republican in form.[165]

It did not take long for the Republican Congress to apply the principles established in the debates of early 1867 to the case of the South. However, it was
not the Republican triumph in the District of Columbia and territory bills, nor
any sort of conspiracy, as often suggested, that prompted Republicans to impose
black suffrage on the South in March 1867.[166] As shown in the previous pages,
Republicans were not firmly united in dealing with the black suffrage issue,
even with the admission of new states. The grave political situation between the
second half of 1866 and early 1867 had given Republicans a chance to unite on
the southern black suffrage issue. The most serious challenge the Republicans

now faced was the ratification of the Fourteenth Amendment. The adoption of the amendment required ratification by at least four of the southern states, plus all of the states then under Republican control; but under Johnson's influence, none of the southern states was willing to ratify the amendment. The failure of the amendment could mean the defeat of congressional reconstruction and, consequently, give Johnson an opportunity to restore his reconstruction program. Calling congressional reconstruction "absolute despotism," Johnson himself stood uncompromisingly against the amendment and the whole principle of congressional reconstruction.[167] Republicans were compelled by the situation to work out a more forceful and decisive policy, with which they hoped to secure not only the ratification of the amendment but also congressional control over Reconstruction.

The primordial form of the Reconstruction Act (H.R. 1143), as introduced by Stevens to the House on February 6, 1867, contained no provision regarding black suffrage. The bill would reorganize the South under the direction of Congress by the national mechanism of federal military enforcement.[168] After a day of fierce and intense debate on the merit of the bill, Ashley, who had fought tirelessly to link black suffrage with the reconstruction of the South since the beginning of the Thirteenth Amendment, offered an amendment to the original bill on February 8. His proposal provided that military rule would cease in a southern state after that state adopted a new constitution which would "secure to all citizens of the United States within said State, irrespective of race or color, the equal protection of the laws, including *the right of the elective franchise*, and [would] ratify the proposed amendment to the Constitution of the United States."[169] The Ashley amendment was crucial in two fundamental ways: it made black suffrage (or impartial suffrage) and ratification of the Fourteenth Amendment a condition for readmission; and, by doing so, it mapped out a more concrete, feasible, and workable plan for the South to be reorganized than the purely military enforcement did.

Four days later, Bingham, the leading voice of Republican moderates, offered a more comprehensive amendment, which conspicuously contained the two essential elements (ratification of the Fourteenth Amendment and black suffrage) offered by Ashley.[170] On the same day, Blaine went a step further: he demanded that the new state constitutions be approved by manhood suffrage in addition to all that was required by Bingham's amendment. The purpose of his proposal, Blaine said, was to "bring Congress up to the declaration of making equal suffrage a condition-precedent to admission," which would be the basis of south-

Table 1.5

Senate Passage of the Reconstruction Bill with Sherman Substitute

| | Vote Distribution | | | |
Party	Yeas	Nays	Not Voting	Total Votes
Republican	27	2	10	39
	(69%)	(5%)	(26%)	(100%)
Democrat	1	7	3	11
	(9%)	(64%)	(27%)	(100%)
Others	1	1	0	2
	(50%)	(50%)		(100%)
Summary	29	10	13	

Source: *CG*, 39 Cong. 2 sess., 1469.

ern restoration.[171] Bingham agreed, adding that his amendment would give the South the opportunity to "act in the premises" voluntarily and in conformity with the federal constitutional amendment. Stevens opposed such linkage. The Ashley amendment was a good one, he commented, but it had "no business here."[172] Under Stevens's pressure, the House accepted his own unamended bill on February 13.[173] But the theories of Ashley, Bingham, and Blaine did not die; the Senate revived them during its discussion of the House bill. The Senate amended the House bill with what is known as the "Sherman substitute," which became the fifth section of the final version of the first Reconstruction Act of 1867. The Sherman substitute incorporated all the essential elements of the Ashley, Bingham, and Blaine proposals in the House.[174] The fifth section, according to Sherman, was "the main and material feature" of the bill, which at its heart was to ask the South to extend the right to vote to "all their male citizens, without distinction of race or color." The outraged Sumner could do little to stop the passage of the amended bill in the Senate.[175]

After adding another section to the bill that barred the disfranchised whites from holding offices, the House Republicans accepted the Senate version.[176] The Senate then accepted the House modifications.[177] On March 2, 1867, despite Johnson's veto, the bill became law, finally making black suffrage the indispensable constitutional requirement for Reconstruction.

Table 1.6
House Acceptance of Senate Amendments (Sherman Substitute)
to the Reconstruction Bill

Party	Vote Distribution			
	Yeas	Nays	Not Voting	Total Votes
Republican	115	6	15	136
	(85%)	(4%)	(11%)	(100%)
Democrat	5	36	2	43
	(12%)	(84%)	(4%)	(100%)
Others	6	4	1	11
	(55%)	(36%)	(9%)	(100%)
Summary	126	46	18	

Source: *CG*, 39 Cong. 2 sess., 1400.

It is not the purpose of this study to repeat the story of how the Reconstruction Act of 1867 was made, which has been well documented in several studies.[178] It is, however, important to point out that the final enactment of black suffrage in the South by the Reconstruction Act was closely connected with the congressional debates of the suffrage legislation in the District of Columbia and the federal territories, in terms of constitutional rationale and political expediency. Those earlier laws established the principle that the federal government could mandate impartial suffrage as a means for the would-be states to organize "a republican form of government." Although many moderate Republicans had opposed this principle on the ground that it interfered with a right traditionally reserved to the states, during the debates of the Reconstruction Act, the moderates – almost voluntarily – applied the radical principle to reorganizing the South and made black suffrage a condition for the new state governments of the South. Although they refused to accept the radical theory that the southern states were "conquered territories," their firm support for black suffrage in the Reconstruction Act indicated that the moderates had surely moved in a direction far more radical than they had originally thought possible. Moderate Republicans did so probably because of the pressure from the radicals, who wanted to punish and remake the South with more radical and extreme measures. But they had come to realize, as John Sherman did, that the only way to reduce Reconstruction radicalism, destroy Johnson's hope for a political resurrection, and pursue a reconstruction that was reasonable enough for their own conscience and safe enough for the party's unity was black suffrage.[179] This move was highly consequential. It would open the way, at least theoretically, for the coming of the Fifteenth Amendment.

The Making of the Fifteenth Amendment

The advancement of the Republican cause in the South encouraged the radical Republicans to push black suffrage into the North. Rejecting the New York *Independent*'s proposal to enfranchise blacks throughout the country by a new constitutional amendment, Sumner told Theodore Tilton, "We cannot wait for the slow process of a constitutional amendt. The change should be at once." He wanted nationwide black enfranchisement "by act of Congress," which was "just as constitutional as the other." Sumner had in mind the coming presidential election of 1868. If Congress could pass a law to make black suffrage national before the election, "every Northern state [would] move into line with the colored vote to strengthen the Republican cause."[180] But early in 1867, Sumner had completely rejected the assertion that suffrage was a "privilege" instead of an essential right. In the meantime, drawing lessons from the ordeal of Reconstruction, he came to the conclusion that black suffrage as a political necessity and black suffrage as a principle were inseparable:

> Without the colored vote, the white unionists would have been left in the hands of the rebel. Loyal govt. could not be organized. The colored vote was a necessity. This I saw at the beginning, & insisted pertinaciously that it should be secured. It was on this ground, rather than principle, that I relied most; but the argument of principle was like a re-inforcement.[181]

George William Curtis, the editor of the Republican *Harper's Weekly*, agreed. He told his audience at the New York state constitutional convention in 1867 that "emancipation could be completed and secured only by the ballot in the hands of the emancipated class" and that "civil rights were a mere mocking name until political power gave them substance."[182] Challenging the racial discrimination in voting in New York, Francis Lieber pointed out "an inconsistency" in the state constitution: that a black American citizen possessing no freehold worth $250 had no right to vote in New York, whereas "foreigners [were allowed] to vote in State elections immediately after their arrival."[183] "It is a barbarous heresy to maintain that a government is made only for individuals of a certain race," Lieber cried. To deny suffrage on the ground of "physical nature" was as absurd as the ancient Crimean prince who taxed people according to the color of their eyes.[184]

In 1867, Republicans in several northern states intended to take the issue of black suffrage to the people. The *Nation* warned that universal suffrage was not "a kind of panacea" and reminded the party that it was not a party of "equal suffrage" but a party "of good government, of virtue, knowledge, and understanding."[185] Women's suffrage activists also pressed the party to commit to their cause, but, as Elizabeth Cady Stanton and Susan B. Anthony found out in Kansas, Republicans were reluctant to risk linking black suffrage to women's voting rights. Determined to resist black suffrage, California Democrats warned voters that the Republican doctrine of universal suffrage would lead to an "Asiatic" influx.[186] Republicans in Maryland acted with extreme caution, but when they decided to endorse universal manhood suffrage in 1867, Democrats were already in control.[187]

The outcomes of the elections revealed a sharp contrast between the North and South. According to James M. McPherson, in the South, with the enactment of the Reconstruction Act, about 735,000 blacks and 635,000 whites were registered to vote; between 10 and 15 percent of the potential white electorate was barred from voting. The turnout of black voters was high, ranging from 70 percent in Georgia to nearly 90 percent in Virginia. Blacks constituted a majority in Mississippi, South Carolina, Louisiana, Alabama, and Florida, and their votes secured the southern ratification of the Fourteenth Amendment and other congressional conditions. In June 1868, Arkansas, North Carolina, South Carolina, Georgia, Louisiana, Alabama, and Florida would be readmitted to Congress.[188] But in the North, the Republican campaign for black suffrage was lost. Ohio voters defeated the Republican constitutional amendment that, following national Republican policy, linked black suffrage and disfranchisement of the supporters of the Confederacy. Voters also defeated black suffrage in Kansas and Minnesota. In April 1868, Michigan voters would also reject a black suffrage amendment for the state's new constitution that Republicans helped to formulate in 1867.[189] Democrats won a majority in both houses of the state legislature in New York, New Jersey, and Ohio. Ohio Republicans lost a federal Senate seat occupied by Ben Wade and only by a narrow margin secured the governorship of Rutherford B. Hayes, who spoke for black suffrage. Republicans also lost gubernatorial races in Connecticut, Maine, and California.[190]

The 1867 elections put a halt to the Republican drive for black suffrage. In John Bigelow's view, that quest had cost the party dearly, given his belief that the "masses" in the North refused to accept black suffrage "without preparation and without the consent of the white population of the South."[191] The *Nation*, now taking an independent stand, warned that northerners were actually concerned more about "the kind of government in which the black man [was] to share than about the precise mode or time in which he [was] to share in it."[192] Facing strong and persistent popular distaste for black suffrage, the Republicans, in William Gillette's words, perceived the course of black suffrage in the North as "hazardous" and hoped to postpone it "until the right occasion."[193] As a result, the Republican platform in 1868 presented a double standard on the issue of black suffrage. While the party pressed the South to accept black suffrage by congressional mandate, it assured northern voters that "the question of suffrage in all the loyal States properly belong[ed] to the people of those States."[194] The obvious contradiction made the party's suffrage policy look ideologically inconsistent, politically expedient, and constitutionally awkward—and it was.

Despite Republican caution, the result of the presidential election of 1868 was by no means encouraging. Although Ulysses S. Grant, the Republican candidate for the presidency, won the office, his victory was only a plurality of slightly more than 300,000 out of 5.7 million votes against Horatio Seymour, who once had been an antiwar Democrat. Of the seven southern states that could vote, the Republican majorities were tenuous, with 17,000 in South Carolina, 12,000 in North Carolina, 4,000 in Alabama, and even less in Arkansas. Louisiana and Georgia, where the Republican vote had been effectively curtailed by violence and intimidation, went overwhelmingly Democratic, and the other five were Republican only by a close margin. The voting results showed that except in the New England states, where Republicans were in control, the party had no dominant majority in other parts of the country. Meanwhile, Democrats gained eleven seats in the House but lost two senators.[195]

The election of 1868 offered some important indications for the Republicans. Since Grant won a plurality of only about 300,000 in an election in which an estimated 500,000 blacks cast their votes for the Republicans, black votes clearly were crucial to his election. Although Iowa and Minnesota adopted black suffrage by referendum in 1868, black men still could not vote in eleven of the twenty-one northern states and all five of the border states. One-sixth of the country's black people lived in these states, and they, as Sumner believed, undoubtedly would have supported the Republicans if they were given the ballot. Referring to Connecticut, Sumner told his colleagues, "There are three thousand fellow-citizens in that state at the call of Congress to take their place at the ballot box. . . . Wherever you most need them, there they are; and be assured they will all vote for those who stand by them in the assertion of Equal Rights."[196] Demands for suffrage reached Congress in the form of petitions from local blacks in such northern states as Pennsylvania and New York. Southern blacks also expressed their desire to have equal suffrage conferred by a constitutional amendment.[197] In the meantime, Republicans had to face the ideological inconsistency in their policy, as Blaine recalled years later, of "something so obviously unfair and unmanly" in imposing black suffrage in the South but leaving it to local discretion in the North. The party became "heartily ashamed" of this double standard in 1868, Blaine claimed, and moved immediately after the election of Grant to formulate the Fifteenth Amendment so that "suffrage, as between the races, [would] by organic law be made impartial in all the States of the Union."[198] Thus, a combination of various factors — political calculations regarding the party's future, the need to resolve the ideological dilemma, fears of a quick Democratic return in the impending elections, and the desire to settle the political status of blacks and secure the achievements of the Republican Reconstruction — finally formed the dynamics for the creation of the Fifteenth Amendment.

As in the debates over the previous laws relating to black suffrage, the discussion of the Fifteenth Amendment bill from January to February 1869 also featured internal disagreements, disruptions, and compromises within the Republican party.[199] By the time the different proposals for a constitutional amendment on black suffrage were introduced into both houses in January 1869, Republicans seemed to agree that something had to be done to consolidate black suffrage in the South and to enable black men to vote in the northern and border states. But the various proposals revealed the differences among the Republicans as to how the amendment should be formulated. Emerging from the measures introduced into both houses and the debates were four versions of the would-be amendment: the first would prohibit both the state and federal governments from denying citizens the right to vote and to hold office on account of race, color, or previous condition of servitude; the second would only forbid the states from doing so; the third would also forbid the states to impose literacy, nativity, and property qualifications on voters; the fourth would simply affirm that all male citizens aged twenty-one or older had the right to vote.[200]

These proposals revealed the Republican disagreement over whether the amendment should be made merely an imposition of restrictions on the state power to regulate suffrage or an affirmation of the fundamental change in the ultimate authority controlling the qualifications for suffrage among the citizens of the United States. In other words, should this amendment focus on providing a pragmatic and expedient solution to the constitutional inconsistency and political urgency confronting the party, or should it be considered a permanent enlargement of national power? Radical Republicans wanted the amendment to confer the right to vote in affirmative language and wipe out race, property, nativity, and literacy qualifications. Moderates wanted no fundamental change in the ultimate authority to grant suffrage, which many of them still regarded as a state right. Some moderate Republicans, especially from the Northeast and from the West, supported black suffrage on the condition that their states would retain some kind of freedom either in conferring suffrage or in setting voting qualifications, such as a nativity test to restrict the Chinese or a literacy test to bar the Irish. They insisted that the amendment be limited to removing the race qualification for voting. And the connotation of the word *race*, as understood by these Republicans, specifically meant "African race," not other nonwhite races, such as the Chinese, who were either born in the United States or might later become American citizens through naturalization.[201]

From the beginning of the debate, radicals tried to enlarge the scope of the amendment. The House debate started with George S. Boutwell's proposal, which provided that "the right of any citizen of the United States to vote [would] not be denied or abridged by the United States by reason of race, color, or previous condition of slavery."[202] Ohio Republican Samuel Shellabarger tried to amend Boutwell's proposal with a substitute conferring suffrage on all males over twenty-one years old, except for former rebels, and to abolish all state literacy and property tests. But the House rejected the substitute by a substantial majority and instead approved Boutwell's wording, which was focused in object and moderate in scope.[203]

The original Senate proposal, introduced by William Stewart in behalf of the Committee on the Judiciary, was similar to the Boutwell proposal, except that Stewart's proposal also forbade the denial of the right to hold office for racial reasons. With the office-holding phrase deleted, the proposal was essentially the final version of the Fifteenth Amendment. Stewart included the office-holding phrase, according to Gillette, in an effort "to elicit southern Republican support."[204] Indeed, it was essentially a moderate bill, as Stewart, a recent halfway radical, knew well from talking to his associates about how limited the party's resources were in support of a radical measure. But other Republicans wanted the bill to be still more explicitly limited in its goal. About ten days after the Senate started debating Stewart's proposal on January 28, Jacob Howard of Michigan proposed to specify that the amendment was to protect the suffrage of "citizens of United States of African descent." But the Senate rejected his plan.[205] Later, the Senate accepted a proposal made by Henry Wilson, who asked to abolish all discrimination or qualifications for voting or holding office because of "race, color, nativity, property, education, or religious belief." The Wilson plan was certainly revolutionary: it placed in the hands of Congress virtually all voting qualifications except age and residence. The *National Anti-Slavery Standard* called it "important, comprehensive."[206] But when this plan, combined with a proposal to reform the electoral college system presented by Indiana Republican Oliver P. Morton, was sent to the House on February 15, the House defeated it right away. In two days, the Senate would also reject the Wilson plan as Morton and other Republicans withdrew their support. Obviously, both houses did not want to give Congress comprehensive power to regulate suffrage.[207]

When the Senate started again with the Stewart proposal on February 17, Howard asked to remove the phrase "by the United States," which he believed contained the notion that Congress could regulate suffrage. Edmunds of Vermont objected. Without saying that Congress had the power to regulate suffrage, he defended the congressional power to establish black suffrage in a careful conceptualization: "If the right to regulate suffrage in any respect belongs to Congress, as in the Territories it does, and in the District of Columbia, then when we prohibit Congress from exercising that right on a particular ground we leave its other powers unimpaired, exactly as they stood before." The Senate eventually rejected the Howard proposal.[208] Understanding Edmunds's points, Joseph Fowler of Tennessee tried to amend the bill by a general declaration that voting and office-holding rights were not to be "denied or abridged by the United States or by any State," with the intention to stop the congressional disfranchisement of former rebels. His attempt was unsuccessful.[209]

James Doolittle, a Republican from Wisconsin, also wanted to terminate white disfranchisement for a different reason: Chinese suffrage. Doolittle believed that with this amendment and revision of the nation's naturalization law (which he mentioned that Sumner was ready to submit), suffrage would be open to the Chinese. Chinese suffrage "in California and Oregon and on all the Pacific slope" would be "as potent as negro suffrage in the States of the South, perhaps more so; for while the negro population of the South [would] be diminishing, in all human probability," the Chinese would be "pouring in upon our western shores by hundreds of thousands." To counterbalance the "policy of extending political power in this Government to the inferior races," Doolittle suggested, Congress had to stop "the disfranchisement and exclusion of members of the superior race, unless they [were] convicted of crimes."[210] After numerous refusals to adjourn, the Senate finally passed the bill by a vote of 35 to 11, with 20 absent, including Sumner, Sherman, Trumbull, Howard, and Yates.[211]

When the Senate bill reached the House, John A. Logan (R-Ill.) moved to strike the office-holding right, because that was a state right. Once blacks had the right to vote, Logan reasoned, they would "take care of the right to hold office."[212] But, pushed by Bingham, the House amended the Senate bill by reinstating the once-defeated Wilson and Shellabarger proposals but deleting from the amendment the words "by the United States." This move dismayed House radicals such as Boutwell, who wanted a limited bill to be passed before the close of the session.[213] On February 24, the joint conference between the House (represented by Boutwell, Bingham, and Logan) and the Senate (represented by Stewart, Roesco Conkling, and Edmunds) produced a compromise: to retain the original Senate bill (Stewart version) but drop the office-holding right.[214] The next day, the House approved the compromise by a vote of 144 to 44, with 35 not voting.[215] In the Senate, however, the conference report was challenged by a mixture of Republicans and Democrats, including Wilson, Pomeroy, Doolittle, Edmunds, Sawyer, Norton, and Warner. Edmunds, who refused to sign the conference report because it struck out the words "to hold office," accused the committee of "merely asserting the shadow while it wiped out the substance." Warner from Alabama was disappointed in the moderate tone of the bill. As the session drew to a close, Republican senators realized that unless the Senate accepted the compromise, as Justin Morrill (R-Vt.) put it, the suffrage amendment would have to be abandoned by this Congress. On

February 26, 1869, the Senate accepted the amendment by a vote of 39 to 13, with 14 absent, including Edmunds, Sumner, Henderson, and Pomeroy.[216]

The final version of the Fifteenth Amendment empowered the federal government to prohibit the states from excluding blacks from voting on account of race, color, and previous condition of servitude. Thus, this amendment constitutionally recognized the principle of political equality between black and white male Americans, as established by the suffrage legislation between 1866 and 1867 and the first Reconstruction Act of 1867. By making black suffrage part of national politics, the Fifteenth Amendment had pushed Reconstruction far beyond the restoration of the old political order in the southern states and, in a way, redefined the rules of American politics and American democracy. It elevated congressional reconstruction, as led by the Republican party, to a point that many prewar radical reformers had never dreamed of being able to achieve.

The amendment, however, did not directly and explicitly confer suffrage on a single black person, in the South or in the North. It did not specify whether the ultimate authority over suffrage belonged to the federal government or state governments. Like the Thirteenth and Fourteenth Amendments, it was essentially the work of moderate Republicans, who had endeavored to balance the need to modify or change the original structure of federal-state relations with the need to retain a structure of some kind. Given their political and ideological

Table 1.7

House Passage of Final Conference Report for the Fifteenth Amendment Bill

| Party | Vote Distribution | | | |
	Yeas	Nays	Not Voting	Total Votes
Republican	140	5	24	169
	(84%)	(2%)	(14%)	(100%)
Democrat	3	38	9	50
	(6%)	(76%)	(18%)	(100%)
Others	1	1	2	4
	(25%)	(25%)	(50%)	(100%)
Summary	144	44	35	

Source: CG, 40 Cong. 3 sess., 1563–64.

Table 1.8

Senate Passage of Final Conference Report for the Fifteenth Amendment Bill

Party	Vote Distribution			
	Yeas	Nays	Not Voting	Total Votes
Republican	38	3	13	54
	(70%)	(6%)	(24%)	(100%)
Democrat	0	8	1	9
		(89%)	(11%)	(100%)
Others	1	2	0	3
	(33%)	(67%)		(100%)
Summary	39	13	14	

Source: CG, 40 Cong. 3 sess., 1641.

limitations, the Republicans seemed unable to come up with any better solution than the Fifteenth Amendment to deal with black suffrage in 1869. Ideologically, the party had not been able to develop a genuine appreciation and respect for blacks' political rights. Undoubtedly, some radical Republicans believed in political equality between white and black Americans and regarded it as essential to the existence of American democracy. But most Republicans were unwilling to accept the radicals' reasoning. Rather, they regarded suffrage as a political privilege that could be granted only to those who were legitimate members of society. To give the freedmen the vote would be to act against the prevailing standard of the social, cultural, and racial values of contemporary America.

The evolution of the Fifteenth Amendment reflected the strengths and weaknesses of American constitutionalism. The idea of equality as pronounced by the Declaration of Independence was the main ideological source for Reconstruction politics, and the Civil War and emancipation had generated an enormous dynamic for realizing that idea. The radical Republicans, as they had sincerely showed, wanted to carry on an idealistic reform with some measures more revolutionary than the Thirteenth, Fourteenth, and Fifteenth Amendments. But they were handicapped from doing so, both politically and constitutionally. To transform black suffrage from a largely political idea of the former abolitionists into a positive constitutional right for every freedman required political resources, historical opportunities, and constitutional mechanisms. But because the party was composed of such diverse interest groups, and because the process of constitutional change required so many compromises inside and outside the party, black men's political rights had been subjected to many confrontations and compromises. Very often, during the process of compromising, the original ideological core in favor of black suffrage was lost or transformed into a purely partisan concern to gain political advantages and to avoid political disadvantages. The compromises would continue after black suffrage was written into the Constitution. Thus, while male black Americans were proclaimed equal voters, the battle to maintain and effectuate their voting rights had just begun.

CHAPTER TWO

The Making of Federal Enforcement Laws, 1870–1872

Adoption of the Fifteenth Amendment and Ensuing Problems

Congress passed the Fifteenth Amendment on February 26, 1869, and it was immediately submitted to the states for ratification. New England states – including Connecticut, where now the Republicans were in control – promptly approved the amendment.[1] However, bitter fights over ratification ensued in the Middle Atlantic states. Radical Republicans in New York had demanded black suffrage at their 1867 state convention, but the subsequent defeat of that year had made them extremely cautious about raising the issue in state politics. Thus, for New York Republicans, the Fifteenth Amendment offered an opportunity to accomplish their earlier goal without whipping up local antiblack sentiments. With control of both houses of the state legislature, Republicans approved the amendment in 1869. When the next Democratic legislature voted to rescind the Republican decision, it was too late.[2] In Pennsylvania, where a radical attempt to revoke the state's black disfranchisement law was defeated in 1868, Republican were encouraged by Grant's election and approved the amendment by a strict party vote in March 1869. New Jersey accepted the amendment almost a year after its ratification, but Delaware rejected the amendment and would not approve it until 1901.[3]

Fearing that the amendment would benefit the Chinese, state legislators in states of the Far West, except in Nevada, rejected the amendment. In California, where the Chinese outnumbered blacks ten to one in 1870, linking the amendment to Chinese suffrage as a Democratic tactic to defeat the amendment was particularly successful. Oregon never took action on the amendment before its ratification was proclaimed.[4] Nevada Republicans managed to approve the amendment only after William Stewart, the state's native son in Washington and the principal framer of the amendment, had assured his associates back home that the amendment meant no enfranchisement for the Chinese by deleting the nativity test from its final version.[5]

In the border and midwestern states, the process of ratification was not uneventful. Kentucky rejected the amendment. In Maryland, the all-Democratic legislature unanimously refused to ratify the Fifteenth Amendment in February 1870, and only when the ratification of the amendment by the requisite twenty-eight states appeared certain did the state pass a black registration bill.[6] Their wartime unity crumbling, Republicans in Ohio managed to approve the amendment by a close vote.[7] Michigan Republicans were glad that the amendment would not "incur the enmity of Massachusetts by interfering with an educational test, or Rhode Island by striking down the nativity qualification, or all the Pacific states by exciting alarm over the possibility of John Chinaman voting himself into office." With dominant majorities in both houses, the Republicans voted to ratify the amendment within a week after it was submitted to the state.[8] Under Grant's pressure, Governor David Butler of Nebraska called a special session of the state legislature, which in February 1870 overwhelmingly ratified the amendment.[9] Other states, including Illinois, Indiana, Kansas, Wisconsin, and Iowa (where black suffrage had already been approved), duly ratified the amendment. Missouri Republicans for some reason forgot to ratify the second section of the amendment in their first ratification in March 1869 and hurriedly reratified the amendment in January 1870.[10]

In the South, all of the former Confederate states, except Tennessee, ratified the amendment within a year.[11] Since black suffrage had already become a practice since 1867, white southerners might have regarded it as a device to enfranchise blacks in the border and northern states rather than as an additional punishment on the South. Ratification nonetheless was a prerequisite for readmission for Texas, Virginia, Mississippi, and Georgia. Their ratification helped secure the required three-fourths majority for turning the amendment into part of the Constitution. On March 30, 1870, Secretary of State Hamilton Fish announced that the Fifteenth Amendment had become law.[12]

Among the northern populace, the passage and ratification of the Fifteenth Amendment produced the feeling that the long struggle against American slavery had finally, really come to an end. During April and May 1870, blacks throughout the country celebrated the ratification of the amendment. In Boston, about three thousand blacks, including the veterans of the Fifty-fourth and Fifty-fifth Massachusetts (Colored) Regiments, participated in the proces-

sion held in Boston Public Park. Black Missourians held celebrations throughout the state, and the procession of several thousand black voters and their
wives and children in St. Louis spanned more than two miles. In Detroit, blacks
carried portraits of Abraham Lincoln, Ulysses S. Grant, and John Brown and
sang verses that ran, "The ballot-box has come, now let us all prepare to vote;
With the party that made us free."[13] A white observer recorded the celebration
held by black Philadelphians on April 26, 1870:

> I took Lombard street at Twelfth and walked down to Fifth. That generally plain
> street looked lively with flags and other decorations. The occupants of the houses
> were mostly out of doors looking happy and important, and displaying rosettes
> and miniature flags.[14]

At the Baltimore celebration, a *New Era* correspondent wrote:

> Wagons draped in bunting and trimmed with evergreens, containing girls dressed
> in white and carrying small flags; Printing press, mounted on a wagon from which
> small sheets containing the text of the Fifteenth Amendment were struck and dis-
> tributed to the crowd as the procession moved along.[15]

Prominent antislavery activists, Republican lawmakers, and black leaders spoke
at the celebrations, all proclaiming the final victory in the revolution against
slavery. Addressing the Baltimore crowd in a letter, William Lloyd Garrison
claimed the final victory of the northern ideology of freedom. With blacks liberated and enfranchised, "the interests of the North [were] as the interests of the
South and the institutions of one section of the country essentially like those of
every other."[16]

To many antislavery veterans, the Fifteenth Amendment ushered the American nation into a new historical epoch, on which Frederick Douglass spoke at a
meeting in Albany on April 22, 1870:

> What does this fifteenth amendment mean to us? I will tell you. It means that the
> colored people are now and will be held to be, by the whole nation, responsible
> for their own existence and their well or ill being. It means that we are placed
> upon an equal footing with all other men. . . . It means that you and I and all of us
> shall leave the narrow places in which we now breathe, and live in the same com-
> fort and independence enjoyed by other men. It means industry, application to
> business, economy in the use of our earnings, and the building up of a solid char-
> acter. . . . It means that color is no longer to be a calamity; that race is to be no
> longer a crime; and that liberty is to be the right of all.[17]

Although not completely satisfied with the final version of the amendment, Wendell Phillips, a leading abolitionist and a radical Republican, shared Douglass's anticipation. Calling it "the grandest and most Christian act ever contemplated or accomplished by any Nation," Phillips believed that the amendment had elevated African Americans from the status of "a lately enslaved and still hated race to the full level of citizenship" and that the amendment was thus "the completion and guaranty of emancipation itself."[18] On April 9, 1870, ten days after the ratification of the Fifteenth Amendment was proclaimed, the American Anti-Slavery Society, of which Phillips was the president, announced the end of its existence. The spirit of the society, Douglass told his audience, would be carried on "through new instrumentalities" that would be devoted to the interests of the Indians, women, and "suffering humanity everywhere."[19]

Many Republican leaders shared the popular feeling that the Fifteenth Amendment settled the issue of black men's voting rights and signaled the end of the party's antislavery mission. Their reactions mingled optimism, relief, and paternalism. Acknowledging that the amendment's ratification was the issue that he had been worried about most since entering the White House, Grant expressed pleasure that black suffrage was "out of politics and reconstruction completed." In his special congratulatory message to the members of Congress, Grant urged the legislative branch to "encourage popular education" of blacks to ensure the better use of their new voting rights.[20] Other Republican leaders gave similar advice. Chief Justice Salmon P. Chase, one of the earliest Republican promoters of black suffrage, urged blacks to acquire faith, virtue, knowledge, patience, temperance, and "brotherly kindness" in order to exercise their political rights intelligently.[21]

For some Republicans, the ratification of the Fifteenth Amendment meant the end of the nation's antislavery history. They saw no need to continue to make race or previous condition of servitude an issue in national politics and urged leniency for the former rebels. In his reply to an invitation from Cincinnati blacks, who were organizing a celebration of the Fifteenth Amendment, Chase suggested that blacks urge Congress to remove the political disability imposed on former rebels in the South by the Fourteenth Amendment. By such actions, Chase stated, blacks could help establish peace, good will, and prosperity throughout the nation.[22] A Boston Republican paper believed that "the amendment would put an end to all the woes and leave the national energies free to adjust the disturbed industries of the country, and to unite in ministering to its highest prosperity and happiness."[23] Frowning on Missouri Republican senator Charles D. Drake's speech during the Georgia readmission debate, the *Chicago Tribune* simply advised the radical Republicans: "Let the colored man alone."[24]

The gratitude blacks demonstrated toward the Republican party seemed to assure the party of their firm support in the future. Watching blacks vote for the first time at a local election in Cincinnati, Governor Rutherford B. Hayes of Ohio recorded that they were "very happy" and voted Republican "almost solid."[25] The newly enfranchised blacks, the New York *Independent* predicted, would reinforce the party's strength both in the North and in the South in the coming congressional and state elections of 1870. The *New York Times* agreed, concluding that if the newly added eight hundred thousand black votes (of which about seven hundred thousand came from the South) were ever "cast solid, it would decide the result of general elections for many years to come."[26] *Harper's Weekly*, another staunch Republican organ, was even more optimistic, envisioning that, in a year or so, the Union would be "wholly restored, equal rights secured, the debts greatly reduced, taxation diminished, and foreign question[s] satisfactorily adjusted."[27]

Despite all the jubilation and optimism generated by the Fifteenth Amendment, Republicans in Congress remained rather cautious about the actual effects of the amendment. For radical Republicans, the loopholes were obvious. Theoretically, the amendment left unchallenged the ultimate authority of the states in regulating voters' qualifications. Its restriction of state power did not go beyond prohibiting exclusion on the basis of race, color, or previous condition of servitude. Other legal restrictions on voting, such as property, residence, and literacy tests, still could be added to state constitutions once the Democrats regained control of the South. Jacob M. Howard (R-Mich.) voiced this concern in the Senate debate over the admission of Virginia. He warned that if the state was allowed to impose a property qualification of two hundred dollars for voting, very few blacks in Virginia could vote and the Fifteenth Amendment would be "of little value."[28]

Republicans in Congress had good reason to worry about whether the political equality promised by the Fifteenth Amendment would be realized. Southern politics in the beginning of the 1870s was characterized not by the peace, good feeling, and prosperity that northerners had expected to see but by the violence, brutality, and disorder caused by Ku Klux Klan activities. Founded in early 1866 and composed mainly of extreme white supremacists and former rebels, the Ku Klux Klan spread throughout the South in late 1869 and 1870. Under the pretext of restoring social order, but really to destroy Republican-controlled state governments, Klansmen used force and terror to attack black voters who voted or would vote for Republican tickets, and whipped and murdered black Republican leaders in their homes. By 1870 the Klan, and such similar organizations as the Knights of the White Camelia and the White Brotherhood, had become deeply entrenched in almost every southern state. Serving as a military force for the Democratic party in the South, the Klan terror aimed both at overthrowing the Republican state governments and at privately persecuting Republican leaders and supporters, black and white. Accordingly, the Klan terror reduced the number of black voters, helping Democrats win control of state legislatures.[29]

Meanwhile, state and local Republicans were restrained by state constitutions from enacting a powerful and effective policy to combat the Klan's activities. Although the Republican government of Arkansas passed anti-Klan laws, they were seldom enforced. One reason for their ineffectiveness was that in many cases the state constitutions denied the governors the authority to suspend the writ of habeas corpus. In March 1870, this situation forced Governor William W. Holden of North Carolina to appeal to President Grant and Congress for federal legislation against the Klan and to punish Klansman by military tribunal. North Carolina, wrote Holden, was "in a State of insurrection," amid Klan outrages on both blacks and whites who supported the Republican party. But the state government could not overcome the terror for the lack of financial and human resources. "If Congress would authorize the suspension by the President of the writ of *habeas corpus* in certain localities, and if criminals could be arrested and tried before military tribunals, and shot," Holden suggested, "we should soon have peace and order throughout all this country."[30]

The intensity of the Klan's activities forced black legislators in Georgia to present a petition in March 1870 to Hiram R. Revels of Mississippi, the nation's first black senator. They declared:

> If elections take place this fall . . . violence and bloodshed will mark the course of such elections, and a fair expression of the will of the people cannot be had. We shall be driven from the polls, as in the Presidential election by armed and organized bands of rebels, and our State given over to the guidance and control of the most extreme men of the Democratic party.[31]

Petitions such as this revealed not only the urgent need to check the Ku Klux terror but also the foreseeable collapse of the Republican governments in the South if the federal government failed to take serious and prompt action to protect black voters. On March 16, 1870, when the Senate discussed the Georgia readmission bill, Revels rose "to plead for protection for the defenseless race" in the South and urged that the Republican party and Congress enforce the recent constitutional amendments. The black senator forcefully argued that black soldiers had rushed to rescue Union armies "thinned by death and disaster" and that the people in the North owed "to the colored race a deep obligation which it [was] no easy matter to fulfill."[32] Other Republican senators from the South warned their colleagues that "every mail" brought the details of "some revolting tragedy" and "that nothing but the most stringent of all laws and regulations [would] check this era of bloodshed and dethrone, this dynasty of the knife and bullet." The southern senators added that the Republican party had to "stand in carrying into effect the reconstruction policy, or the whole fabric of reconstruction, with all principles connected with it, amount[ed] to nothing at all."[33] Southern Democrats openly repudiated the amendment as a dead letter. A leading newspaper in West Virginia deemed that the amendment was "of no effect whatever in any State until the Legislature [made] its constitution and laws to conform to it, or until Congress enact[ed] laws to enforce it."[34]

The Klan terrorism alarmed the Republicans and motivated them to make the enforcement of the Fifteenth Amendment an "absolute necessity."[35] But Republican motivations were also derived from the party's desire to prevent Democratic frauds in the elections of northern cities. Edwards Pierrepont, a U.S. attorney in New York City who later would serve as Grant's third attorney general, expressly hoped that by enforcing the Fifteenth Amendment in New York, Democratic corruption would be reduced and Republican gains secured. In regard to the election of 1870, Pierrepont wrote, "The Democrats will *count* some 55 thousand majority—In this city they *count* at least, 28 thousand more than they poll—Congress *can* pass a law under which we can be protected—the XV amendment gives the *power*; whether Congress has the *courage* I know not; but cowardice never wins." He assured Grant that with enforcement machinery established, the Republicans could save the state, "and not otherwise." Obviously what Pierrepont suggested would link enforcement of the Fifteenth Amendment with the national combat against northern election fraud. Giving a liberal interpretation of the enforcement section (the second) of the amendment, Pierrepont told Grant "that national power [should] be used for national success."[36]

In fact, Pierrepont was not the only one to see the importance of the second section of the Fifteenth Amendment, which empowered Congress to enforce the first section by "appropriate legislation." Oliver P. Morton of Indiana reminded his fellow senators that the second section was "intended to give to Congress the power of conferring upon the colored man the full enjoyment of his right" and that both sections should be construed "in harmony with each other."[37] In effect, many Republicans, as demonstrated later during the debate over the enforcement laws, believed that the Fifteenth Amendment would remain ineffective until and unless it was enforced by further federal laws. Senator John Sherman, usually a moderate Republican, argued for enforcement laws, without which the amendment "would not have the full force and sanction of law." Sherman noted that enforcing the amendment was the Republicans' "imperative duty":

> Otherwise, Democratic judges who enforce the election laws in the different States, will cover themselves under this construction of the Constitution, and the fifteenth amendment will be practically disregarded in every community where there is a strong prejudice against negro voting.[38]

Sherman's argument represented a practical concern: the meaning of the Fifteenth Amendment had to be interpreted and defined by more federal enforcement legislation. In other words, the amendment simply established a principle; what was needed now was an explanation and application of that principle.

There was, however, another pragmatic and immediate concern: enforcement could help the party politically, as revealed by both Sherman and Pierrepont. Given the political tensions between the Democratic-buttressed Klan activities and recently established southern Republicanism, of which the black voting constituency was a part, northern Republicans saw enforcement as an opportunity to develop and consolidate the party's influence among southern voters. Blacks had the right to vote, but they must be made a long-term, loyal, Republican voting population in the South to resist the Democratic recovery that was under way. Republicans also hoped, as the later debates on enforcement laws show, that federal enforcement could help keep northern ballot boxes pure and clean and gave the party a decent chance to win.

Here, as many Republicans believed, partisan and national interests were not in contradiction; rather, they were in full harmony with each other. This was particularly so when the party had just won both a military and political contest with the South and Democrats over an issue of freedom versus slavery, an issue containing enormous moral implications. In fact, during much of the Reconstruction period, many Republicans frequently identified the party's political interests with the nation's interests. Whether the Republican party could shield black men's rights to vote was a test of the strength not only of national authority but also of the quality and endurance of the party's Reconstruction program. The political implication of enforcement, as Carl Schurz put it, was to use national power to impose a change upon the "popular prejudice, so long nourished ... [and] ... naturally arrayed against the enfranchisement of the former slave."[39] Thus, enforcing the Fifteenth Amendment would prevent "a repetition" of the Civil War crisis, Howard said, and maintain "the authority of the Union."[40] The amendment's enforcement was part of an effort to fulfill the political promises of the nation's recent revolution, which the party had led and hoped to continue to lead.

The Making of the Enforcement Act of May 31, 1870

Between May 1870 and June 1872, the Republican-controlled Congress passed five laws directly relating to the legal application of the Fourteenth and Fifteenth Amendments. Three of these laws were known as the "Enforcement Acts" or "Force Acts." Two of the three enforcement acts related specifically to enforcing the Fifteenth Amendment. The other enforcement act, or the "Ku Klux Force Act," and two other federal laws respectively dealt with enforcing the Fourteenth Amendment, amending naturalization laws, and appropriations, but they nonetheless contained provisions concerning enforcement of the Fifteenth Amendment.[41] Correlated, these enforcement laws represented the Republican party's efforts to give substantive meaning to the Fifteenth Amendment, to provide federal machinery for implementing the amendment, and to establish a uniform system of supervision and enforcement at national elections. Constitutionally speaking, these enforcement laws marked the beginning of using national law enforcement to protect citizens' rights in a modern scale.

Throughout the period in which the enforcement laws were debated, the Republican party maintained a dominant majority in Congress. At the second session of the Forty-first Congress, when the first and second enforcement laws were debated and passed, the Senate consisted of sixty-one Republicans, nine Democrats, and two Conservatives; in the House, Republicans outnumbered the sixty-four Democrats by nearly a hundred.[42] Given this political advantage, strengthened by Grant's occupancy of the White House, it seemed that the party would have little difficulty passing an enforcement law. But from the introduction of the first enforcement bill at the second session of the Forty-first

Congress in February 1870 to the passage of the last enforcement law at the second session of the Forty-second Congress in June 1872, intraparty tensions
plagued Republicans in both houses. They heatedly debated several issues: how
extensive enforcement should be; whose voting rights should be protected under the Fifteenth Amendment; how much power the federal enforcement officers should have; whether the president should be authorized to use military
force in their behalf; and whether individual citizens should be punished for
violating the Fifteenth Amendment. On the surface, the internal debates suggested that Republicans differed on policy making. But these debates revealed
a growing, underlying divergence in Republican opinion on the nature of Reconstruction and in political outlook, which would eventually split the party.
These debates further indicated how different groups of Republicans defined
the party's role in protecting black rights under the influence of the political
and economic interests they represented.

The first Republican clash over enforcement occurred when the first enforcement bill came up for discussion in both houses in May 1870. The House
bill (H.R. 1293) was introduced on February 21, 1870, but was not called for
discussion until May 16, 1870. The essential object of the House bill – according to John Bingham, who introduced it – was to enforce the Fifteenth Amendment nationwide. Bingham noted that black suffrage had been denied not only
in the South but also in such northern states as Ohio, his home state.[43] The
House bill confirmed the principle underlying the Fifteenth Amendment, that
racial discrimination against black voters should be removed in all states. It penalized by fine and imprisonment any action by federal and state officers that
obstructed citizens from registering and voting. It punished anyone who prevented, by force and violence, black citizens from exercising the suffrage. Finally, the bill authorized federal circuit judges to hear all cases concerning its
enforcement.[44]

Although brief, the House bill was pointedly unambiguous in direction and
harsh in punishment. Much of it focused on regulating the behavior of federal and state enforcement officers. Clearly, the House bill sought primarily to
punish violations committed by federal and state officials designated to handle
voting and registration matters in states. The bill also included two notable features: the enforcement of black suffrage at all elections, federal, state, or municipal, which expressed a broad interpretation of federal power; and the imposition of punishment upon individual citizens who prevented black voters from
voting. But the bill provided no enforcement machinery other than to designate

federal circuit and district judges to hear cases arising under the bill and considered no military apparatus.[45] The House bill was more declaratory than punitive.

Compared with the House bill, the Senate measure, introduced on April 19, was lengthy and comprehensive. The Senate bill (S. No. 810) grew out of several similar bills introduced by William Stewart, Oliver P. Morton, Charles Sumner, and George F. Edmunds from February to April. Although based on Edmunds's proposal, the final version was heavily reworked by the Committee on the Judiciary.[46] The seventeen-section Senate bill differed radically from the House bill in four respects.[47] First, the Senate bill established the principle that the act of fulfilling voting prerequisites was equivalent to the act of exercising the right to vote, so that any attempt or action by federal and state officials to prevent a black voter from meeting voting requirements was equivalent to an infringement of his right to vote. In other words, whereas the House bill defined illegal practices only as the refusal of federal or state election officials to receive taxes and to assess property for black voters, the Senate bill went much further, making it illegal to block black voters from registering and voting. Second, the Senate bill made it a federal crime for individuals to conspire against a citizen's enjoyment of rights secured by the Constitution and federal laws, including the right to vote. Whereas the House bill only lightly punished individual violations of the Fifteenth Amendment, the Senate bill penalized even individuals who conspired to deprive black voters of any of their civil and political rights. This was particularly important because much of black disfranchisement was carried out in the South by the Ku Klux Klan. Third, the Senate provided substantial enforcement machinery to execute the law. Whereas the House bill would just authorize federal courts to hear cases, the Senate would empower judges to appoint supervisors to watch the process of voting and registration, to make arrests, and to appoint deputies, who were also authorized to make arrests at polls; and it would give the president the power to use federal military force "for the purpose of the more speedy arrest and the trial of persons charged with a violation of this act."[48] Fourth, whereas the House measure pertained only to the Fifteenth Amendment, the Senate bill enforced both that law and the third section of the Fourteenth Amendment, by continuing to disqualify former rebels from holding office and removing those who had already held office. To prevent Klan actions against blacks outside the polling places, the bill also enforced some provisions of the Civil Rights Act of 1866.[49]

Obviously, Senate Republicans were far more perceptive than their House counterparts in detecting the problems in the South. They saw the real obstacle to black suffrage not in the election laws of southern states but in the actual process of practicing registration and voting, where the terrorism of the Ku Klux Klan proved far more dangerous than any statute. Many infringements of black suffrage, Senate Republicans believed, occurred not at the polls but on plantations and highways or other places with an "immediate relation to registration and to voting." Under the House bill, Stewart argued, a mob could "prevent registration, as they ha[d] done over in Virginia, and there [was] no penalty provided."[50] Furthermore, the Republican senators believed that more voting prerequisites would be "invented" to disfranchise black voters once Democrats took over southern state governments. Finally, they saw that the Republican state governments in the South alone could not stop the Klan terror or the rapid development of black disfranchisement by force and that the federal government was obliged to intervene.[51] Thus, the Senate intended an enforcement bill that would provide black voters with more complete protection, to be executed by an adequate federal enforcement machinery. The framers clearly expected the bill to be as comprehensive as possible to stop the rampant Ku Klux Klan, to protect the political rights of blacks, and to defeat Democratic attempts to regain political power in the South.

Both houses started to debate their own enforcement bills in mid-May. After a brief debate, the House passed its bill (H.R. 1293) with an overwhelmingly partisan vote on May 16.[52] In the Senate, the Republicans were virtually in a stalemate: the radicals wished to have a tougher bill, and the moderates wanted a milder bill. So when the House bill reached the Senate, moderate Republicans immediately asked to substitute the House version for the Senate's.[53] On May 18, having seen that it was impossible to neglect the House bill, Stewart, the Republican floor manager for the enforcement issue, agreed to have the House bill brought up for discussion. But as soon as the House bill was presented, Stewart, as urged by Sumner, asked to amend it by striking the original contents and inserting instead the whole Senate bill, under the title of the House bill. By this tactic, the House bill (H.R. 1293) virtually became the Senate bill (S. No. 810).[54]

Democrats wanted neither of the enforcement bills, but they particularly loathed the Senate bill. They saw it as a dangerous enlargement of federal power over states. Denying the existence of "the contingency or occasion for the passage of this act," George Vickers of Maryland argued that "the extension of suffrage to the African race was not intended to enlarge the power of Congress over the white race." For Vickers, the Republican effort to change the South's political habits by using national power would be futile because the ballot could not "elevate the colored man and make him equal to the white." Racial separation and inequality were God's creation, "which neither legislation nor bayonets can demolish."[55] Allen Thurman of Ohio called the Senate bill "inofficious and nugatory." Challenging the bill on legal grounds, Thurman argued that to put trials for election perjury in the hands of federal courts would "take away from the State courts the right to punish offenses" because election perjury was also an offense under many state laws. He also criticized the congressional authorization that the president could use military power to keep order at the polls as putting "a civil order under the military authority in its most vital point."[56] The Democrats regarded the Senate bill as particularly dangerous because it severely punished "not officers of a State at all, mere private individuals, [but] mere trespassers, mere breakers of the peace, mere violators of the State law." John P. Stockton (D-N.J.) charged the Senate measure with creating "a great many new offenses."[57]

However, the Republicans were also divided. A major criticism from the Republican camp was that the Senate bill was too harsh on former rebels and too broad in its scope. Orris S. Ferry of Connecticut, a conservative Republican, asked to remove sections 13 and 14 of the Senate bill concerning the political disability of southern whites. Disqualifying them from suffrage and political offices, Ferry argued, was "in defiance of the principles" upon which the Republican party rested and "simply doing an injury to the whole society."[58] His argument for restoring the political rights of the former rebels was that since the amendments established national citizenship and national political rights, the former rebels should be encouraged to "get out of this sectional isolation and come up to the grandeur of American nationality."[59] Ferry's real concern, however, was that the party should develop a conciliatory policy toward southern whites, from among whom it had to win adherents, or the Republicans would "go down in every Southern State." He deeply distrusted black voters, who, in his view, would "retain the old attachment to the old home and the old master, and those attachments [would] stay with them till they [died]."[60]

Ferry's remarks won support from a group of Republicans from the South, including Hiram R. Revels of Mississippi, who also urged political leniency for southern whites.[61] Frederick A. Sawyer of South Carolina praised Ferry for echoing "the sentiments of the vast majority of the people of the Republican party," adding that continuing the political disability of southern whites would "cut off from the Republican party one of its great elements of strength."[62] Conservative concerns about whether former rebels could hold office reflected their belief that the future of southern Republicanism depended on whites instead of black voters, a belief that would gain widespread acceptance in the party in the late 1870s and 1880s.

Radical Republicans were upset with the moderates and conservatives for advocating a "policy of conciliation."[63] They quickly saw the danger in returning former rebels to political offices. Without black suffrage firmly established in the South, Oliver P. Morton argued, allowing politically disabled whites to hold office would dismantle black suffrage and make the Fourteenth Amendment "a perfect nullity." If Jefferson Davis was allowed to come back to the Senate, Morton warned his colleagues, the black senator Hiram Revels would be driven out of the Senate. Thus the policy of conciliation, cried Morton, was "a mistaken policy that ha[d] failed from the very first." The former rebels, Morton stated, had been "cast in the mold of the rebellion," and in that mold they would remain.[64] Simon Cameron agreed, endorsing a measure that would require the enforcement of black suffrage prior to the removal of white disabilities. The Pennsylvania Republican boss argued that "the Rebels of the war were rebels still."[65]

Although many Republicans opposed restoring the rights of the former rebels to hold office, they were hesitant to commit to an extensive federal law. They feared that protecting black political rights to such a comprehensive degree might supersede the states' right to regulate elections and suffrage. For many, the regulation of suffrage had been and remained a state matter, over which the federal government had no authority except for the color and race qualifications. In their view, enforcement of black suffrage should never go beyond a strict and faithful interpretation of the Fifteenth Amendment.[66] John Sherman, who approved of enforcement but opposed a harsh bill, argued that the second and third sections of the Senate bill were "too vague and indefinite to found an indictment upon." The Fifteenth Amendment should be interpreted strictly, stated Sherman, not to the extent that all other state registration laws would be overruled to protect black voters.[67] Morton, who had opposed the moderate "policy of conciliation" because it restored former rebels to political office, criticized the Senate bill as being "broader than the fifteenth amendment." Morton held that the House bill was basically "confined to the subjects embraced in the fifteenth amendment," but "the provisions of the Senate bill [were] general, without reference to the fifteenth amendment."[68] These Republicans shared some of the Democrats' views on state regulation of suffrage and doubted federal authority to punish individual violators of the Fourteenth and Fifteenth Amendments. Where the line between state and federal authority over these issues remained undefined, these Republicans chose a milder and more restrained enforcement policy.

For the radicals, the states' rights theories were "fallacies," no more than an excuse to deny federal authority to protect the political and civil rights of American citizens. To those who fought the slave power before the war, the term *states' rights* was still an irritating reminder of the cause of the late war. Attacking the call for respecting states' rights, Carl Schurz argued that black liberties and civil rights had been subject to the mercy of the states, rescued by the Republican-led revolution, and placed "under the shield of national protection."[69] In his view, the war and Reconstruction had transformed the constitutional culture of American society, which secured "to the generality of its members . . . to the whole people, and not to a part of them only, the right and the means to cooperate in the management of their common affairs, either directly, or where direct action [was] impossible, by a voluntary delegation of power." Thus, to guarantee the enjoyment of national rights, the national government was obliged to provide adequate protection for its citizens.[70]

Undoubtedly, radical Republicans looked to black suffrage as a major support for the development of Republicanism in the South, but their motivations for enforcing a strong enforcement bill were more complicated than simply gaining political advantage. To be sure, they interpreted the Fifteenth Amendment in the broadest, most idealistic sense. They did so because they saw that black suffrage could be disrupted by various state and individual actions discriminating on account of race or color. However, the radicals refused to see voting rights as isolated from the rest of the political and social context. Rather, the right to vote was an integral part of federal citizenship and closely associated with the exercise of civil rights. Thus the enforcement policy must be made, stated Stewart, to meet "a hundred prerequisites" that could be "invented by the States" and to prevent the Ku Klux Klan from going on plantations and intimidating people. The use of "general language" in the Senate bill, Stewart reasoned, was to cover "any act necessary to qualify the voter to vote" because it was impossible "to enumerate over-specifically all the requirements that might be made as prerequisites for voting."[71] The real differences between the House and Senate bills, observed Matthew H. Carpenter (R-Wis.), was that the former bill would punish a violation already committed "by fine and imprisonment," whereas the latter would "carry out and enforce the principle" of the Fifteenth Amendment and "give effect to the votes of colored persons offered at the polls."[72]

Concerns about the reactionary nature of states' rights theory, the need to consolidate national authority over citizens' political and civil rights, and the broad interpretation of the Fifteenth Amendment supplied the rationale for the Senate bill. There was, however, a problem of time. The radicals wanted to enforce the Fourteenth Amendment and the Civil Rights Act of 1866 in separate bills, but they feared that there was "no time" for separate enforcement measures at the current session.[73]

As a result, several important sections were appended to the Senate bill. One important addition was that private individuals who violated the Fourteenth and Fifteenth Amendments would be punished under this law. This was a remedy to deal with the violence committed by private citizens either individually or in combined form. It was also a device to provide federal protection when a state withheld its protection to a citizen. If "a State by omission neglect[ed] to give to every citizen within its borders a free, fair, and full exercise and enjoyment of his rights," reasoned John Pool, who was a former Whig from North Carolina, it would be the duty of the federal government to "supply" a protection for those rights. This addition, which eventually became the sixth section of the first enforcement act, was the first federal law to penalize individuals for violating the civil rights of other citizens.[74]

Realizing that most southern blacks still depended on the white economy, Republicans included another addition to the bill, which prohibited white employers from preventing blacks from voting by using economic threats, such as unemployment, ejection from rented houses, lands, and other property, or refusing to renew leases or contracts for labor. These threats, Morton argued, were the most effective means for former masters to control the freedmen's votes and "the greatest danger to which the colored people of the South" were exposed. This addition, pushed by both Pool and Morton, became the fifth section of the final bill.[75]

The third important addition was a set of three sections dealing with fraudulent voting practices in northern cities.[76] Referring to the Republican loss in New York City in 1868, Sherman, who proposed the addition, called northern election fraud a grievance that had become "of greater magnitude even than denial of right to vote to colored people." Fraud had enabled Democrats in New York City to control every congressional district and destroyed the purity of the nation's entire electoral system. According to Sherman, northern election fraud had become "a national evil so great, so dangerous, and so alarming in character" that Congress had to "adopt some provisions" to protect itself and the people from the danger arising "from those wholesale frauds."[77] Democrats immediately opposed Sherman's amendments, calling them inappropriate and partisan. But Republicans stood firm, and the amendments were eventually written into the enforcement law.[78] Sherman's sections on election fraud actually opened a new vista for enforcement, which would become a major issue in the debates over the next two enforcement laws and for the next two decades.

After a tiring debate of nineteen hours on May 20, the Senate passed the bill.[79] When the bill returned to the House for concurrence, the House immediately asked for a joint conference to discuss the differences. But the bill remained substantially unchanged and was once again approved by the Senate on May 25.[80] House Democrats tried to filibuster against the measure, which they called "a fatal blow at the State rights." But owing to the Republican majority, the House succeeded in passing the conference report.[81] On May 31, 1870, the bill went into effect with President Grant's approval.[82]

Although the first enforcement act, with twenty-three sections, enforced several clusters of Reconstruction laws, including the Fourteenth and Fifteenth Amendments and the Civil Rights Act of 1866, the focus was on black suffrage. The bill restated the first section of the Fifteenth Amendment in a positive

Table 2.1

Senate Passage of Conference Report for H.R. 1293
(Enforcement Act of May 31, 1870)

Party	Vote Distribution			
	Yeas	Nays	Not Voting	Total Votes
Republican	47	2	11	60
	(78%)	(3%)	(19%)	(100%)
Democrat	0	9	0	9
		(100%)		(100%)
Others	1	0	2	3
	(33%)	(0%)	(67%)	(100%)
Summary	48	11	13	

Source: CG, 41 Cong. 2 sess., 3809.

Table 2.2

House Passage of Conference Report for H.R. 1293
(Enforcement Act of May 31, 1870)

| Party | Vote Distribution | | | |
	Yeas	Nays	Not Voting	Total Votes
Republican	131	1	30	162
	(81%)	(1%)	(15%)	(100%)
Democrat	1	55	8	64
	(2%)	(86%)	(12%)	(100%)
Others	1	2	1	4
	(25%)	(50%)	(25%)	(100%)
Summary	133	58	39	

Source: *CG*, 41 Cong. 2 sess., 3884.

tone, asserting that the right of all U.S. citizens to vote "at any elections by the people" should not be deprived on the basis of race, color, or previous condition of servitude (sec. 1). The bill ordered election officers to give equal opportunity for all voters to meet *any* prerequisites required by the states for voting without racial discrimination (secs. 2 and 3); punished those who obstructed qualified voters by force, bribery, threats, and intimidation (sec. 4); imposed a severe fine and imprisonment upon those who prevented voters from exercising suffrage by threatening to terminate existing financial arrangements with the voters, such as employment, contracts, and tenancy (sec. 5); penalized two or more individuals who, by conspiracy or in disguise, intimidated or injured a citizen with intent to prevent his "free exercise and enjoyment of *any right or privilege* granted or secured to him by the Constitution or laws of the United States" (sec. 6).[83] The bill also provided a mechanism for enforcement, including authority for federal district courts to hear enforcement cases, federal district attorneys and marshals to investigate violations of the Fifteenth Amendment and to make arrests, and the president to use military force to keep order at the polls if needed (secs. 7–13, 19, 23). The second object of the act was to ban fraudulent practices in elections (secs. 20–22). Third, the act continued to bar former rebels from holding political office, essentially a provision contained in the third section of the Fourteenth Amendment (secs. 14–15). Finally, the bill provided that all persons, including immigrants, be given equal civil rights, such as the right to make contracts and to sue, and others secured by the Civil Rights Act of 1866 (secs. 16 – 18).[84] Well aware of the diversity of the bill's objectives, the framers finally entitled it "An Act to enforce the Fifteenth Amendment and for other purposes."[85]

The enforcement bill, known as the Enforcement Act of May 31, 1870, was the first and most important congressional legislation to enforce the Fifteenth Amendment. The four enforcement laws passed thereafter either were a derivation or extension of this act or were aimed at other subjects with suffrage enforcement included as a rider. The act defined the extent to which voting rights would be exercised and protected under the Fourteenth and Fifteenth Amendments. It gave substance to the Fifteenth Amendment and identified the connection between civil and political rights. It extended federal power to those areas the states ignored; although the act provided punishment for individual actions against black suffrage, it did so in the historical context that much of the southern terrorism was committed by conspiracies of allied individuals (Ku Klux Klan members) who went unpunished by state laws. The act was significant also as the first to extend federal enforcement in the North, which signaled the party's effort to establish a national system of election supervision. Constitutionally and federally, it had the potential to be a major step, a quantum leap.

However, the act did cause fear, even among those who pushed it through Congress. Carl Schurz, a staunch supporter, warned his colleagues that federal enforcement of black rights should stop "as soon as the pressure of necessity" ceased. If the Republican party attempted to "carry that revolution much farther in the direction of an undue centralization of power," it "would run against a popular instinct far stronger than party allegiance ha[d] ever proved to be."[86] Not long thereafter, Schurz became a leading spokesman for the liberal Republicans and against the enforcement policy. More conservative Republicans than Schurz were, as expected, equally concerned, if not more so.

Republican disagreements on the Senate and House bills were closely observed by the *New York Times*, which believed that they indicated "the sentiment of the Senate on the question of general amnesty and the policy of the Republican party toward the People of the South."[87] Later the paper asserted that the fight over enforcement showed that Republicans were split into two factions, "the one seeking to inaugurate new and harsh measures toward the South, and the other to secure pacification and to construct some wise and

prudent policy independently of old issues of the war."[88] The *Times* had de-
tected the party's problem, and the problem would not go away.

Black Suffrage, Chinese Suffrage, and the Politics of Making the Naturalization Act of 1870

Although the primary object of the Enforcement Act of May 31, 1870, was to
protect southern black voters from Klan terrorism, several sections of the act
also dealt with fraudulent practices in northern elections. True, the Fifteenth
Amendment neither addressed election fraud nor specifically authorized Congress to provide legislation to correct it. But the reality that northern fraud
could hurt the party as much as southern black disfranchisement, and eventually hurt the whole system of congressional elections, alarmed Republicans. For
such Republicans as Ohioans John Bingham in the House and John Sherman
in the Senate, both from a state inclining toward Democratic control, removing
election fraud in the North was as important as protecting black suffrage in the
South. During the debate over the first enforcement act, they reminded their
colleagues that the fraudulent practices found in the elections in northern cities
could come back to haunt the party.[89] While the Republican party might protect southern black voters with the first enforcement act, the measure was effectively defeated in the North by the Democratic party, which was increasingly
regaining influence over northern voters. The party's loss in New York in the
1868 presidential election also remained a fresh memory: not only did New
York fail to give its electoral votes to Grant and Colfax, but the Democratic party
also won thirteen of the state's thirty-one seats in Congress.[90]

One serious fraudulent practice in northern cities, particularly in New York
City, was that of recent immigrants casting votes by using false naturalization
papers as their certificates of citizenship. Although national citizenship was
constitutionally confirmed and established in 1866 by the Civil Rights Act and
in 1868 by the Fourteenth Amendment, the naturalization of foreign immigrants remained largely the business of the states. Because neither the Fourteenth nor the Fifteenth Amendment clearly conferred the right to vote upon
citizens or made suffrage one of the integral rights of national citizenry, the
states were left to regulate matters of suffrage, including those regarding naturalized aliens.[91] Thus, controlling the naturalization process in places such as

New York City, where immigrants arrived in large numbers, meant controlling new voters.

The Democrats, however, posed a particular threat to the Republicans in New York City, largely because the Democratic machine controlled the bulk of the city's new immigrant votes. In 1868, New York went Democratic by a slim margin of only ten thousand votes, but Tammany Hall had issued at least sixteen thousand vouchers to new immigrants who needed money to cover the expenses for going through the naturalization process. At least partly for that reason, New York's Union League Club had pressed for national legislation to oversee the naturalization process. With the elections of 1870 coming soon, the elimination of fraud in northern elections became an urgent issue for Republicans. Under these circumstances, Republicans in Congress proposed to make naturalization wholly a federal matter and to eliminate such corruption in elections.[92]

The Naturalization Act of 1870, the second of the voting rights enforcement laws between 1870 and 1872, has generally been overlooked in the study of black suffrage legislation, but the law was an important logical connection between the enforcement laws of May 31, 1870, and February 28, 1871. As its primary goal was to amend the existing system of naturalization, the bill seemingly had nothing to do with the Fifteenth Amendment. But during the debate, the bill was extended to enforce federal control over both naturalization and suffrage under the name of the Fourteenth and Fifteenth Amendments. The congressional debate over the bill led to the usual explosion of disagreements among the Republicans on a number of issues: the relation between naturalization, citizenship, and the right to vote; race and qualifications of national citizenship; naturalization and suffrage; and the quality of American democracy. Some of the issues had appeared before, but this debate pushed the party to confront its fundamental dilemma between its avowed idealism for political equality and the practical economic and political interests of the different locales that its members represented.

The naturalization bill was first introduced into the House by Noah Davis, a radical Republican from New York, on June 13, 1870, just two weeks after the first enforcement act became law. The measure, according to Davis, was intended to amend the existing naturalization laws, punish fraudulent practices in the naturalization process, and give federal courts exclusive jurisdiction over controversial cases concerning naturalization. It was a simple, straightforward bill, with no reference to voting rights.[93] Although some Democrats voiced their opposition, the Republican majority voted them down, passing the bill without difficulty.[94]

When the Senate took up the bill a week later, Roscoe Conkling, a Republican leader from New York and a member of the Judiciary Committee, presented the House bill with "an amendment in the nature of substitute."[95] Conkling's substitute was more complicated and substantial than the original House bill. Eleven of the thirteen sections of the bill dealt with naturalization matters, encompassing all the details regarding procedures, manners, fees, qualifications for naturalization and citizenship, and punishment for frauds in the process of naturalization. Like the House bill, it specified that only federal courts were authorized to handle all offenses concerning naturalization practices.[96] But the Conkling bill went beyond the issue of naturalization and stepped into the sphere of voting. In the last two sections, the bill empowered federal district and circuit court judges to designate deputies to be present at all times and places fixed for voter registration in each precinct in cities and towns of more than twenty thousand. These deputies were designated to watch registration, voting, and counting and "to challenge any name proposed to be registered, and any vote offered" (sec. 12). The bill also empowered federal marshals to appoint as many deputies as needed to keep order at the polls and to make all necessary arrests "for any offense or breach of the peace committed in their view" when congressional elections were held (sec. 13). Essentially, the measure would require a naturalized citizen to present his certificate, authorized by a federal court, before voting.[97]

In the long run, Conkling's bill might be understood as a genuine effort to modernize the federal system administering naturalization.[98] In fact, national control of immigration (and naturalization) was also urged by such respectable legal minds as Francis Lieber, who sought the establishment of a national board of immigration to control "the whole immigration business." In two letters to Hamilton Fish in April 1870, Lieber urged upon the secretary of state that it was the national government's duty "to put [immigration control] under national sway and regulation in every respect, morally and physically."[99] Even for the time, the Conkling proposal contained a special constitutional meaning: empowering the federal government to control the process of recruiting new American citizens, since national citizenship was confirmed by the Fourteenth Amendment. The bill's purpose, Conkling explained, was to remove from the states the sole jurisdiction over citizenship and to have the national courts uniformly handle the process of conferring citizenship upon naturalized aliens. The bill, Conkling declared, did "nothing except to purify the process of naturalization, and . . . to render more assured, to appreciate, to set a new value upon the rights of American citizenship." [100] But given the political context of 1870, Conkling might have pushed the bill for a more immediate and perhaps more partisan purpose: to break Democratic control of the voting power in New York City, which was, as Republicans believed, composed of a large number of falsely naturalized aliens.

Neither Conkling nor any other member of the committee explained why the last two sections were added to the bill, but the rationale underlying the arrangement was obvious: to have federal officials present at the polls in populous cities to challenge foreign-born voters who were unlawfully naturalized. Conkling may have calculated that such an arrangement was a logical extension of the first enforcement act, which had provided the federal machinery to enforce black suffrage in the South. Conkling also may have felt that, since the federal government had the power to control naturalization (which in turn would lead to federal citizenship), it was the federal government's duty to review the voting qualifications of naturalized citizens at congressional elections. Whatever the reasoning, the last two sections of the Conkling bill linked the issues of naturalization, citizenship, and suffrage to the first enforcement act. Technically, the two sections regarding federal supervision at elections expanded the substance of the first enforcement act without going beyond its principles. These two sections also became the stepping stone to the Enforcement Act of February 28, 1871, which would give specific attention to northern election fraud.

The Democrats immediately saw the measure as a partisan effort to block their efforts to recruit voters from naturalized citizens in the North and to help reinvigorate the Republican party in New York. [101] But much of the Democratic attack focused on naturalization, especially the power of the states to naturalize aliens. Only Thomas Bayard of Delaware, probably the shrewdest Democratic legal mind in Congress, challenged on constitutional grounds the two sections concerning federal supervision at the polls. He argued that suffrage "may or may not be one of the incidents of citizenship" and depended "entirely on the constitutional regulations of the States" in which naturalized citizens resided. The Fifteenth Amendment only limited states' rights to regulate suffrage on color, race, and previous conditions of servitude, without giving the federal government "unlimited power" to supervise elections.[102] Later, Bayard called the Republican attempt to tack the supervision sections to the naturalization bill "a gross usurpation of a power in no way delegated" to Congress. If Congress had no right to give suffrage (to the aliens), it had no right "to control it in any way whatever."[103]

Despite their vocal opposition, the Democrats were too weak a minority to threaten the bill's passage. The real challenge came from the Republican party itself: many Republicans disliked the bill, and some loathed it. Republicans from the West and Midwest echoed the Democratic charges, calling it "an obstruction to naturalization."[104] The West and Midwest wanted new immigrants, and in many states laws were passed to shorten the residency periods to attract permanent settlement. The lengthy and meticulous process of federal control of naturalization would stop the states from adopting a more liberal policy. Morton of Indiana, usually a supporter of federal action in behalf of black rights, complained about the complicated nature of the proposed naturalization process and asked not to go beyond the House bill.[105] James Howell of Iowa assailed the bill as an effort by New York Republicans to promote their own interests.[106] Others warned that the party's unfriendly attitude toward the naturalized citizens would "quite seriously injure the popularity of the party" among immigrants and at the state and local levels.[107] Obviously, these Republicans wanted to keep state control over naturalization from falling into federal hands. This insistence on states' rights seemed ideologically ironic, since a majority of the party had just upheld federal supremacy over national citizenship.

Under pressure, Conkling agreed to modify his proposal on the basis of the original House bill, but without removing the last two sections, which no Republican challenged. But right before the Senate reached an agreement on the final version of the bill, Charles Sumner rose and proposed to add to the revised Conkling bill a new section: "That all acts of Congress relating to naturalization be, and the same are hereby, amended by striking out the word 'white' wherever it occurs, so that in naturalization there shall be no distinction of race or color."[108]

Long determined to eradicate every piece of racial prejudice in the nation's law, Sumner had prepared to bring his proposal into the Senate before the business of enforcement began. He had told his radical colleagues, "I do not think the work (of antislavery) finished so long as the word 'white' is allowed to play any part in legislation," including those concerning naturalization. And he was very consistent about his antidiscrimination record.[109] Sumner probably considered this as an opportunity to correct existing federal naturalization laws, which had permitted only "free white persons" to be naturalized.[110] His logic was simple: since the Civil Rights Act of 1866 and the Fourteenth Amendment had established a color-blind American citizenship, it was necessary to make corresponding changes in the nation's naturalization laws, which retained racial discrimination. But his proposal unexpectedly became an ideological time bomb that completely destroyed the agreement on the bill and almost killed it.

If Sumner's proposal became law, no foreign immigrants could be barred from applying for naturalization on the basis of color and race. Their naturalization would, after a certain period, enable them to obtain United States citizenship and, consequently, the rights that accompanied it, including the right to vote. For all its moral strength and idealism, such a proposal would win the approval of few Republicans. Even Francis Lieber, who supported strong and uniform national control over immigration, had suggested a law, immediately after the adoption of the Fifteenth Amendment, to prohibit "the immigration of any but white people." Lieber saw a bleak future for the country with large numbers of Germans and Irish in New York and "the Chinese and Japanese in San Francisco."[111] Sumner's proposal outraged Republicans from western states, which were already engaged in heated debates about the issue of Chinese coolie labor, as waves of contracted Chinese workers rushed into the West and Rocky Mountain region. Although the first large-scale anti-Chinese violence in the West was still ten years away, the anti-Chinese sentiment had become phenomenal.[112] In states of the Far West, the Chinese question had been the principal obstacle to ratification of the Fifteenth Amendment. As pointed out earlier, even after the nativity test was deleted, California and Oregon still rejected the amendment, while Nevada ratified it with the understanding that the amendment would not guarantee the enfranchisement of the Chinese.[113] Under such circumstances, accepting Sumner's proposal would mean political suicide for western Republicans, who would engulf Sumner's proposal with fierce criticism and opposition.

William Stewart, who had just led the party's fight for the Fifteenth Amendment and the first enforcement act, was the most vocal. Stewart claimed that he did not oppose protecting the civil rights of Chinese laborers but frowned on naturalizing and subsequently enfranchising them. For Stewart, black enfranchisement was "an act of justice":

> The negro was among us. This was his native land. He was born here. He had a
> right to protection here. He had a right to the ballot here. He was an American
> and a Christian, as much so as any of the rest of the people of the country. He
> loved the American flag. Although he was ignorant, although he had been [a]
> slave, it became important that he should be enfranchised, so that he might pro-
> tect himself in this great strife that we always have and always must have in a free
> government, where every man must take care of himself.[114]

However, Stewart said, the Chinese were entirely different, "pagans in religion, monarchists in theory," who looked "with utter contempt upon all modern forms as dangerous innovations." To enfranchise the Chinese meant to subject the "the political destiny of the Pacific coast" to ignorant Chinese laborers.[115] George H. Williams of Oregon, who later became Grant's attorney general in charge of enforcing the Fifteenth Amendment, asked that the Chinese be excluded from Sumner's proposal. Williams saw Chinese naturalization as a potential threat to free labor ideology and practice in America. The Chinese laborers were an organized labor force, which, in his view, could be equated with southern slavery and turned into an organized political force if they were granted citizenship and suffrage. Williams warned his colleagues that once the Chinese were enfranchised, "the black and white laborers of the country [would] combine to crush the [Republican] party which invites competition with their labor from China" at the next election.[116]

The Republican division over the Chinese issue was ironic. The line used to distinguish radicals from moderates and conservatives on the race issue blurred on the Chinese issue. Sumner was the strongest defender of his proposal. Two of Sumner's comrades were Lyman Trumbull of Illinois and William Sprague of Rhode Island. Trumbull, normally more conservative, charged both Stewart and Williams with racism and reminded them that it was not long "since the color of the skin being black deprived an individual of all his rights."[117] Sprague, a textile manufacturer, supported Sumner's proposal mainly because it would eventually enable America to benefit from cheap Chinese labor. Carl Schurz, once identified as a radical and increasingly a liberal Republican, disagreed with Stewart and Williams but persuaded Sumner to withdraw the proposed color-blind naturalization law because it was "not yet fully matured" and served "to obstruct the passage of the bill."[118]

Henry Wilson, well aware of the controversies then raging about the use of Chinese strikebreakers in Massachusetts, refused to support Sumner's proposal. He regarded the importation of Chinese coolie labor as a "modern slave-trade system" used by big corporations to challenge "the free labor of this country, North and South." He would support voting rights for the Chinese if they voluntarily assimilated into American society. But Wilson doubted that would happen because they were from China, "a country of cheap labor, a country of paganism, a country with a civilization wholly distinct from our own."[119] Oliver P. Morton, who led several major debates over issues of black rights in the Senate, told Sumner that excluding the Chinese from suffrage did not contradict the Declaration of Independence because the Chinese did not have a natural right to enjoy American rights.[120]

The local anti-Chinese pressure, the fear of the revival of slave labor, the anxiety to gain back the free labor support drifting into the Democratic camp, and the dark image of Chinese political culture – all scared the anti-Chinese Republicans and made them put aside the principle of universal political equality and set limits for the enjoyment of American democracy. By then, Republicans must have realized how difficult it was for the party to transform equality as a concept into a universal policy in actual politics. But excluding the Chinese from naturalization prompted a question: If Republicans could prohibit a Chinese alien from becoming an American citizen and obtaining the right to vote because of his race, what was wrong with the Democrats who wanted to exclude blacks from suffrage for the same reason? Democrats and advocates of women's suffrage raised a similar question: Why was it wrong to exclude blacks from voting when women lacked the right to vote? In answering the question, the Republicans pointed to differences in constitutional origins and cultural deficiency (in contrast to the argument of sexual inferiority in justifying their position in denying women the right to vote): blacks were citizens of the United States and entitled to the right to vote; the Chinese as a race were culturally and politically insufficient to acquire the status of American citizenship and therefore be enfranchised. In other words, black suffrage was "an act of justice";[121] Chinese suffrage was "a practical problem," not "a question of principle."[122]

The final votes on the bill were dramatic. Before Sumner's proposal was called for a final vote, Democratic senator Willard Saulsbury of Delaware proposed, in an attempt to defeat the entire bill, excluding both Chinese and Africans from naturalization. The majority of Republicans immediately voted down the amendment.[123] But the Democratic proposal alerted the Republicans.

To show the party's firm stance on black equality and "save the practical good . . . rather than endanger all," Willard Warner of Alabama proposed to add a new section to the current bill so that naturalization could be extended "to the aliens of African nativity and to persons of African descent." The new proposal won Senate approval by a majority of one and became the last section of the Naturalization Act of 1870.[124] Constitutionally, the Warner addition was crucial for opening the door for immigration of Africans, especially those settling in the Caribbean. But since Republican supporters knew well that few Africans were able to come to America then, the section served largely as a political gesture to accord with what Warner called "a ripened public opinion" on black rights rather than a sincere policy to attract Africans to America.[125]

After the vote on Warner's amendment, Lyman Trumbull tried to amend the section by putting "persons born in the Chinese empire" under the protection of Warner's amendment, but the amendment was voted down by a vote of 31 to 9, with 32 not voting. Trumbull's motivation for extending naturalization to the Chinese was complicated. His real purpose seemed to be to defeat the Warner proposal for legitimating African immigration rather than to encourage Chinese naturalization. He thought that allowing Africans to be naturalized would open "the whole continent of Africa, where [were] to be found the most degraded examples of man . . . on the face of the earth, pagans, cannibals, men who worship[ed] beasts, who [did] not compare in intelligence at all with the Chinese."

Table 2.3

Senate Acceptance of Warner's Amendment to H.R. 2201
(Naturalization Act of July 14, 1870)

| Party | Vote Distribution | | | |
	Yeas	Nays	Not Voting	Total Votes
Republican	21	12	27	60
	(35%)	(20%)	(45%)	(100%)
Democrat	0	8	1	9
		(89%)	(11%)	(100%)
Others	0	0	3	3
			(100%)	(100%)
Summary	21	20	31	

Source: CG, 41 Cong. 2 sess., 5176.

Table 2.4

Senate Rejection of Sumner's Amendment to H.R. 2201

(Naturalization Act of July 14, 1870)

| Party | Vote Distribution | | | |
	Yeas	Nays	Not Voting	Total Votes
Republican	12	19	29	60
	(20%)	(32%)	(48%)	(100%)
Democrat	0	7	2	9
		(78%)	(12%)	(100%)
Others	0	0	3	3
			(100%)	(100%)
Summary	12	26	34	

Source: *CG*, 41 Cong. 2 sess., 5177.

Only 8 Republicans (15 percent of the party votes), mostly from the South, stood with Trumbull; the majority of the party (85 percent) either voted against the proposal (24 votes) or abstained (27 votes).[126] When Sumner's proposal came up for a final decision, the majority of Republicans decided not to support Sumner, either by abstaining or by joining the Democratic opposition.[127]

Probably because much of the debate focused on the Chinese question, the two sections regarding federal supervision at the polls were entirely ignored until the last minute. Again, Democrat Thomas Bayard questioned the constitutionality of the two sections. But Bayard's question attracted no attention.[128] Thus, the final version of the naturalization bill remained largely the same as the original House bill, except for the last three sections, which the Senate added.[129] Sections 5 and 6, specifying the duties and powers of federal officials at the polls in large cities, strengthened the provisions prescribed in the first enforcement act. On July 4, 1870, the Senate passed the naturalization bill by a strict party vote of 33 to 8, with 31 not voting. Without the Trumbull and Sumner provisions, more than half of the Republicans (55 percent) approved the bill. While 26 Republicans (43 percent) abstained, only one Republican, Arthur Boreman of West Virginia, voted against H.R. 2201.[130] A few days later, the House accepted the Senate's amendments with an overwhelming partisan vote.[131] On July 14, with President Grant's signature, the bill became law.

The Naturalization Act of July 4, 1870, had no long-term impact on the course of enforcing the Fifteenth Amendment, especially in the South. This was because of its supplementary nature and the brief life of the two enforcement sections, which, in less than one year, would be superseded by the third enforcement act—that of February 28, 1871. But the act significantly linked the issues of suffrage, citizenship, and naturalization. Although the debate once again displayed Republican unity in support of black suffrage and the constitutional settlement of the Civil War, it also revealed the fragility of this unity. It would become more difficult for the party to stand together as various local interests continued to rise in the postwar period.

Watching the debate unfold, Frederick Douglass praised Sumner for upholding the republican principles of political equality on the Chinese question. But the "bitter contest" among the Republicans made the black leader doubt how enduring the party's future policy on black rights would be:

> A bitter contest, I fear, is before us on this question. Prejudice, price of race, narrow views of political economy, are on one, humanity, civilization and sound policy are on the other. In your position I see the value of fixed principles. While others hesitate you go forward. While others are entangled in the meshes of temporary expediency you can promptly move forward in the light and harmony of those principles which are broad, grand and eternal.[132]

The Making of Three Other Enforcement Laws, 1871–1872

The enactment of the first two enforcement laws had a practical purpose: to meet the Democratic challenge in the elections of 1870. To the Republicans, the 1870 elections would be a test of the strength for the presidential election in 1872. Soon after the naturalization law took effect, Grant, writing to Conkling, expressed his concern with the coming elections in New York. He urged that as "the largest" and "certainly the most important state," New York must "secure a fair election" and be "secure to the Republican party."[133] The northern press had predicted that the recently enacted enforcement laws would help the federal government to check the Democratic fraud. Although doubtful about the appointments of election inspectors, the *Chicago Tribune* welcomed the Naturalization Act of July 14, 1870, and its provisions on federal supervision of elections in large cities. The paper held that if the law was "fairly and firmly enforced at the next election, every honest and decent Democrat throughout the land, as well as every Republican, [would] breath freer, in the consciousness that one of the chief dangers to the republic ha[d] been removed."[134]

Federal agencies in New York, led by Noah Davis, who had resigned from the House and become the district attorney of the southern district of New York, prepared to enforce both enforcement laws. On November 7, 1870, the day before the election, Davis and U.S. marshal George H. Sharpe reached an agreement with New York mayor A. Oakey Hall and J. S. Bosworth, representative of the New York City Board of Police, that promised cooperation "in good faith" by the city police. Although this agreement was believed to make federal military interference "wholly unnecessary," New York governor John T. Hoffman still ordered the state's National Guard to get ready for election day. The *New York Times* called the Democratic movement "a Tammany trick."[135] In the meantime, the city's federal election supervisors checked the registry and compiled a list of fifteen thousand "fraudulently registered" names. About five hundred warrants had been prepared for fraudulent voters.[136] On election day, twenty-six were arrested, including a member of the Tammany Hall General Committee. Voter registration in the city was reduced by twenty to thirty thousand. Both the Democratic governor and mayor were elected, but at a reduced majority.[137] Despite the enforcement law, the results of the 1870 elections were less encouraging than Republicans had expected or hoped. Although Democrats in New York City failed to increase their seats owing to the effectiveness of the enforcement laws, upstate Democrats won 4 more congressional seats.[138] Worse, the Democratic strength in the House rose from 69 seats in the third session of the Forty-first Congress to 102 (including 6 conservatives from the South) in the first session of the Forty-second Congress. In the Senate, the Democrats also increased their seats from 11 to 13.[139]

The political situation in the South was equally threatening for the Republicans. With the aid of Klan terrorism, Democrats quickly returned to the center of the southern political stage. In Georgia, Democrats won 80 percent of the seats in the state legislature and most of the congressional seats. General Dudley Du Bois, a leading Georgia Klansman, was elected to Congress from the eastern district, where Klan intimidation was dominant. In Florida, the Republican majority was substantially reduced when black voters were threatened if they voted Republican.[140] Alabama Democrats won the lower house of the state legislature, and Texas Democrats won three of the state's four seats in the House.[141] Meanwhile, the first enforcement act was ineffectively carried out in

the South. President Grant called attention to enforcement but did little to implement the law.[142] Later, Charles Sumner criticized Grant's inaction, and partly
for this reason, he refused to endorse Grant for reelection.[143]

The election left Republicans as alarmed by Democratic gains in the North
as they were by Klan outrages in the South.[144] Although the party maintained
majorities in both houses, a reversal clearly was possible in two years if Republicans remained idle on enforcement. Federal enforcement in New York City in
1870 reduced Democratic frauds and kept peace at the polls, but, as the *New
York Times* admitted, it "did not accomplish very much" to shake the control of
Tammany Hall.[145] Partially because of their initial success in New York and partially because of their technical deficiency, as the *Times* predicted, the first two
enforcement acts needed to be improved and extended nationwide. Soon after
the elections were over and the third session of the Forty-first Congress convened, Republicans began to introduce new bills to amend the first two enforcement acts.[146]

The new enforcement bill (H.R. 2634), as reported by John Bingham from
the House Judiciary Committee on February 15, 1871, aimed at providing technical details regarding enforcement machinery, which were believed missing or
insufficient in the first two enforcement acts. The bill was basically an enlargement of section 20 of the Enforcement Act of May 31, 1870, adding nineteen
sections. The new bill made fraudulent practices in voting and registration a
federal crime and required all state laws regarding congressional elections to
observe the federal law. The bill repealed sections 5 and 6 of the Naturalization
Act of July 14, 1870 (sec. 18), but in its second section reenacted them by providing that in cities with populations of at least twenty thousand a federal judge,
upon request, could appoint two election supervisors in each precinct. The bill
detailed the procedures for circuit and district courts to appoint chief supervisors (secs. 13 and 3); prescribed the payment and duties of supervisors in challenging doubtful voters, inspecting the registry, making arrests, watching voting, registration, and counting (secs. 4 – 6); empowered the supervisors and
marshals to appoint their deputies (secs. 8, 12); and provided for penalties
against offenders who molested enforcement officials and officials who neglected their duties (secs. 7, 9, 10, 11). The bill authorized circuit and federal
courts to hear cases arising under the law and allowed them to be removed from
state to federal courts upon petition (secs. 14 – 17). The last section (19) required written or printed ballots for electing representatives in Congress.[147]

Unlike previous enforcement acts, the new bill provided detailed guidelines.
It explained the duties of the federal enforcement officers and defined crimes
and election fraud, empowered federal courts to hear all cases arising under the
law, and modernized the ballot by requiring written ballots for congressional
elections.[148] The new enforcement bill obviously targeted the states' power to
regulate elections. The political contest of 1870 showed that northern fraud
and southern Klanism were equally detrimental to Republican efforts to maintain the rights of the taxpayers and the party's power. For some, the former was
even more threatening. Any military attempt to overthrow liberties, declared
Illinois Republican Burton C. Cook, was "far more remote than the possibility that the fountain of all law [would] be poisoned and corrupted by such
frauds."[149] The new enforcement bill, in Bingham's view, would equip the national government with the "power of self-preservation" against state laws "acting separately and without violence" to "demolish the national government."[150]

Democrats in both houses saw the bill as the Republican party's "desperate
extremity to retain power." For the Democrats, the legislative power to enforce
the Fifteenth Amendment was only "accessory" to the first provision of the
amendment. Thus it should be "latent, and must forever remain so," as long as
the states took no action against black voters on the basis of color and race. The
enforcement bill would only destroy state sovereignty and "lead to monarchy,

Table 2.5

Senate Passage of H.R. 2634 (Enforcement Act of February 28, 1871)

| Party | Vote Distribution | | | |
	Yeas	Nays	Not Voting	Total Votes
Republican	38	1	22	61
	(62%)	(2%)	(36%)	(100%)
Democrat	0	8	3	11
		(73%)	(27%)	(100%)
Others	1	1	0	2
	(50%)	(50%)		(100%)
Summary	39	10	25	

Source: *CG,* 41 Cong. 3 sess., 1655.

Table 2.6

House Passage of H.R. 2634 (Enforcement Act of February 28, 1871)

Party	Vote Distribution			
	Yeas	Nays	Not Voting	Total Votes
Republican	142	3	22	167
	(85%)	(2%)	(13%)	(100%)
Democrat	1	59	9	69
	(1%)	(86%)	(13%)	(100%)
Others	1	2	1	4
	(25%)	(50%)	(25%)	(100%)
Summary	144	64	32	

Source: *CG*, 41 Cong. 3 sess., 1285.

aristocracy, anarchy and revolution."[151] But the Democrats failed to filibuster against the bill. Both houses passed the bill with strong partisan support, and Grant approved it on February 28, 1871.[152]

While Republicans were fighting to get the third enforcement act past Congress to suppress election fraud in the North, they fought a different battle on the southern front: suppressing the Ku Klux Klan. In 1870 and 1871, Klan terrorism continued to run rampant in the South. A campaign of violence and terrorism against black voters had begun in North and South Carolina. On August 22, 1870, Governor Robert K. Scott of South Carolina apprised Grant of the political situation in his state. According to Scott, the past election in the northern part of the state had an "unusual quietness," which may have been "attributable to the presence of detachments of United States troops at the localities where they were most apprehended"; but in "the upper or more northern communities" where the white population predominated, local opponents of black suffrage initiated a program to "vitiate the Election" by destroying ballot boxes. Reporting the violence at Laurens Courthouse, where state Republican officers were assaulted, Scott described a "general reign of terror and lawlessness" under which "Colored men and women [were] dragged from their homes at the dead hour of night and most cruelly and brutally scourged for the sole reason that they dared to exercise their own opinion upon political subjects." He told Grant that the state militia was poorly equipped and could not combat the experienced Klansmen.[153] By the spring of 1871, a delegation from South Carolina informed Grant that state authorities could no longer maintain order.

Meanwhile, in North Carolina, it was little better; Republican legislators were ousted from the state legislature. Governor Holden was impeached and convicted for misusing martial law.[154] *Harper's Weekly* urged the Republican-controlled Congress to take immediate actions to protect black voters, who would "prevent the national government falling into the hands of the Ku Klux party."[155] Grant also pressed Congress to pass an effective act to control the Klan. Writing to Speaker of the House James Blaine, Grant asked Congress to give "immediate attention" to "a deplorable state of affairs existing in some portions of the South." Even if Congress could only discuss a single subject in the coming session, Grant urged, it should be that of "providing means for the protection of life and property in those sections of the country."[156]

Republicans presented the anti-Klan bill, later known as the Ku Klux Force Act of April 20, 1871, in the House soon after the first session of the Forty-second Congress convened in March 1871. There had been an attempt to bring up the bill when Congress was considering the third enforcement act in mid-February, but some House Republicans, including Blaine and James A. Garfield, joined the Democrats to defeat it, reasoning that it went beyond the limits of congressional power.[157] The Ku Klux Force Act, the fourth enforcement law since 1870, was an amalgam of several propositions. Its main goals were to enforce the Fourteenth Amendment and punish states for depriving U.S. citizens of "any of the rights, privileges, or immunities" protected by federal law. But, notably, the bill also penalized any individuals who violated this law. Again, realizing that antiblack crimes were mostly the work of private individuals (i.e., the Klan) and the state laws were silent on these outrages, Republicans resorted to a broad interpretation of the national authority over the civil rights of national citizenship established by the Fourteenth Amendment. When the South drifted into "a state of anarchy and bloodshed" and the states refused to punish the crimes, William Stoughton (R-Mich.) argued, it was "an extraordinary combination to commit crime" that required "extraordinary legislation for its suppression."[158] The only way to stop the Klan outrages was to enact "strong and vigorous laws ... promptly executed by a firm hand, armed, when need be, with military power."[159]

The debates in both houses were long; indeed, more than eighty House members spoke. The focus was on the extent of congressional power to enforce the Fourteenth Amendment. Most Republicans stood firm with the party's principles, justifying the use of federal power to protect citizens' rights under the Civil War amendments. In the House, James Monroe argued that the amendments were "a natural growth" of the Constitution.[160] Samuel Shellabarger of Ohio, who led the House debate, refuted the Democratic challenge on the bill's constitutionality, declaring that the constitutional revolution to change "an immortal chattel into an immortal citizen . . . [was taking] no step back!"[161] Even moderates such as Henry Dawes of Massachusetts radically argued that the president could enforce the state laws as "an instrument for the enforcement of the United States laws."[162] In the Senate, John Pool further developed the argument he used in the discussion of the first enforcement act in May 1870, adding much more thorough constitutional theories. According to Pool, after the Fourteenth Amendment, national citizenship rested "no longer upon mere implication, but as a substantive thing, with all its incidents subject to the national authority"; the amendment also offered all U.S. citizens a new right — the right to the protection of the laws.[163] On this point, Pool maintained:

> If the States shall fail to secure and enforce this right of the colored man, and deny him protection in the free exercise and enjoyment of it as a citizen of the State, then the United States, by virtue of his national citizenship, must and will, by appropriate legislation, by all the power of its courts, by its land and naval forces, extend over him within the States the shield of the national authority.[164]

In the Senate, Trumbull and Schurz led the Republican opposition. Trumbull supported the principle of enforcement but thought the bill went so far as to become "a general crime code for the States of the Union."[165] Agreeing, Schurz regarded the bill as "an encroachment of the national authority upon the legitimate sphere of local self government." But Schurz's real complaint was that enforcement would be the wrong remedy to stop southern violence, that it would only further division by party lines. Now labeling himself "a liberal Republican," Schurz said that even though the suffering blacks in the South deserved sympathy, he considered "the rights and liberties of the whole American people of still higher importance" than black interests. Evils should not be "cured at the expense of a permanent good."[166]

After many amendments, the House passed the bill on April 6 and the Senate on April 10.[167] After two conferences, both houses approved the bill with a heavy partisan majority on April 19.[168] Grant approved the bill on April 20.

Although shorter, the final version of the measure retained much of its original strength. It authorized federal courts to hear all cases regarding rights in-

Table 2.7

Senate Passage of H.R. 320 (Ku Klux Force Act)

| Party | Vote Distribution | | | |
	Yeas	Nays	Not Voting	Total Votes
Republican	36	2	17	55
	(65%)	(4%)	(31%)	(100%)
Democrat	0	10	3	13
		(77%)	(23%)	(100%)
Others	0	1	1	2
		(50%)	(50%)	(100%)
Summary	36	13	21	

Source: CG, 42 Cong. 1 sess., 831.

fringements under the Civil Rights Act of 1866 (sec. 1), enlarged the president's power to use national military force to suppress domestic disturbances and to suspend the writ of habeas corpus when organized conspiracies were powerful enough to obstruct the execution of the laws (secs. 3 and 4), prohibited Klan members from serving as jurors in federal courts (sec. 5), and punished those who aided criminals penalized under the bill's second section (sec. 6). The act also specified that it would not supersede other enforcement acts (sec. 7). The most important section of the act was the second, which spelled out more than twenty kinds of specific practices defined as illegal, including using force and intimidation to interfere with any citizen's exercise of voting rights in federal elections.[169] This section actually enlarged and extended section 6 of the Enforcement Act of May 31, 1870, which first established the principle of penalizing individual or conspirative violence against rights protected by federal laws but had proved vague and difficult to employ in framing indictments. This section virtually outlawed the Klan and similar groups that conspired to deprive citizens of their political and civil rights.[170]

Given its radical and expansive nature, the Ku Klux Force Act, the fourth enforcement law in a row, probably would have produced the most effective results in suppressing the Klan had it been thoroughly implemented. But the Force Act intensified Republican infighting and, in a sense, accelerated the party's disunity in its policy toward the South. The Force Act passed when the

Table 2.8
House Passage of H.R. 320 (Ku Klux Force Act)

Party	Vote Distribution			
	Yeas	Nays	Not Voting	Total Votes
Republican	93	1	36	130
	(72%)	(1%)	(27%)	(100%)
Democrat	0	67	25	92
		(73%)	(27%)	(100%)
Others	0	6	2	8
		(75%)	(25%)	(100%)
Summary	93	74	63	

Source: CG, 42 Cong. 1 sess., 808.

liberal Republican movement was on the horizon. The liberals, composed mostly of former radical Republicans in the Northeast who were disgusted with the Grant administration's corruption, wanted a conciliatory policy toward the South and due restoration of traditional constitutionalism.[171] Naturally, they became the archopponents of the Force Act within the party. Carl Schurz, one of the founders of the liberal Republican movement and a former supporter of black rights, had vehemently opposed the Force Act. Black suffrage was "a necessary and absolutely logical consequence" of the Civil War and a strategy to enable blacks to protect themselves so that the North could "avoid the necessity of national interference as much as possible." But, Schurz argued, blacks failed to grasp their new rights and ignorantly followed or were driven to follow dishonest political adventurers, who were also responsible for southern political disasters. Instead of continuing to rely on black political power to reconstruct the South, Schurz suggested, the Republican party should now turn to the "good elements" of the South and remove political disabilities imposed by the Fourteenth Amendment on the former rebels.[172] The *Chicago Tribune* ridiculed the Force Act as "attempting to cure a cancer with a compress." The paper blamed the troubles in the South on "the evil fruits of Radicalism" and urged Republicans to abandon enforcement.[173] It was a far cry from the party's traditional radicalism.

Other Republicans, too, worried about going beyond the limits of traditional constitutionalism. Although they welcomed federal assistance in certain economic and financial arenas such as railroad land grants and monetary policy, these Republicans were uncertain as to how far federal authority should go to protect civil and political rights, a sphere previously reserved for state authorities. Sweeping enforcement would eventually lead to the creation of a highly powerful and centralized federal government, which would threaten the local government or lead to political corruption. "We are working on the very verge of the Constitution," stated future president James A. Garfield; "many of our members are breaking over the lines, and, it seems to me, exposing us, to the double danger, of having our work overthrown by the Supreme Court and of giving the Democrats new material for injuring us, on the stump." [174] Even staunch Republican organs such as *Harper's Weekly*, a supporter of enforcement, expressed concerns about how constitutionally endurable the Force Act would be as it crossed the traditional lines on several issues. [175]

These doubts and liberal opposition clearly had a negative effect on the Republican course of enforcement in general and the party's effort to enact another black suffrage enforcement law in 1872 in particular. The original bill (S. No. 791), introduced by Louisiana Republican William Kellogg on March 11, 1872, was essentially supplementary. It provided that circuit court judges would have the power, upon request, to appoint election supervisors to watch the polls and count votes at every local precinct. This would extend the power granted to federal officers in cities and towns with a population of more than twenty thousand, first by the Naturalization Act of July 14, 1870, and then by the Enforcement Act of February 28, 1871. [176] The purpose of the bill was to strengthen federal enforcement in the South, especially in rural areas, and, as Oliver P. Morton declared, to "inspire as much confidence on the part of the country as [was] possible." [177] Senate Democrats tried to defeat the bill by tying it to an amnesty bill then under debate. The majority of Republicans opposed the linkage and managed to rush the bill through the Senate on May 14, 1872. [178] But when the bill reached the House for discussion on May 28, Democrats asked to drop it, for they did "not want an army at the polls to superintend the holding of elections." [179] When John Bingham, the Republican floor manager, tried to save the bill by urging the House to consider it on May 31, many Republicans joined the Democrats in voting not to discuss the bill, hence killing it. [180] On the same day, the House failed to pass another Senate bill (S. No. 656), designed to extend the tenure of the fourth section of the Ku Klux Force Act for another congressional session.[181]

Determined to revive his aborted bill, Kellogg waited for a chance to fight back. When the House civil appropriation bill (H.R. 2705) came to the Senate in early June for endorsement, Kellogg immediately proposed to add to it an amendment that extended to judges of all federal circuit courts the power and authority to supervise elections and appoint supervisors to make arrests at polls. Obviously, Kellogg wanted to "reenact" his aborted bill (S. No. 791).[182] Upset at the strategy of the Republicans who wanted to rush the rider through by enacting a rule limiting each speech to five minutes, Democrats angrily charged the Republicans with preventing "freedom of speech in the Senate."[183] The verbal exchanges between the Republicans and Democrats were heated. If the Republicans wanted to pass the enforcement amendment, Allen Thurman cried, they should "pass it openly, pass it in a manly way."[184] Charles Sumner defended the bill's legality, averring that the appropriation was to carry out existing statutes, which included all the enforcement acts passed by Congress. He even suggested adding provisions from his civil rights bill to the House bill. Having seen two Senate enforcement bills defeated by House Republicans, Sumner was pessimistic about the prospect of passing any further enforcement acts on black suffrage in any future Congress. He told his colleagues, "I trust that at this last moment, when we do seem to have it in our power to secure the equal rights of the colored race, they will not be set aside on a technicality."[185]

The Republicans finally accepted the Kellogg rider with a small majority as the Senate passed H.R. 2705 on June 7.[186] But the House could not agree. On June 8, representatives from both houses met again. After eight hours of discussion, the Senate made some important concessions: although the bill empowered federal judges to name deputies to supervise voting, such appointments would not be made until requested by ten citizens (the original provisions required a request from only two citizens); supervisors must be appointed from the precinct in which they resided; the supervisors would receive no compensation except in cities of twenty thousand inhabitants; and, most crucial, federal marshals appointed to supervise elections were to be prohibited from making any arrests at polls in areas with fewer than twenty thousand inhabitants.[187] Such an arrangement, Garfield admitted, virtually stripped the effectiveness of enforcement laws and made the presence of federal officers merely "a moral challenge" at the polls to the violations of the Fifteenth Amendment.[188]

Table 2.9

House Acceptance of Last Conference Report for H.R. 2705

Party	Vote Distribution			
	Yeas	Nays	Not Voting	Total Votes
Republican	102	1	31	134
	(76%)	(1%)	(72%)	(100%)
Democrat	0	71	27	98
		(72%)	(28%)	(100%)
Others	0	7	1	8
		(88%)	(12%)	(100%)
Summary	102	79	59	

Source: *CG*, 42 Cong. 2 sess., 4456.

When the report of the last joint conference returned to the House, only Shellabarger questioned the power of federal marshals to make arrests; the rest of the Republican majority remained silent on the issue. The bill passed the House on June 8. When the final report reached the Senate, Morton challenged the last concession as making federal supervisors "silent spectators without even the power to challenge a vote." George Edmunds, one of the Senate conferees, explained that the House insisted on "having this provision put in as a means of composing their difference in the other body." Edmunds admitted that the Senate was "forced to assent with a view of getting to an end."[189] Finally, the Senate accepted the report on June 10, the last day of the session.

The enforcement rider in the Civil Appropriation Act of June 10, 1872, was virtually powerless and ineffective. It was, in fact, a retreat from the previous enforcement laws. More important, it was the product of the growing divergence between the still radical Senate and the already moderate and conservative House Republicans on the issue of black suffrage. For Republicans, unity on black suffrage was becoming more and more a thing of the past.

The five enforcement laws passed between 1870 and 1872 demonstrate a dichotomy between political and constitutional arguments within the Republican party. This dichotomy was reflected in three sets of arguments: (1) the necessity to protect the political and civil rights of black Americans versus the breach of

Table 2.10

Senate Acceptance of Last Conference Report for H.R. 2705

| | Vote Distribution | | | |
Party	Yeas	Nays	Not Voting	Total Votes
Republican	38	5	13	56
	(68%)	(9%)	(23%)	(100%)
Democrat	0	12	4	16
		(75%)	(25%)	(100%)
Others	1	0	1	2
	(50%)		(50%)	(100%)
Summary	39	17	18	

Source: *CG*, 42 Cong. 2 sess., 4495.

the tenets of traditional constitutionalism; (2) the necessity to expand federal authority in enforcing federal laws versus the possibility that such an expansion would take away rights reserved to the states, creating a centralized federal government and leading to political corruption; (3) the necessity to protect the rights of newly enfranchised black Americans versus the fear that this protection would damage and abridge the rights of white Americans. These arguments ultimately led to a single question: How far should the federal government go to enforce black suffrage and the Civil War amendments?

Ideologically, radical Republicans viewed black suffrage enforcement as both a political necessity and an obligation of the federal government. Enforcement was crucial to stabilizing and sustaining Republican control at the national and state levels, which they considered an indispensable political guarantee of the nation's general interests. This was neither an ideological misconception by the party nor merely its pretext for expediency. It was a belief that had evolved historically from the events of the Civil War and Reconstruction, through which the strength and possibilities of the national government were tested. The Civil War and Reconstruction created a new national government, epitomized in the Thirteenth, Fourteenth, and Fifteenth Amendments. These amendments gave the nation a new political life, the national government new responsibilities, and the Republican party a new mission: to establish and consolidate a national government immune from the danger of another civil war. Thus, for radical-minded Republicans, Reconstruction was a continuation of the confrontation between the Union and the Confederacy. Creating enforcement laws was crucial to defining the "new birth of freedom" and to defending the war's achievements, including the party's control of the government. Under this circumstance, black suffrage was both an object and a weapon of defense.

More conservative and moderate Republicans took black suffrage with caution and perhaps suspicion. They were less confident than their radical counterparts in black men's political capacity. They accepted emancipation and enfranchisement as legitimate results of the war but were unprepared for drastic changes in traditional federal-state relations. These Republicans shared Democratic fears that the unlimited expansion of the federal government and its power could damage the state governments and that this federal power could be abused by unscrupulous politicians. For them, a comprehensive enforcement of black political and civil rights could fundamentally alter the nature of the American polity and break the checks and balances between federal and state powers. They were deeply troubled by the prospect that unqualified suffrage, as aided by federal enforcement, would turn the traditional republican form of government of free and independent men into a democracy of ignorance and alienation.

These ideological differences were not the only dividing line by which individual Republicans in Congress were labeled "radical," "moderate," or "conservative." In fact, except for Charles Sumner and a few others whose records were consistent, many Republicans had carried with them simultaneously all of these political outlooks. They could be "radical" in discussing one enforcement bill and "moderate" or "conservative" in debating a different bill, or they could switch positions when the same bill was discussed. Political attitudes were not the sole factor that affected the decision making of the Republicans. In effect, because the geographical, economic, and political interests represented by the party members were so diverse, many Republicans had to make decisions on grounds other than the party's proclaimed principles.

However, despite all the ideological confusion and divisive political and economic interests, the Republicans managed to push through five enforcement laws in a short period of two years. Despite the suspicion and infighting, as the voting records on all the laws show, the majority of the party stood united. What cemented the party was not merely its proclaimed principles of justice and equality, or the desire to punish former enemies, or partisan interests, but all of these added together. Republicans were not political angels, and they wanted the enforcement laws to meet the party's pragmatic need to win elections in the North and to protect their black supporters in the South. But at the time, the party's need for self-preservation and expansion was indisputably associated with doing justice to black Americans, defining the contents of the Civil War amendments, constructing a healthy system of national elections, and expanding the federal government's functions in protecting citizens' rights. The enforcement laws carried with them these mixed goals. In this context, the Republicans and their enforcement acts deserve credit for consolidating the political results of the Civil War and opening new possibilities for American democracy.

CHAPTER THREE

The Anatomy of Enforcement, 1870–1876

Enforcement in Action

The sweeping enforcement laws adopted by the Republican Congress between May 1870 and June 1872 helped transform the principles of the Civil War amendments into the actual policies of the federal government. These laws demonstrated the Republican determination to use national power to secure the achievements of the late war, put down political rebellion in the South, guarantee the purity of national elections, and reinforce the party's strength, South and North. While Republicans in Congress cleared the way for federal enforcement, the actual effect of enforcement depended on the thoroughness and efficacy of the federal government. In addition to the party's control of Congress, which would guarantee both financial and political cooperation, the success of the enforcement acts was contingent on several other conditions: a sustaining (northern) public opinion supporting enforcement; an efficient state machinery, judicial and military, to implement the laws and carry out executive orders; and a strong and devoted president who would actively involve himself in planning and executing the laws.

By the time the first enforcement act passed Congress at the end of May 1870, there seemed little doubt that the law would be enforced by President Grant, who had pledged to secure black suffrage. In his inaugural address on March 4, 1869, Grant expressed his concern that as long as states withheld the freedmen's rights to vote, the issue of suffrage would "agitate the public." He had urged all the states to ratify the Fifteenth Amendment, which he considered the only practical solution to the troubles surrounding black suffrage.[1] Although elected as a Civil War hero with the famous slogan "Let us have peace," Grant was not ready to make peace with the Klan in the South. Aware of the

important expansion of federal powers brought about by the recent constitutional amendments and the enforcement acts, he believed that these laws were
made to consolidate the consequences of the Civil War. To an extent, Grant sub-
scribed to the radical Republican argument that maintaining the supremacy of
national authority in a period of political transition was not only proper but
necessary.[2]

Grant, however, acted cautiously and selectively. He would only use federal
military force to aid southern Republicans as a last resort. In July 1870, two
months after the first enforcement act became law, Governor William W.
Holden of North Carolina, in an attempt to counter the Klan raids, raised a
force of volunteers and sent it to the counties of Alamance and Caswell, both
"in a state of insurrection." Worrying that his six-hundred-some men, black
and white, could not deal with the Klan forces, Holden appealed to Grant that
"a regiment of federal troops be at once sent to the State," warning the president that the defeat of Republicanism in North Carolina would be "exceedingly
disastrous." Upon receiving Holden's letter, Grant immediately ordered Secretary of War William W. Belknap to dispatch six companies to Raleigh to "suppress violence and to maintain the law if other means should fail."[3] But despite
the federal aid, North Carolina was lost to the Democrats and Holden impeached for illegally organizing military forces and directing unlawful arrests in
March 1871.[4]

In South Carolina, Grant stood firm with the state Republicans and kept the
federal troops present in that heavily Republican state. Although the anti-Re-
publican Union Reform Party, which Grant termed "the enemies" of the party
that had supported him, had ruthlessly attacked the Republicans, Republicans
retained control in 1870. The "little disturbance . . . experienced in any quarter" may have been "attributable to the presence of detachments of United
States troops at the localities where they were most apprehended," Governor
Robert K. Scott reported.[5] But the Klansmen of the northern part of the state
raided the polls around election day and terrorized black voters.[6] Similar requests also reached Grant from Governor Harrison Reed of Florida, who wrote
in October 1870 to ask for "at least five companies of Federal soldiers" to be
used as "a police force to protect the people against violence in the discharge of
their duties as freemen at the polls" on election day.[7] Grant responded three
days before the election by sending two companies stationed in New Orleans to
Tallahassee. After the election was over, at Reed's request, Grant allowed them
to stay in Tallahassee to protect the Republican legislature until the end of its
first session in February 1871.[8]

In March 1871, watching the southern situation continue to deteriorate, Grant warned that when Congress was not in session, he might use the power given to him by the twelfth and thirteenth sections of the first enforcement act to "protect [South Carolina] and citizens thereof against domestic violence."[9] But the power authorized to the president to aid state governments by the first enforcement act was limited: troops were to be used only "to aid in the execution of judicial process" under the enforcement law. When the radical Republicans failed to secure passage of an earlier version of what became the Ku Klux Force Act, Grant called for anti-Klan legislation, by which he hoped to enlarge presidential power to suppress Klan terrorism and protect southern Republican strength.[10]

The Ku Klux Force Act, which the Democrats united to protest in a signed address, gave Grant the power to use military forces and to suspend the writ of habeas corpus. Armed with the Ku Klux Force Act, Grant was able to cope with the southern challenges with more strength. In October 1871, when Klan violence broke out in several counties in South Carolina, Grant suspended the writ of habeas corpus in the Klan-ridden areas and ordered federal troops to give prompt aid to the enforcement officers. They did so, and about two thousand Klansmen fled the counties. The presence of blue uniforms scared the Klansmen and effectuated enforcement. Alfred Howe Terry, the commander of the federal troops in the seaboard states (from South Carolina to Mississippi, plus Kentucky and Tennessee), reported that in 1870 alone, more than 200 expeditions of federal troops were sent out at the request of state and federal civil authorities. In 1871, 160 operations were reported, not including those in South Carolina to suppress the Klan.[11]

Between 1870 and 1872, federal troops played an important role in battling Klan activities, especially in South Carolina, Mississippi, and Florida. The main task of the troops was to help federal enforcement officers carry out their duties in the troubled areas. The numbers of troops stationed in the South and the aid they provided varied from state to state. The peak number of federal troops stationed in South Carolina during 1870 – 72 was about 1,000 men, with garrisons in nine locations. In Mississippi, there were only 198 federal troops in 1870; the number increased to 559 in 1872 and fell to 46 in 1874.[12] Before the 1870 elections, the southern appeal for military assistance mounted. When Florida requested federal troops, General William T. Sherman informed Grant that recent orders had taken "every company in Dept of the South." The number of troops in the South then was unimpressive, with only one company each in Tennessee and Mississippi, two in Kentucky, six in South Carolina, and sixteen in Alabama.[13] Mostly, the armed forces escorted federal enforcement officials to make arrests. But in places such as South Carolina, where Klan activities were more severe, federal troops participated in arresting criminals.

However, military operations and presidential proclamations suspending habeas corpus were two options employed only in times of emergency. The bulk of enforcement had to be accomplished by the federal courts under the auspices of the newly created Department of Justice. Besides the traditional duties of the attorney general, the department was given new powers, including enforcing federal criminal and civil regulations; supervising legal matters involving Native American affairs, the mails, immigration, and naturalization; and protecting and enforcing "the rights and property of the United States." A solicitor general was created to assist the attorney general, who received the authority to supervise the conduct of all district attorneys and control the financial accounts of the district attorneys, the marshals, and their assistants.[14] The creation of the Justice Department was an attempt to save federal expenses for hiring special counsels and to centralize the management of federal judicial affairs. But from the vantage point of enforcement, this new addition to the federal government helped institutionalize enforcement of the Fourteenth and Fifteenth Amendments in the early 1870s.

Early enforcement was conducted principally under the direction of Grant's second attorney general, Amos Akerman, a New Hampshire – born, Dartmouth-educated Georgia Republican. A former Confederate, Akerman nonetheless became "a dedicated opponent of Klanism" who truly believed in exercising national power to protect the rights of blacks in the South.[15] Akerman assumed his position when enforcing the Fourteenth and Fifteenth Amendments became the responsibility of the Department of Justice.[16] In Akerman's view, Klanism was not simply a form of racial hatred against black citizens; the Klan was an organized crime gang challenging the law and authority of the national government. Using the language of radical Republicans in Congress, he suggested employing "extraordinary means" to strike down the Klan.[17]

Hoping to crush Klanism quickly and efficiently, Akerman urged his subordinates to speed up their handling of enforcement cases against Klansmen. When Klan atrocities occurred in South Carolina in October 1871, Akerman instructed U.S. district attorney D. T. Cobin that the Klan "leaders in the conspiracies" and those who had "contributed intelligence and social influence to these conspiracies" should "be brought to trial and if found guilty by the jury, should be subjected to the sentence of the court." For those whose "criminality

[was] inferior to that of the first class," Akerman asked that they be punished at least by having to submit a written confession.[18] Akerman personally traveled to North Carolina and South Carolina to supervise the implementation of the enforcement acts in 1871. In South Carolina, where he spent two weeks with federal enforcement officers, Akerman took charge of the trials of a dozen of the worst Klan members, who were prosecuted and indicted before predominantly black juries. Shocked by the evidence of the Klan outrages presented to him, Akerman recommended a full-scale application of the recent Ku Klux Force Act to suppress the Klan in South Carolina.[19]

One of the most publicized and reported events during the course of early enforcement was the so-called Great South Carolina Ku Klux Klan Trials, in Columbia, in the winter of 1871 and 1872. The military operations in South Carolina were successful in 1871, and by the end of that year, the federal government had taken into custody approximately six hundred allegedly associated with Klan activities.[20] The large number of suspects undoubtedly increased the already enormous pressure on federal enforcement officers. In addition, the trials would last more than two months, producing proceedings of nearly four hundred pages.[21] Since it was the first time the federal courts handled cases arising under the enforcement acts (specifically, the Enforcement Act of May 31, 1870, and the Ku Klux Force Act of April 20, 1871) on such a large scale, the trials attracted national attention. When the trials opened in Columbia in November 1871, people flocked into the city, and the galleries of the city's large liberty hall, where the trials were to be held, were "exclusively occupied by colored persons of both sexes."[22]

The real importance of the trials was that this would be the first opportunity to test, publicly, the constitutionality of the enforcement acts. Since the passage of the first enforcement act in May 1870, Democrats had sought to repeal all the enforcement laws so far implemented, but unsuccessfully. Given the dominant Republican majority in both houses, a more realistic way to challenge the enforcement laws was in the judicial arena. Thus Democrats relied heavily on the strength of those who were judicially prominent and politically Democratic. The rationale of such strategy was that the Democratic legal experts would influence the interpretation of the enforcement acts and, ideally, invalidate them. In this sense, the trials became a judicial continuation of the national debate on the legality of federal enforcement of the Civil War amendments, which the Democrats had lost in Congress.

Accordingly, both Republicans and Democrats had devoted great attention to

these trials, which were to be conducted jointly presided over by Hugh L. Bond
of Maryland, judge of the Fourth Federal Circuit, and George Seabrook Bryan,
district judge for South Carolina. Although a determined Republican who
wanted to end the Klan terror "even if it [cost him his] life," Bond was careful
and substantive in constitutional reasoning. Bryan was less encouraging, actually leaning to the Democratic views of the enforcement laws. For the federal
government, U.S. attorney Cobin labored painstakingly in preparing the indictments of hundreds of Klan members. The defense team was headed by two
leading Democratic legal minds of the day: Reverdy Johnson and Henry Stanbery. A Civil War Democrat, Johnson had opposed extreme measures of federal
government toward the South throughout the war and demanded restoration of
the former rights and privileges of southern states after the war. As a lawyer, he
was regarded by his contemporaries as unsurpassed in the American bar. Stanbery served as attorney general under President Andrew Johnson and as one of
the president's counsel during his impeachment trial in 1868. Johnson had
nominated him to the Supreme Court, but the Republicans rejected him.[23]

During the trials, Republican and Democratic legal experts rendered long arguments over the constitutionality of the enforcement acts, which were essentially repetitions of the congressional debates but focusing more on the legal
technicality of these laws. On several occasions, the Democratic attorneys challenged the constitutionality of the Enforcement Act of May 31, 1870, particularly sections 3 (prohibiting obstructions to fulfilling prerequisites required for
voting), 4 (forbidding the use of force to obstruct voting and registration), and
6 (penalizing conspiracies against the enjoyment of rights and privileges of citizens). A typical example was the trial of *United States v. Allen Crosby*, which
charged six whites with conspiracy against an African American voting for a Republican candidate for the House under sections 1, 5, 6, and 7 of the Enforcement Act of May 31, 1870, and section 2 of the Ku Klux Force Act. Stanbery,
the chief defense counsel, attempted to quash the case by holding that the
crime had been wrongfully charged. The word *suffrage*, argued Stanbery, was
never specifically mentioned in section 6 of the Enforcement Act of May 31,
1870, so that the conspiracy against the black voter was simply "a domestic
crime" unpunishable by the federal law. Daniel H. Chamberlain, the future governor of South Carolina who at the time served as state attorney general and
one of the prosecutors of the case, replied that the right of suffrage was "secured . . . in the first section of the act": "We have indicted according to the language of the act." Judge Bond, presiding over the trial, reinforced Chamber-

lain's argument by declaring that crimes and offenses defined in later sections of the Enforcement Act of May 31, 1870, were "applicable to all the antecedent sections," including the first one in which the right of suffrage for black citizens was declared. Stanbery then asked that the case go to the Supreme Court. Finally, the trial continued on the valid points while Stanbery and Johnson agreed to have the issue under question taken to the Supreme Court, which never handled this case.[24]

In another case, *United States v. Robert Hayes Mitchell*, Stanbery defended Mitchell, a young Ku Klux Klan member charged with the murder of a black Republican under section 6 of the first enforcement act. The testimony, which took four days and ran to 120 pages in the congressional report, gave strong evidence for the political crimes committed by the Klan in northwestern South Carolina. Again, the Democratic attorneys insisted that section 6 of the Enforcement Act of May 31, 1870, was defective because it did not specify that the right of suffrage was among the "immunities and privileges" protected by that section. Therefore, the indictment was not sustained, and the defective section of the law had to be quashed.[25] Both Stanbery and Johnson knew well that the language of section 6 was general in nature; it prohibited conspiracies to prevent a citizen's "free exercise and enjoyment of any right or privilege granted or secured to him by the Constitution or laws of the United States." The Republicans, as discussed in the previous chapter, inserted this section with the intention of enforcing both the Fourteenth and Fifteenth Amendments. They had anticipated that many crimes against black voters would occur not at the polls but outside the polling places and would be committed not by states' but by individuals' actions. But Johnson and Stanbery chose not to follow the Republican logic and to make that connection. Instead, they hoped to defeat the section by arguing that the generality of its language was incompatible with the nature of the enforcement act. In a way, the Democratic argument foreshadowed the Supreme Court's decision in *United States v. Reese* in 1876, which challenged the legal nicety of section 6 of the Enforcement Act of May 31, 1870.[26] In a much more flamboyant, partisan tone, Johnson attacked federal interference in state affairs: "The war ended and ended so as forever to put an end to what I think was an erroneous construction of the Constitution." The enforcement acts, Johnson declared, "were unconstitutional and violative, not only of the rights of [South Carolina], but of every State in the Union, as well as the rights of the individual citizen." Stanbery again asked that the case be filed with the Supreme Court for a final analysis and decision, but Bond overruled that motion and continued the trial. Mitchell finally pleaded guilty and was sentenced to eighteen months in prison and a fine of one hundred dollars.[27]

The cases put to trial in South Carolina amounted to a small portion of the cases pending. According to historian Lou F. Williams, nearly fifty Klansmen pleaded guilty in the initial court session, and during 1872 nearly a hundred cases terminated in South Carolina. It was a small number when compared with the number of cases untried, which amounted to about twelve hundred in 1872.[28] Although brief, the trials were a success, for they stopped Klan activities and scared Klan members out of the state. But more important was that the trials had demonstrated the federal government's determination to combat Klan terrorism and to protect the rights of black citizens.

The effect of enforcement was also dramatic in other areas such as northern Mississippi, where the Republicans were strong and federal enforcement machinery adequate. By the end of 1870, 45 cases under the enforcement acts had been reported to the attorney general. Thirty-four resulted in convictions, and eleven were either dismissed or nolle prosequi. Meanwhile, 271 cases under the Enforcement Act of May 31, 1870, were pending in federal courts.[29] In 1871, there were 314 criminal cases under the enforcement acts — 206 from the South and 108 from the rest of the country — of which 128 ended in convictions.[30] In 1872, the enforcement cases almost tripled, reaching 856, with 603 coming from the South. The national conviction rate was about 53 percent — 456 out of 856 ended in convictions — but the conviction rate in the South was as high as nearly 90 percent (448 cases out of 603 ended in convictions).[31]

In retrospect, federal enforcement of the Fourteenth and Fifteenth Amendments in the early 1870s was a remarkable episode in the history of Reconstruction. Its historical significance lies not only in its unprecedented use of national and state machinery to protect the political and civil rights of black Americans but also in transforming into action the idea of the supremacy of national authority, as contained in Reconstruction legislation. Most of all, it helped to maintain the political promises of the Thirteenth, Fourteenth, and Fifteenth Amendments.

Enforcement was nonetheless carried out under very difficult circumstances, which probably accounted for its brevity. One of the major problems was the lack of a long-term special task force for enforcement. The Department of Justice and the federal judiciary — the attorney general, district attorneys, federal judges, marshals, and their appointees — carried out enforcement as additional business, in addition to their routine work. Although the president could use force in case of emergency, the process of inviting military assistance was complicated and involved several bureaucracies, including the Justice and War Departments and the White House. Because the command was largely decentralized and communication primitive, the efficiency of enforcement depended on the political judgment and professional discipline of federal enforcement officers.[32]

In addition, prudence was a concern. In a sense, enforcement was a constitutional experiment in the new federal-state relations established by the new constitutional amendments. Anticipating strong local resistance in the field and courtroom, the Department of Justice had to act with great caution. Even Akerman himself would caution his subordinates to perform their duties "in no unnecessary harshness . . . [and] in a decent and gentlemanly manner."[33] Despite giving Akerman a strong hand in suppressing the Klan in October 1871, Grant was reluctant to resort to frequent uses of extreme methods such as the suspension of habeas corpus. Meanwhile, enforcement was interrupted by Grant's decision in December 1871 to dismiss Akerman, whose rulings on certain railroad land grants had displeased influential Republicans connected to such railroad tycoons as Collis P. Huntington and Jay Gould.[34] Gone with Akerman was much of the vigor of federal enforcement. Although Akerman's successor, George H. Williams, a former senator from Oregon, continued the prosecutions, he was more interested in ending the prosecutions of the Klansmen than in revitalizing enforcement.[35]

Another major difficulty was the lack of adequate federal resources, financial and personnel, to sustain enforcement. Large-scale prosecutions and trials like the 1871–72 Ku Klux Klan cases in South Carolina were rare because of funding restraints and shortages in enforcement officers to secure evidence. Although a relatively large number of Klansmen were convicted in South Carolina, few went to prison.[36] Federal officers often found themselves unable to deal with the open defiance of the enforcement laws by local government and, as a result, had to resort to the Department of Justice for more assistance. In 1872, when Democrats in New York were determined to challenge the enforcement acts by using state-appointed election supervisors to confront federal supervisors, George H. Sharpe, the federal marshal of New York's southern district, urged Williams to allow him to appoint more deputy supervisors, because "many of the men appointed to duty . . . were arrested by various local authorities." He added, "The machinery of the election is already being prepared by the municipal authorities, and it is proper that our action should be simultaneous, and so timely as to give information to all good citizens."[37]

The shortage of money presented another serious obstacle: enforcement was

expensive, but Congress was not very generous. During the peak years of enforcement between 1870 and 1872, the expenses of maintaining courts tripled
in South Carolina, quadrupled in the western district of North Carolina, and
rose ten times in Mississippi.[38] Even in places such as New York, where the judiciary budget was adequate at the beginning, inadequate funding became a
major problem when the Ku Klux Force Act enlarged the scope of enforcement.
After the Ku Klux Force Act went into effect, John Davenford, the chief federal
supervisor of elections in the southern district of New York, wrote to Sharpe to
ask for an increase in funding for enforcing the new law, under which, Davenford wrote, he had "at least 100 more election districts . . . to care for." Sharpe,
in turn, forwarded Davenford's request to the attorney general and apprised the
latter that his district needed a "reasonable and proper" increase of the funding
from fifty thousand to seventy-five thousand dollars.[39] The deficiency in funding continued in 1873 and forced Attorney General Williams to ask district attorneys to stop prosecuting cases under the enforcement acts "unless the public
interest imperatively require[d] it."[40]

These difficulties had, in one way or another, contributed to the decline of
federal prosecutions against the Klan and election frauds. In 1873, the attorney
general reported 1,304 enforcement cases, but the conviction rate had dropped
significantly to 36 percent. The number of dismissals of that year doubled the
figure in the preceding year. After 1874, the conviction rate continued to decline. Of 966 reported cases under the enforcement acts, only 102, or fewer
than 10 percent, resulted in convictions. The number of dismissed or quashed
cases reached 864 by 1875, and in 1876 the total number of the cases under the
enforcement acts was 149, of which only 3 resulted in convictions, two of these
in the South. Criminal prosecutions under the enforcement acts continued until the early 1890s, but, as Appendix 7 shows, after 1876, not only did the total
numbers of cases fluctuate, but fewer and fewer convictions were from the
South, where blacks were most often prevented from voting.[41]

The Impact of Liberal Opposition and the 1872 Election on Black Suffrage Enforcement

Financial, administrative, and personnel problems had been the impediments
to long-term enforcement, but a more severe blow to the implementation of the
enforcement laws came from political factionalism within the Republican party.

The liberal Republican movement started in the late 1860s and early 1870s as a faction challenging the political professionalism then appearing in the party. Originally labeling themselves "independents," "reformers," or "true Republicans," the liberals distinguished themselves from the regular, or stalwart, Republicans, whom they despised as representative of increasingly corrupt politics under the leadership of the politically inept Grant. Hardly before Grant's first year in the White House was over, some liberals, such as one of William Sprague's friends, wanted to dissolve the Republican party because "its vitality [was] gone."[42] But this factional counterforce became a national movement by the end of 1871 when it merged with other political forces opposing Grant's renomination for president. Some veteran radical Republicans such as Carl Schurz and George W. Julian became the leaders of the movement, while others, including Charles Sumner and Henry Wilson, were quite sympathetic with its political slogans. It drew substantial support from a group of professionals, academicians, reform-minded businessmen, and influential editors such as Charles Francis Adams Jr. of the *North American Review*, Edwin L. Godkin of the *Nation*, Horace White of the *Chicago Tribune*, and Samuel Bowles of the *Springfield Republican*—and, of course, Horace Greeley of the *New York Tribune*.[43]

As the liberal Republican movement became nationalized, the liberals began to identify more and more with the opposition to further federal enforcement of black suffrage in the South. As briefly discussed in the previous chapter, some liberals, such as Schurz, had strongly supported the first enforcement law in 1870, but by April 1871, Schurz denounced the Ku Klux Force Act and had opposed every enforcement bill ever since. To supporters of the liberal cause, the federal enforcement policy was a "policy of repression"; the only way to save the "fruits of the war" was "a generous cause and an honest capable man at the head of affairs."[44] Ideologically, the liberals might have been nostalgic for such Jeffersonian values as limited government, state sovereignty, individual freedom, and moral politics, but their hatred at the postwar development of machine politics and its consequences—in particular, political corruption and abuse of state and federal patronage by the Grant administration—was partly derived from their personal frustrations in office seeking. They feared that federal enforcement of these postwar amendments would lead to centralization and, inevitably, endless political corruption. "Centralization is the order of the day and centralization breeds corruption and abuses," Charles Francis Adams warned his audience in Quincy, Massachusetts, not long before enforcement was launched in 1870. He saw numerous power-hungry politicians "raving like wolves around the President and heads of Departments, and snap[ping] like hungry hounds at each others' bones."[45]

The liberals also shared a deep fear and distrust of black suffrage. Their feelings became particularly visible after southern violence and disorder broke out in the late 1860s and early 1870s. They regarded enfranchising blacks by national power as a fatal error of Reconstruction. Many accepted the view that the freedmen's ignorance and illiteracy had caused both the corruption of southern Republican governments and the resentment of southern whites. They advocated a national literacy test for all voters.[46] Responding to the liberals' call for a detachment of party politics in the South, the liberal *Nation* declared the "bold" political experiment of black suffrage a failure in 1871 and asked to leave the whole issue of suffrage to the states.[47]

The "let-alone" attitude was shared and voiced by Horace Greeley, the would-be presidential candidate for the liberals in 1872. The onetime radical persuaded Josephine Griffing not to offer charity to blacks because they were "an easy, worthless race, taking no thought for the morrow, and liking to lean on those who befriend[ed] them." Charity would not help to "stimulate them to self reliance."[48] The liberal distrust of blacks' political capacity was a reflection of emerging social Darwinism, a popular subject in liberal journals throughout the 1870s. One article published in the *Nation* in July 1870 applied Darwinism to explain the "question of race" and concluded that the African was "one of the most stationary [races] . . . [and] it [would] require a much longer time than it [was] worth . . . to bring him into the condition of [the white] race."[49] To others, the most fearful thing was not black incapacity in politics but its result. The *Chicago Tribune* argued that partisan politics would reduce voters "to the level of a machine" and every northern voter should "rise above party lines and do his own thinking."[50] Such sentiments were striking and ironic: the liberal fear of what the Yale sociologist William Graham Sumner would later call "a corruption of democracy" echoed the anxieties expressed by Democrats and conservative Republicans during the debate over the black suffrage laws a few years before.[51]

In retrospect, the liberals' concerns were historically legitimate and raised fundamental issues that would challenge the Republican party's black suffrage policy in the years to come. How, for instance, would political equality for blacks be maintained without strong and effective federal enforcement? How long could enforcement be sustained even if the federal government was willing to enforce the laws, given the intensity of political confrontations in the South? How could the party maintain its commitment to black suffrage when institutionally the party had to compete with Democrats to maintain or obtain power at both national and local levels? Finally, how willingly would Republican constituencies support the party's commitment to black suffrage? The liberals had no answers for these questions. In fact, they wanted to remove the element of black suffrage from national politics, or at least lessen its impact. The liberals viewed the regular Republicans' programs as purely expedient, and inevitably such views narrowed their objectives in the 1872 presidential election solely to anti-Grantism.

Anti-Grantism would not help the liberals gain sympathy or support from the regular Republican camp. A mixture of some of the party's founders, second-generation Republicans, and black Republicans, the regulars continued to identify enforcement as the party's responsibility and a political necessity, and they were determined to place it at the top of the party's program in the 1872 election. For regular Republicans, too, the year 1872 signaled no immediate prospect of peace and good feelings. They interpreted the recent atrocities against blacks by the Ku Klux Klan in the South and election frauds committed by Democrats in the North as evidence of political recovery by the former rebels. Retreat from their enforcement policy, one Republican warned party leaders, meant that the country would "go Democratic . . . [and] have another scene of bloodshed."[52] *Harper's Weekly*, then still a major Republican organ in the North, constantly furnished northern readers with detailed and vivid reports of southern disorder and Klan terrorism and reiterated the importance of keeping Republicans in power. One of the weekly's reports on Georgia informed the northern audience that prior to the enforcement, any "unoffending and blameless" Republican was "compelled to sleep with his rifle under his pillow" and that "no language [could] paint too severely" the Klan outrages. "So long as the General government interposed," the writer declared, "the life of the colored voter was safe, or his assassins were punished; the white Republicans for the past year have escaped personal violence from their Democratic neighbors."[53]

To be sure, even among the regular Republicans, few saw the federal enforcement of black rights as a permanent policy; but many believed that, in the period of political transition, federal protection for blacks and Republican control of national power were indispensable. If things remained as now, Grant wrote at the beginning of federal enforcement in 1870, it was "of the utmost importance" that Republicans control the national government. If the party lost control in 1872, Grant warned, it "would lose, largely the results of [its] victories in the field," war pensions and debts would go unpaid, and the Civil War amendments "would be dead letters."[54] Republican thinking certainly contained some idealism about how its control of power would help the southern states and southern people, including black men, grow accustomed to the practice of black enfranchisement. The Republican party, as Massachusetts financier John M. Forbes argued, should firmly hold national power "until the colored populations [were] strong enough to protect themselves": "Give them, for a few years longer, the pen, and the press, and the habit of carrying arms, and of working for themselves before you turn them out to the tender mercies of their old masters, under the plausible guise of 'local self-government.'"[55]

Thus, with the 1872 presidential election came the clash between two Republican notions of the federal role in protecting black rights: the state activism upheld by regular Republicans, and the restrained federal interference in state affairs advocated by liberal Republicans. In 1872 the Democratic party was still far from being competitive. But when it threw its support to Horace Greeley, whom liberal Republicans nominated to challenge the regular Republican candidate, Grant, the presidential election of 1872 became a contest between two factions of the Republican party. Subsequently, the policy of enforcement became a focal point of the election. The "chief questions to be decided" in the presidential election, *Harper's Weekly* announced, were whether "a cruel and desperate minority [should] be allowed to renew its outrages upon the rights and welfare of the whole under the shelter of Mr. Greeley's supporters, or whether it [should] be crushed or broken down by the firm rule of the Republican party and of President Grant."[56]

In many ways, Grant was not the most desirable candidate even for regular Republicans. His patronage policy satisfied few, and his Dominican diplomacy disappointed many. But he benefited greatly from the prevailing political sentiment of 1872, which was characterized by the dominance of sectional animosity and distrust. Grant's Civil War record, the continuing sectional strife and the uncertainty it created, his commitment to federal enforcement of black rights, and, most of all, the support of regular Republicans — all helped him gain support from the party and the populace.[57] Although some veteran Republicans disliked Grant's political style, they still regarded him as the party's best choice in 1872. John Sherman, a longtime opponent of Grant's patronage policy, despite his brother's close relationship with Grant, fully supported his reelection because the "chief interest" of the election was "the preservation of the Republican party," which was "essential to secure the fair enforcement of the results of the war."[58] Writing from Berlin, John Bigelow shared Sherman's view, advising the *New York Tribune* that since popular feeling did not "ask for a change of President this time," the newspaper should not agitate "a permanent opposition to the popular choice, much less to deprive the country of the benefit." It was, Bigelow declared, simply the wrong time "for the Democrats to go to Washington."[59] Amos Akerman, who directed the early phase of enforcement and had been asked to resign as attorney general, enthusiastically supported Grant's reelection as "the speediest way to give permanent tranquility to the South." With Grant in the White House, Akerman assured Republicans, the enforcement policy would continue and "the offenders [would] cease to hope for impunity in crime."[60] Charles Sumner, the all-time champion of black rights, was probably the most distressed when he found that he had to make a choice between Grant, for whose political sincerity and competence he had little respect, and Greeley, a onetime fellow fighter in the war against slavery but a politically changeable man who represented the liberal interest that wished to do away with black issues and reconcile with the South. Sumner wanted to see federal enforcement continued, but he did not want to see Grant reelected. Writing to Carl Schurz, Sumner confided his dilemma:

> I tremble for my country when I contemplate the possibility of this man [Grant] being fastened upon us for another four years. What can be done to make this impossible? I also tremble when I think of reconstruction, with Liberty & Equality, committed for four years to the tender mercies of the Democrats. Which way is daylight?[61]

Under pressure from liberals, regulars, and black Republicans, Sumner could not make up his mind by April 1872 and, as he told Henry W. Longfellow, decided to wait further "when the whole field [was] clear to take that position in which [he could] best serve the country & especially continue to maintain the rights of the African race."[62]

Sumner shared the liberals' frustration and resentment, especially toward the so-called stalwart Republicans, who had been viewed as the maneuverers behind the inept Grant. The stalwarts, identified by their extreme loyalty to the party, were in fact the products of the emerging machine politics of the early 1870s, meaning professionally managed politics. These Republicans were largely the second generation of the party, people who gained their reputations mostly by their professional management of the party affairs at the local and national levels during the Reconstruction years. Among those conventionally identified as such were Roscoe Conkling of New York, Simon Cameron of Pennsylvania, and John A. Logan of Illinois. In later times, William Chandler of New Hampshire and Henry Cabot Lodge of Massachusetts would be added to the list.

These regular managers possessed a political view different from that of the liberals. Both groups saw the profound changes that the Civil War and Reconstruction had brought to the nation's old constitutionalism; both welcomed the party's transformation from a prewar coalition of loosely connected antislavery forces into a nationally structured organization. But where liberals feared the dangers of centralized power and degraded party politics, the regulars saw the potential of the national government and the opportunity for the party to benefit from it. The regular leaders developed a notion of a modern party system — that is, parties were no longer merely a moral club of refined and selected gentleman politicians but an instrument that could effectively mobilize a wide range of interests to gain and consolidate political and economic benefits. These Republicans understood the paradox confronting northern politics in the early 1870s that the liberals had failed to identify: the professionalization of the Republican politics was the very source of political strength that enabled the party to secure both political dominance and the achievements of Reconstruction, including black suffrage. Thus, for these regulars, federal enforcement of the Civil War amendments was an important part of the expanding federal functions and a good opportunity to exercise political influence and patronage.

Among Grant's staunchest supporters were black Republicans. Both the desire for complete liberty and equality and the knowledge that their constitutional rights remained unsecured induced them to side steadfastly with the regular Republicans. At a time when the lives of black voters were subject to Klan terrorism, Republican-led enforcement provided the only hope for black Americans. The party was "the deck" when "all outside" was "the sea," Frederick Douglass said.[63] In May 1872, the convention of black citizens held in New Orleans pledged "unswerving devotion" to the Republican nominee of the Philadelphia convention.[64] For black voters, a presidential candidate's qualifications were rather straightforward: whether he would commit to a continuous enforcement of black rights, and whether he was capable of preventing the reversal of Reconstruction. Black Americans had "no interest in public affairs higher than the freedom and elevation of [their] long[-]enslaved race," Douglass declared in August 1872, but because the country wanted "certainty" and the confidence and repose only certainty could give, blacks had to support regular Republican candidate Grant, who was "pure and simple." Douglass regarded the liberal Republicans' politics of reconciliation as dangerous and their presidential candidate, Greeley, as "many sided, . . . wicked and ambiguous." Undoubtedly, a commitment to enforcing black rights was the major factor that influenced black voters in the 1872 election.[65] Even when Sumner, the paramount supporter of black rights who sympathized with the liberal cause and disputed Grant's policy on Santo Domingo, accused Grant of lacking sincere devotion to the course of enforcing black rights and urged blacks to support Greeley instead of Grant, Douglass refused to take Sumner's advice. In an open letter, Douglass defended Grant's record on black civil rights and called him "a wise, firm, and consistent friend of the just rights of man, without regard to race, color, or previous condition of servitude."[66]

Thus, the enforcement of the Fourteenth and Fifteenth Amendments became the most valuable political capital for Grant and the Republican party in the election of 1872. This had been unmistakably clear to supporters of Grant's reelection. At the Republican convention in Philadelphia on June 5, 1872, Gerrit Smith, a veteran antislavery activist and an influential New York Republican, nominated Grant as the presidential candidate. In his speech, Smith gave special attention to the Ku Klux Force Act, which, he believed, had "done more good in a shorter time than any law ever enacted by the Congress." He again argued that the state governments could not be trusted and black rights could be protected only by the national government. Oliver P. Morton, a leading Senate Republican, linked the party's success to national interests. He argued that the Fourteenth and Fifteenth Amendments were the party's works and that it should continue its efforts until no other party could challenge "the legality or the validity of these amendments" and until blacks had "the full and free enjoyment of their rights."[67]

To ensure popular support, the party pledged to do more. In their platform, Republicans declared that they would continue to enforce the recent constitutional amendments, which could "safely be entrusted only to the party that secured those amendments." They promised that "complete liberty and exact equality in the enjoyment of all civil, political, and public rights" would be maintained throughout the country "by efficient and appropriate State and Federal legislation" and that no racial discrimination would be allowed in the nation's law and government.[68] In his letter of acceptance, Grant also promised to bring "the time when the title of citizen" carried with it "all the protection and privileges to the humbled that it [did] to the most exalted."[69]

With the strong enforcement program between 1870 and 1872, the party's promise of a further commitment to enforce national laws, the popular sentiment to defeat the revival of the southern slave power, popular support from rank-and-file Republicans, and disarray in the liberal and Democratic camps, the Republican party won the 1872 election, "the fairest and most democratic presidential election in the South until 1968." The party carried every northern and western state along with eight southern states. Grant won 3,597,132 popular votes, the largest popular majority of the party in the nineteenth century, and 286 electoral votes, four times more than Greeley's 66. The Republicans also regained a two-thirds majority in the House while securing a similar majority in the Senate. Undoubtedly, the regular Republican victory benefited enormously from the nation's lack of conciliatory sentiment and a strong Republican vote from the South. Years later, historian William Hesseltine would interpret the election as "disapproval of Greeley rather than approval of Grant."[70] That also could mean disapproval of Greeley's policies – and they were vastly different from those of Grant and the regular Republicans.

Oscillation and Disruption of Enforcement

Despite its pledge made before the election, the party's enforcement policy after 1872 proved much less vigorous than in previous years. Indeed, inconsistency and indecision became its chief characteristics. Two related events seriously disrupted the process of enforcement: the economic panic of 1873, and the congressional election of 1874.

The 1873 panic peaked with the collapse of Jay Cooke and Company in New York on the morning of September 18, but several other smaller banking and investment businesses had already been compelled to close their doors earlier. The panic resulted from a series of factors, including inflated European financial markets, insecure investment in the railroad business in the South, investment miscalculations, and lack of national regulatory policies. But when the panic caused the failure of about five thousand businesses with a total capitalization of $228,499,000 involved, it seriously disrupted postwar economic expansion and forced the Republican government to deal with the situation.[71] The panic also triggered tremendous resentment among the working class, which helped give rise to the modern labor movement. In the winter of 1873 and 1874, while New York bankers asked the Grant administration to help the markets recover, workers held massive demonstrations in major northern industrial cities such as New York, Boston, and Chicago to demand greater governmental responsibility for public relief and fair wages. Strikes spread throughout the nation.[72] The economic depression occurred when the federal government was equipped with no constitutional authority or institution to cope with abrupt economic shocks and their social consequences. Neither major party had any positive policy, nor was either prepared to meet the challenge.

A more important consequence of the panic was probably the redirection of national politics. As the old two-party line based on wartime ideologies was dismantling and tension between labor and capital throughout the country increased, a new configuration of sectional and economic interests began to replace the old sectional, racial animosities. When the Republican government took steps toward more economic regulation, the party found itself deeply divided along regional lines on railroad rates, currency, and federal interference with the economy. The eastern, western, and southern states, for example, clashed over railroad rates in December 1873, with the West and South united in demanding national regulation and reasonable railroad rates and the eastern states opposing such regulations. On currency, party lines became even more confusing during the debates. Western and southern congressmen of both parties attempted to transform John Sherman's currency plan into an "inflation bill" so that about sixty-four million dollars in greenbacks and national bank notes could be injected into the financial market. After calculating its consequences, Grant reversed his original stand by vetoing the bill. His veto won the approval of most eastern investors and businesses wishing to see a governmental commitment to specie payment and honest money, but western states felt that their interests had been ignored.[73] The West, declared the *St. Louis Daily Globe*, must throw away "petty localism" and unite "in demanding a scheme for the general good of this section."[74]

The economic disorder and its consequences also benefited the Democrats, who lost no time in exploiting Republican misfortune. In the congressional elections of 1874, Democrats won control of the House of Representatives for the first time since 1856. The number of House Democrats rose from 69 to 169, and Democrats gained 10 new Senate seats. Meanwhile, Democrats returned to power in several southern states, including Arkansas, Alabama, and Texas. Republicans also lost governorships in several important northern states, including New York, Massachusetts (for the first time), Pennsylvania, Illinois, Indiana, and Ohio. Out of the thirty-five states that held elections in 1874, twenty-three went Democratic.[75]

The 1873 panic and 1874 defeat had an enormous impact on the Republican outlook on the future of party politics. These events reinforced or accelerated the shift of the party's attention from the political issues of the late war to economic issues. This evolution, and Democratic opportunism, were not the only reasons the Republicans lost in 1874. Resentment in Republican ranks at the party's economic policies contributed to the defeat, especially in the Midwest. Zachariah Chandler, a party leader from Michigan, informed James G. Blaine that the Republican defeat in the Midwest was due to "discontents and dissatisfaction" from the late financial panic and "the consequent unsettled condition of monetary and business affairs." Because of this and other issues such as temperance, he told the House Speaker, "a large percentage of the Republicans" in Ohio, Michigan, and Indiana simply cast no vote for the Republican candidates "through apathy or indifference."[76] Commenting on the party's defeat and its impact on the 1876 presidential election, a New York paper advised Republicans to "do their utmost" in the remaining months of the present session and, "with unsparing vigor," to push through such measures as a new currency bill, a civil service bill, and a cheap transportation bill.[77] Responding to the defeat in 1874, even veteran Republicans realized that post-1870 economic and social developments would bring more and more challenges that the old party ideology and structure could neither comprehend nor accommodate. Lamenting the Republican defeat and disarray, John Bigelow declared that since the party, established "for the constitutional resistance to the extension of slavery," had emancipated blacks under Lincoln and enfranchised them under Grant, "its *raison d'être* ha[d] ceased."[78]

The panic of 1873 and the 1874 election cast a large shadow over enforcement policy, but the Grant administration and Republican Congress did not immediately abandon enforcement or eliminate black rights as an issue. Grant was never a faithful preacher for racial equality and hardly an ardent fighter for black rights. In his second inaugural address, he pledged to protect the civil rights "which citizenship should carry with it," but he declined the idea of social equality, which was not "a subject to be legislated upon." His announcement that he would seek no legislation "to advance the social status of the colored man, except to give him a fair chance to develop what there [was] good in him," was described by *Harper's Weekly* as "thoroughly in accord with the national policy so emphatically indorsed by the people."[79]

However, Grant was also serious and sincere enough to believe in the federal government's responsibility to protect the rights of national citizenship. He was certainly aware of the consequences of elections with or without black votes. In his sixth annual message, delivered on December 7, 1874, Grant condemned the illegal activities in the latest elections in the South, the use of force and threats to compel black voters to vote according to the wishes of their employers. He reiterated that his administration would continue to enforce the constitutional amendments "with vigor." If the Fifteenth Amendment and the enforcement acts remained unenforced, Grant believed, the "whole scheme of colored enfranchisement [was] worse than mockery and little better than a crime." While he asked Congress to investigate the elections, however, Grant noticed the unpopularity of federal enforcement, which was also "repugnant" to his own feeling, so he cautioned that federal interference in state affairs must be strongly supported by the evidence required by the law.[80]

Grant's enforcement policy was fraught with inconsistency and uncertainty. When violence broke out in Louisiana in 1873 and 1874, Grant dispatched federal troops to help the state Republican government. But when a similar situation occurred in Mississippi, Grant hesitated. In a local election in Warran County (Vicksburg) in August 1874, Democrats defeated Republican candidates by a combination of intimidation and manipulation. Racial disputes took place when the Democrats wanted to control the county government. White mobs declared war against black citizens, who decided to withdraw from the city. By the end of the year, about three hundred blacks and two whites had been killed during the riots. Only after Republican governor Adelbert Ames sent two requests for federal help were troops finally sent to Vicksburg in January 1875 to calm the situation.[81]

While the vigor of enforcement declined after the 1872 election, complaints from southern blacks about Klan violence and Democratic election frauds continued to flow into the White House and Congress. In February 1873, a black voter from Savannah, Georgia, complained to Grant that his vote had been refused by state election officials, who refused to acknowledge his tax payment. The former rebels were fully equipped with muskets and bayonets "to prevent [blacks] from voting." The black Republican also reported difficulties for blacks in obtaining formal education, for there were not enough local schools and "not one third of the colored children" were admitted. The writer asked Grant to look over these examples of local oppression and see if there was "any justice in it."[82] Another Republican voter, whose house was burned down by Klansmen because he voted for Republican tickets, appealed to Grant that the federal government should "give due consideration" to a tough enforcement policy to suppress the Klan and save local Republicans from "lawless desperation or midnight assassins." Because the Democrats had regained their power in many southern locales, the writer believed that seeking redress in a state court "would amount to nothing."[83] In other words, the federal government was the only source from which black voters could seek protection.

Black citizens' demands for federal protection of their political rights mounted after the 1874 election. A large number of letters from Republican voters in southern states vividly described the election frauds committed by local Democrats. In one case, blacks in the parish of Caddo, Louisiana, had been forced by local whites to vote for a Democratic candidate. "We have never voted the Democrat ticket and never will," the black voters wrote, "[but] we can not help it for the way these white people here in these southern states is going on with us. . . . We stay here among them."[84] A Georgia black Republican, whose candidacy for the state legislature was denied by state election officials, detailed to the president how local Democrats had controlled the election through force and fraud:

> Voting Day comes over. Early in the morning seven hundred Colored men & me . . . assemble at the court house and ask for two republican men to be appointed as managers. No, no, cried the Democrats, you can not get any appointed here. The colored continue to gather. We declared that we would not vote unless some man was there that would see that we got a fair election. While we were at the polls the Democrats, to show that they were not going to give a fair election, put a large wood box in the Court house door & nail a rope on the top of it, turn the hallow site in the Court house, shut all the doors of the Court house but the one that the box was in & put all Democratic managers inside & we are [sic] tap the box to receive tickets and hand them to those that was inside. Therefore we saw that they were going to rascal us out of the election. We concluded not to cast a vote to this end. We all left the polls and never voted at all.

"Shall such election as this pass?" the black writer asked. "Is it not in your Power to issue fair election when [the] Governor . . . won't do it? If not, what shall we poor Freedman do?" He asked for another election.[85]

Black complaints sent a warning signal to the Grant administration and the then Republican Congress that the party might lose the next presidential election without further enforcement to guarantee a fair election for black and Republican voters in the South. Grant himself continued to pass the letters from the South on to the Department of Justice and Congress and call for a more powerful enforcement law to guarantee honest elections in the South, particularly in Louisiana, Arkansas, and Mississippi, where the state governments were still under Republican control.[86] Thus, at the last session of the Forty-third Congress, soon after passing Charles Sumner's civil rights bill in January 1875 as a final tribute to the unwavering champion of equal rights who died in 1874,[87] the Republicans immediately launched a campaign for a new enforcement law.

The new enforcement bill (H.R. 4745) was introduced into the House by John Coburn (R-Ind.) on February 18, 1875. The original bill had thirteen sections and largely reinforced federal power over elections—but with important improvements. The bill prohibited any conspiracy, violence, or subversion conducted by individuals or combined individuals to "invade" or "usurp" state governments (secs. 1 and 2), an important measure to sustain Republican state governments in the South, which were under siege from the Democrats. The bill reinforced the provisions in the previous enforcement laws prohibiting any intimidation, bearing of arms, and violence against voters on election days or refusal to deny registration to qualified voters (sec. 3). It also required the states to give "sufficient opportunities" for voters to register (sec. 4). In the meantime, the bill penalized the destruction and concealment of ballot boxes and voter lists (sec. 5). The harshest measure was the sixth section, which imposed a death penalty on those engaged in illegal actions (as listed in the bill) who killed other individuals. Obviously an attempt to deal with election frauds in the southern rural areas, the new bill specifically extended the power of election supervisors in the cities and towns with a population of twenty thousand or more to those functioning in rural counties (secs. 8 and 9). This addition revived the Kellogg proposal (S. No. 791), which the House had killed in 1872. But the bill also provided that enforcement officers created by this bill would receive no federal compensation for their service (sec. 11), a reaffirmation of the provision in the 1872 civil appropriation bill (the last enforcement act between 1870 and 1872). Finally, the bill reinforced the authority of federal district courts to hear the cases under the bill (sec. 7) and restored the president's power to suspend the writ of habeas corpus if necessary—a presidential power under the Ku Klux Force Act of April 20, 1871, which expired in 1872.[88]

Compared with previous laws, the new enforcement bill focused more on the violence and disorders in the rural South. In principle, the bill did not go beyond what had already been enacted by existing laws, except in two places: it extended the power of election supervisors and reinforced presidential power to suspend habeas corpus. But the opposition was strong from both Democrats and Republicans themselves. Much of the two-day debate in the House on February 26 and 27 repeated such familiar themes as whether the national government had the power to oversee the protection of black rights and how they could be best protected. Republican opposition focused on the presidential power to suspend habeas corpus and federal interference with local politics. Conservative Republicans generally shared the view, as uttered by Michigan's George Willard, that the bill was an act of legislative "imperialism" that imposed the political will of one section upon another. Stopping federal interference with local politics, Willard argued, would remove "the habit of the emancipated portion of the [southern] population to rely upon external aid" and give the South a chance to resume home rule, "the kind of rule which for the most part settle[d] disputes, quiet[ed] disturbances, distribute[d] justice between man and man by agencies created by the people right at home in their own township."[89] Henry L. Pierce (R-Mass.) regarded the bill as an attempt to secure 138 electoral votes from southern states. While existing laws were sufficient to accomplish all that was "necessary in the Southern States," Pierce argued, the new force bill, "with cruel and unusual penalties," would only be an unnecessarily "violent remedy."[90]

A distinctive feature of the Republican opposition this time was the growing tendency to interpret southern schemes against black suffrage as a social wrong and to dissuade the party from engaging further in passing legislation that was powerless to correct social wrongs. Joseph R. Hawley, a veteran abolitionist and onetime staunch radical from Connecticut, announced that he was compelled to depart from his "radical associates" on this bill. The power of federal legislation was limited, Hawley was persuaded, and could neither "reach into all the relations of life" nor "directly protect all the rights of humanity."[91] He felt that there should be no further enforcement because the existing laws were sufficient to preserve all the rights under the Constitution. He also had another, perhaps more realistic, reason:

> There are wrongs there that we can never reach in this Hall until we have changed the Constitution of the United States. There is a social, and educational, and moral reconstruction of the South needed that will never come from any legislative halls, State or national; it must be the growth of time, of education, and of Christianity. We cannot put justice, liberty, and equality into the hearts of a people by statutes alone.[92]

After years of fighting for black rights, the historical-minded Hawley probably had come to see the limits of Reconstruction and the futility of further enforcement without substantive changes in southern life. But his remarks unintentionally foreshadowed a rationale underlining the Supreme Court opinions on the *Civil Rights Cases* in 1883 and *Plessy v. Ferguson* in 1896.[93]

The bill's proponents thought that the party should not abandon black voters. To do so, they believed, would mean a total abandonment of the party's ideals and programs. To these Republicans, the politics of Reconstruction was not a dead issue. Charles Albright of Pennsylvania warned his colleagues, "If you give up at this point, what becomes of the boasted fruits and victories of the war? . . . This is not the occasion nor the hour when we should falter or hesitate in the great struggle for the common rights of man." Appealing to fellow Republicans not to retreat, Albright argued that the party could only be strong when it was "bold and aggressive in its policy of right and justice."[94] Again, the bill's supporters argued that enforcing black suffrage was the national government's duty. If the national government and the president were not allowed to suppress the violence and usurpation in Louisiana and Alabama, John Coburn warned, the same crimes would be repeated in other states. And he saw greater threats:

> If there be no restraints, no system of amendment, no regulation that can bind the restless and ambitious leaders in political strife, then our days as a nation are numbered, and the sun of republican government is sinking already beneath the horizon. The twilight and the swift-following deadness of national death are rapidly approaching.[95]

This speech voiced a real sense of danger to radical Republican nationalism and constitutionalism. For the bill's proponents, the bill was the party's last chance to save enforcement, the party's southern allies, and the party itself. Clearly, the incoming House, with the Democrats as a majority, would block every Republican effort to pass any enforcement law. The bill could wait no longer, Illinois Republican Joseph G. Cannon cried: "I have no patience with some gentlemen who admit the necessity for action, but quietly fold their arms, while the blood of the slain cries from the ground and the moan of the widow and orphan are heard as protests against the most foul taking-off of the husband and father, and search with a microscope for a fancied want of power to legislate, or cry conciliation and peace, peace, when there is no peace for those citizens of the United States, if they persist in exercising their rights in voting as they prefer, but the peace of the grave."[96]

Seeing the majority of Republicans reluctant to extend to the president unlimited power to suspend habeas corpus, Benjamin Butler, the outgoing radical, suggested restricting the presidential power to four southern states (Alabama, Mississippi, Louisiana, and Arkansas) and limiting the period during which the power could be exercised to two years (long enough to cover the 1876 presidential election). This suggestion fulfilled the minimum requests of the radicals but satisfied many middle-of-the-road Republicans in the House. On February 27, the House passed the bill (H.R. 4745) by a vote of 135 to 114, with 38 not voting. More than thirty Republicans, including such leading voices such as George F. Hoar, James A. Garfield, and Henry L. Dawes, voted against it.[97] But when the measure went to the Senate, it arrived too late for concrete action. After two readings, the bill was laid on the table.[98]

What effect the new enforcement act would have had obviously is unanswerable. But its death created an opportunity for Democrats to advance their political recovery in a speedier and more aggressive fashion. In the latter half of 1875, southern Democrats launched a sweeping campaign of violence and intimidation, known as the "Mississippi Plan," to control the state election. The Democratic strategy had two steps: to gather all whites into the Democratic party, and to intimidate black voters into voting Democratic or keep them from voting at all. Blacks who voted Republican often were dismissed from their jobs. Later, bribery was applied to buy black votes for Democratic tickets. When black voters refused to submit to Democratic threats, violence was used against them.[99] One witness of the Mississippi Plan later recalled:

> It will be worth any man's life to have a Republican ticket. . . . No one here dare
> be on the ticket if it would cost him his life. . . . I can find no one willing to take
> any place on the ticket from highest to lowest. . . . The policy of the white league
> now seems to be to bring charges against prominent Republicans and execute law
> by the power of the mobs.[100]

The defeat of the new enforcement bill left the Grant administration a lonely fighter at the height of the Democratic comeback in 1875. Grant could offer southern Republicans limited assistance and would do so only after state Republicans had tried and exhausted their own resources. When, in September 1875, Republican governor Adelbert Ames of Mississippi appealed to Grant for aid, federal authority did not offer prompt assistance, despite Grant's earlier assurance of federal aid in time of crisis. Part of the Grant administration's concern was that since enforcement had become increasingly unpopular in the North, dispatching federal troops to Mississippi might not help the Republicans there, but it would definitely create a liability for Republicans in northern states such as Ohio, where Rutherford B. Hayes was winning the governorship. The

Ames government then planned to organize a state militia of black citizens but abandoned the idea for fear that it would lead to a war of the races in the state. Consequently, Democrats won both branches of the Mississippi legislature and threatened to impeach Ames, who was forced to resign in March 1876. As Mississippi fell into Democratic hands, other southern states quickly borrowed the Mississippi Plan as the most effective means to disfranchise blacks and topple the remaining Republican governments.[101]

The failure to pass a new enforcement bill and Grant's inaction toward the Mississippi Plan marked the end of the Republican policy of constructive, aggressive, and active enforcement of black suffrage.[102] Among the factors that contributed to the bill's defeat were the growing doubts about the constitutionality of enforcement, the shift of the party's attention to economic and financial matters, concerns about the negative effect on the 1876 elections, and simply a shortage of time. But party infighting also contributed to the defeat. In the eyes of the liberal- and moderate-minded Republicans, the radical effort to renew enforcement and Grant's call for a tough southern policy were part of the president's scheme for getting a third term. The defeat of the party in 1874, *Chicago Tribune* editor Horace White was convinced, persuaded Grant that he was the man who could "pull the party through in 1876." [103] However, the new enforcement bill would not help the party but only, as Joseph Medill put it, offer Democrats "a club to knock out our brains." Republicans might force the bill through, and that might be justifiable, but it would not be enforceable because the party was "no longer in the majority." Until the people put the Republican party back in power, Medill told Blaine, Republicans had "no business to be making such apparent coercive laws." [104]

It would be fourteen years before Republicans had another chance to regain both houses of Congress and the presidency and to try to enforce the Fifteenth Amendment. Before then, how the party, increasingly faction ridden and interests driven, could maintain unity in keeping alive the idea of federal enforcement of black suffrage would remain a challenge to the incoming generation of Republicans.

The Supreme Court and the Decline of Enforcement

In addition to the Democratic comeback in the House and the defeat of the new enforcement bill in 1875, the prospect for Republican efforts to enforce the Fifteenth Amendment grew even more discouraging as the Supreme Court began to step in and render decisions on the constitutionality of the first enforcement act. In *United States v. Reese* and *United States v. Cruikshank*, the Supreme Court, composed of seven Republicans and two Democrats, challenged sections 3, 4, and 6 of the Enforcement Act of May 31, 1870 – the three most important and substantive provisions regarding federal punishment of voting discrimination on account of race and federal protection of U.S. citizens' civil and political rights. These rulings momentarily but authoritatively closed the political debate between Republicans and Democrats over national authority in protecting black political rights.

Enforcement laws had been a powerful weapon for the lower federal courts to crush Klansmen and protect black voting rights. Federal judges throughout the country were indeed the first judicial examiners and interpreters of the enforcement laws. As the reported cases showed, before the Supreme Court's decisions on *Reese* and *Cruikshank* in 1876, federal district and circuit judges universally upheld the constitutionality of the enforcement laws, especially the first enforcement act. The radicalism of their rulings varied, but they never doubted the power of Congress to enforce black suffrage or challenged the legality of the enforcement laws.[105] The more liberal-minded judges might even have consciously elaborated their own political understanding of the enforcement laws. For instance, in *United States v. Canter et al.* (1870), after affirming the legality of the enforcement law, Judge Leavitt (for southern Ohio) went on to lecture the defendants (who tried to prevent blacks from voting) that admitting blacks into the American polity was a political experiment and that there was a "good reason to hope that the experiment [would] work auspiciously to the promotion of the stability and success of [the nation's] free institutions."[106]

At times, Democratic defense counsel would directly challenge the legality of the enforcement laws, as Johnson and Stanbery did in the 1871–72 South Carolina Ku Klux Klan trials, but federal judges such as Hugh L. Bond in South Carolina stood firm in guarding the laws.[107] Other judges would go even further. In *United States v. Hall et al.* (1871), in which two whites were charged with violating section 6 of the Enforcement Act of May 31, 1870, for disrupting black meetings, circuit court judge William B. Woods (for southern Alabama), later a Supreme Court justice, ruled that the enforcement law provided protection to U.S. citizens for all rights secured by the Constitution, including those enumerated in the first ten amendments originally reserved for people and states. His rationale was that the Fourteenth Amendment reversed the old order of federal and state citizenship and made national citizenship independent of state citizenship. Consequently, he held, a U.S. citizen was entitled to all the privileges and immunities secured by the Constitution, which were also under the protection of laws of Congress; therefore, the 1870 enforcement law could protect freedom of speech and peaceable assembly.[108] Woods's interpretation was a bold one. He actually helped to spell out the substance of the phrase "any right," which had appeared in section 6 of the enforcement act but had never been fully explained by the congressional Republicans who debated it. The Supreme Court, however, would soon correct Woods's interpretation in the *Slaughterhouse* opinion.

Given the strong enforcement momentum in the lower federal courts, the best chance for Democrats to excise the enforcement acts from the nation's lawbooks was to get an opinion from the high court. In the South Carolina trials, Reverdy Johnson and Henry Stanbery had worked hard to force enforcement cases to be transmitted to the Supreme Court, which they hoped would give "the true construction of the Constitution" and, as Stanbery put it, the "most mature consideration" of the enforcement laws.[109] How the high court would respond was uncertain, since the Court was overwhelmingly Republican. But to Democrats, it was better to have the enforcement laws judged by the higher court, where at least two Democratic justices were still serving, than to let them be used as powerful Republican weaponry in elections.

The Democratic calculations made sense, especially when one carefully studies the nine brethren sitting on the high bench in the mid-1870s. Among the nine justices were two Democrats, Nathan Clifford and Stephen J. Field, both avowed opponents of radical Reconstruction. Clifford, a James Buchanan appointee, had "naturally felt little sympathy with the rise and growth of the enlarged views of national authority and federal power." He had always remained, as his biographer put it, "politically orthodox, constitutionally conservative, and temperamentally safe."[110] Field, Lincoln's only Democratic appointment to the Court, had been "driven back into the Democratic camp" when his decisions in the test oath cases had clashed with Republicans.[111]

The Republican justices, three appointed by Lincoln and four by Grant, varied in judicial caliber and partisan loyalty. Samuel F. Miller had been a "strong Lincoln man," but judicially he tended to be independent. When the Fourteenth Amendment was being debated, Miller supported it but denied that it intended black suffrage. In 1869, he openly opposed black suffrage because he believed that "the leaders of the radical party in the gulf states . . . ha[d] been ignorant, and unused to the exercise of political power."[112] David Davis, a close friend of Lincoln's for many years and politically ambitious, actually had opposed Lincoln's Emancipation Proclamation and usually remained "in accord with the prevailing sentiments of his time."[113] Noah H. Swayne, a southern-born Ohio Republican, was Lincoln's first appointee and had proved loyal but of little help in the Republican cause. Among Grant's appointees, Joseph Bradley was vigorous and resourceful. He shared a first-rank judicial reputation with Miller and Field, but he was "a realist, refusing to be diverted by legal fictions or anachronisms."[114] Ward Hunt and William Strong were newer converts to Republicanism and judicially weak. Chief Justice Morrison R. Waite, whom Grant appointed in 1874 only after several others turned down the post, was never politically conspicuous, and judicially his contemporaries considered him second-rate at best.[115] Indeed, the Republican justices had a majority, but their opinions were unlikely to be guided by their party's political needs or, more accurately, by the needs of a certain party faction. Compared with the Republicans in Congress, the Republican justices had more space for independent actions.

However, the questions that the Republican-dominated Court was soon to confront were no less serious than in 1857 when *Dred Scott* was decided. Given that Republicans had passed three new constitutional amendments and a group of federal laws under unusual circumstances, the Court had to contemplate the effect of these laws, not for the time being, or the South, but the whole nation and for years to come. It had to decide how much change should be allowed for the nation's constitutional framework, what kind of federal-state relations should be defined to carry on the new Union, and how best to protect the interests of every citizen, black and white, and the nation. The justices, all keen readers of contemporary politics, had to stretch their historical vision to both the past and future to look for answers.

The Court's first important opinion on the Civil War amendments came in March 1873. In 1869, Louisiana enacted a law authorizing all slaughtering in New Orleans to be confined to the Crescent City Livestock Landing and Slaughter-House Company. About a thousand butchers, who refused to slaughter animals in the mandated abattoir, were out of a job. In their lawsuits against the state of Louisiana, these butchers alleged that the statute violated the Thirteenth Amendment by creating an involuntary servitude and the Fourteenth Amendment by abridging the immunities and privileges of United States citizenship, depriving them of property without due process of law and denying them equal protection of the laws.[116]

The Supreme Court opinion on these suits, known as the *Slaughterhouse Cases*, was principally concerned with interpreting the meaning and scope of the Fourteenth Amendment. Speaking for the 5 – 4 majority, Justice Miller held that the Fourteenth Amendment specified that every citizen had a dual citizenship, national and state. The two citizenships commanded two different sets of privileges and immunities. Miller defined the privileges and immunities of national citizenship as such rights as that of access to Washington, D.C., and to the coastal seaports, the right to protection on the high seas and abroad, the right to use the navigable waters of the United States, the right of assembly and petition, and the privilege of habeas corpus. State citizenship, Miller asserted, included those rights that had "at all times been enjoyed by citizens of the several States" that made up the Union, "from the time of their becoming free, independent, and sovereign." Based on this rationale, Miller concluded that the right to slaughter animals freely in Louisiana was beyond the protection of the national government.[117]

In presenting the dual-citizenship theory, Miller affirmed national citizenship, the positive existence of rights attached to it, and federal power to protect those rights. But in defining the substance of the rights of national citizenship, Miller tried not to cross the traditional boundary of states' rights, since he doubted that the framers of the Fourteenth Amendment intended to "bring within the power of Congress the entire domain of civil rights heretofore belonging exclusively to the States."[118] Here, Miller rejected the interpretation, given by circuit court judge William B. Woods in an 1871 opinion, that the amendment made national citizenship into primary citizenship and commanded all rights secured by the Constitution, including those originally reserved to the states.[119] The Fourteenth Amendment, Miller emphasized, should not be understood as a law designed to "radically change the whole theory of the relations of the State and Federal governments."[120] For Miller, the Fourteenth Amendment neither expanded the national power nor shrank state power over the protection of citizens' civil rights.

Four of Miller's brethren disagreed. Speaking for Chief Justice Chase, Bradley, and Swayne, Field adopted the rationale that radical Republicans frequently employed during the congressional debate on the Fourteenth Amendment. He argued that the amendment was meant to protect the fundamental (natural) rights of life, freedom, and pursuit of happiness, which were "the gifts of the Creator" and not to be conferred, only recognized, by law. A devoted supporter of a free economy, Field held that states must be prevented from denying citizens those fundamental rights.[121] Bradley, in another dissenting opinion, echoed Field's theory and argued that the right not to be deprived of life, liberty, or property without due process of law was secured in the original Constitution and therefore required protection by the federal government. Like Judge Woods, Bradley placed the federal government above the state government in locating the primary responsibility for protecting a citizen's fundamental rights. This was probably due to his belief that the recent amendments were meant to remedy not only slavery but also mischiefs such as "the spirit of insubordination and disloyalty to the National government which had troubled the country for so many years in some of the States."[122] But by a majority of one, Miller's opinion prevailed.

The *Slaughterhouse* opinion won applause from Democrats and northern liberals as a timely support for their fight against the Republican attempt to advance further legislation on civil rights. The *Nation* lauded the opinion for discouraging those "who believed the New Amendments to have introduced very revolutionary principles as to the relations of the State to the General government." The wrongs done to blacks, although to be condemned, could not be "righted by hounding on his old masters to acts of violence and lawlessness by the passage of equally violent and lawless acts of Congress," the weekly asserted.[123] During the debate on the Civil Rights Act of 1875, Representative Milton J. Durham (D-Ky.) calmly assured Republicans that even if Congress passed the bill, the Court would "stay the storm" that threatened "to overthrow the fundamental principles of free government on this continent." His prediction would come true in 1883, when the Court invalidated the law in the Civil Rights Cases.[124]

However, *Slaughterhouse* went far beyond assuring the Democrats an inevitable dead end for the Civil Rights Act of 1875. By proclaiming the Court's fidelity to the original federalism, the decision cleared the way for southern acts of terror that the federal enforcement mechanism had been designed to challenge or hinder. For black Republicans, the decision diminished the federal government's power to protect black rights and negated the essential achievement of the Civil War and Reconstruction. Frederick Douglass commented on *Slaughterhouse* in a letter to his old antislavery comrade Gerrit Smith: "Two citizenships mean no citizenship. The one destroy[s] the other. It is the folly as Franklin would have it, of harness a horse at each end of the wagon. The one defeats the efforts of the other. The nation affirms, the State denies, and there is no progress. The true doctrine is one nation, one country, one citizenship, and one law for all the people."[125]

Inevitably, the *Slaughterhouse* decision also affected federal enforcement of black suffrage. Its strict interpretation of the Fourteenth Amendment and federal power under the postwar constitutional framework laid the foundation for the Court's decisions on *United States v. Reese* and *United States v. Cruikshank* in 1876. They would emasculate the Enforcement Act of May 31, 1870.

The *Cruikshank* case originated from the killing of numerous blacks in the small town of Colfax, Louisiana. Known as the "Grant Parish Massacre," the trouble was a by-product of the state's recently disrupted election in 1872, in which two candidates simultaneously claimed the governorship. William P. Kellogg, a radical Republican originally from Illinois, defeated the fusionist, John McEnery. But when McEnery refused to accept Kellogg's terms for conciliation, two governments were set up in the state, each with its own militia, legislature, and local appointees. On April 13, 1873, about a hundred black citizens of Colfax attended a meeting with the town's Republican sheriff and judge, both recognized by the Kellogg government. A group of armed whites, led by the former sheriff, surrounded them. When the blacks refused to obey the whites' order to leave the courthouse, the whites opened fire on them and set fire to the courthouse. The *New York Times* reported, "The unfortunate colored men were literally roasted alive." [126] After the massacre, the Department of Justice sent J. J. Hoffman to investigate and to secure the evidence. More than a hundred whites were indicted, but only Cruikshank and eight others were caught and brought before the federal circuit court in New Orleans. The first trial in late February and early March 1874 ended with the acquittal of one and left the remaining eight to face a second trial when the jury was unable to reach a verdict. [127]

The second trial started on May 18 and was presided over by circuit justice Joseph Bradley. The indictment, drawn by U.S. district attorney James R. Beckwith, ran to 164 pages and contained thirty-two counts. Beckwith charged Cruikshank and his associates with conspiracy and violence to deprive the blacks of their right to life, a crime punishable under section 6 of the Enforcement Act of May 31, 1870. He also charged them with murdering black citizens, which was punishable under section 7 of the same act.

Beckwith was determined to press the indictment, but Justice Bradley made the indictment impossible. [128] Bradley dismissed all of the indictments on the ground that they lacked precision in criminal description. If Miller's *Slaughterhouse* opinion ranked as the most important on the Fourteenth Amendment in the 1870s, Bradley's opinion on *Cruikshank* in circuit court (for the district of Louisiana) in 1874 should have the same prominence for interpreting the Thirteenth and Fifteenth Amendments. Bradley held that both the Civil Rights Act of 1866 and the Fourteenth Amendment were consequences of the Thirteenth Amendment, which was, in turn, a result of the Civil War. Through the war, Congress acquired "the power not only to legislate for the eradication of slavery, but the power to give full effect to this bestowment of liberty" on four million former slaves. The Civil Rights Act of 1866 was necessary because the abolition of slavery required the federal government and national law to "place the other races on the same plane of privilege as that occupied by the white race."[129] However, following Miller's rationale in *Slaughterhouse*, Bradley stressed that these new powers did not allow Congress to pass laws to punish any offenses except those that aimed "at the deprivation of the colored citizen's enjoyment and exercise of his rights of citizenship and of equal protection of the laws because of his race, color, or previous condition of servitude." Unless the charges were accompanied by an averment that the injury was committed for the reason of race, they could be not sustained in the federal courts.[130]

As debatable as it was, Bradley's interpretation of the Fifteenth Amendment was highly original. The amendment, although "negative in form," conferred "a positive right which did not exist before." The right – "to be exempt from the disability of race, color, or previous condition of servitude, as respects the right to vote" – was "principally intended to confer upon colored citizens the right of suffrage." It was, in his view, "a constitutional extension" of the Civil Rights Act of 1866. But because it was not "an absolute" but "a relative" right, the enforcement of the amendment could not go beyond the boundary of all other amendments: the race line. Any outrage, atrocity, or conspiracy against black citizens, "whether carried on in a guerrilla or predatory form, or by private combinations, or even by private outrages or intimidation," was beyond federal jurisdiction unless the crime was motivated by the reason of race. All other outrages, "whether against the colored race or the white race," were to be handled solely by state courts unless a state by its laws denied to any particular race equality of rights.[131] Bradley dismissed the indictments on several grounds, including the inability of Congress to enforce the right of assembly and lack of evidence showing racial discrimination in state laws. But he principally rejected sections 4 and 6 of the 1870 enforcement act, upon which the main indictments drew. These sections were "general and universal" and went beyond the Fifteenth Amendment. What was missing in these sections was the crime identifier: race, "the essential ingredient" in any crime to be sustainable in federal court under the enforcement act.[132]

In contrast to Miller in *Slaughterhouse*, Bradley was more willing to recognize the substantive changes in American constitutional law. He affirmed the new powers that the federal government acquired through the war and upheld its authority to enforce the new amendments. But he limited the enforcement only to cases involving "war of race." In other words, the federal government could not extend its protection to black rights until it proved that race motivated the offense. What was "war of race"? Bradley gave no definition. His opinion might have gone a step beyond *Slaughterhouse* because it at least acknowledged the possibility that the national government had the power to protect black rights under certain circumstances, but when he left all the "ordinary crimes" to state jurisdiction, Bradley actually sounded a retreat by placing the federal government secondary to the state governments in overseeing the rights of American citizens. Whatever Bradley gave, he took away more, virtually emasculating the Civil War amendments and restoring antebellum constitutionalism.

Nobody present in court was more shocked by Bradley's opinion than Judge William B. Woods. In 1870, when the circuit court in Alabama was presented a charge against a group of young whites at Eutaw who had violently interrupted an assembly of black Republicans, Woods, then heading the court, wrote to seek Bradley's advice on whether such conduct was indictable under section 6 of the newly created Enforcement Act of May 31, 1870. Bradley replied that the right to political assembly was "one of the most sacred rights of citizenship" and could not "be abridged by any State." If there existed a conspiracy to prevent people from exercising the right of suffrage, he said, it was indictable under section 6 of the law. Finally, because of the differing opinions of Bradley and Woods,[133] the case was submitted to the Supreme Court, and the district attorney was instructed to release the accused on bail.[134]

When the *Cruikshank* case went to the Supreme Court, *United States v. Reese* had already been filed for review. The *Reese* case originated in a municipal election held on January 30, 1873, in Lexington, Kentucky. At the election, two election inspectors, Hiram Reese and Matthew Foushee, rejected the vote of William Garner, an African American, even after he produced an affidavit showing that he had offered to pay the poll tax at a certain time and place but had been refused by the city tax collector. Reese and Foushee were then arrested and accused of violating sections 3 and 4 of the Enforcement Act of May 31, 1870. James F. Robinson, the tax collector, was indicted under section 2 of the same act.[135] The case was first tried at the federal circuit court in Louisville and argued by defense attorneys B. F. Buckner and Henry Stanbery.

In early February 1874, circuit judge Halmer H. Emmons and district judge Bland Ballard announced a division of opinion. Consequently, the case was docketed in the Supreme Court and the defendants discharged on five hundred dollars bail.[136]

Like the *Cruikshank* case, which was crucial in deciding that the use of the Enforcement Act of May 31, 1870, in Louisiana could continue, the *Reese* case was important in clarifying the role of the capitation tax required by the city of Lexington, an obvious device to prevent blacks from voting for the Republican party. As soon as the Lexington election was over, a dispatch from there, published in the *New York World*, reported that "the negro population largely outnumber[ed] the whites, but a provision of the city charter requiring the payment of a capitation tax as a prerequisite to the right of suffrage disfranchised about two-thirds of the negro vote and left the Democrats an easy victory."[137] In the meantime, federal enforcement officers in the South pressed the Department of Justice to have the Supreme Court hear the two cases to clear the way for enforcement to continue. Gabriel C. Wharton, the federal prosecutor of the *Reese* case in Louisville, hoped for an early decision "on the validity and proper construction of the statute."[138] Meanwhile, James Beckwith, Wharton's counterpart in New Orleans, told the attorney general that so long as the *Cruikshank* case remained undecided, "any trial in the present condition of affairs [would] simply be an expensive mockery."[139]

The *Reese* case was first argued on January 13 and 14, 1875. Attorney General Williams and Solicitor General S. F. Phillips charged both Reese and Foushee with refusing to receive Garner's vote on account of his race, a violation of section 3 of the Enforcement Act of May 31, 1870. Buckner, the defense counsel, argued that because the section lacked a phrase like "race, color, or previous condition of servitude" to "define the animus of the election officers' wrongful refusal," the indictment could not be sustained. For the same reason, section 4 was also defective and went "entirely beyond the power of enforcing the Fifteenth Amendment"[140] — a point that Bradley had raised in his opinion at the Louisiana circuit court several months before.

When the Court delivered its decision on *Reese* in March 1876, it was obvious that much of Buckner's criticism of sections 3 and 4 had been accepted by all but one justice. Writing for the Court, Chief Justice Waite focused on the constitutionality of the two sections. Section 3, Waite stated, was inappropriate because it did "not in express terms limit the offence of an inspector of elections . . . to a wrongful discrimination on account of race." Section 4 was sub-

ject to the same objection, for in the section the Court found "no words of limitation, or reference even, that [could] be construed as manifesting any intention to confine its provisions to the terms of the Fifteenth Amendment."[141]
Based on this, Waite concluded that "the language" of the two sections did not
"confine their operation to unlawful discriminations on account of race." Since
the Enforcement Act of May 31, 1870, had brought "a most important change
in the election laws," Waite argued, the statute had to be construed strictly and
contain no "double meaning."[142] Since the Court could not reject two sections
that were unconstitutional and retain the rest of the act, "each of the sections
[had to] stand as a whole, or fall altogether." But Waite did *not* suggest a permanent death for the act; he suggested that Congress, instead of repairing the
defective law, make a new law, not enforce an old one. But that would be "no
part of [the Court's] duty," he concluded.[143]

The Court's ruling in *Cruikshank* was delivered soon after *Reese* was made
public. The argument in *Cruikshank* centered on two questions: were the indictments good, and, if good, were they punishable under section 6 of the
Enforcement Act of May 31, 1870? Attorney General Williams and Solicitor
General Phillips held that the defendants had violently disrupted a peaceful
assembly and injured the lives of American citizens. Since the Fourteenth
Amendment guaranteed U.S. citizens the enjoyment and exercise of the immunities and privileges secured by the Constitution, they argued, this conduct was
punishable under section 6 of the act, which enforced the Fourteenth Amendment.[144] The defense counsel argued that the amendment granted the federal
government none of those "acknowledged, pre-existing rights," except "the
very few express limitations imposed upon the States," and that the Constitution nowhere dealt "with the ordinary relations of society," nor did it "under-
take to protect individuals in the several states."[145] Robert Marr, the chief
defense counsel, pleaded with the Court not to alter the principles outlined in
the *Slaughterhouse Cases*; otherwise, he warned, "The shackles will have fallen
in vain from four millions of blacks, who were born slaves, if fetters more
galling are to be rivetted on so many more millions of white people, who were
born free."[146]

The Court did not disappoint Marr. After a long but clear reiteration of the
principal points of the *Slaughterhouse* opinion, Waite, speaking for the whole
Court, turned to concrete questions. He dismissed each count that charged the
defendants with unlawfully hindering blacks from political assembly, because
the right to assembly as a state right existed long before the adoption of the

Constitution.[147] As to the charges that the defendants bore arms in executing the violence, Waite said that Congress could not punish that because the Second Amendment declared that right was not to be infringed.[148] For injuries done to black citizens, Waite said that Congress could offer no help because the rights of life and personal liberty were "natural rights of man"; their protection had become part of state sovereignty when states had been instituted. "Sovereignty, for this purpose, rests alone with the States."[149] Nor could the Fourteenth Amendment offer any further protection because the amendment did not "add anything to the rights of one citizen as against another" but simply furnished "an additional guaranty against any encroachment by the States upon the fundamental rights which belong[ed] to every citizen as a member of society."[150] Citing no evidence of racial prejudice, Waite dismissed the counts charging the defendants with violating the Fifteenth Amendment. Unmistakably and respectfully, the chief justice did not miss the point articulated by Bradley in 1874 in the circuit court.[151]

Waite then dismissed the counts based on section 6 of the Enforcement Act of May 31, 1870, because the section – phrased to provide federal protection for a U.S. citizen's enjoyment of "any right or privilege" secured by the Constitution or federal laws – failed to specify "any particular right" to be protected. Without specifications, a crime or an indictment could not be sustained.[152] Again, Waite did not explicitly invalidate section 6, and he reaffirmed, in a slightly weaker tone, his view in *Reese* that the federal government could enforce black suffrage. But his interpretation of the national protection of civil rights strictly followed *Slaughterhouse* guidelines.

The Court's decisions clearly jeopardized and discouraged enforcement. In the immediate aftermath of *Reese* and *Cruikshank*, federal enforcement declined further. In 1875, when *Reese* and *Cruikshank* were pending, argued, and decided in the Court, the conviction rate in enforcement cases in the South declined to 7 percent (16 out of 205 cases). In 1876, only 2 of 106 cases from the South resulted in convictions. The number of enforcement cases nationwide dropped from 234 in 1875 to 149.[153] As another presidential election year approached, the Court's decisions intensified the political and racial conflict in the southern states. Writing to Chief Justice Waite, Hugh L. Bond called the high court decisions "awful" and warned that politics had "not warmed up here yet and [would] only be the more disagreeable in these southern states as they [grew] warmer." Criticizing the Court's suggestion that a better enforcement law should be created, Bond predicted, "A better congress may make a better law and no one would take a livelier pleasure in executing it there." [154] A federal district attorney in Charleston, South Carolina, described his plight in carrying out his duty as an enforcement officer: "If the red shirts break up meetings by violence, there is no remedy, unless it can be proved to have been done on account of race and color, which can't be proved, because the people can only peaceably assemble under the Constitutional guarantees. . . . It is hard to sit quietly and see such things, with the powerful arm of the government, bound in decisions. With colored men crowding my office, it is hard to make them understand my utter helplessness." [155]

The Court decisions, too, disappointed black leaders, who were left confused as to the real motivations behind the decisions and the federal government's sincerity in enforcement. Replying to a letter inquiring about his opinion of the Court's decisions on the *Reese* and *Cruikshank* cases, Frederick Douglass wrote:

> I am no lawyer – and cannot stop now to give you any defense of the legality of any
> measures adopted by Government to enforce the 15th Amendment. I cannot
> think, however, that Attorney General Taft who is a man learned in the law, has
> made any mistake in the matter. The Constitution has been often invoked to
> shield treason and I rather think it so invoked in the present instance. [156]

The Democrats welcomed the decisions, which they cited whenever the issue of enforcement came up for discussion in subsequent Congresses. They knew what the decisions really meant, as did many Republicans. Speaking of the minds of aloof northern liberals or frustrating independents, the *Nation* predicted before the decisions that although the Fifteenth Amendment could not be openly nullified, it eventually would "only have the efficiency and vitality of a very perfect and muscular corpse." [157]

The *Nation*, however, probably spoke only part of the truth. The *Reese* and *Cruikshank* decisions, delivered as enforcement was losing its supporters, could be interpreted as the Republican Court's response to the North's changed political sentiments and the South's strong resistance rather than merely a pure judicial scrutiny of the enforcement laws. If so, the Court's political response, carved in constitutional language, was never simply a negation of the enforcement or of its objective: the Fifteenth Amendment.

In discussing the impact of the Court's decisions, it is important to note that although the Court, in deciding *Reese* and *Cruikshank*, challenged the constitutionality and technicality of the Enforcement Act of May 31, 1870, and rendered a strict interpretation of the Fourteenth Amendment, in neither case did it strip the federal government of its power to enforce the Fifteenth Amendment.[158] The Court's opinions contained a dual message. On the one hand, it rendered the act virtually powerless by invalidating two of its most important sections (secs. 3 and 4) and by challenging another one (sec. 6). But on the other hand, the Court affirmed that the Fifteenth Amendment created "a new constitutional right"—the right to be exempt from voting discrimination on account of race—and, perhaps more important, agreed that Congress had the power to protect that right. In other words, black suffrage was a constitutionally enforceable right. To use Bradley's words, the "right shall not be denied" meant that "the right shall be enjoyed."[159]

But how should the Court's attitude toward black suffrage enforcement be evaluated? If the Republican justices were truly supportive of black suffrage and wanted to have this law prevail, why did they not follow the argument made by the lonely dissenting Ward Hunt in *Reese*, who argued that the word "aforesaid" in section 3 clearly referred to the racial discrimination contained in sections 1 and 2?[160] If they were indifferent or hostile toward federal protection of black voting rights, why should they vote to allow Congress to make new enforcement laws? Of course, when both opinions were delivered, every justice knew well that with the Democrats' impending control of the House, the chance for a new law was almost zero. What was going on in the minds of the justices? Why did they permit the possibility for a new enforcement law without allowing the existing one to live? Might it be, as historian Michael Les Benedict suggests, that in this way, they could actually reinforce federalism instead of reducing the power of federal government?[161] Might it be, too, because justices like Bradley sincerely believed that the enforcement law simply could not survive on its technicalities?[162] Or, might it be because the Republican justices considered it politically wise and important to secure a judicial affirmation of congressional authority to enforce black suffrage before the Democrats had a chance to repeal the judicially defective enforcement act? While the Republican justices put the enforcement act in doubt, they might have cast their eyes toward the future.

Before the Court delivered the decisions, the Enforcement Act of May 31, 1870, had been adopted in the *Revised Statues* enacted by Congress on June 22, 1874. The three sections of the enforcement act in question (secs. 3, 4, and 6) were divided, revised, and respectively placed in different categories of the *Revised Statutes* in 1875 and later in 1878.[163] In the *Revised Statutes* of 1875 (and 1878), section 3 became sections 2007 and 2008, and section 4 became sections 2009 and 5506. No substantive changes were made to these sections—

nor were any needed, since sections 2007, 2008, and 2009 were placed under the title "Elective Franchise." However, the Court's decisions in 1876 rendered these sections virtually ineffective, as few cases were brought up under them. Section 5506, placed under the title "Crimes against Elective Franchise and Civil Rights of Citizens" in the *Revised Statutes*, remained effective in enforcement and carried with it the legal strength of the original section. Democrats would constantly challenge this section in years to come, and a Democratic Congress eventually would repeal it in 1894.[164] Section 6 of the Enforcement Act of May 31, 1870, which the Court challenged in *Cruikshank*, was placed as section 5508 in the 1875 and later 1878 *Revised Statutes* under the title "Civil Rights." This section later became section 241 of Title 18 in the United States Code and has remained an important provision for the protection of civil rights.[165]

In fact, all of these sections survived despite the Court's decisions. Except for sections 6 and 17 (respectively secs. 5508 and 5510 in the *Revised Statutes*), most of the revised sections of the Enforcement Act of May 31, 1870, would die at the hands of a Democratic Congress in 1894.[166] The Court would take a more affirmative and steadfast attitude in interpreting and defending the Fifteenth Amendment and federal enforcement of black suffrage in later years, as it did in *Ex parte Siebold* (1880), *Ex parte Clarke* (1880), and *Ex parte Yarbrough* (1884).[167] But for the time being, the Supreme Court had done enough to frustrate the enforcement policy of the party responsible for appointing all but one of its members.

CHAPTER FOUR

The Hayes Administration and Black Suffrage, 1876–1880

The Inner Compromise of Republican Principles in 1876

Eighteen seventy-six was the centennial year. On May 10, the International Exhibition of Arts, Manufactures, and Products of the Soil and Mine opened in Fairmount Park, Philadelphia. President Grant gave the opening speech, assuring visitors that the exhibition would not only inspire them with "a profound respect for the skill and taste" of people from other nations but also satisfy them with "the attainments" made by Americans during the preceding one hundred years.[1] The American products at the exhibition impressed foreign visitors, who, one writer reported, joined "in expressions of surprise and admiration at the excellence" of America's manufactures, schools, railroads, newspapers, and "the soundness" of its social life.[2]

Indeed, the year 1876 marked the first major steps toward ultimate American economic supremacy. By that year, the United States had a population of 46 million and possessed about 1.9 billion acres of land, of which 188 million were agriculturally used. Different regions of the nation were linked by railroads that amounted to 76,808 miles of track. Although three-quarters of Americans still lived as farmers, a quarter of a million factories employed 2.5 million workers. And the United States was producing 533,191 tons of steel. Illiteracy among ordinary Americans was reduced. The higher standard of living, hopes for higher pay, and prospects of quick success attracted many immigrants to the United States.[3] All of this indicated the great potential for Americans to make a large stride into the industrial age. Given these circumstances, the 1876 presidential election loomed large.

However, many Republicans found little to cheer about. The party's political record was dismaying. During Grant's second presidency, the party lost its battles on almost every front. The panic of 1873 and its aftermath had divided Republicans over a number of economic issues, including tariff and revenue reforms. The decline in federal aid to railroad construction in the South forced state governments to retreat from their subsidy policy, halting railroad construction in that region. The failure of the Republican Congress to provide aid for internal improvements in the South had contributed to growing southern dissatisfaction, falling economic prosperity, and, politically, the fall of Republican governments in several southern states.[4] In the 1874 elections, the party lost control of the House. In early 1875, the party failed to enact a new enforcement act and could do nothing but helplessly watch the resurgence of Democratic violence against black voters in the South. The Grant administration's inactions on the Mississippi Plan surrendered one of the last remaining southern Republican governments. The Supreme Court decisions in the *Reese* and *Cruikshank* cases of that year virtually shackled the federal government from taking an active and aggressive part in protecting black voters in the South.

Confronted with this situation, many Republicans realized that the 1876 presidential election had to be a turning point for the party's political program. But, compared with its overwhelming success in 1872, the party was less certain that it could carry the 1876 presidential race. First, although the southern question remained a paramount issue of national politics, Civil War fever was waning, and northern interest in the fate of black Americans was fading. Frustrated with the slow progress and constant violence in the South, the North had become increasingly indifferent to southern issues. Meanwhile, other issues, such as civil service reform, currency reform, railroads, and the labor movement, were quickly grabbing national attention and becoming the focus of public concern. Not only did Democrats effectively use these issues for their political purposes, but rank-and-file Republicans also demanded that their party seriously address them. In March 1876, in a letter to Rutherford B. Hayes, then the governor of Ohio, James A. Garfield revealed his fear that the party faithful would divide over the issue of currency reform, prompting bipartisan unity between soft-money men of both parties once Democrats brought the Specie Resumptions Act before Congress. Later, John Sherman, another veteran Ohio Republican, predicted that Republicans in different states might support different measures regarding specie. Sherman urged Hayes to use his influence to write a specie policy to the platform of the Ohio Republican convention.[5] Discontent also prevailed among New Hampshire Republicans: as one of them reported to William E. Chandler, who would help manage the 1876 election, there had been a "tendency to independent thinking," which would be "rapidly developing into independent voting or staying at home on election day."[6] Continuing to address political issues left by the war and Reconstruction (or to use the fashionable term, to wave the "bloody shirt") would be less effective than four years before. "You have got to have a revolution in the republican party with some violence to it," *Springfield Republican* editor Samuel Bowles urged Henry L. Dawes of Massachusetts, "or you will have a revolution out of the party."[7]

By 1876, too, Republicans no longer could deride Democrats as the party of corruption. The Grant administration had been inundated by waves of political scandals that had reduced the party's political and moral credibility to new lows. The administration was first hurt by the exposure of the Whiskey Ring in 1874, when Grant's own secretary was investigated for taking payoffs in return for helping St. Louis distillers avoid taxes.[8] Later, both Attorney General George Williams and Secretary of the Interior Columbus Delano were compelled to resign when members of their families were accused of accepting bribes in return for influencing the policies of these departments. But the most devastating scandal was Secretary of War William W. Belknap's sale of the post tradership in Oklahoma Territory, for which he had accepted bribes (transmitted through his wife) of up to about twenty-one thousand dollars.[9] These scandals effectively demoralized Republicans and thus seriously undermined the party's political credibility.[10] Grant, the party's hero in 1868 and 1872, had lost much of his luster because of these scandals. The idea of a third term, which Grant himself never seriously entertained, seemed even to some of his longtime supporters a potential political disaster. If Grant's third term was to be a contingency for the party, John Sherman said, it would be "an act of suicide" and "disrupt [the] party in every Republican State."[11] Time, scandal, and infighting had also left Republicans bereft of strong, popular leaders.

By then, almost all of the party's legendary figures from the Civil War era had disappeared from the political stage. The death of Thaddeus Stevens in 1868, William Pitt Fessenden in 1869, William H. Seward in 1872, Salmon P. Chase in 1873, Charles Sumner in 1874, and Henry Wilson in 1875 removed the first-generation Republicans who had once served as the party's political heart and soul.[12] Others had either gone liberal—Carl Schurz, Lyman Trumbull, and George W. Julian (who later endorsed the Democrats in 1876)—or never returned to national politics, as Ben Wade and James Ashley (one of the first Republicans to advocate black suffrage in Congress) had been defeated for reelection. George S. Boutwell (a leading black suffrage advocate in the House) and John B. Bingham (virtually a restraining force on the Reconstruction Act and the Fifteenth Amendment) retired. Nonetheless, the party retained a solid core. Still others who had participated in Reconstruction legislation – James A. Garfield, James G. Blaine, William D. Kelley, John Sherman, George Hoar, George F. Edmunds, and Samuel Shellabarger, to name a few – remained regular Republicans. Some of them, like Blaine, would play a leading role in the near future, but none of them was blessed to command the party with the political skills, ideological originality, and personal charisma of the party's dead legends. In addition, the die-hard party loyalists, or stalwarts, or machine politicians – Roscoe Conkling, Oliver P. Morton, Simon Cameron, John A. Logan, and Zachariah Chandler – began to forge a solid inner circle advancing to the party's leadership through professional management and patronage, joined later by people such as William Chandler, Henry Cabot Lodge, and John C. Spooner in the late 1880s. Thus, by 1876, the Republican party was experiencing a generational change in both leadership and political focus. In an age of political mediocrity, issues and personalities assumed a different importance. But precisely because there was no overwhelming personality to unite all of the factions, the party's future looked very uncertain.

In addition, the Democratic party had resurfaced as a much more competitive challenger in 1876 than four years earlier. Then, it had been unable to produce its own candidate and could only collaborate with the liberal Republicans against the regular Republicans. But by 1876, except in Louisiana, South Carolina, and Florida, every other southern state was under Democratic control. In the North, Democratic influence was on the rise. Besides, the Democratic House engaged in vigorous corruption bashing as soon as it met, leading to the explosion of the Belknap affair and disgrace for the Grant administration. Undoubtedly, the Democrats posed a serious challenge to the Republicans. Thus, to win the election, Republicans needed to restructure the party's political agenda, mobilize its old constituencies, attract new supporters, and, in short, form a new united front encompassing all segments of the party, be they regular, stalwart, half-breed, or liberal.

On the one hand, the faction-ridden Republicans seemed helpless. On the other hand, since none of the factions could win the election alone, it was an opportunity to reach compromises and form a new coalition. Of all the factions, the liberal Republicans and the so-called Independents became the party's major targets for recruitment in the North.[13] Having failed to defeat the regular

Republicans in 1872, the liberal Republicans stayed loosely outside the party and, throughout Grant's second term, remained major opponents of the administration. Although staying mostly aloof, the liberals never gave up their hope of reforming the Republican party and its programs. When the 1876 election approached, liberal leaders such as Schurz, Horace White, and William Cullen Bryant returned to the Republican fold, believing that the time had come for them to impose their influence on the party or even to take it over. The liberals saw, unmistakably, the impending election as an opportunity to reorganize the political forces within the Republican party, to revitalize the party's influence through their reform programs, and to give birth to a new political mode for the nation.[14]

One issue on which returning liberals and regular Republicans disagreed was federal enforcement of the rights of southern blacks. The liberals wanted the national government completely disengaged from involvement in black suffrage in the South. Throughout the campaign, leading liberal journals and newspapers blasted the Grant administration's southern policy as unwise and erroneous. For the liberals, black suffrage had been an irritant, a generator of political corruption at the state and national levels, and a threat to the operation of American democracy. They argued that as long as black suffrage remained a national issue, the federal government would always be involved in political controversy and partisan antagonism. The *Springfield Republican* blamed blacks for being ignorant and an "ignorant suffrage," which caused political corruption in the South. Comparing black education in Louisiana and Georgia, the paper found that in the latter, the black school population increased much faster than in the former. It concluded that the Republican government in Louisiana should be condemned for having "stolen and squandered the fund appropriated to school purposes" and that the fate of blacks should be left to their former masters, who "for their own best interest, [would] not [be] allowing a large voting population to grow up in ignorance."[15]

Much of the liberal opposition to enforcement centered on the argument that the federal government had no obligation to help the recently freed and enfranchised blacks. The *Nation* declared that "the Republican party ought not to be allowed to go on one year longer with a misty sense of guardianship towards the negro, but without any clear or defined idea of the legal duties of the relation or the manner of performing them."[16] Liberals also insisted that blacks should no longer be treated as the "nation's wards." The *Chicago Tribune*, which once had advocated federal aid to black voters in the South, changed its tone: "The government is merely the reflection of the sentiment of the people, and the people are not advocating and insisting on any such program. The blacks at the South, like other freemen who want to enjoy a full measure of rights, must strike for themselves when they are assailed."[17]

The liberals did not openly repudiate the principle of political equality as established by the Fifteenth Amendment. They knew that was impossible. They recognized the full citizenship and political rights of blacks. But they no longer wanted the party to carry the burden of black suffrage. The problem was not only the ignorance of black voters but also manipulation by power-hungry Republicans, who had misguided the black voters. The way to stop the abuse of black suffrage, one writer suggested, was to make black votes common property for Republicans and Democrats—that is, to remove black suffrage from the Republican agenda. "The abolition of the color line would be the surest protection of negro suffrage," the author suggested.[18] This proposal, seemingly a device to make black suffrage a local, nonpartisan issue, was in fact part of the liberals' general political guideline that states' rights and sovereignty should be restored. The liberals hoped to navigate the party from the political issues of the Civil War and Reconstruction to other matters they thought more urgent and important, including civil service reform, economic reform, and party realignment.

Regular Republicans clashed with liberals over the party's southern policy and commitment to black rights. Here the term *regular* was a comprehensive term, which included the so-called stalwart, half-breed, and other nonliberal Republicans. These Republicans believed that the party should continue its commitment to black suffrage. While they saw black suffrage as the symbol of the party's highest political achievement during Reconstruction, it also meant that black voters could remain the backbone of the party in the South if their right to vote received federal protection. The Republican intention to protect black suffrage was not simply "waving the bloody shirt" so that the party's political interests could be preserved. Some Republicans sincerely regarded black suffrage as an indisputable result of the late war and Reconstruction, a new infrastructure of American politics that could not be ignored or removed because of the passage of time. In a long essay on American politics, Richard H. Dana Jr., an influential Republican publicist, argued that the post-Reconstruction nation was "based on equal rights of all, with the gift of the unlimited right of suffrage to the whole body of emancipated slaves, in all their ignorance, weakness, credulity, and brutishness." Black rights as secured by the constitutional amendments were part of the plan of Reconstruction, which should be carried out "in accordance with the system of the Republic." Although he urged a more cautious and prudent policy toward the South and an allowance for southern whites "to attempt to regain their control of affairs," Dana declared:

> There is one conviction we hope will be always foremost in the minds and hearts
> of the American people. It is that we owe our first duty to the subject race which
> we have emancipated. The promise of this nation that they shall have freedom
> and civil and political equality is the most sacred promise we ever made. It is the
> most sublime and touching act in our history. Nothing can so much disgrace us as
> to violate it, or palter with it in a double sense. . . . The Republic must keep faith
> with the negro. For this, force — civil certainly, military possibly — must be used.[19]

To some Republican leaders, the Civil War had left a legacy that would affect the course of American history permanently and could never be lightly dismissed. James A. Garfield argued that the country had experienced a "gigantic revolution . . . a revolution of even wider scope . . . than the Revolution of 1776" and that the nation's politics had to be adjusted and changed for a "broad and grand perspective." The revolution dealt with "elements and forces" that had been at work on the continent "more than two hundred and fifty years," Garfield observed, and such a revolution, while completely beyond any individual's control, should be treated "as a force to be studied, as a mandate to be obeyed."[20]

As in the past, the Republican motivation for protecting black suffrage was closely identified with the party's attempt to win elections. Since the beginning of federal enforcement, the defense of political idealism had never been separate from the defense of pragmatic political interests. Although much of the liberal northern press had criticized enforcement, the recent practice of the Mississippi Plan by southern Democrats had aroused the political vigilance of many northern Republicans. The Mississippi Plan demonstrated that blacks could be stripped of their rights if the federal government remained silent. Once black suffrage was denied, Republican hopes for a strong rank and file in the South would also be diminished. To meet "the conspiracy of the slaveholders, open and avowed, to control the nation," some northern Republicans urged their leaders to use federal troops to meet Democratic challenges in the South. One New York Republican urged William E. Chandler, the party's national campaign manager, to push Grant to send "a sufficient supply of troops to South Carolina, Louisiana, North Carolina, Florida & Alabama etc. so as to allow the people to have a fair course of a free vote."[21]

In October 1876, when the Grant administration decided to use "the whole power of the government to prevent murder and to secure an honest and fair election" in states such as South Carolina, the *Chicago Tribune* supported Grant's decision, although the paper soon would reverse its stand.[22] In about three weeks, the paper published three substantial reports and editorials focusing on election violence and frauds committed by southern Democrats. The paper was furious at the southern adoption of the Mississippi Plan, under which "thousands of negroes ha[d] been dismissed from employment; ha[d] been cut off from all means of earning a living for themselves and families," while "murder and assassination of negroes were made a popular pastime" for whites. The paper assailed Mississippi Plan practices as "barbarities that rival[ed] those practiced by the Turks upon the Christians ... [and] a revival of sectionalism in a form more repulsive than even that which existed before the War."[23] Black voters, the *Tribune* reported, were "peaceable, orderly, law-abiding, good citizens, quietly fulfilling their duties under the laws." It argued further:

> They have committed no offense. They have not threatened the rights of others. They have not even defended their own; and now, after years of the suffering, poverty, and degradation of slavery, they are granted the boon of freedom only to find themselves the victim of their own former owners, and reduced to destitution because they are Republicans.[24]

For regular Republicans, the 1876 election was so crucial that it would have a decisive effect on the party's future. Overwhelmed by the fear of losing the presidency, regular Republican leaders effectively used the issue of black rights during the campaign, seeing it as the party's political agenda. Matthew S. Quay, then the chairman of the Republican State Committee of Pennsylvania and a would-be national party organizer, was more concerned with the negative impact of a Democratic presidency on the nation's future. If the Republicans lost, he warned, the "net result of the war" would then be the "substitution of the shot-gun for the slave-whip" in the southern states. "Our billions of treasure will have been spent in vain and our soldiers dead will have died as the fool's death."[25]

Other Republicans couched the issue in similar terms. Seeking to maintain a Republican presidency to stop Democratic aggression, John Sherman perceived the importance of the election long before the campaign started:

> As to the approaching presidential contest, the importance ... cannot be overstated. The election of a Democratic president means a restoration to full power in the Government of the worst elements of the rebel confederacy. The Southern

States are to be organized by violence and intimidation into a compact political power only needing a small fragment of Northern States to give it absolute control, which by a majority rule of the party it will govern the country as it did in the times of Pierce & Buchanan.

If it should elect a President and both Houses of Congress, the constitutional amendments would be destroyed; the freedmen would be nominally citizens but really slaves; numberable claims swollen by perjury would be saddled upon the Treasury; our public credit would be impaired; the powers of the General government would be crippled, and the honors won by our people in subduing rebellion would be subjects of reproach rather than of pride.[26]

The only safeguards to prevent these evils, Sherman suggested, were "the election of a Republican President; and the adoption of a liberal Republican policy which should be fair and even generous to the South but firm in the maintenance of all the rights won by the war." Yet Sherman's proposed Republican policy contained two apparently contradictory yet intrinsically correlated elements, that is, a *liberal*, *fair*, and even *generous* treatment of the South and a *firm* maintenance of black rights established by the Civil War and Reconstruction. Sherman suggested that Rutherford B. Hayes, then the first Republican governor of Ohio elected for three consecutive terms, would be an ideal presidential candidate.[27]

The nomination of Hayes as the Republican candidate at the Cincinnati convention in June 1876 is not a subject of the present study, but what needs to be stressed here is that his selection was largely a compromise between liberal and regular Republicans over the party's policy toward black rights.[28] Among the Republican presidential hopefuls, Blaine was a strong candidate. He led the half-breed Republicans, who did not advocate the abandoning of blacks but were more interested in directing the party toward more economically and financially oriented programs. But Blaine's chances were badly damaged when he was suspected of involvement in a railroad swindle. Benjamin Bristow, a liberal hopeful who established his reputation through his battle against corruption in the Grant cabinet, nonetheless failed to draw an impressive crowd of supporters. The supporters of Roscoe Conkling and Oliver P. Morton, both stalwart representatives, threw their votes to Hayes when they saw that otherwise Blaine would win the nomination.[29]

A substantial proportion of Republicans saw a need to change party policy, but that change was not to be a total reversal or repeal of the party's previous principles. What was most important was to nominate someone who could beat the Democrats. On the last round of balloting at the Cincinnati convention, the

Michigan delegates announced that since Hayes had beaten the Democrats in his own state for three terms, they wanted "to give him a chance to beat another Democratic candidate for the Presidency in the broader field of the United States." The Michigan vote influenced other states and became crucial in securing Hayes's nomination.[30] The day after Hayes's nomination at the Cincinnati Republican convention, the *Louisville Courier-Journal* commented that the defeat of Bristow and large vote cast for Blaine showed that administrative reform was "not a prevailing idea with the Republicans."[31] Hayes's record as a Civil War veteran, his three-term governorship in an important northern state, his distance from Grantism, and the political maneuvers of his campaign managers and advisers — all helped him defeat other, better-known Republican nominees. "Hayes's character and career," the *San Francisco Chronicle* stated, "constitute a platform in themselves."[32] But Hayes's adherence to Republican Reconstruction principles and his expressed moderation on the southern question were the most important factors that enabled him to emerge from relative national political obscurity to become accepted by all the factions of the Republican party.

Hayes's thinking on black rights evolved from his experience with Reconstruction and was shaped by later developments in the South. He supported the Thirteenth and Fourteenth Amendments when he represented Ohio in the House from 1865 to 1867. When he resigned from the House after being nominated for governor of Ohio in July 1867, he campaigned for black suffrage in his state, urging Congress to pass a law to grant black citizens the vote. He was then a firm believer in impartial suffrage and shared much of the prevailing Republican zeal for a constitutional reconstruction. "Our government . . . is not the government of any class, or sect, or nationality, or race," Hayes said in a speech at Lebanon, Ohio; "it is the government of the freeman; and when colored men were made citizens, soldiers, and freemen by our consent and votes, we were stopped from denying them the right of suffrage."[33]

When the Fifteenth Amendment became law in 1870, Hayes hailed it. But he immediately noted that universal education must follow universal suffrage. Although frustrated by what he called "the evil of rule by ignorance" as practiced in the South and some northern cities, he refused to think that the remedy was to restore slavery or disfranchise blacks, which would be "the abandonment of the American principle that all must share in government." He advised his southern friends to "*forget to drive and learn to lead* the ignorant masses around them."[34]

The debates between regular and liberal Republicans over the party's southern policy undoubtedly influenced the formulation of Hayes's thinking on the southern question and black rights. Despite liberal efforts to make reform the party's priority at the Cincinnati convention, Hayes quickly realized that the strongest sentiment shared by the majority of the party in 1876 was still the fear of a Democratic victory and the overthrow of Reconstruction principles. In one of his letters to his campaign manager, William H. Smith, Hayes wrote:

> The drift of the Canvass is plain. The people *do dread* a victory for the United South. They see in it continued trouble — nullification of the amendments — Rebel claims, and schemes. &c, &c, &c, and I think anything which withdraws attention from this issue to merely personal matters is a mistake. The school issue, the civil service issue, the currency issue, &c., are all in point and good, but merely personal issues may well be dropped with a few words of denunciation.[35]

Writing to Garfield, Hayes made clear that the major concern of the election was "not to allow the Rebellion to come into power." This position, he told John Bingham, "would give [the Republicans] the prestige of the attack" and was "in line of a decided and growing public sentiment."[36] In a letter to Carl Schurz, who supported his reelection as governor, Hayes expressed a similar view. He explained to the liberals that he put the southern question first not because he himself was indifferent to reform but simply because the antirebel sentiment dominated the Republican canvass in the West and Northwest.[37] Hayes's use of the southern question, however, was not just to win the election, for he had deep concerns about the consequences of a Democratic victory, which, he believed, would "prove especially calamitous to the South — not to the Colored people alone, but the White people also." He feared that southern Democrats had always regarded black suffrage as "a monstrous wrong" and would "in effect nullify the provisions of the Constitution which secure[d] this right to the colored men."[38] On this point, Hayes shared regular Republicans' concern that the party's southern policy should aim not only at keeping the party in power but also, in William E. Chandler's words, at protecting blacks and saving "the Nation from great peril."[39]

Although some regular Republicans urged him to adopt a strong southern policy similar to Grant's in Louisiana and South Carolina, Hayes never did so. In fact, he had shared much of the liberals' anti-Grant feelings and personally disliked Grant's policies. In March 1875, after he was nominated for the governorship, Hayes privately expressed his concerns about the future of the Republican party:

I do not sympathize with a large share of the party leaders. I hate the corruptionists of whom Butler is leader. I doubt the ultra measures relating to the South, and
I am opposed to the course of General Grant on the third term, the civil service
and the appointment of unfit men on partisan or personal grounds.[40]

Hayes perceived a real need for a different policy toward the South. His liberal-minded advisers kept pushing him to adopt a more generous southern policy and completely drop issues regarding federal enforcement of black suffrage.
Carl Schurz, the original liberal leader, advised Hayes to express himself boldly
on the need for hard currency, southern reconciliation, and civil service reform
in his letter of acceptance. Schurz hinted that such a declaration would help
Hayes win German votes.[41] George William Curtis, whom Hayes respected as
one of the "great political writers," also advised him to be bold in denouncing
the spoils system. Hayes did not do exactly what Curtis expected, but he
promised to try to "hit the nail on the head, and to hit it pretty hard."[42] Meanwhile, Charles Nordhoff, the correspondent for the *New York Herald*, advised
Hayes to write "a temperate, carefully considered, but rather *daring* letter" declaring that "the Southern troubles" were "substantially over" and that "for the
future[,] federal interference in the local affairs of the southern States, always
dangerous & to be deplored, [would] no longer be necessary." The purpose of
doing so, Nordhoff said, was to win the support of southern Whigs and northern
liberals. "The darkies you'll have any how," Nordhoff wrote, "the white whigs
[sic] are what you want to capture." Nordhoff believed that "the lasting harmony" of the South would depend upon a "rearrangement" of parties.[43]

Hayes faced a twofold challenge. At the political level, the achievements of
the Civil War and Reconstruction — political equality, black suffrage, and the
constitutional amendments — were not to be abandoned; these were not only the
party's political capital but also part of the nation's new political heritage. At
the policy level, although the military enforcement policy was regarded as a failure, other alternatives had to be pursued so that black rights could be maintained and the Democratic "united South" destroyed. The tasks that Hayes set
for himself were both admirable and ambitious. He wanted to replace sectional
strife with national harmony, revitalize the party without infringing on the political achievements of the Civil War and Reconstruction, and restore state sovereignty without giving up black rights. But the task was also extremely difficult — and Hayes knew it. Writing to Schurz, Hayes revealed the difficulties in
formulating his southern policy:

My anxiety to *do* something to promote the pacification of the South is perhaps in danger of leading me too far. I do not reflect on the use of the military power in the past. But there is to be an end of all that, except in emergencies which I can't think of as possible again. We must do all we can to promote prosperity there. Education, emigration and immigration, improvements occur to me. But the more I think of it, the more I see in what you say. We must go cautiously and slowly. . . . Perhaps we must be content to leave that to time – taking care not to obstruct time's healing process by injudicious meddling.[44]

The only alternative that seemed possible was to remove federal interference and influence from local affairs in the South. Soon after the Republicans lost control of the House, Hayes realized the ineffectiveness of enforcement. He agreed that a "let-alone policy" seemed "to be the true course" and that the South's future depended largely on "the moderation and good sense of the Southern men in the next House of Representatives."[45] But when Schurz urged him to include in his letter of acceptance a pledge for the right to self-government, Hayes immediately rebuffed the suggestion. The so-called "local self-government, in *that* connection," for Hayes, "seemed to smack of the bowie knife and revolver. 'Local self-government' ha[d] nullified the 15th amendment in several States, and [was] in a fair way to nullify the 14th and 13th."[46] But, given the unpopularity of federal enforcement policy, Hayes had to compromise on this point. In his letter of acceptance, he pledged:

> The moral and material prosperity of the Southern states can be most effectually advanced by a hearty and generous recognition of the rights of all by all – a recognition without reserve or exception. With such a recognition fully accorded, it will be practicable to promote, by the influence of all legitimate agencies of the general government, the efforts of the people of those states to obtain for themselves the blessings of honest and capable local government. If elected, I shall consider it not only my duty, but it will be my ardent wish, to labor for the attainment of this end.[47]

There was no better alternative for Hayes. He would not continue Grant's policy. Neither would he give up blacks or the liberal forces gathered around him. He wanted to secure a southern pledge for black rights while assuring a chance "for the interests and feelings of the well disposed white man" in the South.[48] Hayes's stand on black rights won the support of prominent black leaders. Blanche K. Bruce, the black senator from Mississippi, represented the state to cast the vote for Hayes at the Cincinnati convention. When he returned to the Senate, he sent a special congratulatory note to Hayes:

As the only Representative in the U.S. Senate of more than four million people who are set apart by their fellow citizens as a distinct and separate race, and who have for more than a century toiled as slaves to their brethren, I feel a peculiar pleasure in this first hour of their freedom, in offering these congratulations, and in assuring you that speaking for my race, the Colored people of America will hail the day when all men shall be constrained to adopt your language, in a recent speech at Fremont, to wit: "it is for each man to do what he can to make others happy. That is the prayer and that is the duty of life."[49]

John Langston, then the dean of Howard University's law school, also believed that Hayes's presidency would be sustained by "a healthy public sentiment, in all sections" in this "most critical period of [the] National existence."[50]

In a sense, black voters had no better choice than Hayes. In 1876, partisan spirit still ran high, and, at least for black voters, the contrast between the Republican and Democratic parties was still very conspicuous, especially on issues regarding national protection of black rights. The Republican party remained the only political ally black voters could rely on for the improvement of their condition and the security of their rights. A Democratic victory would be calamitous for blacks in the South. Black leaders were persuaded to give Hayes their full support, because "the triumph of Tilden" was "the triumph of murder as an element in politics."[51] Undoubtedly, black leaders were dissatisfied with Republicans for not giving them full-fledged aid. Despite black emancipation and enfranchisement, by the time of the centennial of the Declaration of Independence, blacks and many whites still saw their country as "a *White Man's Government*." Under such circumstances, black leaders were asked to "support the Republican wing of this white man's government" because they had "more real friends in that party than any where else" and because they could "make this Republican wing of more service than . . . the Confederate-Democratic wing."[52]

One object of Hayes's southern policy was to win over southern whites for the Republicans and dismantle the "solid South," which he considered the main obstacle to national harmony. Privately, he worried about how he would "get support from good men of the South, late Rebels." He saw his "let-alone" policy as the "best disposition towards the Southern people, Rebels and all." Before the election results were decided, Hayes even started to think about appointing a southern Democrat to the cabinet.[53] And Hayes proudly regarded his own policy as a major breakthrough in the party's efforts to develop Republicanism in the South. He complained that party leaders had no faith in charting new paths to unite the South. "It was curious to see the horror of friends," he wrote to Schurz, "when I announced quietly that I meant to appoint at least one Democrat on every State Board."[54]

Thus, long before he withdrew federal troops from Louisiana and South Carolina in April 1877, the decision had been formulated in Hayes's mind. His southern policy and his treatment of black rights reflected the mixed feelings existing among Republicans at that time. The issue of defending black rights was closely related to ending federal interference in local affairs, which, however, endangered black rights, given that federal enforcement was the only powerful deterrent to the violence and terrorism imposed on black voters by local white Democrats in the South. Hayes's southern policy was to try, with the intention of reconciliation, to defederalize the issue of protecting black suffrage.

Given the evolution of Hayes's southern policy, it is wrong to say that his policy totally abandoned blacks and unconditionally surrendered their political rights to southern "home rule." Hayes never openly or privately discussed the idea of America without black suffrage. Even when he admitted the importance of states' rights, he held without exception that equal rights for all Americans was the precondition. He never denied the principles established by the constitutional amendments. Hayes's policy represented a Republican effort to search for a new strategy, not only to develop its forces in the South but also to consolidate the principle of equal rights. The party's goal was to gain support from the South and make the party truly national. But whether such a policy would work would depend largely on how sincerely southern whites would appreciate Hayes's intentions and cooperate with him. Thus, the *North American Review* regarded Hayes's policy as nothing more than a political experiment.[55]

The Experiment of a New Southern Policy

The disputed outcome of the 1876 presidential election is one of the knottiest, most controversial issues in American political history.[56] The main dispute focused on the returns from three southern states — Florida, Louisiana, and South Carolina — where local Republicans charged Democrats with fraud and then threw out questioned Democratic votes and declared both the Hayes electors and the Republican state tickets elected. The Democrats in those states, in turn, accused Republicans of electoral fraud. Each state submitted two sets of returns. This situation compelled Congress to create a special electoral commission to determine which votes were to be counted. Republican leaders were uncertain about the final result until Joseph Bradley, a Republican Supreme Court justice, was named to fill the position left open by the departure of Justice David Davis, an independent.[57] With a majority of one vote, the eight Republicans made the decisions of the commission, which gave the disputed electoral votes to Hayes and declared him president on March 2, 1877.

Between the campaign, the controversy, and Hayes's background, northern public opinion had long expected a change in Republican policy. With Hayes's victory, the *Springfield Republican* immediately urged the new president to cut off "all reliance of the new administration on the past" and to break down "the bridges behind it."[58]

Hayes's inaugural address was in many ways a manifesto of the ideological and political outlook of many northern Republicans, especially toward black rights and federal-state relations. Following the guidelines laid down in his letter of acceptance but using more explicit wording, Hayes's inaugural clearly stated that the national government had "a moral obligation" to "employ its constitutional power and influence to establish the rights of the people it ha[d] emancipated, and to establish and to protect them in the enjoyment of those rights when they [were] infringed or assailed." While Hayes pledged that his administration would "protect the rights of all by every constitutional means," he regarded "honest and efficient local self-government as the true resource" for the southern states to promote "the contentment and prosperity of their citizens."[59] Here, Hayes was trying to distinguish between federal and state responsibilities.

Hayes reminded his audience that the South had been burdened with a social and political revolution for too long and that it was time to take care of "material development." To remove the old political strife, Hayes advocated efforts "to wipe out in . . . political affairs the color line and the distinction between North and South," so that there would not merely be "a united North or a united South, but a united country."[60] Obviously, reconciliation highlighted the address, but Hayes remained committed to his pledge to protect equal rights. He saw the national government's power to guard black emancipation and enfranchisement as constitutionally indisputable.

Hayes's call for obliterating the color line in political affairs seemed to be a response to the liberals' earlier call to abolish the color line of black suffrage, but what he hoped to achieve was a united country on the basis of the Reconstruction principles of equal rights. Hayes's insistence on the federal government's obligation to protect black rights was intellectually coherent with his decision to veto the Democratic Congress's attempt to repeal federal enforcement acts during 1879 – 80. His position was clear to the *Springfield Republican*, which noticed that although Hayes respected the rights of local self-government, he was "determined to surrender none of the equal rights which the war achieved and the constitution secured to all classes." *Harper's Weekly* welcomed Hayes's address and expected it to "command sympathy and support of all men from all the parties."[61]

With the great and sincere ambition to be the president of a united country, Hayes did everything possible to show the South that his policy and political style differed radically from the previous administration's. By the time Hayes was ready to take office, the basic tone of his southern policy was set:

> My course is a firm assertion and maintenance of the rights of the colored people
> of the South to the Thirteenth, Fourteenth and Fifteenth Amendments, coupled
> with a readiness to recognize all Southern people, without regard to past political
> conduct, who will now go with me heartily and in good faith in support of these
> principles.[62]

As part of his effort to rebuild the party's confidence and promote his reform policy, Hayes chose a cabinet that could be characterized as a new departure. None of its members had been closely associated with the previous administration. Several members, most notably Secretary of the Interior Carl Schurz and Secretary of State William M. Evarts, had been liberal Republican leaders. John Sherman was probably the only one close to regular Republican ranks, but Sherman was a major advocate for a "liberal Republican policy." As he had promised, Hayes named Tennessee Democrat David M. Key postmaster general, a source of many federal jobs. Hayes's appointments outraged the regular Republicans, but the liberal Republican organs, which had urged Hayes to include "the best elements" of the Republican party in his administration, hailed the cabinet as evidence that "the rule of partisanship" had been succeeded by "the era of patriotism."[63] When in a local election the Republicans gained more popular support, the *Chicago Tribune* attributed the success to the cabinet selection, which, with the appointment of the liberal Schurz and Democratic Key, "broke through the party machinery, defied the Senatorial autocracy."[64]

The most controversial part of the first phase of Hayes's southern policy was to withdraw the federal troops guarding the statehouses in Louisiana and South Carolina. The politics of withdrawal originated with the outcome of the 1876 election. Republicans Daniel H. Chamberlain of South Carolina and Stephen B. Packard of Louisiana claimed to have been elected governors of their respective states on the basis of essentially the same returns that had placed Hayes in the White House. The Democrats claimed that the returning boards created by the Republican legislatures had, according to the state constitutions, no authority over the returns of the election officers of the precincts and districts. The Democrats claimed on the face of the returns the election of Francis T. Nicholls as governor of Louisiana and Wade Hampton as governor of South Carolina and a sufficient number of candidates to constitute the lawful legislature in each of these states. Consequently, both Packard and Nicholls set up a state government in Louisiana; Chamberlain and Hampton did the same in South Carolina; and each was supported by a legislature claiming to be each state's lawful legislature. The Republican governors and legislatures were installed in the regular statehouses and defended by federal troops within the buildings.[65]

Supposedly, Hayes and the Democratic governments in those two states had agreed that federal recognition of the Democratic governments should be contingent upon Democratic pledges not to repress the states' Republicans and not to deprive blacks of their civil and political equality.[66] But the process of settling the disputes in those two states still demanded sophisticated political handling. Neither the Constitution nor federal statute books provided a ready solution for this situation. Constitutionally, Hayes could have chosen to continue the policy of military enforcement with the Republican governments in those two states. But he chose otherwise.

Many studies of Reconstruction regard military withdrawal as the end of Reconstruction. Historians have variously praised or criticized Hayes for his decision on this issue.[67] Frankly, Hayes had contemplated the rationale for withdrawal as a possible way to end the southern strife long before he entered the White House.[68] The withdrawal was the first test of Hayes's goodwill policy. Hayes believed that southern whites would give blacks full rights when the federal government stopped aiding the local Republican governments. At the same time, Hayes was influenced by demands from the party and the northern business community for a change from military reconstruction.[69] Soon after Hayes's inauguration, many northern merchants urged him to withdraw federal troops from the southern states to end the disorder. Business communities in major northern cities passed resolutions calling for the end of military rule in the South.[70] Northern newspapers reinforced public demand with a series of editorials; *Harper's Weekly* openly declared that the danger that the freedmen "would have been reduced to a condition little better than slavery . . . ha[d] in great measure passed away." It opposed any further use of military force to maintain political stability in the South:

> Twelve years have taught the new citizens their power, and the old citizens the necessity, for their own safety, of friendly relations. . . . If army may be a police any where, it may be so every where. American statesmanship must trust American principles. American principles declare equal rights and demand equal protection. . . . It is not the interest of a single class or race that is to be considered, but the welfare and harmony of all the people in the State.[71]

The article illustrated a great irony of American politics: the theories of equal rights and national protection of equal rights, which radical Republicans had used to achieve black rights, were used now to undermine the practice of these theories.

Some Republicans already had been preparing for withdrawal – logistically and ideologically. Ohio Republican Charles Foster, one of Hayes's closest allies in the House, was asked by Democratic journalist Charles Nordhoff of the *New York Herald* to pass along his "knowledge of the minds of the Democratic side" to Hayes. Nordhoff told Foster that white leaders in Louisiana would "be able to restrain the impatience of the people, and wait in quiet till after March 4th" if Hayes's "accession [would] rid them of the carpetbag government" and he would "keep his hands off the State." Nordhoff believed that the main goal of southern whites was to get rid of local Republican government: "They don't care who is President – not a cent – but they can't stand the Packard government any longer."[72]

When the Louisiana question was discussed on March 16, a majority of Hayes's cabinet members shrank from using federal authority to support one state government against another. Four plans were offered, including a new election in those two states, congressional actions, federal acknowledgment of the Packard and Chamberlain governments, and withdrawal of federal troops.[73] On March 20 the cabinet met again, and the majority, as Hayes recorded, "seemed indisposed to use force to uphold Packard's government." Only Attorney General Devens disagreed, but he was "not decidedly for it." Hayes seriously doubted that the nation would "sustain the policy of upholding a State Government against a rival government, by the use of the force of the United States."[74] Hayes realized that once the federal troops were ordered to withdraw, the Republican governments in both Louisiana and South Carolina would immediately fall, but "the real thing" to be achieved was "safety and prosperity for the colored people." He made clear that his wish was "to restore harmony and good feeling between sections and races." This could only be done by "peaceful methods."[75] However, Hayes moved cautiously and tried to secure the approval of the whole cabinet. Schurz noticed that his superior moved "slowly but surely" and always wanted "to have his wagons together when he marche[d], but [lost] no battles."[76] After Hampton pledged, during a meeting with Hayes in late March, to secure equal rights for both blacks and whites, Hayes ordered the federal troops guarding the statehouse in Charleston back to their barracks. The Hampton government immediately took over Chamberlain's government. In early April, Hayes sent a commission to Louisiana and was advised to order an immediate withdrawal. On April 20, Hayes ordered Secretary of War George W. McCrary to withdraw the federal troops from the Louisiana statehouse.[77] Before he gave up, Packard issued a farewell address in which he lamented that "one by one, the republican state government[s] of the South ha[d] been forced to succumb to force or fraud or policy."[78]

Hayes regarded the withdrawals as "the vital steps" in his attempt "to solve the Southern question." He was confident that his plan would bring the security of black rights. He expected many regular Republicans to condemn his policy, but he would not "worry or scold" if they did because he meant well.[79]

Southern Republicans felt desperate and disheartened at the withdrawal. Even William H. Smith, Hayes's confidant, confessing his own deep feeling for the "good old Republicans," reported to the president that Louisiana Republicans had "manifested a good deal of feeling" and their minds were "filled with doubts" and the future was "not clear to them."[80] Chamberlain, the defeated Republican governor of South Carolina, left the state and moved to New York. He held the Hayes administration responsible for the Republican defeat in the South:

> The Presidential contest also endangered us and doubtless defeated us. The hope of electing Tilden incited our opponents, and the greed of office led the defeated Republicans under Hayes to sell us out. There was just as distinct a bargain to do this at Washington as ever existed which was not signed and sealed on paper. And the South is not to be blamed for it, if anybody is; but rather those leaders, like Evarts, who could never see their Constitutional obligations towards the South until the offices were slipping away from their party.[81]

The response of blacks to the withdrawal was mixed.[82] Many regarded it as a betrayal. Some tolerated it as a necessary step to achieve permanent stability in the South. Others were puzzled but had no choice other than to think that

Hayes's choice was out of necessity and with the best of intentions. Some prominent black leaders — John Langston, the acting dean of Howard University; M. W. Gibbs of Arkansas; John Thomas Rapier of Alabama; J. Wills Menard of Louisiana; Robert Smalls of South Carolina; and John R. Lynch of Mississippi — all pledged their support of Hayes's policy. Frederick Douglass, who had been informed about and endorsed Hayes's view on the southern question, understood that the decision on withdrawal "might rather be considered the President's necessity." Probably thinking about why Lincoln had acted slowly on emancipation, Douglass said, "Statesmen often [are] compelled to act upon facts as they are, and not as they would like to have them."[83] Five days after the Packard government fell, a delegation of Louisiana blacks visited the White House and asked Hayes to continue his support of Packard. Hayes persuaded his black guests in the belief that his policy would only bring them "a happier condition of affairs."[84]

Northern responses to the withdrawal were also mixed. Some defended Hayes's decision, calling it not an abandonment of the principle of equality but simply "an adjustment" of the party's policy. In a letter to P. B. S. Pinchback, Charles Baylor, a New York Republican, explained:

> The north has not lost interest in the cause of Equality of citizenship under the Government as Represented by the Negro citizens of the late Slave States of the Union. *That cause the North will never abandon* not because of any love for the Negro or for the principle, but simply because the Union cannot be maintained as a white man's Democracy based on negro serfdom as its corner stone. It can only be maintained through the vindication of the principle of equality of Citizenship for all men before & under the Law.[85]

He said that the northern "back-down" on the southern question resulted from the bad character of northern political adventurers in the South, "a natural distaste to the use of military power in civil government," and the good faith pledge of the redeemers' government, which the North accepted.[86]

Liberal Republicans applauded Hayes's policy. They shared his optimism and felt that withdrawal would ensure civil and political equality for blacks. "With the realization of President Hayes' hopes and intentions," the *Chicago Tribune* predicted, "the 'bloody shirt' will no longer be a stock in trade for political parties, and the African's place in politics will be as secure as that of the European classes in the North."[87] After Republican governor Chamberlain left the South Carolina statehouse, the *Nation* called the removal of federal troops "the close of the revolutionary period in southern politics."[88] Instead of regarding the withdrawal as a betrayal of blacks, liberals believed that it would help blacks enjoy their rights in a more secure way. Military enforcement had created racial antagonism in the South and given whites the excuse to form a solid South on the color line, explained *Harper's Weekly*. Consequently, withdrawal would only help divide southern whites. The paper argued that Hayes's policy proposed "to abandon nobody and to surrender nothing." The condition of blacks was most satisfactory where the military arm was weakest, the paper said.[89]

Much blunter than *Harper's Weekly*, the *Nation* responded to withdrawal with a sense of relief. It declared that with the fall of the last Republican governments in the South, "the negro [would] disappear from the field of national politics."[90] Many liberal Republicans argued that with the black issue gone, it was time for the party to devote itself to civil service reform. George William Curtis went to Washington to urge more reform. He found that Hayes provided the best "chance in a thousand years" for the reform movement, and the "change in tone and spirit from the late regime [was] total."[91]

Republicans in northern states responded in different ways. Republicans in Massachusetts, Ohio, New Jersey, Pennsylvania, and Wisconsin approved Hayes's decision, but in New York, Iowa, and Maine, where regular Republican forces were strong, opposition was vocal. The New York Republican convention split over whether to endorse Hayes's policy. The Iowa convention adopted a resolution condemning Hayes for abandoning the Republican governments in Louisiana and South Carolina and asserting that he had conceded too much to the states' rights movement. The United States, the resolution declared, was a nation, not a league, and federal enforcement of the laws should be resumed to protect citizens' rights. The *Nation* regarded the Iowa resolution as the "mere factious desire to keep the party organization in power."[92]

One of the great ironies of the debates between the regular and liberal Republicans on Hayes's withdrawal decision was that both sides tried to use the theory of nationalism and protection of equal rights. Both sides applied the theory in different contexts. Whereas the Iowa resolution called on the party to protect citizens' rights because the nation was a nation, not a league, George William Curtis of New York argued that mutual respect and confidence between the races was the root of national greatness. At the New York Republican convention, Curtis said:

> I don't believe there is one honest republican who will say that President Hayes is not doing just what he pledged himself to do. He is showing to the South that the forces and elements of the republican party of the North are not hostile or

vindictive toward any section of the country. He is engaged in showing that we are pledged to equal rights for all citizens and he is endeavoring to promote mutual respect and confidence, the only vital root of national greatness. His southern policy tends to show that the republican party is a national party.

Despite their differences on the policy toward the South, northern Republicans agreed that the nation and equal rights must be respected. They might have played with the idea, but the idea was well entrenched in the postwar ideology of the Republican party.[93]

Hayes's policy aroused particular resentment among the old radical Republicans. Several veteran abolitionists, including William Lloyd Garrison and Wendell Phillips, accused Hayes of betraying the faith of the Republican party. Ben Wade, the radical from Ohio, called his failure to protect the emancipated blacks a crime.[94] Grant's attorney general Amos T. Akerman, who had fought against the Ku Klux Klan in 1870–71, took a dim view of Hayes's conciliatory policy. He believed that Democrats would give Hayes "some surface compliments and accept office from him and then laugh at him for his folly . . . in letting them take him in."[95] The more conservative Thurlow Weed approved of Hayes's policy of withdrawal but not of his abandonment of southern Republicans. Weed argued that "the protection should simultaneously have been extended to Govrs. Chamberlain and Packard and to all trustworthy Republicans in the three Southern States to which the president [was] indebted for his election."[96]

To more radical Republicans, Hayes's policy was "treachery." A New Hampshire Republican wrote to party leader William E. Chandler, "Every day of Hayes' administration makes true Republicans appreciate more & more the sterling qualities of Gen. Grant." He urged Chandler to take the lead in the fight against Hayes and his appeasement policy: "A little thunder & lighting will generally clean an unhealthy atmosphere. Best of all it hit Hayes [in the] head."[97]

The divisions between different factions of the Republican party were encapsulated in their opinions of Hayes's policy. Zachariah Chandler, the chairman of the National Republican Committee, planned to call a meeting of the committee in late July to find out how the group should respond to Hayes's policy. In his letter to William E. Chandler, he expressed his view:

> My own opinion is that something should be done to arrest the destruction of the Republican Party by the Administration and perhaps it can be done better by the National Committee than in any other way.

Perhaps a strong resolution expressing a want of confidence in the Cabinet as at present constituted, or in certain member of it, would open the President's eyes and pave the way for a change for the better. His policy has killed the party in the Gulf states and put it in a minority in a majority of the other states North, as well as South, at least for the time being.

It seems to me that some effort ought to be made to effect a change in the policy of the Administration.

I do not believe that the Republican party will endorse the doctrine that a successful mob constitutes a state government or a government of any kind.

I wish that you would write to some of the members of the National Committee that you are best acquainted with, and get their views, or perhaps what would be better urge your own.[98]

The Republican committee reacted to the call for a meeting with indifference. Zachariah Chandler complained that there were "so many weak policy men on the Committee . . . besides the members from the Southern States who seem[ed] to have lost their courage altogether." But he believed that the majority of the party in both Ohio and Michigan opposed Hayes's policy. He stated, "The administration had the power to aid the Republican party in the South in its struggle for existence, but it chose the other course and the party vanished into thin air."[99]

Regular Republicans, in despair at the policy, hoped to keep the Republican majority in the Senate closely united as the last front for the party. Realizing that Hayes was trying to get Republican senators' support, William E. Chandler asked Zachariah Chandler to influence Michigan Republican senator Isaac P. Christancy not to side with the president. "Could you have him enlightened as to what the Republicans of your State think about the Hayes southern policy by letter from people whose opinions he would respect . . . [and] make a sentiment which shall lead its Senators to be among the foremost in the Radical column?" William Chandler wrote.[100] Zachariah Chandler shared his anxieties, but he believed that Christancy was well aware that the policy of the administration was "almost universally condemned by the republicans" in his state. But, even so, he added, severe criticism had been "refrained from with the hope that the President would in turn discover his mistakes and pursue a different course, one that would tend to save, rather than destroy the republican party." The nation's prospects were gloomy: "The South has gone beyond hope. I see no other course to pursue but to constitute the North and protect the national treasury and the national honor."[101]

On December 3, 1877, Hayes delivered his annual message and defended his policy as "the wisest in the presence of this emergency." The withdrawal of federal troops was "no less a constitutional duty and requirement, under the circumstances existing at the time, than it was a much-needed measure for the restoration of local self-government and the promotion of national harmony." Hayes repeated his pledge to protect the civil and political rights of blacks and to secure "immediate repression and sure punishment by the national and local authorities, within their respective jurisdictions, of every instance of lawlessness and violence toward them."[102]

Probably because the National Republican Committee failed to reach a consensus on Hayes's policy, William E. Chandler, a committee member, published an open letter on December 26, 1877, on the "so-called Southern policy of the administration of President Hayes." Addressing New Hampshire Republicans, Chandler accused Hayes of betraying the "radical platform pledging federal power to protect human rights and lawful governments at the South." With reports and news excerpts principally from the *New York Tribune*, Chandler sketched the process through which Hayes's associates, including John Sherman, Charles Foster, and Stanley Matthews, and southern white leaders worked out an agreement to abandon the Packard government in Louisiana before the confirmation of Hayes's presidency.[103]

However, despite the noble talk, what concerned Chandler most were the annihilation of the Republican party in the South and the division of the party in the North. Hayes's policy, he thought, was suicidal. Chandler simply did not think that a united nation and national harmony could be achieved by surrendering the Republican party in the South. He believed that the party would still be an effective weapon in politics. This belief directly contradicted the liberals' call for the reorganization of parties or the end of partisan politics. In a sense, Hayes shared much of that conviction. Thus, to Chandler, the fall of the southern Republicans was a dangerous sign for the party's future in national politics:

> The Republican party has lived long, and survived many assaults and many treasons, only because it has been a party founded upon high principles, animated by lofty sentiment, courageously acting up to noble convictions. If it now disgraces its record, and endorses or fails to repudiate the Hayes surrender, its voters will leave it by thousands; its days are numbered; it will die a deserved and an unhonored death.[104]

Chandler's letter was printed by New York papers. Staunch regular Republicans in the North warmly received it. Zachariah Chandler called it "a ringing slashing and yet trustful statement" that would "open the eyes of some people." He demanded that "the drifting policy" be abandoned or the party would be "lost in a boundless sea of irresolution and contempt."[105] Garrison, the old abolitionist, hailed Chandler's letter as "a judicial presentation of the facts in the case—a faithful reminder of pledges sacredly made, and shamefully broken." Garrison blasted Hayes's explanation for his decisions and cautioned the North that the South was "still rebellious at heart though wearing the mask of submission."[106] In another letter, Garrison cheered Chandler with this sentiment: "As the most disheartening occurrences during the anti-slavery conflict invariably were overruled for good, so I believe a saving reaction is ultimately to succeed the present defection in the Republican ranks."[107] The liberals, however, saw little damage that Chandler's letter could do to Hayes's policy and predicted that it would hasten "the mutual understanding of the friends of the administration."[108]

The Chandler letter pushed Republican differences in formulating a post-Reconstruction southern policy to the extreme. The dispute between regular and liberal Republicans was principally about how best to develop the party's influence in the South. The party was more concerned about partisan development than about black rights, although its members had not hesitated to use the pretext of defending black rights.

Republican Defense of the Enforcement Policy

Despite the resentment in his party, Hayes believed that his intentions were good and his policy was working. On a goodwill tour to New England, Ohio, and the South in the summer and fall of 1877, Hayes continued to preach reconciliation and racial harmony. Wherever he went, he "tried to impress the people with the importance of harmony between different sections, States, classes, and races, and to discourage sectionalism and race and class prejudice."[109] Aware of local displeasure with his policy, Hayes cautiously told his audience that what he wanted in his presidency "was to do something for the whole country and for all its inhabitants."[110] In Jeffersonville, Indiana, Hayes gave a similar talk, saying his duty was to promote the equal welfare and happiness of all sections of the country and to secure "the equality of all men of all races."[111] In the South, Hayes was welcomed. In an address delivered in the capital of Tennessee, Nashville, Hayes defended his southern policy. He was pleased to see, "after almost six months' trial, that the majority of the people of the South—the white people of the South – ha[d] no desire to invade the rights of the colored people so as to make it at all necessary to have Federal bayonets in their midst."[112] In Atlanta, Hayes called slavery "a crime of our fathers," but, with civil and political equality for all citizens, Hayes believed, sectional and color lines could be removed from American politics.[113]

But Hayes's triumph was short-lived, if it ever lived at all. Before the year ended, Hayes's policy was losing momentum, even among prominent blacks who had supported it. As part of his effort to set an example for recognition of equal rights, at the beginning of his administration, Hayes named a few well-known blacks to patronage positions. He appointed Frederick Douglass the United States marshal for the District of Columbia. Hayes believed that Douglass's appointment had "more significance than a personal remembrance of that distinguished gentleman."[114] Douglass agreed with Hayes on this point and felt that his appointment would "be gratifying to a large class of the American people of all colors."[115] Hayes also asked his subordinates to appoint more blacks to "diminish race prejudice."[116]

These efforts were genuine on Hayes's part but useless in the eyes of such northern black sympathizers as Thomas K. Beecher. "You do not benefit the blacks by decorating Fred. Douglass with a Marshalship!" wrote the brother of Henry Ward Beecher, who actually opposed federal protection for blacks and advocated that the black man take his own chances because one did not "bless his state by translating a field hand into a legislator."[117] But, after the Republican governments fell, blacks were seldom appointed to important posts. P. B. S. Pinchback, already retired from active politics and extremely disappointed about the negative effect of Hayes's policy, wrote to the president:

> Under the administration of your predecessor when the need of representation in the Federal service was less urgent than now, the colored element never had less than three good appointments in this city; among which, at different times, were Post master, Surveyor, Collector of Internal Revenue, Naval Officer, and appraiser, and Pension Agent, in which capacities I believe they acquitted themselves creditably. Now, with our political condition materially changed, and by your act in part, we have only one or two good positions, and those in point of the representation character of the men filling them, too insignificant to be considered in that category.[118]

At the same time, black suffrage was restricted in many southern states where Democrats triumphed. Georgians added restrictions to their state's new constitution, such as one year of residence (originally six months were required), a strict registration system, and full payment of taxes for the current year (originally only the tax for the previous year was required). In the meantime, racial discrimination was practiced in schooling. *Harper's Weekly* found "no harsh treatment of the negro" and added that these restrictions, "guards of the suffrage, far from being extravagant or unjust, tend[ed] both to purify the ballot and to settle the population," but the purpose of adding the new restrictions was obviously to prevent black suffrage.[119] In South Carolina, racial tension was not lessened by Hayes's policy. In October 1878, Joseph H. Rainy, the black representative from South Carolina, told Hayes that in Sumter and other counties, white Democrats resorted to intimidation and violence to prevent black voters from organizing for elections. Hayes admitted that, despite his nonpartisan policy, "the division there [was] still on color line." But he believed that there was "no political principle in dispute between them." He wrote further, "The whites have the intelligence, the property, and the courage which make power. The negroes are for the most part ignorant, poor, and timid. My view is that the whites must be divided there before a better state of things will prevail."[120] Texas newspapers reported that at a local election in Marshal, Democrats bulldozed the usual Republican majority of the county from 1,500 votes to 150, had the votes counted by a "committee of citizens," and declared their candidates' victories with the support of "an armed mob."[121] By late October, Hayes realized that "the bother in the South" was "ugly in many ways." He decided to make "a clear, firm and accurate statement of the facts as to Southern outrages."[122]

However, the congressional election of 1878 dealt Hayes a heavy blow and sentenced his policy of reconciliation to death. Before the election, Hayes had expected a favorable result, although he sensed that "probably the Dem. [would] have both Houses of Congress" for the first time since 1858, and he was right.[123] During the election, southern Republicans captured only three House seats and none in the Senate, and "the southern wing of the party virtually disappeared." Only 62 of 294 southern counties with black majorities went Republican, compared with 125 in 1876. Of the 155 counties whose population was less than 5 percent black, the Republicans carried only 9, 3 less than in 1876. No Republican governor was elected in the South.[124] While interpreting the elections in the North as "stronger than in any off year since the war," Hayes admitted that his party did not have a victorious share in the South. The president realized that the South was "substantially solid" against the party and that the "poor, ignorant, and timid" blacks could not "stand alone against the whites." [125]

The election results not only dismayed Hayes but also changed his views of the South, transforming his optimism for a united nation into a determination to defend Republican principles. In subsequent weeks, Hayes learned that in South Carolina, Louisiana, and other southern states, "grave charges" were made that the constitutional provisions that guaranteed equal citizenship had been "practically nullified; that by fraud or force or intimidation, colored citizens ha[d] been disfranchised." [126] On November 12, 1878, the *Washington National Republican* interviewed Hayes on the election and his southern policy. He expressed his disappointment and indignation at the southern betrayal of his goodwill policy:

> Of the personal and partisan sacrifices I made in this effort, and of the consequent interruption of certain relations which had previously existed between myself and some of my supporters, I have nothing to say just now. But it appears that the leaders who made these pledges either did not exert themselves to keep them or were unable to do so. In fact, I am reluctantly forced to admit that the experiment was a failure. The first election of importance held since it was attempted has proved that fair elections with free suffrage for every voter in the South are an impossibility under the existing condition of things. [127]

Hayes explained that his cabinet decided to take "the most determined and vigorous action" against the southern outrages, not because the Republican party was "the sufferer" but "because free suffrage and freedom of political rights" had been interfered with. Still, Hayes did not think the Democratic governors in South Carolina and Louisiana should be held responsible for the outrages and insisted that they tried but failed to repress the violence. [128] On December 2, Hayes delivered his second annual message, which historian Stanley Hirshson correctly called "a far cry from his inaugural." After condemning the fraud and intimidation in Louisiana and South Carolina, the president asked Congress to "make an adequate appropriation to enable the executive department to enforce the laws." [129] Under the direction of the Department of Justice, federal enforcement officers arrested twenty-three white South Carolinians for violating the Fifteenth Amendment. On December 2, 1878, Attorney General Charles Devens reported to Congress that unlawful combinations, violence, and "ballot-box stuffing" in several southern states had prevented "the colored people from exercising their right of suffrage." As violent resistance to federal enforcement increased in the South, the determined attorney general asked Congress to give "some addition to the anticipated expenses" for his department, to "protect officers of the United States and witnesses summoned on its behalf against causeless prosecutions, and to enable them to transfer the examination of them to the courts of the United States."[130]

The election was a crisis, which defeated Hayes's reconciliatory southern policy and yet offered an opportunity for the Republicans to achieve unity, even temporarily, to deal with the common threat from the South. Once again, black suffrage became the centripetal force to pull the party together. In fact, different Republicans had different agendas on their mind before the elections. For people like Blaine, resisting the rise of greenbackism and guarding the "honest money" policy were a major concern, although when he spoke about the division between the parties, his message was clear: Republicans were "composed mainly of the Loyal Union men, who contracted the debt to subdue the Rebellion," with "the other embracing all the bad elements that sought to overthrow" the government.[131] Although never forgetting black rights, Hayes placed "a sound constitutional currency" atop the party agenda.[132] But, for antislavery veterans like Garrison, the fight to maintain "a gold basis as against an inflated and irredeemable paper currency" was only secondary to the federal protection of the "personal and political rights" of four million black Americans. If otherwise, it would "reverse the scale of values" and "place money and its uses above man and his liberty."[133]

Despite all this, after the election, different Republicans began to speak in a united voice, denouncing the Democratic victory in the South as a usurpation of black political power. On December 11, 1878, Blaine proposed a resolution in the Senate, asking Congress to investigate southern election frauds. One point that Blaine emphatically addressed, to the applause of the northern press, was the actual disequilibrium of voting power between the northern and southern white population. As a result of the frauds that deprived southern blacks of voting rights, 65,000 whites in the South elected one representative while, in the North, 132,000 elected one representative; thus, the vote cast by a former Confederate was twice as powerful and influential as the vote cast by a Union veteran from the North. One consequence of this imbalance, the *Chicago Tribune* commented, was that the "great financial, commercial, agricultural, and industrial interests of New England, Eastern, Middle, and Western States" might thus be made subject to "the absolute dictation" of the South.[134] Blaine's speech also made a scary revelation that the Republicans had not seriously considered: once the South effectively disarmed black voting power through fraud and violence, black suffrage, intended to shield blacks from political oppression and help the Republican party expand in the South, could be turned against blacks and Republicans as southern Democrats reaped the benefits of extra voting power by disfranchising blacks. The injustice done to the Negro, Blaine stated, was "also injustice to the white man."[135] Rejecting the idea that Blaine's speech was merely another waving of the "bloody shirt," the *Troy Budget* believed that the Maine senator had "struck out a comparatively new path" by connecting the black disfranchisement in the South and the reduction of the voting strength in the North.[136] Agreeing, a New York Republican held that this connection had theoretically advanced the party's principles of justice.[137] Fearing the repetition of the Democratic frauds in the 1880 presidential election, the New York *Independent* urged enactment of laws "within the limits of the Constitution" to protect rights of all the people.[138]

Other Republicans worked to bring black disfranchisement to public attention. Garrison urged William Chandler to push party leaders to move vigorously in Congress, because "they generally seemed disposed to handle the Southern question very gingerly." That only a few Republican leaders addressed black suffrage in Congress dismayed Garrison: "Alas for the vacant seats in the Senate and House of Representatives of Sumner, and Wilson, and Wade and Morton, and Thaddeus Stevens!" He asked Chandler to arrange public meetings for Elizabeth L. Palmer, the wife of a Republican legislator in South Carolina, "to testify before Northern audiences, both as eye-witnesses and as victims who ha[d] experienced in their persons the brutality and proscription meted out to loyalty by the Confederate ruffians."[139] Calling black suffrage "the leading question" in politics, deposed Republican governor Daniel H. Chamberlain of South Carolina warned the North that Democratic supremacy in the South was "the result of the violent exclusion or fraudulent suppression of the colored vote."[140]

Once again, the debate over black suffrage was revived. In March 1879, the *North American Review* invited prominent Republican and Democratic leaders to debate the function and meaning of black suffrage. All of the Democrats assailed black suffrage, arguing that blacks were incompetent to exercise the vote because of their ignorance. The two Republican participants, Blaine and Garfield, defended black suffrage. Reflecting on the recent violence against blacks and the loss of the Republican seats in Congress, Blaine vowed: "If the question were again submitted to the judgment of Congress, I would vote for suffrage in the light of experience with more confidence than I voted for it in the light of an experiment." Disputing the Democratic charge of black ignorance, Garfield enumerated black accomplishments in the postemancipation period. "Suffrage is the sword and shield of our law," he argued, "on every ground of private right, of public justice, and national safety, the negro ought to have been enfranchised."[141]

Despite all the Republican talk, enacting a new enforcement law was nothing more than wishful thinking. In fact, after the 1878 election gave Democrats control of both houses in the Forty-sixth Congress, Republicans only had the chance to defend the existing enforcement laws. Democrats had long wanted to get rid of the enforcement laws, which they had always interpreted as partisan leverage to serve Republican interests. Indeed, a congressional committee, headed by Pennsylvania Democrat William A. Wallace, had been formed to investigate the election of 1878; it concluded that the use of the federal enforcement law to supervise congressional elections had been a pretense. Knowing that they would control both houses in the next Congress, House Democrats delayed all action on a number of appropriation bills in the last session of the Forty-fifth Congress, including ones to support the army in enforcing laws and to pay deputy marshals who had served at elections in 1878. The purpose of the delays was to disable the enforcement laws in the next Congress.

The Democratic majority in the Forty-sixth Congress, however, was a limited one. In the House the Democrats had a majority of nineteen, and in the Senate the Democrats led the Republicans by nine. The Democratic majority was still short of the two-thirds required to pass new legislation to repeal the existing enforcement acts. What the Democrats hoped to do, as demonstrated later, was to carry out their repeal plan by using a technique that the Republicans used in the debate on the civil appropriation bill (the last enforcement act) in 1872, that is, to insert riders – substantive legislation – into appropriation bills.[142] Under such circumstances, the only way Republicans could prevent the riders from becoming law was the presidential veto power. Thus, the battle over the appropriation bills between 1879 and 1880 became a test of Hayes's political conscience and determination in guarding the principles of the nation and, indirectly, his party. Realizing his responsibility, Hayes vowed not to give up the enforcement acts, for "the people [would] not allow this [Democratic] revolutionary course to triumph."[143]

Soon after the special session convened on March 18, 1879, the Democrats went into action. First they reintroduced into the House the aborted army appropriation bill (H.R. 1), in which they inserted in section 6 clauses amending two sections of the enforcement law. The two sections targeted were sections 2002 and 5528 of the *Revised Statutes*. Section 2002 originated in a federal law passed on February 25, 1865, which allowed the U.S. military and other federally armed civilians to be "where any general or special election" was held "in any State" when there was a necessity "to repel the armed enemies of the United States, or to keep the peace at the polls." Section 5528 originated from the same law but contained the penalty for violating the conditions of employing the armies. The Democratic army appropriation bill proposed to amend both sections by removing the phrase "or keep the peace at the polls," so that federal military forces could not be called to aid federal enforcement officers in supervising elections.[144] The rider became the focus of a month-long debate between the Democrats and Republicans. Democratic floor manager William A. J. Sparks of Illinois pretentiously said that the purpose of the repeal was to save money, but other Democrats were blunter about their motivations. Alexander H. Stephens, Democratic representative from Georgia and once the vice president of the Confederacy, called the military presence at the polls one of "the relics and vestiges" of the late war, deserving to be buried with the past.[145]

The Republicans were prepared. On March 19, one day after the session started, Republican leaders in Congress and Hayes's secretary of state, William Evarts, met to discuss how to resist the Democratic repeal. According to Garfield, who was present, without mentioning the name of Hayes, Evarts made clear that the party must guard the principle that voting was "not to be obstructed, but that fraudulent voting [was] to be punished." But Evarts indirectly suggested to congressional leaders that, if the election supervisor provisions could be retained, the Republicans might give up the sections on federal marshals, for he was not so sure that the empowerment of marshals at the polls was "wise." But Garfield thought that the Republicans were not "in a temper to give up any part of the election laws in this struggle." He believed that any concession the party made "would probably weaken [it] in the fight."[146]

On the day the Democrats introduced their measures, the Republican executive committee met again and agreed upon "a program of resistance." It included four options: preventing any Democratic bill (on amending the enforcement laws) from being discussed (on a point of order), amending it by imposing the same restrictions on state military forces at elections, voting against the bill containing the rider, and "no filibustering except to procure sufficient time for debate."[147] During the debate, the Republicans focused their arguments on the unconstitutionality of the rider, which they branded a counterrevolution against the established authority of the national government and the president, an attempt to repeal federal power established by the Civil War, and a destruction of the national defense of the purity of the ballot box.[148] The "ablest" Republican speech was given by Garfield, who structured his argument on the rationale that the rider was legislative coercion imposed by Democrats on the executive branch—an action revolutionary and "destructive" to the "free consent of all the powers that unite to make laws." While Hayes later conveniently adopted this rationale in his vetoes,[149] Henry L. Muldrow (D-Miss.), hearing Garfield's accusation, responded that they were just imitating what the Republicans did with the civil sundry appropriation bill of 1872.[150]

At certain points, the debate went back to the original question of whether the Fifteenth Amendment had conferred on blacks the right of suffrage. As expected, Democrats supported their argument by citing the Supreme Court's *Reese* decision.[151] Harry White (R-Pa.) insisted that, despite *Reese*, Congress could still prevent racial discrimination in voting. Without this protection, riots might occur and "the colored man [might] be stoned and driven by a yelling mob from the polls in sight of a United States official or garrison."[152] The debate reached a high point when Senator William P. Frye, a radical Republican from Maine, harshly charged the Democrats with attempting to disfranchise black voters:

There were a half dozen dusky faces in this House in the last Congress. Where are the dusky faces now? You say that the places that knew them once shall know them no more forever. Why? Because you have "captured the Capitol," and you say that you will keep it. You say that no troops shall be used at the polls to keep the peace, and that the solid South will continue solid. . . . Now, do not laugh till you have won. You have not won yet. You are still in a state of glorious uncertainty. You have not repealed the law affording protection to voters at the polls yet. You have not repealed the election laws yet, and you will not repeal them until you have removed the present Executive from his chair.[153]

Despite Republican efforts, the army appropriation bill (H.R. 1) passed the House on April 5, by a partisan vote of 148 to 122.[154] It was an intense moment, with 270 of 286 members participating in the vote. All Republicans voted against the bill, whereas "nearly every Democrat" voted for it. Garfield was pleased with Republican unity and expected that, with "fine fighting trim," the party would "educate the public to the rascality proposed by the democrats."[155]

When the bill reached the Senate, Republicans continued the fight lost in the House. Blaine, who sat on the committee, tried to amend the rider so as to

Table 4.1

House Passage of H.R. 1

Party	Vote Distribution			
	Yeas	Nays	Not Voting	Total Votes
Republican	2	121	9	132
	(2%)	(91%)	(7%)	(100%)
Democrat	143	1	7	151
	(95%)	(1%)	(4%)	(100%)
Others	3	0	0	3
	(100%)			(100%)
Summary	148	122	16	

Source: CR, 46 Cong. 1 sess., 270.

allow federal troops to "keep the peace at the polls." But he was outvoted by two Democrats on the committee.[156] Leading the Senate Republican debate, John A. Logan made a passionate speech deploring the southern violence that deprived blacks of the substance of their liberties. He indirectly criticized Hayes's reconciliatory southern policy by pointing out its consequences: "We have taken a serpent to our bosoms which, as it becomes warmed by the generous fires of sympathy, will sting us to death." The Republican party, he declared, would not "relinquish" any of its principles established through the suffering of the war and would "never abandon" the three Reconstruction amendments.[157] Henry L. Dawes, usually a moderate, interpreted the rider as a Democratic scheme to accomplish what they had failed to do with bullets.[158] Conkling backed Dawes's argument and, in a three-hour speech, called the rider a Democratic device to "turn the idea of the sovereignty of the nation into a laughing-stock and a by-word."[159] In turn, Democrats spoke bitterly about how Republicans had humiliated them in 1865 by inserting these two provisions. Again, interpreting both *Cruikshank* and *Reese* according to their understanding, they argued that since the United States had no voters of its own, it had no right to send troops to watch the polls.[160] Finally, the bill passed the Senate on April 25, 1879, with a strict partisan vote of 41 to 30. All Republicans stood against the bill.[161]

When the bill came to the White House, Hayes immediately vetoed it on the ground that section 6 violated "the meaning and spirit of the Constitution" and

Table 4.2

Senate Passage of H.R. 1

| Party | Vote Distribution | | | |
	Yeas	Nays	Not Voting	Total Votes
Republican	0	29	3	32
		(90%)	(10%)	(100%)
Democrat	38	0	2	40
	(95%)		(5%)	(100%)
Others	3	1	0	4
	(75%)	(25%)		(100%)
Summary	41	30	5	

Source: *CR*, 46 Cong. 1 sess., 913.

would "deprive the civil authority of the United States of all power to keep the peace at congressional elections." The more important consequence of the bill was the dysfunction of the presidential power in national affairs. "The new doctrine, if maintained, will result in a consolidation of unchecked and despotic power in the House of Representatives," Hayes declared. "A bare majority of the House will become the Government."[162] Traditional evaluations of Hayes's veto message tend to argue that he was motivated by his determination to maintain executive independence. But, given the debates over the enforcement laws and the close working relations between the president and Republican leaders in Congress, it is equally clear and probably more important that Hayes was determined to sustain federal enforcement of black suffrage. In his veto message, he defended the enforcement as "safeguards" for "impartial, just, and efficient" elections and maintained that these laws should "be so nonpartisan and fair in their operation that the minority . . . [would] have no just grounds to complain."[163] As he noted in his diary a few months before his veto, Hayes felt that he had to resist "to the last extremity" the Democratic effort to repeal the enforcement acts because the enforcement legislation was so important to "protect the elections, to secure the purity, the honesty, the sanctity of the ballot-box."[164]

The House failed to override Hayes's veto. The vote to turn it was 120 to 110, with 55 not voting. Not a single Republican voted with the Democrats. Instead, 104 Republicans (79 percent of the party votes) voted nay and 27 abstained.[165]

Table 4.3
House Passage of H.R. 1382

Party	Vote Distribution			
	Yeas	Nays	Not Voting	Total Votes
Republican	4	89	38	131
	(3%)	(68%)	(29%)	(100%)
Democrat	118	1	32	151
	(78%)	(1%)	(21%)	(100%)
Others	3	0	0	3
	(100%)			(100%)
Summary	125	90	70	

Source: CR, 46 Cong. 1 sess., 1094–95.

But House Democrats soon tried again, bringing up another bill (H.R. 1382), called "an act to prohibit military interference at elections." Unlike the rider in H.R. 1, this bill was confined to the issue of prohibiting the use of federal troops except on application from the state. But it specifically repealed all other laws inconsistent with it.[166] George M. Robeson (R-N.J.) tried to offer a substitute that would allow the president to call on the army to enforce the Constitution and "to overcome forcible obstruction to the execution of laws," but the House rejected it.[167] On May 6, the House passed the bill by a strict partisan vote of 125 to 99.[168] Three days later, after a futile resistance by the Republicans, the bill passed the Senate.[169]

When the bill was introduced into the House, Hayes asked Samuel Shellabarger, a close Republican friend from Ohio, to help him understand how the bill would affect the enforcement of election laws. Shellabarger quickly provided him with a long, detailed analysis. The bill, in Shellabarger's view, "would *not* repeal, *out-right*," the presidential use of federal troops to execute general laws but would repeal only "such laws as authorized such army to be 'brought to or employed' at an Election place." He continued:

> The whole purpose of the act is to serve a *notice* upon all Thugs – Ku Klux – Roughs – Repeaters and Rioters – that there shall be *one* place and *one* time at which the president and his officers shall be, if not powerless, then at least exceptionally and purposely *weak*, for the enforcement of a certain special law or class

Table 4.4
Senate Passage of H.R. 1382

Party	Vote Distribution			
	Yeas	Nays	Not Voting	Total Votes
Republican	0	22	10	32
		(69%)	(31%)	(100%)
Democrat	31	0	9	40
	(78%)		(22%)	(100%)
Others	2	1	1	4
	(50%)	(25%)	(25%)	(100%)
Summary	33	23	20	

Source: CR, 46 Cong. 1 sess., 1189.

of laws. That it is a *notice* that on congressional Election days, at Election places, the selected place, where mobs, disorders and crime, wholly destructive of all Elections, shall not be approached or interfered with by that *kind* of a *posse* . . . the result then . . . is that . . . the power to call on the military to aid . . . can not be done . . . on federal election day. . . . The pending bill is either an attempt to strip the president of this constitutional right to decide as to when he shall so use the army or else it is a repeal of all such laws & either is indefeasible.[170]

In the meantime, Garfield, still generous with his advice to Hayes on the issue, was happy to report that the president was "fully in line with his party."[171] On May 12, 1879, citing the relevant federal laws and precedents that Shellabarger's memo provided, Hayes called the bill "a menace" and vetoed it on the ground that the independence of the national government should never be hampered.[172] Watching the House Democrats once again fail to override his veto, Hayes was pleased. "'The use of troops at the polls' is a favorite battle cry of our opponents, utterly without any foundation in recent facts," Hayes informed New York Republican leader Edwin D. Morgan, "and yet if not fully understood [it may be] capable of mischief."[173]

While Congress was debating the army appropriation bill (H.R. 1) and the military interference bill (H.R. 1382), House Democrats prepared another bill (H.R. 2) to appropriate legislative, executive, and judicial expenses for the next year. In this measure, Democrats inserted a rider to reduce the number and power of federal election supervisors, deputy supervisors, and marshals. They also removed a number of important powers of federal enforcement officers, including the power to arrest, inspect poll records, examine voter eligibility, and participate in counting the ballot. Specifically, the bill proposed to repeal several important sections of the *Revised Statutes*, including five sections – 2016, 2018, 2020, 2027, and 5522 – of the Enforcement Act of February 28, 1871 (respectively, sections 4, 5, 7, 13, and 10), dealing with federal supervision of registration and voting, punishment of fraud, and payment for enforcement officers. The bill also proposed to repeal three other sections – 2028, 2029, and 2030 – from the Republican rider of the Civil Sundry Appropriation Act of June 10, 1872, regarding enforcement in rural areas. The bill also proposed to amend sections 2017 and 2019, both also originating from the 1871 law.[174] Obviously, Democrats intended to invalidate the most comprehensive federal election law up to that time.

Republicans in both houses did their best to resist the bill.[175] Harry White, one of most vocal Republican protesters in the House, tried to stop the bill by challenging the propriety of placing the rider in the bill. But the House ignored him. On April 26, it passed the bill, 141 to 120.[176] About a month later, on May 20, the Senate accepted the bill, 37 to 27.[177] Holding that the bill contained the same political purposes as the previous two, Hayes issued a third veto

Table 4.5

House Passage of H.R. 2

Party	Vote Distribution			
	Yeas	Nays	Not Voting	Total Votes
Republican	1	119	12	132
	(1%)	(90%)	(9%)	(100%)
Democrat	137	1	13	151
	(91%)	(1%)	(8%)	(100%)
Others	3	0	0	3
	(100%)			(100%)
Summary	141	120	25	

Source: *CR*, 46 Cong. 1 sess., 960.

Table 4.6
Senate Passage of H.R. 2

		Vote Distribution		
Party	Yeas	Nays	Not Voting	Total Votes
Republican	0	26	6	32
		(81%)	(19%)	(100%)
Democrat	35	0	5	40
	(88%)		(12%)	(100%)
Others	2	1	1	4
	(50%)	(25%)	(25%)	(100%)
Summary	37	27	12	

Source: *CR*, 46 Cong. 1 sess., 1484–85.

on May 29, contending that the legislation denied the federal government the ability to make its supervision of elections "effectual."[178] Again, when Hayes's veto message reached the House, the 131 Republicans stood together to defeat the Democratic attempt to override the veto.[179]

In the remaining month of the session, Democrats made two more attempts to repeal the enforcement acts. The first (H.R. 2252) was a bill to create appropriations for judicial expenses. Again, Democrats inserted a rider, disallowing the use of any federal money "to pay any salaries, compensation, fees, or expenses under or in virtue of title 26 of the Revised Statutes." The bill forbade the federal government from making any contract for future payment until an appropriation to meet this payment had been made by law — an attempt to prevent future appropriation for enforcement expenses. In the third section, the Democrats provided that blacks could not be disqualified from being jurors, a gesture to show their intention to guarantee black rights.[180] But the denial of payment virtually deprived the election supervisors and their deputies of the compensation for their service. Since the election laws could not be repealed for the moment, cutting off the payment of the enforcement officers, as the bill's floor leader, John A. McMahon (D-Ohio), put it, would "effect the purpose."[181] Garfield called the bill "an attempt to accomplish by indirection" what could not be done "by an open and plain repeal." When he proposed to modify the

Table 4.7

House Passage of Conference Report for H.R. 2252

| | Vote Distribution | | | |
Party	Yeas	Nays	Not Voting	Total Votes
Republican	0	80	51	131
		(61%)	(39%)	(100%)
Democrat	102	1	49	152
	(67%)	(1%)	(32%)	(100%)
Others	0	0	3	3
			(100%)	(100%)
Summary	102	81	103	

Source: *CR*, 46 Cong. 1 sess., 2185–86.

bill, a group of Democrats interrupted him by crying from their seats, "Vote!"[182] With their majority, Democrats succeeded in passing the conference report of the bill first in the House on June 19 and then in the Senate on June 21. Hayes issued his fourth veto on June 23, notifying Congress that he would tolerate no bill denying the federal government "even the civil authority to protect congressional elections."[183]

Three days after failing to override Hayes's veto on H.R. 2252, Democrats forced the House to consider another bill (H.R. 2382) that would compensate federal marshals and their deputies for the current year (1879–80) but deny it subsequently.[184] By this time, even some Democrats had tired of this endless repeal battle. The bill rushed through the House on June 27 and the Senate the next day, with many members from both houses abstaining from votes.[185] Hayes's fifth veto killed the bill.[186] The president again consulted with his Ohio friend Garfield, who suggested that Hayes stress that the marshals functioned as "the only policy" of the federal government. On June 30, Hayes announced his veto to stop the framers of the bill from seeking "a radical, dangerous, and unconstitutional change" in the character of the nation's institutions.[187]

With Hayes's fifth veto, Congress adjourned, and the marshals were left with no funding. The inability of Congress to make appropriations for marshals and their deputies caused "much anxiety" among those affected, both federal en-

Table 4.8
Senate Passage of Conference Report for H.R. 2252

Party	Vote Distribution			
	Yeas	Nays	Not Voting	Total Votes
Republican	0	16	16	32
		(50%)	(50%)	(100%)
Democrat	29	0	11	40
	(73%)		(27%)	(100%)
Others	2	1	1	4
	(50%)	(25%)	(25%)	(100%)
Summary	31	17	28	

Source: *CR*, 46 Cong. 1 sess., 2257.

forcement officers and "private parties." And, Attorney General Charles Devens reported, if this continued, the interest of the United States "would be seriously deranged." Despite the "embarrassment under which they labored," Devens reported, federal enforcement officers nonetheless had "struggled to perform their duties faithfully" and met "no important practical difficulty," except in a few instances when the fiscal deficiency compelled the marshals to postpone their service.[188] Even so, the attorney general still received scores of letters from his subordinates, asking for an explanation. Thus, as soon as the second session of the Forty-sixth Congress convened on December 1, 1879, Devens made an urgent request to Congress for an appropriation of six hundred thousand dollars to compensate the marshals.[189] Once again, he emphasized that the functions of the marshals and their deputies were indispensable to stop fraudulent election practices such as "ballot-box stuffing." He argued that these offenses struck "at the very foundation of republican government."[190]

The partisan battle over the appropriation for enforcement resumed in early March when Representative John McMahon (D-Ohio) introduced a deficiency bill (H.R. 4924). As an action to supply "certain deficiencies in the appropriations" for federal government expenses, the bill included a fund of six hundred thousand dollars for the payment of the fees and expenses of the U.S. marshals and their general deputies earned during the fiscal year ending June 30, 1880,

Table 4.9
House Passage of H.R. 2382

		Vote Distribution		
Party	Yeas	Nays	Not Voting	Total Votes
Republican	0	68	63	131
		(52%)	(48%)	(100%)
Democrat	89	1	62	152
	(59%)	(1%)	(40%)	(100%)
Others	0	0	3	3
			(100%)	(100%)
Summary	89	69	128	

Source: *CR*, 46 Cong. 1 sess., 2397–98.

but it denied payment for the special deputy marshals, who were assigned to assist the marshals and their general deputies at elections. These special deputies, McMahon argued, were "creatures unknown to the law except when appointed for an election for Representatives about to take place."[191] Undoubtedly, this was another Democratic attempt to weaken the Enforcement Act of February 28, 1871, which allowed U.S. marshals to appoint special deputies to supervise congressional elections.

Familiar arguments were repeated in both houses. Thomas Reed, the would-be Republican boss, called the bill a political measure to "trample down the safeguards" for the upcoming presidential election in 1880.[192] Democrats responded that their action was to "shield . . . the purity of elections from the power of corrupt and debauched partisans."[193] Democrats managed to get the bill through both houses by the end of April by their sheer majority voting power.[194] On May 4, 1880, Hayes vetoed the bill with the familiar but sharp criticism of the Democratic scheme to repeal the enforcement acts, which he called "indispensable to fair and lawful elections."[195]

The Democrats refused to budge. They packed a new attempt to change the enforcement acts into a bill introduced into the Senate on May 6, two days after Hayes's veto. The bill (S. No. 1726), "regulating the pay and appointment of special deputy marshals," allowed payment for deputy marshals but removed the power of appointing the deputies from the U.S. marshals to the judges of

Table 4.10
Senate Passage of H.R. 2382

| | Vote Distribution | | | |
Party	Yeas	Nays	Not Voting	Total Votes
Republican	0	15	17	32
		(47%)	(53%)	(100%)
Democrat	26	0	14	40
	(65%)		(35%)	(100%)
Others	0	0	4	4
			(100%)	(100%)
Summary	26	15	35	

Source: *CR*, 46 Cong. 1 sess., 2413.

the circuit courts.[196] This removal materially changed the regulations provided by sections 2021, 2022, 2023, 2024, and 2028 of the *Revised Statutes* (all originating from the Enforcement Act of February 28, 1871, except 2028, which was originally from the Civil Appropriation Act of 1872), which authorized U.S. marshals to appoint special deputy marshals as needed and placed the special deputy marshals under the direction of the marshals who appointed them. Having the deputy marshals appointed by circuit court judges for the next congressional election, as the bill proposed, would make the process of the appointments more difficult, since circuit courts normally met after the process of registration for voting. In such cases, U.S. marshals were virtually made powerless to carry out their duties.[197] Thus, Republicans saw the bill as "a sheer deception."[198] The Democratic purpose, as the antienforcement *Nation* pinpointed, was to stop the appointments of deputy marshals as a source of political patronage, since a U.S. marshal was "always a partisan, and often a rabid partisan," and was rarely appointed for "anything but his partisanship."[199] On June 15, one day after the bill passed both houses,[200] Hayes vetoed it, reasoning that it completely changed the present election laws by substituting new officers unknown to the existing laws. The real problem with the bill was, in Hayes's words, its "discrimination against the authority of the United States," as the bill restricted the deputy marshals from making arrests when crimes were committed at elections.[201]

Hayes seemed to have no better alternative when he decided to seek a compromise with the white leadership in the South at the beginning of his presidency. The pressure from both liberal and conservative Republicans, the bad political reputation of the Grant administration, the political controversies inherent in using the federal army in the South, and the determination of southern Democrats to resist enforcement forced him to seek a different policy toward the South. Hayes's presidency was born out of a complicated process of political negotiations, compromises, and calculations, which, in effect, kept him from continuing a strong enforcement policy. But Hayes was not passive. Instead, he willingly and ambitiously engaged in formulating a new southern policy featuring reconciliation. He might have been politically naive to think that the nation could be united under his goodwill policy, but his sincerity in seeking national unity on the basis of the new constitutionalism was genuine. Probably because of his sincerity and faith in his reconciliation blueprint, Hayes did not break his promises after becoming president. He virtually could not do so, given the way his cabinet was formulated and his own thinking on the southern question.

Hayes did not, however, intentionally try to abandon the principles established by the postwar amendments. Nor did he seek to surrender the constitutionality of black political rights in the face of violent southern opposition. He sought cooperation from the southern state governments, which he naively believed would respect black rights. When he realized that his reconciliation policy could secure neither respect for the rights of black citizens nor the vigorous development of the party in the South, he firmly stood by the enforcement acts. Although enforcement was never effective during his administration, his vetoes — seven of them — of the Democratic bills between 1879 and 1880 were crucial in retaining the enforcement acts in the nation's lawbook and, perhaps more important, keeping the idea of enforcement alive.

It must also be noted that during the fight over the enforcement laws between 1879 and 1880, Republicans presented an unprecedented solid unity. As demonstrated by the tables in this chapter, unusually strong and close cooperation existed between various factions of the party and between congressional Republicans and Hayes. This gave the Republicans an institutional leverage to defeat Democratic attempts to repeal the enforcement acts, even though the latter had a simple majority in both houses. But what made the cooperation possible, or held the party together, was the party's determination to maintain the principles of new constitutionalism, which the politics of the Republican party had conveniently identified as its political lodestar. The day after he issued his last veto, Hayes assailed "the attempt of the Democratic Party in Congress, in the Supreme Court and in the Country at large to reestablish the State Rights doctrine of Calhoun and the Rebellion," and he declared that the Republican party must carry on "the resistance to these reactionary movements."[202] Hayes would be gone from office, but the principle that he had sought to uphold would survive.

FRANCHISE.

"And Not This Man?"

Harper's Weekly, August 5, 1865, page 489.

"MUSTERED OUT" COLORED VOLUNTEERS AT
LITALE ROCK, ARKANSAS.
Harper's Weekly, May 19, 1866, page 308.

THE GEORGETOWN ELECTION – THE NEGRO AT THE BALLOT-BOX.
Harper's Weekly, March 16, 1867, page 172.

WE ACCEPT THE SITUATION.
Harper's Weekly, April 13, 1867, page 240.

"THE FIRST VOTE."
Harper's Weekly, November 17, 1867, cover.

WHY "THE NIGGER IS NOT FIT TO VOTE."

Harper's Weekly, October 24, 1868, cover.

UNCLE SAM'S THANKSGIVING DINNER.
Harper's Weekly, November 20, 1869, page 745.

XVTH AMENDMENT.—"Shoo Fly, don't Bodder me!"
Harper's Weekly, March 12, 1870, page 176.

SHALL WE CALL HOME OUR TROOPS?

"We intend to beat the Negro in the battle of life, and defeat means one thing—
EXTERMINATION."—*Birmingham (Alabama) News*

Harper's Weekly, January 9, 1875, page 37.

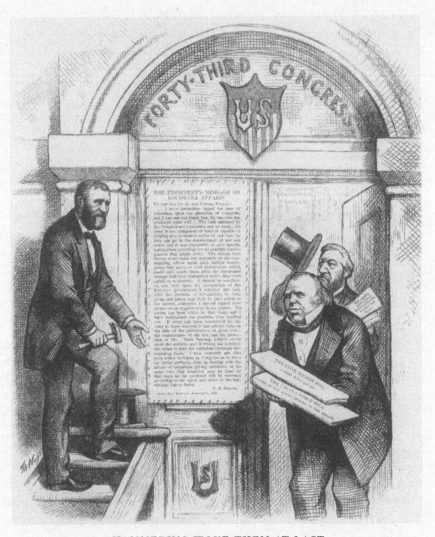

HAMMERING WOKE THEM AT LAST.

U.S.G. "Thank you! My duties are perfectly clear now, and I will execute them
according to the spirit and letter of the law, without *fear* or *favor*."

Harper's Weekly, March 27, 1875, cover.

"IS *THIS* A REPUBLICAN FORM OF GOVERNMENT? IS *THIS*
PROTECTING LIFE, LIBERTY, OR PROPERTY? IS *THIS* THE EQUAL
PROTECTION OF THE LAWS?"
Harper's Weekly, September 2, 1876, page 712.

"HE WANTS A CHANGE TOO."
Harper's Weekly, October 28, 1876, page 872–73.

ANOTHER "FEDERAL INTERFERENCE."

THE STRUGGLE BETWEEN ATHENA HYGEIA AND YELLOW JACK.

Harper's Weekly, April 19, 1879, page 308–9.

THE REPUBLICAN NATIONAL CONVENTION AT CHICAGO.
Harper's Weekly, June 19, 1880, page 392–93.

THE FRIEND OF THE FREEDMEN.

"Now, that we have made them free, we will stand by these black allies! We will stand
by them until the sun of liberty shall shine with equal ray upon every man, back or
white throughout the Union!"—GENERAL GARFIELD, August 6, 1880.

Harper's Weekly, October 23, 1880, page 685.

THE "PRACTICAL" POLITICIAN'S LOVE FOR THE NEGRO.
Harper's Weekly, July 25, 1885, page 473.

RELIEVING ("BAYONET") GUARD.
U.S.A. "Keep the Peace at the Polls."
C.S.A. "WE'LL KEEP IT!"
Harper's Weekly, May 31, 1879, page 432.

CHAPTER FIVE

The Survival of a Principle, 1880–1888

The Revival of Black Suffrage in the Election of 1880

The political calendar of the Republican party in 1880 seemed to have been turned back to 1872. The party's principal objective was neither to achieve reconciliation with the South nor to commit to civil service reform, both of which had been the main parts of the party's platform four years earlier. The "first duties of the Nation," the Republican platform of 1880 declared, were "the equal, steady and complete enforcement of laws, and the protection of all . . . citizens in the enjoyment of all privileges and immunities guaranteed by the Constitution." Condemning southern Democrats for obstructing "the freedom of suffrage" through fraud, the Republicans vowed to divide the "solid South . . . by the peaceful agencies of the ballot." To preserve the "fruits of the costly victories," the platform pledged, Republicans would uphold the supremacy of the Constitution and federal authority to determine "the boundary between the powers delegated and those reserved" by the states.[1]

Compared with the party's call for national harmony in 1876, the 1880 platform sounded like a declaration of war against the white South. Why did the Republican party, after four years of seeking cooperation from the white South, give up its policy of pacification and return to the tactics that the Democrats would ridicule as waving "the bloody shirt"? What made the party subscribe to the protection of citizens' rights of suffrage as its first duty after virtually leaving it to the states four years earlier?

The resurgence of the Republican emphasis on federal protection of suffrage grew out of the failure of Hayes's southern policy. When he ordered the withdrawal of federal troops from the Louisiana and South Carolina statehouses in 1877, Hayes had hoped that the white South, in turn, would guarantee equal rights for all citizens and respect for federal authority. But no miracle happened. Much of the South was still under the firm control of the Democratic party. Black voters in the South remained disfranchised by force and fraud. Indigenous Republicanism was suppressed, unable to mobilize voters under the political terror of the Democrats and local white supremacists.

The withdrawal of federal troops from the South cleared the way for Democratic political advancement at the national level as well. During the 1878 congressional elections, Democrats took control of the Senate and, combined with their majority in the House (won in 1874), captured Congress for the first time since 1856. In 1879, immediately after gaining control of Congress, they attempted to repeal the enforcement acts. Although Hayes's vetoes prevented success, the possibility remained that the enforcement acts might be repealed, especially if the Democrats captured the White House in the coming election of 1880.

During the 1878 congressional elections, southern Republicans and black voters experienced another wave of intimidation, fraud, and violence. According to historian Robert M. Goldman, election violence and fraud were common in the entire South but particularly serious in South Carolina, Alabama, and Louisiana. Postelection trials and prosecutions of some kind were carried out in almost every southern state, but owing to strong support for the defendants, convictions were rare. By 1880, cases relating to the 1878 elections were quietly dropped and gave way to new cases arising from the 1880 presidential election.[2] Throughout the four years of the Hayes administration, the numbers of the enforcement cases remained very low. In 1877, 133 out of the total 234 enforcement cases were from the South, but only 6 resulted in convictions. Meanwhile, more than 300 cases of a similar nature were pending in the federal courts. In 1878, the national figure for the enforcement cases dropped to 26, the lowest in the history of enforcement. Although 23 cases were from the South, all were eventually dismissed. In 1879, the attorney general reported 146 criminal cases under the enforcement acts – 93 from the South – but again, the conviction rate was still low.[3]

In the opinion of both regular and black Republican leaders, Hayes's policy of reconciliation was at least partially responsible for the aggressive comeback of the Democratic party. Watching the Democrats try repeatedly to repeal the enforcement acts, Frederick Douglass reversed his support of Hayes's experiment of extending reconciliation to the South, for such an experiment only gave the Democrats a chance "in establishing a solid south."[4]

Although few regular Republican leaders had shared Hayes's enthusiasm for voluntary southern compliance with the terms of guaranteed black suffrage, most of them were still willing to give the president a chance to try his goodwill policy. But open opposition within the party, led by William E. Chandler, started after the 1878 election. Other party leaders, such as James A. Garfield, James G. Blaine, and George F. Hoar, were less blunt but by no means more lenient toward Hayes's goodwill policy. After the 1878 elections were over, Blaine submitted a resolution to the Senate urging Congress to investigate the Democratic suppression of black votes in the South, which, he believed, had brought the Democrats more congressional seats than they should have.[5] In March 1880, in a debate on black suffrage organized by the *North American Review*, Blaine condemned southern Democrats for nullifying black suffrage "by indirect and unlawful means" in the recent elections. He argued that black suffrage was above partisan interests: "[It] must become our practice."[6] Hoar, another Senate Republican leader, told his Massachusetts constituents that the party should not divert its attention from the issue of black suffrage but should make it the paramount issue of the election.[7] In a way, this preelection rhetoric on black suffrage was not so much an appeal to the Republican conscience as an effort by party leaders (or presidential hopefuls) to formulate the political leitmotif for the coming presidential campaign. At least, President Hayes would think so. The outgoing president admitted that the defeat of his policy had led to the revival of the Republican party's antisouthern sentiment: "The failure of the South to faithfully observe the Fifteenth Amendment is the cause of the failure of all efforts toward complete pacification." And, Hayes wrote, it was "on this hook that the bloody shirt" now hung.[8]

Making black suffrage a central issue in the 1880 Republican campaign, however, was not merely a pragmatic response to the political advance of the Democratic party. Regular Republican leaders shared a much deeper concern. For them, the 1880 election projected a new contest between the old North and the old South. With the aggressive comeback of the Democratic South, Republican leaders saw that the South, once defeated and subdued, was now fully revived and reorganized into a new political entity. The practice of black disfranchisement through violence and fraud demonstrated the arrogance of the old South rejecting the terms of Reconstruction and, more serious, its potential to reverse those terms. "The franchise intended for the shield and defense of the negro," Blaine argued, "has been turned against him and has vastly increased the power of those from whom he has nothing to hope and everything

to dread." The once defeated slave power not only had imposed political slavery on the former slaves but, by usurping the voting power of black men, would
also impose political tyranny on the North.[9] Thus, for Republican leaders, the
struggle against the solid South was a continuation of the struggle against the
old slave power.

Despite their rhetorical commitment to black suffrage, Republicans confronted the challenge to transform their oral commitment to black suffrage enforcement into an agreed-upon party policy. This was no easy task, especially
when the Republicans were divided on other issues. Here, once again, was a
case of the faction-unity complex of party politics. To defeat the Democrats in
the election, various Republican factions first had to reach inner compromises
and form a coalition. It was easier to meet the inner expectations of all factions
when the party confronted overwhelming and compelling situations or when
the party had a candidate whose political qualifications were exceedingly better
than others, as with those in 1860, 1864, 1868, and 1872. But when the circumstances were less overwhelming, when none of the factional candidates was
clearly supreme, and, very important, when the issues and factional interests to
be dealt with multiplied, the result of the contest among various party factions
became less certain. Thus, the party coalition might rely heavily on whatever
consensus the factions reached on the issues, and the hopeful with the least factional identity might become the ideal candidate. This was what happened with
the Republican party in 1880.

There were essentially four identifiable Republican groups (or factions) in
1880: the liberals, the stalwarts, the half-breeds, and those not identified with
the previous three groups. The liberals were the residuals of early Liberal Republicanism, and many would later become the "mugwumps" of the 1880s. The
liberals argued that the party should commit itself to a number of issues directly
related to the nation's economic development, including tariff reduction, the internal revenue system, civil service reform, national aid to education, and internal improvements. Federal protection of black rights was not on the liberal
agenda. In a pamphlet issued by a group of New York Republicans calling a
party conference in April 1880, these so-called independent Republicans re-
volted against the pro-Grant Republican force and asserted that a political party
was "a cooperation among voters to secure the practical enactment into legislation of political conviction set forth as its platform." They believed that a
Republican could refuse to follow any party nomination or action that was
"against his private judgment." The document declared, "If his party no longer

represents its professed principles in practical workings, it is his duty to vote against it."[10] The liberals had played a major role in helping to formulate Hayes's goodwill policy toward the South in 1876, but they had no dominant voice in the party in 1880. They were, as James G. Blaine would later ridicule them, "noisy but not numerous, pharisaical but not practical, ambitious but not wise, pretentious but not powerful."[11] Even so, the liberals nonetheless voiced the waning of northern interest in the issues left by the Civil War. And their pressure for solving economic problems clearly showed a stronger alliance between northern Republicans and business interests, which would become a dominant force in shaping the party's course in the 1880s and early 1890s. The liberals preferred to select their nominees from four candidates who themselves were not liberals: George F. Edmunds, William Windom, Joseph R. Hawley, and William B. Allison.[12]

The stalwarts were those regular Republicans committed to electing Ulysses S. Grant for a third term in 1880. Headed by such Republican machine politicians as Roscoe Conkling of New York, John A. Logan of Illinois, and J. Donald Cameron of Pennsylvania, the stalwarts consisted of Republicans from the South and several northern states. Motivated by the wartime spirit and demanding a strong commitment to party discipline, they wanted to make no concessions to southern Democrats and regarded Republican control of the national government as the only way to defend the achievements of the Civil War and Reconstruction, which would include southern Republicanism. They were really modern politicians who sought to achieve results through the effective use of the party network and to secure partisan loyalty through political patronage.[13]

Those regular Republicans ridiculed by the stalwarts as "half-breeds" for being deficient in party loyalty were led by James G. Blaine, whom Hayes had defeated for the nomination in 1876. Although unwilling to affiliate with the liberals, the half-breeds wanted to sever the party from the political scandals of the earlier Grant administration. The half-breeds paid more attention to economic development in the North, but their main goal was to establish a strong national government, which would direct the nation's political and economic affairs according to northern interests. Like the liberals, the half-breeds also were strongly opposed to Grant's nomination for presidency, which they believed would damage the party's image and hurt its chances of winning the election.[14] Although the stalwarts and half-breeds were committed to a tough policy toward the South, their dispute jeopardized the chance for a united party and, consequently, the possibility of reviving the party's commitment to black political rights in the South.

The fourth group of Republicans really was not an identifiable faction because it had no leader. Politically, these Republicans, among whom were party veterans James A. Garfield, George F. Edmunds, and perhaps John Sherman, shared many of the concerns expressed by all three other factions, but they probably wanted more than any of those groups to keep the party together.

Thus, the unity of the party remained uncertain when it convened in Chicago on June 2, 1880. In addition to Grant and Blaine, several names were placed in nomination, including John Sherman, Hayes's secretary of the treasury; George F. Edmunds, a radical leader in the Senate; William Windom, a senator from Minnesota; and Elihu B. Washburne, minister to France. But the main contest was between Grant and Blaine. Both the stalwart and half-breed camps had gathered a substantial number of supporters, but neither commanded a majority of the delegates required for nominating its desired candidate. The three-hundred-odd stalwarts voted solidly for Grant, and a comparable number of the half-breeds stood behind Blaine. None of the other candidates could draw votes from the two leading candidates. The deadlock continued through the first thirty-five ballots and was not broken until the thirty-sixth, when 399 votes suddenly went to James A. Garfield, whose name was not originally placed in nomination and went unmentioned until the thirty-fourth ballot. Most supporters of Blaine and several minor candidates voted for Garfield, while the 306 Grant supporters remained intact until the end of the balloting.[15] According to Norman E. Tutorow, who studied the balloting in great detail, in the first thirty-five ballots, Grant's foes waited patiently for a chance to break up his 306 votes, with the expectations that they could prevent a third term for Grant and nominate their own favorite candidates. Not until the last ballot did all of Grant's opponents narrow their original expectations to a single goal: to defeat the third-term presidency. Then they were able to combine their votes to secure Garfield's nomination.[16] What really happened between the thirty-fifth and thirty-sixth ballots may remain a myth of political psychology, but what really mattered was that the foundation for a new Republican unity had been achieved.

A real dark horse candidate, Garfield was acceptable to all the factions. Blaine called his nomination a "not unwelcome one" and assured Garfield that his supporters would provide him with "the reliable strong background" his administration needed "for success."[17] Hayes, the outgoing president, who had hoped to see John Sherman succeed him rather than Grant or Blaine, was obviously pleased with the selection of his fellow Ohioan because it enabled "the hostile factions to come together."[18] Generous oral support also came from the stalwart Republicans, who were disappointed about their inability to nominate Grant for another term but happy to see Blaine a loser—not to mention that their man, Chester A. Arthur, was chosen to be Garfield's running mate. Congratulating Garfield, John A. Logan pledged, "The men who stood by Grant's banners will be seen in the front of this contest on every field."[19]

Various reasons have been cited to explain why Garfield could finally command the party's support at the convention: his longtime service as a House Republican leader; his record in the Civil War and Reconstruction; his skill at molding the party ethos at the Chicago convention; and the good impression derived from his first speech appealing for party unity at the convention.[20] But no historian has better explained Garfield's nomination than E. V. Smalley did in his article for the *Atlantic Monthly* in August 1880. College educated, a Civil War veteran, a career Republican representing one of the most important northern states in the House, Garfield was the only candidate who could unite all factions of the party because his well-balanced political style and his understanding of the American system represented "the strong, average good sense, patriotism, liberality, tolerance, and progressive impulses of the republican organization." Valued for his knowledge of industrial and economic questions, Garfield was regarded as the right man for the time when the nation began to enter "an era of remarkable material development," during which the questions of politics would be "mainly of an economic nature." Smalley also believed that although Garfield was never "ultra-partizan," he could be trusted for "his steady republicanism and his broad views of the scope of national authority steadfastly to maintain the results of the war as they affect the integrity of the Union and the equal citizenship of all its inhabitants."[21]

Although Garfield's nomination was important, even crucial, to unify Republicans at the Chicago convention and to guarantee victory in the 1880 presidential election, it did not end the factional infighting. Whether the party could unite and win the election largely depended on Garfield's skills at handling the demands of the party's factions and balancing their interests. Thus, the way Garfield was nominated meant that, at best, he could only be a skillful mediator of the party's factions. Garfield himself was fully aware of these divisions. Although he personally opposed the idea of a three-term presidency and disliked the dictatorship of the stalwart leaders, he dealt cautiously with these issues, believing that the settlement of principles was "more important than the fate of any candidate."[22]

Following the party's platform, Garfield's letter of acceptance, issued on July 10, reflected much of the political temper of regular Republicans. The letter characterized the question of respecting and implementing national election laws as the foremost issue. It stressed the freedom of ballots. It denounced the state supremacy doctrine, "which so long crippled the functions of the national government." Repeating the old Republican rhetoric, Garfield argued that no peace and prosperity would be restored until "every citizen, rich or poor, white or black, [was] secure in the free and equal enjoyment of every civil and political right guaranteed by the Constitution and the laws." He regarded political equality, the free migration of laborers, and social and industrial contentment as the preconditions to economic prosperity. He pointed out that the evil afflicting the South was Democratic repression of freedom and intolerance of southern Republican "political opinion and action."[23] Like the platform, Garfield's letter also discussed other issues — national aid to education, national finances, tariff, material development, Chinese immigration, and civil service reform — in such an order as to make civil service reform the last item on the agenda, which reflected the party platform that Garfield played a large role in writing. Finally, Garfield stressed that the Chicago platform and his arguments were not the "temporary devices of a party to attract votes and carry an election." He declared, "They are deliberate convictions, resulting from a careful study of the spirit of our institutions, the events of our history, and the best impulses of our people."[24]

Garfield's letter was well received by Republicans at large. His strong attitude on federal enforcement of black rights won praise from such stalwart leaders as John A. Logan, who called the letter "an able document" and "a wise, judicious, sound paper." Obviously, Garfield gave full attention to the regular Republican agenda. The tone of his letter was meant to harmonize the divided party.[25] With his letter and other thoughtful political arrangements, Garfield quickly obtained trust and support from stalwart and half-breed Republican leaders. The choice of Arthur, a Conkling protégé, as his running mate and his later appointment of Blaine as his secretary of state demonstrated Garfield's skill at balancing the interests of major party factions.

In August 1880, in New York City's Fifth Avenue Hotel, Garfield and Arthur had a conference with Republican leaders. The participants included Blaine,

Logan, Sherman, William McKinley, Murat Halstead, William E. Chandler, Henry L. Dawes, J. Donald Cameron, Levi Morton, and Thomas Platt. The meeting secured a consensus on major political issues, including patronage, economics, and, most of all, the party's southern policy. On the last point, Republican leaders agreed: Hayes's southern policy of conciliation should be abandoned; the party should pledge assistance to all southern Republicans in their efforts to win back state power; and no concession should be made to Democrats in the South. Largely because of Garfield's skill at political engineering, the Republican party was finally united before the election.[26]

This political engineering was important, for it helped Garfield and Arthur win the 1880 election. The Republican victory, however, did not come easily. The turnout was one of the highest of the century (more than 78 percent), but the result was one of the closest in history. Garfield and Arthur won 214 electoral votes, only 59 more than Democratic candidate Winfield Scott Hancock and his running mate, William English. Hancock could have won the election with a total of 190 if New York's 35 electoral votes had gone to him. But Garfield's popular majority was only 9,464 (4,454,416 to Hancock's 4,444,952). Garfield carried almost every northern and western state (except New Jersey, Nevada, and five of the six votes in California). Hancock carried every southern state. Garfield's popular vote in the South fell behind that of his party in 1876, but his proportional vote was slightly higher, and the number of counties he carried was about the same as that of Hayes. In the South in 1876, Republicans polled 740,708 popular votes, or 40.34 percent of the total cast, and carried 201 of the 928 counties. In 1880, they gathered 671,826 popular votes, or 40.84 percent of the total, and captured 206 of the 943 counties.[27] Meanwhile, Republicans won the House but failed to regain the Senate. Garfield believed that the loss of the Senate was caused by Democratic whisperings tying him to the Crédit Mobilier scandal, and the Democrats' circulation of the forged "Morey letter," calling him soft on restriction of the Chinese immigrants, which had been publicized a month before the election.[28]

The election indicated that by 1880, the wartime scars of sectional confrontation still had not healed. Rather, there remained, in the words of New York governor Alonzo B. Cornell, "a square division of the old free States against the Slave States."[29] To Grant, Garfield's election meant that the country had escaped "a calamity."[30] Others regarded the Republican victory as the real defeat of Hayes's southern policy. George W. Marton, a New York office seeker, wrote to William E. Chandler, "The days of namby-pambyism are about over."[31] Expectations ran high: as William Dodge declared, with Garfield in the White House, the nation would "never see a Solid South again."[32]

Black Republicans shared much of the party's joy at Garfield's election. For some black Republican leaders, Garfield was not the best choice, but at least he was not the worst. Although they had little influence in the process of selecting the party's leaders, blacks placed their hopes for equal rights in Republican hands and would support any Republican leader who promised to protect their rights. In Washington, D.C., Frederick Douglass helped organize a political club in the name of Garfield and Arthur to express their support.[33] In his campaign for Garfield, Douglass emphatically placed national protection of black rights as the most important task for Republicans, who were "bound by their histories and characters" to pursue the course.[34] After Blanche K. Bruce campaigned in Indiana for Garfield, he reported to Garfield that Republicans there were united and the "colored people [were] thoroughly aroused" and would be found "working" on election day. He assured Garfield that black citizens were pleased with his nomination because of his record and the prospect that he would exercise his "constitutional power to protect their brothers" in the South.[35] Garfield's election was, to blacks, an assurance of federal protection of suffrage and other rights. They saw that, as John Langston wrote, Garfield's election had fixed "Freedom, Free Principles, and the perpetuation of the union . . . beyond any future opportunity for change or disturbance."[36]

Promises Unfulfilled

Could Garfield fulfill all of these expectations? Although black suffrage was a familiar subject to Garfield and, since the beginning of Reconstruction, he had been involved in many key battles over the issue, his record in support of black suffrage legislation was marked by moderation and occasional inconsistency. Garfield, however, had never opposed the idea of federal protection of black suffrage. At the end of the Civil War, deeply impressed by black soldiers' "act of freedom," Garfield was one of the first Republicans to ask for immediate black enfranchisement. One of the few Republicans who saw the connections between black suffrage and fulfillment of the tenets of American political democracy, Garfield considered black suffrage the only device to remove the gap between the original Constitution and the Declaration of Independence and genuinely and permanently to secure blacks' freedom and other rights.[37] In his House

speech on the Freedmen's Bureau bill in early 1866, Garfield argued that nothing was "more dangerous to a republic than to put into its very midst four million people stripped of the rights of citizenship, robbed of the right of representation, but bound to pay taxes to the government."[38]

Despite his radical rhetoric, Garfield always remained prudent and moderate,
sometimes even conservative, when black suffrage was discussed. The standard
he set for himself during Reconstruction was "to be a radical and not be a fool."
He constantly derided his radical counterparts as impractical.[39] Between 1870
and 1872, Garfield was a House Republican leader and supported most of the
party's measures to enforce the Fourteenth and Fifteenth Amendments, except
the civil appropriation bill of June 10, 1872, which included an enforcement
rider.[40] In 1874, when Grant decided to use federal troops to intervene in election disputes in Louisiana and protect the Republican government there, Garfield opposed it as politically unwise and constitutionally unacceptable to have
federal soldiers marching into the state legislative hall and "expelling members
at the point of the bayonet."[41] In November 1876, when the election disputes in
three southern states – South Carolina, Louisiana, and Florida – led to a deadlock in the returns of the presidential election, Garfield, at Grant's request, went
to New Orleans to watch the recounting of the election results. There, hearing
"a remarkable statement by a delegation on the outrages and intimidation practiced by Democrats in Mississippi," Garfield wrote to his wife:

> If half they tell is correct, the election in that state was an outrage on good gov-
> ernment beyond endurance. . . . I hope the disclosure of the facts will result in
> awakening our people to the necessity of putting national elections under the
> control of national officers, and bring the result under national supervision.[42]

Writing to his close friend Burke Hinsdale, Garfield condemned the Democratic fraud and declared that the only cure for electoral crimes was to defeat
the criminals whenever it could be "lawfully done."[43]

Like many other regular Republicans of his day, Garfield was reluctant to
commit himself to strong military action in the South, preferring that enforcement be carried out through federal courts. That may have partially explained
why he wanted to give Hayes's southern policy a chance for "a fair trial" and refrained from any open denunciation of the president's policy when it failed.[44]
But when Democrats in Congress tried to repeal the enforcement acts in 1879
and 1880, Garfield commanded the Republican defense in the House and
played an important role in influencing Hayes's decisions to veto the Democratic bills.[45]

Compared with people like Conkling and Schurz, Garfield understood and appreciated black suffrage in a more genuine political and intellectual sense, but he was unsure as to the best way to ensure black men's right to vote without intensifying racial and political tensions in the South. He saw the issue as involving not only racial tensions between blacks and whites but also the competition between the Republican and Democratic parties. His anxiety over the issue of black suffrage was revealed in a 1876 letter to Burke Hinsdale:

> The future of the negro is a gloomy one unless some new method can be introduced to adjust him to his surroundings. His labor is indispensable to the prosperity of the South. His power to vote is a mortal offense to his late masters. If they control it, it will be not only a wrong to him but a dangerous increase of their power. If he votes against them, as he almost universally inclines to do, he will perpetuate the antagonism which now bears such baneful fruit. I am tangled in the meshes of this strange problem.[46]

Essentially, in 1880, Garfield faced a challenge much like the one Hayes had four years earlier: how could the party best protect and perpetuate black suffrage in the South without further rending sectional sentiments? And how, through federal protection of black suffrage, could Republican strength in the South be enhanced and the party's victory in the next election guaranteed? Formulating a reasonable southern policy, at the heart of which black suffrage was to be placed, was a real challenge to Garfield.

Garfield's alternatives were limited. His predecessors had tried several means of enforcing black suffrage in the South and removing sectionalism from national politics, but they had achieved little. In Garfield's judgment, both Grant's use of federal troops to assist southern Republican governments and Hayes's appeasement to let southern Democratic governments take care of black suffrage without efficient federal supervision were failures. He particularly disliked the latter, which he termed "a confession of [the party's] weakness." Concession would not help to revitalize southern Republicanism.[47]

The manner by which Garfield was chosen as the party's presidential candidate also limited his initiatives in policy making. Since he was elected as a dark horse, commanding none of the party's major factions, he had to be even handed, at least politically, in treating the views presented to him by various faction leaders on black suffrage and the South. Compared with his predecessors, Garfield was deprived of many privileges of leadership, let alone that he faced a Democratic Senate. Although not entirely successful and respected during their administrations, Grant and Hayes were at least able to take some

radical steps in formulating their own policies toward the South. Whatever
southern policy Garfield might pursue, he had to consider whether it could secure the support of the party's major factions, rather than whether it would
work effectively in promoting black suffrage in the South.

Republicans, at least within the regular camps, agreed on the principle of
federal protection of black suffrage but not on policy. Each faction regarded
Garfield as the representative of its interests. The liberals urged Garfield to follow Hayes's course and drop black suffrage as an issue from his southern policy
and, as the *Springfield Republican* put it, "let natural causes work a natural
cure." The *Nation* agreed that reconciliation between property holders, between the North and South, was "a matter of paramount importance."[48] The
North American Review printed an article that demanded an immediate termi-
nation of federal aid to black suffrage and argued that black suffrage had
benefited the Republicans in all presidential elections since Reconstruction but
denied the choice of the white Americans who "made America what it [was]."[49]
Carl Schurz, retiring from the Hayes administration, warned Garfield not to be
ruled by bosses or to neglect liberal programs.[50]

The stalwarts wanted to be tough with the South. William E. Chandler, the
mastermind of the 1880 election, advised Garfield that his political survival and
success depended on honest administration, positive efforts to promote the
country's material interests, and "fidelity to northern sentiment" in handling
sectional issues. Believing that these were the preconditions for the party to win
again in 1884, Chandler asked Garfield to treat the issue of black suffrage seriously, but his main concern was located in the next election. He told Garfield:

> What we can do to protect suffrage remains to be considered, that we are sacredly
> bound to do all we can there is no doubt. I trust that your inaugural will speak
> forcibly to that effect. If you do not let the deep and undying sentiments of the
> northern people receive under your administration any such shock as President
> Hayes inflicted they will bear the Republican party through the fight of 1884 more
> easily and triumphantly than they did through that of 1880.[51]

Although Garfield sought advice on his southern policy from various sources,
he seemed most influenced by the views of Albion W. Tourgee. A carpetbagger
Republican in the South during Reconstruction, Tourgee had recorded the Republican fight against the Ku Klux Klan in his well-known *A Fool's Errand*
(1879) and would argue for racial equality in the famous *Plessy* case in 1896. In
a fourteen-page reply to Garfield, Tourgee discussed what he considered the

roots and cure of the problem of the solid South. According to Tourgee, the so-
called solid South was not a political party or a voluntary organization with a
concrete existence. Rather, it was "an institution, a belief," and "a common
sentiment" that was "solidly anti-reconstruction, anti-negro equality, anti-
everything that the Republican Party ha[d] done in or toward the South." The
solid South, Tourgee stated, was ideologically and culturally "a legitimate out-
growth of Slavery" that identified itself with the Democratic party simply because Democrats reflected its political demands. Since the solid South was a
deep-rooted political culture based on slavery, Tourgee argued, it could not be
easily eliminated by party politics.

In a way, Tourgee seemed to agree with what the Supreme Court said in the
Cruikshank decision in 1876 and would say in the *Civil Rights Cases* (1883) and
Plessy (1896): legislation was powerless to remove societal racism. However,
Tourgee advised Garfield not to follow Hayes's reconciliation policy but to support southern Republicans instead of wooing the Democrats. "Rescue Republicans," he cried, "not appoint nor consider the appointment of any one for any
Federal position in those states, who is not openly and professedly a Republican." He urged Garfield to "lead, organize and dignify the Republican party of
the South, to give [it] a tolerably fair election four years from this time." In addition, he suggested that the federal government aid black education in the
South.[52]

Tourgee's reasoning on the solid South and his call for national aid to black
education struck Garfield deeply. After all, Garfield himself was a thinking
politician. Two weeks later when Garfield wrote to Burke A. Hinsdale, his longtime friend and the president of Hiram College, the president-elect outlined his
thoughts on blacks and the southern question in language and logic identical to
those expressed in Tourgee's letter. Garfield suspected that offering patronage
to southern Democrats would help his administration:

> In my opinion the real trouble can be summed up in this: Our government is a
> modern republic; the South was rooted and grounded in feudalism based on slav-
> ery; and the destruction of slavery has not yet destroyed the feudalism which it
> caused. Nothing but time can complete its dissolution. I do not know a better way
> to treat that people than to let them know that this is a modern free government,
> and only men who believe in it, and not in feudalism, can be invited to aid in ad-
> ministering it; then give the South, as rapidly as possible, the blessings of general
> education and business enterprise; and trust to time and these forces to work out
> the problem.[53]

On March 4, 1881, Garfield unveiled his southern policy in his inaugural address. He devoted almost half of his address to issues concerning black rights and the South. He hailed the emancipation and enfranchisement of black Americans, which, he believed, had "freed" the nation from "the perpetual danger of war and dissolution" and "added immensely to the moral and industrial forces" of its people. He condemned the practice of black disfranchisement in the South and elegantly argued that "no middle ground" existed "between slavery and equal citizenship." Despite his pledge to guarantee blacks the right to vote, his solution was to promote national aid to black education. Voters' ignorance would lead to fraud and corruption in elections and, eventually, to "the fall of the republic." Universal education was a national responsibility and not a southern issue; it had to be enforced by law and with national resources. Garfield had only one sentence appealing for sectional reconciliation: "We may hasten or we may retard, but we cannot prevent, the final reconciliation." He placed civil service reform behind other issues – economic development, currency reform, and religious freedom – and held that the primary duty of that reform was in the legislative branch.[54]

Despite his eloquence on the importance of black suffrage and the meaning of the recent revolutionary changes in the Constitution, Garfield's program on black suffrage offered little that was concrete and innovative. He promised to apply the force of law to protecting pure and free suffrage, but he gave no indication as to the means and extent of executing his promises. The only innovative feature of his suffrage policy was his support for national aid to black education. To an extent, Garfield may have been influenced by Tourgee's view on black education, yet he might also have shared the liberal Republican complaint that the ignorance of black voters was mainly responsible for southern political corruption. Meeting a black delegation from Alabama before his inaugural, Garfield promised to aid blacks on political and economic issues, but he asked black leaders to work hard to improve black education because there was "a great deal of force" in Democratic charges that the ignorance of black voters had caused corruption. He promised that his administration would help remove "the last obstacle" in adjusting the troublesome question that blacks and their late condition had "given to this country."[55] Theoretically Garfield's black suffrage policy was consistent with the rationale of the party's earlier programs: to use national resources and power to aid blacks in obtaining and defending their rights.

Still, Garfield needed to come up with some measures to ensure black suffrage and the development of southern Republicanism. In 1880 the party failed to carry the South, but in such states as Florida, North Carolina, Virginia, and Tennessee, the Democrats won only by a marginal majority. In North Carolina, a shift of 2 percent of the total votes would have made the state Republican. To win these states in the next election, Republicans had to get more white votes in alliance with black votes.[56]

Meanwhile, southern Democrats began to compete with Republicans for control of black votes. According to historian Justus Doenecke, Democrats of the black belt frequently defeated their opponents by courting or coercing blacks, who sometimes gave them support. The black belt Democrats found black suffrage an asset as long as they could control it. Democrats also gave offices to blacks in return for their tacit support. Thus, in 1880, eleven blacks entered the lower house of Louisiana and four the upper house.[57] Obviously, the Democratic wooing of black votes was not a sincere acceptance of the political equality of black Americans but more a tactic to suppress the growth of Republicanism in the Deep South. As long as black suffrage was severely limited, Democrats would take advantage of it to serve their interests. But the Democratic use of black votes had other effects. It further reduced black suffrage to a pure instrument of expediency in the partisan struggle for power. This situation might have forced Republican leaders to look for other potential partners from the Democratic camp to help promote their cause in the South.

Political developments in the South in 1880 inspired some Republican leaders to think of forming an alliance between southern Republicans (black and white) and anti-Bourbon Democrats. The anti-Bourbon forces became quite visible in certain southern states by the late 1870s. William Mahone, a leader of Virginia's Readjuster – a movement advocating the repudiation of a portion of the state's debt – was elected to the Senate in 1879 by a legislature composed mostly of the Readjusters.[58] The Readjusters did not support Garfield's election in 1880, but they realized that they needed Republican help to win the state election in 1881. At the same time, Republicans urgently needed to maintain a majority in the Senate so that the party could control the confirmation of federal appointees. By 1880, Republicans regarded federal appointments in the South as the only powerful and feasible device to promote the party's programs. Thus, securing a Republican majority in the Senate "was essential, even vital to the success of the work now again commenced of securing a free and honestly counted ballot at the south."[59]

William E. Chandler urged Garfield to make a deal with Mahone so that he could be counted as a vote for the Republican party in the Senate. Bourbon Democrats would not "consent to the confirmation of officers" who would

"faithfully and courageously labor to abolish those crimes as political agencies."
Democratic obstruction of Republican appointments in the South, Chandler
warned, would prevent the appointees from exerting themselves "to prevent
that fatal suppression of free suffrage to which they owe[d] their position and
the local ascendancy of their party." He went on:

> It will be utterly impossible to put the weight of the federal administration on the
> side of free political action at the south unless the federal appointees in every
> southern state can be placed in their offices against and in spite of the hostility
> and adverse votes of the democratic senators from that state.[60]

Chandler advised Garfield that "no time should be lost in ascertaining" by "direct honorable communication" if Mahone was willing "to sustain the administration." Chandler knew that the party had to pay a price for this communication, but he argued that it would be better "to lose part of the federal
appointments in one southern state in order to maintain federal power unconditionally in all the others, than to be obliged to surrender about all control in
all the states to the senators therefrom."[61]

A Republican-Readjuster alliance became particularly tempting for both
sides after the Forty-seventh Congress convened on March 1, 1881. The Senate
had thirty-seven Republicans, thirty-seven Democrats, one independent who
announced that he would vote with the Democrats, and Mahone, who had not
said how he would vote. Since the Republican vice president could only cast a
tie-breaking vote, Mahone would determine which party would organize the
Senate. Several Republican senators predicted that Mahone would act with
their party and called his cooperation "vital as the beginning of a southern
break-up."[62] But Mahone agreed to cooperate with the Republicans on the condition that the party recognize his vote by securing federal appointments in Virginia for his supporters. After a deadlock and negotiation, Mahone announced
that he would vote with the Republicans.

Garfield was reluctant to accept the deal with Mahone. In 1876, when asked
to push Hayes to pursue a conciliatory policy toward the South in return for cooperation with the Republican government, he refused. He had since remained
doubtful about the Democrats' real motivations for pushing such cooperation.
In 1879, when black voters sided with the Readjusters to elect Mahone to the
Senate, Garfield thought it was a mistake for black voters because "in doing so
they inflicted a serious if not fatal wound upon the honor of prosperity of Virginia."[63] Garfield wanted to break up the solid South, but not at such a high
price that Republican appointees were to be removed to make room for Ma-

hone's Readjusters in Virginia. Garfield worried that such a political deal might be "the open door to larger consequences in the South," but it was "marred by the apparent advantages to him and to the Republicans which his affiliation [brought]." He predicted that if he made concessions to Mahone, his own policy to help Virginia Republicans would become "unusually difficult."[64] What Garfield wanted was cooperation with the Readjusters if they would guarantee black suffrage in Virginia. He was skeptical that the Republican-Readjuster alliance would accomplish the political goals of the Republican party.[65]

Garfield's concern over the consequences of possible Republican-Readjuster cooperation was more complicated than simply losing Republican political gains in Virginia. He had long advocated an alliance between northern and southern business and industry as a way to break the solid South. But the failure of Hayes's reconciliation policy had taught him a lesson, and he had little faith in the political integrity of southern politicians, Bourbon or Readjusters. The thing he feared most was that cooperation with Mahone would lead the public to believe that he was for repudiation, which he had strongly denounced in his inaugural address. When a group of Virginia Republicans, including an African American, told Garfield that they would combine with Mahone on state issues to secure protection for blacks, Garfield agreed but stressed that it should be done only if they could "secure the good" they were seeking "without endorsing repudiation in any way."[66]

Thus, when Garfield died on September 19, 1881, about two months after he was struck by the bullets fired at Union Station in Washington by the frustrated office seeker Charles J. Guiteau, Garfield had formulated no definite and feasible southern policy. No coherent plan was made to improve federal enforcement of black suffrage in the South. No action was taken to strengthen southern Republicanism. He had neither the time nor the resources to take any positive action on his long-range plan on black education. His dislike for the repudiators prevented him from fully recognizing Mahone as the party chieftain in Virginia. Nothing had been done for blacks except a few appointments, which he had made under pressure.[67] Because of his short time in office, his lack of initiative, his concerns about political integrity, and deficient support from congressional Republicans, Garfield's southern policy was confined to oscillating between different possibilities: federal aid to black education, an alliance with the Readjusters in Virginia, and tough enforcement policy. Thus, upon his death, as Stanley Hirshson concludes, Garfield left his successor nothing substantial and concrete to follow.[68] But although Garfield never had the chance to demonstrate his true potential for finding a middle ground on the issue — his was indeed a presidency that might have been — he stood firmly by the Republican promise to guard black political rights.

Uncertainty and Defeat

Garfield died as Lincoln had. Aside from the vast difference in their times, the two Republican leaders shared other similarities. Both men were original, if different in degree, in conceptualizing the new meaning of American constitutionalism. Both were accurate in reading the political mind of their party. Both could hold the party's factions together. Both left office with no concrete policy but only indications on black rights. Both left successors of vastly different antecedents and commitments. Even the unfriendly *Nation* realized that Garfield's death removed "the natural, legitimate chieftainship of the Republican party" and would inevitably lessen the "feeling of party allegiance among leaders and followers which ordinarily [was] one of the strongest elements of the cohesion" of the party.[69] Just as a few radical Republicans saw Lincoln's death as an opportunity to reform the South, some Republicans regarded Garfield's death as fortunate in the sense that "the influences which surrounded him would have made it impossible to live up to the people's idea of him."[70]

Like Andrew Johnson, whom Lincoln picked to be a symbol of the balanced distribution of power and party unity, Chester A. Arthur was selected by Garfield to be his running mate in 1880 only as a gesture to woo the support of stalwart Republicans. When he was nominated at the Chicago convention, Arthur was regarded as no more than "a ward politician," and "no one anticipated the importance of the gift thus handed to him." Arthur's vice presidency was understood, at least by the *Nation*, as an unintended device to lessen his political mischief. Everyone, including Garfield and Arthur, would agree with the *Nation*'s ominous comment that the chance that Garfield, "if elected, [might] die during his term of office" was "too unlikely a contingency to make any provision for."[71]

Because he was "placed in so embarrassing a position" and went into power "under such tragic circumstances," Arthur was urged by his Republican friends not to make immediate and abrupt changes in Garfield's cabinet to avoid "producing any serious results to the country or to the party."[72] Unprepared for the presidency, Arthur was in no position to initiate any new policy. Thus, in his first address as president, which had only three paragraphs, Arthur said nothing about the future except to assure the nation, "No demand for speedy legislation has been heard; no adequate occasion is apparent for an unusual session of Congress."[73]

The tone of Arthur's policy toward southern blacks was revealed in his first annual message, which was delivered three months after he became president. He referred to black suffrage, but his focus was solely on black education. "Many who now exercise the right of suffrage are unable to read the ballot which they cast," Arthur said. "Upon many who had just emerged from a condition of slavery were suddenly devolved the responsibilities of citizenship in that portion of the country most impoverished by war." Arthur suggested that education of blacks could be done "by local legislation and private generosity" and supplemented by such aid as could be "constitutionally afforded by the National Government."[74] The northern press, including the *Atlantic Monthly*, noticed the unusual absence of a Republican paragraph on the South and thought that the party had discarded the "bloody shirt."[75]

Compared with Garfield, Arthur was in an even more difficult position from which to launch an inspiring or inspired black suffrage policy. Originally an antislavery Whig, Arthur had been an active and efficient party worker since the founding of the Republican party. The peak of his career had been as the collector of the Port of New York, responsible for collecting two-thirds of the nation's tariff revenue. Unlike Garfield, who had been involved in many important national debates on black political rights, Arthur had no record in this respect. Nor had he given any in-depth thought to black rights. Thus, it was not strange to see that on several occasions, Arthur would refuse to speak out in favor of black rights.[76]

Meanwhile, Arthur faced another challenge: the ineffectiveness of the enforcement acts in the South. During and after the 1880 presidential election, the Department of Justice received numerous reports of violations of the enforcement laws. Garfield's attorney general reported to Congress that, in 1881, 166 of 342 cases under the election laws ended in convictions. Of the 166 there were 95 from the South, about 58 percent of the total number.[77] When Arthur's attorney general, Benjamin Brewster of Pennsylvania, came to office, he instructed district attorneys to prosecute every election case with a nonpartisan spirit, but owing to the strong influence of local politics and jury prejudice, most of the cases were declared mistrials. In 1882 Brewster reported 256 cases under elections laws, but only 32 ended with convictions, and the southern conviction rate dropped to 19 percent (23 out of 154 cases ended in convictions).[78]

When the 1882 congressional election approached, Arthur directed Brewster to handle enforcement of election laws in several southern states such as Georgia, Alabama, and Texas, where the independent movement grew fast. Although federal officers arrested some Bourbon ringleaders, convictions could not be secured. Brewster asked federal officers to carry out to the letter all regulations governing the registration of voters and called for the immediate arrest of state or local officers who obstructed, hindered, or interfered with these rules. This strategy failed. After the summer of 1882, federal enforcement officials in the South received little aid from the Justice Department.[79]

In search of a workable southern policy, Arthur turned to an option that Garfield had hesitated to use: forming a coalition of the Democratic Readjusters and independents, southern Republicans, and southern blacks. Doubtful that African Americans alone could prevent the Democratic advance, he urged blacks to unite with anti-Bourbon Democrats, because "a permanently defeated Republican party [was] of little value in any State, North or South"; "if any respectable body of men" waged war on the Bourbon Democracy, "with reasonable prospects of success," it was to be sustained. Since the majority of Readjusters and independents were former Democrats disgruntled with their party's economic policies, Arthur saw them as a more detrimental wedge to break Democratic hegemony in the South and as a new force to revive southern Republicanism at the same time. Arthur's southern policy then focused on a single object: to prevent the old slave power from recovering, even at the cost of sacrificing the prospect of establishing a permanent Republican force in the South.[80]

Arthur's coalition policy induced criticism, especially from southern Republicans and blacks, who regarded it as achieving nothing more than subordinating them to the former rebels. Frederick Douglass expressed his deep disappointment with the party's policy: "It is sad just now to see the once great and powerful Republican [party] — which had done so much for our Country, for humanity and civilization being now literally stabbed to death — assassinated by men who have hitherto been its staunch defenders."[81] The Republican *New York Tribune* also found Arthur's appeasement of southern Readjusters and independents intolerable. By contrast, William E. Chandler was among those who defended Arthur's policy as a great step "against Bourbon Democracy in favor of free speech, free education, free suffrage, and an honest counting of ballots."[82]

The Republican search for cooperation with southern anti-Bourbon forces did not proceed unconditionally. Republicans required that the southerners recognize and respect black suffrage. Republican leaders saw the division between Bourbon and readjustment Democrats over economic issues as an opportunity to drive a wedge into the solid South. "A great popular revolt at the South against Bourbon democratic rule and practices" could be a great opportunity to dismantle the old slave power. Cooperation with anti-Bourbon forces became especially urgent as the 1882 congressional election neared. Republican leaders such as Chandler, who was supposedly masterminding Arthur's southern policy, hoped that an alliance with them would enable Republicans to regain control of the House in the election.[83] The alliance between the Republicans and the Readjusters, however, must be preconditioned by the latter's recognition of black voting rights. Writing to Blaine, Chandler best expressed the rationale for Arthur's policy toward these southern Democrats:

> It is our imperative duty to get them if they can be obtained by honest and honorable means. . . . Every independent democrat or coalition candidate at the South fully and sincerely pledges himself in favor of a free vote, an honest count, the obliteration of race distinctions and popular education by a common school system; while in every case the Bourbon democratic candidate is in fact against all these principles and depends for his success upon their suppression.[84]

Arthur's strategy, however, did not fundamentally alter the situation. In 1882, although the South sent 8 anti-Bourbon Democrats (4 more than in 1880) and 8 Republicans to the House, the new House had 200 Democrats to 119 Republicans. In the Senate, the Republican margin was only 4. In local elections, the independents gained over the Republicans. The Republican-Readjuster alliance showed some effect on the election results, especially in Virginia, from which 6 of the 8 newly elected independents came; the others were from North Carolina and Mississippi. In the North, the Republican party lost Ohio because of the temperance issue, the defection of German Americans, and dissatisfaction with the boss system. Grover Cleveland, the mayor of Buffalo, won the New York governorship. In Pennsylvania, 100,000 Republican independents defected, and in Massachusetts, Republicans stayed home and let Democratic candidate Ben Butler be elected the governor.[85]

This small gain from the Readjuster-Republican-black coalition was in line with a prediction made by the northern press and some liberal Republican leaders that the political capital of the "solid South" (or the "bloody shirt") had been exhausted. The *Atlantic Monthly* noted that "the party line became vague and confusing" and "the party spirit" was at a "low ebb." The magazine argued that political questions no longer divided the parties: "The old parties are speedily to give place to new ones . . . the signs of the times point to new groupings of political forces upon new questions, chiefly economic in their character."[86]

For Carl Schurz, the party contests in 1882 had a completely new meaning and began a completely new phase in American political history. He asserted that the issue of the "solid South" had been "practically eliminated" from party contests. For him, a new party system was inevitable. With his usual keen political sense, Schurz noted that post – Civil War America had rapidly become an industrial, prosperous, and complex society. In this new society, social forces had substantially expanded and reorganized on the basis of economic interests. "We have a people with new social organization, new wants, and new grievances and new aspirations," he said, "and becoming more and more accustomed to look to a central authority for things which formerly were not considered within the range of its functions." These social and economic changes imposed an urgent need for change upon the existing parties, which appeared "scarcely fitted for the appreciation and treatment" of the situation.[87]

Some southern intellectuals agreed on the need for change but offered a different response: the black vote had to be divided. Atticus G. Haywood, president of Emory College, argued that the Readjuster-Republican-black alliance in Virginia showed that parties would "ere long become confusedly mixed" and that "the negro vote in due time [would] be courted, divided and counted," although to eliminate racial prejudice would take time.[88] Thus partisan contests for national power became more severe and had a more practical goal for each party. Since neither party commanded an absolute majority of popular votes and both were "minority parties of nearly equal organized strength," it became crucial for both to win the "independent voters" for success. Under such circumstances, the southern question changed from one of defending or depriving blacks of their political rights into a partisan struggle over winning their votes.

Harper's Weekly echoed Schurz's analysis. Now a liberal organ, the weekly, assessing Grover Cleveland's victory in New York, claimed that his election indicated the disappearance of distinctive partisan issues. It argued that "no fundamental principles of government, no measures of administrative policy" divided the parties. Politics was transformed from a struggle between parties to a conflict among "factions within the parties, not of the parties with each other." Thus, the paper advised, any "extreme partisan position [was] unwise." With the age of partisan politics over, the nation had entered "an era of personal politics," by which it meant that actual political division between parties would disappear.[89]

The Republican loss in 1882 seemed to close Arthur's brief experiment of forming a coalition with southern anti-Bourbon elements and left the party in disarray. The party had temporarily united under Garfield in 1880, but his death left Republicans leaderless. As a tried and true stalwart, Arthur could not fit into Garfield's shoes. Although Arthur tried to take an approach different from that of his old stalwart associates, his leadership was handicapped by his lack of ability and vision and by a lack of respect from Congress and his party. After the 1882 election, Arthur backed the ultimately successful civil service reform act, but otherwise he administered the office "in a business-like way" and left "questions of policy for his party to determine, without his interference." In 1884, the *Atlantic Monthly* observed that the Republican party had suffered "a hopeless disintegration," with no party discipline enforced and an "ineffectual" appeal to party feeling from its supporters.[90]

The disarray of the regular Republicans left an opening for the once silenced voice of the former liberal Republicans, now called the "mugwumps." This group included the old intellectual liberals and members of the post – Civil War generation of Republicans, who were mostly concerned with commercial and economic development in the North and South. A group of the liberals met in New York City in February 1884 and appointed a committee to organize for the election. The committee decided that the presidency should be kept within the Republican party, but it aimed at nominating a candidate who would commit to advance "the cause of Administrative Reform." Calling themselves "Republicans within the Republican party," the liberals wanted to get rid of the old issues of sectional disputes and black rights.[91] They sought civil service reform, peace on the American continent, and the global extension of American "moral and commercial influence"; and finally, as liberal leader Frederick Holls put it, "without abridging the rights of any citizen, all undue interference on the part of the federal officials, with local, state, or national politics" was to be forbidden.[92]

Nonetheless, the liberals had no chance in 1884. It was James G. Blaine's turn. The leader of the half-breed Republicans had not lost his constituency since his defeat for the 1880 nomination. Garfield's death helped restore Blaine to his natural prominence in the regular Republican camp. Most of his stalwart rivals were gone. Conkling had resigned from the Senate in 1881 over a patronage dispute with Garfield. Ulysses S. Grant was dying. J. Don Cameron was too young and parochial to be a challenger. The two potential stalwart leaders – John A. Logan and Arthur – were no real threat: Arthur had been president for too short a time with too small a constituency to win enough support; Logan could be recruited as a running mate. Thus the 1884 Republican campaign was a Blaine campaign. According to Stanley Hirshson, many powerful Republicans believed that since "Southern industrialists and planters increasingly favored protection," a high tariff platform "would induce a large number of Redeemers to desert the Democracy."[93] With this in mind, Blaine supporters sought to play down the race question and stress economic issues in the coming campaign. Their goal was still to control the national government, but their strategy was to play the economic card rather than the card of black rights. As the country quickly moved into an age of industrialization, Blaine Republicans saw that northern and southern interests could be united on economic issues while disagreeing on the political issues of the late war.[94]

The stalwarts did not completely withdraw at the 1884 convention. Logan, regarded by some regulars as the Republican "Back Bone," remained the only hope for restoring the party's commitment to black rights in the South.[95] One letter from Illinois criticized the party leadership for being blind "to the fatal result of the overthrow of free suffrage in the South." The writer urged Republican leaders to uphold free suffrage rather than give full attention to the tariff issue.[96] Although Blaine supporters constituted a large portion of the party's delegates at the Chicago convention in 1884, Republican leaders managed to arrange an intraparty compromise to ensure that the major factions were properly represented and to enhance the party's chances of victory. As a result, after the convention nominated Blaine for president, Logan was named for the second place to represent "the three quarters of a million men who lately wore blue" in the Civil War.[97]

Overwhelmed by anxiety to win northern voters, the Republican party ranked the importance of the contemporary issues and put economics at the top of its platform: tariff, protection of labor, civil service reform, foreign policy, and the southern question. In the last paragraph, the party promised:

We extend to the Republicans of the South, regardless of their former party affiliations, our cordial sympathy, and pledge to them our most earnest efforts to promote the passage of such legislation as will secure to every citizen, of whatever race or color, the full and complete recognition, possession and exercise of all civil and political rights.[98]

Not every regular Republican was happy with the platform. Charles A. Boutella, a congressman from Maine, bluntly criticized the Blaine Republicans for treating black rights too lightly:

> You are the best judge of what is politics, but if I were to speak on national issues you know I should assign more prominence and importance to the overthrow of popular government in the South. . . . I don't think the two closing resolutions of our Chicago platform put this case any too strongly. I recognize your pointed reference to the ballot, but would have preferred not to have had the settled policy of Southern prescription referred to as "exceptional" and "occasional." I should also place the establishment of political and civil rights and the indication of the ballot as the foremost issue—taking precedence of mere material and economic questions.[99]

Black suffrage, however, received a great deal of attention in Logan's acceptance speech. Besides eloquently defending the historical significance of black suffrage and fiercely condemning Democratic fraud and intimidation against black voters, Logan agreed that black education was important, but he argued:

> It is the duty of the National Government to go beyond resolutions and declarations on the subject, and to adopt such measures as may lie in its scope, to secure the absolute freedom of National election everywhere. . . . In accordance with the spirit of the last resolution of the Chicago Platform, measures should be taken at once to remedy this great evil, in as short a time as the case admits.[100]

Despite all such efforts, the Republicans were beaten in the 1884 presidential election. The shaky party unity of three factions was unable to overcome the diversity of their commitments. Blaine lost to Democratic nominee Grover Cleveland, a popular governor of New York, known as a fiscal conservative and civil service reformer, by a very close margin, 4,911,017 to 4,848,334; 219 electoral votes, including New York's 36, went to Cleveland. Some contemporary observers believed that Blaine's conservative stance on civil service reform caused his defeat. But Blaine blamed fraud by southern Democrats, who "had unjustly intimidated over a million black voters away from the polls and thereby carried enough states to steal the close election."[101] To some Republicans, however, the defeat was a psychological irritation more than a real political loss. William Chandler considered the Democratic victory short-lived: "Every dog may have his day, but that of the treasonable northern democracy allied with southern suppressers [sic] of free suffrage by fraud and murder will be a short one."[102] In Ohio, John Sherman also tried to reinvigorate the Republican cause by calling for black rights. But his motivation was challenged by his largely apolitical brother William Sherman, who castigated the Republicans for not enforcing black suffrage when they had the chance.[103]

Of course, the reduced Republican commitment to black rights – the failure to wave "the bloody shirt" – was not the only reason for the defeat. As the United States moved into the age of industrialization and commercial expansion, the political and economic demands of voters also diversified. Therefore, it became increasingly difficult for a party to maintain its constituencies.

However, the 1884 Republican campaign does provide a good example of the faction-unity complex, especially in contrast with the case of 1880. Why did the party not make its foremost commitment to black rights, as in 1880, since, as Blaine later realized, southern black votes were so crucial to victory? Probably because the party's perception of black suffrage had changed. With a new generation coming into the party, Republicans no longer might have seen black voters as their only ally in the South. The efforts to build an alliance with southern Readjusters practically legitimated this perception. In addition, stressing black education as a fundamental way to help black voters, as Garfield and Arthur did, also helped divert the party's attention from the more immediate political needs of blacks. Finally, that the tariff, immigration, and labor issues split Republicans as well as Democrats might have made party leaders cast their eyes on the votes of their previous foes. In any case, in 1884, as Frederick Douglass commented, the Republican party "forgot for the moment its high mission as the party of great moral ideas, and sought victory on grounds far below its ordinary level." The party "made the body more important than the soul; national prosperity more important than national justice."[104] Douglass was savvy enough to know the working secret of the American party system:

> Parties, like men, must act in the living present or fail. It is not what they have done or left undone in the past that turns the scale, but what they are doing, and mean to do now. The result shows that neither the past good conduct of the Republican party nor the past bad conduct of the Democratic party has had much to do with the late election.[105]

But what would be the acts (or issues) that would enable the party to "act in the living present" and "turn the scale"? Who would be the judges of these acts and who would arbitrate the judgments?

The Supreme Court and the Federal Protection of Black Rights in the 1880s

The Republican defeat in 1884 did not end federal enforcement. An essential support for Republican enforcement of the Fifteenth Amendment came from the enforcement acts passed in the early 1870s. As discussed in Chapter 3, several sections (3, 4, and 6) of the Enforcement Act of May 31, 1870, were challenged by the Supreme Court in its *Reese* and *Cruikshank* decisions in 1876, but the Court did not invalidate the whole law. In fact, the enforcement acts had been incorporated into the *Revised Statutes* — a compilation of public laws that were "general and permanent in their nature" — which was first published in 1875 under the authorization of Congress. Sections 3 and 4 of the Enforcement Act of May 31, 1870, both of which would be struck down by the Court in 1876 for lacking the definition of the crimes created under the sections, had become sections 2007, 2008, 2009, and 5506 of the 1875 edition of the *Revised Statutes*. And section 6, another section in question, had been placed as section 5508.[106]

On March 2, 1877, Congress named George S. Boutwell, a radical Republican who had participated in the making of the Fifteenth Amendment and other black suffrage laws, commissioner to prepare a new edition of the *Revised Statutes*. His job was to "incorporate into the text of the first edition of the statutes all the amendments" made since December 1, 1873. He was given no power "to change the substance or to alter the language of the existing edition of the Revised Statutes, nor could he correct any errors or supply any omissions therein except as authorized by the several statutes of amendment." He reported that he incorporated "several hundred" specific amendments in the new edition.[107] According to Boutwell, he "framed and reported the amendments to the Revised Statutes, which were afterwards incorporated in the edition of 1878." In preparing the new edition, which contained "a reference to the decisions of the Supreme Court," Boutwell said that he "was compelled to read all the opinions of the Court from the beginning of the Government, so far, at least, as to understand the character of each opinion."[108] When the new edition of *Revised Statutes* was published in September 1878, sections 2007, 2008, 2009, 5506, and 5510 remained unchanged. In his annotations, however, Boutwell made the point that these sections were addressed by the 1876 *Reese* and *Cruikshank* opinions of the Supreme Court.[109] All other sections of the enforcement acts also appeared in the new edition.[110] Thus, by incorporating the questioned sections into the *Revised Statutes*, Congress technically met the challenge presented by the Court and, with a minor rearrangement, kept alive the invalidated sections of the first enforcement act.[111]

The *Revised Statutes* provided a legal basis for the federal courts to continue prosecuting violations of the enforcement acts. Prosecutions under the enforcement laws continued between 1881 and 1888, although the conviction rates remained low. In 1883, of 287 enforcement cases, 201 were from the South, but only 12 cases resulted in convictions. The national number of the enforcement cases for 1884 was 190 – 160 from the South, 30 from the rest of the country – but 26 cases (of which the South shared 17) ended in convictions.[112] But the *Reese* and *Cruikshank* decisions did have a strong negative impact on the decisions made by lower federal judges. In its 1877 decision on *United States v. White*, James White's indictment under section 5511 of the *Revised Statutes* for procuring "certain persons to vote more than once," the District Court of Southern Ohio dismissed several counts because no averment was made to show that the offender prevented blacks from voting on account of race. The court opinion, modeled after *Reese*, stated that the right to vote was derived not from the Constitution but from the state and that Congress could not punish discrimination in voting unless it was on account of race.[113] On other occasions, lower court judges did their best to avoid the negative impact of the *Reese* decision and tried to make the best use of it to support federal enforcement. William B. Woods, U.S. circuit court judge for Louisiana, in deciding *United States v. Goldman et al.* (1878), stood by the principle that Congress had the power to protect voters at the elections of its members. The Supreme Court's statement in *Reese* and *Cruikshank* that the United States had no voters of its own, according to Woods, referred "solely to voters at an election for state officers."[114]

One question arising from lower court decisions was how to define the boundary between federal and state enforcement officers in carrying out their respective duties at elections. Because most elections were mixed – that is, elections for congressional, state, and local elections were held simultaneously –

voters would cast several ballots at the polls on election day. The supervision of elections then became a problem, especially for federal enforcement officials authorized by law to challenge only fraudulent behavior occurring in voting for congressional representatives, not other offices. This left room for the state election officers to avoid and even refuse federal challenges at the elections. In dealing with the confusion, some lower federal courts narrowly defined the duties of federal enforcement officials. In *United States v. Gitma* (1879), district judge Robert W. Hughes ruled that the enforcement acts (secs. 2017, 2019, 2020, and 2022) authorized federal election supervisors to be in the room with election judges but did not give "marshals, in the absence of supervisors, the powers and duties of supervisors proper." Therefore, the duties of the marshals were "not those of supervisors of elections, but merely those of conservators of the peace at the polls." This kind of ruling limited the functions of federal marshals to assisting election supervisors.[115]

In 1880, the Supreme Court rendered two opinions, *Siebold* and *Clarke*, that upheld the constitutionality and superiority of the enforcement acts, displaying a judicial and political temper radically different from that of *Reese* and *Cruikshank*. *Ex parte Siebold* was argued on October 24, 1879, and decided on March 8, 1880. The case involved the arrest and conviction of Albert Siebold, a Baltimore state-appointed election judge, and his associates, who were charged with violations of sections 5515 and 5522 of the *Revised Statutes* for hindering the duties of federal supervisors at the congressional election on November 15, 1878. Petitioning for a writ of habeas corpus, Siebold argued that although the federal government had the right to enforce its own election laws, it could not punish state officials for neglect of a state duty.[116] The Court's 7–2 majority opinion, as delivered by Justice Joseph P. Bradley, rejected the idea of dual sovereignty concealed in Siebold's argument, holding (1) that although states might make laws regarding congressional elections, federal laws on the same subject (in this case, the enforcement acts) were "constitutionally paramount" and *pro tanto* superseded the state laws; and (2) that the federal government had no power to punish a state-appointed election official, unless he violated federal election laws while performing a mixed state and national duty.[117] The Court, however, carefully limited this power of federal punishment to congressional elections and disallowed its use in purely state or local elections. Two Democratic justices, Field and Clifford, dissented. Justice Field accepted Siebold's argument and reasoned that the federal government could not impose duties on state officials.[118]

Ex parte Clarke, argued before the Court at the same time, involved the conviction of Augustus F. Clarke, a state-appointed election judge in Cincinnati. He was indicted and convicted for allowing the sealed poll books of an 1878 congressional election to be broken open, a violation of both the state election law of Ohio and section 5515 of the federal *Revised Statutes* (sec. 22 of the Enforcement Act of May 31, 1870). As with Siebold, Clarke petitioned for a writ of habeas corpus on the ground that a federal circuit court had no jurisdiction in the premises. In deciding the case, the 7–2 majority opinion simply followed the rationale of *Siebold*. Again, Clifford and Field dissented.[119]

These two opinions, joined by every Republican justice and delivered in the midst of congressional Democrats' execution of their repeated attempts to repeal and reduce the enforcement acts, were welcome news to Republican leaders. Garfield described them as "a sweeping affirmation of the constitutionality of the legislation in controversy between Republicans and Democrats in 1879–80."[120] Calling the decisions "masterly opinions," Hayes expected future cases in this category to follow the principles laid down by these two opinions.[121] Garfield, in his inaugural address in 1881, would repeat the essence of the Court's rulings.[122]

The Supreme Court's liberal view on enforcement continued in its decision in *Ex parte Yarbrough* in 1884. Jasper Yarbrough, a Georgian Klansman, and his seven associates were arrested and convicted under sections 5508 and 5520 of the *Revised Statutes* (respectively sec. 6 of the Enforcement Act of May 31, 1870, and sec. 2 of the Ku Klux Force Act of 1871) for using violence and force to prevent Berry Saunders, a black man, from voting at a congressional election. The defendants petitioned for a writ of habeas corpus on the ground that a federal court had no jurisdiction over the offense committed by private citizens.[123] Speaking for the unanimous Court, Justice Samuel Miller, who wrote the *Slaughterhouse* opinion in 1873, broadly interpreted the Fifteenth Amendment and substantially revised the Court's standing on federal power to enforce black suffrage, as expressed by *Reese* in 1876. Miller acknowledged the reasoning in *Reese*—that the Fifteenth Amendment gave "no affirmative right to the colored man to vote"—but he argued that, "under some circumstances," the amendment might "operate as the immediate source of a right to vote." He continued:

> In all cases where the former slave-holding States had not removed from their Constitutions the words "white man" as a qualification for voting, [the Fifteenth Amendment] did, in effect, confer on him the right to vote, because, being para-

mount to the State law, and a part of the State law, it annulled the discriminating word *white*, and thus left him in the enjoyment of the same right as white
persons. . . .

In such cases this fifteenth article of amendment does, *proprio vigore*, substantially confer on the negro the right to vote, and Congress has the power to protect
and enforce that right.[124]

Miller rejected the defendants' petition on the practical ground that the acts
of Yarbrough and his associates were "too common in one quarter of the country and [gave] omen of danger from lawless violence."[125] Since congressional
elections were "the very sources of power" for the federal government, it could
not allow congressional elections to "be poisoned by corruption or controlled
by violence and outrage, without legal restraint." The right to vote was not to be
placed "at the mercy of the combinations of those who respect no right but
brute force, on the one hand, and unprincipled corruptionists on the other."[126]

Yarbrough advanced the interpretation of the Fifteenth Amendment to the
utmost limit in its fourteen-year history. Together with *Siebold* and *Clarke*, it
helped consolidate several constitutional principles under debate – the constitutionality of black suffrage and federal power to enforce it, federal power to
supervise congressional elections, and the supremacy of federal election laws
over cases relating to national elections. To what extent these decisions helped
strengthen federal enforcement, or the Republican party in the subsequent
elections, was unclear. But these decisions set guidelines for lower federal
courts in their handling of similar cases. In *Ex parte Geissler* (1880), for example, the Circuit Court of the Northern District of Illinois closely followed
the *Siebold* ruling and strongly defended the rights of federal election supervisors. Both state and federal governments affected the lives of citizens, the
court opinion said, but "when the question of nationality and of the rights of
the United States as a nation" arose and had to be decided, then the national
power and sovereignty overrode what was "sometimes called the sovereignty of
the state."[127] In *United States v. Seaman* (1885), the Circuit Court of the Southern District of New York decided against the conviction of a voter who was
arrested for fraudulent voting at a mixed election because no averment was
shown that he was trying to cast the vote for a congressman. In a negative way,
the court used *Siebold* as the basis for its reasoning,[128] and the Circuit Court of
the East District of Missouri rendered a similar opinion in *United States v. Morrissey* in 1887.[129]

Although the Supreme Court liberally interpreted federal power to protect black political rights, it stood firmly behind its earlier restrictive interpretation of the federal power to protect black civil rights. In *United States v. Harris* (1883)—a case involving an indictment of R. G. Harris and a group of white farmers from Crockett County, Tennessee, for beating several blacks and killing one, a grave violation of section 5519 of the *Revised Statutes* (sec. 2 of the Ku Klux Force Act)—the Court ruled that the beating and murder did not constitute a federal offense because the white yeoman mob's action was a private one; and although the state of Tennessee's failure to prevent it was regrettable, no federal crime was involved. Citing both *Reese* and *Cruikshank*, the Court's majority opinion, delivered by Republican justice William B. Woods, reaffirmed that the Fourteenth and Fifteenth Amendments applied only to state actions and concluded that section 5519 had no "constitutional authority."[130] As the court remained consistent, so did Republican organs.

Applauding *Harris* for striking down "the Centralism of Liberty" and the "Imperialism of Equal Rights," the *Nation*, a longtime foe of the Ku Klux Force Act, asserted that the Court's ruling settled "the point forever that the Fourteenth Amendment merely add[ed] new limitations upon State action" but did "not change in any way the fundamental structure of the Government."[131] *Harper's Weekly* believed that the decision uttered "the true doctrine of national supremacy." It argued that the enforcement acts, which were designed to "magnify the national authority" at the close of the war, might be preferable to the destruction of slavery, but, in "a calmer time," "the laws passed under that humane impulse" were found to be "incompatible with strict constitutional authority."[132]

The major blow, however, came from the *Civil Rights Cases* decided in the same year. Reviewing five cases arising under the Civil Rights Act of 1875 and involving denials of access to public accommodations and facilities for black citizens, the Court ruled that the Fourteenth Amendment applied only to state law, not to persons or activities private in nature. Writing for the 8–1 majority, Justice Bradley, who had recently spoken for the Court in *Siebold* and *Clarke*, found the Civil Rights Act of 1875 unconstitutional because the Fourteenth Amendment prohibited only state abridgment of civil rights and gave no power to Congress to protect blacks from discrimination by private individuals. Bradley also rejected the applicability of the Thirteenth Amendment, which in his view only meant to eliminate "badges of slavery," not to prohibit racial discrimination in "an inn, a public conveyance, or a theatre." Following the *Slaughter-*

house Cases and *Cruikshank*, Bradley argued that antidiscrimination laws should be enacted by states themselves.[133] Hayes's appointee John Marshall Harlan was the only dissenter. Attacking the majority's narrow view of the Thirteenth and Fourteenth Amendments, Harlan argued that the Thirteenth Amendment gave the federal government power to legislate in the area of civil rights for blacks, which was part of the freedom of a U.S. citizen.[134] But his opinion was unavailing.

Republicans reacted strongly. Shortly after the deliberation of the *Civil Rights Cases*, Senate Republican leader George F. Edmunds introduced two bills. He made clear that his first bill (S. No. 15) was specifically designed to remedy the damage caused by the Court's invalidation of the Civil Rights Act of 1875 and to protect "the colored citizens of the United States" because in some states, "wicked and cruel and prejudicial" distinctions were still made "against them in respect of their civil rights." His second bill (S. No. 16) was "further to protect the constitutional rights of citizens," including "the right to a free vote and a fair count." Despite pleas for immediate consideration and swift action, both bills died in the Judiciary Committee.[135]

Meanwhile, Frederick Douglass and other black leaders waged a war of words with northern newspapers over the decision. In Douglass's view, the *Civil Rights Cases* ruling was "a step backward" and "a concession to a prejudice" that belonged to "an extinct institution and places."[136] African Americans all over the country held protest meetings, and blacks in Chicago called for a general strike. The resolution passed at the National Convention of Colored Citizens in Louisville in October 1883 condemned Democrats for continuing the course set up "years ago by that archvillain Chief Justice Taney," but it also attacked the Republicans as unfriendly.[137] While the *New York Times* deemed blacks' call for protest "silly talk," the *Chicago Tribune* criticized Douglass for misinterpreting the Court's intention. "[Blacks] battle for their rights in contact with the world just as white men must do," the *Tribune* argued; any special code for blacks' protection "would virtually take them out of the ranks of equal citizenship."[138] Responding to the *Tribune* attack, Douglass disputed the racial argument and declared that his concern was not merely blacks' rights but the human rights under the protection of the government:

> I never was antislavery because of my color – had I been I should have been less than half antislavery – but my antislavery being based broadly upon manhood I have been a thoroughgoing abolitionist. I am charged all over the country with

attacking the decision of the Supreme Court on the Civil Rights Bill. I am not
ashamed of that attack. That decision is [a] surrender of the main result of
the war.[139]

Why did the Court affirm federal enforcement of black suffrage while invalidating federal protection of black civil rights? In a speech delivered in May
1887 at the University of Michigan, Justice Miller offered an explanation: the
Reconstruction amendments contained a "pervading" sentiment for "a strong
national Government," but the Court did "not see in those amendments any
purpose to destroy the main features of the general system." The framers of
these amendments, Miller argued, "still believed that the existence of the States
with powers for domestic and local government, including the regulation of
civil rights – the rights of person and of property – was essential to the perfect
working" of the nation's "complex form of government," though they had
"thought proper to impose additional limitations on the States and to confer
additional power on that of the nation."[140] Recalling *Slaughterhouse* as the "el-
ementary decision" in determining "the effect of the three new Constitutional
amendments" on federal-state relations, Miller said that such relations might be
considered now as settled, "with the exception of the specific provisions in
them for the protection of the personal rights of the citizens and people of the
United States." Miller believed that the "necessity of the great powers conceded
by the Constitution *originally* to the Federal Government, and the equal necessity of the autonomy of the States and their power to regulate their domestic affairs, remain[ed] as the great features" of the nation's complex form of government.[141] However, Miller did not specify what were the "personal rights" under
the protection of the national government.

Thus, twenty years after the enactment of the nation's first civil rights law,
Miller and his Republican colleagues (except John Marshall Harlan) had not
traveled far in terms of national protection of black civil rights. As to national
protection of black political rights, the Court gave favorable opinions, not
merely affirming black men's rights to vote but increasingly to purify the electoral process. Political purity, reasoned Miller in *Yarbrough*, was crucial to the
existence of the federal government:

> In a republican government, like ours, where political power is reposed in repre-
> sentatives of the entire body of the people, chosen at short intervals by popular
> elections, the temptations to control these elections by violence and by corruption
> is a constant source of danger.[142]

In any case, the Supreme Court rulings in *Siebold*, *Clarke*, and *Yarbrough* were constitutionally and politically significant. These decisions, rendered when further legislation on enforcement became impossible, thus served as the constitutional basis for the continuation of the enforcement acts during the 1880s. Technically, they reinforced at least some Reconstruction concepts and laid the legal foundation for Republicans to enact the federal election bill (the "Lodge Force Bill") after the party regained power in 1888.

CHAPTER SIX

The Rise and Fall of Reenforcement, 1888–1891

Stalemate on Federal Enforcement of Black Suffrage, 1884–1890

The Democratic victory in 1884 was not the end of the Republican cause of federal enforcement. The three major Supreme Court decisions of the early 1880s—*Siebold*, *Clarke*, and *Yarbrough*—not only maintained the constitutionality of enforcement but also compelled the incoming Cleveland administration to do more than pay lip service to continue the use. In his inaugural address, Cleveland, the first Democratic president since the outbreak of the Civil War, acknowledged the validity of black emancipation and enfranchisement and pledged that his administration would protect "the freedmen in their rights or their security in the enjoyment of their privileges under the Constitution and its amendments."[1] Before the midterm elections of 1886, Cleveland ordered his attorney general, Augustus H. Garland, to execute "the Statutes of the United States touching the appointment of Supervisors of Election and special deputy marshals, and the performance of their duties and their compensation." The attorney general urged his subordinates to understand the enforcement laws but instructed them to perform their duties "without infringing upon the rights of any citizen," in a manner that was to be "firm and at the same time free from an unnecessary display of authority."[2]

However, enforcement during the Democratic interregnum was not very effective, although the federal enforcement laws were constitutionally functional and the Cleveland administration made use of these laws. In November 1885, after the Knights of Labor in Wyoming massacred twenty-eight Chinese miners, Cleveland ordered federal troops to put down the Knights-organized "insurrection." Twenty-seven members of the mob were indicted under the Ku Klux Force Act of 1871, but eventually local juries found all of them innocent.[3] In

216

1885, out of 283 enforcement cases, there were 81 convictions, only 2 of them from the South. In this year, criminal prosecutions under the enforcement acts (or the "Election Laws," an expression used since 1882) from northern states for the first time since 1871 surpassed those from the South.[4] In 1886, the national number of election law cases dropped to 47, and none of the 6 convictions were from the South, where the total number of the cases amounted to 8. In 1887, there were 96 cases in total, but only 2 cases, both being dismissed, reported from the South. In 1888, the number of the election law cases rose to 131, of which 14 were reported from the South. But, again, only 1 of the 25 convictions was from the South.[5]

Meanwhile, Republicans and Democrats in Congress engaged in a protracted but largely fruitless battle over the fate of the enforcement laws. Republicans wanted to revitalize these laws, whereas Democrats simply wanted to eliminate them. The battle began at the end of Hayes's administration and may have directly resulted from his vetoes of Democratic attempts to repeal the enforcement laws in 1879 and 1880. In December 1880, when the third session of the Forty-sixth Congress met, Henry M. Teller, a Republican senator from Colorado who later served as President Arthur's secretary of the interior, introduced a bill (S. No. 1870) concerning the elections of House members.[6] In the same session, Thomas Turner, a Kentucky Democrat, also introduced into the House a bill (H.R. 6653) to prevent fraud and corruption in presidential and congressional elections.[7] But none of the bills ever resurfaced from the committees. On December 5, 1881, four days after the first session of the Forty-seventh Congress began, Teller introduced a similar bill (S. No. 92),[8] and ten days later Henry Neal (R-Ohio) put before the House a bill (H.R. 1281) providing punishment against bribery at elections.[9] House Democrats responded instantly when Jesse H. Finley of Florida proposed a bill (H.R. 1972) to amend sections 5511, 5512, and 5515 of the *Revised Statutes*, a core part of the original enforcement acts.[10] Later that year, John R. Lynch, a black Mississippian, introduced a bill (H.R. 6203) to amend federal election laws, but no action was taken.[11] In 1882, Leonidas C. Houk, a Republican from Tennessee, in his bill (H.R. 6935) urged Congress to preserve the purity of elections and punish crimes against free ballots.[12] Bills of a similar nature continued to be presented to the House at the first session of the Forty-eighth Congress, but the House remained silent on the enforcement laws. But none of the bills was brought up for debate by either party.[13]

In December 1884, soon after the Democrats won the presidential election and a majority of Congress, they moved against enforcement again. Alexander M. Dockery, a Missouri Democrat, introduced two bills (H.R. 7535 and H.R. 7536) respectively asking the House to repeal the federal acts that authorized the appointment of election supervisors and deputy marshals.[14] Another Democrat, Fassett J. Follett of Ohio, followed up with a bill (H.R. 7647) proposing to repeal sections 2011 to 2031 inclusive, section 5521, and part of section 689 of the *Revised Statutes*, the essentials of the Enforcement Act of February 28, 1871.[15] Follett's bill was among the first Democratic bills to specify what sections of the enforcement laws they intended to repeal and, in a way, to signal the Democratic goal of removing the enforcement laws from the federal books. All these sections mentioned in Follett's bill would indeed be repealed in 1894, when Democrats controlled every branch of the federal government. But this was impossible in 1884, when Republicans still controlled the Senate. In the meantime, their local constituents reminded Republicans in Congress of other threats to enforcement. They warned that Cleveland's federal appointees, many of whom had been Confederate officers, might impair rather than improve the federal enforcement of the election laws.[16] One petition sent to John Sherman complained that some citizens in the South "for a series of years, and during the late election for President and Vice-President" were "kept away from the polls by threats and acts of violence and bloodshed, a system of ruffianism unrebuked by the governments."[17]

The Forty-ninth Congress continued to witness a mixed effort by both Republican and Democratic members in the House to seek congressional action to punish frauds and offenses against free ballots.[18] While Democrats kept introducing bills to repeal the enforcement laws,[19] Republican attempts to improve the election laws grew out of the frustration that the federal laws became increasingly ineffective under a Democratic presidency.[20] Charles H. Grosvenor, an Ohio Republican in the House, noted that the average number of voters in each congressional district in five southern states was 16,214, whereas in all the northern states the number was 35,149. He believed that intimidation, bribery, and fraud were among the abuses of the ballot, but he also emphasized that "ignorance and indifference on the part of the voters, both white and black," were responsible for the discrepancy. He suggested that Congress refuse to seat anyone whose "certificate of election" did not "state the vote and show that a certain proportion of the voters in the district voted, either for or against him."[21] Grosvenor again raised the political imbalance that had united Republicans against the Democratic attempt to repeal the election laws in 1879 – 80, and the federal mechanism of reviewing the process of voting and counting. These questions would become the main concerns of the "force bill" in 1890.

In the meantime, William E. Chandler, who had long been involved in designing the party's campaign strategy, began turning his attention to forming party unity in pushing a new election law. In February 1887, Chandler wrote to Republican friends in several southern states, including Louisiana, Florida, Mississippi, and South Carolina, asking them to collect information on state election laws. He assured his informants that their information would be used "in consultation with others desirous of devising some method of securing just and fair elections" in their state.[22] Southern Republican leaders lauded him as "one of the few leaders" who had sought "to keep the party awakened to its great principles and high moral duties and who saw the consequences of temporizing with enemies, forsaking supporters and waiving vital issues," but they had little confidence in expecting any serious results. Responding to Chandler's request for proposals to amend existing laws and to remedy election frauds in the South, E. M. Brayton doubted that his suggestions could be of any real use because the party was "crushed beyond the power of any agency of the old leaders to give it vitality, protection and a fair field."[23]

In December 1887, soon after he was elected to the Senate by the New Hampshire legislature, Chandler introduced a bill (S. No. 429) for federal control of elections in Mississippi, Louisiana, South Carolina, and Florida. Chandler knew that his measure had little chance of passing Congress, or even emerging from committee, but he intended to make the bill a declaration that his party wanted "to limit the suppression of the suffrage to elections for State officers and give . . . free suffrage for national officers."[24] Congratulating Chandler for presenting the bill, a Texas Republican hoped that Congress would pass the bill and bring about "the political justice" people had "for a long time been deprived of right" in Texas.[25]

However, hopes for passing a new enforcement bill in 1887 were minimal. E. M. Brayton was right in a sense when he charged the party with losing its high morals and principles in the 1880s, but the party was unable to push for a new enforcement law because it controlled no institutional mechanism to carry out its efforts. Since Democrats recaptured the House in 1874, the two parties rotated control of the federal government. In 1877, when Hayes entered the White House, he faced the Forty-fifth Congress, where Democrats controlled the House by a majority of 13 and the Republicans retained the Senate with a plurality of only 3. The 1878 elections paved the way for Democrats to control both houses in the next Congress, but their pluralities (6 in the Senate and 19 in the House) were too small to override the vetoes of the Republican Hayes. In 1881, Democrats maintained a small majority of 12 in the House, but the temporary coalition between the Republicans and Virginia Readjuster William Mahone denied the Democrats control of the Senate. In 1883, at the opening of the Forty-eighth Congress, while 197 Democrats stood in the House, dwarfing their Republican counterparts by 79, they became a minority in the Senate, 2 behind the Republican 38. When Democrats won both the presidency and the House in 1884, they had no luck in subduing the Senate Republican majority, which would last through the entire Cleveland administration.[26]

Throughout this period, neither party simultaneously controlled all three federal branches. Turnover in Congress was so frequent that neither of the parties could have a durable base to pursue its agenda. Thus, fluctuation produced a political stalemate, and the very institutional mechanism that blocked the Republicans from renewing or improving the earlier enforcement acts was the same mechanism that also prevented the Democrats from eliminating the existing enforcement laws.

The stalemate certainly intensified congressional confrontations over elections laws. As the 1888 presidential election neared, Republicans worked hard to enhance the laws and Democrats to reduce their strength. In addition to Chandler's bill, at least four Congressmen, Republican and Democratic, introduced bills relating to election laws during the first session of the Fiftieth Congress.[27] The intensive manner in which bills were introduced in 1888 indicated that frauds and bribery in elections had become a main concern for both parties. Both realized that the current laws could not meet the challenge of misconduct in national elections and that new laws would have to be formulated. This concern forecast the Republican political agenda for the coming presidential election and a bitter fight between Republicans and Democrats over the new election law to be brought up for discussion in 1890 and 1891.

The Election of 1888 and Black Suffrage

The 1888 presidential election, in William E. Chandler's words, was "of greatest importance." It was the party's chance to regain the executive branch and, more crucial, to restructure the cause of enforcement, which was vital to both the party and the nation. Probably with some exaggeration, but obviously with grave seriousness, Chandler warned that another Democratic victory in the presidential election would the make that party's rule "permanent," and "an appeal to arms sooner or later would be inevitable."[28]

Compared with that of 1884, the political situation in 1888 was more complicated and divisive, and neither Democrats nor Republicans had any key cards. Both parties confronted a series of issues that deeply divided the nation's political forces, including labor-capitalist disputes, taxation, silver, antitrust and antimonopoly movements, temperance, and, most important, the rise of new political parties as a result of general distrust and discontent with the sincerity and commitment of both parties. The Cleveland administration had an unimpressive political record. Because Republicans controlled the Senate and Democrats were divided, Democratic attempts to pass a moderate tariff bill and a bill to reduce internal revenue taxes in 1886 were defeated. Meanwhile, Cleveland, whose election was due largely to his civil service reform pledge and who wanted to carry out his campaign pledge, encountered great resentment from his own party when he charged that Collector Hedden of the New York Customs House was violating the spirit of the Civil Service Act and had him investigated. Cleveland's veto of a Democratic pension bill – a gesture to show the Democrats' patriotism – further alienated him from his party.[29] More serious, the administration failed to solve the problem of inefficiency of the monetary system; this had affected the practical interests of the agricultural population in the midwestern and western states, which desired more efficient circulation of currency and resented the monetary monopoly of the Northeast.[30] Urban problems, centering on the conflicts between the labor class and industrialists, created the basis for the development of the Socialist movement. During the race for New York City mayor in 1886, Henry George, the author of *Progress and Poverty*, campaigned as a labor candidate, beat Republican Theodore Roosevelt, and was only thirty thousand votes behind Democratic candidate Abram S. Hewitt, whose victory allegedly depended on fraudulent counting.[31] The United Labor Party, formed in February 1887 and split into two parties in the 1888 election, offered no threat to Republicans and Democrats in any real sense, but popular resentment gathered under the flag of a third party gave both parties a warning that could not be simply overlooked.

For Republicans, however, the challenge of 1888 was more severe. For the first time since 1856, they would campaign as an opposition party, an unaccustomed role. Although the lack of a presiding administration created an opportunity for many presidential hopefuls, it also increased the party's difficulties in forming an organizational center around which different factions might compromise and form new coalitions. Likewise, since no Republican policies had been put into effect in the past few years, various factions argued over the best campaign platform to win the election.[32] Once again in 1888, Republicans engaged in an internal debate as to whether federal enforcement of black rights and enforcement laws should be put atop the party's agenda and whether this issue could help the party win the election.

For the radicals – those who wanted to see the party continue its enforcement policy[33] – the party had to take federal enforcement of black rights and protection of purity of congressional elections as its foremost issues. Federal protection of black suffrage, argued John J. Ingalls of Kansas, a new radical recruit, was the party's "paramount issue," before which "tariffs, taxes, currency and surplus [shrank] and dwindle[d] into nothingness."[34] Following the party's earlier ideological argument, radicals held that black suffrage remained an unsolved fundamental challenge for the nation and that whether a legally qualified voter could safely cast his vote and have his vote honestly counted was a matter of "vital principle." Denouncing the election of Francis T. Nichols as Louisiana governor, Chandler challenged the election returns of the Louisiana gubernatorial election in 1888 and accused the Democrats of false counting and killing black voters. Reiterating the rhetoric of the first-generation radicals, Chandler warned that without suffrage, black freedom was "a mockery and a snare," and with black suffrage "permanently suppressed," the condition for southern blacks would "grow worse and worse." He challenged the nation, and especially the North, not to treat the issue of black suffrage with indifference.[35] Attempting to form the party's coalition under the Civil War ideology, Chandler untiringly reminded the party of its past:

> If the Republicans of the North, who prescribed universal suffrage as the last and final condition of the settlement with the South for its causeless and bloody rebellion, and embodied this condition in the fifteenth amendment of the Constitution, have not the fidelity, persistency, and courage to demand and secure its observance, but submit to its nullification by the oligarchy which now rules both the North and the South; and if they thus abandon the colored people to the wrongs and oppressions which now encompass them, they will deserve no better fate than to have the whips and the fetters from which Abraham Lincoln freed the bondmen applied to their own backs and clasped upon their own limbs.[36]

Most of the radical concerns were pragmatic. The Fifteenth Amendment, Ingalls reasoned, gave the South thirty-eight additional members of Congress, but if the North let the former rebels continue to disfranchise blacks, the additional thirty-eight House seats, which belonged to black voters, would continue to be stolen by the Democrats and the North would be subdued to southern voting superiority. With only forty-eight northern electoral votes, Ingalls warned, the South would be able to win control of the national government, reconstruct the Supreme Court, and "eliminate the negro as an element in the political problem."[37] Ingalls's warning was echoed by Chandler, who saw that Democratic control of the national government threatened "the manufacturing and all other industries of the North." Democratic control of the White House meant "to hold in its hands the decision of all . . . national questions, those of foreign policy, tariff, finance, internal improvements, and all expenditures."[38] The revival of the old slave power, one southern Republican wrote, would prevail to "degrade labor . . . so that a poorly paid tenant might be substituted for slave labor in the cotton fields of the South."[39] According to the radicals, black suffrage therefore was the party's base for launching any other programs and its principal source for regaining and maintaining control of the federal government. The North had to unite to compel "southern masters to desist from their attempt perpetually to rule through crimes against the black man and against the Constitution."[40]

Other Republicans, however, wished to "unify and harmonize" the party by playing down old wartime issues, or getting rid of the "bloody shirt." Although James G. Blaine declined to lead the party this time, he actually showed the way for his followers, who faithfully pushed forward his strategy. Reading the nation's political mind and attempting to lure support from business-oriented supporters from the South and new voters nationwide, these Republicans saw party success as depending on tariff protection, revenue reform, and federal aid to internal improvements in the South, issues closely related to economic immediacy and practicality. Such thinking might have been partially inspired by Cleveland's call for tariff changes, but it was indeed a realistic approach for getting voters.[41] James S. Clarkson of Iowa, who later became the vice chairman of the party's national committee, argued that with the development of nation's economy, the existence and strength of a political party depended on how the party would attract new recruits. In Clarkson's view, the Republican party in the 1880s was no longer composed of romantic social reformers and Union army soldiers of the Civil War era but of a postwar generation of businessmen whose interests and demands had to be satisfied by the party's programs. Clarkson argued that the party should not stick to its heroic past and old principles such as black rights. Rather, it should look beyond the old issues and attract new constituents by stressing economic and financial issues.[42]

The probusiness, protariff argument had a large number of supporters. These included the party's old independent elements such as Whitelaw Reid, new industrialist recruits like Stephen Benton Elkin and Marcus A. Hanna, and old stalwarts such as John Sherman and William D. Kelley.[43] Kelley, a vocal proponent of black suffrage in the 1860s and now taking the nickname "pig iron" for his strong support of the American iron and steel industry, believed that the issue of black suffrage had lost its power to attract new voters. The color line, these men felt, should be supplanted by the economic line. The unfitness of blacks for political responsibilities and their unreliability as a political partner were popular topics in many northern newspapers.[44]

Although tariff and other economic concerns would dominate the party's agenda for 1888, the intraparty debate over the southern question made its way into the 1888 convention. Clarkson opposed putting any bloody shirt slogans in the platform, contending that it would only harm efforts to attract newcomers. Other members of the Republican national committee, such as Albert J. Beveridge of Indiana and Ingalls, insisted on addressing the southern question. These radical Republicans believed that black disfranchisement could not be allowed to continue and political equilibrium between sections had to be restored.[45]

The final version of the 1888 Republican platform leaned heavily toward economic and financial issues. The platform gave a balanced presentation of the party's view on each of the important economic and social issues of the day. It pledged the party's determination to support protection of home industry and oppose Cleveland's free trade policy, denounced the importation of Chinese labor "alien" to the nation's "civilization and constitution," rejected the practice of monopoly of trade, and promised support for the homestead policy. The platform also denounced the inefficiency of Democratic foreign policy and recommended appropriation for improving the nation's naval forces. At the end, the platform promoted temperance and morality and repeated its commitment to civil service reform.[46]

Not forgotten, the radical argument for black suffrage and federal enforcement was accepted by the platform and placed atop the party's programs. In contrast with the 1884 platform, which only briefly promised federal enforcement of equal suffrage at the end, the Republican platform of 1888 gave elaborate attention to the issue. Pledging its devotion to the Constitution and "the autonomy reserved to the States under the Constitution," the platform vowed to protect "the personal rights and liberties" of all U.S. citizens, "especially the supreme and sovereign right of every lawful citizen, rich or poor, native or foreign born, white or black, to cast one free ballot in public elections, and to have that ballot duly counted." The platform went on:

> We hold the free and honest popular ballot and the just and equal representation of all the people to be the foundation of our Republican government and demand effective legislation to secure the integrity and purity of elections, which are the fountains of all public authority. We charge that the present Administration and the Democratic majority owe their existence to the suppression of the ballot by a criminal nullification of the Constitution and laws of the United States.[47]

It is important to note several modifications of the party's suffrage stance. First, equal suffrage instead of black suffrage was emphasized, although black suffrage was intended to be the object of attention. Second, although the party charged Democrats with election fraud, the conventional tone of sectional animosity, as in 1880 and even in 1884, was absent. The call for "a free ballot and a fair count" aimed more at securing the purity of elections and eliminating fraudulent practices at the polls, South and North, than at reviving federal enforcement of black suffrage in the South. The election frauds in northern cities, where large numbers of foreign immigrants lived and voted, presented a problem no less urgent than black disfranchisement in the South and probably even more threatening as it spread nationwide. Thus, the Republican demand for "effective legislation to secure the integrity and purity of elections" implied two objectives: to reinforce black suffrage in the South, and, more important, to reform the current mechanism of federal supervision of congressional elections nationwide by reducing corruption to a minimal level. Even so, the northern press reacted negatively to the Republican platform. A *Springfield Republican* editorial accused the party of creating "an unfortunate and unnatural color line in politics," which was "the prime cause of all the recent troubles in the South."[48]

Compared with the suffrage policies announced by five other parties in the race, the Republican party distinguished itself for its firm commitment to both the principle of equal suffrage and federal responsibility in securing the purity of elections. The platform of the American party—a political and ideological heir of the Know-Nothing party of 1856—accepted equal suffrage for U.S. citizens but condemned the practice in seventeen states of allowing the foreign-born to vote without obtaining citizenship first and demanded literacy as a qualification for voting.[49] The Prohibition party also supported the imposition of educational qualifications on voters, although it held that suffrage should not

rest on "mere circumstance of race, color, sex or nationality."[50] The Union Labor platform supported women's suffrage but left to the states the control of suffrage regulation.[51] Denouncing both Republicans and Democrats as corrupt
and "unworthy of the suffrage" who did not "live upon public plunder," the
United Labor platform emphatically asked for the adoption of the Australian
system of voting to secure "the effectual secrecy of the ballot" and to do away
with money politics.[52] Democrats entirely avoided the issue of voting and election fraud and simply gave a vague pledge of its "devotion to a plan of government regulated by a written Constitution, strictly specifying every granted
power and expressly reserving to the States or people the entire ungranted
residue of power" in the platform.[53]

The Republican convention, held in Chicago on July 7–9, 1888, nominated
Benjamin Harrison, a former senator from Indiana and Civil War veteran, with
New Yorker Levi P. Morton as his running mate. By 1888, the heads of all the
major conventional factions of the party had retired from politics. The party's
only recognizable flag bearer, James G. Blaine, declined the opportunity after
seeing that he could not command unanimous party support.[54] After Blaine's
withdrawal, the nomination was left to a group of the party's "favorite sons"–
loyal and well connected to the party but not outstanding in political distinction or charisma. This group included John Sherman, a veteran suitor for the
presidency; William B. Allison, a rising Republican star from Iowa; William
McKinley, an avowed protectionist from Ohio; Walter Q. Gresham, an Illinois
jurist preferring free trade; and Benjamin Harrison, the grandson of "Old
Tippecanoe." Harrison's selection came amid relative peacefulness. Unlike
Garfield, he was not chosen as a dark horse candidate. But like Garfield, he was
nominated to break a deadlock between the forces behind Sherman and other
candidates; consequently, he had little control over the direction of the party's
platform.[55]

Even though Harrison left the campaign to be managed by the party's national committee, headed by Matthew S. Quay of Pennsylvania and James
Clarkson of Indiana, he did speak about protecting black rights. In his acceptance letter, Harrison stressed that black people asked not for special protection from the government but only for "the common rights of American citizenship." He warned that the party would get no support from black voters
unless their plight of disfranchisement was addressed.[56] But Harrison was prudent and later, under the influence of Quay and his committee, decided that
he should "say nothing that would be an impediment in the way of the cam-

paign."[57] Meanwhile, Harrison's running mate, Morton, said nothing about the issue of the South.[58]

After the convention, the national committee concentrated on the tariff issue, hoping to extract new blood from business circles to support the party. The radical Republicans criticized the national committee for using the tariff issue and trying to remove or belittle the matter of suffrage enforcement. The committee's "cowardly" attitude toward the South, John Spooner of Wisconsin argued, would only lead to the domination of "the old conspiracy of the South and its system of labor against the system of free and dignified labor of the north."[59] Chandler simply refused to follow the committee's program and raised the issue of suppression of black votes in the South by leading an investigation challenging the credentials of Randall L. Gibson, a Democrat from Louisiana.[60] The radicals urged Harrison not to confine his leadership to the party's pledge for protection, which, Albion W. Tourgee wrote, was only "the secondary impulse" and, *as a sentiment*, had never won a popular election." He encouraged Harrison to "avow a deliberate purpose to get out the negro vote" and adopt an aggressive campaign style to "conquer Mississippi, Louisiana and South Carolina – in all of which there [was] an average of 60 percent black Republicans – and to help the Republicans in North Carolina and Virginia." Only by such a campaign, Tourgee believed, would Harrison achieve "distinctiveness, originality and character."[61]

Nonetheless, Republicans won the 1888 election. Cleveland led Harrison slightly in popular votes, but he had only 168 electoral votes, 65 behind Harrison's 233. Harrison captured both New York and Indiana, two doubtful but crucial states for the Republicans. Among southern states, only West Virginia went Republican, but elsewhere the results were close. While Cleveland won several southern states by a small margin, Harrison received more southern ballots than any Republican presidential candidate since the end of Reconstruction. In the meantime, Republicans from southern and border states increased their seats in the House, giving the party a majority. Together with the holdover majority in the Senate and on the Supreme Court, the Republican party, for the first time since 1875, would control every branch of the national government.[62]

The Republican victory in 1888, achieved on the basis of the party's unity, was regarded by historian Robert D. Marcus as "largely a historical accident."[63] Democratic disunity, anti-South rhetoric, effective use of local Republican clubs and networks, diffusion of opposition – all helped Republicans win the election. But the party's pledges on a number of issues, including the protective

tariff, federal aid to education, and welfare for the Union veterans, were probably more effective in securing its victory over the Democrats in 1888. These
pledges appealed strongly to Middle Atlantic and New England voters, as well as
to some of the constituencies of two labor parties. In the meantime, Republicans skillfully blended the party's tariff policy, hostility to importation of contract labor, and the desire for further business expansion with its principles of
patriotism and nationalistic pride.[64] The trump card held by the party was the
magic word *protection*, which, as Kentucky Republican William O. Bradley
spelled out in seconding Harrison's nomination at the Chicago convention,
meant protection to American industries, "the persecuted people of the South,"
southern children "laboring in ignorance," and soldiers "who shed their blood
upon the fields of battle that this Nation might live." The party, as Bradley
pointedly indicated, wanted to combine its Civil War heritage as glorified by
Abraham Lincoln with the Whiggish "American System" of internal improvement dreamed by Henry Clay.[65]

The Republican victory in 1888 restored the party's confidence and created
new expectations. However, success meant different things to different Republicans. For the protariff wing, the party's good fortune was due to its tariff policy. Southerners voted for the party not because it had a heroic Civil War record,
nor for its support for black rights, but because of its economic policy and the
prosperity that could be derived from it. Many Republicans asked their party to
turn its tariff promise into concrete legislation, so that the new recruits could
become permanently loyal to the party. As soon as the presidential vote was
cast, a "high private" of the Republican party offered advice to Matthew S.
Quay, the chairman of the national committee, on how to consolidate the
party's gain:

> The republican party managers must begin at once *through the present organiza-*
> *tions* to nurse up the party strength by means of confirming the recruits obtained
> in this election — some merely voting with us on the tariff issue and in their own
> minds for this once only. These new recruits are plastic material and can mostly
> be permanently secured by issue and rational treatment, *and through the channels*
> *of the present organizations*, if you will take the proper means of setting that phase
> in motion. . . . The other thought is that plan should be made, when the republi-
> can administration gets in power to frame a tariff bill in accordance with the *prac-*
> *tical views of manufacturers*. . . . This plan carried out in the spirit of courtesy and
> friendliness will secure not only doubtful men but even democrats who can ap-

preciate the fostering care of a protective government. . . . In short now is the time
to secure the building up of the republican party and nurse it for a still greater
triumph in 1892.[66]

Some southern Republicans lent their support to the protariff argument and
tried to influence Harrison in formulating his southern policy in a way that emphasized economic development. One Texas delegate to the Republican convention advised Harrison to adopt a policy that would let the South correct its
course "without any irritating legislation." He argued that time would improve
conditions for blacks and increase their fitness to vote, but, meanwhile, solid
white votes might be divided on economic and local issues.[67] A group of "native
white Republicans and old line Union men" told Harrison that Democrats
would use any tough anti-South policy to "stir race strife and perpetuate Bourbon power" in the South. They told the president-elect, "Success of republican
principles and peace between the races, justice to the negro, and material prosperity in South Carolina can only be reached through the leadership and support of intelligent and liberal white people."[68] The chairman of the Republican
Executive Committee of Kentucky expressed the same opinion. With the North
"always doubtful" in the struggle "between the parties of order and disorder,"
the South was "always in a position to hold the balance of power." But if the
South remained "solid," disorder, revolution, and war would "be always imminent." Thus, to assure peace in the South, "Republican armies, physical armies,
armies of intellect and common sense, armies of education and progress" had
to be "recruited and placed in the field in the South . . . to support the law of the
Nation."[69]

For radical Republicans, however, the 1888 victory created a great opportunity to solve the black suffrage problem once and for all. In fact, during the
campaign, black disfranchisement continued. As one of George Hoar's correspondents reported, Ku Klux Klanism revived in Washington County, Texas,
where black and white Republicans were either prevented from voting or compelled to vote the Democratic ticket. Radicals believed that had blacks been allowed to vote, the party's victory would have been more impressive.[70] Southern
Republicans asked party leaders to address the election frauds in the Senate
and questioned the qualifications of Democratic senators who had been recently elected. E. B. Brayton, the Republican leader of South Carolina, wrote to
Chandler that since 1882, there had been no general registration for voting,

contributing to black disfranchisement. "Abundant and irrefutable" proof was found that state registration officers tried to impede and delay the registration of new and old voters. He called the immediate enactment of an election bill "the key to the situation."[71]

As with the protariff Republicans, radical Republicans regarded immediate legislation as vital to consolidating and enhancing the political capital gained from the recent election. The way to do so was to pass a new election law as soon as possible. A few days after the 1888 election, one Massachusetts Republican lawyer urged Hoar, the chairman of the Senate Committee on Privileges and Elections, to "take the lead in this great work of securing the purity and freedom of elections." Impatient for the party action, he even sent Hoar a draft of a new election law, in which he suggested the establishment of "a Board of Commissioners of Elections" to be responsible for appointing district election commissioners, settling the contested votes, and issuing certificates of elections. He suggested national adoption of the Australian ballot system, separate dates for national and state elections, and popular election of senators.[72] Hoar must have taken these suggestions seriously: not only were several of them incorporated into the Senate election bill he prepared in 1890, but, as Hoar's biographer, Richard E. Welch Jr., noted, in December 1889 Hoar also broached the idea of separate registration and voting time for congressional elections.[73]

Radical Republicans tried to influence the formulation of southern policy, a subject that Harrison had avoided during the campaign. When Harrison asked Chandler for advice on the nation's political future, the New Hampshire Republican saw an opportunity to elaborate his view of the South, which he called "not extreme or unreasonable." Expressing an understanding of Harrison's recent remarks that there was no southern question, Chandler assured the president-elect:

> It seems to me there is no southern question except the question whether the 15th amendment of the Constitution shall be obeyed, like all other portions of that instrument. The North has no other issue with South. The North has no animosity toward the South; on the contrary it is full of kindly feelings which have been expressed in many ways; but it can never consent to a permanent nullification of the 15th amendment. . . .
>
> To be sure it will be asserted that obedience to the 15th amendment will result in "negro supremacy" in the South, especially in Louisiana, Mississippi, and South Carolina. This is the great bugbear. But the results of impartial suffrage under the 15th amendment must be accepted by the South whatever they may be.

Many troubles must arise from the existence in the same community of the two races. But they are not, therefore[,] to be allowed to co-exist the one as the superior, the other as the subject race. They must live on terms of political equality and the consequences must be patiently borne.

In each of the three States above mentioned, however, I have discovered that the race issue is purposely kept alive by the white Democrats as the only means of retaining the Democratic party in political power. They do not want the blacks to divide between the two parties. They will not allow the whites to [be] so divided. If both races should divide, politically, they know the result would inevitably be a Republican majority in the State. Therefore, they keep up the cry of "negro supremacy."[74]

Chandler advised Harrison that, since federal troops could no longer be used to enforce the constitutional amendments, "the machinery of the courts" was of "utmost importance." And Harrison was to appoint an "able and courageous" attorney general, who would at all events "be an actor and not a conservative let-alone-policy man." He urged Harrison that if the Republican party wanted to remain in power in 1892, it had to "begin to do some things immediately," something to show the country the differences between the Democrats and Republicans.[75]

In addition to Chandler's full-fledged advice, Harrison also received other advice on the issue of black suffrage. One federal judge from Mississippi advised Harrison to pursue a policy of decoloring black suffrage – that is, dividing black votes between Democrats and Republicans – and then "the white race" would "divide and wisely control" public affairs.[76] Leading woman suffragist Susan B. Anthony, writing to Harrison, welcomed the Republican party's returning to "its original attitude as the defender" of the political freedom but urged the president-elect to include women's suffrage in his inaugural address.[77] John M. Langston, a black leader, urged Harrison to pay attention to conditions for blacks in the South.[78] Fully aware of the conflicting opinions regarding the party's southern policy, Harrison promised to do his best to keep the party in power. "I am very deeply sensible of the perplexities that are lying in ambush along my path," Harrison confided to Hoar. "I know the limitations that rest upon a President elected by a party, and can only hope that my friends will judge considerately the honest attempt that I shall make to establish our party so firmly in the confidence of the people as to secure a Republican secession."[79] Thus, when he delivered his inaugural address on March 4, 1889, Harrison prudently followed the guidelines in the party's platform. He insisted upon the

freedom of the ballot as the condition of national life and emphasized the necessity for the exercise of every power vested in Congress and the executive
branch for securing that freedom. But, obviously as a result of persuasion from
southern protectionists, Harrison suggested that an alliance between protectionists and blacks in the South in a friendly and cooperative manner would secure the political interests of both groups.[80]

It appeared that Harrison wanted to give balanced treatment to both the enforcement and tariff issues. His main objective was to restore strong federal
protection of black suffrage so as not to scare away the new recruits from the
South, who would be rewarded for their loyalty with favorable legislation in tariff and currency reform. Whether Harrison and his party would be able to
achieve this goal depended largely on the political consciences and skills of the
Republican legislators.

The Making of the Lodge Bill in the House

The Fifty-first Congress convened with an obvious Republican advantage. The
party had a 173 – 156 majority in the House and exceeded the Democrats by 10
in the Senate. This setting promised at least an institutional possibility for Republicans to pass the legislation they desired, including a new election law. As
soon as the first session convened, both houses received a great number of bills
from Republican members concerning enforcement or revision of the existing
election laws.[81] Meanwhile, many rank-and-file Republicans suggested legislation on the subject or sent their own bills to Congress. Stephen Hackworth of
Topeka, Kansas, wrote to Hoar and urged that federal courts take up all trials
relating to controversial election cases. Meanwhile, Ebenezer Wakeley, a lawyer
from Chicago, assured Chandler that the federal government had the authority
to enforce black suffrage, for "all the power over the destiny of the Freedmen,
outside and beyond the war amendments, [was] in the General Government,
and not in the states."[82]

The Senate designated George F. Hoar, William E. Chandler, and John C.
Spooner to work out the bill. Hoar, one of the remaining original makers of the
enforcement acts, began to consider the question of a new national election law
soon after Harrison's inauguration. Although by no means a radical Republican
in any measure, Hoar lacked neither faith nor determination in federal power to
protect black suffrage and to keep the polls clean.[83] Chandler, one of the few

Republicans with the old stalwart blood in his veins, was the leading advocate for enforcing the Fifteenth Amendment. Spooner was relatively new to the Senate but by no means inexperienced with the subject. Having failed to get the Senate to consider his bills strengthening the election laws in the Fiftieth Congress, Spooner now believed the time had come for passing a new election bill.[84] The House manager of the new election law was Henry Cabot Lodge, a rising star in the Massachusetts Republican circle and former Harvard historian. Lodge, who was too young to take part in making the Reconstruction laws, was not unfamiliar with the party's glorious past and its legends, including Charles Sumner, a frequent guest at his father's house on Boston's Beacon Street.[85]

Essentially, the new election law had to accomplish two old objectives: to terminate Democratic suppression of southern Republican votes, especially black votes, and to provide a more effective mechanism for eliminating fraudulent practices at congressional elections throughout the nation. But, from the beginning, the Republican managers disagreed on the precedence of one objective to the other and on the best strategy to achieve both goals. Senate Republican managers held that the new law should limit its scope only to those sections where such a law was needed most — namely, the South — and that the best way to do it was to enhance the existing enforcement acts. Hoar proposed to pass a bill providing federal enforcement "in particular districts where its aid was invoked" by voters. Originally, Hoar had followed John Sherman's suggestion and proposed to separate congressional and state elections. He abandoned the proposal when many Republicans opposed it as too costly and involving too much bureaucratic work. After consulting Republicans in both houses, Hoar then decided to make the new law an updated or improved version of the old enforcement acts of the 1870s. The most crucial revision he proposed was the creation of a federal canvassing board with ultimate authority to settle disputes over returns between federal and state election enforcement officers.[86]

Chandler personally favored "a much broader law than the extension of the Supervisors' Law." He wanted to follow the radical suggestion made by Albion W. Tourgee to take "the whole power of conducting the election of representatives in Congress out of the hands of State officers and [commit] it entirely to federal officials," but he realized that it was impossible to do so. The difficulty in enacting a "universal" and "newly-devised" election law, Chandler told House Speaker Thomas Reed, was not only in the extraordinary expenses to be paid by the national treasury for the operation of the law in each of the

325 congressional districts throughout the nation but also in the potential Republican revolt against the idea that the federal government should "take the Congressional elections entirely out of the hands of State officials in all of the States" simply because elections in some southern states were "unfair and not free." Thus, Chandler believed that Hoar's bill had "the practical merit of being the method upon which" Republicans were most likely to reach an agreement "so as to secure its passage."[87]

Spooner agreed, admitting that he and his fellow Republicans were "distinctively nationalists" but their lawmaking had to be kept "within reasonable bounds," for "a national election law, to be operative throughout the whole country, would be intolerable."[88] Aware that House Republicans might have a different view or strategy on formulating the new law, which might be a radical one, Chandler was confident that through a joint conference, they would "reconcile all conflicting views." But the most important thing for the party was to pass a new election law. "The necessity is upon the Republican party, and the sooner the shock of the conflict begins in the House or the Senate or both, the better for us all."[89]

Lodge, the House manager of the election law, thought differently. For Lodge, enabling southern blacks to vote in congressional elections was important because "since the fall of the reconstruction governments, the entire Republican vote, both black and white, ha[d] been practically suppressed" to such an extent that "in some states no effort [was] made even to cast the vote."[90] But the best way to eliminate southern suppression of black votes was to carry out comprehensive ballot reform. By 1889, election frauds had become such a political epidemic that, in addition to the adoption of the Australian ballot system by several states, more than twenty-two state legislatures were scheduled to discuss measures of ballot reform, and four-fifths of the governors in their messages condemned corruption and fraud at the polls.[91] Lodge shared the pragmatic concerns of the Senate Republicans that black votes were important to secure the party's influence in the South, but his pragmatism rested on a much broader and nationalistic basis. Representing a new generation of reform-minded Republicans, Lodge inherited elements of Sumner's conventional New England radicalism but was equally blessed with a good understanding of the political modernity. He believed that the best way to secure partisan interests was to move partisan programs beyond partisan interests. In a letter to E. B. Hayes, Lodge revealed his thoughts about the new election law. Passing any law simply to "protect the negro" in southern elections, in Lodge's view, was "out of the question."

The country does not want a force bill or anything resembling it. Still less do we want anything sectional, but the country is very much aroused on the question of ballot reform and I believe will stand by a bill to introduce the Australian system at all Congressional elections until all the states are willing to adopt the system themselves. On this line I am confident that I shall win. It is the most important public question at this moment and on this issue of ballot reform and purity at elections. I propose to make my fight and not on any narrow scheme of supporting the voters in certain southern districts.[92]

Lodge had his practical concerns as he noted that the North was tired of reviving wartime sectional animosity. He informed the northern audience that the new election law was "neither to raise a 'war issue' nor [was] it waving the 'bloody shirt'" but to fight the existing evils of election frauds, which was "a question of to-day." He reminded the North that "a fraudulent Congressional election in South Carolina directly affect[ed] the rights of voters in New York and Massachusetts." Thus:

The only effective remedy for these evils, so far as Congressional elections are concerned, must be found in a national election law. The day for sectional legislation on this subject, if it ever existed, has completely gone by. Any law, to be effective, must be national, and, above all, must be in harmony with the great and vital movement for pure elections which is rapidly assuming an overwhelming importance in the minds of the people.[93]

Lodge's nonpartisan rationale would gain support from Spooner, who was convinced that the new law had to be "so framed that the people [could] see in it nothing of partisanship, and the unmistakable purpose upon the part of the Republican party to secure a free ballot and a fair count."[94] Given the intense interparty competition, the sincerity of a nonpartisan stand might be questioned, and the self-proclaimed nationalism might be seen only as a tactic to disguise the party's hidden agenda and win enough support, in and out of the party, to pass the bill. But no matter the ultimate purpose of the party, the Republican framers of the new election bill realized that, if the party sincerely wanted to solve election problems in the South and North, the new laws had to be made in such a way that partisan interests were the least of the motivations behind it. In other words, Republicans had to treat the law as a long-term national policy to perpetuate an orderly practice of political democracy rather than as a temporary, expedient measure for obtaining immediate gains. Lodge, at least, regarded this as the opportunity to reform thoroughly the nation's election system. And he would include in his bill such measures as national adoption of the Australian ballot system and separation of congressional elections from state and local elections.[95]

Despite their differences, Republican managers in both houses shared one fundamental belief: that federal authority to enforce free suffrage at national elections had to be reaffirmed and consolidated through the new law. The party would not interfere with "local concerns" or "set ignorance above intelligence," Lodge said; he continued:

> But we do say that the clauses of the constitution ought to be carried out, and carried out in good faith. No people at the close of a great and bloody war can afford to write into its constitution that no man shall be deprived of his vote on account of race, color or previous condition of servitude, and stand by and see that made a dead letter.[96]

After several communications and exchanges, Senate Republican managers gave the House the right of way to initiate the bill but reserved the right to amend it.[97] On June 19, 1890, Lodge reported to the House the federal election bill H.R. 11045, amending and supplementing the election laws of the United States and providing for more efficient enforcement.[98] The lengthy bill — seventy-five pages and fifty-seven sections and later famed as the "Lodge Force Bill" after its author — was a compromise among the Republican managers. The bill, as Lodge put it, was "an extension and improvement" of the "legislation of 1870 and 1871."[99] Privately, Lodge was dissatisfied with the measure, which did not go as far as he wanted to see it go. He considered it "a half-way measure" but trusted that "good [would] come from this election law."[100]

The Lodge bill, as explained by Lodge and more substantively demonstrated by the Senate substitute, contained several provisions that substantially revised the existing enforcement acts, especially the Enforcement Act of February 28, 1871, the principal election law.[101] First, the bill provided that a chief election supervisor representing the federal government could be installed for each judicial circuit of the country. Under the 1871 law, the circuit court would appoint election supervisors in response to requests filed by the citizens of the district shortly before congressional elections. The Lodge bill authorized the chief supervisor, once appointed by the court, to accept applications from citizens asking for federal supervision of elections, to inform the court of the necessity of opening for business transactions during the election period, and to appoint three supervisors, not more than two from any political party, for each voting precinct. This provision, in effect, transferred the power originally placed with the circuit court to the chief supervisor, whose tenure could be terminated only by the court for misconduct.

Second, the Lodge bill expanded the duties of the federal supervisors. The 1871 law specified their duties as attending registration and voting, challenging and making a list of doubtful voters, and watching the count. The new bill enumerated more than ten kinds of duties for a federal supervisor, including new ones: inspecting the registration lists; verifying a doubtful voter's name, identity, and residential information; placing an oath before a voter when his qualifications were challenged; making a list of all voters; making and certifying statements of the votes cast in his election district; and assisting the court in preventing illegal immigrants from voting. With the new bill, the federal supervisors were given greater space than before to scrutinize and examine such documents as the poll lists and votes, which were normally under the control of state election officers.

The third revision, perhaps the most important one, was that the Lodge bill authorized the establishment of a United States Board of Canvassers, composed of three men – citizens of good standing – appointed by the circuit court. The board was charged with examining and returning the votes as transmitted to it by the federal supervisors. If the board's certificate agreed with that of the state officials, the candidate holding both would become a member of the House. If they differed, that of the board, on a majority decision, was prima facie evidence of election. A contestant could appeal the board's decision to a circuit court; in the event of a reversal, the candidate certified by the court went to Congress. No such board was authorized in the earlier enforcement laws.[102] This provision was revolutionary. It gave the federal government the final authority to decide contested elections. Theoretically, it adopted the principle of the Supreme Court's *Siebold* decision (1880) – which the Republican lawmakers repeatedly cited – that state election laws yielded to the supremacy of federal election laws when the two were in conflict.[103] Predicting that this feature would be "dreaded and hated" and "bitterly fought" by southern Democrats, John C. Spooner hoped the bill could restore his party "to its old-time vigor." Before Lodge presented the bill to the House, Spooner explained the bill's rationale to a friend:

> [It is to ensure that] the Government is present at every election, and at every polling place, to see precisely what is done by State officials, and that when the election closes the Federal official will have a poll list and a statement of the votes cast, and that the canvass of the votes is to be made by a Federal board, thus

depriving the partisan State Governors in the south of the power, which they have heretofore abused, of issuing certificates of election.[104]

Lodge, too, stressed the bill's constitutionality, backed by the Fifteenth Amendment and the recent Court decisions in *Siebold* and *Yarbrough*. The bill's leading goal, Lodge argued, was to secure the "publicity" of the process and results of congressional elections. Dismissing Democratic accusations that the bill was partisan, Lodge skillfully employed Charles Sumner's phrase to defend its nationalistic nature:

> It was said many years ago by a distinguished statesman of my own State that freedom was national and slavery sectional. So it may be said with equal truth that honest elections are national and dishonest elections are sectional. If an impure ballot-box was a universal condition the frame of the national Government could not long endure.[105]

Lodge did not hesitate to admit that his bill was partially intended to enforce black suffrage in the South. Blacks, Lodge argued, had fought in the Civil War and "died in the trenches and on the battle-field by hundreds for the Government." They deserved "some better reward." Lodge was also bothered by "prefixing qualifying adjectives" to the word "American." Without knowing that he was forecasting and discrediting the twentieth-century debate over the racialization of American identity, Lodge tried to give a "pure and simple" American definition:

> If a man is not satisfied to be an American pure and simple and to abandon the prefixes which denote race distinctions, then he is better outside this country than in it. . . . We have clothed [blacks] with the attributes of American citizenship. We have put in their hands the emblem of American sovereignty. Whether wisely or unwisely done is of no consequence now; it has been done and it is irrevocable.[106]

Following Lodge, Jonathan H. Rowell of Illinois argued that black suffrage was a double-edged experiment but a necessary step after the war. Ignorant suffrage was evil but was "nothing in comparison with the evil of a subject class." Like Lodge, Rowell also gave statistical evidence to show the southern suppression of black votes.[107] Harrison Kelley, a Kansas Republican whom New York Democrat Charles Turner called "a new John Brown of Kansas," argued that the bill was not tough enough: "The battles of liberty have not all been fought nor all been won."[108]

As expected, the Democratic attack concentrated on the federal authority to decide disputed returns. Democrats argued that by empowering the federal courts to decide them, state election laws were virtually nullified. The bill, as James W. Covert (D-N.Y.) charged, was based "on an unrepublican, an undemocratic, and an un-American distrust of the people and officers selected by them." Its purpose was to "get into the hands of the Republican party the whole election machinery of the States . . . dragging it into the filth of partisan politics." Democrats believed that under the control of the chief supervisors, federal courts would sacrifice judicial integrity to politics.[109] Criticizing the bill for creating a huge state machinery of enforcement for partisan purposes, Hilary A. Herbert (D-Ala.) complained that enforcing the bill would be beyond the financial capacity of the federal government and likened the manner in which the supervisor controlled elections to the French dictator Louis Napoléon.[110] Meanwhile, William S. Holman (D-Ind.) offered a legalist critique. Since both circuit judges and the chief supervisors they chose were political appointments and would hold office for life, the bill would produce "autocratic power" and keep Republicans in control.[111]

Democrats also attacked the *Siebold* and *Yarbrough* decisions. William Breckinridge of Kentucky doubted that "the dictum of any judge uttered in an opinion and announcing the decision of that court in a private litigation between private citizens" should be used to "bind the consciences and judgments of the members of Congress." With a "shrewd politician, clothed with Federal authority" at the polls, he said, racial tension would arise, trade would be interrupted, and bankruptcies would follow.[112]

Several Republicans joined the Democrats in denouncing the bill. Herman Lehlback of New Jersey argued that it invaded states' rights and would cause unnecessary conflicts between federal enforcement officers and local voters.[113] Surprisingly, opposition also came from southern Republicans, who refused to admit that blacks were politically oppressed. Instead of seeing that the bill would lend them political muscle, southern Republicans viewed it as a sectional measure. Speaking from the vantage point of regional interests, Hamilton G. Ewart, a North Carolina Republican, regarded the Lodge bill as harmful to southern (white) Republicanism. He indicated that since new southern political forces like the Farmers' Alliance were no longer threatened by "the Bourbon Democrat scarecrow of negro supremacy," a Republican call for enforcing black suffrage would be equally unwise and ineffective, because it would destroy southern Republicanism. He believed that breaking the solid South required

Table 6.1

House Passage of H.R. 11045 (the Lodge Bill)

Party	Vote Distribution			
	Yeas	Nays	Not Voting	Total Votes
Republican	154	2	16	172
	(90%)	(1%)	(9%)	(100%)
Democrat	0	147	8	155
		(95%)	(5%)	(100%)
Others	1	0	0	1
	(100%)			(100%)
Summary	155	149	24	

Source: *CR*, 51 Cong. 1 sess., 6940–41.

not the traditional party line but "the great doctrine of protection." The Lodge bill would only "make Republican success at the South in the future an absolute impossibility."[114] Hamilton Dudley Coleman of Louisiana, lecturing his northern brethren that the South wanted "peace, progress, and prosperity" instead of black suffrage, urged them to give up the bill and "open the ranks of the Republican party" to other recruits from southern society, namely the former Confederate supporters.[115]

The House debate on the Lodge bill began on June 26. But before the discussion started, Republicans succeeded in securing the rule for a quick debate by a strictly partisan vote on June 19.[116] Thus, despite all the opposition, Republican managers were able to close the debate after a week. On July 2, the House passed the bill (H.R. 11045), 155 to 149. Two Republicans, Coleman of Louisiana and Lehlback of New Jersey, voted with Democrats against it. The Democrats, now a minority, united to vote against it.[117]

Blacks responded enthusiastically to the Lodge bill. Robert H. Terrel, a law student at Howard University, urged blacks to support the Lodge bill. He regarded it as "more to the Negro than the mere fulfillment of a platform pledge," explaining:

[The election bill is] an evidence that the great common sense of the nation, its sympathies, and the robust qualities of American patriotism are combining to assist the Negro to a complete political assimilation. It is not only the duty of a government to protect the lives of its citizens, but it is the duty of every citizen to see that his fellow citizen is allowed the honest and effective exercise of his civil and political rights.[118]

The northern liberal and independent press denounced Lodge's bill even before its passage. The *Springfield Republican* held that a new federal election law would only create "election commotions in the South in consequence of the wholesale enfranchisement of ignorant creatures" and place southern whites "in mental bondage."[119] After the bill passed the House, the old liberal Republicans mercilessly tore it apart. Calling it "the most reckless, mischievous and wicked measure" of his time, Schurz believed that its purpose was to assure that the protectionists could "gain some more Congressmen in negro districts to pass more tariffs in their interests."[120] Watching the Lodge bill go to the Senate, the *Springfield Republican* hoped that "conservative sentiment" there would "prevent action on the bill." But, as the paper worried, when "aggressiveness, ardor and party discipline" were "on the side of extreme measures," there was "danger that a hesitating opposition" would be "swept away by the current."[121]

The Federal Election Bill (the Lodge Bill) in the Senate

Ideally, the Senate Republican managers of the bill expected quick passage and, with Harrison's approval, to put it into effect before the 1890 election. The situation in the South required such a law, as black Republican leader Robert Smalls reported to Chandler on July 22. "Nothing short of its passage will ever give us our rights as guaranteed to us by the Constitution," the former congressman from South Carolina wrote. Smalls reported that in Beaufort County only about two thousand of the six thousand Republicans were registered under the state laws, which made it difficult for the voters to renew their certificates. If this continued, he stated, no more than two thousand voters in that county could vote in the coming congressional election. Smalls warned that it would "be a great mistake should the Senate fail to pass the bill."[122] In the meantime, Mississippi adopted a new state constitution that limited suffrage by imposing a poll tax and literacy test on voters, disregarding the limitations placed on the state when readmitted after the war.[123]

On August 7, George F. Hoar, who chaired the Senate Committee on Privileges and Elections, reported that the majority of his committee favored the

House bill, with an amendment in the nature of a substitute.[124] But, right before the Senate could discuss the Lodge bill, Matthew S. Quay and J. Donald Cameron, two Republican senators from Pennsylvania known for their protariff attitude and canny politics, moved to postpone action on the Lodge bill until the short session so that the Senate could act on the McKinley tariff bill. Quay and Cameron convinced Senate Republican leaders that the McKinley bill was an immediate necessity for the party in the coming election of 1890, whereas the election bill could wait.[125]

Quay's maneuver jeopardized the election bill's chances. Hoar, the bill's sponsor, was also concerned about the tariff issue, but he did not want to see the enforcement issue disposed of without prospects for consideration in the near future. Oliver H. Platt of Connecticut and Spooner, both supporters of the measure, strongly condemned Quay.[126] The angry Hoar cried that rather than have constitutional government overthrown for the sake of protecting their southern investments, "the people of Massachusetts would prefer to have their factories burned and to live on codfish and 50 cents a day."[127] Under pressure from the bill's managers, the Republican caucus reached an agreement, signed by those at the conference, pledging to take up "on the first day of the next session the Federal Election Bill, and to keep it before the Senate to the exclusion of other legislative business, until it [could] be disposed of by a vote." Party leaders also agreed on a second point, that is, to press for a rule change to secure the bill's passage.[128] The second point was noted earlier by Platt, who believed that the bill's success depended on whether they could "change the rules."[129]

The move by Quay and Cameron was, in a sense, a response to the northern business temper. The *Springfield Republican* anticipated a wave of opposition from the northern business sector, which would help defeat the bill. "The business men of the North cannot afford to have the old sectional rancor between the two sections revived," the paper said, "[and] cannot afford to have their increasingly profitable business relations with the South disturbed."[130] In effect, the party stressed the tariff issue to win support not only from the business class but also from other classes, including working-class voters.

The postponement of the election bill greatly angered its supporters. Both the *New York Tribune* and *Philadelphia Press* denounced Quay's move and called on Republican senators to repudiate it. Lodge also protested against the Senate decision to delay consideration of the election bill. He wrote to Harrison and asked the president to step in:

The resolution of Senator Quay places us in a very dangerous position. Its adoption will in my judgment be not only disastrous to the Tariff bill for the sake of which it is said to have been introduced, but it will be ruinous at the polls. To defeat the Election bill now would be an abandonment of a pledge to which the Republican party is bound by every law of honor[,] good faith and public duty. I wish it would be possible for you to exert some direct and public influence in behalf of the bill. If you do so it would have I think a very decisive effect.[131]

The issue was not really a matter of timing — that is, when to discuss the election bill. It was a matter of party discipline and moral commitment. The House could pass the bill with a slim majority, owing largely to the strong leadership of new House Speaker Thomas Reed, who introduced the new quorum rule and strictly enforced it. The Senate decision to postpone debate on the Lodge bill, the *Nation* observed, simply demonstrated "the collapse of the new program of government devised by 'Tom' Reed and adopted at his orders by the Republicans in the House." The postponement in the first place made the bill's chances in the Senate look "gloomy."[132]

The Senate passed the McKinley tariff bill by a strict party-line vote in early September, and the House approved the law a few days before the Congress adjourned on October 1, only five weeks away from the off-year election. However, the tariff act — a generous grant of power to the president to negotiate trade conventions and modify tariff duties without congressional oversight — did not help the party in the election. The party lost control of the House and lost it by a large margin. With the Republicans carrying only 88 out of 235 seats, Democrats won control of the House by the largest margin since 1875. Fortunately, Republicans retained a majority in the Senate and thus prevented any Democratic legislation.[133]

Analyzing the results of the 1890 election, James S. Clarkson attributed the party's defeat to several reasons: Democratic distortion and misinterpretation of the McKinley tariff act, "soreness and sulking over national or local offices or appointments," the "usual lukewarmness in off years," the ineffectiveness of party's propaganda, and the indifference of rank-and-file Republicans, who simply stayed home on election day. But, in Clarkson's view, the real challenge for Republicans, not only during the past election but more so in the 1892 presidential election, was the Farmers' Alliance, which had been growing fast in the western and southern states. The farmers suffered from real grievances as the nation's financial system failed to help them out of debt or benefit them. "The farmer can no longer be held by the argument of Protection and home market alone," Clarkson warned; "he is going to make trouble in politics, at the expense of the dominant party, until the banking facilities of the country are made as good for him as for the business men or tradesmen of the city and town"; "the Alliance movement will remain till the evil is cured."[134] If Clarkson's analysis was not all that accurate, he definitely was correct in pinpointing the Populist movement as a main reason for the Republican defeat in the Midwest and the South. True, the McKinley tariff act was given too little time to test its full strength before the election, but the outcome, in effect, denied the legitimacy of the tariff issue as the basis for the party's grand coalition, as the protariff and probusiness Republican leaders had believed it to be.

Whatever caused the defeat, it sent Harrison reeling. Dismayed, he told a friend that if the Populists could hold "full one half" of Republican voters in such states as Kansas and Nebraska, the party's future was "not cheerful." He indicated that the party should adopt a policy "liberal enough to include more than a class however large and estimable that class may be."[135] Even before the election, Harrison had been dubious about relying on protectionism as the sole basis for the development of southern Republicanism and the party coalition. He saw a vigorous federal enforcement bill as important to prevent Democratic intimidation in the border states and help to create a permanent protariff majority in the South.[136] Harrison might have been thinking that to deal with the Democrats in the 1892 election, Republicans had to try to unite all the anti-Democratic forces, including the Populists.

Not long after the 1890 election, Harrison began to pay attention to the election bill and even asked his secretary to collect relevant information for him. The Department of Justice informed the president that "no enforcement" of the Enforcement Act of February 28, 1871, had "ever occurred in Georgia, Mississippi, in the northern District of Alabama."[137] In the meantime, local Republican leaders such as Harrison Reed in Florida reported that no Republican efforts could be made in his district "to prepare the way for '92": "There is no possibility of securing freedom & equal rights without federal assistance."[138] In his message to Congress on December 1, 1890, Harrison renewed his plea for the passage of the force bill. To those who doubted its effectiveness, Harrison pointed to the character of its opposition. For those who held the measure to be unconstitutional, a new exercise of power, and an invasion of states' rights, he referred them to Supreme Court decisions affirming the validity of such legislation and to the enforcement acts of 1870–71, by which the Congress had established certain practices for the election of representatives. He affirmed the point made by Lodge: "Such a law should be absolutely nonpartisan and impartial." [139]

Partially because of the pressure from Harrison and partially because of the early caucus agreement, the Republican leaders unanimously decided to bring the bill up for discussion on December 2, the first day of the second session of the Fifty-first Congress. [140] The Republican members of the Committee on Privileges and Elections examined the Senate bill, discussed it among themselves, and proposed and agreed to a large number of modifications. After the Republicans reached agreement, the bill was sent to the full committee (including Democrats George Gray of Delaware and James L. Pugh of Alabama). The committee had stricken from the House bill the section imported from the civil rights chapter of the *Revised Statutes* that might be construed as authorizing the use of troops at the polls and generally to enforce the provisions of this proposed law. The committee had eliminated the house-to-house canvass provided by the House bill. It also agreed to remove the section relating to juries in federal courts. The committee had cut down the House bill by removing and condensing a large number of sections, diminishing its size by fifteen to twenty pages. [141]

The Senate version of the election bill, according to Hoar and Spooner, retained the essence of the Lodge bill but modified it in three areas. First, the House measure contained a provision for revising the laws regarding the summoning and impaneling of juries in federal courts; the Senate bill struck it because it was unwise "to incorporate a provision on that subject, distinct and separate from the subject of elections." Second, the Senate bill contained "stringent and strict provisions to prevent excessive fees on the part of the local officers." [142] Third, the Senate bill omitted "a good many minute regulations as to conduct of the officers, where they should sit in reference to the State officers and so on, which had been proposed in the House bill." [143]

Senate Democrats tried in every possible way to block the discussion of the bill. Their attacks were similar to those of their House counterparts but much harsher. David Turpie of Indiana charged that the bill projected "an entire reversal of the respective political positions of the two races" in the South. He called northern Republicans hypocrites because the "suppression of the colored vote in the North" was a "thing without question, actual, unconditional, and absolute." [144] James Pugh vowed that since the "repeal of the fifteenth amendment" was impossible, "all the friends of white supremacy" had to join efforts to "make it as harmless as possible."[145] Arthur Gorman of Maryland challenged the lifetime appointment of the chief supervisor, who fit "in no place in the mechanism" of the government.[146] James George of Mississippi, which had recently accomplished what C. Vann Woodward terms the "Second Mississippi Plan" to disfranchise black men, argued that if the bill became law, all state election officers would be virtually converted into federal officers.[147] Determined to filibuster, Democrats constantly interrupted the discussion and, when the Republicans pressed for a vote, foiled the scheme by leaving the Senate chamber, preventing a quorum from assembling.

Republican opposition came mainly from western states, where the party had lost many seats in the recent election. William Stewart of Nevada led the western fight against the election bill. In Stewart's opinion, even if the bill became law, southern sentiment would make it unenforceable. Reviewing the history of enforcement, the author of the final version of the Fifteenth Amendment and floor manager of the first enforcement act in 1870 argued that federal enforcement would not help uplift blacks if they did not acquire "education, position and property." Time and endurance, Stewart advised, were the remedy for racial prejudice against black voters. While still claiming to be "a friend of the negro," Stewart declared that on this bill he had to break with his party.[148]

Seeing the party's unity to pass the law falling apart, Spooner came to the rescue. In a long speech on December 20, Spooner defended the bill's constitutionality and rejected the Democratic charges point by point. The bill, Spooner declared, was aimed at every spot in the nation, but the South was where the proposed law was "especially needed." He referred to the recent imposition of a literacy test by Mississippi's constitution as the second "Mississippi plan" to deprive blacks of their voting rights. Spooner also criticized Stewart's argument that southern sentiment would block enforcement. Those "sworn to duty under the Constitution" should never bow to the old southern sentiment.[149]

Spooner may have been right to locate partisan disagreement on the election bill in the fundamental fact that Democrats belonged "to the strict constructionists" of the Constitution.[150] But the same could not be said of the revolt of western Republicans, led by Stewart and motivated by the determination to defend local economic interests and to punish Harrison's breach of his pledge to aid the West on currency issues. Money had been one of the issues that cut across the party line since the Hayes administration. There had long been a crusade by the western mining states to push the federal government to include silver in full-bodied federal coinage so that the region could expect a higher price for its product and, consequently, greater prosperity. The western states supported Harrison's nomination in 1888 with the understanding that he was a friend of silver, although he never committed to free coinage of silver.[151] In June 1890, Senate silverites tried to add a free-silver amendment to the Sherman Silver Purchase Act, which allowed the government to purchase 4.5 million ounces of silver each month, but the amendment was defeated in the House under the leadership of the antisilver Speaker Thomas Reed. When the silverites were persuaded to vote for a compromise version of the silver purchase bill, they were assured of a reward: a free-coinage bill in a later session.[152] The Republican defeat in 1890 was interpreted by some members of the silver bloc – silver senators from the major mining states of Nevada, Colorado, Idaho, and other new western states that the Republican Congress had brought into the Union – as a mandate for a free-coinage bill. In addition, they were infuriated to learn that Harrison was less committed to the free-coinage issue than they had expected, and they interpreted his hesitation as a breach of his early pledge. With time running out in the short lame-duck session of Congress, silver Republicans were anxious to get the free-coinage issue settled, even at the expense of the election bill to which they had earlier committed themselves.[153]

This probably explained the legislative coup d'état on January 5, 1891, in the Senate. The month-long fruitless debate on the election bill had already bat-

Table 6.2

Senate Vote on Stewart's Motion

| Party | Vote Distribution | | | |
	Yeas	Nays	Not Voting	Total Votes
Republican	8	29	14	51
	(16%)	(57%)	(27%)	(100%)
Democrat	26	0	11	37
	(70%)	(0%)	(30%)	(100%)
Summary	34	29	25	

Source: CR, 51 Cong. 2 sess., 912–13.

tered the morale of Republicans, some of whom had no particular feeling about the bill from the beginning. When Hoar moved to discuss the bill, Stewart rose and moved to discuss S. No. 4675, the free-coinage bill. Despite Hoar's angry protest, the Senate voted 34 to 29 to put aside the election bill and pick up the silver bill.

Among the 34 yea votes were eight Republicans: Stewart and John P. Jones of Nevada, William J. McConnell and George L. Shoup of Idaho, Leland Stanford of California, Henry M. Teller and Edward O. Wolcott of Colorado, and William D. Washburn of Minnesota.[154] All but one of these Republicans had pledged in a written statement to stand for the election bill until the vote in the Senate. "The Lodge bill," the *Nation* announced, "had been buried by a bargain between the Democrats and free silverites."[155] Writing after the silver Republicans had their way, Spooner informed his Wisconsin friends that the election bill was sidetracked "by the Confederates and a few alleged Republicans."[156] The "weakness" in the party's ranks, he told another friend, prevented the party from adopting a rule to limit the debate, rendering the bill's quick passage "impractical."[157] But he vowed that his party would renew the fight "as soon as the silver bill [was] disposed of." He predicted that more deserters might block the bill, but he maintained, "We will at least put the fellows where they must show their hands."[158]

The free-coinage bill passed the Senate but failed in the House, where many northeastern Republicans were not ready to abandon the gold standard. After the free-silver issue was dropped on January 16, Hoar immediately moved to resume debate on the election bill. Democrats did everything possible to prolong or disable the debate. While those present kept introducing impossible amendments and suggestions, others simply wandered in the galleries outside the Senate, preventing a quorum. At one point, only thirty-four senators answered a roll call.[159] Stewart moved to recommit the election bill to the Committee on Privileges and Elections, but his suggestion was rejected. The Senate, however, ran into a stalemate when it voted on whether to table the amendment made by John H. Reagan (D-Tex.), and the debate began anew only after Vice President Levi P. Morton cast a party-line vote to break the 33 – 33 tie.[160]

Republicans realized that unless they could change the rule of the debate, the bill would die of the Democratic filibustering. On January 22, Nelson Aldrich of Rhode Island, chairman of the Rules Committee, reported out the resolution for stopping debate, which he had introduced in December. This resolution allowed any senator to demand closure after a bill had been under con-

Table 6.3

Senate Refusal to Table Wolcott's Motion

| Party | Vote Distribution | | | |
	Yeas	Nays	Not Voting	Total Votes
Republican	34	6	11	51
	(67%)	(12%)	(21%)	(100%)
Democrat	0	29	8	37
		(78%)	(22%)	(100%)
Summary	34	35	19	

Source: *CR*, 51 Cong. 2 sess., 1740.

sideration for a reasonable length of time and, further, allowed the vote on the
bill if the demand was seconded by a majority of senators present.[161] As the
Senate began to debate the Aldrich resolution, Wolcott, one of the eight silver
Republican defectors in January, suddenly interrupted Democrat John Tyler
Morgan of Alabama, who was speaking against Aldrich's resolution, and moved
to consider S. No. 12500, making an apportionment of House members. When
the managers of the election bill moved to table Wolcott's proposal, the Senate
rejected that request by a vote of 34 to 35, with 19 abstaining.

A few minutes later, the Senate accepted Wolcott's motion by a reversed vote
of 35 to 34, with the same 19 not voting. Analysis of the votes shows that the
Democrats were joined by the Republicans from the silver states of Colorado
and Nevada (Jones, Stewart, Teller, and Wolcott) and by J. Donald Cameron of
Pennsylvania and William Washburn of Minnesota.[162] "Too angry to write,"
Spooner condemned the "legislative supremacy" of the "Confederacy and the
Western Mining Camps." He spoke bitterly about Stewart and others who betrayed "the Republican party and the rights of citizenship for silver."[163] The
election bill was never again brought up.

The death of the election bill brought to an end a memorable era in the history
of the Republican party. From December 1863, when James M. Ashley of Ohio
first tried to incorporate black suffrage into a reconstruction bill, the party had
come a long way to reach the Lodge bill. In more than twenty-five years, against
all odds, the party managed to put into the Constitution the Fifteenth Amend-

Table 6.4
Senate Acceptance of Wolcott's Motion

| | Vote Distribution | | | |
Party	Yeas	Nays	Not Voting	Total Votes
Republican	6	34	11	51
	(12%)	(67%)	(21%)	(100%)
Democrat	29	0	8	37
	(78%)		(22%)	(100%)
Summary	35	34	19	

Source: *CR*, 51 Cong. 2 sess., 1740.

ment, enact a series of enforcement laws, secure the constitutionality of federal enforcement, succeed in resisting Democratic attempts to repeal the enforcement laws, and forge the dynamics to push for a more effective enforcement bill. During this time, the party had expanded its commitment from merely enforcing black suffrage to establishing a comprehensive and meticulously designed national system of election supervision, something both ideologically and institutionally embedded in the spirit of the Civil War amendments. However, by January 1891, the Republican party was unable to continue its commitment to black suffrage and federal enforcement. The cause had to be put aside for something else.

Why? Several reasons quickly come to mind: the betrayal by the silver Republicans; the fear within Republican ranks of the revival of radical Reconstruction; the deterioration of the party's political conscience and moral commitment; agrarian upheaval in the West and South, which enhanced the negative image of blacks as an economic competitor for poor whites and pressed the Republicans for more financial legislation; and, last but not least, the conventional suspicion and resistance about empowering the federal government to move into the political spheres of the states.

All of this may be persuasive in explaining the party's failure to enact the election law in 1891. But the election bill failed because of more fundamental problems that plagued the party from the beginning of the 1888 presidential campaign and, probably, even further back. It is perhaps more enlightening to analyze why the Lodge bill failed in light of why, in 1870 and 1871, Republicans succeeded in pushing through the first enforcement laws. First, ideological impulses for black suffrage were not the primary motivation for many Republican congressmen, or for many party leaders, during the campaign of 1888. The same cannot be said of the early 1870s, although ideology was not the only force behind the Republican party. Few of the 1890 Republicans maintained the same degree of faith in and commitment to black suffrage as the first-generation party leaders. The survivors of the older generation – Edmunds, Hoar, Sherman – had limited influence; Stewart only helped to dismantle the cause. In 1890, ideological commitment was no longer a holding power as in the 1870s.

Second, although in both periods Republicans expected some pragmatic, immediate, and direct outcomes to be generated from their efforts to enforce the Fifteenth Amendment, the enforcement program weighed differently in the party's political agenda. In the early 1870s, enforcing the Fifteenth Amendment (which included protecting the southern Republican governments and preventing the quick comeback of the Democrats) was one of the party's major policies in securing control of the federal government. In the late 1880s and early 1890s, reenforcement of the Fifteenth Amendment (which included upholding black suffrage and expanding federal supervision at the polls) was perceived by many as only one of the options available for the party to employ to consolidate its power and perpetuate its influence. As the political locus shifted from the traditional North-versus-South pattern to a more complicated cluster of economic and political conflicts across geographical divisions, the cause of enforcement was reduced to a national issue of regional effect, instead of being a regional issue of national importance.

Third, the party's strength in Congress in the early 1870s differed from the later period. At the third session of the Forty-first Congress, in which the Enforcement Act of February 28, 1871, was passed, Republicans had an absolute majority in both houses and a determined president sitting in the White House.[164] But in the Fifty-first Congress, the Republican majority in both houses was slim. Thanks to Thomas Reed's majestic control, the House passed the Lodge bill. But in the Senate, the defection of a few silver Republicans could become detrimental to the whole cause of enforcement, which had come a long way through thick and thin. Even with a majority, the party in 1891 had no real institutional guarantee for the election bill.

Politically speaking, the Republican party in 1891 still functioned as a vehicle of certain political and economic interests as it did back in 1871. Precisely because of its function as a means of gathering, transmitting, and promoting the interests of certain segments of society, the party had a life. To sustain that life and maintain its vitality, the party had to be responsive to the demands of its new recruits, who did not live in the party's past. Although the party's commitment to black rights declined after the end of Reconstruction, the party had never been pushed, as it was in 1891, to make a conscious decision as to whether to abandon the cause of enforcing the Fifteenth Amendment. When the Republicans did make that decision, the party closed the chapter of its political activism in behalf of black rights in the nineteenth century.

Equality Deferred, 1892–1910

After the Lodge bill failed to pass the Senate in January 1891, the northern press speculated that federal enforcement of the Fifteenth Amendment was doomed. The *Nation* commented that since the issue of enforcement had dogged the party for so long, many Republicans would "be glad to get rid of a system" that had been "tried in the balance and found wanting." The weekly predicted that the Lodge bill's defeat would improve Democratic chances of winning the next election.[1] In their platform in 1892, the Democrats claimed that the Lodge bill's defeat gave their party a mandate to repeal the enforcement acts. Federal enforcement policy, Democrats warned, "if sanctioned by law, would mean dominance of a self-perpetuating oligarchy of office-holders." During the 1892 campaign, the Democratic press thoroughly exploited the issue of the force bill.[2]

Vowing not to "relax its efforts" to pursue "the integrity of the ballot and the purity of elections," the Republicans in their platform cautiously placed enforcement of federal election laws as the last principle of its domestic policies. The whole platform, devoted to the protective tariff, trade, monetary reform, and foreign relations, only made a one-sentence denunciation of the southern outrages "perpetrated upon American citizens for political reasons."[3] Black Republican leader John R. Lynch of Mississippi was invited to speak in Chicago on the importance of maintaining the party's stance on the federal election bill, but the party's determination to pursue the issue remained vague, as Harrison, who won renomination, evaded a clear and straightforward endorsement of the bill.[4] Part of the Republican caution arose from the tactical concern that a strong commitment to the federal election bill would hurt the so-called fusion between the Republicans and Populists in the South. As the Populist movement expanded into the South in the early 1890s, Republicans saw an opportunity to break the Democratic dominance in that region. But neither the Populists nor the Republicans were genuinely committed to cooperation in principle.[5]

At the same time, Democratic intimidation and fraud continued to prevail in the South and blocked either Populists or Republicans from carrying the region. The 1892 presidential election resulted in a Republican defeat. Harrison was about 400,000 popular votes behind Democrat Grover Cleveland, who also led Harrison in electoral votes, 277 to 145. Twenty-two electoral votes went to James B. Weaver of Iowa, the Populist candidate, who also won about one million popular votes.[6] The policies of the Harrison administration were mainly responsible for popular disaffection and desertion, especially in the North. Both the McKinley tariff and the force bill became Democratic targets. Cleveland won the South and four important northern states—New York, New Jersey, Connecticut, and Indiana. Democrats regained control of the Senate and House, although in the latter the margin was not so impressive.[7] For the first time since the Civil War, Democrats controlled both the legislative and executive branches of the federal government. Such control offered them the long-sought chance to repeal the enforcement laws.

Democrats began their repeal battle soon after they won the House and defeated the federal election bill. On July 19, 1892, the House authorized its last investigation of federal election laws. The committee submitted a report in early 1893, recommending the repeal of the enforcement acts. The reasons for the repeal were that (1) the enforcement acts were useless to prevent or punish crime, since no conviction had resulted from trials under these laws; (2) enforcement was too expansive; (3) these laws were partisan by nature and used for partisan purposes; and (4) enforcement interfered with the voting rights of qualified voters.[8] Repeal, however, was impossible in the Fifty-second Congress, since Republicans still controlled the Senate. Once the Fifty-third Congress convened, however, Democrats introduced bills to remove the enforcement acts from federal law books.

On September 11, 1893, Henry St. George Tucker of Virginia, speaking for the House Committee on the Election of the President, Vice-President, and Representatives in Congress, introduced H.R. 2331, proposing "to repeal all statutes relating to supervisors of elections and special deputy marshals, and for other purposes."[9] Specifically, the bill intended to repeal sections 2002 and 2005–2020 inclusive, under the title "Elective Franchise" of the *Revised Statutes*, all provisions relating to the appointment, qualifications, power, duties, and compensation of federal supervisors of elections. Tucker's bill also proposed to remove sections 2021–2031, relating to the appointments, duties, and compensation of special deputies. He also asked to repeal sections 5506,

5511–5515 (inclusive), and 5520–5523 (inclusive), under the title "Crimes" of the *Revised Statutes*, provisions relating to the punishment of frauds and crimes under the enforcement acts.[10]

The bill was so comprehensive and thorough that it intended to eliminate all of the five enforcement laws enacted by the Republican Congress between 1870 and 1872.[11] These laws, according to Tucker, were beyond the constitutional boundaries allowed to Congress in regulating suffrage. Citing section 4 of Article I of the Constitution, Tucker argued that the original right of suffrage rested with the states, where the power to regulate suffrage should originate.[12] Other Democrats backed Tucker by denouncing the enforcement laws as "the curse of Cromwell." Josiah Patterson of Tennessee concluded that the black race for the moment was "incapable of self-government," that universal black suffrage was "impracticable."[13] John L. McLaurin of South Carolina supported the repeal because southern blacks "were never better treated, were never better prosperous, and never cared less for politics than now." What blacks needed, he stated, was to be let alone to work out their own destiny.[14]

House Republicans formed a united front to resist the bill. Republican challenge focused on two points: the enforcement acts were legitimate constitutional results of the Civil War and Reconstruction and crucial to the purity of national elections. Adopting the party's Civil War ideology, Morriot Brosius of Pennsylvania argued that since suffrage was a "constitutional mode of expression" involving the consent of the governed, the national government had the right to regulate it. The enforcement acts were the outcome of the altered conditions of the nation's politics, which required "additional safeguards, [and] the extension of Federal functions." The Democratic defense of the repeal, in his view, simply showed that the state sovereignty theories of John Calhoun had "had an asylum in the minds of only those who never [forgot] and rarely learn[ed] anything."[15]

Once, the Supreme Court opinion on *Yarbrough* became a weapon for Republicans. Charles Daniels of New York reminded Democrats of the unanimous decision that supported federal power to protect black voting rights.[16] When William H. Denson (D-Ala.) referred to the *Yarbrough* decision to show the North's distrust of the South and denied federal power to supervise elections, George Ray of New York, leading the Republican force on the House floor, immediately engaged in an intense verbal exchange with Denson over the functions of the federal government. Ray saw the Democratic bill as a counterrevolutionary effort to reverse the outcome of the late war.[17] In a major speech on

October 6, Ray reinforced Republican charges that southern states had openly disfranchised blacks and insisted on federal power to secure the purity of federal elections. States might die, but the nation would live, Ray concluded.[18] Republicans made several attempts to amend the bill with the intention to save at least part of the enforcement acts, but the Democratic majority rejected their proposals.[19] On October 10, the Democratic majority passed the bill (H.R. 2331) by a vote of 201 to 102, with 50 abstaining. Of the 126 available Republican votes, an overwhelming majority voted against the bill.[20]

When H.R. 2331 reached the Senate, Republicans managed to delay discussion until the second session of the Fifty-third Congress.[21] Immediately after the second session convened on December 4, 1894, Democrats forced the Senate to discuss the bill. The Senate Committee on Privileges and Elections, headed by former Confederate Zebulon B. Vance of North Carolina, recommended the House bill without amendment. William E. Chandler, whom illness had prevented from defending the federal election bill in the Fifty-first Congress and was now determined to save the enforcement laws, insisted that the opinion of the Republican minority be presented to the Senate.[22] A dozen Republican senators spoke in the two-month debate, trying to prevent or scale down the repeal. George F. Hoar, one of the remaining Republicans who had participated in making the enforcement acts in the early 1870s, defended the laws "as a matter of course" derived from experience. In responding to the

Table 7.1

House Passage of H.R. 2331

| Party | Vote Distribution | | | |
	Yeas	Nays	Not Voting	Total Votes
Republican	0	102 (81%)	24 (19%)	126 (100%)
Democrat	194 (89%)	0	25 (11%)	219 (100%)
Others	7 (88%)	0	1 (12%)	8 (100%)
Summary	201	102	50	

Source: CR, 53 Cong. 1 sess., 2378.

Democratic claim of states' rights to control suffrage, Hoar lectured the Democrats with a line of thinking that in every sense matched the 1870 radical Republican rationale:

> We are a nation, not a league of nations. In regard to matters which are within our national domain we are a sovereign, not a league of sovereigns, although the States undoubtedly, in my judgment, have very large powers of sovereignty, and one of the things which is purely national is the United States House of Representatives. The members of that body do not represent States as do the Senators; they represent districts of the United States and the people thereof in their relation to and as a part of the national legislative power. Therefore, in all logic and in all reason the function of choosing those is a national function, the superintendence of that function is a national duty, securing that right is a national obligation.[23]

Chandler submitted an amendment to the bill, which required the appointment of a poll watcher representing candidates for congressional positions at the request of one hundred resident voters. His purpose was to make a contingency in case existing federal enforcement laws were wiped out. The ultimate object, Chandler said, was "to make this a paramount right under the national law" that "each candidate for Congress may have a watcher at the registration place and at each polling precinct." Orville Platt (R-Conn.) supported Chandler's amendment and believed that its operation would add no expenses to the federal government.[24] For James Wilson of Iowa, preservation of the 1870 enforcement acts meant more than retaining the ideology of Republican Reconstruction and the Fourteenth and Fifteenth Amendments. He believed that "the sections of the Revised Statutes relating to Federal elections" should be preserved because the southern constitutional campaign against black enfranchisement was unfolding. Wilson cited the Mississippi constitution of 1892 (in which one provision required voters to understand the state constitution before they could vote), arguing that the real purpose of the repeal was to remove federal election officers from the states so that they could carry out the Mississippi Plan.[25]

Henry Cabot Lodge strengthened the Republican protest by giving a learned historical review of the enforcement acts. He argued that during the debate on the federal election bill in the Fifty-first Congress, even the Democrats recognized the constitutionality of federal enforcement and that the Court decisions on *Siebold* and *Yarbrough* had clarified the point. Lodge also attacked the literacy requirement in the Mississippi constitution of 1892, which disfranchised the black man not because he was "ignorant" but because he was "black." To give a black person his vote in theory but take it away from him in practice, Lodge cried, was "the worse of all oppressions."[26]

William Stewart of Nevada, the author of the final version of the Fifteenth Amendment and Republican floor leader for the first enforcement act in 1870, was, ironically, one of the only two Republicans who supported the repeal of the enforcement acts. Since his departure from the party line in the Fifty-first Congress, Stewart had become so obsessed with the silver question that even during his speech on H.R. 2331 he could not help but constantly return to the subject; his Republican colleagues had to keep him focused on the enforcement laws. He offered no substantive argument either for or against repeal except his repeated theories about remonetizing silver. Eventually, he would vote with the Democrats.[27]

Watching Stewart's defection "with feelings of no ordinary regret," Chandler continued the fight until the very last minute. To demonstrate the deterioration of the conditions of southern blacks, Chandler read a recent speech by Frederick Douglass in Washington, D.C., exposing the mob rule under which blacks lived.[28] But on February 7, 1894, the Senate passed H.R. 2331, 39 to 28, with 17 absences. Only two Republicans, Stewart of Nevada and William A. Peffer of Kansas, voted for the bill. Twenty-eight Republicans (72 percent of the party's total votes) voted against it, while another 9 did not vote. Of the 43 Democratic

Table 7.2

Senate Passage of H.R. 2331

Party	Vote Distribution			
	Yeas	Nays	Not Voting	Total Votes
Republican	2	28	9	39
	(5%)	(72%)	(23%)	(100%)
Democrat	35	0	8	43
	(80%)		(18%)	(100%)
Others	2	0	0	2
	(100%)			(100%)
Summary	39	28	17	

Source: CR, 53 Cong. 2 sess., 1999.

votes, 35 voted for the bill, 8 abstained, and none voted against it.[29] On February 8, President Cleveland approved the bill, and all sections concerned with the repeal act, forty in all, ceased to be the law of the land.[30]

The political battle against enforcement was over; judicial action was close behind. In 1903, in *James v. Bowman*, the Supreme Court invalidated section 5507 of the *Revised Statutes* (which was originally sec. 5 of the Enforcement Act of May 31, 1870) because it purported to prohibit individual action, whereas the Fifteenth Amendment banned actions only "by the United States or by any State." This section and several others — 5516 (sec. 11 of the Enforcement Act of May 31, 1870), 5509 (sec. 7 of the same law), and 5518 and 5519 (sec. 2 of the Ku Klux Force Act of April 20, 1871) — were repealed by Congress in March 1909. In March 1911, Congress repealed section 1786 of the *Revised Statutes* (sec. 14 of the Enforcement Act of May 31, 1870), 1787 (sec. 15 of the same law), 699 (secs. 16 and 18 of the same law and sec. 1 of the Ku Klux Force Act of April 20, 1871), 645 (sec. 17 of the Enforcement Act of February 28, 1871), 800 (sec. 5 of the Ku Klux Force Act), and 629 (secs. 1 and 6 of the same law). Of all the sections of the Republican-made enforcement laws, only three — 2204, 5508, and 5510 (respectively secs. 1, 6, and 17 of the Enforcement Act of May 31, 1870) — have survived and have been retained in the modern-day *United States Code*.[31]

The removal of the enforcement laws from federal statute books also removed the legal basis for federal interference in elections and left the enforcement of the Fifteenth Amendment to the states. Southern states had long regarded the enforcement acts as federal codes restricting states' power in regulating elections; now they began an open and unrestricted movement to disfranchise black voters, which had been under way since the early 1880s.[32] Mississippi took the lead. In August 1890, the Mississippi constitutional convention, which the recently victorious Democrats dominated, decided on several devices to curtail black suffrage. The suffrage article of the new state constitution allowed illiterate voters to register only after they demonstrated a satisfactory understanding of the state constitution (as judged by the state registrar). The new suffrage article also imposed a one-year residence requirement in the precinct and payment of a two-dollar poll tax annually for two years before the election.[33] The Mississippi constitution, which the Republicans in the Senate called a new "Mississippi Plan," proved effective not only in disfranchising black voters but also in blocking the Populists who had worked to challenge the Democrats by forging a new party among the poor white Mississippian farmers. According to J. Morgan Kousser, the new constitution reduced black turnout "from about 30 percent in the 1888 presidential race to virtually nothing thereafter."[34]

Other southern states followed suit. Between 1895 and 1910, seven followed the Mississippi scheme to enhance their suffrage restrictions or invent new ones to reduce and eliminate black votes. The Ben Tillman – led Democrats of South Carolina, where the eight-box law was adopted in 1882 as a device to confuse black voters, proposed to confine suffrage to those who paid a poll tax six months before the election and who were literate or owned three hundred dollars' worth of taxable property. Meanwhile, a literary test was imposed on illiterates who had applied for permanent registration as voters before 1898.[35] In Louisiana, where two earlier laws already had substantially reduced black votes by 1897, a new state constitution became law in 1898. Among other things, it established the "grandfather" plan, intending to disqualify black voters while providing a mechanism to qualify desirable white voters. Under the new state constitution, only 2.9 percent of black adult males were registered to vote in 1902 and 1.1 percent in 1904.[36] In 1901, despite the resistance of black voters, Alabama adopted the "old soldier" and "grandfather" plans in its constitution. The next year, Virginia Democrats proclaimed a new state constitution with a suffrage plan practically similar to that of the Alabama constitution.[37] In 1908, Georgia adopted new suffrage regulations in its state constitution on the basis of the Alabama model. The new Georgia suffrage measure, as with its counterparts in other southern states, was designed to evade the Fifteenth Amendment without legally violating it. Its purposes were to place great discretionary power in the hands of local election and registration officials to determine the legal qualifications of voters and, ultimately, to repeal the Fifteenth Amendment in act, if not in fact.[38]

The effects of black disfranchisement were profound and comprehensive. In the 1896 presidential election, about 130,000 blacks in Louisiana registered to vote, and black registrants were in the majority in twenty-six parishes. In 1900, two years after the state constitution went into effect, only 5,320 blacks registered as qualified voters, a decline of 96 percent from 1896. The new Georgia state constitution reduced black registration from 28.3 percent in 1904 to 4.3 percent in 1910.[39] In the meantime, the total turnout in the South also declined. According to the leading study of black disfranchisement of the period, an average 64 percent of the southern adult males turned out to vote in the elections in the 1880s; this figure increased to 73 percent in the first half of 1890s. But by 1910, the southern turnout declined to an average of 30 percent. Thus, the proclaimed system of political democracy had been virtually transformed into a system of political oligarchy.[40]

Watching Democrats ruthlessly impose new suffrage codes in the South from 1890 to 1910, the Republican party could do very little to challenge or resist the process of disfranchisement. The defeat of the federal election bill in 1891 and the repeal of the enforcement acts in 1894 removed the constitutional and political basis on which the party's cause of black suffrage had rested since 1870. Republicans had attempted to promote cooperation with the Populists, but their success was moderate and temporary.[41] In 1894, owing largely to Democratic failures in managing domestic issues, Republicans won back both branches of Congress, but with Cleveland in power, the Republican majority in Congress could do no more than frustrate Democratic plans.[42]

The 1896 presidential campaign proved no better. It was essentially a battle over financial issues, especially the silver question. Although the party's headquarters maintained a "Colored Bureau," its platform made only a passing mention of citizens' right to a free ballot and fair count. The split of the coalition of Democrats, free-silver Republicans, and Populists, the heavy financial contributions made by the northeastern industrialists, and the astute campaign style of the party's nominee, William McKinley—all helped secure the Republicans' final victory.[43]

Once again, Republicans controlled Congress and the presidency in March 1897, when the Fifty-fifth Congress convened. And this Republican dominance of the national power would continue until 1910, when Democrats finally regained control of the House. But this fourteen-year Republican restoration to federal power brought no major Republican policies intending to restore to black men the right to vote. True, in 1896, the Republican party gained great power—leading the Democrats in the House, by 204 to 113, and in the Senate, by 47 to 33—to act, but McKinley, despite his early record of supporting black rights, was cautious about bringing the issue of race back into national politics.[44] Instead of arousing sectional confrontation, McKinley did his best to promote the sentiment of conciliation. In an address to the Georgia legislature on December 14, 1898, McKinley declared that sectional lines no longer marred "the map of the United States." Under such guidelines, McKinley remained silent on race issues, even when pressed to give federal protection to blacks threatened with lynching.[45] During McKinley's presidency, Republicans in Congress made no serious efforts to deal with the issue of black disfranchisement in the South.

The 1900 Republican campaign gave more than a passing mention to the issue of black voting rights. Responding to the new suffrage restrictions in several southern state constitutions, the platform condemned the devices as "revolutionary" in defiance of the Fifteenth Amendment. But while wanting black support at the party's nomination, McKinley failed to mention the need to remedy black disfranchisement in his second inaugural address.[46]

If any of the Republican presidents during this period should have cared about black suffrage, McKinley was probably the one. He had fought not only in the Civil War but also for the earlier Republican legislation on black rights in Congress. But his silence on black voting rights revealed how much the Republican party had traveled away from wartime sentiments and political outlook. The Republican victories in 1896 and 1900 were won without the southern support. The return of the northeastern states to the Republican camp and the addition of the western states might have induced some Republicans to the belief that black suffrage was no longer useful or politically expedient.

Theodore Roosevelt, who succeeded the slain McKinley in September 1901, intended to reinvigorate the party's cause to break the solid South, but he relied on a few trusted men in various states and was not very successful, even though he won the 1904 presidential election. Once again, the Republican success rested on the party's grip of the Northeast, Midwest, and border states.[47] In Congress, black suffrage was discussed or mentioned only when Democrats introduced resolutions to repeal the Fifteenth Amendment and the reduction provision of the Fourteenth Amendment.[48] Occasionally, Republicans would call for investigations of suffrage restrictions, as Charles Dick of Ohio and Edgar D. Crumpacker of Indiana did respectively in 1901 and 1902, or make a speech to defend the Fifteenth Amendment, as Edward de V. Morrell of Pennsylvania did in 1904. But neither the president nor Congress was prepared to fight.[49]

The most important action in the Republican fight on black suffrage was probably the measure presented by Senator Thomas C. Platt of New York on December 7, 1904. Platt's proposal required enforcement of the representation reduction provision of the Fourteenth Amendment—that is, to reduce the House seats for those states that, in federal elections, denied the right to vote to males twenty-one or over for causes not permitted in the Constitution. But Roosevelt considered the enforcement proposal unwise.[50]

Roosevelt was more articulate about the race question in his second term, but no more active. After consulting such leaders as Booker T. Washington, his onetime guest at the White House, Roosevelt spoke of the "Negro Problem" at a Lincoln Day dinner in February 1905. He criticized northern indifference toward the South and urged equal treatment of blacks before the law, but he also insisted that the "backward race" must be trained without harming the high civilization of the "forward race."[51] However, the president took no real action to correct black disfranchisement. W. E. B. Du Bois, then teaching at Atlanta University and involved in founding the Niagara Movement, clashed with Roosevelt's do-nothing policy. The movement published a pamphlet in 1907 calling on northern blacks to vote against Roosevelt. In March 1908, Du Bois himself announced his intention to support Democrat William J. Bryan, for "an avowed enemy" was "better than [a] false friend."[52]

In retrospect, the defeat of the federal election bill in 1891 signaled the end of Republican activism and commitment to enforcing the Fifteenth Amendment. The repeal of the enforcement acts in 1894 closed that chapter in the history of Reconstruction. By the time the party regained the institutional mechanisms for enforcement between 1896 and 1910, the momentum and vigor were gone. More important, by the 1890s, the nation's political and economic conditions had so changed that the issue of race no longer held its original vitality in party politics.

Historically speaking, the fall of black suffrage enforcement was sadly inevitable. First, the Republican party had never truly united in establishing and enforcing black suffrage. The party's prewar disagreement over how black freedom and equality should be defined continued throughout the war and Reconstruction. Many Republicans accepted black suffrage only when it became indispensable to postwar political reorganization. But when enforcement was required to maintain the usefulness of the Fifteenth Amendment, the party was torn between those who insisted on a firm and comprehensive enforcement program, those who preferred only limited federal assistance to the freedmen, and those who opposed the idea of enforcement. This confusion was further complicated by the changing positions of the Republican lawmakers, who also acted according to local interests.

In addition, Republicans maintained black suffrage as both an ideological commitment and a pragmatic leverage to generate political benefits. In actual party politics, the latter function weighed more than the former, although the former had never been completely ignored or abandoned. Consequently, enforcement laws were made in response to particular political situations more than to a belief in the need to set up permanent federal protection of black men's rights. In turn, each Republican administration from Grant to Harrison had to respond to popular and internal pressures on the issue of black suffrage, which were the main sources from which their policies regarding enforcement were formulated. Although these Republican administrations contributed to maintaining the principle of black suffrage, each also contributed to the fall of the cause, as demonstrated by Grant's inconsistency, Hayes's political naïveté about the South, Garfield's lack of timely action, Arthur's wishful thinking on the Republican-Readjuster alliance, and Harrison's concession to the tariff Republicans.

Correlatedly, black suffrage enforcement was carried out in a period when the essence of American constitutionalism was being redefined. As shown in the previous chapters, many Republican lawmakers were reluctant to move too far beyond the original federal-state structure. The times required an active federal role in mapping out the new national political order, but the Republicans who composed the main portion of the federal political landscape could neither ignore nor escape their commitments to local and regional constituencies. Such concerns had formed the core of the Republican conservatism, presenting major challenges to the party's enforcement and reenforcement programs.

It is, however, a remarkable fact that, given the historical circumstances under which black suffrage was established and enforced and the inertia associated with party politics and constitutional practice, enforcement of black suffrage remained on the federal statute books for nearly a quarter of the century. How did it manage to survive? What impact did it have on later constitutional developments regarding black rights in the United States? In discussing the history of black suffrage enforcement, it is important to remember that the Republican-supported idea of political equality between black and white men, like the ideas of black emancipation and citizenship, drew its original ideological strength from the Declaration of Independence. The idea of equal rights before the law, as derived from the party's prewar free labor ideology, provided an ideological foundation for Republican policies regarding black civil and political rights. But the party never could have engineered its programs to establish and enforce black suffrage without the victory of the Republican-led Union in the Civil War. The Union's victory, together with black participation and emancipation, enabled the party to transform the idea of equal civil and political

rights only for white American men into the idea of equal rights for all American men, black and white. This ideological transformation materialized in the
three postwar constitutional amendments, which in turn became the constitutional basis and requirement for enforcing black voting rights.

Equally important were two other results of the Civil War: the establishment
of national authority over citizens' civil and political rights, and Republican
control of the national power in the postwar period. Both provided institutional
mechanisms to consolidate the war's results. The party's control of federal
power induced it to identify its cause as the cause of the nation. The very notion
that the government must protect the rights of its citizens was an important
idea shared by every Republican administration during this period, although
not every one of them sincerely made efforts to enforce it. Even during the
Democratic interval between 1885 and 1889, the Cleveland administration had
to pledge its commitment to enforcing the Fifteenth Amendment, or at least go
through the motions. The Republican Congresses and administrations did their
best in 1870s and 1880s to block the Democratic attempts to repeal the enforcement laws. The Supreme Court, although opposed to federal legislation
enforcing social equality, also offered important constitutional support to national protection of black voting rights, especially in early 1880s. All of this had
a great deal to do with the institutional mechanisms that maintained the legality of the idea of enforcement.

The repeal of the enforcement laws in 1894 ended Republican enforcement,
but the Democrats were unable to repeal the Fifteenth Amendment, which
provided a vital and viable constitutional source for African Americans to regain their political rights in the twentieth century. The spirit of early federal
enforcement and the Fifteenth Amendment per se became the basis for the
African American struggle to regain franchise in the twentieth century. When
Booker T. Washington was advocating the idea of industrial education as a way
to elevate African Americans from poverty and social discrimination, W. E. B.
Du Bois and his colleagues in the Niagara Movement firmly believed that black
reenfranchisement was the only sure way to rebuke oppression and discrimination imposed on blacks. Under the pressure of the recently founded National
Association for the Advancement of Colored People (NAACP), the Supreme
Court in *Guinn and Beal v. United States* (1915) invalidated the grandfather
scheme used by several southern states to deny black men the right to vote.[53] In
1924, the NAACP succeeded in presenting a white primary case to the Court. In

Nixon v. Herson (1927), the Supreme Court held that the Texas white primary statute violated the Fourteenth Amendment. The white primary was eventually declared impossible under the Fifteenth Amendment by the Court in *Smith v. Allwright* (1944).

About the same time, the NAACP began to launch a series of programs seeking legal protection of the rights guaranteed by the Fourteenth and Fifteenth Amendments. The NAACP's courtroom struggles for black rights were, up to and after the *Brown v. Board of Education* decision in 1954, crucial in compelling federal and state governments to respect and recognize the constitutionality of the amendments. These struggles, together with other black protests throughout the 1930s and 1940s, also helped to forge the political momentum for the civil rights movement of the 1950s and 1960s, through which African Americans would eventually regain the right to vote. If the Republican party was only partly successful in its all too often halfhearted efforts to protect black political rights in the late nineteenth century, it laid the groundwork for the reenfranchisement of African Americans and a new transformation of American democracy in the twentieth century.

APPENDIX ONE

ENFORCEMENT ACT OF
MAY 31, 1870

Chap. CXIV.—*An Act to enforce the Right of Citizens of the United States to vote in the several States of this Union, and for other Purposes.*

Be it enacted by the Senate and house of Representatives of the United States who are or shall be otherwise qualified by law to vote at any election by the people in any State, Territory, district, county, city, parish, township, school district, municipality, or other territorial subdivision, shall be entitled and allowed to vote at all such elections, without distinction of race, color, or previous condition of servitude; any constitution, law, custom, usage, or regulation of any State or Territory, or by or under its authority, to the contrary notwithstanding.

Sec. 2. And be it further enacted, That if by or under the authority of the constitution or laws of any State, or the laws of any Territory, any act is or shall be required to be done as a prerequisite or qualification for voting, and by such constitution or laws persons or officers are or shall be charged with the performance of duties in furnishing to citizens an opportunity to perform such prerequisite, or to become qualified to vote, it shall be the duty of every such person and officer to give to all citizens of the United States the same and equal opportunity to perform such prerequisite, and to become qualified to vote without distinction of race, color, or previous condition of servitude; and if any such person or officer shall refuse or knowingly omit to give full effect to this section, he shall, for every such offense, forfeit and pay the sum of five hundred dollars to the person aggrieved thereby, to be recovered by an action on the case, with full costs, and such allowance for counsel fees as the court shall deem just, and shall also, for every such offense, be deemed guilty of a misdemeanor, and shall, on conviction thereof, be fined not less than five hundred dollars, or be imprisoned not less than one month and not more than one year, or both, at the discretion of the court.

Sec. 3. And be it further enacted, That whenever, by or under the authority of the constitution or laws of any State, or the laws of any Territory, any act is or shall be required to [be] done by any citizen as a prerequisite to qualify or entitle him to vote, the offer of any such citizen to perform the act required to be done as aforesaid shall, if it fail to be carried into execution by reason of the wrongful act or omission aforesaid of the person or officer charged with the duty of receiving or permitting such performance or offer to perform, or acting thereon, be deemed and held as a performance in law of such act; and the person so offering and failing as aforesaid, and being otherwise qualified, shall be entitled to vote in the same manner and to the same extent as if he had in fact performed such act; and any judge, inspector, or other officer of election whose duty it is or shall be to receive, count, certify, register, report, or give effect to the vote of any such citizen who shall wrongfully refuse or omit to receive, count, certify, register, report, or give effect to the vote of such citizen upon the presentation by him of his affidavit stating such offer and the time and place thereof, and the name of the officer or person whose duty it was to act thereon, and that he was wrongfully prevented by such person or officer from performing such act, shall for every such offense forfeit and pay the sum of five hundred dollars to the person aggrieved thereby, to be recovered by an action on the case, with full costs, and such allowance for counsel fees as the court shall deem just, and on conviction thereof, be fined not less than five hundred dollars, or be imprisoned not less than one month and not more than one year, or both, at the discretion of the court.

Sec. 4. And be it further enacted, That if any person, by force, bribery, threats, intimidation, or other unlawful means, shall hinder, delay, prevent, or obstruct, or shall combine and confederate with others to hinder, delay, prevent, or obstruct, any citizen from doing any act required to be done to qualify him to vote or from voting at any election as aforesaid, such person shall for every such offense forfeit and pay the sum of five hundred dollars to the person aggrieved thereby, to be recovered by an action on the case, with full costs, and such allowance for counsel fees as the court shall deem just, and shall also for every such offense be guilty of a misdemeanor, and shall, on conviction thereof, be fined not less than five hundred dollars, or be imprisoned not less than one month and not more than one year, or both at the discretion of the court.

Sec. 5. And be it further enacted, That if any person shall prevent, hinder, control, or intimidate, or shall attempt to prevent, hinder, control, or intimidate, any person from exercising or in exercising the right of suffrage, to whom the right of suffrage is secured or guaranteed by the fifteenth amendment to the Constitution of the United States, by means of bribery, threats, or threats of depriving such person of employment or occupation, or of ejecting such person from rented house, lands, or other property, or by threats of refusing to renew leases or contracts for labor, or by threats of violence to himself or family, such person so offending shall be deemed guilty of a misdemeanor, and shall, on conviction thereof, be fined not less than five hundred dollars, or be imprisoned not less than one month and not more than one year, or both, at the discretion of the court.

Sec. 6. And be it further enacted, That if two or more persons shall band or conspire together, or go in disguise upon the public highway, or upon the premises of another, with intent to violate any provision of this act, or to injure, oppress, threaten, or intimidate any citizen with intent to prevent or hinder his free exercise and enjoyment of any right or privilege granted or secured to him by the Constitution or laws of the United States, or because of his having exercised the same, such persons shall be held guilty of felony, and, on conviction thereof, shall be fined or imprisoned, or both, at the discretion of the court,—the fine not to exceed five thousand dollars, and the imprisonment not to exceed ten years,—and shall, moreover, be thereafter ineligible to, and disabled from holding, any office or place of honor, profit, or trust created by the Constitution or laws of the United States.

Sec. 7. And be it further enacted, That if in the act of violating any provision in either of the two preceding sections, any other felony, crime, or misdemeanor shall be committed, the offender, on conviction of such violation of said sections, shall be punished for the same with such punishments as are attached to the said felonies, crimes, and misdemeanors by the laws of the State in which the offense may be committed.

Sec. 8. And be it further enacted, That the district courts of the United States, within their respective districts, shall have, exclusively of the courts of the several states, cognizance of all crimes and offenses committed against the provisions of this act, and also, concurrently with the circuit courts of the United States, of all causes, civil and criminal, arising under this act, except as herein otherwise provided, and the jurisdiction hereby conferred shall be exercised in conformity with the laws and practice governing United States courts; and all crimes and offenses committed against the provisions of this act may be prosecuted by the indictment of a grand jury, or, in cases of crimes and offenses not infamous, the prosecution may be either by indictment or information filed by the district attorney in a court having jurisdiction.

Sec. 9. And be it further enacted, That the district attorneys, marshals, and deputy marshals of the United States, the commissioners appointed by the circuit and territorial courts of the United States, with powers of arresting, imprisoning, or bailing offenders against the laws of the United States, and every other officer who may be specially empowered by the President of the United States, shall be, and they are hereby, specially authorized and required, at the expense of the United States, to institute proceedings against all and every person who shall violate the provisions of this act, and cause him or them to be arrested and imprisoned, or bailed, as the case may be, for trial before such court of the United States or territorial court as has cognizance of the offense. And with a view to afford reasonable protection to all persons in their constitutional right to vote without distinction of race, color, or previous condition of servitude, and to the prompt discharge of the duties of this act, it shall be the duty of the circuit courts of the United States, and the superior courts of the Territories of the United States, from time to time, to increase the number of commissioners, so as to afford a speedy and convenient means for the arrest and examination of persons charged with a violation of this act; and such commissioners are hereby authorized and required to exercise and discharge all the powers and duties conferred on them by this act, and the same duties with regard to offenses created by them by this act, and the same duties with regard to offenses created by this act as they are authorized by law to exercise with regard to other offenses against the laws of the United States.

Sec. 10. And be it further enacted, That it shall be the duty of all marshals and deputy marshals to obey and execute all warrants and precepts issued under the provisions of this act, when to them directed; and should any marshal or deputy marshal refuse to receive such warrant or other process when tendered, or to use all proper means diligently to execute the same, he shall, on conviction thereof, be fined in the sum of one thousand dollars, to the use of the person deprived of the rights conferred by this act. And the better to enable the said commissioners to execute their duties faithfully and efficiently, in conformity with the Constitution of the United States and the requirements of this act, they are hereby authorized and empowered, within their districts respectively, to appoint, in writing, under their hands, any one or more suitable persons, from time to time, to execute all such warrants and other process as may be issued by them in the lawful performance of their respective duties, and the persons so appointed to execute any warrant or process as aforesaid shall have authority to summon and call to their aid the bystanders or posse comitatus of the proper county, or such portion of the land or naval forces of the United States, or of the militia, as may be necessary to the performance of the duty with which they are charged, and to insure a faithful observance of the fifteenth amendment to the Constitution of the United States; and such warrants shall run and be executed by said officers anywhere in the State or Territory within which they are issued.

Sec. 11. And be it further enacted, That any person who shall knowingly and wilfully obstruct, hinder, or prevent any officer or other person charged with the execution of any warrant or process issued under the provisions of this act, or any person or persons lawfully assisting him or them from arresting any person for whose apprehension such warrant or process may have been issued, or shall rescue or attempt to rescue such person from the custody of the officer or other person or persons, or those lawfully assisting as aforesaid, when so arrested pursuant to the authority herein given and declared, or shall aid, abet, or assist any person so arrested as aforesaid, directly or indirectly, to escape from the custody of the officer or other person legally authorized as aforesaid, or shall harbor or conceal any person for whose arrest a warrant or process shall have been issued as aforesaid, so as to prevent his discovery and arrest after notice or knowledge of the fact that a warrant has been issued for the apprehension of such person, shall, for either of said offenses, be exceeding six months, or both, at the discretion of the court, on conviction before the district or circuit court of the United States for the district or circuit in which said offense may have been committed, or before the proper court of criminal jurisdiction, if committed within any one of the organized Territories of the United States.

Sec. 12. And be it further enacted, That the commissioners, district attorney, the marshals, their deputies, and the clerks of the said district, circuit, and territorial courts shall be paid for their services the like fees as may be allowed to them for similar services in other cases. The person or persons authorized to execute the process to be issued by such commissioners for the arrest of offenders against the provisions of this act shall be entitled to the usual fees allowed to the marshal for an arrest for each person he or they may arrest and take before any such commissioner as aforesaid, with such other fees as may be deemed reasonable by such commissioner for such other additional services as may be necessarily performed by him or them, such as attending at the examination, keeping the prisoner in custody, and providing him with food and lodging during his detention and until the final determination of such commissioner, and in general for performing such other duties as may be required in the premises; such fees to be made up in conformity with the fees usually charged by the officers of the courts of justice within the proper district or county as near as may be practicable, and paid out of the treasury of the United States on the certificate of the judge of the district within which the arrest is made, and to be recoverable from the defendant as part of the judgment in case of conviction.

Sec. 13. And be it further enacted, That it shall be lawful for the President of the United States to employ such part of the land or naval forces of the United States, or of the militia, as shall be necessary to aid in the execution of judicial process issued under this act.

Sec. 14. And be it further enacted, That whenever any person shall hold office, except as a member of Congress or of some State legislature, contrary to the provisions of the third section of the fourteenth article of amendment of the Constitution of the United States, it shall be the duty of the district attorney of the United States for the district in which such person shall hold office, as aforesaid, to proceed against such person, by writ of quo warranto, returnable to the circuit or district court of the United States in such district, and to prosecute the same to the removal of such person from office; and any writ of quo warranto so brought, as aforesaid, shall take precedence of all other cases on the docket of the court to which it is made returnable, and shall not be continued unless for cause proved to the satisfaction of the court.

Sec. 15. And be it further enacted, That any person who shall hereafter knowingly accept or hold any office under the United States, or any State to which he is ineligible under the third section of the fourteenth article of amendment of the Constitution of the United States, or who shall attempt to hold or exercise the duties of any such office, shall be deemed guilty of a misdemeanor against the United States, and, upon condition thereof before the circuit or district court of the United States, shall be imprisoned not more than one year, or fined not exceeding one thousand dollars, or both, at the discretion of the court.

Sec. 16. And be it further enacted, That all persons within the jurisdiction of the United States shall have the same right in every State and Territory in the United States to make and enforce contracts, to sue, be parties, give evidence, and to the full and equal benefit of all laws and proceedings for the security of person and property as is enjoyed by white citizens, and shall be subject to like punishment, pains, penalties, taxes, licenses, and exactions of every kind, and none other, any law, statute, ordinance, regulation, or custom to the contrary not-withstanding. No tax or charge shall be imposed or enforced by any State upon any person immigrating thereto from a foreign country which is not equally imposed and enforced upon every person immigrating to such State from any other foreign country; and any law of any State in conflict with this provision is hereby declared null and void.

Sec. 17. And be it further enacted, That any person who, under color of any law, statute, ordinance, regulation, or custom, shall subject, or cause to be subjected, any inhabitant of any State or Territory to the deprivation of any right secured or protected by the last preceding section of this act, or to different punishment, pains, or penalties on account of such person being an alien, or by reason of his color or race, than is prescribed for the punishment of citizens, shall be deemed guilty of a misdemeanor, and, on conviction, shall be punished by fine not exceeding one thousand dollars, or imprisonment not exceeding one year, or both, in the discretion of the court.

Sec. 18. And be it further enacted, That the act to protect all persons in the United States in their civil rights, and furnish the means of their vindication, passed April nine, eighteen hundred and sixty-six, is hereby re-enacted; and sections sixteen and seventeen hereof shall be enforced according to the provisions of said act.

Sec. 19. And be it further enacted, That if at any election for representative or delegate in the Congress of the United States any person shall knowingly personate and vote, or attempt to vote, in the name of any other person, whether living, dead, or fictitious; or vote more than once at the same election for any candidate for the same office; or vote at a place where he may not be lawfully entitled to vote; or vote without having a lawful right to vote; or do any unlawful act to secure a right or an opportunity to vote for himself or any other person; or by force, threat, menace, intimidation, bribery, reward, or offer, or promise thereof, or otherwise unlawfully prevent any qualified voter of any State of the United States of America, or of any Territory thereof, from freely exercising the right of suffrage, or by any such means induce any voter to refuse to exercise such right; or compel or induce by any such means, or otherwise, any officer of an election in any such State or Territory to receive a vote from a person not legally qualified or entitled to vote; or interfere in any manner with any officer of said elections in the discharge of his duties; or by any of such means, or other unlawful means, induce any officer of an election, or officer whose duty it is to ascertain, announce, or declare the result of any such election, or give or make any certificate, document, or evidence in relation thereto, to violate or refuse to comply with his duty, or any law regulating the same; or knowingly and wilfully receive the vote of any person not entitled to vote, or refuse to receive the vote of any person entitled to vote; or aid, counsel, procure, or advise any such voter, person, or officer to do any act hereby made a crime, or to omit to do any duty the omission of which is hereby made a crime, or attempt to do so, every such person shall be deemed guilty of a crime, and shall for such crime be liable to prosecution in any court of the

United States of competent jurisdiction, and, on conviction thereof, shall be punished by a fine not exceeding five hundred dollars, or by imprisonment for a term not exceeding three years, or both, in the discretion of the court, and shall pay the costs of prosecution.

Sec. 20. And be it further enacted, That if, at any registration of voters for an election for representative or delegate in the Congress of the United States, any person shall knowingly personate and register, or attempt to register, in the name of any other person, whether living, dead, or fictitious, or fraudulently register, or fraudulently attempt to register, not having a lawful right so to do; or do any unlawful act to secure registration for himself or any other person; or by force, threat, menace, intimidation, bribery, reward, or offer, or promise thereof, or other unlawful means, prevent or hinder any person having a lawful right to register from duly exercising such right; or compel or induce, by any of such means, or other unlawful means, any officer of registration to admit to registration any person not legally entitled thereto, or interfere in any manner with any officer of registration in the discharge of his duties, or by any such means, or other unlawful means, induce any officer of registration to violate or refuse to comply with his duty, or any law regulating the same; or knowingly and wilfully receive the vote of any person not entitled to vote, or refuse to receive the vote of any person entitled to vote, or aid, counsel, procure, or advise any such voter, person, or office to do any act hereby made a crime, every such person shall be deemed guilty of a crime, and shall be liable to prosecution and punishment therefor, as provided in section nineteen of this act for persons guilty of any of the crimes therein specified: Provided, That every registration made under the laws of any State or Territory, for any State or other election at which such representative or delegate in Congress shall be chosen, shall be deemed to be a registration within the meaning of this act, notwithstanding the same shall also be made for the purposes of any State, territorial, or municipal election.

Sec. 21. And be it further enacted, That whenever, by the laws of any State or Territory, the name of any candidate or person to be voted for as representative or delegate in Congress shall be required to be printed, written, or contained in any ticket or ballot with other candidates or persons to be voted for at the same election for State, territorial, municipal, or local officers, it shall be sufficient prima facie evidence, either for the purpose of indicting or convicting any person charged with voting, or attempting or offering to vote, unlawfully under the provisions of the preceding sections, or for committing either of the offenses thereby created, to prove that the person so charged or indicted, voted, or attempted or offered to vote, such ballot or ticket, or committed either of the offenses named in the preceding sections of this act with reference to such ballot. And the proof and establishment of such facts shall be taken, held, and deemed to be presumptive evidence that such person voted, or attempted or offered to vote, for such representative or delegate, as the case may be, or that such offense was committed with reference to the election of such representative or delegate, and shall be sufficient to warrant his conviction, unless it shall be shown that any such ballot, when cast, or attempted or offered to be cast, by him, did not contain the name of any candidate for the office of representative or delegate in the Congress of the United States, or that such offense was not committed with reference to the election of such representative or delegate.

Sec. 22. And be it further enacted, That any officer of any election at which any representative or delegate in the Congress of the United States shall be voted for, whether such officer of election be appointed or created by or under any law or authority of the United States, or by or under any State, territorial, district, or municipal law or authority, who shall neglect or refuse to perform any duty in regard to such election required of him by any law of the United States, or of any State or Territory thereof; or violate any duty so imposed, or knowingly do any act thereby unauthorized, with intent to affect any such election, or the result thereof; or fraudulently make any false certificate of the result of such election in regard to such representative or delegate; or withhold, conceal, or destroy any certificate of record so required by law respecting, concerning, or pertaining to the election of any such representative or delegate; or neglect or refuse to make and return the same as so required by law; or aid, counsel, procure, or advise any voter, person, or officer to do any act by this or any of the preceding sections made a crime; or to omit to do any duty the omission of which is by this or any of said sections made a crime, or attempt to do so, shall be deemed guilty of a crime and shall be liable to prosecution and punishment therefor, as provided in the nineteenth section of this act for persons guilty of any of the crimes therein specified.

Sec. 23. And be it further enacted, That whenever any person shall be defeated or deprived of his election to any office, except elector of President or Vice-President, representative or delegate in Congress, or member of a State legislature, by reason of the denial to any citizen or citizens who shall offer to vote, of the right to vote, on account of race, color, or previous condition of servitude, his right to hold and enjoy such office, and the emoluments thereof, shall not be impaired by such denial; and such person may bring any appropriate suit or proceeding to recover possession of such office, and in cases where it shall appear that the sole question touching the title to such office arises out of the denial of the right to vote to citizens who so offered to vote, on account of race, color, or previous condition of servitude, such suit or proceeding may be instituted in the circuit or district court of the United States of the circuit or district in which such person resides. And said circuit or district court shall have, concurrently with the State courts, jurisdiction thereof so far as to determine the rights of the parties to such office by reason of the denial of the fight guaranteed by the fifteenth article of amendment to the Constitution of the United States, and secured by this act.

Approved, May 31, 1870.

Source: Statutes at Large 16 (1870): 140 – 46.

NATURALIZATION ACT OF
JULY 14, 1870

Chap. CCLIV.—*An Act to amend the Naturalization Laws and to punish Crimes against the same, and for other Purposes.*

Be it enacted by the Senate and House of Representatives of the United States of America in Congress assembled. That in all cases where any oath, affirmation, or affidavit shall be made or taken under or by virtue of any act or law relating to the naturalization of aliens, or in any proceedings under such acts or laws, and any person or persons taking or making such oath, affirmation, or affidavit, shall knowingly swear or affirm falsely, the same shall be deemed and taken to be perjury, and the person or persons guilty thereof shall upon conviction thereof be sentenced to imprisonment for a term not exceeding five years and not less than one year, and to a fine not exceeding one thousand dollars.

Sec. 2. And be it further enacted, That if any person applying to be admitted a citizen, or appearing as a witness for any such person, shall knowingly personate any other person than himself, or falsely appear in the name of a deceased person, or in an assumed or fictitious name, or if any person shall falsely make, forge, or counterfeit any oath, affirmation, notice, affidavit, certificate, order, record, signature, or other instrument, paper, or proceeding required or authorized by any law or act relating to or providing for the naturalization of aliens; or shall utter, sell, dispose of, or use as true or genuine, or for any unlawful purpose, any false, forged, ante-dated, or counterfeit oath, affirmation, notice, certificate, order, record, signature, instrument, paper, or proceeding as aforesaid; or sell or dispose of to any person other than the person for whom it was originally issued, any certificate of citizenship, or certificate showing any person to be admitted a citizen; or if any person shall in any manner use for the purpose of registering as a voter, or as evidence of a right to vote, or otherwise, unlawfully, any order, certificate of citizenship, or certificate, judgment, or exemplification, showing such person to be admitted to be a citizen, whether heretofore or hereafter issued or made, knowing that such order or certificate, judgment, or exemplification has been unlawfully issued or made; or if any person shall unlawfully use, or attempt to use, any such order or certificate, issued to or in the name of any other person, or in a fictitious name, or the name of a deceased person; or use, or attempt to use, or aid, or assist, or participate in the use of any certificate of citizenship, knowing the same to be forged, or counterfeit, or ante-dated, or knowing the same to have been procured by fraud, or otherwise unlawfully obtained; or if any person, and without lawful excuse, shall knowingly have or be possessed of any false, forged, ante-dated, or counterfeit certificate of citizenship, purporting to have been issued under the provisions of any law of the United States relating to naturalization, knowing such certificate to be false, forged, ante-dated, or counterfeit, with intent unlawfully to use the same; or if any person shall obtain, accept, or receive any certificate of citizenship known to such person to have been procured by fraud or by the use of any false name, or by means of any false statement made with intent to procure, or to aid in procuring, the issue of such certificate, or known to such person to be fraudulently altered or ante-dated; or if any person who has been or may be admitted to be a citizen shall, on oath or affirmation, or by affidavit, knowingly deny that he has been so admitted, with intent to evade or avoid any duty or liability imposed or required by law, every person so offending shall be deemed and adjudged guilty of felony, and, on conviction thereof, shall be sentenced to be imprisoned and kept at hard labor for a period not less than one year nor more than one thousand dollars, or both such punishments may be imposed, in the discretion of the court, And every person who shall knowingly and intentionally aid or abet any person in the commission of any such felony, or attempt to do any act hereby made felony, or counsel, advise, or procure, or attempt to procure the commission thereof, shall be liable to indictment and punishment in the same manner and to the same extent as the principal party guilty of such felony, and such person may be tried and convicted thereof without the previous conviction of such principal.

Sec. 3. And be it further enacted, That any person who shall knowingly use any certificate of naturalization heretofore granted by any court, or which shall hereafter be granted, which has been, or shall be, procured through fraud or by false evidence, or has been or shall be issued by the clerk, or any other officer of the court without any appearance and hearing of the applicant in court and without lawful authority; and any person who shall falsely represent himself to be a citizen of the United States, without having been duly admitted to citizenship, for any fraudulent purpose whatever, shall be deemed guilty of a misdemeanor, and upon conviction thereof, in due course of law, shall be sentenced to pay a fine of not exceeding one thousand dollars, or be imprisoned not exceeding two years, either or both, in the discretion of the court taking cognizance of the same.

Sec. 4. And be it further enacted, That the provisions of this act shall apply to all proceedings had or taken, or attempted to be had or taken, before any court in which any proceeding for naturalization shall be commenced, had, or taken, or attempted to be commenced; and the courts of the United States shall have jurisdiction of all offenses under the provisions of this act, in or before whatsoever court or tribunal the same shall have been committed.

Sec. 5. And be it further enacted, That in any city having upwards of twenty thousand inhabitants, it shall be the duty of the judge of the circuit court of the United States for the circuit wherein said city shall be, upon the application of two citizens, to appoint in writing for each election district or voting precinct in said city, and to change or renew said appointment as occasion may require, from time to time, two citizens resident of the district or precinct, one from each political party, who, when so designated, shall be, and are hereby, authorized to attend at all times and places fixed for the registration of voters, who, being registered, would be entitled to vote for representatives in Congress, and at all times and places for holding elections of representatives in Congress, and for counting the votes cast at said elections, and to challenge any name proposed to be registered, and any vote offered, and to be present and witness throughout the counting of all votes, and to remain where the ballot-boxes are kept at all times after the polls are open until the votes are finally counted; and said persons and either of them shall have the right to affix their signature or his signature to said register for purposes of identification, and to attach thereto, or to the certificate of the number of votes cast, and [any] statement touching the truth or fairness thereof which they or he may ask to attach; and any one who shall prevent any person so designated from doing any of the acts authorized as aforesaid, or who shall hinder or molest any such person in doing any of the said acts, or shall aid or abet in preventing, hindering, or molesting any such person in respect of any such acts, shall be guilty of a misdemeanor, and on conviction shall be punished by imprisonment not less than one year.

Sec. 6. And be it further enacted, That in any city having upwards of twenty thousand inhabitants, it shall be lawful for the marshal of the United States for the district wherein said city shall be, to appoint as many special deputies as may be necessary to preserve order at any election at which representatives in Congress are to be chosen; and said deputies are hereby authorized to preserve order at such elections, and to arrest for any offense or breach of the peace committed in their view.

Sec. 7. And be it further enacted, That the naturalization laws are hereby extended to aliens of African nativity and to persons of African descent.

Approved, July 14, 1870.

Source: Statutes at Large 16 (1870): 254 – 56.

APPENDIX THREE

ENFORCEMENT ACT OF
FEBRUARY 28, 1871

Chap. XCIX.—*An act to amend an Act approved May thirty-one, eighteen hundred and seventy, entitled "An Act to enforce the Rights of Citizens of the United States to vote in the several States of the Union, and for other Purposes."*

Be it enacted by the Senate and House of Representatives of the United States of America in Congress assembled, That section twenty of the "Act to enforce the rights of citizens of the United States to vote in the several States of this Union, and for other purposes," approved May thirty-one, eighteen hundred and seventy, shall be, and hereby is, amended so as to read as follows:—

"Sec. 20. And be it further enacted, That if, [at] any registration of voters for an election for representative or delegate in the Congress of the United States, any person shall knowingly personate and register, or attempt to register, in the name of any other person, whether living, dead, or fictitious, or fraudulently register, or fraudulently attempt to register, not having a lawful right so to do; or do any unlawful act to secure registration for himself or any other person; or by force, threat, menace, intimidation, bribery, reward, or offer, or promise thereof, or other unlawful means, prevent or hinder any person having a lawful right to register from duly exercising such right; or compel or induce, by any of such means, or other unlawful means, any officer of registration to admit to registration any person not legally entitled thereto, or interfere in any manner with any officer of registration in the discharge of his duties, or by any such means, or other unlawful means, induce any officer of registration to violate or refuse to comply with his duty or any law regulating the same; or if any such officer shall knowingly and wilfully register as a voter any person not entitled to be registered, or refuse to so register any person entitled to be registered; or if any such officer or other person whose duty it is to perform any duty in relation to such registration or election, or to ascertain, announce, or declare the result thereof, or give or make any certificate, document, or evidence in relation thereto, shall knowingly neglect or refuse to perform any duty required by law, or violate any duty imposed by law, or do any act unauthorized by law relating to or affecting such registration or election, or the result thereof, or any certificate, document, or evidence in relation thereto, or if any person shall aid, counsel, procure, or advise any such voter, person, or officer to do any act hereby made a crime, or to omit any act the omission of which is hereby made a crime, every such person shall be deemed guilty of a crime, and shall be liable to prosecution and punishment therefor as provided in section nineteen of said act of May thirty-one, eighteen hundred and seventy, for persons guilty of any of the crimes therein specified: Provided, That every registration made under the laws of any State or Territory for any State or other election at which such representative or delegate in Congress shall be chosen, shall be deemed to be a registration within the meaning of this act, notwithstanding the same shall also be made for the purposes of any State, territorial, or municipal election."

Sec. 2. And be it further enacted, That whenever in any city or town having upward of twenty thousand inhabitants, there shall be two citizens thereof who, prior to any registration of voters for an election for representative or delegate in the Congress of the United States, or prior to any election at which a representative or delegate in Congress is to be voted for, shall make known, in writing, to the judge of the circuit court of the United States for the circuit wherein such city or both, guarded and scrutinized, it shall be the duty of the said judge of the circuit court, within not less than ten days prior to said registration, if one there be, or, if no registration be required, within not less than ten days prior to said election, to open the said circuit court at the most convenient point in said circuit. And the said court, when so opened by said judge, shall proceed to appoint and commission, from day to day and from time to time, and under the hand of the said circuit judge, and under the seal of said court, for each election district or voting precinct in each and every such city or town as shall, in the manner herein prescribed, have applied therefor, and to revoke, change, or renew said appointment from time to time, two citizens, residents of said city or town, who shall be of different political parties, and able to read and write the English language, and who shall be known and designated as supervisors of election. And the said circuit court, when opened by the said circuit judge as required herein, shall therefrom and thereafter, and up to and including the day following the day of election, be always open for the transaction of business under this act, and the powers and jurisdiction hereby granted and conferred shall be exercised as well in vacation as in term time; and a judge sitting at chambers shall have the same powers and jurisdiction, including the power of keeping order and of punishing any contempt of his authority, as when sitting in court.

Sec. 3. And be it further enacted, That whenever, from sickness, injury, or otherwise, the judge of the circuit court of the United States in any judicial circuit shall be unable to perform and discharge the duties by this act imposed, it shall be his duty, and he is hereby required, to select and to direct and assign to the performance thereof, in his place and stead, such one of the judges of the district courts of the United States within his circuit as he shall deem best; and upon such selection and assignment being made, it shall be lawful for, and shall be the duty of, the district judge so designated to perform and discharge, in the place and stead of the said circuit judge, all the duties, powers, and obligations imposed and conferred upon the said circuit judge by the provisions of this act.

Sec. 4. And be it further enacted, That it shall be the duty of the supervisors of election, appointed under this act, and they and each of them are hereby authorized and required, to attend at all times and places fixed for the registration of voters, who, being registered, would be entitled to vote for a representative or delegate in Congress, and to challenge any person offering to register; to attend at all times and places when the names of registered voters may be marked for challenge, and to cause such names registered as they shall deem proper to be so marked; to make, when required, the lists, or either of them, provided for in section thirteen of this act, and verify the same; and upon any occasion, and at any time when in attendance under the provisions of this act, to personally inspect and scrutinize such registry, and for purposes of identification to affix their or his signature to each and every page of the original list, and of each and every copy of any such list of registered voters, at such times, upon each day when any name may or shall be received, entered, or registered, and in such manner as will, in their or his judgement, detect and expose the improper or wrongful removal therefrom, or addition thereto, in any way, of any name or names.

Sec. 5. And be it further enacted, That it shall also be the duty of the said supervisors of election, and they, and each of them, are hereby authorized and required, to attend at all times and places for holding elections of representatives or delegates in Congress, and for counting the votes cast at said elections; to challenge any vote offered by any person whose legal qualifications the supervisors, or either of them, shall doubt; to be and remain where the ballot-boxes are kept at all times after the polls are open until each and every vote cast at said time and place shall be counted, the canvass of all votes polled be wholly completed, and the proper and requisite certificates or returns made, whether said certificates or returns be required under any law of the United States, or any State, territorial, or municipal law, and to personally inspect and scrutinize, from time to time, and at all times, on the day of election, the manner in which the voting is done, and the way and method in which the poll-books, registry-lists, and tallies or check-books, whether the same are required by any law of the United States, or any State, territorial, or municipal law, are kept; and to the end that each candidate for the office of representative or delegate in Congress shall obtain the benefit of every vote for him cast, the said supervisors of election are, and each of them is, hereby required, in their or his respective election districts or voting precincts, to personally scrutinize, count, and canvass each and every ballot in their or his election district or voting precinct cast, whatever may be the indorsement on said ballot, or in whatever box it may have been placed or be found; to make and forward to the officer who, in accordance with the provisions of section thirteen of this act, shall have been designated as the chief supervisor of the judicial district in which the city or town wherein they or he shall serve shall be, such certificates and returns of all such ballots as said officer may direct and require, and to attach to the registry list, and any and all copies thereof, and to any certificate, statement, or return, whether the same, or any part or portion thereof, be required by any law of the United States, or of any State, territorial, or municipal law, any statement touching the truth or accuracy of the registry, or the truth or fairness of the election and canvass, which the said supervisors of election, or either of them, may desire to make or attach, or which should properly and honestly be made or attached, in order that the facts may become known, any law of any State or Territory to the contrary notwithstanding.

Sec. 6. And be it further enacted, That the better to enable the said supervisors of election to discharge their duties, they are, and each of them is, hereby authorized and directed, in their or his respective election districts or voting precincts, on the day or days of registration, on the day or days when registered voters may be marked to be challenged, and on the day or days of election, to take, occupy, and remain in such position or positions, from time to time, whether before or behind the ballot-boxes, as will, in their judgment, best enable them or him to see each person offering himself for registration or offering to vote, and as will best conduce to their or his scrutinizing the manner in which the registration or voting is being conducted; and at the closing of the polls for the reception of votes, they are, and each of them is, hereby required to place themselves or himself in such position in relation to the ballot-boxes for the purpose of engaging in the work of canvassing the ballots in said boxes contained as will enable them or him to fully perform the duties in respect to such canvass provided in this act, and shall there remain until every duty in respect to such canvass, certificates, returns, and statements shall have been wholly completed, any law of any State or Territory to the contrary notwithstanding.

Sec. 7. And be it further enacted, That if any election district or voting precinct in any city, town, or village, for which there shall have been appointed supervisors of election for any election at which a representative or delegate in Congress shall be voted for, the said supervisors of election, or either of them, shall not be allowed to exercise and discharge, fully and freely, and without bribery, solicitation, interference, hinderance, molestation, violence, or threats thereof, on the part of or from any person or persons, each and every of the duties, obligations, and powers conferred upon them by this act and the act hereby amended, it shall be the duty of the supervisors of election, and each of them, to make prompt report, under oath, within ten days after the day of election, to the officer who, in accordance with the provisions of section thirteen of this act, shall have been designated as the chief supervisor of the judicial district in which the city or town therein they or he served shall be, or the manner and means by which they were, or he was, not so allowed to fully and freely exercise and discharge the duties and obligations required and imposed by this act. And upon receiving any such report, it shall be the duty of the said chief supervisor, acting both in such capacity and officially as a commissioner of the circuit court, to forthwith examine into all the facts thereof; to subpoena and compel the attendance before him of any witnesses; administer oaths and take testimony in respect to the charges made; and prior to the assembling of the Congress for which any such representative or delegate was voted for, to have filed with the clerk of the House of Representatives of the Congress of the United States all the evidence by him taken, all information by him obtained, and all reports to him made.

Sec. 8. And be it further enacted, That whenever an election at which representatives or delegates in Congress are to be chosen shall be held in any city or town of twenty thousand inhabitants or upward, the marshal of the United States for the district in which said city or town is situated shall have power, and it shall be his duty, on the application, in writing, of at least two citizens residing in any such city or town, to appoint special deputy marshals, whose duty it shall be, when required as provided in this act, to aid and assist the supervisors of election in the verification of any list of persons made under the provisions of this act, who may have registered, or voted, or either; to attend in each election district or voting precinct at the times and places fixed for the registration of voters, and at all times and places when and where said registration may by law be scrutinized, and the names of registered voters be marked for challenge; and also to attend, at all times for holding such elections, the polls of the election in such district or precinct. And the marshal and his general deputies, and such special deputies, shall have power, and it shall be the duty of such special deputies, to keep the peace, and support and protect the supervisors of elections in the discharge of their duties, preserve order at such places of registration and at such polls, prevent fraudulent registration and fraudulent voting thereat, or fraudulent conduct on the part of any officer of election, and immediately, either at said place of registration or polling-place, or elsewhere, and either before or after registering or voting, to arrest and take into custody, with or without process, any person who shall commit, or attempt or offer to commit, any of the acts or offenses prohibited by this act, or the act hereby amended, or who shall commit any offense against the laws of the United States: Provided, That no person shall be arrested without process for any offense not committed in the presence of the marshal or his general or special deputies, or either of them, or of the supervisors of election, or either of them, and, for the purposes of arrest or the preservation of the peace, the supervisors of election, and each of them, shall, in the absence of the marshal's deputies, or if required to assist said deputies, have the same duties and powers as deputy marshals: And provided further, That no person shall, on the day or days of any such election, be arrested without process for any offense committed on the day or days of registration.

Sec. 9. And be it further enacted, That whenever any arrest is made under any provision of this act, the person so arrested shall forthwith be brought before a commissioner, judge, or court of the United States for examination of the offenses alleged against him; and such commissioner, judge, or court shall proceed in respect thereto as authorized by law in case of crimes against the United States.

Sec. 10. And be it further enacted, That whoever, with or without any authority, power, or process, or pretended authority, power, or process, or any State, territorial, or municipal authority, shall obstruct, hinder, assault, or by bribery, solicitation, or otherwise, interfere with or prevent the supervisors of election, or either of them, or the marshal or his general or special deputies, or either of them, in the performance of any duty required of them, or either of them, or which he or they, or either of them, may be authorized to perform by any law of the United States, whether in the execution of process or otherwise, or shall by any of the means before mentioned hinder or prevent the free attendance and presence at such places of registration or at such polls of election, or full and free access and egress to and from any such place of registration or poll of election, or in going to and from any such place of registration or poll of election, or to and from any room where any such registration or election or canvass of votes, or of making any returns or certificates thereof, may be had, or shall molest, interfere with, remove, or eject from any such place of registration or poll of election, or of canvassing votes cast thereat, or of making returns or certificates thereof, any supervisor of election, the marshal, or his general or special deputies, or either of them, or shall threaten, or attempt, or offer so to do, or shall refuse or neglect to aid and assist any supervisor of election, or the marshal or his general or special deputies, or either of them, in the performance of his or their duties when required by him or them, or either of them, to give such aid and assistance, he shall be guilty of a misdemeanor, and liable to instant arrest without process, and on conviction thereof shall be punished by imprisonment not more than two years, or by fine not more than three thousand dollars, or by both such fine and imprisonment, and shall pay the costs of the prosecution. Whoever shall, during the progress of any verification of any list of the persons who may have registered or voted, and which shall be had or made under any of the provisions of this act, refuse to answer, or refrain from answering, or answering shall knowingly give false information in respect to any inquiry lawfully made, such person shall be liable to arrest and imprisonment as for a misdemeanor, and on conviction thereof shall be punished by imprisonment not to exceed thirty days, or by fine not to exceed one hundred dollars, or by both such fine and imprisonment, and shall pay the costs of the prosecution.

Sec. 11. And be it further enacted, That whoever shall be appointed a supervisor of election or a special deputy marshal under the provisions of this act, and shall take the oath of office as such supervisor of election or such special deputy marshal, who shall thereafter neglect or refuse, without good and lawful excuse, to perform and discharge fully the duties, obligations, and requirements of such office until the expiration of the term for which he was appointed, shall not only be subject to removal from office with loss of all pay or emoluments, but shall be guilty of a misdemeanor, and on conviction shall be punished by imprisonment for not less than six months nor more than one year, or by fine not less than two hundred dollars and not exceeding five hundred dollars, or by both fine and imprisonment, and shall pay the costs of prosecution.

Sec. 12. And be it further enacted, That the marshal, or his general deputies; or such special deputies as shall be thereto specially empowered by him, in writing, and under his hand and seal, whenever he or his said general deputies or his special deputies, or either or any of them, shall be forcibly resisted in executing their duties under this act, or the act hereby amended, or shall, by violence, threats, or menaces, be prevented from executing such duties, or from arresting any person or persons who shall commit any offense for which said marshal or his general or his special deputies are authorized to make such arrest, are, and each of them is hereby, empowered to summon and call to his or their aid the bystanders or posse comitatus of his district.

Sec. 13. And be it further enacted, That it shall be the duty of each of the circuit courts of the United States in and for each judicial circuit, upon the recommendation in writing of the judge thereof, to name and appoint, on or before the first day of May, in the year eighteen hundred and seventy-one, and thereafter as vacancies may from any cause arise, from among the circuit court commissioners in and for each judicial district in each of said judicial circuits, one of such officers, who shall be known for the duties required of him under this act as the chief supervisor of elections of the judicial district in and for which he shall be a commissioner, and shall, so long as faithful and capable, discharge the duties in this act imposed, and whose duty it shall be to prepare and furnish all necessary books, forms, blanks, and instructions for the use and direction of the supervisors of election in the several cities and towns in their respective districts; to receive the applications of all parties for appointment to such positions; and upon the opening, as contemplated in this act, of the circuit court for the judicial circuit in which the commissioner so designated shall act, to present such applications to the judge thereof, and furnish information to said judge in respect to the appointment by the said court of such supervisors of election; to require of the supervisors of election, where necessary, lists of the persons who may register and vote, or either, in their respective election districts or voting precincts, and to cause the names of those upon any such list whose right to register or vote shall be honestly doubted to be verified by proper inquiry and examination at the respective places by them assigned as their residences; and to receive, preserve, and file all oaths of office of said supervisors of election, and of all special deputy marshals appointed under the provisions of this act, and all certificates, return, reports, and records of every kind and nature contemplated or made requisite under and by the provisions of this act, save where otherwise herein specially directed. And it is hereby made the duty of all United States marshals and commissioners who shall in any judicial district perform any duties under the provisions of this act, or the act hereby amended, relating to, concerning, or affecting the election of representatives or delegates in the Congress of the United States, to, from time to time, and with all due diligence, forward to the chief supervisor in and for their judicial district all complaints, examinations, and records pertaining thereto, and all oaths of office by them administered to any supervisor of election or special deputy marshal, in order that the same may be properly preserved and filed.

Sec. 14. And be it further enacted, That there shall be allowed and paid to each chief supervisor, for his services as such officer, the following compensation, apart from and in excess of all fees allowed by law for the performance of any duty as circuit court commissioner: For filing and caring for every return, report, record, document, or other paper required to be filed by him under any of the provisions of this act, ten cents; for affixing a seal to any paper, record, report, or instrument, twenty cents; for entering and indexing the records of his office, fifteen cents per folio; and for arranging and transmitting to Congress, as provided for in section seven of this act, any report, statement, record, return, or examination, for each folio, fifteen cents; and for any copy thereof, or of any paper on file, a like sum. And there shall be allowed and paid to each and every supervisor of election, and each and every special deputy marshal who shall be appointed and shall perform his duty under the provisions of this act, compensation at the rate of five dollars per day for each and every day he shall have actually been on duty, not exceeding ten days. And the fees of the said chief supervisors shall be paid at the treasury of the United States, such accounts to be made out, verified, examined, and certified as in the case of accounts of commissioners, save that the examination or certificate required may be made by either the circuit or district judge.

Sec. 15. And be it further enacted, That the jurisdiction of the circuit court of the United States shall extend to all cases in law or equity arising under the provisions of this act or the act hereby amended; and if any person shall receive any injury to his person or property for or on account of any act by him done under any of the provisions of this act or the act hereby amended, he shall be entitled to maintain suit for damages therefor in the circuit court of the United States in the district wherein the party doing the injury may reside or shall be found.

Sec. 16. And be it further enacted, That in any case where suit or prosecution, civil or criminal, shall be commenced in a court of any State against any officer of the United States, or other person, for or on account of any act done under the provisions of this act, or under color thereof, or for or on account of any right, authority, or title set up or claimed by such officer or other person under any of said provisions, it shall be lawful for the defendant in such suit or prosecution, at any time before trial, upon a petition to the circuit court of the United States in and for the district in which the defendant shall have been served with process, setting forth the nature of said suit of prosecution, and verifying the said petition by affidavit, together with a certificate signed by an attorney or counsellor at law of some court of record of the State in which such suit shall have been commenced, or of the United States, setting forth that as counsel for the petition[er] he has examined the proceedings against him, and has carefully inquired into all the matters set forth in the petition, and that he believes the same to be true, which petition, affidavit, and certificate shall be presented to the said circuit court, if in session, and, if not, to the clerk thereof at his office, and shall be filed in said office, and the cause shall thereupon be entered on the docket of said court, and shall be thereafter proceeded in as a cause originally commenced in that court; and it shall be the duty of the clerk of said court, if the suit was commenced in the court below by summons, to issue a writ of certiorari to the State court, requiring said court to send to the said circuit court the record and proceedings in said cause; or if it was commenced by capias, he shall issue a writ of habeas corpus cum causa, a duplicate of which said writ shall be delivered to the clerk of the State court, or left at his office by the marshal of the district, or his deputy, or some person duly authorized thereto; and thereupon it shall be the duty of the said State court to stay all further proceedings in such cause, and the said suit or prosecution, upon delivery of such process, or leaving the same as aforesaid, shall be deemed and taken to be moved to the said circuit court, and any further proceedings, trial, or judgment therein in the State court shall be wholly null and void; and any person, whether an attorney or officer of any State court, or otherwise, who shall thereafter take any steps, or in any manner proceed in the State court in any action so removed, shall be guilty of a misdemeanor, and liable to trial and punishment in the court to which the action shall have been removed, and upon conviction thereof shall be punished by imprisonment for not less than six months nor more than one year, or by fine not less than five hundred nor more than one thousand dollars, or by both such fine and imprisonment, and shall in addition thereto be amenable to the said court to which said action shall have been removed as for a contempt; and if the defendant in any such suit be in actual custody on mesne process therein, it shall be the duty of the marshal, by virtue of the writ of habeas corpus cum causa, to take the body of the defendant into his custody, to be dealt with in the said cause according to the rules of law and the order of the circuit court, or of any judge thereof in vacation. And all attachments made and all bail or other security given upon such suit or prosecution shall be and continue in like force and effect as if the same suit or prosecution had proceeded to final judgment and execution in the State court. And if upon the removal of any such suit or prosecution it shall be made to appear to the said circuit court that no copy of the record and proceedings therein in the State court can be obtained, it shall be lawful for said circuit court to allow and require the plaintiff to proceed de novo, and to file a declaration of his cause of action, and the parties may thereupon proceed as in actions originally brought in said circuit court; and on failure of so proceeding judgment of non prosequitur may be rendered against the plaintiff, with costs for the defendant.

Sec. 17. And be it further enacted, That in any case in which any party is or may be by law entitled to copies of the record and proceedings in any suit or prosecution in any State court, to be used in any court of the United States, if the clerk of said State court shall, upon demand and the payment or tender of the legal fees, refuse or neglect to deliver to such party certified copies of such record and proceedings, the court of the United States in which such record and proceedings may be needed, on proof by affidavit that the clerk of such State court has refused or neglected to deliver copies thereof on demand as aforesaid, may direct and allow such record to be supplied by affidavit or otherwise, as the circumstances of the case may require and allow; and thereupon such proceeding, trial, and judgment may be had in the said court of the United States, and all such processes awarded, as if certified copies of such records and proceedings had been regularly before the said court; and hereafter in all civil actions in the courts of the United States either party thereto may notice the same for trial.

Sec. 18. And be it further enacted, That sections five and six of the act of the Congress of the United States approved July fourteen, eighteen hundred and seventy, and entitled "An act to amend the naturalization laws, and to punish crimes against the same," be, and the same are hereby, repealed; but this repeal shall not affect any proceeding or prosecution now pending for any offense under the said sections, or either of them, or any question which may arise therein respecting the appointment of the persons in said sections, or either of them, provided for, or the powers, duties, or obligations of such persons.

Sec. 19. And be it further enacted, That all votes for representatives in Congress shall hereafter be by written or printed ballot, any law of any State to the contrary notwithstanding; and all votes received or recorded contrary to the provisions of this section shall be of none effect.

Approved, February 28, 1871.

Source: Statutes at Large 16 (1871): 433 – 40.

APPENDIX FOUR

ENFORCEMENT ACT OF
APRIL 20, 1871
(THE KU KLUX FORCE ACT)

Chap. XXII.—*An Act to enforce the Provisions of the Fourteenth amendment to the Constitution of the United States, and for other Purposes.*

Be it enacted by the Senate and House of Representatives of the United States of America in Congress assembled, That any person who, under color of any law, statute, ordinance, regulation, custom, or usage of any State, shall subject, or cause to be subjected, any person within the jurisdiction of the United States to the deprivation of any rights, privileges, or immunities secured by the Constitution of the United States, shall, any such law, statute, ordinance, regulation, custom, or usage of the State to the contrary notwithstanding, be liable to the party injured in any action at law, suit in equity, or other proper proceeding for redress; such proceeding to be prosecuted in the several district or circuit courts of the United States, with and subject to the same rights of appeal, review upon error, and other remedies provided in like cases in such courts, under the provisions of the act of the ninth of April, eighteen hundred and sixty-six, entitled "An act to protect all persons in the United States in their civil rights, and to furnish the means of their vindication"; and the other remedial laws of the United States which are in their nature applicable in such cases.

Sec. 2. That if two or more persons within any State or Territory of the United States shall conspire together to overthrow, or to put down, or to destroy by force the government of the United States, or to levy war against the United States, or to oppose by force the authority of the government of the United States, or by force, intimidation, or threat to prevent, hinder, or delay the execution of any law of the United States, or by force to seize, take, or possess any property of the United States contrary to the authority thereof, or by force, intimidation, or threat to prevent any person from accepting or holding any office or trust or place of confidence under the United States, or from discharging the duties thereof, or by force, intimidation, or threat to induce any officer of the United States to leave any State, district, or place where his duties as such officer might lawfully be performed, or to injure him in his office, or to injure his person while engaged in the lawful discharge of the duties of his office, or to injure his property so as to molest, interrupt, hinder, or impede him in the discharge of his official duty, or by force, intimidation, or threat to deter any party or witness in any court of the United States from attending such court, or from testifying in any matter pending in such court fully, freely, and truthfully, or to injure any such party or witness in his person or property on account of his having so attended or testified, or by force, intimidation, or threat to influence the verdict, presentment, or indictment, or any juror or grand juror in any court of the United States, or to injure such juror in his person or property on account of any verdict, presentment, or indictment lawfully assented to by him, or on account of his being or having been such juror, or shall conspire together, or go in disguise upon the public highway or upon the premises of another for the purpose, either directly or indirectly, of depriving any person or any class of persons of the equal protection of the laws, or of equal privileges or immunities under the laws, or for the purpose of preventing or hindering the constituted authorities of any State from giving or securing to all persons within such State the equal protection of the laws, or shall conspire together for the purpose of in any manner impeding, hindering, obstructing, or defeating the due course of justice in any State or Territory, with intent to deny to any citizen of the United States the due and equal protection of the laws, or to injure any person in his person or his property for lawfully enforcing the right of any person or class of persons to the equal protection of the laws, or by force, intimidation, or threat to prevent any citizen of the United States lawfully entitled to vote from giving his support or advocacy in a lawful manner towards or in favor of the election of any lawfully qualified person as an elector of President or Vice-President of the United States, or as a member of the Congress of the United States, or to injure any such citizen in his person or property on account of such support or advocacy, each and every person so offending shall be deemed guilty of a high crime, and, upon conviction thereof in any district or circuit court of the United States or district or supreme court of any Territory of the United States having jurisdiction of similar offenses, shall be punished by a fine not less than five hundred nor more than five thousand dollars, or by imprisonment, with or without hard labor, as the court may determine, for a period of not less than six months nor more than six years, as the court may determine, or by both such fine and imprisonment as the court shall determine. And if any one or more persons engaged in any such conspiracy shall do, or cause to be done, any act in furtherance of the object of such conspiracy, whereby any person shall be injured in his person or property, or deprived of having and exercising any right or privilege of a citizen of the United States, the person so injured or deprived of such rights and privileges may have and maintain an action for the recovery of damages occasioned by such injury or deprivation of rights and privileges against any one or more of the persons engaged in such conspiracy, such action to be prosecuted in the proper district or circuit court of the United States, with and subject to the same rights of appeal, review upon error, and other remedies provided in like cases in such courts under the provisions of the act of April ninth, eighteen hundred and sixty-six, entitled "An act to protect all persons in the United States in their civil rights, and to furnish the means of their vindication."

Sec. 3. That in all cases where insurrection, domestic violence, unlawful combinations, or conspiracies in any State shall so obstruct or hinder the execution of the laws thereof, and of the United States, as to deprive any portion or class of the people of such State of any of the rights, privileges, or immunities, or protection, named in the Constitution and secured by this act, and the constituted authorities of such State shall either be unable to protect, or shall, from any cause, fail in or refuse protection of the people in such rights, such facts shall be deemed a denial by such State of the equal protection of the laws to which they are entitled under the Constitution of the United States; and in all such cases, or whenever any such insurrection, violence, unlawful combination, or conspiracy shall oppose or obstruct the laws of the United States or the due execution thereof, or impede or obstruct the due course of justice under the same, it shall be lawful for the President, and it shall be his duty to take such measures, by the employment of the militia or the land and naval forces of the United States, or of either, or by other means, as he may deem necessary for the suppression of such insurrection, domestic violence, or combination; and any person who shall be arrested under the provisions of this and preceding section shall be delivered to the marshal of the proper district, to be dealt with according to law.

Sec. 4. That whenever in any State or part of a State the unlawful combinations named in the preceding section of this act shall be organized and armed, and so numerous and powerful as to be able, by violence, to either overthrow or set at defiance the constituted authorities of such State, and of the United States within such State, or when the constituted authorities are in complicity with, or shall connive at the unlawful purposes of, such powerful and armed combinations; and whenever, by reason of either or all of the causes aforesaid, the conviction of such offenders and the preservation of the public safety shall become in such district impracticable, in every such case such combinations shall be deemed a rebellion against the government of the United States, and during the continuance of such rebellion, and within the limits of the district which shall be so under the sway thereof, such limits to be prescribed by proclamation, it shall be lawful for the President of the United States, when in his judgment the public safety shall require it, to suspend the privileges of the writ of habeas corpus, to the end that such rebellion may be overthrown: Provided, That all the provisions of the second section of an act entitled "An act relating to habeas corpus, and regulating judicial proceedings in certain cases," approved March third, eighteen hundred and sixty-three, which relate to the discharge of prisoners other than prisoners of war, and to penalty for refusing to obey the order of the court, shall be in full force so far as the same are applicable to the provisions of this section: Provided further, That the President shall first have made proclamation, as now provided by law, commanding such insurgents to disperse: And provided also. That the provisions of this section shall not be in force after the end of the next regular session of Congress.

Sec. 5. That no person shall be a grand or petit juror in any court of the United States upon any inquiry, hearing, or trial of any suit, proceeding, or prosecution based upon or arising under the provisions of this act who shall, in the judgment of the court, be in complicity with any such combination or conspiracy; and every such juror shall, before entering upon any such inquiry, hearing, or trial, take and subscribe an oath in open court that he has never, directly or indirectly, counselled, advised, or voluntarily aided any such combination or conspiracy; and each and every person who shall take this oath, and shall therein swear falsely, shall be guilty of perjury, and shall be subject to the pains and penalties declared against that crime, and the first section of the act entitled "An act defining additional causes of challenge and prescribing an additional oath for grand and petit jurors in the United States courts," approved June seventeenth, eighteen hundred and sixty-two, be, and the same is hereby, repealed.

Sec. 6. That any person or persons, having knowledge that any of the wrongs conspired to be done and mentioned in the second section of this act are about to be committed, and having power to prevent or aid in preventing the same, shall neglect or refuse so to do, and such wrongful act shall be committed, such person or persons shall be liable to the person injured, or his legal representatives, for all damages caused by any such wrongful act which such first-named person or persons by reasonable diligence could have prevented; and such damages may be recovered in an action on the case in the proper circuit court of the United States, and any number of persons guilty of such wrongful neglect or refusal may be joined as defendants in such action: Provided, That such action shall be commenced within one year after such cause of action shall have accrued; and if the death of any person shall be caused by any such wrongful act and neglect, the legal representatives of such deceased person shall have such action therefor, and may recover not exceeding five thousand dollars damages therein, for the benefit of the widow of such deceased person, if any there be, or if there be no widow, for the benefit of the next of kin of such deceased person.

Sec. 7. That nothing herein contained shall be construed to supersede or repeal any former act or law except so far as the same may be repugnant thereto; and any offenses heretofore committed against the tenor of any former act shall be prosecuted, and any proceeding already commenced for the prosecution thereof shall be continued and completed, the same as if this act had not been passed, except so far as the provisions of this act may go to sustain and validate such proceedings.

Approved, April 20, 1871.

Source: Statutes at Large 17 (1871): 13–15.

APPENDIX FIVE

ENFORCEMENT RIDER IN THE CIVIL APPROPRIATION ACT OF JUNE 10, 1872

Chap. CDXV.—*An act making Appropriation for sundry civil Expenses of the Government for the fiscal Year ending June thirtieth, eighteen hundred and seventy-three, and for other Purposes.*

Be it enacted by the Senate and House of Representatives of the United States of America in Congress assembled, That the following sums be, and the same are hereby, appropriated, for the objects hereinafter expressed, for the fiscal year ending June thirtieth, eighteen hundred and seventy-three, viz.:

. . .

JUDICIARY

For defraying the expenses of the courts of the United States, including the District of Columbia; for jurors and witnesses, and expenses of suits in which the United States are concerned, of prosecutions for offenses committed against the United States; for the safe-keeping of prisoners; and for the expenses which may be incurred in the enforcement of the act, relative to the right of citizens to vote, of February twenty-eighth, eighteen hundred and seventy-one, or any acts amendatory thereof or supplementary thereto, three million two hundred thousand dollars; of which sum two hundred thousand dollars shall be available for the expenses incurred during the present fiscal year, the said act being hereby supplemented and amended so as to further provide as follows: "That whenever, in any county or parish, in any congressional district, there shall be ten citizens thereof of good standing who, prior to any registration of voters for an election for representative in Congress, or prior to any election at which a representative in Congress is to be voted for, shall make known, in writing to the judge of the circuit court of the United States for the district wherein such county or parish is situate, their desire to have said registration or election both guarded and scrutinized, it shall be the duty of the said judge of the circuit court, within not less than ten days prior to said registration or election, as the case may be, to open the said court at the most convenient point in said district; and the said court, when so opened by said judge, shall proceed to appoint and commission, from day to day, and from time to time, and under the hand of the said judge, and under the seal of said court, for such election district or voting precinct in said congressional district, as shall, in the manner herein prescribed, have been applied for, and to revoke, change, or renew said appointment from time to time, two citizens, residents of said election district or voting precinct in said county or parish, who shall be of different political parties, and able to read and write the English language, and who shall be known and designated as supervisors of election; and the said court, when opened by the said judge as required herein, shall, therefrom and thereafter and up to and including the day following the day of the election, be always open for the transaction of business under this act; and the powers and jurisdiction hereby granted and conferred shall be exercised, as well in vacation as in term time; and judge, sitting at chambers, shall have the same powers and jurisdiction, including the power of keeping order and of punishing any contempt of his authority, as when sitting in the court: *Provided,* That no compensation shall be allowed to the supervisors herein authorized to be appointed, except those appointed in cities or towns of twenty thousand or more inhabitants. And no person shall be appointed under this act as supervisor of election who is not at the time of his appointment a qualified voter of the county, parish, election district, or voting precinct for which he is appointed. And no person shall be appointed deputy-marshal under the act of which this is amendatory, who is not a qualified voter at the time of his appointment, in the county, parish, district, or precinct in which his duties are to be performed. And section thirteen of the act of which this is an amendment shall be construed to authorize and require the circuit courts of the United States in said section mentioned to name and appoint, as soon as may be after the passage of this act, the commissioners provided for in said section, in all cases in which such appointments have not already been made in conformity therewith. And the third section of the act to which this is an amendment shall be taken and construed to authorize each of the judges of the circuit courts of the United States to designate one or more of the judges of the district courts within his circuit to discharge the duties arising under this act or the act to which this is an amendment. And the words 'any person' in section four of the act of May thirty-first, eighteen hundred and seventy, shall be held to include any officer or other person having powers or duties of an official character under this act or the act to which this is an amendment: *Provided.* That nothing in this section shall be so construed as to authorize the appointment of any marshals or deputy-marshals in addition to those heretofore authorized by law: *And provided further.* That the supervisors herein provided for shall have no power or authority to make arrests or to perform other duties than to be in the immediate presence of the officers holding the election, and to witness all their proceedings, including the counting of the votes and making of a return thereof. And so much of said sum herein appropriated as may be necessary for said supplemental and amendatory provisions is hereby appropriated from and after the passage of this act."

. . .

Approved June 10, 1872.

Source: Statutes at Large 17 (1872): 347-49.

APPENDIX SIX

SECTIONS FROM THE ENFORCEMENT ACTS IN THE *REVISED STATUTES*, THEIR REPEALS, AND AMENDMENTS

Enforcement Law	Original Section	Section in *Rev. Stat.*	Explanation
1870 May 31	1	2004	Retained as sec. 1972 under Title 42 in the *United States Code 1988 Edition*
		629	Repealed on March 3, 1911 (*Statutes at Large*, 36:1168)
	2	2005	Repealed on February 8, 1894 (*Statutes at Large*, 28:36)
		2006	Repealed on February 8, 1894 (*Statutes at Large*, 28:36)
		629	Repealed on March 3, 1911 (*Statutes at Large*, 36:1168)
	3	2007	Repealed on February 8, 1894 (*Statutes at Large*, 28:36)
		2008	Repealed on February 8, 1894 (*Statutes at Large*, 28:36)
		629	Repealed on March 3, 1911 (*Statutes at Large*, 36:1168)
	4	2009	Repealed on February 8, 1894 (*Statutes at Large*, 28:36)
		5506	Repealed on February 8, 1894 (*Statutes at Large*, 28:37)
		629	Repealed on March 3, 1911 (*Statutes at Large*, 36:1168)
	5	5507	Repealed on March 4, 1909 (*Statutes at Large*, 35:1153)
	6	5508	Amended on March 4, 1909 (*Statutes at Large*, 35:1092); retained as sec. 241 under Title 18 of *United States Code 1994 Edition*

Enforcement Law	Original Section	Section in *Rev. Stat.*	Explanation
	7	5509	Repealed on March 4, 1909 (*Statutes at Large*, 35:1153)
	8	1022	Amended on March 4, 1909 (*Statutes at Large*, 5:1092–93)
		629	Repealed on March 3, 1911 (*Statutes at Large*, 36:1168)
	9	1982	Amended on March 4, 1909 (*Statutes at Large*, 5:1092–93, 1139, 1141–42)
		1983	Transfer of duties; on May 28, 1896 (*Statutes at Large*, 29:184)
	10	1984	
		1985	
		5517	Amended on March 4, 1909 (*Statutes at Large*, 5:1092–93)
	11	5516	Repealed on March 4, 1909 (*Statutes at Large*, 35:1154)
	12	1986	Amended on May 28, 1896 (*Statutes at Large*, 29:179,184); March 3, 1905 (ibid., 33:1207); February 26, 1919 (ibid., 40:1182)
		1987	
	13	1989	
	14	563	Repealed on March 3, 1911 (*Statutes at Large*, 36:1168)
		629	Repealed on March 3, 1911 (*Statutes at Large*, 36:1168)
		1786	Amended on March 3, 1911 (*Statutes at Large*, 36:1167)
	15	1787	Repealed on March 3, 1911 (*Statutes at Large*, 36:1168)
	16	563	Repealed on March 3, 1911 (*Statutes at Large*, 36:1168)
		629	Repealed on March 3, 1911 (*Statutes at Large*, 36:1168)
		641	Repealed on March 3, 1911 (*Statutes at Large*, 36:1168)
		699	Repealed on March 3, 1911 (*Statutes at Large*, 36:1168)

Enforcement Law	Original Section	Section in *Rev. Stat.*	Explanation
		1977	Application extended; June 15, 1880 (*Statutes at Large*, 21:204)
		2164	
	17	5510	Amended on March 4, 1909 (*Statutes at Large*, 35:1092); retained as sec. 242 under Title 18 of the *United States Code 1994 Edition*
	18	563	Repealed on March 3, 1911 (*Statutes at Large*, 36:1168)
		629	Repealed on March 3, 1911 (*Statutes at Large*, 36:1168)
		641	Repealed on March 3, 1911 (*Statutes at Large*, 36:1168)
		699	Repealed on March 3, 1911 (*Statutes at Large*, 36:1168)
		722	Amended, March 4, 1909 (*Statutes at Large*, 5:1088–1159); March 3, 1911 (ibid., 36:1087–1169)
	19	5511	Repealed on February 8, 1894 (*Statutes at Large*, 28:37)
	20	5512	Repealed on February 8, 1894 (*Statutes at Large*, 28:37)
	21	5514	Repealed on February 8, 1894 (*Statutes at Large*, 28:37)
	22	5515	Repealed on February 8, 1894 (*Statutes at Large*, 28:37)
	23	563	Repealed on March 3, 1911 (*Statutes at Large*, 36:1168)
		629	Repealed on March 3, 1911 (*Statutes at Large*, 36:1168)
		2010	Repealed on February 8, 1894 (*Statutes at Large*, 28:37)
1871 February 28	1	5512	Repealed on February 8, 1894 (*Statutes at Large*, 28:36)
		5513	Repealed on February 8, 1894 (*Statutes at Large*, 28:36)

Enforcement Law	Original Section	Section in *Rev. Stat.*	Explanation
	2	2011	Repealed on February 8, 1894 (*Statutes at Large*, 28:36)
		2012	Repealed on February 8, 1894 (*Statutes at Large*, 28:36)
		2013	Repealed on February 8, 1894 (*Statutes at Large*, 28:36)
	3	2014	Repealed on February 8, 1894 (*Statutes at Large*, 28:36)
	4	2016	Repealed on February 8, 1894 (*Statutes at Large*, 28:36)
	5	2017	Repealed on February 8, 1894 (*Statutes at Large*, 28:36)
		2018	Repealed on February 8, 1894 (*Statutes at Large*, 28:36)
	6	2019	Repealed on February 8, 1894 (*Statutes at Large*, 28:36)
	7	2020	Repealed on February 8, 1894 (*Statutes at Large*, 28:36)
	8	2021	Repealed on February 8, 1894 (*Statutes at Large*, 28:36)
		2022	Repealed on February 8, 1894 (*Statutes at Large*, 28:36)
	9	2023	Repealed on February 8, 1894 (*Statutes at Large*, 28:36)
	10	5522	Repealed on February 8, 1894 (*Statutes at Large*, 28:36)
		5523	Repealed on February 8, 1894 (*Statutes at Large*, 28:36)
	11	5521	Repealed on February 8, 1894 (*Statutes at Large*, 28:36)
	12	2024	Repealed on February 8, 1894 (*Statutes at Large*, 28:36)
	13	2025	Repealed on February 8, 1894 (*Statutes at Large*, 28:36)
		2026	Repealed on February 8, 1894 (*Statutes at Large*, 28:36)

Enforcement Law	Original Section	Section in *Rev. Stat.*	Explanation
		2027	Repealed on February 8, 1894 (*Statutes at Large*, 28:36)
	14	3689	Partially repealed on February 8, 1894 (*Statutes at Large*, 28:36)
	15	629	Repealed on March 3, 1911 (*Statutes at Large*, 36:1168)
	16	643	Partially repealed on February 8, 1894 (*Statutes at Large*, 28:37)
		646	Repealed on March 3, 1911 (*Statutes at Large*, 36:1168)
	17	645	Repealed on March 3, 1911 (*Statutes at Large*, 36:1168)
		950	
	19	27	Amended on February 14, 1899 (*Statutes at Large*, 30:830)
1871 April 20	1	563	Repealed on March 3, 1911 (*Statutes at Large*, 36:1168)
		629	Repealed on March 3, 1911 (*Statutes at Large*, 36:1168)
		699	Repealed on March 3, 1911 (*Statutes at Large*, 36:1168)
		1979	
	2	563	Repealed on March 3, 1911 (*Statutes at Large*, 36:1168)
		629	Repealed on March 3, 1911 (*Statutes at Large*, 36:1168)
		699	Repealed on March 3, 1911 (*Statutes at Large*, 36:1168)
		1980	
		5336	Repealed on March 4, 1909 (*Statutes at Large*, 35:1153)
		5406	Repealed on March 4, 1909 (*Statutes at Large*, 35:1153)
		5407	Repealed on March 4, 1909 (*Statutes at Large*, 35:1153)
		5518	Repealed on March 4, 1909 (*Statutes at Large*, 35:1154)

Enforcement Law	Original Section	Section in *Rev. Stat.*	Explanation
		5519	Repealed on March 4, 1909 (*Statutes at Large*, 35:1154)
		5520	Repealed on February 8, 1894 (*Statutes at Large*, 28:37)
	3	5299	
	5	800	Repealed on March 3, 1911 (*Statutes at Large*, 36:1168)
		801	Repealed on March 3, 1911 (*Statutes at Large*, 36:1168)
		822	Repealed on March 3, 1911 (*Statutes at Large*, 36:1168)
		629	Repealed on March 3, 1911 (*Statutes at Large*, 36:1168)
	6	629	Repealed on March 3, 1911 (*Statutes at Large*, 36:1168)
		1981	
1872 June 10	1	2015	Repealed on February 8, 1894 (*Statutes at Large*, 28:36)
		2028	Repealed on February 8, 1894 (*Statutes at Large*, 28:36)
		2029	Repealed on February 8, 1894 (*Statutes at Large*, 28:36)
		2030	Repealed on February 8, 1894 (*Statutes at Large*, 28:36)
		2031	Repealed on February 8, 1894 (*Statutes at Large*, 28:36)

Sources: United States, *Revised Statutes at Large* (Washington, D.C.: U.S. Government Printing Office, 1875), 348–52, 353–61, 1073–78; *Second Edition of Revised Statutes of the United States* (Washington, D.C.: U.S. Government Print Office, 1878), in *Statutes at Large* 18, pt. 1 (1878): 347–57, 1067–72, 1146–57, 1085; *Statutes at Large* 28, pt. 1 (1894): 36–37; ibid., 35, pt. 1 (1909): 1092–93, 1153–59; ibid., 36 (1911): 1168–69; United States, *United States Code 1988 Edition* (Washington, D.C.: U.S. Government Printing Office, 1989), 16:340–44; United States, *United States Code 1994 Edition* (Washington, D.C.: U.S. Government Printing Office, 1995), 9:69; United States, Library of Congress, *Index to the Federal Statutes, 1874–1931; General and Permanent Law Contained in the Revised Statutes of 1874 and Volumes 18–46 of the Statutes at Large*, ed. Walter H. McClenon and Wilfred C. Gilbert (Washington, D.C.: U.S. Government Printing Office, 1933), 165–69, 367–69, 1222–23, 1264–65.

CRIMINAL PROSECUTIONS UNDER ENFORCEMENT ACTS, 1870–1894, BY SECTION AND YEAR

Year	South[b]	North[c]	Others[d]	National
		Number of Cases (Convictions/Dismissals[a])		
1870	16 (0/16)	15 (15/0)	28 (17/11)	59 (32/27)
1871	206 (108/98)	27 (11/16)	81 (9/72)	314 (128/186)
1872	603 (448/155)	27 (6/21)	226 (2/224)	856 (456/400)
1873	1,148 (466/682)	33 (2/31)	123 (1/122)	1,304 (469/835)
1874	890 (97/793)	12 (4/8)	4 (1/63)	966 (102/864)
1875	216 (16/200)	4 (0/4)	15 (2/12)	234 (18/216)
1876	108 (2/106)	1 (1/0)	43 (0/43)	152 (3/149)
1877	133 (6/127)	40 (26/14)	61 (6/55)	234 (38/196)
1878	23 (0/23)	1 (0/1)	2 (0/2)	26 (0/26)
1879	93 (14/79)	15 (9/6)	38 (17/21)	146 (40/106)
1880	53 (0/53)	1 (0/1)	16 (1/15)	70 (1/69)
1881	177 (95/82)	132 (69/63)	33 (8/25)	342 (166/176)
1882	154 (23/131)	72 (3/69)	31 (6/25)	257 (32/225)
1883	201 (12/189)	66 (32/34)	20 (6/13)	287 (50/237)
1884	160 (17/143)	8 (2/6)	22 (7/15)	190 (26/164)
1885	107 (1/106)	173 (79/94)	3 (1/2)	283 (81/202)
1886	8 (0/8)	30 (1/29)	9 (5/4)	47 (6/41)
1887	2 (0/2)	62 (34/28)	32 (11/21)	96 (45/51)
1888	14 (1/13)	19 (4/15)	98 (20/78)	131 (25/106)
1889	22 (11/11)	256 (60/196)	136 (55/81)	414 (126/288)
1890	42 (8/34)	51 (15/36)	213 (67/213)	306 (90/216)
1891	19 (0/19)	80 (23/57)	96 (23/73)	195 (46/149)
1892	12 (1/11)	100 (10/90)	2 (2/20)	134 (13/121)
1893	17 (0/17)	123 (40/80)	1 (10/71)	221 (50/171)
1894	25 (0/25)	44 (20/24)	14 (1/13)	83 (21/62)

Sources: Annual Report of the Attorney General of the United States, House Executive Documents, 41 Cong. 3 sess., no. 90; 43 Cong. 1 sess., no. 6; 2 sess., no. 7; 44 Cong. 1 sess., no. 14; 2 sess., no.

20; 45 Cong. 2 sess., no. 7; 3 sess., no. 7; 46 Cong. 2 sess., no. 8; 3 sess., no. 9; 47 Cong. 1 sess., no. 4; 2 sess., no. 8; 48 Cong. 1 sess., no. 9; 2 sess., no. 12; 49 Cong. 1 sess., no. 7; 2 sess., no. 8; 50 Cong. 1 sess., no. 7; 2 sess., no. 7; 51 Cong. 1 sess., no. 7; 2 sess., no. 7; 53 Cong. 2 sess., no. 7; 3 sess., no. 7; *Senate Executive Documents*, 42 Cong. 3 sess., no. 32. Table model and pre-1877 figures consulted in Everette Swinney, "Suppressing the Ku Klux Klan: The Enforcement of the Reconstruction Amendments, 1870-1874" (Ph.D. diss., University of Texas at Austin, 1966), 363 – 64; William Gillette, *Retreat from Reconstruction, 1869-1879* (Baton Rouge: Louisiana State University Press, 1979), 43.

Note: The reports of the attorney general used such terms as "Enforcement Act of May 31, 1870" (for the 1870 report), "Enforcement Acts" (for 1871 – 80 reports), and "Election Laws" (for 1881 – 94 reports).

[a] Dismissals include acquittals and cases that were nolled, discontinued, or quashed.

[b] The ten southern states (Alabama, Arkansas, Florida, Georgia, Louisiana, Mississippi, North Carolina, South Carolina, Texas, Virginia).

[c] The remaining Union states (California, Connecticut, Illinois, Indiana, Iowa, Kansas, Massachusetts, Michigan, New Hampshire, New Jersey, New York, Ohio, Pennsylvania, Rhode Island, and Idaho Territory).

[d] This group includes border states (Delaware, Kentucky, Maryland, Missouri, Tennessee, West Virginia), federal territories, and new states (Colorado, Dakota, Montana, Nebraska, Nevada, New Mexico, Oklahoma, Oregon, Utah, Washington, Wisconsin, Wyoming, and District of Columbia).

STRENGTH DISTRIBUTION OF THE MAJOR PARTIES IN THE FEDERAL GOVERNMENT, 1861–1909

Year	President (Party)	Cong.	House Rep/Dem	Senate Rep/Dem
1861–65	A. Lincoln (R)	37	105/43	1/10
		38[a]	102/75	36/9
1865–69	A. Johnson (R)	39	149/42	2/10
		40	143/49	42/11
1869–77	U. S. Grant (R)	41	49/63	56/11
		42	134/104	52/17
		43	194/92	49/19
		44	169/109	45/29
1877–81	R. B. Hayes (R)	45	40/153	39/36
		46	130/149	33/42
1881	J. A. Garfield (R)	47	47/135	37/37
1881–85	C. A. Arthur (R)	48	118/197	38/36
1885–89	G. Cleveland (D)	49	140/183	43/34
		50	152/169	39/37
1889–93	B. Harrison (R)	51	66/159	39/37
		52	88/235	47/39
1893–97	G. Cleveland (D)	53	127/218	38/44
		54	244/105	43/39
1897–1901	W. McKinley (R)	55	204/113	47/34
		56	185/163	53/26
1901–9	T. Roosevelt (R)	57	97/151	55/31
		58	208/178	57/33
		59	250/136	57/33
		60	222/164	61/31

Source: Samuel Charles Patterson, Roger H. Davidson, and Randall B. Ripley, *A More Perfect Union: Introduction to American Government* (Pacific Grove, Calif.: Brooks/Cole, 1989), app. C.

[a] In this Congress, the majority party is marked as "Unionist Party."

ABBREVIATIONS

CG	*Congressional Globe*
Collected Works	Abraham Lincoln. *The Collected Works of Abraham Lincoln.* Edited by Roy P. Basler. New Brunswick, N.J.: Rutgers University Press, 1953 – 55.
CR	*Congressional Record*
CSP	*The Papers of Charles Sumner* (on microfilm), Larmont Library, Harvard University
CU	Columbia University Library
FDP	Frederick Douglass. *The Frederick Douglass Papers.* Edited by John W. Blassingame and John R. McKivigan. 5 vols. New Haven: Yale University Press, 1979 – 91.
Federal Cases	*The Federal Cases: Comprising Cases Argued and Determined in the Circuit and District Courts of the United States; from the Earliest Time to the Beginning of Federal Reporter, Arranged Alphabetically by the Titles of the Cases, and Numbered Consecutively.* St. Paul: West, 1894 – 97.
Federal Reporter	*Federal Reporter: Cases Argued and Determined in the Circuit and District Courts of the United States.* St. Paul: West, 1881 – 91.
HPC	Rutherford B. Hayes Presidential Center, Fremont, Ohio
HT	Huntington Library, San Marino, California
HU	Houghton Library, Harvard University
KKK Report	United States. Congress. Joint Select Committee on the Condition of Affairs in the Late Insurrectionary States. *Report of the Joint Select Committee Appointed to Inquire into the Condition of Affairs in the Late Insurrectionary States, So Far as Regards the Execution of Laws, and the Lives and Property of the Citizens of the United States and Testimony Taken* (South Carolina, vol. 3), 42 Cong. 2 sess. Reprinted as vol. 5 of the *Ku Klux Klan Conspiracy.* Washington, D.C.: U.S. Government Printing Office, 1872.
LC	Manuscripts Division, Library of Congress
Messages and Papers	United States. President. *A Compilation of the Messages and Papers of the Presidents of the United States.* Edited by James D. Richardson. Washington, D.C.: U.S. Government Printing Office, 1896 – 99.
MHS	Massachusetts Historical Society, Boston
NA	National Archives
NHHS	New Hampshire Historical Society, Concord, New Hampshire
NYPL	New York Public Library

Selected

Letters   Charles Sumner. *The Selected Letters of Charles Sumner.* Edited by Beverly Wilson Palmer. 2 vols. Boston: Northeastern University Press, 1990.

Statutes

at Large   United States. *The Statutes at Large and Proclamations of the United States of America ... edited by George P. Sanger.* Vol. 16 (Dec. 1869 to Mar. 1871), Vol. 17 (Mar. 1871 to Mar. 1873). Boston: Little, Brown, 1871–73; United States. *The Statutes at Large of the United States ... edited, printed, and published under the authority of an act of Congress, and under the direction of the Secretary of State.* Vol. 18, pt. 3 (Dec. 1873 to Mar. 1875), to Vol. 49, pt. 2 (Jan. 1935 to June 1936). Washington, D.C.: U.S. Government Printing Office, 1875–1936.

UR   University of Rochester Library

U.S.   *United States Supreme Court Reports*

NOTES

Introduction

1. According to Eric Foner, 267 blacks were among the 1,000 delegates to the constitutional conventions of 1867–69 that created the postwar state governments for the southern states. During Reconstruction, 683 blacks served in the lower houses of state legislatures, and 112 served in the state senates. P. B. S. Pinchback served briefly as the governor of Louisiana. At the national level, in addition to black senators and congressmen, there were black ambassadors. Blacks also held numerous federal positions. Eric Foner, *Freedom's Lawmakers: A Directory of Black Office-holders during Reconstruction* (New York: Oxford University Press, 1993), xiv–xv; also see Paul Finkelman, introduction to *African Americans and the Right to Vote*, vol. 6 of *Race, Law, and American History, 1700–1990*, ed. Paul Finkelman (New York: Garland, 1992), viii.

2. Although I use "black suffrage" more frequently than "black male suffrage" in the following pages, it should be understood that both terms indicate black male suffrage.

3. Samuel Denny Smith, *The Negro in Congress, 1870–1901* (1940; reprint, Port Washington, N.Y.: Kennikat, 1966), 4–6.

4. J. Morgan Kousser, *The Shaping of Southern Politics: Suffrage Restriction and the Establishment of the One-Party South, 1800–1910* (New Haven: Yale University Press, 1974), 182–224; Paul Lewinson, *Race, Class, Party: A History of Negro Suffrage and White Politics in the South* (1932; reprint, New York: Russell & Russell, 1963), 79–97; Finkelman, introduction to *African Americans and the Right to Vote*, xiii–ix; Frederic D. Ogden, *The Poll Tax in the South* (Birmingham: University of Alabama Press, 1958), 1–31.

5. John W. Burgess, *Reconstruction and the Constitution, 1866–1876* (New York: Charles Scribner's Sons, 1902), 245; Claude G. Bowers, *The Tragic Era* (Cambridge: Riverside Press, 1929), 307-8; Bernard A. Weisberger, "The Dark and Bloody Ground of Reconstruction Historiography," *Journal of Southern History* 25 (November 1959): 428; Walter L. Fleming, *Sequel of Appomattox: A Chronicle of the Reunion of the States* (New Haven: Yale University Press, 1919), 292. For early general accounts of Reconstruction and federal enforcement of black suffrage, see also William Archibald Dunning's *Essay on the Civil War and Reconstruction and Related Topics* (1897; reprint, New York: Harper & Row, 1965) and *Reconstruction, Political and Economic, 1865–1877* (New York: Harper & Brothers, 1907).

6. A. Caperton Braxton, *The Fifteenth Amendment: An Account of Its Enactment* (1903; reprint, Lynchburg, Va.: J. P. Bell, 1934), 16-26. See also Kirk H. Porter, *A History of Suffrage in the United States* (Chicago: University of Chicago Press, 1918).

7. William Watson Davis, "The Federal Enforcement Acts," in *Studies in Southern History and Politics Inscribed to William Archibald Dunning . . . by His Former Pupils*, ed. James W. Garner (1914; reprint, Port Washington, N.Y.: Kennikat, 1964), 205-28. For mixed concerns argument, see

John Mabry Mathews, *Legislative and Judicial History of the Fifteenth Amendment* (Baltimore: Johns Hopkins Press, 1909), 118.

8. William Gillette, *The Right to Vote: Politics and the Passage of the Fifteenth Amendment* (Baltimore: Johns Hopkins University Press, 1965); William Gillette, *Retreat from Reconstruction, 1869–1879* (Baton Rouge: Louisiana State University Press, 1979), 442. For similar views, see Howard K. Beale, "On Writing Reconstruction History," *American Historical Review* 45 (July 1940): 819; James M. McPherson, *The Struggle for Equality: Abolitionists and the Negro in the Civil War and Reconstruction* (Princeton: Princeton University Press, 1964), 430; Phyllis F. Field, *The Politics of Race in New York: The Struggle for Black Suffrage in the Civil War Era* (Ithaca, N.Y.: Cornell University Press, 1982), 230; and Leslie H. Fishel Jr., "Northern Prejudice and Negro Suffrage, 1865–1870," *Journal of Negro History* 39 (January 1954): 8–26.

9. LaWanda Cox and John H. Cox, "Negro Suffrage and Republican Politics: The Problem of Motivation in Reconstruction Historiography," *Journal of Southern History* 33 (August 1967): 303–30. Another two very important general accounts of Reconstruction that directly reversed the interpretations of the Dunning school are Kenneth Stampp's *The Era of Reconstruction, 1865–1877* (New York: Vintage, 1965) and William R. Brock's *An American Crisis: Congress and Reconstruction, 1865–1877* (New York: St. Martin's, 1963). Both Stampp and Brock viewed the radical Reconstruction as a true reform effort of the Republican party in the postwar years.

10. Eric L. McKitrick, *Andrew Johnson and Reconstruction* (Chicago: University of Chicago Press, 1960), 55-56; Michael Les Benedict, *A Compromise of Principle: Congressional Republicans and Reconstruction, 1863–1869* (New York: W. W. Norton, 1974), 326-27.

11. Everette Swinney, *Suppressing the Ku Klux Klan: The Enforcement of the Reconstruction Amendments, 1870–1877* (New York: Garland, 1987), 87.

12. Stephen Cresswell, "Enforcing the Enforcement Acts: The Department of Justice in Northern Mississippi, 1870–1890," *Journal of Southern History* 53 (August 1987): 421-40.

13. James E. Sefton, *The United States Army and Reconstruction, 1865–1877* (Baton Rouge: Louisiana State University Press, 1967), esp. chaps. 10–11.

14. William Gillette, *Retreat from Reconstruction*, esp. chaps. 2–7.

15. Eric Foner, *Reconstruction: America's Unfinished Revolution, 1863–1877* (New York: Harper & Row, 1988), chaps. 9–11.

16. Roger Alan Cohen, "The Lost Jubilee: New York Republicans and the Politics of Reconstruction and Reform, 1867–1878" (Ph.D. diss., Columbia University, 1976), 55, 76. For a good study on the politics of black suffrage at the state level in the North, see James C. Mohr, ed., *Radical Republicans in the North: State Politics during Reconstruction* (Baltimore: Johns Hopkins University Press, 1976); see also Richard O. Curry, ed., *Radicalism, Racism, and Party Realignment: The Border States during Reconstruction* (Baltimore: Johns Hopkins University Press, 1969).

17. John G. Sproat, *"The Best Men": Liberal Reformers in the Gilded Age* (1968; reprint, Chicago: University of Chicago Press, 1982).

18. Patrick Riddleberger, "Republican Abandonment of the Negro during the Reconstruction," *Journal of Negro History* 45 (April 1960): 88-102.

19. Harold M. Hyman, *A More Perfect Union: The Impact of the Civil War and Reconstruction on the Constitution* (New York: Alfred A. Knopf, 1973), 437–38, 530.

20. Harold M. Hyman and William M. Wiecek, *Equal Justice under Law: Constitutional Development, 1835 – 1875* (New York: Harper & Row, 1982), 512 – 13.

21. Robert J. Kaczorowski, *The Politics of Judicial Interpretation: The Federal Court, Department of Justice, and Civil Rights, 1866 – 1876* (New York: Oceana, 1985), xiii – xiv.

22. Vincent P. De Santis, *Republicans Face the Southern Question: The New Departure Years, 1877 – 1897* (Baltimore: Johns Hopkins University Press, 1959); Stanley P. Hirshson, *Farewell to the Bloody Shirt: Northern Republicans and the Southern Negro, 1877 – 1893* (Bloomington: Indiana University Press, 1962).

23. Richard E. Welch Jr., "The Federal Election Bill of 1890: Postscripts and Prelude," *Journal of American History* 52 (December 1965): 511 – 26.

24. Robert M. Goldman, *"A Free Ballot and a Fair Count": The Department of Justice and the Enforcement of Voting Rights in the South, 1877 – 1893* (New York: Garland, 1990).

Chapter One. The Road to the Fifteenth Amendment, 1860 – 1870

1. For major studies of the origins of the Republican party, see Eric Foner, *Free Soil, Free Labor, Free Men: The Ideology of the Republican Party before the Civil War* (New York: Oxford University Press, 1970); William E. Gienapp, *The Origins of the Republican Party, 1852 – 1856* (New York: Oxford University Press, 1987); Tyler Anbinder, *Nativism and Slavery: The Northern Know Nothings and the Politics of the 1850s* (New York: Oxford University Press, 1992); Michael F. Holt, *Forging a Majority: The Formation of the Republican Party in Pittsburgh, 1848 – 1860* (New Haven: Yale University Press, 1969).

2. I notice the difficulties and inconsistency, as demonstrated by several major studies of the Civil War and Reconstruction period, in defining such terms as *radical, conservative,* and *moderate* Republicans. For instance, in his study of the Republican party before the Civil War, Eric Foner includes in his list of radical Republicans Charles Sumner, Thaddeus Stevens, Francis Gillette, Henry Wilson, John Andrew, Salmon P. Chase, Ben Wade, Jacob Howard, and Zachariah Chandler. The British historian W. R. Brock, in his study of Reconstruction, adds a few more names to the radical group, such as Timothy Howe, William P. Fessenden, J. W. Grimes, William D. Kelley, George S. Boutwell, Elihu B. Washburn, and James F. Wilson. Eric L. McKitrick, in his classic account of 1865 – 66 politics, credits William Pitt Fessenden with erecting the Fourteenth Amendment but labels him a leader of moderate Republicans in Congress. Michael Les Benedict, supported by a painstaking research of congressional voting records, marks Fessenden as a "consistent conservative" Republican from the Thirty-eighth to Fortieth Congress. Realizing the shifts in the voting behavior of the Republicans, William Gillette in his in-depth study of the politics and passage of the Fifteenth Amendment wisely uses the *radical* and *moderate* labels specifically to indicate the differences in Republican attitudes toward the desirability of black suffrage.

In this study, the term *radical Republicans* is used as a working definition to describe those Republicans who tended to advocate and support more radical changes in race relations in addition to the abolition of slavery. It needs to be made clear that the radicals did not share or possess the same degree of radicalism on every agenda of Reconstruction politics. In fact, as the following pages

show, radicals and moderates shifted when the issues of black enfranchisement and federal enforcement of black suffrage were discussed.

See Foner, *Free Soil*, 281-85; Hans L. Trefousse, *The Radical Republicans: Lincoln's Vanguard
for Racial Justice* (New York: Alfred A. Knopf, 1969), 1-34; William R. Brock, *An American Crisis:
Congress and Reconstruction, 1865-1867* (New York: St. Martin's, 1963), 86-90; Eric L. Mc-
Kitrick, *Andrew Johnson and Reconstruction* (Chicago: University of Chicago Press, 1960); Michael
Les Benedict, *A Compromise of Principle: Congressional Republicans and Reconstruction,
1863-1869* (New York: W. W. Norton, 1974), 21-58; David H. Donald, *The Politics of Reconstruc-
tion, 1863-1867* (Baton Rouge: Louisiana University Press, 1965), 29-33; William Gillette, *The
Right to Vote: Politics and the Passage of the Fifteenth Amendment* (Baltimore: Johns Hopkins Uni-
versity Press, 1965), 47-48 n. 6. For a detailed and critical roll call study of House members' voting behavior on important Reconstruction issues from 1863 to 1869, see John Lockhart McCarthy,
"Reconstruction Legislation and Voting Alignments in the House of Representatives, 1863-1869"
(Ph.D. diss., Yale University, 1971).

3. William H. Furness to Charles Sumner, Philadelphia, December 10, 1860, *CSP*; Sumner is
quoted from an autograph document, undated, Charles Sumner Papers, LC; James M. Ashley, Addresses delivered at Craneville, Ohio, January 27, 1859, and at Charloe, Ohio, January 31, 1859,
quoted in *Duplicate Copy of the Souvenir from the Afro-American League of Tennessee to Hon.
James M. Ashley of Ohio*, ed. Benjamin W. Arnett (Philadelphia: Publishing House of the A.M.E.
Church, 1894), 16-17, 24. For a perceptive discussion of radical Republican thinking on the eve
of the Civil War, see Herman Belz, *Emancipation and Equal Rights: Politics and Constitutionalism
in the Civil War Era* (New York: W. W. Norton, 1978), esp. xv.

4. Lydia Maria Child to Charles Sumner, Wayland, December 26, 1859; Woodbury Davis to
Charles Sumner, Portland, February 10, 1860, *CSP*; Charles Sumner to the duchess of Argyll (Elizabeth Georgiana Campbell), Washington, December 14, 1860, Charles Sumner Papers, HT.

5. September 4, 1860, Edward Bates, *The Diary of Edward Bates, 1859-1966*, ed. Howard K.
Beale (1933; reprint, New York: Da Capo, 1971), 141; Foner, *Free Soil*, 264-66; James M. McPher-
son, *Battle Cry of Freedom: The Civil War Era* (New York: Oxford University Press, 1988), 159;
Welles to Lincoln, Hartford, December 10, 1860, Gideon Welles Papers, HT.

6. Trumbull had made similar remarks at the Republican convention in 1856 that the Republican party was not for "the welfare of the Negro" but "for the protection of the laboring whites, for
the protection [of whites] and [their] liberties." Address of Senator Lyman Trumbull, delivered in
Chicago, August 7, 1858, quoted from Leon F. Litwack, *North of Slavery: The Negro in the Free
States, 1790-1860* (Chicago: University of Chicago Press, 1961), 268; McPherson, *Battle Cry*, 159.

7. Ben Wade's remarks (March 7, 1860), *CG*, 36 Cong. 1 sess., 1860, appendix, 150-55; Lincoln's reply to Stephen Douglas in the first Lincoln-Douglas Debate, August 21, 1858, *Collected
Works*, 3:13-36, esp. 16.

8. Republican Party Platform of 1860, Kirk H. Porter and Donald Bruce Johnson, eds., *National
Party Platforms, 1840-1964* (Urbana: University of Illinois Press, 1966), 31-33.

9. Historians have presented different arguments on the nature of the Republican party's prewar
ideology. Malcolm Moos argues that although the slavery issue galvanized the party into action, liberal capitalism was "a cohesive force in bringing together the elements that formed the Republican
party and giving it the staying power to last out more than one or two political engagements." Eric

Foner, while recognizing that a number of ideas had been essential to Republican ideology, argues that the deep-seated concern was the expansion of the idea of free labor. Foner points to "the creation and articulation of an ideology which blended personal and sectional interest with morality so perfectly that it became the most potent political force in the nation. The free labor assault upon slavery and southern society, coupled with the idea that an aggressive Slave Power was threatening the most fundamental values and interests of the free states, hammered the slavery issue home to the northern public more emphatically than an appeal to morality alone could ever have done." William Gienapp agrees with Foner that free labor did have a distinguishing role in Republican ideology, but he argues that it did so only after 1857. He believes that the dominant force of the party's political outlook before and around 1856 was the idea of republicanism. Malcolm Moos, *The Republicans: A History of Their Party* (New York: Random House, 1956), 39–40; Foner, *Free Soil*, 309–10; Gienapp, *Origins of the Republican Party*, 353–57, 364–65.

10. Foner, *Free Soil*, 291.

11. Wilson's remarks (April 12, 1860), *CG*, 36 Cong. 1 sess., 1860, pt. 2:1684; Litwack, *North of Slavery*, 270-72.

12. Abraham Lincoln, "Speech at Peoria, Illinois," *Illinois Journal*, October 21, 1854, reprinted in *Collected Works*, 247-83, esp. 256.

13. "Unpalatable Counsel," *New York Tribune*, September 22, 1855.

14. Gilbert Thomas Stephenson, *Race Distinctions in American Law* (New York: D. Appleton and Co., 1910), 281–341; James C. Mohr, *The Radical Republicans and Reform in New York during Reconstruction* (Ithaca, N.Y.: Cornell University Press, 1973), 205; for voting requirements in colonial times, see Robert J. Dinkin, *Voting in Revolutionary America: A Study of Elections in the Original Thirteen States, 1776–1789* (Westport, Conn.: Greenwood, 1982), chap. 2; see also Kirk H. Porter, *A History of Suffrage in the United States* (Chicago: University of Chicago Press, 1918), chaps. 2, 3, and 4; Charles H. Wesley, "Negro Suffrage in the Period of Constitution-Making, 1787–1865," *Journal of Negro History* 32 (April 1947): 154–60; Edward Price, "The Black Voting Rights in Pennsylvania, 1780–1900," *Pennsylvania Magazine of History and Biography* 100 (July 1976): 356–73, esp. 363; Marion Thompson Wright, "Negro Suffrage in New Jersey, 1776–1875," *Journal of Negro History* 33 (April 1948): 174–76.

15. Robert R. Dykstra, "Bright Radical Star," in *Radical Republicans in the North: State Politics during Reconstruction*, ed. James C. Mohr (Baltimore: Johns Hopkins University Press, 1976), 168; Ronald P. Formisano, "The Edge of Caste: Colored Suffrage in Michigan, 1827–1861," *Michigan History* 56 (Spring 1972): 19–41; Paul Finkelman, "Prelude to the Fourteenth Amendment: Black Legal Rights in the Antebellum North," *Rutgers Law Journal* 17 (1986): 477–79; Litwack, *North of Slavery*, 271.

16. In 1860, Lincoln won 54 percent of the vote in New York, but the black suffrage amendment received only 37 percent, virtually all from the Republicans. McPherson, *Battle Cry*, 225; Frederick Douglass, "Equal Suffrage Defeated," *Douglass' Monthly* (December 1860) (reprint, New York: Negro Universities Press, 1969), 369; Litwack, *North of Slavery*, 91; Phyllis F. Field, *The Politics of Race in New York: The Struggle for Black Suffrage in the Civil War Era* (Ithaca, N.Y.: Cornell University Press, 1982), 187–219; Mohr, *Radical Republicans and Reform*, 205.

17. Russell Evrett to Thomas Haines Dudley, Pittsburgh, April 17, 1860, Thomas Haines Dudley Papers, HT.

18. Frederick Douglass, "What the Black Man Wants," speech delivered at the Thirty-second Annual Meeting of the Massachusetts Anti-Slavery Society in Boston on January 26, 1865, in William D. Kelley, Wendell Phillips, and Frederick Douglass, *The Equality of All Men before the Law Claimed and Defended in Speeches by Hon. William D. Kelley, Wendell Phillips, and Frederick Douglass* (Boston: Rand and Avery, 1865), ser. 3, 37; see also *FDP*, 4:59–69.

19. MS of speech, marked "1861," in S. B. Anthony Papers, LC, quoted in McPherson, *Struggle for Equality*, 226–27; see also 221–59 for northern abolitionists' attitudes toward black civil and political rights.

20. Lieber to Sumner, New York, December 19, 1861; Lieber to Bates, New York, June 8, 1862, Lieber Papers, HT. For a lucid and perceptive discussion of the Union responses to the runaway slaves during the Civil War, see Ira Berlin, "The Black Military Experience, 1861–1867," in *Freedom: A Documentary History of Emancipation, 1861–1867*, ser. 2, *The Black Military Experience*, ed. Ira Berlin (London: Cambridge University Press, 1982), 1–34; see also Harold M. Hyman, *The Radical Republicans and Reconstruction, 1861–1870* (Indianapolis: Bobbs-Merrill, 1967), lxiii.

21. Lieber to Sumner, New York, April 29, 1862, Lieber Papers, HT.

22. Bigelow to Bowen, September, 1862, John Bigelow Papers, NYPL, quoted from Margaret Antoinette Clapp, *Forgotten First Citizen: John Bigelow* (1947; reprint, New York: Greenwood, 1968), 176–77.

23. United States, *Official Opinions of the Attorneys General of the United States*, 10:387–89, quoted from Marvin R. Cain, *Lincoln's Attorney General Edward Bates of Missouri* (Columbia: University of Missouri Press, 1965), 223–24; Samuel E. Sewall to Charles Sumner, Melrose, December 28, 1862, *CSP*, reel 27.

24. The Bates-Lieber exchanges on suffrage and citizenship are summarized from Bates to Lieber, Washington, October 10, October 21, November 22, 1862; Lieber to Bates, October 25, November 25, 1862, Lieber Papers, HT.

25. Bates to Lieber, Washington, October 10, 1862, Lieber Papers, HT. Lieber possessed a much more progressive and liberal view on possible constitutional changes. He saw that the war had brought an opportunity to redefine constitutionalism and rights. "No advance of mankind can be imagined without the change, expansion or contraction of old rights and the addition of new ones," Lieber declared. He defined a right as "a well-founded claim of man on man" but added, "Every claim that man makes on man must be a moral claim." Since slavery was immoral, the "old claim" had to be abolished or the "new claim" had to be established: "that is to say, laws of abolition or laws of establishment must be enacted." Lieber to Bates, New York, October 18, 1862, Lieber Papers, HT.

26. Julian's remarks (January 14, 1862), *CG*, 37 Cong. 2 sess., 1862, pt. 1:327–32; see also Patrick W. Riddleberger, *George Washington Julian Radical Republican: A Study in Nineteenth-Century Politics and Reform* (Indianapolis: Indiana Historical Bureau, 1966), 166; Hyman, *Radical Republicans*, 38–50.

27. In March 1862, Lincoln hoped that Congress would pass a measure to authorize the states to initiate and administer compensated emancipation. On July 14, 1862, Lincoln asked Congress to authorize the issuance of governmental bonds to states that adopted a compensated emancipation program. *Collected Works*, 5:144–46, 317–18; see also *CG*, 37 Cong. 2 sess., 1862, pt. 4:3322–23, 3340; Ira Berlin, "Black Military Experience," 1–34; Belz, *Emancipation and Equal Rights*, 38-39.

28. Bates had favored the speedy deportation of freed slaves as a necessary component of the administration's emancipation program. Bates is quoted in Cain, *Lincoln's Attorney General*, 213.

29. George B. McClellan to Lincoln, July 7, 1862, in Edward McPherson, ed., *The Political History of the United States of America, during the Great Rebellion* . . . (Washington, D.C.: Philip and Solomons, 1864), 385.

30. David Donald, *Lincoln Reconsidered: Essays on the Civil War Era* (1956; reprint, New York: Vintage, 1989), 106.

31. Historian Barbara J. Fields emphasizes that the slaves' voluntary actions of running away from plantations preceded Lincoln's call for their emancipation and that such actions demonstrated the slaves' political consciousness for gaining freedom by their own efforts during the early period of the Civil War. She argues that "their experience with slave owners . . . made slaves see Lincoln as the emancipator before he saw himself that way. . . . It was the slaves' acting on that foreknowledge that forced Lincoln to become the emancipator." Barbara J. Fields, "Slavery, Race, and Ideology in the United States of America," *New Left Review*, 181 (May/June, 1990): 111.

32. Berlin, "Black Military Experience," 10 – 15, esp. 14 – 15; Eric Foner, *Reconstruction: America's Unfinished Revolution, 1863 – 1877* (New York: Harper & Row, 1988), 8.

33. August 3, 1862, Salmon P. Chase, *Inside Lincoln's Cabinet: The Civil War Diary of Salmon P. Chase*, ed. David H. Donald (New York: Longmans, Green, and Co., 1954), 105 – 6.

34. Frederick Douglass, "The Proclamation and a Negro Army: An Address Delivered in New York, New York, On 6 February 1863," in *FDP*, 3:550 – 51.

35. Frederick Douglass, "The Present and Future of Colored Race in America," *Douglass' Monthly* (June 1863): 833-36.

36. Frederick Douglass, "Emancipation, Racism and the Work Before US: An Address Delivered in Philadelphia, Pennsylvania, On 4 December 1863," *Proceedings of the Thirtieth Anniversary Meeting of the American Anti-Slavery Society*, in *FDP*, 3:598 – 609, esp. 608 – 9; for Lincoln's Gettysburg Address, see *Collected Works*, 7:17 – 23.

37. *Proceedings of the National Convention of Colored Men Held in Syracuse, New York, October 4 – 7, 1864; With the Bill of Wrongs and Rights and Address to the American People* (1864; reprint, Wilmington, Del.: Scholarly Resources, 1974), 14 – 15, 46 – 61; see also *FDP*, 3:598 – 609.

38. *Christian Recorder*, December 19, 1863, quoted from James M. McPherson, *The Negro's Civil War: How American Negroes Felt and Acted during the War for the Union* (New York: Pantheon Books, 1965), 274 – 75.

39. J. B. Roudanez and Arnold Bertonneau to Lincoln, Senate, and the House of Representatives, Washington, March 10, 1864; J. B. Roudanez and Arnold Bertonneau and free colored population of La. to A. Lincoln, Senate, and House of Representatives, New Orleans, January 5, 1864, originals in NA (38 Congress, ser. 467), copies found at the archives of the Freedmen and Southern Society Project, Department of History, University of Maryland, College Park. At least on two occasions between 1863 and 1864 when Frederick Douglass spoke of black suffrage, Republican leaders were sharing the platform with him. On December 4, 1864, when Douglass gave his speech at the American Anti-Slavery Society in Philadelphia, Henry Wilson and several Republicans were present. At the reception for Jean-Baptiste Roudanez and Arnold Bertonneau on April 12, 1864, in Boston, Douglass urged the Republican leaders present – Sumner, Kelley, and others – to exert their "influence, not so much for the abolition of slavery . . . but for the complete, absolute, unqualified enfranchisement of the colored people of the South." Black leaders' opinions were also

widely circulated through *Douglass' Monthly* and other black publications. Frederick Douglass, "Representatives of the Future South: An Address Delivered in Boston, Massachusetts, On 12 April 1864," in *FDP*, 4:24–31; also see *FDP*, 3:598, for other Republican-black contact.

40. Douglass, "Emancipation, Racism, and The Work Before US: An Address Delivered in Philadelphia, Pennsylvania, On 4 December 1863," *Liberator*, 29 January 1864, reprinted in *FDP*, 3:605.

41. Sumner to the duchess of Argyll, Boston, September 8, 1863, Charles Sumner Papers, HT.

42. *CG*, 38 Cong. 1 sess., 1864, pt. 3:2615 (Daniel Morris's statement).

43. Ibid., 1864, pt. 4:2989 (Isaac N. Arnold's statement).

44. Section 2 of Article 1 of the original Constitution provided that the members of the House should be "chosen every second Year by the People of the several States" and the qualifications of the electors for the House members should be the same as those "requisite for Electors of the most numerous Branch of the State Legislature." Section 4 of the same article provided that, while each state should prescribe the "Times, Places and Manner of holding Elections for Senators and representatives," the Congress "may at any time by Law make or alter such Regulations, except as to the Places of chusing Senators." During the congressional debates regarding black suffrage (and its enforcement) in the 1870s and 1880s, both proponents and opponents of black suffrage (and its enforcement) cited these two sections as the most important constitutional sources to develop their arguments on the laws regarding black enfranchisement and federal authority to enforce election laws. The constitutional sections are quoted from Alfred H. Kelly, Winfred A. Harbison, and Herman Belz, *The American Constitution: Its Origins and Development*, 2 vols. (1965; reprint, New York: W. W. Norton, 1991), app. 3.

45. Lieber's constitutional amendments contained the following parts: Amendment A (Article XIII) provided, "Every native of this Country (except sons of aliens whom the Law may exempt and Indians not taxed) and every naturalized citizen owes plenary allegiance to the government of the United States, and is entitled to and shall receive, its protection at home and abroad due by every government to its citizens or subjects"; Amendment B (Article XIV) dealt with treason; Amendment C was on the crime of sedition; Amendment D (Article XVI) empowered Congress to pass laws for trials of treason in the states where state judicial machinery was disrupted by the rebellion; Amendment E (Article XVIII) and F (Article XVIII) respectively dealt with abolishing slavery and slave trade; Amendment G provided, "No human being shall be excluded from the courts of justice as parties to actions, as indicated for offenses or crimes or as witness on account of race or colour." Francis Lieber, *Amendments of the Constitution, Submitted to the Consideration of the American People . . .* (New York: Loyal Publication Society, 1865); see also Lieber to Charles Sumner, New York, March 5, 1864; Lieber to Martin R. Thayer, New York, February 3, 1864, Lieber Papers, HT.

46. Gideon Welles to "My Dear Sir," Washington, August 25, 1863, Welles Papers, HT.

47. Bates to Lieber, Washington, October 8, 1863, Lieber Papers, HT.

48. William Stewart, a Nevada Republican who later would be asked to draft the final version of the Fifteenth Amendment, told an audience at Dayton, Nevada, that he did not like black people, but if it was "necessary for loyal men in the South to have Negro vote [*sic*] to secure the election of Union Men," he was ready and willing to give it to them because a "loyal Negro had a better right to vote than a disloyal white man." *Gold Hill Daily News*, September 26, 1865, quoted from Russell Elliott, *Servant of Power: A Political Biography of Senator William M. Stewart* (Reno: University of Nevada Press, 1983), 58.

49. Ashley's bill aimed at amending the Constitution to prohibit slavery, or involuntary servitude, in all the states and territories (December 14, 1863). *CG*, 38 Cong. 1 sess., 1863, pt. 1:19; Ashley's bill providing provisional military governments (December 21, 1863), ibid., 70; Herman Belz, *Reconstructing the Union: Theory and Policy during the Civil War* (Ithaca, N.Y.: Cornell University Press, 1969), 181. In his first reconstruction bill introduced on March 12, 1862, Ashley intended to emancipate all slaves, confiscate public lands of Confederate states, and "lease or give" such lands to "slaves so emancipated." The bill also explicitly barred those who held military and political offices of the Confederacy from voting in the process of reorganization; however, the bill said nothing about whether black men could be counted as "loyal persons" who would be allowed to vote and serve as jurors in the Union-occupied districts in the South. The bill was rejected by the majority of the Republicans in the House. Years later, Ashley recalled that all the later reconstruction bills passed by Congress were "not as safe, nor as desirable, as [his] original bill." He felt that the Republicans in Congress then "fell short of our duty to the black men." James M. Ashley to Benjamin W. Arnett, [November 1892], in *Duplicate Copy of the Souvenir from the Afro-American League of Tennessee to Hon. James M. Ashley of Ohio*, ed. Benjamin W. Arnett (Philadelphia: Publishing House of the A.M.E. Church, 1894), 360 – 62; for Ashley's first reconstruction bill of March 12, 1862, and House vote of the bill, see ibid., 363 – 69.

50. When the Wade-Davis bill was first proposed as a substitute for the Ashley reconstruction bill, the Republicans in Congress could not agree on the terms of black suffrage. The bill was discussed again in July 1864 when the proposed Senate bill No. 16 (which later became the Thirteenth Amendment to the Constitution) was defeated in the House. The Wade-Davis bill differed from Lincoln's 10 Percent Plan on several points: instead of requiring only 10 percent of the voters to take an oath of allegiance to begin the process, it required 50 percent; instead of allowing this group to elect new state officers, it mandated the election of delegates to a constitutional convention; it enfranchised only those who could take the "iron-clad oath" swearing that they had never voluntarily supported the rebellion; and it enacted specific legal safeguards for the freedmen's liberty, which were to be enforced by federal courts. But the Wade-Davis bill confined suffrage only to whites. Benedict, *Compromise of Principle*, 70 – 83; John Hay, *Lincoln and the Civil War in Diaries and Letters of John Hay*, ed. Tyler Dennet (New York: Dodd, Mead, & Co., 1939), 120-21; Belz, *Reconstructing the Union*, 227; James M. McPherson, *Ordeal by Fire: The Civil War and Reconstruction* (New York: Alfred A. Knopf, 1982), 405.

51. Charles Sumner, *Charles Sumner, His Complete Works*, 15 vols. (Boston: Lee and Shepard, 1900), 8:237–39, 242; Charles Sumner, *Memoir and Letters of Charles Sumner*, ed. Edward L. Pierce, 4 vols. (Boston: Roberts Brothers, 1893), 4:183; David H. Donald, *Charles Sumner and the Rights of Man* (New York: Alfred A. Knopf, 1970), 180 – 81.

52. In his speech in the Senate on March 28, 1864, Lyman Trumbull stressed that to make Lincoln's proclamation effective and "to get rid of" slavery, there had to be some more efficient way than by the proclamations that had been issued. Ohio Republican John Sherman agreed and further stated that a constitutional amendment was needed because the president had no "constitutional power . . . to emancipate slaves beyond his military lines" and that "a mere proclamation" of emancipation could at any time be "modified, changed, or revoked." Lincoln, while facing a challenge from some Republican lawmakers to his authority over reconstruction, also urged Congress not to miss this historic opportunity to abolish slavery. The constitutional amendment alone, Lincoln said, could "meet and cover all cavils." *CG*, 38 Cong. 1 sess., 1864, pt. 2:1313 (proposed

amendment), 1313 – 14 (Trumbull's remarks), 1315 (Sherman's remarks); Abraham Lincoln, "Reply to Committee Notifying Lincoln of His Renomination," June 9, 1864, reprinted in *Collected Works*, 380; LaWanda Cox, *Lincoln and Black Freedom: A Study in Presidential Leadership* (Urbana: University of Illinois Press, 1985), 11; James M. McPherson, *Ordeal by Fire*, 392.

53. Sumner's remarks (April 8, 1864), *CG*, 38 Cong. 1 sess., 1864, pt. 2:1479 – 83; Alan P. Grimes, *Democracy and the Amendments to the Constitution* (Lexington, Mass.: Lexington Books, 1978), 36.

54. Sumner's amendment (April 8, 1864), *CG*, 38 Cong. 1 sess., 1864, pt. 2:1483; for Senate debate on Sumner's amendment, see 1483 – 90; Sumner to George William Curtis, April 13, 1864, in *Selected Letters*, 2:233 – 34.

55. *CG*, 38 Cong. 2 sess., 1865, pt. 1:139 – 40.

56. Thirty-eighth Congress, H.R. No. 602, December 15, 1864, House of Representatives File of Printed Bills, National Archives, quoted in Herman Belz, "Origins of Negro Suffrage during the Civil War," *Southern Studies* 17 (1978): 126, also see 122 – 27; Du Bois, *Black Reconstruction*, 158; C. Peter Ripley, *Slaves and Freedmen in Civil War Louisiana*, 173. Ashley resubmitted his earlier bill including black suffrage. Ibid., 280 – 81 (January 16, 1865); Herman Belz, "Origins of Negro Suffrage during the Civil War," *Southern Studies* 17 (Summer 1978): 126 – 27.

57. *CG*, 38 Cong. 2 sess., 1865, pt. 1:281 – 91; Belz, "Origins of Negro Suffrage," 127 – 28.

58. *CG*, 38 Cong. 2 sess., 1865, pt. 2:937.

59. *CG*, 38 Cong. 2 sess., 301, 1002, 1091, 1101, 1110, 1129; Belz, *Reconstructing the Union*, 253 – 55.

60. The proposed Thirteenth Amendment passed the Senate without difficulty but failed to pass the House at the end of the first session of the Thirty-eighth Congress in June 1864. It was not until January 1865, when the second session of the Thirty-eighth Congress convened, that the Thirteenth Amendment was brought up for reconsideration in the House by James M. Ashley. By then, northern victory was almost at hand, and the Republicans had won a majority of both houses of Congress and the presidency. After strenuous lobbying by Lincoln, who wanted to make the amendment a bipartisan bill, several Democrats switched to support the amendment and helped to secure its final passage on January 31, 1865. Lincoln approved it on February 1, 1865. Ratification of the amendment by the necessary twenty-seven states was completed on December 6, 1865. Six former Confederate states ratified the amendment as a condition of readmission by Congress. Grimes believes that the ratification of the amendment would have been impossible if the mandatory requests for ratification had not been imposed on the former Confederate states. *CG*, 38 Cong. 1 sess., 1864, pt. 2:1458, 1864; pt. 4:2939 – 41, 2945, 2960, 2989 – 90, 3357; 2 sess., 1864 – 65, pt. 1:53, 139 – 50, 214 – 17, 480, 531; Grimes, *Democracy and the Amendments*, 39.

61. Chase to J. M. McKim, November 20, 1865, quoted from Harold M. Hyman and William M. Wiecek, *Equal Justice under Law: Constitutional Development, 1835 – 1875* (New York: Harper & Row, 1982), 394.

62. Michael Hahn, *Manhood the Basis of Suffrage: Speech before the National Equal Suffrage Association of Washington, November 17, 1865*, Washington, *National Republican* (pamphlet given by Charles Sumner as a gift to Harvard College Library), found in the Widener Library, Harvard University.

63. Lincoln to Michael Hahn, March 13, 1864, in *Collected Works*, 7:243; Grady McWhiney, ed.,

Reconstruction and the Freedmen (Chicago: Rand McNally, 1963), 8; for information on Lincoln's meeting with black representatives from New Orleans, see *FDP*, 4:24–31.

64. *Collected Works*, 8:399-405.

65. Writing to John Bright, Sumner complained about Lincoln's hesitation on black suffrage: "Mr. Lincoln is slow in accepting truths. I have reminded him that if he would say the word [about black suffrage] we might settle this question promptly & rightly. He hesitates." Sumner to Bright, Washington, March 13, 1865, *Selected Letters*, 2:273–74.

66. In reporting to Lieber his recent meeting with Lincoln, Sumner said that he had assured the president of "the duty of harmony between Congress & the Executive" and discussed the idea of passing a reconstruction bill granting suffrage to all citizens regardless of color in the South. "If this arrangement is carried out it will be an immense political act," Sumner wrote. In April 1865, Sumner further noted, "The more I have seen of the Presdt. the more his character in certain respects has risen, & we must all admit that he has said something better than any body else could have said them." But he was obviously worried about Lincoln's current policy. Chase was glad to see that Lincoln "at length openly" avowed limited black suffrage in his last public address, but he also noted that Lincoln was not ready for universal suffrage. Sumner to Lieber, Washington, December 18, 1864; Sumner to Richard Cobden, March 27, 1865; Sumner to Chase, April 10 and 12, 1865, *Selected Letters*, 2:258–59, 279, 282–83; April 12, 1865, Chase, *Inside Lincoln's Cabinet*, 266.

67. James A. Bayard, a Democrat, feared that Lincoln's death would "be made the pretext for much wrong and oppression" to be imposed on the South by some who did "not regret & reprobate it half as much" as he. Bayard to S. M. L. Barlow, Washington, April 19, 1865, Barlow Papers; Lieber to Charles Sumner, New York, April 15, 1865, Lieber Papers, HT; Henry Winter Davis to Edward McPherson, May 27, 1865, quoted from Gerald S. Henig, *Henry Winter Davis: Antebellum and Civil War Congressman from Maryland* (New York: Twayne, 1973), 243.

68. On the evening of April 30, 1865, Sumner had a long conversation with Johnson on black suffrage, and at the end of the meeting, Johnson assured Sumner, "There is no difference between us." Sumner to the duchess of Argyll, Washington, May 1, 1865, Charles Sumner Papers, HU.

69. On another occasion, Sumner told Francis W. Bird that he and Chase had passed their views on black suffrage on to Johnson, who was "well-disposed" and saw "the rights and necessities of the case." About the same time, Sumner informed Wendell Phillips that Johnson even authorized Chase, who was taking a private trip to several southern states, to "set on foot movements for reorganization by all loyal citizens without distinction of color." Sumner predicted that Johnson would soon speak about black suffrage. Sumner to George L. Stearns, Washington, May 4, 1865; Sumner to Bird, Washington, April 25, 1865; Sumner to Phillips, Washington, May 1, 1865, *CSP*, reel 79; see also *Selected Letters*, 2:298–99.

70. Chase to Johnson, Beaufort Harbor, North Carolina, May 7, 1865, Charleston, South Carolina, May 12, 1865, in Andrew Johnson, *The Papers of Andrew Johnson*, ed. Paul H. Bergeron (Knoxville: University of Tennessee Press, 1989), 8:41, 57–58, 63–64.

71. Foner, *Reconstruction*, 183; McPherson, *Ordeal by Fire*, 498-99.

72. Lewis D. Campbell to Andrew Johnson, Hamilton, Ohio, May 8, 1865; Johnson's reply to Delegation of Black Ministers, May 11, 1865, in Johnson, *Papers of Andrew Johnson*, 8:45–48, 61–62.

73. Sumner to Carl Schurz, Boston, June 22, 1865, in *CSP*, reel 79. In another letter to the

duchess of Argyll, Sumner said that Johnson had broken his promise to Chase and himself. Sumner to the duchess of Argyll, Boston, June 20, 1865, *CSP*, reel 79.

74. Chase to Charles Sumner, Cincinnati, June 25, 1865, in *CSP*, reel 79.

75. John M. Forbes to N. M. Beckwith, Boston, June 25, 1865, in John Murray Forbes, *Letters and Recollections of John Murray Forbes*, ed. Sarah Forbes Hughes, 2 vols. (Boston: Houghton Mifflin, 1900), 2:143–44.

76. Jacob M. Howard to Sumner, Detroit, June 22, 1865, *CSP*, reel 33.

77. Sumner to Chase, June 25, 1865, *CSP*, reel 79.

78. Davis's proposal would be used as a model in the discussion of the second section of the Fourteenth Amendment. Davis to Sumner, June 20, 1865, in Henig, *Henry Winter Davis*, 244.

79. Emphasis added. Sumner to George Bancroft, Senate Chamber, February 1865, *Selected Letters*, 2:269–70.

80. Sumner to John Bright, Washington, March 13, 1865, *Selected Letters*, 2:273–74.

81. Gideon Welles to Charles Sumner, Washington, June 30, 1865, *CSP*, reel 33.

82. Bates was convinced that the radicals' push for black suffrage was to gain political profits. He particularly loathed Chase's devotion to black suffrage, which he interpreted as a device to make himself "a feasible candidate for the next presidency." "Poor man!" Bates wrote. "The eagerness of his appetite makes him eat poison; and if I am any prophet, he will die of it. The worst feature of it is that those headlong partizans are upsetting the constitution and destroying the States." June 21, 1865, in Bates, *Diary of Edward Bates*, 489; Welles diary, June 22, 1865, in McWhiney, *Reconstruction and the Freedmen*, 13–14.

83. Cox to James A. Garfield, Columbus, July 21, 1865, James A. Garfield Papers, LC (microfilm), reel 12.

84. James Harlan to Charles Sumner, Washington, June 15, 1865, *CSP*, reel 33.

85. C. E. Lippincott to Lyman Trumbull, Meridian, August 29, 1865, Lyman Trumbull Papers, LC (microfilm), reel 17.

86. J. W. Phelps to Charles Sumner, Brattleboro, January 2, 1865, *CSP*, reel 32.

87. Morton's view was, however, challenged by the Republican press of his home state. The *Indiana True Republican* stated that to expect the freedmen to acquire property and education and to learn about the exercise of political power when their former masters controlled absolute power was "as unnatural and as cruel as committing the lamb to the tender mercies of the wolf." Morton to Andrew Johnson, November 12, 1865, Johnson MSS, 81, quoted in Howard K. Beale, *The Critical Year: A Study of Andrew Johnson and Reconstruction* (New York: Harcourt, Brace, 1930), 178; *Indiana True Republican*, October 5, 1865, in Riddleberger, *George Washington Julian*, 215.

88. Lieber wished to see the right to vote extended to black soldiers and literary and propertied blacks, but he opposed extending suffrage to every citizen, including women. Lieber to Sumner, New York, February 21, 1865, *CSP*, reel 79; Lieber to Sumner, New York, November 25, 1865, Lieber Papers, HT.

89. Connecticut Republicans brought black suffrage to a referendum only after they were assured by a state court's opinion that a free black was a citizen of both the state and the United States. Such a ruling made the Republicans feel assured of local support for black political rights. John Niven, "Connecticut, Poor Progress in the Land of Steady Habits," in Mohr, *Radical Republicans in the North*, 28; McPherson, *Ordeal by Fire*, 501; Gillette, *Right to Vote*, 25-27.

90. The referendum votes on black suffrage were, in Connecticut, for: 27,217 (45 percent), against: 33,489 (55 percent); in Minnesota, for: 12,170 (45 percent), against: 14,840 (55 percent); in Wisconsin, for: 46,588 (46 percent), against: 55,591 (54 percent). McPherson, *Ordeal by Fire*, 501–2.

91. The bill was originally drafted by the House Judiciary Committee, chaired by James F. Wilson (R-Iowa), and introduced by William D. Kelley (R-Pa.). *CG*, 39 Cong. 1 sess., 1866, pt. 1:162; Kenneth Larry Tomlinson, "Indiana Republicans and the Negro Suffrage Issue, 1865–1867" (Ph.D. diss., Ball State University, 1971), 92.

92. Hayes to his wife, January 10, 1866, in Rutherford B. Hayes, *Diary and Letters of Rutherford Birchard Hayes*, ed. Charles R. Williams, 5 vols. (Columbus: Ohio Archeological and Historical Society, 1922–26), 3:12–13.

93. The bill passed the House 116 to 54. *CG*, 39 Cong. 1 sess., January 16, 1866, pt. 1:311.

94. The Senate debate was led by Ben Wade (R-Ohio), who introduced the Senate bill (S. No. 1). The Senate bill contained a section punishing those who refused to accept the votes from qualified voters, a point that was to be included in the enforcement acts of the Fifteenth Amendment in 1870 and 1871. *CG*, 39 Cong. 1 sess., 1865–66, pt. 1:1, 162, 231; pt. 3:3433–35, 3453.

95. Given the overwhelming opposition of local residents who had rejected black suffrage 812 to 1 in Georgetown and 6,591 to 35 in the city of Washington, the effort to introduce the bill might be regarded, as suggested by LaWanda and John H. Cox, as a manifestation of Republican moral commitment to black political rights or, as Kenneth L. Tomlinson argues, as an experiment to find a solution to the representation dilemma. In light of these two arguments, which in fact do not contradict each other, I see this as a radical effort to set up a precedent of establishing black suffrage by national authority. Such a tactic would be used again in January 1867 when black suffrage in the District of Columbia and federal territories was debated again. LaWanda Cox and John H. Cox, "Negro Suffrage and Republican Politics: The Problem of Motivation in Reconstruction Historiography," in *Journal of Southern History* 33 (August 1967): 303–30, esp. 317; Tomlinson, "Indiana Republicans and the Negro Suffrage Issue," 92.

96. Garfield to Hinsdale, Washington, December 11, 1865, in James A. Garfield and Burke A. Hinsdale, *Garfield-Hinsdale Letters: Correspondence between James Abram Garfield and Burke Aaron Hinsdale*, ed. Mary L. Hinsdale (1949; reprint, New York: Kraus Reprint Co., 1969), 76–77; Wilson to Sumner, September 9, 1865, Charles Sumner Papers, HU, quoted from Ernest McKay, *Henry Wilson: Practical Radical: A Portrait of a Politician* (Port Washington, N.Y.: Kennikat, 1971), 194.

97. South Carolina and Mississippi, the first two states to enact these codes toward the end of 1865, placed the most discriminatory and severe restrictions upon the freedmen. Mississippi required all blacks to possess, each January, written evidence of employment for the coming year. Laborers leaving their jobs before their contracts expired would forfeit pay already earned and, as under slavery, be subject to arrest by any white citizen. Blacks were forbidden to rent land in urban areas. South Carolina forbade blacks from becoming members of the state militia or, without written permission from a district judge or magistrate, from keeping a firearm, sword, or other military weapon. Louisiana prohibited the freedmen from leaving their jobs after choosing their employers. The codes also provided that all disputes between employers and employees should be settled by the former. *Laws of Mississippi*, 1865, 82; *Acts of the General Assembly of Louisiana Regulating*

Labor, Extra Session, 1865, 3; quoted in Henry Steele Commager, ed., *Documents of American History, Volume I: to 1898* (New York: Appleton-Century-Crofts, 1963), 452 – 57; Foner, *Reconstruction,* 199 – 200; McPherson, *Ordeal by Fire,* 511 – 12; McWhiney, *Reconstruction and the Freedmen,* 10 – 11.

98. For perceptive assessments of the Republican radicalism in the making of the civil rights bill, see Robert J. Kaczorowski, *The Nationalization of Civil Rights: Constitutional Theory and Practice in a Racist Society, 1866 – 1883* (New York: Garland, 1987), esp. chaps. 1 and 2; Robert J. Kaczorowski, "To Begin the Nation Anew: Congress, Citizenship, and Civil Rights after the Civil War," *American Historical Review* 92 (February 1987): 45 – 68; see also Foner, *Reconstruction,* 243 – 44.

99. *CG,* 39 Cong. 1 sess., 1866, pt. 2:1291 – 92, appendix 158; Hayes to Lucy Hayes, March 22, 1866, in Hayes, *Diary and Letters,* 3:21.

100. *CG,* 39 Cong. 1 sess., 1866, pt. 2:1679; *Messages and Papers,* 6:398, 405.

101. William Stewart first voted to sustain Johnson's veto of the Freedmen's Bureau bill in February but voted to override Johnson's veto on the civil rights bill. He justified his vote by arguing that Johnson had promised not to veto the bill. Even John Sherman felt betrayed by Johnson's decision. Writing to his brother, he said that Johnson "was elected by the Union party for his openly expressed radical sentiments," and now he sought to "rend to pieces" the party. "He may, by a coalition with Copperheads and rebels, succeed, but the simple fact that nine tenths of them who voted for him do not agree with him, and that he only controls the other tenth by power entrusted to him by the Union party will damn him forever." *CG,* 39 Cong. 1 sess., 1079 – 82, 1103 – 6, 2422 – 29, 2798 – 2803; Elliott, *Servant of Power,* 57 – 60; John Sherman to William T. Sherman, July 8, 1866, Washington, D.C., in John Sherman and William Tecumseh Sherman, *The Sherman Letters; Correspondence between General and Senator Sherman from 1837 to 1891,* ed. Rachel Sherman Thorndike (New York: Charles Scribner's Sons, 1894), 276 – 77.

102. Sumner to the duchess of Argyll, Washington, December 26, 1865, Charles Sumner Papers, HT; James G. Blaine, *Twenty Years of Congress: From Lincoln to Garfield with a Review of the Events Which Led to the Political Revolution of 1860,* 2 vols. (Norwich, Conn.: Henry Bill, 1884 – 86), 2:245.

103. Hayes to Murat Halstead, Washington, February 2, 1866, Hayes, *Diary and Letters,* 3:16.

104. This concern was explicitly articulated by Thaddeus Stevens when he introduced the representation proposal to the House on January 31, 1866. He said that his committee realized that the states had the right, and always had had it, "to fix the elective franchise within their own States" and that if that right was taken away, few states would vote for the amendment of regulating representation. *CG,* 39 Cong. 1 sess., 1866, pt. 1:536.

105. Roscoe Conkling (R-N.Y.) asked to insert "male" in the resolution. Justin S. Morrill (Whig-Vt.) asked to exclude those who could not read and write from legal voters. United States, Congress, *The Journal of the Joint Committee of Fifteenth on Reconstruction, 39th Congress, 1865 – 1867,* ed. Benjamin B. Kendrick (New York: Columbia University Press, 1914), 41.

106. The amended proposal provided that representation in the House be based on population but added, "Whenever the elective franchise shall be denied or abridged in any State on account of race, creed or color, all persons therein of such race or color shall be excluded from the basis of representation." *CG,* 39 Cong. 1 sess., 1866, pt. 1:535 – 36.

107. Emphasis added. United States, Congress, *Journal of the Joint Committee,* 50 – 51, 53;

William E. Nelson, *The Fourteenth Amendment: From Political Principle to Judicial Doctrine* (Cambridge: Harvard University Press, 1988), 49.

108. Before Bingham made this substitution, several amendments to his proposal were presented to the committee, but all retained the words "political rights." United States, Congress, *Journal of the Joint Committee*, 61.

109. William E. Nelson argues that the change of wording might be attributed to three explanations: the draftsmen's neglect of the precision of the language, concern about opposition to black suffrage, and their intention to distinguish between equal protection in the rights of persons and rights of citizens. I believe that concern was mostly about the constitutionality of the federal authority to grant suffrage. Nelson, *The Fourteenth Amendment*, 51 – 52, 100 – 104. For Bingham's explanation, see *CG*, 39 Cong. 1 sess., 1866, pt. 3 : 2542.

110. Sumner confessed that "for a long time" he was "perplexed by the subtlety" of suffrage as a privilege but not as a right. "The more I think of it, the more it seems to me, an essential right," he concluded. "Starting with this principle from our Declaration of Independence, I see no other conclusion, than that every citizen, having a proper residence, must be a voter." Sumner to John Bright, Washington, May 27, 1867, *Selected Letters*, 2 : 397 – 98.

111. The text of Robert Dale Owen's plan for the Fourteenth Amendment was published in 1875 and read:

> Article XIV
>
> Section 1. No discrimination shall be made by any State, nor by the United States, as to the civil rights of persons, because of race, color, or previous condition of servitude.
>
> Section 2. From and after the fourth day of July, eighteen hundred and seventy-six, no discrimination shall be made by any State nor by the United States, as to the enjoyment, by classes of persons, of the right of suffrage, because of race, color, or previous condition of servitude.
>
> Section 3. Until the fourth day of July, eighteen hundred and seventy-six, no class of persons, as to the right of any of whom to suffrage discrimination shall be made by any State, because of race, color, or previous condition of servitude, shall be included in the basis of representation.
>
> Section 4. Debts incurred in aid of insurrection, or of war against the Union, and claims of compensation for loss of involuntary service or labor, shall not be paid by any State nor by the United States.
>
> Section 5. Congress shall have power to enforce, by appropriate legislation, the provisions of this article.

Robert Dale Owen, "The Political Results from the Varioloid," *Atlantic Monthly* 35 (June 1875): 660 – 70; United States, Congress, *Journal of the Joint Committee*, 83 – 84, 297.

112. In his 1875 recollection, Owen recorded his conversation with Thaddeus Stevens the day after the joint committee rejected his proposal. According to Stevens (as recalled by Owen), on April 21, 1866, the joint committee voted to carry Washburne's motion that Owen's plan be reported to the House on Monday, April 23. The committee carried the motion with all the Republican votes in the committee except one. When the vote was taken on April 22, William Fessenden "happened to be absent . . . that day, sick of the varioloid, but was reported convalescent." Thus, in Stevens's

words, "some one suggested that he would probably be well in a few days, and that it would seem a lack of courtesy if the most important report of the session should be made without his agency." Stevens thought that the "presentation of a great public measure" should not be delayed, but, as the House chairman of the committee, he refrained from being "uncivil" to the Senate chairman by raising no objection and thought a few days would make no difference. But when the committee's work on the Owen proposal leaked out, Republican members from New York, Illinois, and Indiana "held, each separately, a caucus to consider whether equality of suffrage, present or prospective, ought to form a part of the republican programme for the coming canvass." Stevens recalled that "by inconsiderable majorities" each of these caucuses decided that black suffrage "ought to be excluded from the platform; and they communicated these decisions" to the committee. Thus, on April 29, when the committee reconsidered Owen's plan, it decided to reject its reference on black suffrage. "Our committee hadn't backbone enough to maintain its ground," Stevens told Owen. The angry Owen cursed Fessenden's varioloid, which he believed "changed the whole policy of the country." Owen, "Political Results from the Varioloid," 664–66.

113. Several Republicans, including William Pitt Fessenden and Charles Sumner, tried to insert political rights, in explicit language, in the first section before April 30, 1866. Hayes also confirmed that the congressional policy was "to leave to the States the question of suffrage," but "in the District and the Territories" it was "for Congress to lay down the rule." Hayes himself supported suffrage for all but felt that all new voters should "be able to write and read." For different proposals, see *CG*, 39 Cong. 1 sess, 1866, pt. 1:362, 702; pt. 2:1034. For the final version of the committee's joint resolution, a work mostly done by Bingham, see ibid., 2286. For Hayes's remarks, see R. B. Hayes to Lucy Hayes, March 15, 1866, Washington, in Hayes, *Diary and Letters*, 3:25.

114. Howard made this comment during the Senate debate over whether black suffrage should be required for the admission of Nebraska on December 19, 1866. Reverdy Johnson (D-Md.) confirmed Howard's statement, saying that in the committee (of which he was a member) "except by one or two gentlemen" who seemed to be "in advance of the age," all agreed that the federal government had no power to regulate the right of suffrage in the states. *CG*, 39 Cong. 2 sess., 1866, pt. 1:185, 190.

115. *CG*, 39 Cong. 1 sess., 1866, pt. 3:2462.

116. Ibid., 2459.

117. Ibid., 2462.

118. Ibid., 2532.

119. Raymond said that he had voted against Owen's proposal. Ibid., 2502.

120. Ibid., 2510.

121. Hayes to Lucy Hayes, Washington, June 14, 1866, in Hayes, *Diary and Letters*, 3:27.

122. *CG*, 39 Cong. 1 sess., 1866, pt. 4:3042, 3149.

123. McKitrick, *Andrew Johnson and Reconstruction*, 332; McPherson, *Ordeal by Fire*, 517-18.

124. *CG*, 39 Cong. 1 sess., 1866, pt. 4:3148.

125. Ashley said that he never would have voted the second and third sections of the amendment "if each had stood alone." James M. Ashley to Gerrit Smith, Toledo, November 9, 1866, Gerrit Smith Papers, box 1, Syracuse University Library.

126. Charles Sumner to Moncure D. Conway, Washington, July 30, 1866, *Selected Letters*, 2:374-75.

127. Andrew Jackson Hamilton, the Unionist leader and provisional governor of Texas, effectively argued this point in a speech in Boston in December 1866. Hamilton argued that suffrage was "the basis of personal and civil rights" and a "vital principle of Republican Government." The continuous denial of the right to vote to black citizens was a denial of constitutional responsibility by the federal government: "We are not dealing now with the rights of *slaves* under *State* authority, but with the rights of *free citizens* of the United States under the guarantees of its Constitution." A. J. Hamilton, *"Suffrage and Reconstruction," The Duty of the People, the President, and Congress. by Hon. A. J. Hamilton, of Texas, Delivered at the Invitation of the Impartial-Suffrage League, at the Tremont Temple in Boston, December 3, 1866* (Boston: Impartial-Suffrage League, 1866), 11–13.

128. Hayes to Lucy Hayes, Washington, March 15, 1866, Hayes, *Diary and Letters*, 3:25.

129. Charles Sumner to Theodore Tilton, Senate Chamber, June 6, 1866, *Selected Letters*, 2:371.

130. Patrick W. Riddleberger, *1866: The Critical Year Revisited* (Carbondale: Southern Illinois University Press, 1979), 189–92; Donald E. Reynolds, "The New Orleans Riot of 1866, Reconsidered," *Louisiana History* 5 (Winter 1964): 5–27; McKitrick, *Andrew Johnson and Reconstruction*, 422–27.

131. James Speed to Francis Lieber, Louisville, November 22, 1866, Lieber Papers, HT.

132. Frederick Douglass's address, September 4, 1866, *FDP*, 4:131–32.

133. Foner, *Reconstruction*, 267.

134. *CG*, 39 Cong. 1 sess., 1866, pt. 4:3433–35, 3453; for a concise discussion on the Republican motivations for introducing the first black suffrage bill for the District of Columbia, see F. William Nicklas, "William D. Kelley: The Congressional Years, 1861–1890" (Ph.D. diss., Northern Illinois University, 1983), 169–74.

135. *CG*, 39 Cong. 2 sess., 1866–67, pt. 1:41 (Wilson's remarks), 78 (Brown's remarks).

136. Ibid., 40–41.

137. Ibid., 102–3.

138. Ibid., 62, 82.

139. Ibid., 62, 103.

140. Ibid., 64.

141. Ibid., 107.

142. Yates also mentioned that popular feeling in the North had been "against universal amnesty as well as for universal suffrage." *CG*, 39 Cong. 2 sess., 1866–67, pt. 1:56, 63.

143. Ibid., 40.

144. Ibid., 66.

145. The vote for the Cowen amendment was 9 yeas, 37 nays, and 6 absent. Ibid., 84.

146. Ibid., 109.

147. Johnson's veto was based on four reasons: (1) the bill was against the popular will of the District of Columbia, and its enactment would increase antagonism between races; (2) the bill violated the right of local government, since most northern states still withheld suffrage from blacks; (3) the bill degraded the quality of American elections; (4) the bill endangered popular liberty by encroaching on the executive department. Ibid., 103–6.

148. The vote in the Senate was 29 to 10, with 10 abstentions. Of the 38 Republican votes in the Senate, 28 (74 percent) voted to overturn Johnson's veto, 4 Republicans voted for the veto, and 6 did not vote. Ibid., 313. In the House, the vote was 113 to 38, with 41 not voting. Only 6 Repub-

licans out of 138 voted for the veto, 28 abstained, and the rest, 104 (75 percent), voted to override the veto. Ibid., 344.

149. Ibid., 103.

150. The bills regarding the admissions of Nebraska (S. No. 456) and Colorado (S. No. 462) were introduced into Senate by Ben Wade at the beginning of the session. Ibid., 13, 36.

151. There were two proposals regarding how such a condition would be imposed. The "Edmunds amendment," named for its author, George F. Edmunds, simply asked that the condition of impartial suffrage be imposed in the congressional law for admitting Nebraska (and later Colorado) without the assent of the state legislature. The "Boutwell amendment," proposed by George S. Boutwell of the House, requested the same condition but further provided that the state legislature would accept this condition "by proclamation." The "Boutwell amendment" was technically less direct in carrying out this imposition. Senator Brown had also proposed an amendment similar to Boutwell's. Ibid., 122 (Sumner), 162 (Brown), 535 (Lawrence).

152. Ibid., 162.

153. Ibid., 185 (Howard), 190 (Johnson).

154. Ibid., 215, 332.

155. Ibid., 338 – 39.

156. Ibid., 329.

157. The Senate vote on its own version of the bill was 24 to 15, with 13 not voting. Twenty-two Republicans (58 percent of the total party votes) voted yeas, 7 voted nays, and 9 did not vote. Ibid., 358, 364.

158. Ibid., 448 – 49 (statements of Broomall), 449 (statements of Blaine), 450 (statements of John Bingham), 472 – 74 (statements of Boutwell), 478 (statements of Stevens).

159. The House vote was 103 to 55, with 33 abstentions. Ninety-four Republicans (69 percent of the 137 total party votes) voted for the bill, 18 voted against it, and 25 were absent. Ibid., 481.

160. The Senate vote on the concurrence was 28 to 14, with 10 abstentions. Twenty-six Republicans (68 percent) voted to accept the House version of the bill, 6 voted against it, and 6 abstained from voting. Four Republicans who either voted against the Edmunds amendment or abstained from the voting switched their votes to support the House version. Ibid., 487.

161. During the brief discussion, Howard suggested that the bill should cover all future cases, meaning, the territories to be organized in the future. Under Ashley's leadership, the House accepted the Senate's minor revision without debate. Ibid., 382, 408, appendix, 181 (the text of the bill), 890.

162. *CG*, 39 Cong. 2 sess., 1867, pt. 2:851 – 52, 821, 818 – 20.

163. The Senate repassed S. No. 456 with a vote of 31 to 9 with 12 not voting. Twenty-eight Republicans voted to override the veto, 3 did not vote with party's majority, and 7 abstained. Ibid., 1096. House Republicans were more united in overriding Johnson's veto, with 110 (80 percent of the party votes) voting yeas, 8 nays, and 19 not voting. Ibid., 1121 – 22.

164. Nine Republicans (24 percent of the party's total votes) joined 9 Democrats and 1 independent in support of Johnson's veto, 4 abstained, and 27 challenged the presidential decision. Ibid., pt. 3:1928.

165. *CG*, 39 Cong. 2 sess., 1867, pt. 1:474.

166. Kirk H. Porter in his history of American suffrage suggested that the suffrage requirement

in the Reconstruction Act of 1867 was a sign of congressional conspiracy. As the previous pages show, such an observation is baseless. In fact, the suffrage provision had been suggested by both radicals and moderates during the discussion. John Sherman was mainly responsible for its final version. But Sherman's intention was more to direct a way for the political reorganization of the former Confederate states than merely to punish them. Porter, *History of Suffrage*, 174.

167. Andrew Johnson, Second Annual Message to Congress, December 3, 1866, *Messages and Papers*, 5:445–59, esp. 445–46; McPherson, *Ordeal by Fire*, 521.

168. The bill, as reported by Stevens in behalf of the joint Select Committee on Reconstruction in February, had five sections covering the following subjects: dividing the former Confederate states into five military districts and imposing military authority there (sec. 1), assignment of military commanders in those districts (sec. 2), duties of the military authorities (sec. 3), suspending the writs of habeas corpus for those under military custody (sec. 4), and enforcement procedures (sec. 5). *CG*, 39 Cong. 2 sess., 1867, pt. 2:1037.

169. Emphasis added. Ashley's amendment had two parts. The first part ordered the return of property seized or confiscated by the federal military forces to the loyal southerners. The second part was on black suffrage and ratification of the Fourteenth Amendment as quoted in the text. Ibid., 1106.

170. The first section of Bingham's amendment required the southern states to ratify the Fourteenth Amendment and present to Congress "a constitution of government" that would "secure equal and impartial suffrage to the male citizens of the United States, twenty-one years of age, resident therein, without distinction of race or color." Ibid., 1177.

171. Ibid., 1182.

172. Ibid., 1211–12 (Bingham), 1214 (Stevens).

173. Blaine moved that the original bill be recommitted to the judiciary committee with instructions that it be reported back to the House immediately with his amendment added. His proposal was first supported (with a majority of 7) and then defeated. Kendrick believed that Stevens's moving speech changed the minds of sixteen Republicans who switched their support to Stevens in the second vote. Ibid., 1210 (statements of Stevens), 1213 (statements of Blaine), 1215 (votes on Blaine's proposal and the bill); United States, Congress, *Journal of the Joint Committee*, 405–6. The House accepted the original version of H.R. 1143 by a vote of 109 to 55 with 26 not voting. One hundred and two Republicans (75 percent of the party votes) voted yeas, 16 voted nays, and 18 abstained. Ibid., 1215.

174. For the text of the Sherman substitute, see Ibid., 1459.

175. Ibid., 1462.

176. When the Senate bill reached the House on February 19, 1867, the House voted to ask for a conference and appointed Stevens, Shellabarger, and Blaine as conferees. But the Senate, after a lengthy debate, refused the House request for conference and insisted on its amendments to the House bill. The House again discussed the bill, and Shellabarger offered an amendment (which was based on an amendment offered by James Wilson of Iowa) that reinstated impartial suffrage and barred those disfranchised by the third section of the Fourteenth Amendment from holding offices. Ibid., pt. 3:1555–70, pt. 2:1399–40. For the final text of the act, see ibid., appendix, 197–98.

177. The Senate concurred in the Shellabarger amendment, which would become the sixth section in the final version of the Reconstruction Act, by a vote of 35 to 7 with 10 abstaining. Thirty-

one Republicans (82 percent of the party votes) approved the final version of the bill, 6 abstained, and only 1 voted nay. Ibid., pt. 3:1645.

178. For example, McKitrick, *Andrew Johnson and Reconstruction*, 473 – 85; Benedict, *Compromise of Principle*, 210 – 43; Kenneth Stampp, *The Era of Reconstruction, 1865 – 1877* (New York: Vintage, 1965), and Brock, *An American Crisis.*

179. John Sherman admitted, during the discussion of the Reconstruction Act, "I did nothing but reduce and group the ideas of others, carefully leaving open to the South in it but general suffrage. This they must take, and the only question is whether they will take it in their own way by their own popular movements, or organize provisional governments. I hope and trust they will learn wisdom from the past. . . . The president has only to forward and inforce the law [sic] as they stand. He ought not to, and must not stand in the way of the determined movement to recognize the States. He had his way and it failed; he ought now fairly to try the Congressional way." John Sherman to William T. Sherman, Washington, March 7, 1867, Sherman and Sherman, *The Sherman Letters*, 289 – 90.

180. Sumner to Theodore Tilton, Washington, April 18, 1867, *Selected Letters*, 2:393 – 94.

181. Sumner to John Bright, Washington, May 27, 1867, *Selected Letters*, 2:397 – 98.

182. George William Curtis, *[A Speech of] George William Curtis at the New York State Constitutional Convention, 1867* (Rochester: New York State Constitutional Convention Campaign Committee, 1867), 7 – 10.

183. Francis Lieber, *Reflections on the Changes Which May Seem Necessary in the Present Constitution of the State of New York* (New York: New York Union League Club, 1867), 26 – 28.

184. Lieber by this time had come to accept, as Sumner did, that suffrage was part of the essential right attached to citizenship. He admitted that different races or different groups within the same races were "of different superiority" and the white race in Europe and America seemed "to be the highest race," but "slowness in falling in the rank of civilization" did not "of itself prove natural inferiority"; most important, "Whatever this difference of groups or races may be it does in no degree affect humanity in man." There should be no differentiations when the rights of man were discussed. Lieber refused to go so far as to regard voting as a natural right because voting required "Intelligence, Independence, Character and ability, interest in and identification with community." But Lieber opposed denying suffrage to blacks on a racial basis: "Who will deny that our colored people have a more abiding interest in the community than thousands and thousands of floating white men who are allowed to vote." Lieber to Theodore Williams Dwight, New York, July 18, 1867, Lieber Papers, HT.

185. "The Republican Troubles," *Nation*, October 31, 1867, 314 – 15.

186. Foner, *Reconstruction*, 312 – 13. William S. Burns to Henry Huntley Haight, Hammondsport, October 28, 1867, Henry Haight Papers, HT. Even Francis Lieber, who supported black suffrage, opposed extending suffrage to Chinese in California but "not on the account of their cheekbones being higher . . . , or their skin being yellow." Lieber to Theodore Williams Dwight, New York, July 18, 1867, Lieber Papers, HT.

187. Charles L. Wagandt, "Redemption or Reaction?: Maryland in the Post – Civil War Years," in *Radicalism, Racism, and Party Realignment: The Border States during Reconstruction*, ed. Richard O. Curry (Baltimore: Johns Hopkins University Press, 1969), 146 – 87.

188. McPherson, *Ordeal by Fire*, 535; Foner, *Reconstruction*, 314.

189. Willis F. Dunbar and William G. Shade, "The Black Man Gains the Vote: The Centennial of 'Impartial Suffrage' in Michigan," *Michigan History* 56 (Spring 1972): 42 – 57, esp. 47.

190. Felice A. Bonadio, "Ohio: A 'Perfect Contempt of All Unity,'" in Mohr, *Radical Republicans in the North*, 89 – 91; Foner, *Reconstruction*, 314 – 15; Gillette, *Retreat from Reconstruction*, 9.

191. John Bigelow to W. H. Huntington, The Squirrels, November 4, 1867, in John Bigelow, *Retrospection of an Active Life*, 4 vols. (New York: Doubleday, Page & Co., 1909 – 13), 4:117.

192. Editorial, "The Remaining Work of the Republican Party," *Nation*, January 28, 1869.

193. In Ohio, Republicans blamed their defeat on the black suffrage amendment. Although few Republicans openly opposed black suffrage, they tended to avoid the issue in the state legislature. Bonadio, "Ohio," 91; Gillette, *Right to Vote*, 27.

194. *Proceedings of the National Union Republican Convention* (Chicago, 1868), 84; Porter and Johnson, *National Party Platforms*, 39 – 40.

195. According to Charles H. Coleman, Grant won 63.1 percent of the popular votes in New England states, 50.5 in the middle states, 41.1 in the loyal slave states, 54.6 in the midwestern states, and 50.6 in the far western states. Charles H. Coleman, *The Election of 1868: The Democratic Effort to Regain Control* (New York: Columbia University Press, 1933), 363 – 65; McPherson, *Ordeal by Fire*, 544 – 45; Foner, *Reconstruction*, 338 – 45; Everette Swinney, *Suppressing the Ku Klux Klan: The Enforcement of the Reconstruction Amendments, 1870 – 1877* (New York: Garland, 1987), 21.

196. *CG*, 40 Cong. 3 sess., 1869, pt. 2:904.

197. Ibid., pt. 1:378 – 79.

198. Blaine, *Twenty Years of Congress*, 2:412 – 13.

199. William Gillette's *The Right to Vote: Politics and the Passage of the Fifteenth Amendment* remains a standard work for the study of the Fifteenth Amendment, especially in documenting the daily procedures and debates of the amendment. For the purpose of the present chapter, I will concentrate on discussing the issues that were mostly debated and coherently related to the questions derived from earlier legislation on black suffrage.

200. For various proposals for the Fifteenth Amendment, see *CG*, 40 Cong. 3 sess., 1868 – 69, pts. 1 – 2: 378 – 79, in particular, 379 (proposal by Stewart), 542 (revised proposal from the Senate's judicial committee), 708 (proposal by Pomeroy), 1305 (proposal by Doolittle), 1306 (proposal by Fowler), 1308 (proposal by Howard), 1425 (proposal by Bingham). McPherson, *Ordeal by Fire*, 545.

201. This point was brought up by James R. Doolittle (R-Wis.) during the Senate debate. *CG*, 40 Cong. 3 sess., 1869, pt. 2:1305. Additional debate on this issue was carried to the first session of the Forty-first Congress when the Naturalization Act of 1870 was debated. In addition, in the Supreme Court's opinion on the *Ex parte Yarbrough* case (1884), Justice Miller stated that the Fifteenth Amendment was "mainly designed for citizens of African descent." See *Ex parte Yarbrough*, 110 U.S. 651 (1884).

202. *CG*, 40 Cong. 3 sess., 1869, pt. 1:726.

203. The vote for Shellabarger's amendment was 62 yeas, 125 nays, 35 not voting. The vote for Boutwell's proposal was 150 yeas, 42 nays, 31 not voting. Ibid., 744 – 45; Gillette, *Right to Vote*, 54.

204. The original Stewart proposal read: "Art. 15, The right of citizens of the United States to vote and hold office shall not be denied or abridged by the United States, or any State, on account of race, color, or previous condition of servitude. And Congress shall have power to enforce

the provisions of this article by appropriate legislation." *CG*, 40 Cong. 3 sess., 1869, pt. 1:379. Gillette, *Right to Vote*, 55.

205. *CG*, 40 Cong. 3 sess., 1012; Gillette, *Right to Vote*, 59.

206. "The Senate – The Amendment," *National Anti-Slavery Standard*, February 13, 1869, 2.

207. *CG*, 40 Cong. 3 sess., 1029 (debate and vote on Wilson proposal), 1042 (Morton plan), 1226 (House rejection), 1295 (Senate rejection); Gillette, *Right to Vote*, 59 – 63, 65.

208. George H. William (R-Oreg.) supported the Howard amendment and regarded it as "a plain and explicit explanation" of what the moderate Republicans meant. *CG*, 40 Cong. 3 sess., 1304 (Howard), 1305 (Edmunds), 1309 (Williams), 1311 (Senate vote).

209. Ibid., 1306.

210. Doolittle proposed an amendment that read: "Nor shall any citizen be so denied, by reason of any alleged crime, unless duly convicted thereof according to law." The Senate rejected his amendment by a vote of 13 yeas, 30 nays, and 23 absent. Ibid., 1305.

211. Ibid., 1318.

212. Ibid., 1426.

213. The Bingham amendment read: "The right of citizens of the United States to vote and hold office shall not be denied or abridged by any State on account of race, color, nativity, property, creed, or previous condition of servitude." The motivations for this amendment were mixed, probably dominated by the intention to defeat the suffrage amendment by prolonging the discussion between the two Houses. The House accepted the Bingham amendment by a vote of 92 yeas, 70 nays (including Boutwell and Broomall, and Shellabarger), and 60 not voting. It accepted the resolution by a vote of 140 yeas, 37 nays, and 46 not voting. *CG*, 40 Cong. 3 sess., 1869, pt. 2:1428.

214. Ibid., pt. 3:1563.

215. Ibid., 1563 – 64.

216. Ibid., 1641.

Chapter Two. The Making of Federal Enforcement Laws, 1870 – 1872

1. John Niven, "Connecticut, Poor Progress in the Land of Steady Habits," in *Radical Republicans in the North: State Politics during Reconstruction*, ed. James C. Mohr (Baltimore: Johns Hopkins University Press, 1976), 43 – 44; William Gillette, *The Right to Vote: Politics and the Passage of the Fifteenth Amendment* (Baltimore: Johns Hopkins University Press, 1965), 119 – 30.

2. James C. Mohr, "New York: The De-Politicization of Reform," in Mohr, *Radical Republicans in the North*, 71 – 75.

3. Edward Price, "The Black Voting Rights Issue in Pennsylvania, 1700 – 1900," *Pennsylvania Magazine of History and Biography* 100 (July 1976): 363; David Montgomery, "Pennsylvania: An Eclipse of Ideology," in Mohr, *Radical Republicans in the North*, 56 – 57; Thomas A. Sanelli, "The Struggle for Black Suffrage in Pennsylvania, 1838 – 1870" (Ph.D. diss., Temple University, 1977), 239 – 99; Gillette, *Right to Vote*, 113 – 19; Marion Thompson Wright, "Negro Suffrage in New Jersey, 1776 – 1875," *Journal of Negro History* 33 (April 1948): 218 – 23.

4. California eventually ratified the amendment on April 3, 1962. Oregon rejected the amendment on October 26, 1870, and finally approved it on February 24, 1959. Gillette, *Right to Vote*,

84 – 85, 155 – 58; Alan P. Grimes, *Democracy and the Amendments to the Constitution* (Lexington, Mass.: Lexington Books, 1978), 58.

5. Nevada was the first state to ratify the Fifteenth Amendment. Stewart was instrumental in the ratification process by putting pressure on his friends back home, warning that the state might lose federal patronage if it failed to ratify the amendment favored by President-elect Grant. Stewart's telegram on the deletion of nativity qualification from the amendment was a timely assurance to his fellow Nevadans, who were obviously worried about the local resistance to Chinese suffrage. The Nevada legislature approved the amendment on March 31, 1869, by a vote of 23 to 16 in the assembly and 14 to 6 in the Senate. Stewart's attitude toward the Chinese suffrage issue would be more thoroughly expressed during the discussion of the Naturalization Act in July 1870. Gillette, *Right to Vote*, 84, 157 – 58; Russell Elliott, *Servant of Power: A Political Biography of Senator William M. Stewart* (Reno: University of Nevada Press, 1983), 63 – 64.

6. Jean H. Baker, *The Politics of Continuity: Maryland Political Parties from 1858 to 1870* (Baltimore: Johns Hopkins University Press, 1973), 177 – 79, 202 – 3; Charles L. Wagandt, "Redemption or Reaction?: Maryland in the Post – Civil War Years," in *Radicalism, Racism, and Party Realignment: The Border States during Reconstruction*, ed. Richard O. Curry (Baltimore: Johns Hopkins University Press, 1969), 146 – 87.

7. According to Felice A. Bonadio, by 1868 the Republican party in Ohio faced a deep division, with the younger members of the party becoming increasingly disaffected by the older members' attitudes toward party loyalty, political corruption, and tariff reform. By the summer of 1869, these new Republicans formed the Citizens Reform party, which had become a balance-holding power in the state legislature. This development could be understood as part of the Liberal Republican movement, which was rising in the North. But it was the older Republicans in the state legislature who helped ratify the Fifteenth Amendment. Felice A. Bonadio, "Ohio: A 'Perfect Contempt of All Unity,'" in Mohr, *Radical Republicans in the North*, 94 – 100; Gillette, *Right to Vote*, 86, 143 – 44.

8. *Detroit Advertiser-Tribune*, February 27, 1869, quoted from Willis F. Dunbar and William G. Shade, "The Black Man Gains the Vote: The Centennial of 'Impartial Suffrage' in Michigan," *Michigan History* 56 (Spring 1972): 52.

9. Knowing that the Nebraska legislature would not meet until 1871, Grant urged David Butler to call the legislature "in extra session" to ratify the Fifteenth Amendment. Explaining his urgency, Grant wrote that he wished "to see a question of such great national importance brought to an early settlement, in order that it [might] no longer remain an open issue, and a subject of agitation before the people." On February 17, 1870, as soon as the legislature approved the amendment with only five votes against, Butler immediately informed Grant of the result via telegram. Grant to David Butler, Washington, November 23, 1869, Ulysses S. Grant, *The Papers of Ulysses S. Grant*, ed. John Y. Simon, 20 vols. (Carbondale: Southern Illinois University Press, 1967 – 95), 20:15 – 16.

10. *CG*, 41 Cong. 2 sess., 1870, pt. 2:1074, 1388; Kenneth Larry Tomlinson, "Indiana Republicans and the Negro Suffrage Issue, 1865 – 1867" (Ph.D. diss., Ball State University, 1971), 213 – 32; Gillette, *Right to Vote*, 84 – 85; Margaret L. Dwight, "Black Suffrage in Missouri, 1865 – 1877" (Ph.D. diss., University of Missouri, 1978), 113 – 14.

11. For details regarding the southern ratification, see Gillette, *Right to Vote*, 96 – 97.

12. The Proclamation of the Secretary of State (Hamilton Fish) and Grant's message to the Senate and House, in *Messages and Papers*, 7:55 – 57.

13. Elijah W. Smith, "Freedom's Jubilee"; B. F. Roberts, "Celebration of the Fifteenth Amendment in Boston"; "The Celebration in Detroit"; Washington *New Era*, April 28, 1870; Dwight, "Black Suffrage in Missouri," 116–24.

14. "The Fifteenth Amendment Celebration in Philadelphia," *New Era*, May 5, 1870.

15. "The Fifteenth Amendment: The Grand Celebration in Baltimore on the 19th," *New Era*, May 26, 1870.

16. Among the speakers of the Baltimore celebration were Republican judge Hugh Bond, Republican representative Horace Maynard of Tennessee, Republican senator Frederick A. Sawyer of South Carolina, Frederick Douglass, and John M. Langston, later the dean of the Department of Law, Howard University. *New Era*, May 26, 1870.

17. "Speech of Frederick Douglass at Tweddle Hall, Albany, April 22, 1870," *New Era*, May 5, 1870; see also *FDP*, 4:270–71.

18. Phillips admitted to disappointment with the Senate's decision to remove the right to take office from the final version of the Fifteenth Amendment. He wished the senators who handled the amendment were "a little more *politicians*– and a little less *reformers*." Wendell Phillips, "The Constitutional Amendment," *National Anti-Slavery Standard*, March 20, 1869; "Congress," *National Anti-Slavery Standard*, February 20, 1869; LaWanda Cox and John H. Cox, eds., *Reconstruction, the Negro, and the New South* (Columbia: University of South Carolina Press, 1973), 106–7.

19. *Anti-Slavery Standard*, May 29, 1870; Frederick Douglass, *The Life and Writings of Frederick Douglass*, ed. Philip S. Foner, 4 vols. (New York: International Publishers, 1950–55), 4:45; "The Disbandment of the Forces," *New Era*, April 28, 1870.

20. Grant speech to a crowd at the White House, April 1, 1870, Grant, *Papers*, 20:137–38; Grant to Elihu B. Washburne, Washington, January 28, 1870, Ulysses S. Grant, *General Grant's Letters to a Friend, 1861–1880* (1897; reprint, AMS, 1973), 64–65; *Messages and Papers*, 6:55–56.

21. Quoted from Chase's letter to the black citizens of the City of Cincinnati, "Judge Chase, Letter from Him in regard to the Fifteenth amendment–He Advocates Universal amnesty," *Chicago Tribune*, April 14, 1870.

22. Ibid.

23. *Boston Advertiser*, January 25, March 1, 1869, and April 1, 1870, quoted from Edith Ellen Ware, *Political Opinion in Massachusetts during Civil War and Reconstruction* (New York: Columbia University Press, 1916), 181–82.

24. "Partisan Legislation," *Chicago Tribune*, April 21, 1870.

25. April 4, 1870, in Rutherford B. Hayes, *Diary and Letters of Rutherford Birchard Hayes*, ed. Charles R. Williams, 5 vols. (Columbus: Ohio Archeological and Historical Society, 1922–26), 3:94.

26. Editorial, New York *Independent*, February 24, 1870; "The Colored Vote," *New York Times*, May 17, 1870.

27. "The New Year," *Harper's Weekly*, January 8, 1870.

28. *CG*, 41 Cong. 2 sess., 1870, pt. 1:600.

29. For studies on the Klan activities during this period, see Allen W. Trelease, *White Terror: The Ku Klux Klan Conspiracy and Southern Reconstruction* (New York: Harper & Row, 1971); Michael Perman, *Reunion without Compromise: The South and Reconstruction, 1865–1868* (Cambridge: Cambridge University Press, 1973); George C. Rable, *But There Was No Peace: The Role of Violence in the Politics of Reconstruction* (Athens: University of Georgia Press, 1984), 60–80, 85–100.

30. W. W. Holden to U. S. Grant, March 10, 1870, in Grant, *Papers*, 20:211–12; Trelease, *White Terror*, 191–273; Eric Foner, *Reconstruction: America's Unfinished Revolution, 1863–1877* (New York: Harper & Row, 1988), 342–44, 425–30.

31. *Atlanta Constitution*, March 16, 1870, quoted from Edmund L. Drago, *Black Politicians and Reconstruction in Georgia: A Splendid Failure* (Baton Rouge: Louisiana State University Press, 1982), 57–58.

32. Revels's statements seemed to respond to the petition sent to him by the Georgia black legislators, but he made no direct reference to the petition in his speech. *CG*, 41 Cong. 2 sess., 1870, pt. 3:1987.

33. Ibid., pt. 4:3669 (George E. Spencer of Alabama); 3613 (John Pool of North Carolina).

34. Ibid., 3568.

35. Ibid., 3568 (statement of John Sherman).

36. Pierrepont to Grant, New York, May 19, 1870, Grant, *Papers*, 20:426–27.

37. *CG*, 41 Cong. 2 sess., 1870, pt. 4:3670.

38. Ibid., 3568.

39. Ibid., 3608.

40. Ibid., 3610–11.

41. The five laws to be discussed in this chapter are (1) act of May 31, 1870, *Statutes at Large* 16 (1870): 140–46 (enforcing voting rights of U.S. citizens); (2) act of July 14, 1870, *Statutes at Large* 16 (1870): 254–56 (amending naturalization laws); (3) act of February 28, 1871, *Statutes at Large* 16 (1871): 433–40 (amending act of May 31, 1870); (4) act of April 20, 1871, *Statutes at Large* 17 (1871): 13–15 (enforcing provisions of the Fourteenth Amendment); and (5) act of June 10, 1872, *Statutes at Large* 17 (1872): 347 (appropriation for sundry civil expenses of the government). For the convenience of discussion, I will call all of these laws "enforcement acts/laws." For the texts of the first four laws and the relevant text of the last law, see Appendixes 1–5 of this study.

42. These numbers are calculated from *CG*, 41 Cong. 2 sess., v–xi. The Republican figure includes John Pool of North Carolina, whose party affiliation was identified as Whig. *Biographic Directory of the American Congress, 1774–1989* (Washington, D.C.: U.S. Government Printing Office, 1989), 1469.

43. *CG*, 41 Cong. 2 sess., 1870, pt. 2:1459, 1812; pt. 3:3503.

44. The House bill had ten sections. Its first section extended federal enforcement of the Fifteenth Amendment "at any Federal, State, county and municipal, or other elections." Violations would be punished by a fine of five hundred to five thousand dollars or imprisonment of one to three years. Sections 2 and 9 provided punishment for any individuals who prevented black voters from voting by force and violence. Sections 3 to 8 penalized state and federal officers who refused to register black voters, or prevented black voters from casting their votes, or refused to receive taxes from black voters if the taxes were prerequisites for voting or registration. Section 10 gave federal district courts the power to hear cases arising under the law. Ibid., pt. 4:3504–5.

45. Ibid.

46. Ibid., pt. 2:1584; pt. 3:2808; pt. 4:2942.

47. The bill had 17 sections. Sections 1 to 5 prohibited federal and state officials or any individuals from preventing black voters from exercising their rights to vote, to register, and to fulfill the prerequisites of voting. Violations would be punished by fine or imprisonment or both. Section 6 authorized federal courts to hear cases under this law. Sections 8 to 10 empowered federal district

courts to appoint election commissioners (later called "supervisors"), described the duties of the commissioners, and provided fees for the arrests they would make at the polls. Sections 11 and 12 authorized the president to direct the enforcement and to use military force, when necessary, to aid the enforcement. Sections 13 and 14 asked to remove those barred by the third section of the Fourteenth Amendment from holding office and continue to bar them from holding offices. Sections 15 to 17 enforced the rights prescribed by the Civil Rights Act of 1866. Ibid., pt. 4:3561–62.

48. Ibid., 3561.

49. Ibid., 3559–61.

50. Ibid., 3559.

51. Ibid., 3559.

52. The vote was strictly by party, with 131 yeas (all Republicans), 43 nays (42 Democrats and 1 Republican), and 53 not voting (34 Republicans, 18 Democrats, and 1 Conservative). Ibid., 3504.

53. John Sherman had suggested considering the House bill as a substitute. Ibid., 3518.

54. Ibid., 3560–62.

55. Ibid., 3481, 3484.

56. Ibid., 3487–88.

57. Ibid., 3568.

58. Ibid., 3490.

59. Ibid., 3490.

60. Ibid., 3490.

61. This was the only speech Revels made in the whole debate over the enforcement act. Revels's term in the Senate was very brief (February 25, 1870, to March 3, 1871), and he was placed on an insignificant committee on education and labor. During his term, Revels introduced three bills on Mississippi's economy and mixed education in Washington, D.C. None of them became law. Revels also introduced eighteen petitions, many of which asked for removal of political disabilities for white Mississippians. As to enforcing the Fifteenth Amendment, Revels seemed to respond coldly to the radical Senate bill, although in his first speech, made on March 16, 1870, on the Georgia readmission bill, he strongly demanded federal protection to support the state government. Revels was the only black representative in the entire Congress when the first and second enforcement acts were debated, but he was absent from final voting of both acts. Ibid. (speeches of Hiram R. Revels), pt. 3:1986–88; pt. 4:3520; Samuel Denny Smith, *The Negro in Congress, 1870–1901* (Chapel Hill: University of North Carolina Press, 1940), 20; Maurine Christopher, *Black Americans in Congress* (New York: Thomas Y. Crowell, 1976), 9.

62. *CG*, 41 Cong. 2 sess., 1870, pt. 4:3517–18.

63. Again, the use of *radical* or *moderate* in this chapter is confined to defining Republicans' stance on enforcement. In other words, these terms are used as working terminology. People switched their positions on the issue from time to time, even during the discussion of the same bill, as Oliver P. Morton, John Pool, and Carl Schurz did. *Radical Republicans* refers to those Republicans who tended to support a harsher policy toward the South and a more expansive power for the federal government to enforce the Fifteenth Amendment. *Moderates* or *conservatives* refers to those who tended to have only limited federal enforcement and to let the states comply with the amendments with a minimum of federal interference.

64. *CG*, 41 Cong. 2 sess., 1870, pt. 4:3489.

65. Ibid., 3519.

66. Even Morton himself acknowledged that suffrage was still "completely under the control of the several States": "except we have taken away their power to deny suffrage on account of race, color, or previous condition of servitude." Ibid., 3569–70.

67. Ibid., 3570.

68. Morton would change his position as the debate went on. He would offer an additional provision on May 20 to the bill that penalized individuals who prevented blacks from voting or registration. Ibid., 3570, 3678.

69. Ibid., 3608.

70. Ibid., 3608–9.

71. Ibid., 3658.

72. Ibid., 3563.

73. Ibid., 3658 (statements of Stewart).

74. Here, the term *individuals* would include both private individuals and those individuals who were officials but functioned as individuals. This section has never been repealed and has instead remained as an important civil rights law in the federal lawbook. See more discussion on this issue in Chapter 3. Ibid., 3613.

75. Ibid., 3612, 3678.

76. These sections were added as sections 21, 22, and 23 to the enforcement act. Ibid., 3663–64.

77. Ibid., 3664.

78. Ibid., 3664–65 (statement of Eugene Casserly), 3672 (statement of Sumner).

79. The majority of the Republicans finally agreed with the Senate amendments to the House bill. The Senate passed the bill by a vote of 43 to 8 with 21 abstaining. Joseph S. Fowler, a Union Republican, voted nay, 17 abstained, and the rest voted yeas. Ibid., 3690.

80. In his report to the Senate, Stewart, who headed the senatorial representation of the joint conference, said that the report did not "change any of the essential features of the bill as it passed the Senate, but [only to] make it a little more harmonious." Ibid., 3753–54 (William Stewart). The vote was overwhelmingly partisan, with 48 yeas (all Republicans), 11 nays (10 Democrats and 1 Union Republican), and 13 absent (1 Conservative and 10 Republicans, including Hiram R. Revels, Carl Schurz, and Henry Wilson). Ibid., pt. 5 : 3809.

81. Ibid., 3884.

82. For a complete text of the bill, see Appendix 1.

83. Emphasis added. There was no specification to the term "any right or privilege." But given the context of the debates (especially the statement of John Pool, who proposed this section), these "rights" meant those secured by the Fourteenth and Fifteenth Amendments and the Civil Rights Act of 1866. Voting was included. This section was strongly opposed by Democrats and moderate Republicans during the debate and would be challenged by the Supreme Court in its 1876 *United States v. Cruikshank* decision. But no action was taken by the Court regarding this section. This provision was first incorporated into the *Revised Statutes* in 1875 and again in 1878 as section 5508 under the title Civil Rights Law. It remains as section 241 of Title 18 in the United States Code. For more detailed discussion, see Chapters 3 and 5. See also Appendix 6.

84. Section 16 provided that same right should be applied to all persons in the United States,

citizen or alien, who should enjoy "the full and equal benefit of all laws and proceedings for security of person and property" as was enjoyed "by white citizens" and should be subject to equal punishment and taxation. No unequal taxation should be imposed by any state upon foreign immigrants. Section 17 provided that no unequal punishment should be imposed upon a foreigner because of his color or race. Section 18 declared that the Civil Rights Act of 1866 would be enforced by this enforcement bill. *CG*, 41 Cong. 2 sess., appendix, 651–53.

85. *Statutes at Large* 16 (1870): 140–46.

86. *CG*, 41 Cong. 2 sess., 1870, pt. 4:3609.

87. "The Fifteenth Amendment," *New York Times*, May 18, 1870.

88. "What Shall We Do Next?" *New York Times*, May 18, 1870, 4. The *Times* sympathized with the moderate House bill, which effected the contemplated purpose and there stopped, but the Senate bill was a "needless elaboration [of] all the points in the House bill." "Enforcing the Fifteenth Amendment," *New York Times*, May 23, 1870.

89. *CG*, 41 Cong. 2 sess., 1870, pt. 4:3664.

90. Everette Swinney, *Suppressing the Ku Klux Klan: The Enforcement of the Reconstruction Amendments, 1870–1877* (New York: Garland, 1987), 103–4; Robert A. Horn, "National Control of Congressional Elections" (Ph.D. diss., Princeton University, 1942), 153–54. It should be added that the Democratic candidate in 1868, Horatio Seymour, had been the state's governor; this favorite son status may have contributed to his victory.

91. Before the Civil War, there was no uniform regulation imposed by the federal government on enfranchising an alien before or after he was naturalized or declared the intention to be naturalized. Although Congress had declared its authority over establishing "an uniform rule of naturalization" by the act of March 26, 1790 (*Statutes at Large* 1 (1790): 103–4) and had subsequently passed laws establishing terms for naturalization, it acted very cautiously in this area. Both the strong states' rights sentiments and conventional practice of naturalizing immigrants under states' rule accounted for some of the congressional caution. But the lack of federal machinery contributed to the virtual laissez-faire state of the matter. The process of naturalization was largely left to the states, as was enfranchisement of aliens.

Alien suffrage varied from state to state. In 1848, the Wisconsin constitution gave an alien the right to vote once he declared his intention for naturalization. Indiana in 1850 allowed an alien to vote one year after declaring his intention, but he would wait for five years before he could be naturalized. Illinois tried to extend the franchise to aliens, but the proposal was defeated in 1848 by a narrow margin. The Michigan constitution of 1850 admitted only white male citizens to the suffrage after a short residence of six months in the state and disallowed foreigners to vote. The Kentucky constitution of 1850 required two-year residence for an alien to vote. In 1857, Minnesota imposed a six-month residence requirement on foreign immigrants who wanted to vote. In 1859, Oregon began to allow aliens to vote after declaring their intention and living in the state one year, an additional six months to that required for the natives; but Chinese, blacks, and mulattoes were specifically excluded from the suffrage. In 1859, Massachusetts amended its constitution to require an alien to live in the state for two years after naturalization in order to vote. In the middle states the foreigner was being enticed with brief residence periods and even the franchise itself. Kirk H. Porter, *A History of Suffrage in the United States* (Chicago: University of Chicago Press, 1918), 113–34; James H. Kettner, *The Development of American Citizenship, 1608–1870* (Chapel Hill:

University of North Carolina Press, 1978), 344 – 45; Edward P. Hutchinson, *Legislative History of American Immigration Policy, 1789–1965* (Philadelphia: University of Pennsylvania Press, 1981), 11– 46, esp. 45 – 46.

92. *New York Times*, October 26, 1868; Albie Burke, "Federal Regulation of Congressional Elections in Northern Cities, 1871–1894" (Ph.D. diss., University of Chicago, 1968), 36 – 37.

93. Davis's bill had only four sections. The first provided for punishment for fraudulent and false oaths, affirmation, and affidavits in relation to the naturalization of aliens; the second punished false conduct in applying for citizenship; the third punished the use of naturalization certificates falsely obtained; and the fourth provided that the U.S. courts would hear cases relating to the act. *CG*, 41 Cong. 2 sess., 1870, pt. 5:4366 – 67.

94. As with the first enforcement act, the vote on Davis's proposal was strictly partisan, with 130 yeas, 47 nays, and 53 not voting. Ibid., 4368.

95. Ibid., pt. 6:4835.

96. The first eleven sections of the bill can be summed as follows: the first five sections detailed the procedures, residence qualifications, methods, time, and place to apply for naturalization by aliens. The sixth and seventh sections proposed regulations regarding the use of the citizenship certificates and the naturalization of the children of naturalized citizens. Section 8 authorized that certificates of citizenship be uniformly issued by federal courts. Section 9 punished fraudulent uses of the certificates. Section 10 punished those who disturbed the commission of federal judges. Section 11 regulated fees for naturalization. Ibid., 4835 – 36.

97. Ibid., 4835 – 36.

98. According to Frank G. Franklin, the issue of establishing a uniform rule of naturalization in the United States was raised in the constitutional convention in 1787, but the idea was rejected. In all the naturalization laws made before 1861, the authority to process naturalization was given to the state and federal courts, but in practice, naturalization was conducted mainly by individual states. The Naturalization Act of 1790, the nation's first, permitted *free white persons* to be naturalized after two years' residence in the United States, "upon application to any common law court of record in the state where they had resided for one year." The Naturalization Act of 1795 required a longer residence and a preliminary declaration of intention and renunciation of former allegiance and of any title of nobility, but retained the color requirement. The act specified that "the supreme, superior, district or circuit court of some one of the states or of the territories . . . or a circuit of district court of the United States" was empowered to naturalize aliens. Ibid., 70 –71. The Naturalization Act of 1798, which was produced under the fear that the United States might get involved in the European war, only amended the length of the residence requirement. Ibid., 93. The Naturalization Act of 1802 again kept the color requirement and required a registration of all aliens in the office "of some federal or state court." Ibid., 107. The subsequent naturalization acts of 1813 and 1824 made no substantial change in authority. Several attempts were made in 1845 and in the late 1850s to amend the naturalization laws, but no bill passed Congress. Emphasis added. Frank George Franklin, *The Legislative History of Naturalization in the United States* (Chicago: University of Chicago Press, 1906), 48 –107, esp. 48, 70 –71, 93, 107.

99. Lieber to Hamilton Fish, New York, April 3, April 15, 1870, Lieber Papers, HT.

100. *CG*, 41 Cong. 2 sess., 1870, pt. 6:5120 –21.

101. Ibid., 4837 (statement of Willard Saulsbury), 4838 – 40 (statement of George Vickers).

102. Ibid., 5114 – 15 (statement of Thomas Bayard).

103. Ibid., 5176.

104. Ibid., 5115 – 17 (statement of Oliver P. Morton).

105. Ibid., 5115 – 17.

106. Ibid., 5118.

107. Ibid., 5118 – 19 (statement of Carl Schurz).

108. Ibid., 5121.

109. Sumner's letter to the Committee of the Anti-Slavery Society, Senate Chamber, April 8, 1870, in *National Anti-Slavery Standard*, April 16, 1870.

110. The first naturalization act, passed by Congress in 1790, said that only "free white persons" could be naturalized as American citizens. Although naturalization laws were changed several times, no proposal had ever been raised to remove the word *white*. Sumner was the first senator to challenge racial discrimination in naturalization. For the interpretations of "free white persons" and cases concerning this provision, see Luella Gettys, *The Law of Citizenship in the United States* (Chicago: University of Chicago Press, 1934), 62 – 69.

111. Lieber to Hamilton Fish, New York, April 3, April 15, 1870, Lieber Papers, HT.

112. According to Roger Daniels, significant Chinese migration to the United States began with the California gold rush of 1849 and ended with the passage of the Chinese Exclusion Act in May 1882. The total number of Chinese entering the United States during this period was nearly 300,000; about 100,000 Chinese arrived from 1849 to 1870. Stanford M. Lyman offers a smaller figure. According to his calculation, during the unrestricted period of Chinese immigration (1852 – 1882), 100,000 Chinese men and 8,848 Chinese women entered the United States. But both authors agree that more than 90 percent of these Chinese were adult males.

The Chinese issue started as a regional concern in the early 1860s, but it soon became a national issue as California Republicans lost control of the state in 1867 owing partly to their resolution in favor of voluntary immigration, which the voters interpreted as a "pro-Chinese" statement. Thus, between 1868 and 1871, California Republicans opposed Chinese immigration and called on the federal government to halt it. By July 1870, some anti-Chinese demonstrations and mass meetings had been held in San Francisco and put pressure on the state lawmakers, who enacted anti-Chinese legislation and ordinances at the state and municipal levels. The first large-scale anti-Chinese riot occurred in Denver on October 31, 1880. Roger Daniels, *Asian America: Chinese and Japanese in the United States since 1850* (Seattle: University of Washington Press, 1988), 9 – 80, esp. 9, 29, 39, 69; Stanford M. Lyman, *The Asian in the West* (Reno: Western Studies Center, Desert Research Institute, University of Nevada, 1970), 18, 27 – 28.

113. Gillette, *Right to Vote*, 54, 77 – 78, 154 – 58.

114. *CG*, 41 Cong. 2 sess., 1870, pt. 6:5152.

115. Ibid., 5150.

116. Ibid., 5158.

117. Ibid., 5164.

118. Schurz opposed all the racial remarks made by Stewart and Williams against the Chinese immigrants. He saw no threat from the growth of the Chinese population. Instead of rejecting the Chinese, Schurz suggested that efforts be made in the direction of Americanizing the Chinese laborers and facilitating them "with new wants" by the time they were returning to China. Once these

Chinese went home to "propagandize" the American way of consumption in China, they would "gradually create markets there" for U.S. products. Sprague saw the Chinese labor force as part of a growing international economic system, which would bring to the United States much-needed profits and cheap labor. Whereas Stewart and Williams appeared more like provincial politicians, Schurz and Sprague were surely among the best minds of the Republican party in projecting the globalization of American economy, which would be partly materialized in the next century, although not quite in China. Ibid., 5159–60 (Schurz), 5170–71 (Sprague).

119. Ibid., 5161–62.

120. Ibid., 5175.

121. Ibid., 5152 (William Stewart).

122. Ibid., 5158 (George H. Williams).

123. Ibid., 5160.

124. Warner thought the Republican opposition to Sumner's proposal wise on the Senate's part, equivalent to Lincoln's decision to postpone issuing his Proclamation of Emancipation until the right time. The vote was 21 yeas (all Republicans), 20 nays (12 Republicans and 8 Democrats), and 31 not voting (27 Republicans, 1 Democrat, and 3 Independents). Sumner, Trumbull, Zachariah Chandler, Morton, and Sprague were among the supporters; Conkling, Wilson, Stewart, and Williams voted against the proposal. Revels was absent in this voting. Ibid., 5176.

125. Morton made clear that there were some who had come from the West Indian islands who were "desirous of being naturalized, but so far as Africa [was] concerned," there were none that would come. Ibid., 5177.

126. The eight Republicans who voted with Trumbull for the amendment were Reuben E. Fenton of New York, Joseph S. Fowler of Tennessee, Alexander McDonald of Arkansas, Samuel C. Pomeroy of Kansas, Benjamin F. Rice of Arkansas, Thomas J. Robertson of South Carolina, William Sprague of Rhode Island, and Sumner of Massachusetts. Ibid., 5177.

127. Three more Republicans, Timothy O. Howe of Wisconsin, Justin S. Morrill of Vermont, and Thomas W. Osborn of Florida, joined the nine Republicans (including Trumbull himself) who supported Trumbull's amendment to vote for Sumner's proposal. Several leading Republicans, including Stewart, Williams, Conkling, Zachariah Chandler, and Wilson, voted against the Sumner proposal. Ibid., 5177.

128. Bayard's question was finally referred to the Committee of the Whole and had no further result. Ibid., 5176–77.

129. For the complete text of the act, see Appendix 2.

130. *CG*, 41 Cong. 2 sess., 5177.

131. The final vote of the House on H.R. 2201 was 132 to 53, with 45 not voting. One hundred and thirty-one Republicans (81 percent of the party votes) approved the Senate modification, 29 abstained, and only 1 disagreed. No Democrat voted for the bill. Ibid., 5441.

132. Douglass to Sumner, Rochester, July 6, 1870, in Frederick Douglass, *Life and Writings*, 3:222–23.

133. U. S. Grant to Roscoe Conkling, August 22, 1870, Roscoe Conkling Papers, LC.

134. "The Law against Election Frauds," *Chicago Tribune*, October 19, 1870.

135. "An Agreement Entered into by the Federal and City Authorities," *New York Times*, November 8, 1870, 1.

136. "The Registry Frauds," *New York Times*, November 8, 1870, 2.

137. *New York Times*, November 2, 9, 1870.

138. Democrats in New York City had six seats in the House, and the number remained unchanged in 1870 elections, but the total number of New York Democratic seats in the House rose from twelve in the Forty-first Congress to sixteen in the Forty-second Congress. Swinney, *Suppressing the Ku Klux Klan*, 107, 111.

139. According to the published roster of the third session of the Forty-second Congress, of 75 senators, 63 were Republicans (including John Pool of North Carolina, who was identified as a Whig but normally voted with the Republicans), 11 were Democrats, and 1 was a Conservative. In the House, there were 171 Republicans, 69 Democrats, and 4 Conservatives. In the first session of the Forty-second Congress, the total number of the senators was 73, of which 57 were Republicans, 1 Whig (Pool), 1 Conservative (John W. Johnston of Virginia), and 13 Democrats. In the House, there were 136 Republicans, 96 Democrats, who could expect assistance from 6 southern Conservatives, and 1 Independent. *CG*, 41 Cong. 3 sess., pt. 1:v–xi; 42 Cong. 1 sess., pt.1:v–xii.

140. Trelease, *White Terror*, 241–42.

141. According to Eric Foner, the defeat of the Republican party was due to a cluster of factors. In Georgia and Alabama, Democrats took advantage of the Republican infighting and demoralization. Violence was important but varied from state to state. In Missouri, West Virginia, Virginia, and Tennessee, the party split. In the Deep South, violence played a more significant role. But around 1870, the Klan "devastate[d] the Republican organization in many local communities." Foner, *Reconstruction*, 441–44; see also Trelease, *White Terror*, 273.

142. Trelease, *White Terror*, 385–86.

143. Charles Sumner to Gerrit Smith, Nahant, August 20, 1871, in *Selected Letters*, 2:569–70. Sumner and Grant also differed substantially on diplomatic issues, especially on the latter's intent to annex the Dominican Republic; such differences eventually led to Sumner's removal as chairman of the Senate Foreign Relations Committee. For details, see David H. Donald, *Charles Sumner and the Rights of Man* (New York: Alfred A. Knopf, 1970), 435–97.

144. Of the newly elected 124 members of the House, 60 were Democrats, 33 were from northern and western states, 27 from southern and border states. Democrats were particularly strong in New York, Pennsylvania, Tennessee, and Kentucky. Of the 64 incoming Republicans, only 10 were from the South.

145. "Our Worthy Masters—As Before," *New York Times*, November 9, 1870.

146. "The General Result," *New York Times*, November 10, 1870, 1; *CG*, 41 Cong. 3 sess., 1870, pt. 1:170 (John Charles Churchill and Thomas A. Jenckes), 378 (Churchill), 1014 (Roscoe Conkling).

147. *CG*, 41 Cong. 3 sess., 1871, appendix, 342–45; *Statutes at Large* 16 (1871): 433–40.

148. Gillette, *Retreat from Reconstruction*, 26.

149. *CG*, 41 Cong. 3 sess., 1871, pt. 2:1280–81.

150. Ibid., 1284–85.

151. Ibid., pt. 3:1641 (Eugene Casserly), 1639 (George Vickers); pt. 2:1273 (Stephen L. Mayhem), 1277–79 (Michael Kerr).

152. Revels, the only black senator, recorded his vote as yea. Ibid., pt. 2:1285; pt. 3:1655.

153. Scott to Grant, RG 107, NA, in Grant, *Papers*, 20:249–51.

154. Foner, *Reconstruction*, 431–44; Gillette, *Retreat from Reconstruction*, 92.

155. "The Ku Klux Klan," *Harper's Weekly*, April 1, 1871, 282.

156. Grant to James G. Blaine, Washington, March 9, 1871, Ulysses S. Grant Papers, ser. 2, LC.

157. Trelease, *White Terror*, 387–88.

158. *CG*, 42 Cong. 1 sess., 1871, pt. 1:322.

159. Ibid., 448 (Benjamin F. Butler).

160. Ibid., 370 (James Monroe).

161. Ibid., 519.

162. Ibid., 477.

163. Ibid., pt. 2:607–8.

164. Ibid., 609.

165. Ibid., 579.

166. Ibid., 687–88.

167. The House passed the bill with a vote of 118 to 91, with 18 not voting. Ibid., 522. The Senate passed the bill by a vote of 45 to 19, with 6 not voting. Ibid., 709.

168. The final vote on the conference report of the bill in the House was 93 yeas (all Republicans), 74 nays (all Democrats), and 63 not voting (49 Republicans and 14 Democrats). Ibid., 831. In the Senate, the vote was 36 yeas (all Republicans), 13 nays (all Democrats and Conservatives), and 21 absent (20 Republicans and 1 Democrat). Ibid., 808.

169. These practices included conspiracies by force or threat to overthrow the government of the United States, to prevent the execution of any law of the United States, to prevent anyone from accepting or holding federal office, to injure federal officers and their property, to deter any party or witness in any federal court from testifying, to influence the verdict and indictment of any juror, to go in disguise on the public highway to deprive directly and indirectly any person "of equal protection of the laws, or of equal privileges or immunities under the laws," to prevent "any citizen of the United States lawfully entitled to vote from giving his support or advocacy in a lawful manner towards or in favor of the election of any lawfully qualified person as an elector of President or Vice President of the United States, or as a member of the Congress of the United States." Ibid., appendix, 335–36.

170. *Statutes at Large* 17 (1971): 13–15; for the text of this law, see Appendix 4.

171. The relations between the liberal Republican movement and enforcement are discussed in the next chapter. For details on the intellectual and political origins of the Liberal Republican movement, see John G. Sproat, *"The Best Men": Liberal Reformers in the Gilded Age* (1968; reprint, Chicago: University of Chicago Press, 1982), 3–71; also see Earle Dudley Ross, *The Liberal Republican Movement* (New York: Henry Holt, 1919).

172. *CG*, 42 Cong. 1 sess., 1871, pt. 2:687–90.

173. "The South and Its Ailments," *Chicago Tribune*, February 19, 1871.

174. Garfield to Burke Hinsdale, March 30, 1871, Letterbooks, Garfield Papers, LC, quoted from Gillette, *Retreat from Reconstruction*, 52.

175. "The Ku Klux Bill," *Harper's Weekly*, April 15, 1871, 330.

176. Before Kellogg introduced his bill (S. No. 791), several bills were introduced into both houses to amend the previous enforcement laws. *CG*, 42 Cong. 2 sess., 1871–72, pts. 1–2:24 (Henry B. Anthony), 59 (George Hoar), 318 (Frederick T. Frelinghuysen), 1115 (Thomas Boles), 1558 (William P. Kellogg), 1588 (Henry W. Corbett), and 1773 (Hale Sypher).

177. Ibid., 1872, pt. 4:3319.

178. Ibid., 3322 (George Edmunds), 3322–23 (Thomas Norwood and Eugene Casserly), 3420 (Henry B. Anthony, Lyman Trumbull, Thomas J. Robertson, and John Sherman), and 3421 (Sumner). The passage of the bill was strictly partisan. Thirty-five of the 36 yeas were from the Republicans, 12 of the 17 nays from the Democrats. Ibid., 3431.

179. Ibid., pt. 5:3934 (statement of James Beck).

180. Ibid., 4103.

181. The Ku Klux Force Act (April 20, 1871) provided that the fourth section, which empowered the president to suspend the writ of habeas corpus if necessary, would terminate after the one regular congressional session. The Senate passed the bill on May 21, 1872, but when the vote was called in the House, James A. Garfield and other Republicans joined with Democrats to defeat it. Ibid., pt. 4:3431; pt. 5:3932.

182. Ibid., pt. 5:4361–62 (William Kellogg).

183. Ibid., 4366 (Allen Thurman).

184. All the leading Democrats and Republicans in the Senate joined the debates. Ibid., 4362 (Allen Thurman), 4363 (Eugene Casserly), 4363 (William Kellogg), 4364 (Roscoe Conkling), 4389 (John Sherman).

185. Ibid., 4393.

186. The Senate passed the bill by a vote of 32 yeas, 11 nays, and 31 not voting. Ibid., 4398.

187. Ibid., 4440 (report of Garfield in the House), 4495 (report of Cole in the Senate).

188. Ibid., 4454.

189. Ibid., 4495.

Chapter Three. The Anatomy of Enforcement, 1870–1876

1. The wording on suffrage in Grant's inaugural address is different from that in the draft of the address. In the draft, Grant wrote,

> Unequal suffrage in the different states is a question which will likely agitate the public mind so long as it ~~continues~~ remains unsettled. I would suggest on this subject to the consideration [sic] of Congress and the people that it be taken out of politics by making suffrage ~~equal~~ uniform, all over the United States so far as it applies to, legislative & executive offices.

In the text of the address, the same paragraph read,

> The question of suffrage is one which is likely to agitate the public so long as a portion of the citizens of the nation are excluded from its privileges in any state. It seems to me very desirable that the question should be settled now, and I entertain the hope and express the desire that ~~the~~ it may be by the ratifyication of the fifteenth article of amendment to the Constitution.

U. S. Grant, "Draft Inaugural Address," "Inaugural Address," March 4, 1869, in Ulysses S. Grant, *The Papers of Ulysses S. Grant*, ed. John Y. Simon, 20 vols. (Carbondale: Southern Illinois University Press, 1967–95), 19:138–42.

2. When the German federation was formed in February 1871, Grant hailed it as a reproduction of "the best feature[s]" of the U.S. Constitution. He told Congress that German unification would bring "great masses of thoughtful and free people under a single government." Ulysses S. Grant to the Senate and House of Representatives, February 7, 1871, *Messages and Papers*, 7:120–21.

3. Grant to W. W. Holden, Long Branch, July 22, 1870, Grant, *Papers*, 20:210. Grant's telegraph to William W. Belknap, Long Branch, July 22, 1870, RG 94, NA, cited from Grant, *Papers*, 20:211; Holden to Grant, July 20, 1870, RG 94, NA, Grant, *Papers*, 210–11. Allen W. Trelease, *White Terror: The Ku Klux Klan Conspiracy and Southern Reconstruction* (New York: Harper & Row, 1971), 208–25; George C. Rable, *But There Was No Peace: The Role of Violence in the Politics of Reconstruction* (Athens: University of Georgia Press, 1984), 104–5.

4. Holden to U. S. Grant, May 20, 1871, Washington, RG 59, NA, in Grant, *Papers*, 20:213.

5. Grant to Daniel H. Chamberlain, Long Branch, August 22, 1870, in ibid., 20:248; Robert K. Scott to Grant, October 22, 1870, RG 107, NA, cited from ibid., 20:249–51.

6. William K. Scott to Grant, October 22, 1870, ibid., 20:249–51; William B. Hesseltine, *Ulysses S. Grant, Politician* (New York: Dodd, Mead, & Co., 1935), 239–40.

7. Harrison Reed to Grant, RG 94, NA, in Grant, *Papers*, 20:466. On November 1, 1870, Senator Thomas W. Osborn from Florida also made a similar request to Grant. Ibid.

8. William T. Sherman to Henry W. Halleck, Louisville, November 5, 1870; Reed to Grant, November 17, 1870; Belknap to Reed, November 22, 1870; in ibid., 20:466–67.

9. Grant, "Proclamation," March 24, 1871, *Messages and Papers*, 7:132–33.

10. Ulysses S. Grant to James G. Blaine, Washington, March 9, 1871, Ulysses S. Grant Papers, ser. 2, reel 3, LC; William S. McFeely, *Grant: A Biography* (New York: W. W. Norton, 1981), 368–69; William Gillette, *Retreat from Reconstruction, 1869–1879* (Baton Rouge: Louisiana State University Press, 1979), 37; James E. Sefton, *The United States Army and Reconstruction, 1865–1877* (Baton Rouge: Louisiana State University Press, 1967), 224.

11. Sefton, *United States Army*, 228.

12. Ibid., 224; Stephen Cresswell, "Enforcing the Enforcement Acts: The Department of Justice in Northern Mississippi, 1870–1890," *Journal of Southern History* 53 (August 1987): 425.

13. William T. Sherman's telegraph to Grant, November 2, 1870, RG 94, NA, quoted from Grant, *Papers*, 20:466.

14. The former duties of the attorney general included authorizing public building; maintaining federal courthouses; promoting public health; codifying federal statutes; and naming, with congressional approval, members of federal boards and commissions. The new department was also responsible for settling claims by or against the United States; supervising the use and sale of federal lands, and handling internal revenue and customs matters. *Statutes at Large* 16 (1870): 162; Homer Cummings and Carl McFarland, *Federal Justice: Chapters in the History of Justice and the Federal Executive* (New York: Macmillan, 1937), 222–29; Robert Michael Goldman, *"A Free Ballot and a Fair Count": The Department of Justice and the Enforcement of Voting Rights in the South, 1877–1893* (New York: Garland, 1991), 45–48.

15. McFeely, "Amos T. Akerman: The Lawyer and Racial Justice," in *Region, Race, and Reconstruction*, ed. J. Morgan Kousser and James McPherson (New York: Oxford University Press, 1982), 408; Everette Swinney, *Suppressing the Ku Klux Klan: The Enforcement of the Reconstruction Amendments, 1870–1877* (New York: Garland, 1987), 182; McFeely, *Grant*, 368; Eric Foner,

Reconstruction: America's Unfinished Revolution, 1863–1877 (New York: Harper & Row, 1988), 457; Lou Falkner Williams, "The Great South Carolina Ku Klux Klan Trials, 1871–1872" (Ph.D. diss., University of Florida, 1991), 92.

16. Akerman was nominated by Grant on June 16, 1870, forty-six days after the first enforcement act went into effect. Grant to the Senate, June 16, 1870, Grant, *Papers*, 20:174.

17. Amos T. Akerman to B. D. Silliman, November 9, 1871, Amos T. Akerman Papers, quoted from McFeely, *Grant*, 372; Foner, *Reconstruction*, 457.

18. Amos T. Akerman to D. J. Cobin (U.S. attorney in South Carolina), November 10, 1871, Attorney-General Instruction Books, bk. C, 28–30, Department of Justice, RG 60, NA.

19. Williams, "Great South Carolina Ku Klux Klan Trials," 93–94.

20. Ibid., 102–3.

21. United States, Congress, Joint Select Committee on the Condition of Affairs in the Late Insurrectionary States, *Report of the Joint Select Committee Appointed to Inquire into the Condition of Affairs in the Late Insurrectionary States, So Far as Regards the Execution of Laws, and the Lives and Property of the Citizens of the United States and Testimony Taken* (South Carolina, vol. 3), 42 Cong. 2 sess (reprinted as vol. 5 of the *Ku Klux Klan Conspiracy*, Washington, D.C.: U.S. Government Printing Office, 1872 [*KKK Report*]), 1799–1810; see also Kermit L. Hall, "Political Power and Constitutional Legitimacy: The South Carolina Ku Klux Klan Trials, 1871–1872," *Emory Law Journal* 32 (Fall 1984): 923–51.

22. *KKK Report*, no. 22, 42 Cong. 2 sess., 5:1622; Charles Fairman, *Reconstruction and Reunion, 1864–1888* (New York: Macmillan, 1971), 200.

23. *National Encyclopedia of American Biography*, 4:372.

24. *KKK Report*, 5:1621, 1630, 1638–39, 1643, 1654.

25. For Stanbery's argument on *United States v. Robert Hayes Mitchell*, see *KKK Report*, 5:1658–60.

26. *United States v. Reese* (1876) is discussed in detail in the latter part of this chapter.

27. *KKK Report*, 5:1858–60, 1818–20; Fairman, *Reconstruction and Reunion*, 206–8.

28. Williams's study on the South Carolina Ku Klux Klan trials provides a detailed, analytical account of the background, process, and outcomes of the trials. Williams, "Great South Carolina Ku Klux Klan Trials," 237–38.

29. William Gillette lists fifty-nine cases under the enforcement acts in 1870. Thirty-two, all from border and northern states, resulted in convictions; all sixteen cases from the South, and eleven from border states, resulted in dismissals. I found only forty-three cases listed under the Enforcement Act of May 31, 1870, and none of them was from the South. There were only two cases, both resulting in conviction, that were under the Naturalization Act of July 14, 1870. Amos T. Akerman, *Annual Report of the Attorney General of the United States for the Year 1870*, in *House Executive Documents*, 41 Cong. 3 sess., no. 90; *Senate Executive Documents*, 42 Cong. 3 sess., no. 32 (actual numbers of the 1870 cases are listed); Gillette, *Retreat from Reconstruction*, 43.

30. *Annual Report of the Attorney General*, in *House Executive Documents*, 42 Cong. 2 sess., no. 55; 3 sess., no. 32, 24–27 (1871 case numbers).

31. *Annual Report of the Attorney General*, in *House Executive Documents*, 42 Cong. 3 sess., no. 32. For details of the regional distributions of the cases convicted and dismissed during this period, see Appendix 7.

32. Stanley F. Horn, "National Control of Congressional Elections" (Ph.D. diss., Princeton University, 1942), 180 – 81; Sefton, *United States Army*, 225 – 26.

33. Amos T. Akerman to D. J. Cobin, November 10, 1871, Attorney General Instruction Books, bk. C, 47 – 48, RG 60, NA.

34. Foner, *Reconstruction*, 458; McFeely, *Grant*, 373.

35. Williams, "Great South Carolina Ku Klux Klan Trials," 238 – 43.

36. Swinney, *Suppressing the Ku Klux Klan*, 267 – 68; Sefton, *United States Army*, 225.

37. George H. Sharpe to George H. Williams, September 18, 1872, Department of Justice, Source-Chronological Files, box 567, RG 60, NA.

38. United States Treasury Department, an Account of the Receipts and Expenditures of the United States, 41 – 42 Cong. (1871 – 73); serials 1565, 1651, 1807, quoted from Swinney, *Suppressing the Ku Klux Klan*, 184.

39. John Davenford to George H. Sharpe, February 28, 1872; Sharpe to George H. Williams, March 25, 1872; Department of Justice, Source-Chronological files, box 567, RG 60, NA.

40. Williams to William H. Smith et al., February 5, 1873, Attorney General Instruction Books, bk. C, 645, Department of Justice, RG 60, NA.

41. Gillette, *Retreat from Reconstruction*, 45.

42. Henry Johns to William Sprague, August 24, 1869, William Sprague Papers, Rare Books and Manuscripts Library, Columbia University; Earle Dudley Ross, *The Liberal Republican Movement* (New York: Henry Holt, 1919), 2 – 44, esp. 24 – 33.

43. John G. Sproat, *"The Best Men": Liberal Reformers in the Gilded Age* (1968; reprint, Chicago: University of Chicago Press, 1982), 12 – 23, 36 – 44; Ross, *Liberal Republican Movement*, 48 – 58.

44. Green Clay to Henry Wilson, March 1, 1871, Henry Wilson Papers, LC.

45. Charles F. Adams, *The Double Anniversary: '76 and '63: A Fourth of July Address Delivered at Quincy, Mass.* (Boston: W. M. Parsons Lunt, 1869), 11 – 16.

46. Carl Schurz, *The Reminiscences of Carl Schurz*, 3 vols. (New York: McClure, 1907 – 8), 3:318 – 24; Sproat, *"The Best Men,"* 32; Stanley P. Hirshson, *Farewell to the Bloody Shirt: Northern Republicans and the Southern Negro, 1877 – 1893* (Bloomington: Indiana University Press, 1962), 126 – 27.

47. "The Problem at the South," *Nation*, March 23, 1871, 192 – 93.

48. Horace Greeley to Josephine S. W. Griffing, September 7, 1870, Josephine Sophie White Griffing Papers, CU.

49. "The Race Question," *Nation*, July 21, 1870, 39.

50. *Chicago Tribune*, September 13, 1872.

51. William Graham Sumner, the Yale sociologist, supported expanding suffrage but would later dispute the idea of equal rights in politics: "It is, however, in my judgment, a corruption of democracy to set up the dogma that all men are equally competent to give judgment on political questions; and it is a still worse perversion of it to adopt the practical rule that they must be called upon to exercise this ability on all questions as the regular process for getting those questions solved. The dogma is false, and the practical rule is absurd." William G. Sumner, "Politics in America, 1776 – 1876," *North American Review* 122 (January 1876): 47 – 87.

52. S. Eliot Lane to George Williams, July 4, 1872, Department of Justice, Source-Chronological Files, RG 60, NA.

53. "Mr. Greeley's Supporters in Georgia," *Harper's Weekly*, September 28, 1872, 757–58.

54. Grant to O. P. Morton, Washington, October 20, 1870, Grant, *Papers*, 20:312–13.

55. John M. Forbes to Charles Sumner, August 10, 1872, in John Murray Forbes, *Letters and Recollections of John Murray Forbes*, ed. Sarah Forbes Hughes, 2 vols. (Boston: Houghton Mifflin, 1900), 2:178–82.

56. "Mr. Greeley's Supporters in Georgia," *Harper's Weekly*, September 28, 1872, 757–58.

57. McFeely, *Grant*, 380–81; Hesseltine, *Ulysses S. Grant*, 269–77.

58. John Sherman to William T. Sherman, Paris, August 2, 1872, John Sherman and William Tecumseh Sherman, *The Sherman Letters: Correspondence between General and Senator Sherman from 1837 to 1891*, ed. Rachel Sherman Thorndike (New York: Charles Scribner's Sons, 1894), 338–39. Sherman was angry with Grant for withdrawing the appointment of W. B. Thrall, one of Sherman's associates, in December 1870. Sherman described his meeting with Grant on this matter as "very unpleasant" and stated, "Whatever may be the consequences to me personally I will no longer submit to this gross and shameless abuse of public patronage without an effort to check it." John Sherman to W. B. Thrall, December 2, 1870, John Sherman Papers, LC.

59. John Bigelow to Whitelaw Reid, Berlin, July 21, November 22, 1871, John Bigelow Papers, NYPL.

60. Amos T. Akerman's letter, *Harper's Weekly*, August 24, 1872, 651.

61. Charles Sumner to Carl Schurz, Boston, September 25, 1871, April 25, 1872, *Selected Letters*, 2:573–74.

62. Sumner to Henry W. Longfellow, Senate Chamber, April 25, 1872, *Selected Letters*, 2:585–87.

63. *Harper's Weekly*, June 22, 1872, 482–83; see also F. William Nicklas, "William D. Kelley: The Congressional Years, 1861–1890" (Ph.D. diss., Northern Illinois University, 1983), 294–95.

64. *Harper's Weekly*, May 11, 1872, 363.

65. *Chicago Tribune*, May 30, 1872; Frederick Douglass to Amy Post, Washington, July 18, 1872, Frederick Douglass Papers, UR; Grant also received a strong endorsement from blacks in Missouri, who would vote for the first time at a presidential election. See Margaret L. Dwight, "Black Suffrage in Missouri, 1865–1877" (Ph.D. diss., University of Missouri, 1978), 155–57.

66. Frederick Douglass's letter, *Harper's Weekly*, August 24, 1872, 651.

67. Republican National Convention, *Proceedings of the National Union Republican Convention*, reported by Francis H. Smith (Washington, D.C.: Gibson Brothers, 1872), 13.

68. Ibid., 51–53; Kirk H. Porter and Donald Bruce Johnson, eds., *National Party Platforms, 1840–1964* (Urbana: University of Illinois Press, 1966), 46–47.

69. Grant to Heouss Settle, Washington, June 11, 1872, Ulysses S. Grant Papers, ser. 2, reel 3, LC.

70. Vincent P. De Santis, *Republicans Face the Southern Question: The New Departure Years, 1877–1897* (Baltimore: Johns Hopkins University Press, 1959), 21; James M. McPherson, *Ordeal by Fire: The Civil War and Reconstruction* (New York: Alfred A. Knopf, 1982), 567–72; Hesseltine, *Ulysses S. Grant*, 308.

71. Hesseltine, *Ulysses S. Grant*, 308–40, esp. 322–25.

72. Ibid., 327–29; Foner, *Reconstruction*, 521–22.

73. Foner, *Reconstruction*, 521–22; Hesseltine, *Ulysses S. Grant*, 335–37.

74. "The West and the Speakership," *St. Louis Daily Globe*, September 27, 1873, clippings in James G. Blaine Papers, reel 17, LC.

75. Gillette, *Retreat from Reconstruction*, 246 – 47; McPherson, *Ordeal by Fire*, 592; Foner, *Reconstruction*, 523.

76. Zachariah Chandler to James G. Blaine, Senate Chamber, November 12, 1874, James G. Blaine Papers, reel 8, LC.

77. "The Last Chance," *New York Graphic*, December 1874, clippings in James G. Blaine Papers, reel 16, LC.

78. John Bigelow to J. W. Parsons, November 18, 1874, John Bigelow Papers, NYPL.

79. "The Second Term," *Harper's Weekly*, March 22, 1873, 218.

80. *Messages and Papers*, 7:284 – 303, esp. 296 – 98.

81. Adelbert Ames to Ulysses S. Grant, telegram, December 19, 1874, Source-Chronological Files, box 2, RG 60, NA; Gillette, *Retreat from Reconstruction*, 150 – 51.

82. G. W. Marshall to Grant, Savannah, Georgia, February 3, 1873, Source-Chronological Files, box 1, RG 60, NA.

83. Joseph T. Hatch to Grant, January 21, 1873, New Orleans, ibid.

84. Caddo Committee of Colored Republicans to Grant, December 5, 1874, ibid., box 2.

85. A. Fremy to Ulysses S. Grant, La Grange, Georgia, October 27, 1874, ibid.

86. Gillette, *Retreat from Reconstruction*, 281 – 82.

87. The Civil Rights Act of 1875 was first proposed by Charles Sumner in May 1870 and intended to prohibit racial discrimination in schools, juries, and all forms of transportation and public accommodations in the United States. It was, in Sumner's words, "the final measure for the safeguard of . . . colored fellow-citizens." The Senate passed the bill in May 1874, which to some was a tribute to Sumner, who had died two months earlier. In February 1875, when the bill came to the House, the school section was cut. Even without the school section, the Civil Rights Act stood as a powerful challenge to racial discrimination. It was the last of the important Reconstruction laws enacted by the Republican party but was declared unconstitutional by the Supreme Court in 1883. Sumner to Edward L. Pierce, December 27, 1871, *Selected Letters*, 2:577; McPherson, *Ordeal by Fire*, 576 – 77.

88. *CR*, 43 Cong. 2 sess., 1875, 3, pt. 2:145; pt. 3:1748 – 49.

89. Ibid., 1838 – 39.

90. Ibid., 1885 – 86.

91. Ibid., 1855.

92. Ibid., 1853.

93. Hawley was not alone in this regard. When the civil rights bill was debated in Congress, Joseph Medill of the *Chicago Tribune* had advised Republicans not to pursue the bill, which had "done no good but much harm": "Legislation is never useful against social or race prejudices." Medill to James G. Blaine, Chicago, February 14, 1875, James G. Blaine Papers, reel 8, LC.

94. *CR*, 43 Cong. 2 sess., 1875, 3, pt. 3:1840 – 49.

95. Ibid., 1834.

96. Ibid., 1902.

97. Ibid., 1906, 1929 (passage of Butler's amendment), 1935 (passage of the bill); Gillette, *Retreat from Reconstruction*, 291.

98. *CR*, 43 Cong. 2 sess., 1875, 3, pt. 3:1936 – 37, 1939 – 40, 2035.

99. Buford Satcher, *Blacks in Mississippi Politics, 1865 – 1900* (Washington, D.C.: University Press of America, 1978), 124.

100. A letter addressed to A. Warver, who was chairman of the State Republican Executive Committee in Jackson County, Mississippi, October 22, 1875; found in document collection titled "U.S. Senate, 44 Cong. Select Committee to Investigate Elections in Mississippi, 1875–1876," NYPL.

101. Gillette, *Retreat from Reconstruction*, 155–63; Foner, *Reconstruction*, 559–63; McPherson, *Ordeal by Fire*, 594–95.

102. Students of Reconstruction agree that 1875 was the turning point of the Republican party's enforcement program. Eric Foner argues that "1875 marked a milestone in the retreat from Reconstruction." William Gillette concludes that "the year 1875 was the turning point for Reconstruction. The emasculation of civil rights, the defeat of the force bill, the backdown in Louisiana and Arkansas, the inaction in Mississippi, and the string of Republican defeats in local contests in the South, all were markings along the road to retreat." Foner, *Reconstruction*, 563; Gillette, *Retreat from Reconstruction*, 294–95.

103. Horace White to James Blaine, Chicago, November 17, 1874; Joseph Medill to Blaine, Chicago, February 14, 1875, James G. Blaine Papers, reel 8, LC.

104. Joseph Medill to James Blaine, Chicago, February 14, 1875, James G. Blaine Papers, reel 8, LC.

105. These cases included *Ex parte McIllwee*, 16 *Federal Cases* (1870): 147–48; *Charge to Grand Jury*, 30 *Federal Cases* (1870): 987–90; *McKay v. Campbell*, 16 *Federal Cases* (1870): 157–60; *United States v. Canter et al.*, 25 *Federal Cases* (1870): 281–82; *United States v. Quinn*, 27 *Federal Cases* (1870): 673–80; *United States v. Hall et al.*, 26 *Federal Cases* (1871): 79–82; *United States v. Crosby et al.*, 25 *Federal Cases* (1871): 701–14; *Harrison v. Hadley, et al.*, 11 *Federal Cases* (1873): 649–54; *Seeley v. Knox*, 21 *Federal Cases* (1874): 1014–16.

106. *United States v. Canter et al.*, 16 *Federal Cases* (1870): 147–48.

107. *United States v. Crosby*, 25 *Federal Cases* (1871): 701–14.

108. *United States v. Hall et al.*, 26 *Federal Cases* (1871): 79–82.

109. *KKK Reports*, 5:1821, 1643.

110. Leon Friedman and Fred L. Israel, eds., *The Justices of the United States Supreme Court, 1789–1969: Their Lives and Major Opinions* (New York: R. R. Bowker, 1969), 967.

111. Carl Bent Swisher, *Stephen J. Field: Craftsman of the Law* (Washington, D.C.: Brookings Institution, 1930), 268.

112. Friedman and Israel, *Justices*, 1015; Samuel Miller correspondence, February 6, 1866, August 29, 1869, quoted from Charles Fairman, *Mr. Justice Miller and the Supreme Court, 1862–1890* (Cambridge: Harvard University Press, 1939), 191–94.

113. Friedman and Israel, *Justices*, 1051.

114. Ibid., 1199.

115. C. Peter Magrath, *Morrison R. Waite: The Triumph of Character* (New York: Macmillan, 1963), 2–22.

116. *Slaughterhouse Cases*, 83 U.S. 36 (1873).

117. Ibid.

118. Ibid.

119. For Woods's opinion, see *United States v. Hall et al.*, 26 *Federal Cases* (1871):79–82.

120. *Slaughterhouse Cases*, 83 U.S. 36 (1873).

121. Ibid.

122. Ibid., 123.

123. "The Civil-Rights Bill," *Nation*, September 17, 1874, 180 – 81.

124. *CR*, 43 Cong. 1 sess., 1874, 2, pt. 1:420 – 21.

125. Frederick Douglass to Gerrit Smith, Washington, July 3, 1874, Gerrit Smith Papers, box 11, Syracuse University Library.

126. *New York Times*, April 16, 1873; Charles Fairman, *Reconstruction and Reunion, 1864– 1888*, part 2 (New York: Macmillan, 1971), 261 – 62; Foner, *Reconstruction*, 550.

127. Fairman, *Reconstruction and Reunion*, 265.

128. Counts 1 to 16 charged the band's offenses under section 6 of the enforcement act for depriving the blacks of their right to life. Counts 17 to 32 repeated the charges but added the charge of murder punishable under section 7. *United States v. Cruikshank et al., 25 Federal Cases* (1874): 708.

129. Ibid., 711.

130. Ibid., 712.

131. Ibid., 714.

132. Ibid., 715 – 16.

133. Fairman, *Reconstruction and Reunion*, 186 – 88. For the Eutaw incident, see Trelease, *White Terror*, 271-73.

134. George H. Williams to James Beckwith, July 11, 1874, quoted from Cummings and McFarland, *Federal Justice*, 245.

135. Fairman, *Reconstruction and Reunion*, 226 – 28.

136. Ibid., 229 – 30.

137. *New York World*, January 31, 1873.

138. Gabriel C. Wharton to George H. Williams, November 10, 1873, RG 60, NA, quoted from Fairman, *Reconstruction and Reunion*, 229.

139. James Beckwith to Williams, October 27, 1874, Department of Justice Manuscripts, quoted from Cummings and McFarland, *Federal Justice*, 245.

140. B. F. Buckner, *Supreme Court of the United States. The United States, Plaintiff in Error, vs. Hiram Reese and Matthew Foushee, Defendants in Error. Brief for Defendants in Error* (n.p., n.d.) [found at Columbia Law School Library], 9, 31.

141. *United States v. Reese*, 92 U.S. 219 – 20 (1876).

142. Ibid., 218 – 19.

143. Ibid., 221.

144. Geo. H. Williams and S. F. Phillips, *Transcript of Record. Supreme Court of the United States. In the Supreme Court of the United States. The United States vs. William J. Cruikshank, William D. Irwin, and John P. Hadnot. No. 609. In Error to the Circuit Court of the United States for the District of Louisiana. Brief for the United States* (n.p., 1875?) [found at Columbia Law School Library], 2 – 27.

145. R. H. Marr, *Supreme Court of the United States. No. 609. The United States, Plaintiffs in Error, versus Cruikshank, Irwin and Hadnot. Argument for Defendants* (n.p., dated as "February 1875") [found at Columbia Law School Library], 24 – 32.

146. Other defense counsel, John A. Campbell and David Dudley Field, also wrote briefs or statements for the defendants, addressing the same arguments as expressed in Marr's brief. David

Dudley Field, *Supreme Court of the United States. The United States Against William I. Cruikshank and Two Others. Points and Brief of Mr. David Dudley Field for the Defendants* (New York: John Polhemus, 1875) [found at Columbia Law School Library]; John A. Campbell, *Supreme Court of the United States. No. 609. United States vs. Wm. J. Cruikshank et al. Conspiracy and Banding in Grant Parish, La. Brief for Defendants* (no city: Clark & Hofeline, Book and Job Printers, 1875?) [found at Columbia Law School Library].

147. *United States v. Cruikshank*, 92 U.S. 551–52 (1876).

148. Ibid., 553.

149. Ibid.

150. Ibid., 554.

151. Ibid., 555–56.

152. Ibid., 558–59.

153. Gillette, *Retreat from Reconstruction*, 43.

154. Hugh L. Bond to Morrison R. Waite, August 20, 1876, Morrison R. Waite Papers, box 7, LC.

155. L. C. Northrop to Charles Devens, January 14, 1879. Source-Chronological File, NA, quoted from Magrath, *Morrison R. Waite*, 133.

156. Frederick Douglass to an unidentified person, October 17, 1876, Frederick Douglass Papers, UR.

157. "Who Are the Friends of Negro Suffrage?" *Nation*, January 25, 1877, 53–54.

158. I agree with Robert Goldman's observation that the *Reese* and *Cruikshank* decisions "did leave intact congressional power to protect black voting rights in the South." Goldman, *"Free Ballot,"* 22.

159. *United States v. Cruikshank*, 25 *Federal Cases* (1874): 712.

160. Hunt criticized the majority opinion, by which "good sense [was] sacrificed to technical nicety, and a sound principle carried to an extravagant extent." *United States v. Reese*, 92 U.S. 238–56.

161. Benedict believes that the Court's decisions intended to reinforce dual federalism rather than reduce federal power. For details of his argument, see Michael Les Benedict, "Preserving Federalism: Reconstruction and the Waite Court," *Supreme Court Review* (1978): 39–79.

162. According to Fairman, who studied the docket of the *Reese* case, Bradley also noticed that the word "aforesaid" in section 3 could indicate the reason of "wrongful act," but he immediately wrote on the margin of the case, "Ought it not then to appear that the inspector knew the facts it referred to? The subject is beset with difficulties." Bradley found section 4 helpless because it did not "confine the offence" on account of race. Fairman, *Reconstruction and Reunion*, 243.

163. Section 5595 of the *Revised Statutes* repealed all acts passed before December 1, 1873, and "any portion of which" was "embraced in any section of said revision." But section 5598 provided that "all offenses committed [prior to the repeal], and all penalties or forfeitures under any statute embraced" in the revision could be prosecuted to a conclusion. *Revised Statutes* (1875): 354, 1073; *Statutes at Large* 18, pt. 1 (1878): 353–55, 1067–68, 1085; Fairman, *Reconstruction and Reunion*, 254–55.

164. Section 5506 of the *Revised Statutes* reads: "Every person who, by any unlawful means, hinders, delays, prevents, or obstructs, or combines and confederates with others to hinder, delay, prevent, or obstruct, any citizen from doing any act required to be done to qualify him to vote, or

from voting at any election in any State, Territory, district, county, city, parish, township, school-district, municipality, or other territorial subdivision, shall be fined not less than five hundred dollars, or be imprisoned not less than one month nor more than one year, or be punished by both such fine and imprisonment." Compared with the original section 4 (see Appendix 1), the most obvious change made in the revised version was the substitution of the words "as aforesaid" for the phrase "in any State, Territory, district, county, city, parish, township, school-district, municipality, or other territorial subdivision" that was originally placed in section 1 of the Enforcement Act of May 31, 1870. Section 5506, however, did not have the phrase "without distinction of race, color, or previous condition of servitude," which was also in the original section 1. *Revised Statutes* (1875): 354, 1073; *Statutes at Large* 18, pt. 1 (1878): 353, 1067–68.

165. By an act of March 2, 1877, George H. Boutwell of Massachusetts, a former radical Republican in the House, was appointed as the commissioner to prepare a new edition of the 1875 *Revised Statutes*. Although Boutwell noticed the decisions of the Supreme Court on both *Reese* and *Cruikshank*, he made no changes of the wording of all the sections in question in the new edition of the *Revised Statutes*. *Statutes at Large* 18, pt. 1 (1878): 353, 1067–68. Section 5508 was not repealed by the Democratic Congress in 1894 and, after a rearrangement, has survived and become section 241 (Conspiracy against rights) in Chapter 13 (Civil Rights) under Title 18 (Crimes and Criminal Procedure) in *United States Code*. *Statutes at Large* 35, pt. 1 (1909): 1092; United States, *United States Code 1994 Edition*, vol. 9 (Washington, D.C.: U.S. Government Printing Office, 1995), 69.

166. For further discussion of this subject, see Epilogue.

167. For discussion of these cases, see Chapter 5.

Chapter Four. The Hayes Administration and Black Suffrage, 1876–1880

1. "Our Centennial," *Harper's Weekly*, May 27, 1876, 422.

2. James D. McCabe, *The Illustrated History of the Centennial Exhibition* (Philadelphia: National Publishing Co., 1876), 3–6, 241–67, 433–59.

3. Ari Hoogenboom, *The Presidency of Rutherford B. Hayes* (Lawrence: University Press of Kansas, 1988), 1–3.

4. Mark W. Summers, *Railroads, Reconstruction, and the Gospel of Prosperity: Aid under the Radical Republicans, 1865–1877* (Princeton: Princeton University Press, 1984), 285.

5. Garfield to Hayes, Washington, March 2, 1876, *Election of 1876* (a selection of Rutherford B. Hayes Papers, LC), microfilm, reel 1, CU; Sherman to Hayes, Washington, March 18, 1876, Rutherford B. Hayes Papers, HPC.

6. C. Dow to William E. Chandler, Rolliusford, New Hampshire, April 4, 1876, William E. Chandler Papers, box 17, NHHS.

7. Samuel Bowles to Henry L. Dawes, Springfield, March 2, 1876, Dawes Papers, LC.

8. William S. McFeely, *Grant: A Biography* (New York: W. W. Norton, 1981), 404–16; William B. Hesseltine, *Ulysses S. Grant, Politician* (New York: Dodd, Mead, & Co., 1935), 378–88.

9. Hesseltine, *Ulysses S. Grant*, 396; James M. McPherson, *Ordeal by Fire: The Civil War and Reconstruction* (New York: Alfred A. Knopf, 1982), 596; for a good discussion of the Belknap scandal,

see Richard E. Welch Jr., *George Frisbie Hoar and the Half-Breed Republicans* (Cambridge: Harvard University Press, 1971), 48–50; see also McFeely, *Grant*, 427–29.

10. Commenting on the Belknap affair, Hinsdale attributed the exposure of the scandal to the Democratic House's intense investigations. He believed that the scandal hurt "in a good many ways" and would hurt at the ballot box in the fall. Hinsdale to Garfield, Irvington, Indiana, March 9, 1876, in James A. Garfield and Burke A. Hinsdale, *Garfield-Hinsdale Letters: Correspondence between James Abram Garfield and Burke Aaron Hinsdale*, ed. Mary L. Hinsdale (1949; reprint, New York: Kraus Reprint Co., 1969), 329.

11. John Sherman to A. M. Burns, January 21, 1876, *Election of 1876*, reel 1, CU.

12. Among other less prominent Republicans, both radical and moderate, who had left the national political stage by 1876 were John Curtiss Underwood of Virginia (died in 1873), who helped draft the state constitution of Virginia in 1867 guaranteeing equal rights for both blacks and whites; and James W. Grimes of Iowa (died in 1872), who was a strong foe of slavery but remained moderate on Reconstruction issues. In the meantime, other controversial Republican figures, including Horace Greeley, the liberal presidential candidate for 1872, and former president Andrew Johnson died in 1872 and 1875 respectively.

13. Writing to John Sherman, New York Republican John Cochrane raised the question of securing the undecided liberal votes for Hayes. "I should not doubt of his carrying the State," Cochrane wrote. "But a large section of [the liberals] have gone to Tilden, many are in suspense, but by far the largest part of them will support the Cincinnati ticket." Cochrane said that he accepted Hayes as "the limit & end of Liberalism" and was directing his "efforts to bring the Liberals to this position." But, he emphasized, the liberals needed strengthening: "The weak souls among them are troubled with the devices of the enemy. They need a strong, irreproachable non-partisan state ticket to confirm the statement that the National Candidates are *sound*." John Cochrane to John Sherman, New York, July 31, 1876, Hayes Papers, HPC.

14. Carl Schurz, *The Reminiscences of Carl Schurz*, 3 vols. (New York: McClure, 1907–8), 3:365–70. George William Curtis most emphatically expressed the liberals' political ambition. He wrote to Hayes, "Should you be elected and your administration should adhere to the platform of your letter, there would be, it seems to me, a reconstruction of parties, as after the election of Jefferson." George William Curtis to Hayes, Ashfield, Massachusetts, September 10, 1876, Hayes Papers, HPC.

15. Editorial, "Education and Politics at the South," *Springfield Republican*, January 1, 1877.

16. "What Is Our Duty to the Negro?" *Nation*, January 11, 1877, 22–23.

17. "The Race Issue," *Chicago Tribune*, December 13, 1876.

18. William Henry Trescot, "The Southern Question," *North American Review* 123 (October 1876): 279.

19. Richard H. Dana Jr., "Points in American Politics," *North American Review* 124 (January 1877): 26–30.

20. Quoted from Trescot, "The Southern Question," 266–67.

21. John Binny told Hayes that he took a number of actions to urge Republican leaders to put pressure on various fronts in order to secure a Republican victory. John Binny to Hayes, New York, October 2, 1876, *Election of 1876*, reel 3, CU.

22. William E. Chandler to Rutherford B. Hayes, New York, October 12, 1876, *Election of 1876*, reel 3, CU; "Gov. Chamberlain's Proclamation," *Chicago Tribune*, October 9, 1876.

23. "The President's Proclamation," *Chicago Tribune*, October 19, 1876.

24. "A Cry for Help," *Chicago Tribune*, October 30, 1876.

25. Matthew S. Quay to Rutherford B. Hayes, August 22, 1876, Matthew S. Quay Papers, LC.

26. John Sherman to A. M. Burus, Washington, January 21, 1876, *Election of 1876*, reel 1, CU.

27. Ibid.

28. For details of Hayes's nomination, see Hoogenboom, *Presidency of Rutherford B. Hayes*, 13–19; Kenneth E. Davison, *The Presidency of Rutherford B. Hayes* (Westport, Conn.: Greenwood, 1972), 20–34.

29. Davison, *Presidency of Rutherford B. Hayes*, 33–35.

30. Ibid., 31.

31. *Louisville Courier-Journal*, June 17, 1876.

32. *San Francisco Chronicle*, June 17, 1876; John Sherman, who nominated Hayes at the Cincinnati convention, described Hayes as "always sensible, industrious and true to his convictions and the principles and tendencies of his party." On the currency question, Hayes was "thoroughly sound" but was "not committed to any particular measure so as to be disabled from co-operating with any plan" that might "promise success." Sherman believed that Hayes was "as trustworthy as any one named" on issues regarding "protection for all in equal rights . . . and the observance of the public faith." John Sherman to A. M. Burus, January 21, 1876, *Election of 1876*, reel 1, CU.

33. Hayes's speech delivered at Lebanon, Ohio, on August 5, 1867, quoted from Russell H. Conwell, *Life and Public Services of Governor Rutherford B. Hayes* (Boston: Franklin Press, 1876), 232–46.

34. Rutherford B. Hayes to Guy M. Bryan, Fremont, July 27, 1875, in Rutherford B. Hayes, *Diary and Letters of Rutherford Birchard Hayes*, ed. Charles R. Williams, 5 vols. (Columbus: Ohio Archeological and Historical Society, 1922–26), 3:263.

35. Rutherford B. Hayes to W. Henry Smith, Columbus, October 5, 1876, *Election of 1876*, reel 3, CU.

36. Hayes to James A. Garfield, August 5, 1876; Hayes to John A. Bingham, Columbus, September 5, 1876; Hayes Papers, HPC.

37. Hayes to Carl Schurz, Columbus, August 9, 1876; Hayes to George William Curtis, Columbus, September 4, 1876, ibid.

38. Hayes to Guy M. Bryan, Fremont, November 23, 1876, ibid.

39. William E. Chandler correspondence, February 9, 1877, quoted from Stanley P. Hirshson, *Farewell to the Bloody Shirt: Northern Republicans and the Southern Negro, 1877–1893* (Bloomington: Indiana University Press, 1962), 25–26.

40. March 28, 1875, Hayes, *Diary and Letters*, 3:269.

41. Hans L. Trefousse, *Carl Schurz, a Biography* (Knoxville: University of Tennessee Press, 1982), 228.

42. Hayes to W. M. Dickson, May 3, 1876, Hayes, *Diary and Letters*, 3:318; Hayes to George William Curtis, Columbus, July 10, 1876, George William Curtis Papers, HU.

43. Charles Nordhoff to Hayes, Washington, June 28, 1876, Hayes Papers, HPC.

44. Hayes to Carl Schurz, February 4, 1877, Hayes, *Diary and Letters*, 3:413.

45. Hayes to Guy M. Bryan, July 27, 1875, ibid., 3:286.

46. Hayes's letter of acceptance is quoted from Keith Ian Polakoff, *The Politics of Inertia: The Election of 1876 and the End of Reconstruction* (Baton Rouge: Louisiana State University Press, 1973), 104 – 5.

47. Ibid., 105.

48. Hayes to George William Curtis, Columbus, July 10, 1876, Curtis Papers, HU.

49. Blanche K. Bruce to Hayes, June 25, 1876, Washington, Hayes Papers, HPC.

50. John M. Langston to Hayes, Washington, February 12, 1877, ibid.

51. W. W. Dedrick, a U.S. attorney in the southern district of Mississippi, wrote to Blanche K. Bruce about the frauds committed by local Democrats in the last presidential election: "Hayes has a right [to] be declared President having received 185 Electoral Votes. To doubt or hesitate on this proposition is to be damned." W. W. Dedrick to Blanche K. Bruce, January 21, 1877, Blanche K. Bruce Misc. MSS, ibid.

52. Charles Baylor to P. B. S. Pinchback, July 7, 1876, Pinchback Misc. MSS, ibid.

53. February 17, 1877, Hayes, *Diary and Letters*, 3:416 – 17.

54. Hayes to Carl Schurz, Columbus, July 24, 1876, Hayes Papers, HPC.

55. *North American Review* 123 (October 1876): 426 – 67.

56. The disputed election of 1876 is a subject of many studies, including C. Vann Woodward, *Reunion and Reaction: The Compromise of 1877 and the End of Reconstruction* (Boston: Little, Brown, 1951); Polakoff, *Politics of Inertia*; Jerome L. Sternstein, "The Sickles Memorandum: Another Look at the Hayes-Tilden Election-Night Conspiracy," *Journal of Southern History* 32 (1966): 342 – 57; Michael Les Benedict, "Southern Democrats in the Crisis of 1876 – 1877: A Reconsideration of *Reunion and Reaction*," *Journal of Southern History* 46 (1980): 489 – 524; George Rable, "Southern Interests and the Election of 1876: A Reappraisal," *Civil War History* 26 (1980): 347 – 61.

57. Learning that Bradley had been chosen to be the fifth judge on the commission, William E. Chandler wrote, "The tribunal is consolidated now and there is no danger of defeat. Cautious & subdued as I have been made by the ups & downs of the last six months I feel that the result is now inevitable. Hayes will be president. He can be looking for a Cabinet and writing his inaugural!" Bradley's selection broke the equilibrium of the commission and gave the Republicans a one-vote majority. William E. Chandler to "My dear sir," February 9, 1877, Hayes Papers, HPC.

58. *Springfield Republican*, March 2, 1877.

59. Hayes, Inaugural Address, March 5, 1877, *Messages and Papers*, 7:442 – 47.

60. Ibid.

61. *Springfield Republican*, March 6, 1877; *Harper's Weekly*, March 17, 1877, 202.

62. February 18, 1877, Hayes, *Diary and Letters*, 3:417.

63. *Springfield Republican*, January 30, 1877.

64. "National Influence in Local Politics," *Chicago Tribune*, April 5, 1877.

65. John W. Burgess, *The Administration of President Hayes* (New York: Charles Scribner's Sons, 1916), 71 – 87.

66. Eric Foner summarizes the deal between Hayes's men and the southern Democratic governments: "Several days before the congressional election commission announced the results of the

disputed election returns, four southern Democrats met with five Ohio Republicans at Washington's Wormley House. Hayes's confidante Stanley Matthews announced that the new President intended to recognize Nicholls as Louisiana's governor and pursue a policy of noninterference in southern affairs, while Nicholls' emissary, Col. Edward A. Burke, pledged to avoid reprisals against the state's Republicans and recognize the civil and political equality of blacks. Similar discussions with Hampton's representatives soon followed." Eric Foner, *Reconstruction: America's Unfinished Revolution, 1863–1877* (New York: Harper & Row, 1988), 580; also see Davison, *Presidency of Rutherford B. Hayes*, 43–44.

67. John W. Burgess evaluated Hayes's policy as a courageous move. Burgess, *Administration of President Hayes*, 88; Rayford W. Logan argues that Hayes's policy avoided another civil war between the North and South at the cost of abandoning blacks' civil and political equality. Rayford W. Logan, *The Betrayal of the Negro, from Rutherford B. Hayes to Woodrow Wilson* (1954; reprint, New York: Collier Books, 1968), 45. A more perceptive interpretation of Hayes's policy is given by Kenneth Davison, who saw it as the product of the political situation of the day and "his own antebellum education and inherited beliefs." Davison, *Presidency of Rutherford B. Hayes*, 142–43.

68. For a long time, Hayes was reluctant to support Grant's enforcement policy. In early 1875, he privately said that he did not "sympathize with a large share of the party leader" and expressed his doubt about the effect of Grant's "ultra measures relating to the South." March 28, 1875, Hayes, *Diary and Letters*, 3:269.

69. Hayes noticed that "both houses of Congress and the public opinion of the country [were] plainly against the use of the army to uphold either claimant to the State government in case of contest." March 23, 1877, Hayes, *Diary and Letters*, 3:429.

70. Hirshson, *Farewell to the Bloody Shirt*, 32; Vincent P. De Santis, *Republicans Face the Southern Question: The New Departure Years, 1877–1897* (Baltimore: Johns Hopkins University Press, 1959), 84–85.

71. *Harper's Weekly*, March 31, 1877, 242.

72. Charles Nordhoff to Charles Foster, February 15, 1877, Hayes Papers, HPC.

73. March 16, 1877, Rutherford B. Hayes, *Hayes: The Diary of a President*, ed. T. Harry Williams (New York: D. McKay, 1964), 83–84.

74. March 20, 1876, ibid., 84.

75. March 23, 1877, ibid., 85.

76. Carl Schurz to Charles H. Grosvenor, March 29, 1877, Charles H. Grosvenor Papers, CU.

77. Rutherford B. Hayes to George W. McCrary, April 20, 1877, Hayes Papers, HPC.

78. *Springfield Republican*, April 26, 1877.

79. Hayes diary, April 22, 1877; Rutherford B. Hayes to William D. Bickham (the mayor of Dayton), April 22, 1877; Rutherford B. Hayes to William M. Dickson, April 22, 1877; Hayes, *Diary and Letters*, 3:430, 432.

80. William H. Smith to Rutherford B. Hayes, April 22, 1877, ibid., 3:432.

81. Daniel H. Chamberlain to William Lloyd Garrison, June 11, 1877, quoted from Walter Allen, *Governor Chamberlain's Administration in South Carolina: A Chapter of Reconstruction in the Southern States* (New York: G. P. Putman's Sons, 1888), app. 3, 504.

82. Vincent P. De Santis, "The Republican Party and the Southern Negro, 1877–1897," *Journal of Negro History* 45 (April 1960): 75–81.

83. On February 17, 1877, Hayes met with Frederick Douglass and James Poindexter and told them his views on the southern question. "They approved," Hayes recorded. "Mr. Douglass gave me many useful hints about the whole subject." Hayes diary, February 18, 1877, Hayes, *Diary and Letters*, 3:417; Frederick Douglass's later remarks were quoted from McPherson, *Ordeal by Fire*, 604; Michael Les Benedict, *The Fruits of Victory: Alternatives in Restoring the Union, 1865–1877* (Lanham, Md.: University Press of America, 1986), 74.

84. *Springfield Republican*, April 26, 1877.

85. Charles Baylor to P. B. S. Pinchback, April 16, 1877, copy in Hayes Papers, HPC.

86. Ibid.

87. "National Influence in Local Politics," *Chicago Tribune*, April 5, 1877.

88. "The Republican Party in South Carolina," *Nation*, April 19, 1877, 230–31.

89. "The Southern Question," *Harper's Weekly*, April 14, 1877, 282; "The President and the Southern Policy," ibid., April 21, 1877, 302.

90. "The Political South Hereafter," *Nation*, April 5, 1877, 202–3.

91. George William Curtis to "Effie," July 22, 1877, George William Curtis Papers, HU.

92. "The President and the Party," *Nation*, July 5, 1877, 4–5; "The New York Republican Convention," *Harper's Weekly*, September 22, 1877, 738; De Santis, *Republicans Face the Southern Question*, 129; Hirshson, *Farewell to the Bloody Shirt*, 38.

93. *Springfield Republican*, October 11, 1877.

94. *Washington Star*, April 23, 1877, quoted from Logan, *Betrayal of the Negro*, 31.

95. Akerman is quoted from Keith Ian Polakoff, "Rutherford B. Hayes," in *The Presidents: A Reference History*, ed. Henry Graff (New York: Charles Scribner's Sons, 1984), 313–14.

96. Thurlow Weed to Vivus W. Smith, October 22, 1877, New York, Thurlow Weed Papers, UR.

97. Geo. W. Marston to William E. Chandler, New York, January 6, 1878, William E. Chandler Papers, box 17, NHHS.

98. Zachariah Chandler to William E. Chandler, Detroit, July 26, 1877, ibid.

99. Zachariah Chandler to William E. Chandler, Detroit, August 7, 1877, ibid.

100. William E. Chandler to Zachariah Chandler, November 19, 1877, Zachariah Chandler Papers, reel 4, LC.

101. Zachariah Chandler to William E. Chandler, November 22, 1877, William E. Chandler Papers, box 17, NHHS.

102. *Messages and Papers*, 7:458–80.

103. William E. Chandler, *Letters of Mr. William E. Chandler Relative to the So-Called Southern Policy of President Hayes . . .* (Concord, N.H.: Monitor and Statesman Office, 1878), 1–37, copy at NHHS.

104. Ibid., 4–5, 23.

105. Zachariah Chandler to William E. Chandler, Detroit, December 28, 1877, William E. Chandler Papers, box 17, NHHS.

106. William Lloyd Garrison to William E. Chandler, Boston, January 21, 1878, in Chandler, *Letters*, 38–48.

107. William Lloyd Garrison to William E. Chandler, Roxbury, February 22, 1878, William E. Chandler Papers, box 17, NHHS.

108. George William Curtis to Rutherford B. Hayes, January 2, 1878, Hayes Papers, HPC.

109. August 26, 1877, Hayes, *Diary and Letters*, 3:442–43.

110. Hayes's speech note at the train platform, Tilton, New Hampshire, August 22, 1877, the "Negro" bound volume, Hayes Papers, HPC.

111. Hayes's speech at Jeffersonville, Indiana, September 18, 1877, ibid.

112. Hayes's speech in Nashville, Tennessee, September 19, 1877, ibid.

113. Hayes's speech at the Markham House, Atlanta, Georgia, September 22, 1877, ibid.

114. Hayes's reply to a delegation of the African Methodist Episcopal Church in the White House on March 23, 1877, ibid.

115. Frederick Douglass to John Sherman, Washington, March 13, 1877, ibid.

116. Hayes to John E. King (collector of New Orleans), Washington, May 7, 1877, Hayes Papers, HPC.

117. Thomas K. Beecher to James G. Blaine, Elmira, April 9, 1877, James G. Blaine Papers, reel 8, LC.

118. On February 8, 1878, Pinchback was appointed Internal Revenue agent by Commissioner Green G. Raum. P. B. S. Pinchback to Rutherford B. Hayes, New Orleans, January 29, 1878, Hayes Papers, HPC; James Haskins, *Pinckney Benton Stewart Pinchback* (New York: Macmillan, 1973), 240.

119. *Harper's Weekly*, September 22, 1877, 739.

120. October 1, 1878, Hayes, *Diary and Letters*, 3:501–2.

121. Hirshson, *Farewell to the Bloody Shirt*, 45–50; Hoogenboom, *Presidency of Rutherford B. Hayes*, 73.

122. Hayes to J. M. Comly, Washington, October 29, 1878, Hayes Papers, HPC; October 26, 1878, Hayes, *Diary and Letters*, 3:505.

123. Hayes to J. M. Comly, October 29, 1878, Hayes Papers, HPC.

124. Hirshson, *Farewell to the Bloody Shirt*, 48; Davison, *Presidency of Rutherford B. Hayes*, 141.

125. November 6, 1878, Hayes, *Diary and Letters*, 3:508–9.

126. November 6, November 12, 1878, ibid., 3:508–9.

127. According to the *New York Tribune*, an interviewer from the *National Republican* interviewed Hayes on November 12. The *Tribune* published the interview on November 13. The *Tribune* correspondent mentioned that the same interview would appear in the *Republican* on the same day (November 13). *New York Tribune*, November 13, 1878, quote from LaWanda Cox and John H. Cox, eds., *Reconstruction, the Negro, and the New South* (Columbia: University of South Carolina Press, 1973), 137–40.

128. *National Republican*, November 13, 1878.

129. Hirshson, *Farewell to the Bloody Shirt*, 50–51; *Messages and Papers*, 7:492–507.

130. Charles Devens, *Annual Report of the Attorney-General*, 1878, in *House Executive Documents*, 45 Cong. 3 sess., no. 7, 18–19; Cox and Cox, *Reconstruction, the Negro, and the New South*, 140–42.

131. Blaine to Geo. C. Gorham, Augusta, September 16, 1878, Blaine Papers, reel 7, LC.

132. Hayes listed several objectives that the Republicans wanted to achieve: "1. A sound constitutional currency, specie and paper, both equal in value to gold. 2. A maintenance of the public credit. 3. Equality of rights for all States and for all the citizens of all the States. 4. We are opposed

to inflation and repudiation. 5. We are opposed to all revolutionary schemes hostile to the stability of the Government. 6. We are opposed to Communism, Socialism[,] repudiation, & inflation." November 6, 1878, Hayes, *Hayes: The Diary of a President*, 169.

133. William Lloyd Garrison to William E. Chandler, Tarrytown, New York, September 23, 1878, William E. Chandler Papers, NHHS.

134. "The Disfranchisement of the Blacks," *Chicago Tribune*, December 13, 1878, clipping in Blaine Papers, LC.

135. Blaine's speech in the Senate, quoted from the *Philadelphia Inquirer*, December 12, 1878, clipping in Blaine Papers, LC.

136. "The Southern Debate," *Troy Budget* (New York), December 16, 1878, clipping in Blaine Papers, reel 16, LC.

137. John Cochrane to James G. Blaine, New York, December 17, 1878, Blaine Papers, reel 8, LC.

138. "The Conciliated South," *Independent*, December 12, 1878; "The Speech of Senator Blaine," *Independent*, December 19, 1878, clippings in Blaine Papers, LC.

139. William Lloyd Garrison to William E. Chandler, January 30, 1879, William E. Chandler Papers, NHHS.

140. D. H. Chamberlain, "Reconstruction and the Negro," *North American Review* 128 (February 1879): 160–75.

141. James G. Blaine et al., "Ought the Negro to Be Disfranchised? Ought He to Have Been Enfranchised?" *North American Review* 128 (March 1879): 225–83.

142. Leonard D. White, *The Republican Era: 1869–1901: A Study in Administrative History* (New York: Macmillan, 1958), 38; Albie Burke, "Federal Regulation of Congressional Elections in Northern Cities, 1871–1894" (Ph.D. diss., University of Chicago, 1968), 224–28.

143. March 9, 1879, Hayes, *Diary and Letters*, 3:528–29.

144. The bill was titled "making appropriations for the army for the fiscal year ending June 30, 1880." *CR*, 46 Cong. 1 sess., 1879, pt. 1:82–83 (statement of William A. J. Sparks), 103; *Revised Statutes* (1875), 353, 1077.

145. *CR*, 46 Cong. 1 sess., 1879, 9, pt. 1:103 (Sparks), 113 (Stephens).

146. March 19, 1879, James A. Garfield, *The Diary of James A. Garfield*, ed. Harry James Brown and Frederick D. Williams, 4 vols. (East Lansing: Michigan State University Press, 1981), 4:202.

147. March 27, 1879, Garfield, *Diary*, 4:206–7.

148. *CR*, 46 Cong. 1 sess., 1879, 9, pt. 1:103 (Omar D. Conger), 115 (Jeptha D. New), 116–18 (James A. Garfield); 181 (Harry White); 208 (Hiram Barber).

149. Ibid., 116–18; March 29, 1879, Garfield, *Diary*, 4:208; *New York Times*, March 30, 1879.

150. *CR*, 46 Cong. 1 sess., 1879, 9, pt. 1:146.

151. Ibid., 218 (John Morgan Bright).

152. *CR*, 46 Cong. 1 sess., 1879, 9, pt. 1:181.

153. Ibid., 153.

154. Ibid., 270.

155. Garfield to William H. Smith, Washington, April 5, 1879, Hayes Papers, HPC; April 5, 1879, Garfield, *Diary*, 4:211–12.

156. *CR*, 46 Cong. 1 sess., 1879, 9, pt. 1:417.

157. Ibid., 439–42.

158. Ibid., 600.

159. Ibid., 803 – 5. It is important to note that all factions of the Republicans united in defending the election laws during this period. Conkling's speech attracted the Republicans from the House, including Garfield, who normally had no admiration at all for the self-conscious New Yorker. Again, Garfield did not fail to notice the "little touches" of Conkling's "self-consciousness": "He spoke from notes without reading and when he completed the sheet of notes, he tore it up into small bits and threw them on the floor – taking some time to do it." But still, Garfield praised Conkling's speech: "[It was] a very strong and complete presentation of our views and entirely in accord with the position I took in my first speech." April 24, 1879, Garfield, *Diary*, 4:222.

160. *CR*, 46 Cong. 1 sess., 1879, 9, pt. 1:601.

161. Ibid., 913.

162. Hayes, veto message, April 29, 1879, *Messages and Papers*, 7:523 – 32, esp. 526 – 28.

163. Ibid., 528.

164. March 18, 1879, Hayes, *Diary and Letters*, 3:529 – 30. On April 26, 1879, before he released his veto message, Hayes had a long conference with Garfield and gave an advance copy of his message to the latter to prepare the Republican resistance to the Democratic override. Garfield diary, April 26, 1879, James A. Garfield Papers, reel 2, LC.

165. *CR*, 46 Cong. 1 sess., 1879, 9, pt. 1:1014 – 15.

166. The bill provided: "It shall not be lawful to bring to, or employ at, any place where a general or special Election is being held in a State any part of the Army or Navy or the United States, unless such force be necessary to repel the armed enemies of the United States or to enforce Section 4, Article 4 of the Constitution of the United States and the laws made in pursuance thereof upon the application of the Legislature or the executive of the State where such force is to be used; and so much of all laws as is inconsistent herewith is hereby repealed." *CR*, 46 Cong. 1 sess., 1879, 9, pt. 1:1049 (George Ladd), 1092 (Proctor J. Knott).

167. Ibid., 1092.

168. Ibid., 1094 – 95.

169. The vote in the Senate was 33 yeas and 23 nays, with 20 absent. Ibid., 1189.

170. Samuel Shellabarger's memo to Hayes, May 1879, Hayes Papers, HPC. (No specific date. Since the bill, marked as "Forty-Six Congress, Tuesday, May 6," was attached and Shellabarger also discussed the content of the Senate version of the bill on the same page, the memo should be dated between May 7 and 10, that is, after the Senate started debating it on May 7 and before Hayes vetoed it on May 12).

171. Garfield to Crete Garfield [wife], May 10, 1879, Margaret Leech and Harry J. Brown, *The Garfield Orbit* (New York: Harper & Row, 1978), 171.

172. Hayes's remarks on verso of Shellabarger's memo, Hayes Papers, HPC; Hayes, veto message, May 12, 1879, *Messages and Papers*, 7:532 – 36.

173. Hayes to Edwin D. Morgan, Washington, May 15, 1879, Hayes Papers, HPC. The House failed to override Hayes's veto, 128 to 97, with 60 not voting. Only 2 Republicans voted with the Democrats; others (98 percent of the party votes) either voted against or abstained. *CG*, 46 Cong. 1 sess., 1298.

174. *Statutes at Large* 18, pt. 1 (1878): 353 – 57, 1067 – 70; *CR*, 46 Cong. 1 sess., 1879, 9, pt. 1:492.

175. H.R. 2 was introduced into the House on April 1 and debated for nearly four weeks. Then the bill went to the Senate, which debated it for about two weeks before voting on it on May 22. Because the bill was comprehensive and long, a substantial proportion of the debates in both houses was on other issues of the bill. For debates specifically on the removal of the enforcement provisions, see *CR*, 46 Cong. 1 sess., 1879, 9, pt. 1:142 (John D. C. Atkins), 487–501 (Harry White), 521–35 (William D. Kelley), 646–58 (Peter V. Deuster), 742–96 (William P. Frye), 914–60 (Warren Keifer and James A. Garfield). Also see 1204–20 (James G. Blaine and George H. Hoar), 1238–56 (William B. Allison and William Windom), and pt. 2:1413–30 (George F. Edmunds and John A. Logan).

176. *CR*, 46 Cong. 1 sess., 1879, 9, pt. 1:960. The House passed H.R. 1 on the same day. The two votes were similar, especially in the strength of Republican opposition.

177. Ibid., 1484–85.

178. Hayes, veto message, May 29, 1879, *Messages and Papers*, 6:4536–40.

179. The House vote was 114 to 93, with 78 not voting; 92 Republicans (70 percent of the party votes) voted nay, and another 39 abstained. *CR*, 46 Cong. 1 sess., 1879, 9, pt. 2:1711.

180. Ibid., 1892–93.

181. Ibid., 1893.

182. Ibid., 1894, 1899.

183. Hayes, veto message, June 23, 1879, *Messages and Papers*, 7:541–44.

184. The House failed to override Hayes's veto on H.R. 2252 with a vote of 102 to 78, with 106 not voting. Again, no Republicans voted with the Democrats. More and more Democrats began to abstain, probably realizing that they had no chance to win. *CR*, 46 Cong. 1 sess., 1879, 9, pt. 2:2292, 2357.

185. Ibid., 2397–98, 2413.

186. House Democrats again failed to override Hayes's veto. The vote was 85 to 63, with 138 members not voting. *CG*, 46 Cong. 1 sess., 1879, pt. 2:2442–43.

187. Garfield diary, June 29, 1879, Garfield Papers, reel 2, LC; Hayes, veto message, June 30, 1879, *Messages and Papers*, 6:545–47.

188. *The Annual Report of the Attorney General*, December 1, 1879, *House Executive Documents*, 46 Cong. 2 sess., no. 8, 15.

189. Ibid., 15.

190. Ibid., 17.

191. *CR*, 46 Cong. 2 sess., 1880, 10, pt. 2:1350, 1515–16.

192. Ibid., 1701.

193. Ibid., 1700 (statement of C. B. Simonton).

194. Ibid., pt. 3:2500–03. The Senate passed the bill with amendments on April 1 by a vote of 35 to 21, with 20 not voting. As before, no Republicans supported the bill. Ibid., 2027.

195. Hayes, veto message, May 4, 1880, *Messages and Papers*, 7:591–92; *CR*, 46 Cong. 2 sess., 1880, 10, pt. 3:2987.

196. *CR*, 46 Cong. 2 sess., 1880, 10, pt. 4:3053, 3413.

197. Ibid., 3516 (Roscoe Conkling).

198. Ibid., 4432 (Joseph W. Keifer).

199. "The Week," *Nation*, May 27, 1880, 393.

200. The House passed the bill with amendments on June 11 by a vote of 110 to 85 with 97 not

voting. Of the 135 Republican votes, 82 voted nays, 51 abstained, and 2 voted yeas. *CR*, 46 Cong. 2 sess., 1880, 10, pt. 5:4452. The Senate agreed on the House amendments on June 14, ibid., 4454, 4509.

201. Hayes, veto message, June 15, 1880, *Messages and Papers*, 7:592–98.

202. Hayes's autographed note, June 16, 1880, in the Garfield Papers, Letters Received, vol. 76, no. 44, LC; copy found in Hayes Papers, HPC.

Chapter Five. The Survival of a Principle, 1880–1888

1. *Proceedings of Republican National Convention*, rept. Eugene Davis (Chicago: Jno. B. Jeffery Printing and Publishing House, 1881), 161–62; Kirk H. Porter and Donald Bruce Johnson, eds., *National Party Platforms, 1840–1964* (Urbana: University of Illinois Press, 1966), 60–62.

2. Robert Michael Goldman, *"A Free Ballot and A Fair Count": The Department of Justice and the Enforcement of Voting Rights in the South, 1877–1893* (New York: Garland, 1990), 72–96.

3. *Annual Report of the Attorney-General* in *House Executive Documents*, 45 Cong. 2 sess., no. 7; 3 sess., no. 7; 46 Cong. 2 sess., no. 8; 3 sess., no. 9. For details on regional distributions, see Appendix 7.

4. Frederick Douglass's speech, October 30, 1879, *FDP*, 4:539–40.

5. James Blaine, "Southern Abuse of Elective Franchise," December 2, 1878, in James G. Blaine, *Political Discussions, Legislative, Diplomatic, and Peculiar, 1856–1886* (Norwich, Conn.: Henry Bill, 1887), 201–9; Thomas H. Sherman, *Twenty Years with James G. Blaine: Reminiscences by His Private Secretary* (New York: Grafton Press, 1905), 66–75.

6. James Blaine, "Ought the Negro to Be Disfranchised? Ought He to Have Been Enfranchised?" Blaine, *Political Discussions*, 278–99.

7. Hoar's remarks were in a letter from William E. Chandler to Hayes. In the letter, Chandler commented on Hayes's recent speech at Yale College and quoted an excerpt from Hoar's speech at Faneuil Hall, Boston. Chandler to Hayes, New York, July 3, 1880, Hayes Papers, HPC.

8. July 21, 1880, Rutherford B. Hayes, *Diary and Letters of Rutherford Birchard Hayes*, ed. Charles R. Williams, 5 vols. (Columbus: Ohio Archeological and Historical Society, 1922–26), 3:651.

9. Sherman, *Twenty Years with James G. Blaine*, 74; James G. Blaine, *Twenty Years of Congress: From Lincoln to Garfield with a Review of the Events Which Led to the Political Revolution of 1860*, 2 vols. (Norwich, Conn.: Henry Bill, 1886), 670–71.

10. Leading members of these so-called independent Republicans included R. R. Rowker, F. W. Whitridge, Geo. Haven Putnam, Henry S. Van Duzer, Geo. Walton Green, and Felix Kaufman. Pamphlet, titled "Invitation for a Republican conference on April 21 at Albany"; memo of Frederick W. Holls, n.d., attached to the invitation; both documents found in Frederick W. Holls Papers, box 11, CU.

11. James G. Blaine to James A. Garfield, Washington, December 16, 1880, James A. Garfield Papers, reel 81, LC (microfilm at CU).

12. A letter signed by Matthew Hale, A. N. Cole, Henry Randall Waite, Ethan Allan, S. S. Guy, and C. W. Gardard, found in Frederick W. Holls Papers, box 11, CU.

13. David M. Jordan, *Roscoe Conkling of New York: Voice in the Senate* (Ithaca, N.Y.: Cornell

University Press, 1971), 321–29; George Frederick Howe, *Chester A. Arthur: A Quarter-Century of Machine Politics* (New York: Frederick Ungar, 1935), 100–104.

14. Years later, Blaine claimed that his faction did not oppose Grant the person, only the idea of the third term, which, he believed, would have destroyed the two-term tradition of the executive branch established by the example of George Washington. There was "no fear that General Grant would abuse a trust," Blaine would argue later, but since "the limit of two terms had become an unwritten part of the code of the Republic," the people felt disregarding the principle "might entail dangers which they would not care to risk" and "believed that the example of Washington if now reinforced by the example of Grant would determine the question for the future, and assure a regular and orderly change of rulers, which is the strongest guarantee against the approach of tyranny." Blaine, *Twenty Years of Congress*, 2:658; Justus D. Doenecke, *The Presidencies of James A. Garfield and Chester A. Arthur* (Lawrence: Regents Press of Kansas, 1981), 13–14.

15. For details of each ballot at the convention, see Norman E. Tutorow, *James Gillespie Blaine and the Presidency: A Documentary Study and Source Book* (New York: Peter Lang, 1989), 52–59; James Pickett Jones, *John A. Logan, Stalwart Republican from Illinois* (Tallahassee: University Presses of Florida, 1982), 136.

16. Tutorow, *James Gillespie Blaine*, 200–273.

17. James G. Blaine to James A. Garfield, Washington, December 16, 1880, Garfield Papers, reel 81, LC; Blaine, *Twenty Years of Congress*, 2:666.

18. Hayes to Garfield, Washington, July 8, 1880, Hayes Papers, HPC.

19. *Proceedings of the Republican National Convention*, 296; Jones, *John A. Logan*, 137.

20. Garfield maintained a prominent role in the convention. He chaired the Rules Committee and oversaw the drafting of the platform. He skillfully rejected Conkling's proposal to eject delegates who would not pledge in advance to support any nominee the convention chose. He nominated Sherman in a moving address, in which he appealed to party unity rather than referring to Sherman's candidacy. Justus D. Doenecke, *Presidencies of James A. Garfield and Chester A. Arthur* (Lawrence: Regents Press of Kansas, 1981), 20–21.

21. E. V. Smalley, "The Republicans and Their Candidate," *Atlantic Monthly* 46 (August 1880): 259–63.

22. Garfield strongly opposed Conkling's suggestion on the unit rule, which would have required unconditional support for the party's candidate once nominated, but refused to confront Grant's supporters and declined to make a speech against the third term presidency of Grant. May 29, 30, 1880, James A. Garfield, *The Diary of James A. Garfield*, ed. Henry James Brown and Frederick D. Williams, 4 vols. (East Lansing: Michigan State University Press, 1981), 4:424–25; Doenecke, *Presidencies of James A. Garfield and Chester A. Arthur*, 20–21.

23. After talking about the South, the Republican platform declared the party's economic policy. It revealed the party's policy on high tariffs, veterans' pensions, improvement of American seacoasts and harbors, immigration of Chinese, land grants to railroads and corporations, and opposition to polygamy. The platform praised Hayes's policy and spoke about the party having "transformed 4,000,000 human beings from the likeness of things to the rank of citizens." The issue of civil service reform was given no attention in the first draft and was added to the platform only after an amendment was made by Baker of Massachusetts. Blaine, *Twenty Years of Congress*, 2:664–65; for the original platform, see *Proceedings of the Republican National Convention*, 161–62.

24. James A. Garfield, "Letter Accepting the Nomination for the Presidency," *The Works of James Abram Garfield*, ed. Burke A. Hinsdale, 2 vols. (Boston: James R. Osgood and Co., 1882–83), 2:782–87.

25. John A. Logan to Garfield, Chicago, July 27, 1880, Garfield Papers, reel 60, LC, microfilm at CU.

26. Stanley P. Hirshson, *Farewell to the Bloody Shirt: Northern Republicans and the Southern Negro, 1877–1893* (Bloomington: Indiana University Press, 1962), 80–81; Doenecke, *Presidencies of James A. Garfield and Chester A. Arthur*, 27.

27. Thomas C. Reeves, *Gentleman Boss: The Life of Chester Alan Arthur* (New York: Alfred A. Knopf, 1975), 204; Vincent P. De Santis, *Republicans Face the Southern Question: The New Departure Years, 1877–1897* (Baltimore: Johns Hopkins University Press, 1959), 101; Hirshson, *Farewell to the Bloody Shirt*, 86; Doenecke, *Presidencies of James A. Garfield and Chester A. Arthur*, 29–30.

28. Learning about his presidential victory, Garfield thanked William E. Chandler for his organizational work and believed that the Republicans could have won the Senate "but for the Morey forgery." He asked for prosecution of the forgery in order "to prevent the recurrence of such a crime." Garfield to Chandler, Mentor, November 8, 1880, Chandler Papers, box 18, NHHS.

29. Alonzo B. Cornell to Andrew White, Albany, November 1, 1880, Andrew White Papers, reel 28, CU.

30. Grant to Garfield, New York, November 11, 1880, Garfield Papers, reel 105, LC, microfilm at CU.

31. Geo. W. Marton to William E. Chandler, New York, December 15, 1880, William E. Chandler Papers, box 18, NHHS.

32. William E. Dodge to James A. Garfield, New York, November 3, 1880, Letters of James A. Garfield (microfilm), CU.

33. Douglass told Sherman that black Republicans would do the same for him if he were the candidate. Douglass to John Sherman, Washington, June 14, 1880, Garfield Papers, reel 54; John Langston to James A. Garfield, Mentor, August 31, 1880, Garfield Papers, reel 63, LC, microfilm at CU.

34. Frederick Douglass's speech at Elmira, New York, August 3, 1880, *FDP*, 4:565.

35. Bruce to Garfield, Indianapolis, September 27, 1880, Garfield Papers, reel 65, LC, microfilm at CU.

36. Douglass to James McCormick Dalzell, Washington, D.C., November 9, 1880, Frederick Douglass Papers, UR; John Langston to Garfield, November 15, 1880, Garfield Papers, reel 17, LC, microfilm at CU.

37. James A. Garfield, "Suffrage and Safety," an oration delivered at Ravenna, Ohio, July 4, 1865, *Works of James Abram Garfield*, 1:86–94.

38. Garfield's speech in the House of Representatives, February 1, 1866, ibid., 1:108–15.

39. Garfield to Burke A. Hinsdale, Washington, January 1, 1867, James A. Garfield and Burke A. Hinsdale, *Garfield-Hinsdale Letters: Correspondence between James Abram Garfield and Burke Aaron Hinsdale*, ed. Mary L. Hinsdale (1949; reprint, New York: Kraus Reprint Co., 1969), 88.

40. See Chapter 2.

41. Garfield to Burke A. Hinsdale, Washington, January 7, 1875, Garfield and Hinsdale, *Garfield-Hinsdale Letters*, 309.

42. James A. Garfield to Mrs. Garfield, New Orleans, November 20, 1876, in Margaret Leech and Harry J. Brown, *The Garfield Orbit* (New York: Harper & Row, 1978), 288 – 89.

43. Garfield to Hinsdale, Washington, November 11, 1876; New Orleans, December 4, 1876, Garfield and Hinsdale, *Garfield-Hinsdale Letters*, 341 – 46.

44. Garfield then wanted to run for the Senate, but under Hayes's suggestion, he agreed to "make the sacrifice" by staying in the House to give Hayes a needed hand. James A. Garfield to Burke A. Hinsdale, Washington, December 18, 1876, ibid., 368 – 69.

45. March 5, 1879, Garfield, *Diary*, 4:193.

46. Garfield to Hinsdale, Columbus, December 4, 1876, Garfield and Hinsdale, *Garfield-Hinsdale Letters*, 346.

47. Garfield to Hinsdale, Mentor, December 30, 1880, ibid., 469 – 70.

48. *Springfield Republican*, October 20, 1880; "Mr. Conkling's Speech at the Academy of Music," *Nation*, September 23, 1880.

49. H. H. Chalmers, "The Effect of Negro Suffrage," *North American Review* 132 (March 1881): 239 – 48.

50. Carl Schurz to Garfield, Washington, January 15, 1881, Garfield Papers, reel 85, LC, microfilm at CU.

51. William E. Chandler to Garfield, Washington, February 17, 1881, Garfield Papers, LC, microfilm at CU.

52. Albion W. Tourgee to Garfield, Philadelphia, December 11, 1880, Garfield Papers, reel 18, LC, microfilm at CU. For Tourgee's view on national aid to black education, see Albion W. Tourgee, "Aaron's Rod in Politics," *North American Review* 122 (February 1881): 139 – 62.

53. Garfield to Hinsdale, Mentor, December 30, 1880, Garfield and Hinsdale, *Garfield-Hinsdale Letters*, 469 – 70.

54. James A. Garfield, Inaugural Address, March 4, 1881, *Works of James Abram Garfield*, 2:789 – 95; *Messages and Papers*, 8:6 – 12.

55. January 11, 1881, Garfield, *Diary*, 4:524 – 25, 17n.

56. Doenecke, *Presidencies of James A. Garfield and Chester A. Arthur*, 50.

57. Ibid., 108 – 9.

58. Hirshson, *Farewell to the Bloody Shirt*, 94 – 95.

59. Chandler's memo to Garfield, November 12, 1880, Garfield Papers, reel 106, LC, microfilm at CU.

60. Ibid.

61. Ibid.

62. Chandler to Garfield, Washington, February 19, 1881, Garfield Papers, reel 19, LC, microfilm at CU.

63. Garfield to Hinsdale, Washington, December 18, 1876, Garfield and Hinsdale, *Garfield-Hinsdale Letters*, 347 – 48; Hirshson, *Farewell to the Bloody Shirt*, 95.

64. March 15, 1881, Garfield, *Diary*, 4:558 – 59.

65. February 5, 1881, ibid., 4:540 – 41.

66. Ibid.

67. Garfield did try to continue one segment of Hayes's policy: appointing African Americans to federal posts. When there was a movement opposed to extending Frederick Douglass's appointment

as U.S. marshal for the District of Columbia, the highest federal position Hayes had given to a black Republican, Douglass urged Garfield to stand up to "this gloomy shadow of an ancient barbarism" of racial prejudice. Later, Douglass withdrew his request for reappointment when he learned that Garfield intended to give the marshalship to one of the president's close friends. But Garfield promised to appoint Douglass recorder of deeds in the District of Columbia. Before Garfield fulfilled his promise, Democrats, to ridicule the Republicans, accused his administration of discrimination against blacks in federal appointments. Democratic senator Brown said: "The last administration did give Hon. Frederick Douglass, who is a man of great intelligence and power, the position of marshal of the District of Columbia, but if the reports be correct he was not invited to do all the honors at the White House that have generally been performed by the marshal of the District of Columbia . . . that he will have to give way to a white man who can attend to all those honors and duties. . . . You have seven cabinet ministers. More than one-fourth of the whole republican population of the United States, if all the colored people are to be counted as republicans, is colored; and yet there is no man among them who is considered worthy by your party to represent that fourth in the cabinet of seven?" Brown concluded that all of the Republican talk about black suffrage was not from love of blacks but "to try to republicanize the South by the use of the negro." Frederick Douglass to Joseph Dottin Husbands, Washington, January 17, 1881, Frederick Douglass Papers, UR; Douglass to Garfield, Washington, December 18, 1880, Garfield Papers, reel 81; Douglass to Garfield, Washington, April 2, 1881, Garfield Papers, reel 95, LC; Douglass to Hayes, Washington, July 1881, Hayes Papers, HPC.

68. Hirshson, *Farewell to the Bloody Shirt*, 78, 98.

69. Editorial, "President Garfield's Death," *Nation*, September 22, 1881, 228.

70. J. C. B. Davis to Hamilton Fish, Brevoort House, September 23, 1881, Chester A. Arthur Papers, reel 3, LC.

71. "The Week," *Nation*, June 17, 1880, 445.

72. John L. Cadwalader to Hamilton Fish, New York, September 20, 1881, Arthur Papers, reel 3, LC; E. D. Morgan to Arthur, Newport, August 22, 1881, Arthur Papers, reel 1, LC.

73. Chester A. Arthur, Inaugural Address, September 22, 1881, *Messages and Papers*, 8:33–34.

74. Chester A. Arthur, First Annual Message, December 6, 1881, *Messages and Papers*, 8:37–65.

75. E. V. Smalley, "The Political Situation," *Atlantic Monthly* 49 (March 1882): 393–99; Reeves, *Gentleman Boss*, 265–67.

76. In early 1882, Daniel Alexander Payne, a senior bishop of the African Methodist Episcopal Church, was expelled from a Florida train because he refused to ride in a segregated car. When black leaders asked the Arthur administration to see to the matter under the Civil Rights Act of 1875, Attorney General Benjamin Brewster promised to pursue the matter but made no effort to do so. On another occasion, Arthur and Brewster coldly rejected the plea of John W. Niles, an African American who raised funds to colonize fellow black citizens to Alaska and was jailed by the state policemen, who also confiscated his fund. After the Supreme Court, in the *Civil Rights Cases* of 1883, ruled that the Civil Rights Act of 1875 was unconstitutional, several bills were introduced into Congress to replace the dead act, but Arthur showed no support for them. Hirshson, *Farewell to the Bloody Shirt*, 101–5.

77. *Annual Report of the Attorney-General* in *Senate Executive Documents*, 47 Cong. 1 sess., no. 4, 11–25.

78. *Annual Report of the Attorney General* in *House Executive Documents*, 47 Cong. 2 sess., no. 8, 22–24; Goldman, *"Free Ballot,"* 111–25.

79. Hirshson, *Farewell to the Bloody Shirt*, 101–5; Goldman, *"Free Ballot,"* 140–51.

80. Arthur's talk with a prominent African American from Georgia appeared in the *Mobile Daily Register*, January 27, 1882, quoted from Hirshson, *Farewell to the Bloody Shirt*, 109.

81. Frederick Douglass to Mrs. Sara Jane (Clarke) Lippincott, October 9, 1880, Frederick Douglass Papers, UR.

82. *New York Tribune*, October 26, 1882; Chandler to Whitelaw Reid, December 17, 1883, Reid Papers, LC, quoted from Hirshson, *Farewell Bloody Shirt*, 114.

83. Chandler to Whitelaw Reid, December 17, 1883, Reid Papers, LC, quoted from Hirshson, *Farewell to the Bloody Shirt*, 111, 114.

84. Chandler to Blaine, New York, October 2, 1882, Chandler Papers, LC.

85. De Santis, *Republicans Face Southern Question*, 178–79; Doenecke, *Presidencies of James A. Garfield and Chester A. Arthur*, 99–100; Hirshson, *Farewell to the Bloody Shirt*, 115–16.

86. Smalley, "The Political Situation," 393–99.

87. Carl Schurz, "Party Schisms and Future Problems," *North American Review* 134 (May 1882): 431–55.

88. *Springfield Republican*, September 19, 1881.

89. *Harper's Weekly*, January 6, 1883, 2.

90. E. V. Smalley, "Political Field," *Atlantic Monthly* 14 (January 1884): 126.

91. Participants at the New York conference included Francis C. Barlow, Joseph W. Harper Jr., Henry E. Tremain, Grange Sard Jr., George Walton Green, Alfred C. Barnes, Sigismund Kaufmann, Henry W. Sprague, Frederick W. Holls, Alfred T. White. Francis C. Barlow to Andrew White, New York, March 4, 1884; letter from Republican conference committee, New York, March 31, 1884; Andrew White Papers, reel 38, Cornell University Library.

92. Frederick William Holls to James G. Blaine, New York, June 16, 1884, Blaine Papers, reel 9, LC.

93. Hirshson, *Farewell to the Bloody Shirt*, 144.

94. John Roach to Blaine, New York, June 12, 1884, Blaine Papers, reel 9, LC; Hirshson, *Farewell to the Bloody Shirt*, 124.

95. A. T. Wood to John A. Logan, Mt. Sterling, Kentucky, February 16, 1883, Logan Papers, container 3, LC.

96. A torn letter to John A. Logan, Woodhill, Illinois, July 26, 1884, ibid., container 4.

97. G. C. Hendrix to Andrew White, New York, May 7, 1884, Andrew White Papers, reel 39, Cornell University Library; Thos. V. Cooper, *Campaign of '84* (Chicago: Baird & Dillon, 1884), 79.

98. Republican Platform of 1884, Porter and Johnson, *National Party Platforms*, 72–74.

99. Charles A. Boutella to Blaine, Washington, July 14, 1884, Blaine Papers, reel 10, LC.

100. Logan, acceptance speech, undated, Logan Papers, container 4, LC.

101. *New York Times*, November 19, 1884.

102. *Springfield Republican*, July 9, 1885.

103. William T. Sherman to John Sherman, October, 1885, in John Sherman and William Tecumseh Sherman, *The Sherman Letters: Correspondence between General and Senator Sherman from 1837 to 1891*, ed. Rachel Sherman Thorndike (New York: Charles Scribner's Sons, 1894), 367–68.

104. Frederick Douglass, address delivered at the twenty-third anniversary celebration of the emancipation of slaves in the District of Columbia, April 16, 1885, in *FDP*, 5:178.

105. Ibid.

106. *Revised Statutes* (Washington, D.C.: U.S. Government Printing Office, 1875), 354, 1073.

107. George S. Boutwell, preface, *Second Edition of Revised Statutes of the United States* (Washington, D.C.: U.S. Government Printing Office, 1878), in *Statutes at Large* 18, pt. 1 (1878): v–vi.

108. George S. Boutwell, *Reminiscences of Sixty Years in Public Affairs*, 2 vols. (1902; reprint, New York: Greenwood, 1968), 2:285.

109. *Statutes at Large* 18, pt. 1 (1878): 353, 1067–68.

110. For a complete list of the sections of the enforcement acts as listed in the 1878 edition of *Revised Statutes* [in *Statutes at Large* 18, pt. 1 (1878)], see Appendix 6.

111. Section 5506 actually maintained the original intention of the Republican lawmakers, that is, to punish individuals who used force or conspiracy against black voters. *Statutes at Large* 18, pt. 1 (1878): 353, 1067.

112. *Annual Report of the Attorney-General* in *House Executive Documents*, 48 Cong. 1 sess., no. 8, 7–8, 44–45; 48 Cong. 2 sess., no. 12, 7–8, 48–49.

113. *United States v. White*, 28 *Federal Cases* (1877): 546–50.

114. *United States v. Goldman et al.*, 25 *Federal Cases* (1878): 1350–54.

115. *United States v. Gitma*, 25 *Federal Cases* (1878): 1323–24.

116. *Ex parte Siebold*, 100 U.S. 371–99 (1880).

117. Ibid.

118. Ibid.

119. *Ex parte Clarke*, 100 U.S. 399–422 (1880); *United States v. Clarke*, 25 *Federal Cases* (1879): 453–54.

120. James A. Garfield, "Obedience to Law the First Duty of Congress," speech delivered in the House of Representatives, March 17, 1880, *Works of James A. Garfield*, 2:723–24.

121. Hayes to Frank Hatton, August 24, 1880, Washington, Hayes Papers, HPC.

122. Garfield, Inaugural Address, March 4, 1881, *Works of James A. Garfield*, 2:788–95.

123. *Ex parte Yarbrough*, 110 U.S. 651–53 (1884).

124. Ibid., 664–65.

125. Ibid., 667.

126. Ibid.

127. The case involved a charge against a federal election supervisor, Geissler, who was imprisoned for having used force to stop a doubtful voter. The court opinion decided that Geissler was acting in line of duty and justified his right as an election supervisor to arrest fraudulent voters. *Ex parte Geissler*, 4 *Federal Reporter* 188–92 (1880).

128. *United States v. Seaman*, 23 *Federal Reporter* 147–53 (1885).

129. *United States v. Morrissey*, 32 *Federal Reporter* 147–53 (1887).

130. *United States v. Harris*, 106 U.S. 633–44 (1883).

131. "The Force Bill in the Supreme Court," *Nation*, January 25, 1883, 74.

132. "The Civil Rights Decision," *Harper's Weekly*, February 3, 1883, 66.

133. *Civil Rights Cases*, 109 U.S. 3–26 (1883).

134. Ibid., 26–62; Eugene Gressman, "The Unhappy History of Civil Rights Legislation," *Michigan Law Review* 50 (1952): 1323–58.

135. *CR*, 48 Cong. 1 sess., 1883, 15, pt. 1:12.

136. "The Social Rights Decision," *Chicago Tribune*, October 20, 1883.

137. "The Late Colored Convention," *Harper's Weekly*, October 27, 1883, 674.

138. "The Negroes," *Chicago Tribune*, October 23, 24, 1883; "Social Rights of the Blacks," ibid., October 24, 1883.

139. Douglass to Alphonso Alva Hopkins, Washington, November 6, 1883, Frederick Douglass Papers, UR.

140. "The State Rights Issue Settled," *Nation*, July 21, 1887, 46.

141. Ibid.

142. *Ex parte Yarbrough*, 110 U.S. 666 – 67 (1884).

Chapter Six. The Rise and Fall of Reenforcement, 1888 – 1891

1. Grover Cleveland, Inaugural Address, March 4, 1885, *Messages and Papers*, 8:299 – 303.

2. Cleveland to Augustus Garland, Instructions, October 5, 1886; Augustus Garland to U.S. Marshals, Instructions, October 15, 1886, quoted from Robert Michael Goldman, *"A Free Ballot and a Fair Count": The Department of Justice and the Enforcement of Voting Rights in the South, 1877–1893* (New York: Garland, 1990), 174 – 75.

3. Robert C. McMath Jr., *American Populism: A Social History, 1877–1898* (New York: Hill and Wang, 1993), 121.

4. There were 173 cases from the North, and 79 ended in convictions. Of the 3 cases reported from the border states, only 1 resulted in conviction. *Annual Report of the Attorney General* in *House Executive Documents*, 49 Cong. 1 sess., no. 7, 7 – 8, 52 – 57.

5. *Annual Report of the Attorney General* in *House Executive Documents*, 49 Cong. 2 sess., no. 8, 7 – 8, 24 – 25; 50 Cong. 1 sess., no. 7, 4 – 5; 2 sess., no. 7, 4 – 5.

6. *CR*, 46 Cong. 3 sess., 1880, 11, pt. 1:33.

7. Ibid., 270 – 71.

8. *CR*, 47 Cong. 1 sess., 1881, 13, pt. 1:5.

9. Ibid., 172.

10. Ibid., 212.

11. Ibid., 1882, 13, pt. 4:3946.

12. *CR*, 47 Cong. 2 sess., 1882, 14, pt. 1:17.

13. *CR*, 48 Cong. 1 sess., 1883, 15, pt. 1:82 (Leopold Morse, D-Mass.), 115 (Leonard Houk).

14. *CR*, 48 Cong. 2 sess., 1884, 16, pt. 1:57.

15. Ibid., 83.

16. Alvin P. Hovey, a Union army general during the Civil War and a future U.S. senator representing Indiana, was particularly concerned about the consequences of Cleveland's appointments of many southern Democrats to federal positions, including federal election officers. Ibid., 1885, 16, pt. 2:1191.

17. Ibid., 1244.

18. *CR*, 49 Cong. 1 sess., 1885, 17, pt. 1:122 (George F. Hoar, R-Mass.), 379 (H.R. 436, proposed by William Steel Homan, D-Ind.), 485 (H.R. 2370, introduced by Houk, R-Tenn.). *CR*, 49 Cong. 2 sess., 1886, 18, pt. 1:386 (H.R. 10252, introduced by Martin I. Townsend, R-N.Y.).

19. Polk Laffoon (D-Ky.), for example, introduced a bill to repeal certain sections of the *Revised Statutes* relating to congressional elections. *CR*, 49 Cong. 1 sess., 1886, 17, pt. 4:3613.

20. "Taking Care of the Ballot," *Springfield Republican*, July 6, 1886.

21. Ibid.

22. Chandler to Horatio Birbee, George McKee, E. M. Brayton, William P. Kellogg, N. Goff, E. McPherson, and others, February 19, 1887, William E. Chandler Papers, container 75, LC; see also Stanley P. Hirshson, *Farewell to the Bloody Shirt: Northern Republicans and the Southern Negro, 1877–1893* (Bloomington: Indiana University Press, 1962), 152–53.

23. Brayton to Chandler, April 22, May 29, 1887, William E. Chandler Papers, container 75, LC.

24. *CR*, 50 Cong. 1 sess., 1887, 19, pt. 1:29; *Statesman*, December 15, 1887, quoted from Leon Burr Richardson, *William E. Chandler, Republican* (New York: Dodd, Mead & Co., 1940), 390–91.

25. I. Houston to Chandler, December 20, 1887, William E. Chandler Papers, LC.

26. Samuel Charles Patterson, Roger H. Davidson, and Randall B. Ripley, *A More Perfect Union: Introduction to American Government*, 4th ed. (Pacific Grove, Calif.: Brooks/Cole, 1989), Appendix C.

27. *CR*, 50 Cong. 1 sess., 1888, 19, pt. 1:211 (H.R. 1346, by William S. Holman, D-Ind.); 230 (H.R. 1825, by Leonidas C. Houk), 319 (H.R. 3363, by Polk Laffoon); and 489 (H.R. 5055, by Charles Townsend, R-Pa.).

28. Blanton Duncan's statement, found in William E. Chandler Papers, container 77, LC.

29. Henry Jones Ford, *The Cleveland Era: A Chronicle of the New Order in Politics* (New Haven: Yale University Press, 1919), 108–17.

30. Ford, *The Cleveland Era*, 105–7.

31. Ibid., 140.

32. Robert D. Marcus, *Grand Old Party: Political Structure in the Gilded Age, 1880–1896* (New York: Oxford University Press, 1971), 101–15, esp. 101.

33. Again, the term *radical Republicans* used here is a working definition specifically to describe those Republicans who, for various reasons, wanted the party to carry on a strong enforcement program. These so-called radical Republicans were not completely identical, either by political origins or ideological views, with the radical Republicans of the Civil War and Reconstruction period, although the two groups' political views might share some common features.

34. John J. Ingalls, "Fetichism in the Campaign," *North American Review* 146 (June 1888): 655–56.

35. William E. Chandler's speech on the recent Louisiana election (August 23, 1888), *CR*, 50 Cong. 1 sess., 1888, 19, pt. 8:7878.

36. Ibid.

37. Ingalls, "Fetichism in the Campaign," 655–56.

38. *CR*, 50 Cong. 1 sess., 1888, 19, pt. 8:7878.

39. Asa E. Stratton to William E. Chandler, Jasper, Alabama, May 19, 1888, William E. Chandler Papers, container 77, LC.

40. William E. Chandler, "Our Southern Masters," *Forum* 5 (July 1888): 508–20.

41. Homer E. Socolofsky and Allen B. Spetter, *The Presidency of Benjamin Harrison* (Lawrence: University Press of Kansas, 1987), 12; Marcus, *Grand Old Party*, 104–5; George H. Mayer, *The Republican Party, 1854–1966*, 2d ed. (New York: Oxford University Press, 1967), 214–15; Harry J.

Sievers, *Benjamin Harrison, Hoosier Statesman: From the Civil War to the White House, 1865 –
1888* (New York: University Publishers, 1959), 314.

42. "The 'Bloody Shirt' Symbol," *Nation*, January 26, 1888, 64.

43. Mayer, *Republican Party*, 214 – 15.

44. Hirshson, *Farewell to the Bloody Shirt*, 145 – 48.

45. Ibid., 159 – 67.

46. George Francis Dawson, *The Republican Campaign Text-Book for 1888* (New York: Brentano's, 1888), 1; "Republican Platform of 1888," in *National Party Platforms, 1840 –1964*, ed. Kirk H. Porter and Donald Bruce Johnson (Urbana: University of Illinois Press, 1966), 79 – 83.

47. "Republican Platform of 1888," 79 – 83.

48. *Springfield Republican*, July 7, 1888.

49. "American Platform of 1888," in Porter and Johnson, *National Party Platforms*, 75 – 76.

50. "The Prohibition Platform of 1888," in ibid., 79.

51. "The Union Labor Platform of 1888," in ibid., 84.

52. "United Labor Platform of 1888," in ibid., 85.

53. "Democratic Platform of 1888," in ibid., 76 – 78.

54. Marcus, *Grand Old Party*, 106 – 25, esp. 113 – 15; Sievers, *Benjamin Harrison*, 311 – 28, esp. 327 – 28; Socolofsky and Spetter, *Presidency of Benjamin Harrison*, 8 – 10.

55. Marcus, *Grand Old Party*, 116 – 25; Sievers, *Benjamin Harrison*, 336 – 56.

56. Benjamin Harrison to Matthew Quay, September 12, 1888, Matthew Quay Papers, LC; *New York Tribune*, September 12, 1888; Hirshson, *Farewell to the Bloody Shirt*, 164.

57. Harrison to George F. Hoar, Indianapolis, November 26, 1888, Benjamin Harrison Papers, reel 13, LC.

58. Hirshson, *Farewell to the Bloody Shirt*, 166.

59. John C. Spooner to J. V. Quarles, October 10, 1888, Letterbooks, vol. 6, 271; John C. Spooner to H. C. Payne, October 11, 1888, Letterbooks, vol. 6, 301 – 2; quoted from Edward A. White, "The Republican Party in National Politics, 1888-1891" (Ph.D. diss., University of Minnesota, 1941), 371; Marcus, *Grand Old Party*, 136 – 38.

60. Hirshson, *Farewell to the Bloody Shirt*, 162.

61. Tourgee to Harrison, Mayville, New York, June 29, 1888, Harrison Papers, reel 9, LC.

62. Socolofsky and Spetter, *Presidency of Benjamin Harrison*, 14 – 15; Hirshson, *Farewell to the Bloody Shirt*, 166 – 67; Meyer, *Republican Party*, 220.

63. Marcus, *Grand Old Party*, 150.

64. Richard E. Welch Jr., *The Presidencies of Grover Cleveland* (Lawrence: University Press of Kansas, 1988), 93 – 97; Socolofsky and Spetter, *Presidency of Benjamin Harrison*, 12 – 14; Marcus, *Grand Old Party*, 138 – 50.

65. *Official Proceedings of the Republican National Convention, held at Chicago, June 19, 20, 21, 22, 23, and 25, 1888* (Minneapolis, Minn.: C.W. Johnson, 1903), 208 – 13; Sievers, *Benjamin Harrison*, 352.

66. Moses A. Herrick to Matthew S. Quay, Boston, November 7, 1888, Matthew S. Quay Papers, LC.

67. E. H. Terrell to Benjamin Harrison, Texas, December 31, 1888, Harrison Papers, reel 14, LC.

68. J. B. Hyde and others to Benjamin Harrison and Republican senators, Greenville County, South Carolina, January 1889, George F. Hoar Papers, box 105, MHS.

69. Augustus E. Wilson to Harrison, Louisville, Kentucky, February 4, 1889, Harrison Papers, reel 17, LC.

70. Stephen A. Hackworth to Hoar, Topeka, November 13, 1888, Hoar Papers, box 103, MHS.

71. Brayton to Chandler, December 17, 1888, William E. Chandler Papers, container 77, LC.

72. Harry J. Cole to Hoar, Haverhill, Massachusetts, November 22, 1888, Hoar Papers, box 103, MHS.

73. Richard E. Welch Jr., *George Frisbie Hoar and the Half-Breed Republicans* (Cambridge: Harvard University Press, 1971), 146.

74. Chandler to Benjamin Harrison, Washington, December 22, 1888, Harrison Papers, reel 14, LC.

75. Chandler to Harrison, Washington, December 22, 1888, Harrison Papers, reel 14, LC. To what extent Harrison took Chandler's advice remained unknown. But it is clear that he requested Chandler's opinion to prepare for his inaugural address. On the same day Chandler wrote to him, Harrison was still seeking advice from other Republican sources. Later, according to *New York World*, Harrison called support of black voting rights important, and he vowed not to appoint anyone who would not enforce the Fifteenth Amendment. Harrison to Murat Halstead, Indianapolis, December 22, 1888, ibid.

76. Robert A. Hill to Harrison, Oxford, Mississippi, December 18, 1888, ibid., reel 14.

77. Susan B. Anthony and May Wright Sewall to Benjamin Harrison, Indianapolis, June 30, 1888, ibid., reel 9.

78. Langston to Harrison, Washington, February 4, 1889, ibid., reel 17.

79. Harrison to Hoar, Indianapolis, November 26, 1888, ibid., reel 13.

80. Benjamin Harrison, Inaugural Address, March 4, 1889, *Messages and Papers*, 8:5440–49; also see Vincent P. De Santis, *Republicans Face the Southern Question: The New Departure Years, 1877–1897* (Baltimore: Johns Hopkins University Press, 1959), 196–97; Malcolm Moos, *The Republicans: A History of Their Party* (New York: Random House, 1956), 175–76.

81. *CR*, 51 Cong. 1 sess., 1889–90, 21, pts. 1–3:100 (S. No. 206 and S. No. 207, by John C. Spooner), 102 (S. No. 302, by William E. Chandler), 136 (S. No. 109, by Chandler), 250 (H.R. 605, by Charles H. Grosvenor), 254 (H.R. 798, by Leonidas C. Houk), 638 (H.R. 5175, by John F. Lacey), 871 (H.R. 5985, by William D. Kelley), 1899 (H.R. 7211, by Louis E. McComas), 2285 (H.R. 8242, by Henry Cabot Lodge).

82. Stephen A. Hackworth to Hoar, January 8, 1889, Hoar Papers, box 105, MHS; Ebenezer Wakeley to Chandler, Chicago, January 8, 1889, William E. Chandler Papers, container 77, LC.

83. Welch, *George Frisbie Hoar*, 146.

84. Spooner to A. J. Turner, December 11, 1889; Spooner to Harrison Reed, December 14, 1889; bound correspondence, container 8, Spooner Papers, LC.

85. John Garraty, *Henry Cabot Lodge: A Biography* (New York: Alfred A. Knopf, 1953), chaps. 1–2; Karl Schriftgiesser, *The Gentleman from Massachusetts* (Boston: Little, Brown, 1944), chap. 2.

86. Chandler's memo to Thomas Reed, April 29, 1890, William E. Chandler Papers, container 81, LC; George F. Hoar, *Autobiography of Seventy Years*, 2 vols. (New York: Charles Scribner's Sons, 1908), 2:154–55.

87. Chandler's memo to Reed, April 29, 1890, William E. Chandler Papers, container 81, LC.

88. Spooner to Geo. W. Esterly, December 25, 1889, Spooner Papers, container 8, LC. Spooner explained that he opposed the Blair education bill because it imposed quasi-federal supervision of

schools and regulated the jury system of the states. He began "to see the necessity of putting on the brakes a little, in order that the line which separate[d] the constitutional powers and functions of the Federal government from those of the States be not too much battered down." Spooner to A. J. Turner, December 11, 1889.

89. Chandler's memo to Reed, April 29, 1890, William E. Chandler Papers, container 81, LC.

90. Henry Cabot Lodge, "Honest Elections," *Frank Leslie's Illustrated Newspaper*, May 3, 1890, found in Henry Cabot Lodge Papers, bound volume 98, MHS.

91. *Springfield Republican*, May 11, 1889.

92. Lodge to E. B. Hayes, January 9, 1890, Lodge Papers, MHS.

93. Lodge, "Honest Elections."

94. Spooner to John Luchsinger, March 16, 1890, Spooner Papers, container 9, LC.

95. Lodge to E. B. Haskell, August 8, 1890, Lodge Papers, MHS.

96. Lodge's speech as reported by *Portland Journal*, August 20, 1890, Lodge Scrapbooks, vol. 97, Lodge Papers, MHS; see also *Springfield Republican*, August 21, 1890.

97. John C. Spooner to Albion W. Tourgee, April 23, 1890, Spooner Papers, container 109, LC; Hoar, *Autobiography of Seventy Years*, 2:152; Welch, *George Frisbie Hoar*, 147.

98. *CR*, 51 Cong. 1 sess., 1890, 21, pt. 7:6286.

99. Ibid., 6540–41.

100. Lodge to E. B. Haskell, August 8, 1890, Lodge Papers, MHS.

101. The Lodge bill was not printed in the *Congressional Record*, but Lodge gave a substantive explanation of the bill. However, the full text of the Senate substitute for the Lodge bill–a condensed version of the original bill with no essential changes–was printed in the *Record*. My discussion of the contents of the two versions of the Lodge bill is based on the available sources of the *Record*. *CR*, 51 Cong. 1 sess., 1890, 21, pt. 7:6538–44; 51 Cong. 2 sess., 1890, 22, pt. 1:22–26.

102. *CR*, 51 Cong. 1 sess., 1890, 21, pt. 7:6538–44; 51 Cong. 2 sess., 1890, 22, pt. 1:22–26; for the Enforcement Act of February 28, 1871, see *CG*, 41 Cong. 3 sess., appendix, 342–45.

103. *United States v. Siebold*, 100 U.S. 371–99 (1880).

104. Spooner to George Farnam, May 8, 1890, Spooner Papers, Letterbooks, container 109, LC.

105. *CR*, 51 Cong. 1 sess., 1890, 21, pt. 7:6540.

106. Ibid., 6544.

107. Ibid., 6554–56.

108. Ibid., 6884–85.

109. *CR*, 51 Cong. 1 sess., 1890, 21, pt. 7:6561 (Henry St. George Tucker), 6595–6601 (James W. Covert), 6673–74 (William McAdoo).

110. Ibid., 6762–65.

111. Ibid., 6845–46.

112. Ibid., 6853–57.

113. Ibid., 6560.

114. Ibid., 6689.

115. Ibid., 6772–73.

116. The vote was 136 yeas, 127 nays, and 64 not voting. Ibid., 6505–11.

117. Ibid., 6940–41.

118. Robert H. Terrel, speech manuscript, dated 1889, Terrel Papers, LC.

119. *Springfield Republican*, December 16, 1889.

120. Carl Schurz, *Speeches, Correspondence, and Political Papers of Carl Schurz*, ed. Frederic Bancroft, 6 vols. (New York: G. P. Putnam's Sons, 1913), 5:73 – 80.

121. *Springfield Republican*, July 7, 1890.

122. Robert Smalls to Chandler, Beaufort, South Carolina, July 25, 1890, William E. Chandler Papers, container 81, LC.

123. Walter L. Fleming, ed., *Documentary History of Reconstruction: Political, Military, Social, Religious, Educational, and Industrial, 1865 to the Present Time* (Cleveland: Arthur H. Clark, 1906 – 7), 450.

124. *CR*, 51 Cong. 1 sess., 1890, 21, pt. 9:8277 – 78.

125. Ibid., 8466, 8488, 8678, 8694, 8724, 8777, 8842; De Santis, *Republicans Face the Southern Question*, 208 – 9; Mayer, *The Republican Party*, 227 – 30.

126. *Philadelphia Press*, August 1890; *Nation*, August 24, 1890, 141.

127. Hoar to John Sherman, August 26, 1890, John Sherman Papers, LC, quoted from Hirshson, *Farewell to the Bloody Shirt*, 222.

128. Hoar, *Autobiography of Seventy Years*, 2:155 – 56.

129. Oliver H. Platt to William E. Chandler, July 22, 1890, William E. Chandler Papers, LC.

130. *Springfield Republican*, July 28, 1890.

131. Lodge to Harrison, August 18, 1890, Lodge Papers, MHS.

132. "The Republican Fiasco," *Nation*, August 21, 1890, 144 – 45.

133. Socolofsky and Spetter, *Presidency of Benjamin Harrison*, 50 – 51; Mayer, *The Republican Party*, 228; Ford, *The Cleveland Era*, 158, 162. There would be 235 Democrats and 88 Republicans in the House when the Fifty-second Congress convened in 1891. The 47 Senate Republicans would exceed the Democrats by 8.

134. James S. Clarkson to Harrison, Asheville, North Carolina, November 26, 1890, Harrison Papers, LC.

135. Harrison to Howard Cole, Washington, November 17, 1890, Harrison Papers, reel 29, LC, microfilm at CU.

136. Harrison to Whitelaw Reid, September 27, 1888, Reid Papers, LC, quoted from Mayer, *The Republican Party*, 227 – 28.

137. O. P. Highboard (private secretary of attorney general) to E. W. Halford (Harrison's private secretary), Washington, November 15, 1890, Harrison Papers, LC.

138. Harrison Reed to E. W. Halford, South Jacksonville, Florida, November 26, 1890, Harrison Papers, reel 29, LC.

139. Harrison, Second Annual Message, December 1, 1890, *Messages and Papers*, 9:107 – 29, esp. 128 – 29.

140. Chandler diary, December 1, 1890, William E. Chandler Papers, NHHS.

141. *CR*, 51 Cong. 2 sess., 1890, 22, pt. 1:169; Hoar, *Autobiography of Seventy Years*, 2: 154 – 56.

142. *CR*, 51 Cong. 2 sess., 1890, 22, pt. 1:48 – 50 (Hoar).

143. Ibid., 168 (Spooner).

144. Ibid., 50 – 54.

145. Ibid., 75 – 76.

146. Ibid., 206.

147. Ibid., 286. The Mississippi Constitution of 1890 was amended to grant suffrage only to those who met the state residence requirement (two years), paid the poll tax (two dollars per year), could read or understand any section of the state constitution, and were free from criminal records. John Hope Franklin observes that "while the 'understanding clause' was, on the face it, applicable to whites and blacks alike and could be used to disfranchise one group or the other, it was clear that in practice it was intended to enfranchise illiterate whites. Negroes were to be disfranchised by the literacy act." Mississippi Constitution, 1890, secs. 241, 243, 244, 249, 251, quoted from John Hope Franklin, "Legal Disfranchisement of Negro," *Journal of Negro Education* 26 (Spring 1956): 243–44; C. Vann Woodward, *Origins of the New South, 1877–1913* (1951; reprint, Baton Rouge: Louisiana State University Press, 1971), 321.

148. *CR*, 51 Cong. 2 sess., 1890, 22, pt. 1:674–88.

149. Ibid., 712–34.

150. Ibid., 724.

151. Elmer Ellis, *Henry Moore Teller: Defender of the West* (Caldwell, Idaho: Caxton Printers, 1941), 180; Fred Wellborn, "The Influence of the Silver-Republican Senators, 1889–1891," *Mississippi Valley Historical Review* 14 (1927–28): 465; Socolofsky and Spetter, *Presidency of Benjamin Harrison*, 55–56.

152. Wellborn, "Influence of Silver-Republican Senators," 468; Socolofsky and Spetter, *Presidency of Benjamin Harrison*, 58–59.

153. Ellis, *Henry Moore Teller*, 191; Mayer, *The Republican Party*, 229; Socolofsky and Spetter, *Presidency of Benjamin Harrison*, 57; H. Wayne Morgan, *From Hayes to McKinley: National Party Politics, 1877–1896* (Syracuse: Syracuse University Press, 1969), 343; Wellborn, "Influence of Silver-Republican Senators," 466–67.

154. *CR*, 51 Cong. 2 sess., 1891, 22, pt. 1:912–13.

155. "Death of the Republican Party," *Nation*, January 8, 1891, 24.

156. Spooner to Isaac P. Sturgeon, January 12, 1891, Letterbook, Spooner Papers, LC.

157. Spooner to David William, January 11, 1891, Letterbook, ibid.

158. Spooner to General M. Griffin, January 11, 1891, Letterbook, ibid.

159. *CR*, 51 Cong. 2 sess., 1891, 22, pt. 2:1431–43.

160. Ibid., 1461.

161. Ibid., pt. 1:819; pt. 2:1468, 1651–53, 1667–82, 1706; Dorothy Ganfield Fowler, *John Coit Spooner: Defender of Presidents* (New York: University Publishers, 1961), 156–57.

162. *CR*, 51 Cong. 2 sess., 1891, 22, pt. 2:1740.

163. Spooner to J. Rusk, January 27, 1891, quoted from Fowler, *John C. Spooner*, 157–58.

164. For details of the party strengths from 1870s and 1890s, see Appendix 8.

Epilogue. Equality Deferred, 1892–1910

1. *Nation*, October 13, 1893.

2. "Democratic Platform of 1892," in *National Party Platforms, 1840–1964*, ed. Kirk H. Porter and Donald Bruce Johnson (Urbana: University of Illinois Press, 1966), 159–60; Vincent P. De

Santis, *Republicans Face the Southern Question: The New Departure Years, 1877–1897* (Baltimore: Johns Hopkins University Press, 1959), 231–33.

3. "Republican Platform of 1892," in Porter and Johnson, *National Party Platforms*, 93–95.

4. *New York Times*, September 6, 1892; De Santis, *Republicans Face the Southern Question*, 231–32.

5. C. Vann Woodward, *Origins of the New South, 1877–1913* (1951; reprint, Baton Rouge: Louisiana State University Press, 1971), 258, 275–76; De Santis, *Republicans Face the Southern Question*, 229.

6. Homer E. Socolofsky and Allen B. Spetter, *The Presidency of Benjamin Harrison* (Lawrence: University Press of Kansas, 1987), 199–200; George H. Mayer, *The Republican Party, 1854–1966*, 2d ed. (New York: Oxford University Press, 1967), 234–38.

7. Socolofsky and Spetter, *Presidency of Benjamin Harrison*, 200; Donald Marquand Dozer, "Benjamin Harrison and the Presidential Campaign of 1892," *American Historical Review* 54 (October 1948): 66, 68–69; H. Wayne Morgan, *From Hayes to McKinley: National Party Politics, 1877–1896* (Syracuse: Syracuse University Press, 1969), 423–24, 436, 441; George Harmon Knoles, *The Presidential Campaign and Election of 1892* (Stanford: Stanford University Press, 1942), 138, 178, 181–98, 207–8, 216, 229–30.

8. *House Executive Reports*, 52 Cong. 2 sess., no. 2365, 199–200; Robert A. Horn, "National Control of Congressional Elections" (Ph.D. diss., Princeton University, 1942), 284–85.

9. *CR*, 53 Cong. 1 sess., 1893, 25, pt. 2:1395, 1634.

10. Ibid., 1893.

11. Of the sections to be repealed, 2005–2009 (inclusive), 5506–5507, 5509, 5516–5517, 5511–5515 (inclusive), and 2010 were from the Enforcement Act of May 31, 1870; 2011, 2014–2027 (inclusive), and 5521–5523 (inclusive) originated from the Enforcement Act of February 28, 1871; 5518–5520 were from the Ku Klux Force Act of April 20, 1871; and 2028–2030 originated from the legislative rider of the Civil Appropriation Act of June 10, 1872. *Statutes at Large*, 18, pt. 1 (1878): 352–57, 1067–72; United States, Library of Congress, *Index to the Federal Statutes, 1874–1931 . . .*, ed. Walter H. McClenon and Wilfred C. Gilbert (Washington, D.C.: U.S. Government Printing Office, 1933), 1223, 1264.

12. *CR*, 53 Cong. 1 sess., 1893, 25, pt. 2:1804.

13. Ibid., 1989.

14. Ibid., 1947.

15. Ibid., 1817–20.

16. Ibid., 1859–63.

17. Ibid., 2025, 2033 (Denson); 2033–37 (Ray).

18. Ibid., 2230–2231 (Ray); 2228–29 (Josiah Hicks).

19. John F. Lacey of Iowa proposed an amendment to retain sections 5506, 5511, 5513–5515, and 5520. Ibid., 2375. Julius C. Burrows of Michigan moved that sections 2205–2210 be maintained. Ibid., 2375–77.

20. Ibid., 2378.

21. Ibid., 2368.

22. *CR*, 53 Cong. 2 sess., 1893, 26, pt. 1:224; 1894, 26, pt. 1:707.

23. Ibid., 1894, 26, pt. 1:929–30.

24. Ibid., 925–26 (Chandler), 926 (Platt).

25. Ibid., pt. 2:1228–31.

26. Ibid., 1313–20.

27. Ibid., 1893, 26, pt. 1:164–65; Russell Elliott, *Servant of Power: A Political Biography of Senator William M. Stewart* (Reno: University of Nevada Press, 1983), 169.

28. *CR*, 53 Cong. 2 sess., 1894, 26, pt. 2:1859–63.

29. Ibid., 1999.

30. *Statutes at Large* 28, pt. 1 (1894): 36–37.

31. *James v. Bowman*, 190 U.S. 127 (1903); Charles V. Hamilton, *The Bench and the Ballot: Southern Federal Judges and Black Voters* (New York: Oxford University Press, 1973), 39; for 1909 repeals and amendments, see *Statutes at Large* 35, pt. 1 (1909): 1153–59, 1092–93; for 1911 repeals, see ibid., 36 (1911): 1168–69; for the modern placement of section 2004, see section 1971 under Title 42 in United States, *United States Code 1988 Edition* (Washington, D.C.: U.S. Government Printing Office, 1989), 16:340–44; for placements of sections 5508 and 5510, see sections 241 and 242 under Title 18 in United States, *United States Code 1994 Edition* (Washington, D.C.: U.S. Government Printing Office, 1995), 9:69. For details of all the repeals and amendments, see Appendix 6.

32. For a detailed account of the development of black disfranchisement in various southern states in the 1880s, see J. Morgan Kousser, *The Shaping of Southern Politics: Suffrage Restriction and the Establishment of the One-Party South, 1880–1910* (New Haven: Yale University Press, 1974), esp. chaps. 1, 4–5; see also Paul Lewinson, *Race, Class, and Party: A History of Negro Suffrage and White Politics in the South* (London: Oxford University Press, 1932), chaps. 3 and 4, for the political settings of black disfranchisement.

33. Clark Leonard Miller, "'Let Us Die to Make Men Free': Political Terrorism in Post-Reconstruction Mississippi, 1877–1896" (Ph.D. diss., University of Minnesota, 1983), 556–642, esp. 595–628; William Alexander Mabry, "Disfranchisement of the Negro in Mississippi," *Journal of Southern History* 4 (1933): 318–33; Kousser, *Shaping of Southern Politics*, 139–43.

34. Miller, "'Let Us Die to Make Men Free,'" 595–628, 635–42; Kousser, *Shaping of Southern Politics*, 143–44.

35. Ibid., 50, 149–51; David Duncan Wallace, *The South Carolina Constitution of 1895* (Columbia: Bureau of Publications, University of South Carolina, 1927), 34; Frank B. Williams Jr., "The Poll Tax as a Suffrage Requirement in the South, 1870–1901," *Journal of Southern History* 18 (November 1952): 483–89.

36. Walter L. Fleming, ed., *Documentary History of Reconstruction: Political, Military, Social, Religious, Educational, and Industrial, 1865 to Present Time* (Cleveland: Arthur H. Clark, 1906–7), 452; Amasa M. Eaton, "The Suffrage Clause of the New Constitution of Louisiana," *Harvard Law Review* 13 (1899): 3–17; Kousser, *Shaping of Southern Politics*, 152–65, esp. 162–65.

37. Joseph Matt Brittain, "Negro Suffrage and Politics in Alabama since 1870" (Ph.D. diss., Indiana University, 1958), 125–43, 149–55; Kousser, *Shaping of Southern Politics*, 170, 178–81; Lewinson, *Race, Class, and Party*, 84.

38. Kousser, *Shaping of Southern Politics*, 220–21; Lewinson, *Race, Class, and Party*, 85–87; Janice Evelyn Christensen, "The Constitutional Problems of National Control of the Suffrage in the United States" (Ph.D. diss., University of Minnesota, 1952), 196.

39. Lewinson, *Race, Class, Party*, 81; Kousser, *Shaping of Southern Politics*, 223.

40. Kousser, *Shaping of Southern Politics*, 224; W. Dean Burnham, "Party Systems and the Political Process," in *The American Party Systems: Stages of Political Development*, ed. William N. Chambers and Walter D. Burnham, 2d ed. (New York: Oxford University Press, 1975), 301.

41. De Santis, *Republicans Face the Southern Question*; John Dittmer, *Black Georgia in the Progressive Era* (Urbana: University of Illinois Press, 1977), 90.

42. Democratic representation in the House was substantially reduced from 218 in the Fifty-third Congress to 105 in the Fifty-fourth Congress, in which the Republicans had a plurality of 39 in the House and 4 in the Senate. Mayer, *Republican Party*, 242 – 43; Samuel Charles Patterson, Roger H. Davidson, and Randall B. Ripley, *A More Perfect Union: Introduction to American Government*, 4th ed. (Pacific Grove, Calif.: Brooks/Cole, 1989), C – 5; Stanley L. Jones, *The Presidential Election of 1896* (Madison: University of Wisconsin Press, 1964), 31 – 32.

43. Jones, *Presidential Election of 1896*, 276 – 96; Mayer, *Republican Party*, 251 – 56; Porter and Johnson, *National Party Platforms*, 109.

44. Richard B. Sherman, *The Republican Party and Black America: From McKinley to Hoover* (Charlottesville: University Press of Virginia, 1973), 3 – 4.

45. Copy of the speech in McKinley Papers, quoted from Sherman, *Republican Party and Black America*, 11, 16.

46. "Republican Platform of 1900," Porter and Johnson, *National Party Platforms*, 123; Sherman, *Republican Party and Black America*, 20 – 21.

47. Sherman, *Republican Party and Black America*, 23 – 51; Mayer, *Republican Party*, 272 – 87; Lewis L. Gould, *The Presidency of Theodore Roosevelt* (Lawrence: University Press of Kansas, 1991), 132 – 46.

48. *CR*, 57 Cong. 1 sess., 3248 (statements of William W. Kitchin of North Carolina, Oscar W. Underwood of Alabama, and Thomas W. Harwick of Georgia).

49. Ibid., 58, 2746; 58 Cong. 1 sess., 165, 236; 58 Cong. 2 sess., 1270 – 78, 4258 – 63; Sherman, *Republican Party and Black America*, 75.

50. *CR*, 58 Cong. 3 sess., 47; *New York Times*, December 8, 1904; Sherman, *Republican Party and Black America*, 76.

51. "Address at the Lincoln Dinner of the Republican Club of the City of New York, February 13, 1905," in Theodore Roosevelt, *The Works of Theodore Roosevelt*, 20 vols. (New York: Charles Scribner's Sons, 1926), 16:342 – 50; Sherman, *Republican Party and Black America*, 53.

52. Elliott M. Rudwick, "The Niagara Movement," *Journal of Negro History* 42 (July 1957): 177 – 95; Sherman, *Republican Party and Black America*, 77.

53. *Guinn Beal v. United States*, 238 U.S. 347 (1915).

SELECTED BIBLIOGRAPHY

PRIMARY SOURCES

MANUSCRIPT COLLECTIONS

Allison, William Boyd. Papers. Library of Congress.

Arthur, Chester Alan. Papers. Library of Congress (on microfilm at Columbia University Library).

Bancroft, George. Papers. Cornell University Library.

Barlow, Samuel. Papers. Huntington Library.

Barney, Hiram. Papers. Huntington Library.

Bigelow, John. Papers. New York Public Library.

Blaine, James G., and Family. Papers. 1777–1945. Library of Congress (on microfilm at Harvard University Library).

Callender, Guy Stevens. Papers. Huntington Library.

Cameron, Simon. Papers. Library of Congress.

Chandler, William E. Papers. Library of Congress.

Chandler, William E. Papers. New Hampshire Historical Society, Concord, New Hampshire.

Chandler, Zachariah. Papers. Library of Congress.

Conkling, Roscoe. Papers. Library of Congress.

Conkling, Roscoe. Papers. Syracuse University Library.

Conway, Moncure D. Papers. Houghton Library, Harvard University.

Crapo, William Wallace. Papers. Massachusetts Historical Society.

Curtis, George William. Papers. Houghton Library, Harvard University.

Dawes, Henry L. Papers. Library of Congress.

Douglass, Frederick. Papers. Library of Congress.

Douglass, Frederick. Papers. Rush Rhees Library, University of Rochester.

Dudley, Thomas Haines. Papers. Huntington Library.

Edes, H. H. Papers. Massachusetts Historical Society.

Fiske, John. Papers. Huntington Library.

Forbes, John M. Papers. Houghton Library, Harvard University.

Garfield, James A. Papers. Library of Congress (on microfilm at Columbia University Library).

Gay, Sydney Howard. Papers. Rare Books and Manuscripts Library, Columbia University.

Godkin, Edward Lawrence. Papers. Houghton Library, Harvard University.

Grant, Ulysses S. Papers. Library of Congress (on microfilm at Columbia University Library).

Greeley, Horace. Papers. New York Public Library.

Griffing, Josephine Sophie White. Papers. Rare Books and Manuscripts Library, Columbia University.

Grosvenor, Charles H. Papers. Rare Books and Manuscripts Library, Columbia University.

Haight, Henry. Papers. Huntington Library.

Hale, John P. Papers. New Hampshire Historical Society.

Harrison, Benjamin. Papers. Library of Congress (on microfilm at Columbia University Library).

Hayes, Rutherford B. Papers. Library of Congress.

Election of 1876 (selection from Rutherford B. Hayes Papers in the Hayes Memorial relating to 1876 election). Library of Congress (on microfilm at Columbia University Library).

Hayes, Rutherford B. Papers. Rutherford Birchard Hayes Presidential Center, Fremont, Ohio.

Hoar, George F. Papers. Massachusetts Historical Society.

Hoar, George F. Papers. Houghton Library, Harvard University.

Holls, Frederick William. Papers. Rare Books and Manuscripts Library, Columbia University.

Lieber, Francis. Papers. Huntington Library.

Lodge, Henry Cabot. Papers. Massachusetts Historical Society.

Logan, John A. Papers. Library of Congress.

McCall, Ansel James, Family. Papers. Cornell University Library.

McCulloch, Hugh. Papers. Library of Congress.

Phillips, Wendell. Papers. Houghton Library, Harvard University.

Pinchback, P. B. S. Papers. Rutherford Birchard Hayes Presidential Center, Fremont, Ohio.

Post Family. Papers. Rush Rhees Library, University of Rochester.

Quay, Matthew S. Papers. Library of Congress.

Ray, Charles. Papers. Huntington Library.

Schurz, Carl. Papers. Rare Books and Manuscripts Library. Columbia University.

Seward, William Henry. Papers. Rush Rhees Library, University of Rochester.

Sherman, John. Papers. Library of Congress.

Sherman, John. Papers. Rutherford Birch Hayes Presidential Center, Fremont, Ohio.

Smith, Gerrit. Papers. Syracuse University Library.

Smith, Goldwin. Papers. Cornell University Library.

Spooner, John C. Papers. Library of Congress.

Sprague, William. Papers. Rare Books and Manuscripts Library, Columbia University.

The Papers of Charles Sumner (microfilm). Harvard and Columbia University Libraries.

Sumner, Charles. Papers. Houghton Library, Harvard University.

Sumner, Charles. Papers. Huntington Library.

Sumner, Charles. Papers. Library of Congress.

Terrel, Robert Heberton. Papers. Library of Congress.

Trumbull, Lyman. Papers. Library of Congress.

Wade, Benjamin, Papers. Library of Congress.

Waite, Morrison R. Papers. Library of Congress.

Weed, Thurlow. Papers. Rush Rhees Library, University of Rochester.

Welles, Gideon. Papers. Huntington Library.

White, Andrew. Papers. Cornell University Library.

Wilson, Henry. Papers. Library of Congress.

PUBLISHED COLLECTIONS OF PAPERS, WORKS, DIARIES,
LETTERS, MEMOIRS, REPORTS, AND DOCUMENTS

Bates, Edward. *The Diary of Edward Bates, 1859–1966.* Edited by Howard K. Beale. Washington, D.C.: U.S. Government Printing Office, 1933.

Berlin, Ira, ed. *Freedom: A Documentary History of Emancipation, 1861–1867.* Ser. 2, *The Black Military Experience.* London: Cambridge University Press, 1982.

Bigelow, John. *Retrospection of an Active Life.* 4 vols. New York: Doubleday, Page, & Co., 1909–13.

Blaine, James G. *Political Discussions, Legislative, Diplomatic, and Peculiar, 1856–1886.* Norwich, Conn.: Henry Bill, 1887.

——. *Twenty Years of Congress: From Lincoln to Garfield with a Review of the Events Which Led to the Political Revolution of 1860.* 2 vols. Norwich, Conn.: Henry Bill, 1884–86.

Blaine, James G., Mrs. *Letters of Mrs. James G. Blaine.* Edited by Harriet S. Blaine Beale. New York: Duffield and Co., 1908.

Boutwell, George S. *Reminiscences of Sixty Years in Public Affairs.* 2 vols. 1902. Reprint, New York: Greenwood, 1968.

Chandler, William E. *Letters of Mr. William E. Chandler Relative to the So-Called Southern Policy of President Hayes, Together with a Letter to Mr. Chandler of Mr. William Lloyd Garrison.* Concord, N.H.: Monitor and Statesman Office, 1878.

——. *Louisiana Election and Southern Election Outrages: Speech of Hon. William E. Chandler, of New Hampshire, in the United States Senate, August 23 and 24, 1888.* Washington, D.C.: N.p., 1888.

Chase, Salmon P. *Inside Lincoln's Cabinet: The Civil War Diary of Salmon P. Chase.* Edited by David H. Donald. New York: Longmans, Green, and Co., 1954.

Commager, Henry Steele, ed. *Documents of American History.* New York: Appleton-Century-Crofts, 1963.

——. *Fifty Basic Civil War Documents.* Princeton: D. Van Nostrand, 1965.

Conkling, Alfred R. *The Life and Letters of Roscoe Conkling, Orator, Statesman, Advocate.* New York: Charles L. Webster & Co., 1889.

Conwell, Russell H. *Life and Public Services of Governor Rutherford B. Hayes.* Boston: Franklin Press, 1876.

Douglass, Frederick. *The Frederick Douglass Papers.* Edited by John W. Blassingame and John R. McKivigan. 5 vols. New Haven: Yale University Press, 1979–91.

——. *The Life and Writings of Frederick Douglass.* Edited by Philip S. Foner. 4 vols. New York: International Publishers, 1950–55.

Duplicate Copy of the Souvenir from Afro-American League of Tennessee to Hon. James M. Ashley of Ohio. Edited by Benjamin W. Arnett. Philadelphia: Publishing House of the A.M.E. Church, 1894.

Fleming, Walter L., ed. *Documentary History of Reconstruction: Political, Military, Social, Religious, Educational, and Industrial, 1865 to the Present Time.* Cleveland: Arthur H. Clark, 1906–7.

Forbes, John Murray. *Letters and Recollections of John Murray Forbes.* Edited by Sarah Forbes Hughes. 2 vols. Boston: Houghton Mifflin, 1900.

Garfield, James A. *The Diary of James A. Garfield.* Edited by Harry James Brown and Frederick D. Williams. 4 vols. East Lansing: Michigan State University Press, 1981.

——. *The Works of James Abram Garfield.* Edited by Burke A. Hinsdale. 2 vols. Boston: James R. Osgood and Co., 1882–83.

Garfield, James A., and Burke A. Hinsdale. *Garfield-Hinsdale Letters: Correspondence between James Abram Garfield and Burke Aaron Hinsdale.* Edited by Mary L. Hinsdale. 1949. Reprint, New York: Kraus Reprint Co., 1969.

Grant, Ulysses S. *General Grant's Letters to a Friend, 1861–1880.* 1897. Reprint, New York: AMS, 1973.

——. *The Papers of Ulysses S. Grant.* Edited by John Y. Simon. 20 vols. Carbondale: Southern Illinois University Press, 1967–95.

Hay, John. *Lincoln and the Civil War in Diaries and Letters of John Hay.* Edited by Tyler Dennet. New York: Dodd, Mead, & Co., 1939.

Hayes, Rutherford B. *Diary and Letters of Rutherford Birchard Hayes.* Edited by Charles R. Williams. 5 vols. Columbus: Ohio Archeological and Historical Society, 1922–26.

——. *Hayes: The Diary of a President, 1875–1881.* Edited by T. Harry Williams. New York: David McKay, 1964.

Hoar, George F. *Autobiography of Seventy Years.* 2 vols. New York: Charles Scribner's Sons, 1908.

Johnson, Andrew. *The Papers of Andrew Johnson.* Vols. 8, 9. Edited by Paul H. Bergeron. Knoxville: University of Tennessee Press, 1989, 1991.

Lincoln, Abraham. *Abraham Lincoln: A Documentary Portrait through His Speeches and Writings.* Edited by Don E. Fehrenbacher. New York: New American Library of World Literature, 1964.

——. *The Collected Works of Abraham Lincoln.* Edited by Roy P. Basler. 9 vols. New Brunswick, N.J.: Rutgers University Press, 1953–55.

McPherson, Edward. *The Political History of the United States during the Period of Reconstruction, April 15, 1865–July 15, 1870.* New York: Da Capo, 1872.

National Encyclopedia of American Biography.

Porter, Kirk H., and Donald Bruce Johnson, eds. *National Party Platforms, 1840–1864.* Urbana: University of Illinois Press, 1966.

Proceedings of Republican National Convention. Reported by Eugene Davis. Chicago: Jno. B. Jeffery Printing and Publishing House, 1881.

Schurz, Carl. *The Reminiscences of Carl Schurz.* 3 vols. New York: McClure, 1907–8.

——. *Speeches, Correspondence, and Political Papers of Carl Schurz.* Edited by George Bancroft. 6 vols. New York: G. P. Putnam's Sons, 1913.

Sherman, John. *Recollections of Forty Years in the House, Senate, and Cabinet.* 1895. Reprint, New York: Greenwood, 1968.

Sherman, John, and William Tecumseh Sherman. *The Sherman Letters: Correspondence between General and Senator Sherman from 1837 to 1891.* Edited by Rachel Sherman Thorndike. New York: Charles Scribner's Sons, 1894.

Sherman, Thomas H. *Twenty Years with James G. Blaine: Reminiscences by His Private Secretary.* New York: Grafton Press, 1928.

Smith, Theodore Clarke. *The Life and Letters of James Abram Garfield.* 2 vols. New Haven: Yale University Press, 1925.

Sumner, Charles. *Charles Sumner, His Complete Works.* 15 vols. Boston: Lee and Shepard, 1900.

——. *Memoir and Letters of Charles Sumner.* Edited by Edward L. Pierce. Boston: Roberts Brothers, 1893.

——. *The Selected Letters of Charles Sumner.* Edited by Beverly Wilson Palmer. 2 vols. Boston: Northeastern University Press, 1990.

Welles, Gideon. *Diary of Gideon Welles.* Edited by Howard K. Beale. New York: W. W. Norton & Co., 1960.

GOVERNMENT PAPERS AND DOCUMENTS, OFFICIAL PUBLICATIONS, AND LEGAL DOCUMENTS

Unpublished

Buckner, B. F. "Supreme Court of the United States. The United States, Plaintiff in Error, vs. Hiram Reese and Matthew Foushee, Defendants in Error. Brief for Defendants in Error." N.d. Found at Columbia Law School Library.

Campbell, John A. "Supreme Court of the United States. No. 609. United States vs. Wm. J. Cruikshank et al. Conspiracy and Banding in Grant Parish, La. Brief for Defendants." [Clark & Hofeline, Book and Job Printers, 1875?] Found at Columbia Law School Library.

Field, David Dudley. "Supreme Court of the United States. The United States Against William I. Cruikshank and Two Others. Points and Brief of Mr. David Dudley Field for the Defendants." New York: John Polhemus, 1875. Found at Columbia Law School Library.

Marr, R. H. "Supreme Court of the United States. No. 609. The United States, Plaintiffs in Error, versus Cruikshank, Irwin and Hadnot. Argument for Defendants." Dated as "February 1875." Found at Columbia Law School Library.

United States. Congress. Senate. "U.S. Senate, 44th Congress Select Committee to Investigate Elections in Mississippi, 1875–1876" (Manuscripts Collection). New York Public Library.

——. Department of Justice. Attorney General's Official Letterbooks. Record Group 60. National Archives, Washington, D.C.

——. Department of Justice. Letters Received from United States Attorneys. Record Group 60. National Archives, Washington, D.C.

——. Department of Justice. Letters Sent by the Department of Justice: General and Miscellaneous, 1870–90. Record Group 60, National Archives, Washington, D.C.

——. Department of Justice. Letters Sent by the Department of Justice to Executive Officers and to Members of Congress, 1871–1904. Record Group 60, National Archives, Washington, D.C.

——. Department of Justice. Letters Sent by the Department of Justice to Judges and Clerks, 1874–1904. Record Group 60, National Archives, Washington, D.C.

——. Department of Justice. Source-Chronological File, RG 60, NA.

Williams, Geo. H., and S. F. Phillips. "Transcript of Record. Supreme Court of the United States. In the Supreme Court of the United States. The United States vs. William J. Cruikshank, William D. Irwin, and John P. Hadnot. No. 609. In Error to the Circuit Court of the United States for the District of Louisiana. Brief for the United States." [1875?] Found at Columbia Law School Library.

Published

Congressional Globe, 37th–42d Congresses.

Congressional Record, 43d–53d Congresses.

House Executive Documents, 41st–53d Congresses.

Senate Executive Documents, 41st–46th Congresses.

Digest of Decisions of the United States Circuit and District Courts, from 1789 to 1880, As Contained in the Thirty Volumes of the Federal Cases. Edited by Members of the Editorial Staff of the National Reporter System. St. Paul: West, 1898.

The Federal Cases: Comprising Cases Argued and Determined in the Circuit and District Courts of the United States; from the Earliest Time to the Beginning of Federal Reporter, Arranged Alphabetically by the Titles of the Cases, and Numbered Consecutively. Books 8, 11, 14, 16, 21, 26 – 30. St. Paul: West, 1894 – 97.

Federal Reporter: Cases Argued and Determined in the Circuit and District Courts of the United States. Vols. 4, 6, 9, 16, 22, 23, 25, 32, 35 – 38, 41 – 44. Saint Paul: West, 1881 – 91.

McPherson, Edward, ed. *The Political History of the United States of America, during the Great Rebellion, from November 6, 1860, to July 4, 1864; including a classified summary of the legislation of the second session of the Thirty-sixth Congress, the three sessions of the Thirty-seventh Congress, the first session of the Thirty-eighth Congress, with the votes thereon, and the important executive, judicial, and politico-military facts of that eventful period: together with the organization, legislation, and general proceedings of the rebel administration.* Washington, D.C.: Philip and Solomons, 1864.

United States. *The Statutes at Large and Proclamations of the United States of America from . . . edited by George P. Sanger.* Vol. 16 (Dec. 1869 to Mar. 1871), Vol. 17 (Mar. 1871 to Mar. 1873). Boston: Little, Brown, 1871 – 73.

———. *The Statutes at Large of the United States from . . . edited, printed, and published under the authority of an act of Congress, and under the direction of the Secretary of State.* Vol. 18, pt. 3 (Dec. 1873 to Mar. 1875) – Vol. 49, pt. 2 (Jan. 1935 to June 1936). Washington, D.C.: U.S. Government Printing Office, 1875 – 1936.

———. *United States Code Annotated.* St. Paul: West, 1969.

United States. Attorney General. *Official opinions of the Attorneys General of the United States, Advising the President and Heads of Departments in Relation to Their Official Duties.* 12 vols. Washington: A. Farnham, 1852 – 70.

United States. Congress. *Biographical Directory of the United States Congress, 1774 – 1989, the Continental Congress, September 5, 1774, to October 21, 1788, and the Congress of the United States, from the First through One Hundredth Congresses, March 4, 1789, to January 3, 1989, inclusive.* Washington, D.C.: U.S. Government Printing Office, 1989.

———. Congress. *Revised Statutes of the United States, Passed at the First Session of the Forty-third Congress, 1873 – '74 . . .* Washington, D.C.: U.S. Government Printing Office, 1875.

———. Congress. *Second Edition. Revised Statutes of the United States, Passed at the First Session of the Forty-third Congress, 1873 – '74 . . .* Washington, D.C.: U.S. Government Printing Office, 1878. Published also as *Statutes at Large* 18, pt. 1 (1878).

———. Congress. Joint Committee on Reconstruction. *The Journal of the Joint Committee of Fifteen on Reconstruction, 39th Congress, 1865 – 1867.* Edited by Benjamin B. Kendrick. Studies in History, Economics, and Public Law edited by the Faculty of Political Science of Columbia University, vol. 62. New York: Columbia University Press, 1914.

———. Congress. Joint Select Committee on the Condition of Affairs in the Late Insurrectionary States. *Report of the Joint Select Committee Appointed to Inquire into the Condition of Affairs in the Late Insurrectionary States, So Far as Regards the Execution of Laws, and the Lives and Property of the Citizens of the United States and Testimony Taken* (South Carolina, Vol. 3). 42 Cong. 2 sess. Reprinted as Vol. 5 of the *Ku Klux Klan Conspiracy.* Washington, D.C.: U.S. Government Printing Office, 1872.

——. Library of Congress. *Index to the Federal Statutes, 1874 – 1931; General and Permanent Law Contained in the Revised Statutes of 1874 and Volumes 18 – 46 of the Statutes at Large.* Edited by Walter H. McClenon and Wilfred C. Gilbert. Washington, D.C.: U.S. Government Printing Office, 1933.

——. President. *A Compilation of the Messages and Papers of the Presidents of the United States.* Edited by James D. Richardson. 10 vols. Washington, D.C.: U.S. Government Printing Office, 1896 – 99.

United States Circuit Court (4th Circuit). *Proceedings in the Ku Klux Trials at Columbia, S.C. in the United States Circuit Court, November Term, 1871.* 1872. Reprint, New York: Negro Universities Press, 1969.

United States Supreme Court. *United States Reports: Cases Argued and Adjudged in the Supreme Court of the United States.* Boston: Little, Brown, 1876 – 91.

ARTICLES, SPEECHES, AND BOOKS ON CONTEMPORARY POLITICS

Adams, Charles F., Jr. *The Double Anniversary: '76 and '63: A Fourth of July Address Delivered at Quincy, Mass.* Boston: W. M. Parsons Lunt, 1869.

Akerman, Amos Tappan. *Reconstruction: Extracts from Speech Delivered at Atlanta, Georgia, September 1st, 1870.* Washington, D.C.: Union Republican Congressional Committee, 1870.

Allen, Walter. *Governor Chamberlain's Administration in South Carolina: A Chapter of Reconstruction in the Southern States.* New York: G. P. Putnam's Sons, 1888.

Bancroft, Frederic A. *A Sketch of the Negro in Politics, Especially in South Carolina and Mississippi.* New York: J. F. Pearson, 1885.

Brooks, Francis Augustus. "A Review of the Federal Elections or Force Bill Now before the United States Senate, Reprinted from the *Boston Post* of January 16, 1890." Boston: N.p., 1890.

Butler, Benjamin Franklin. *The Negro in Politics: Review of Recent Legislation for His Protection-Defense of the Colored Man against All Accusers.* Lowell, Mass.: Marden & Rowell, Books and Job, 1871.

Cooper, Thos. V. *Campaign of '84.* Chicago: Baird & Dillon, 1884.

Curtis, George William. *Speech of George William Curtis at the New York State Constitutional Convention, 1867.* Rochester: New York State Constitutional Convention Campaign Committee, 1867.

Dana, Richard H., Jr. "Points in American Politics." *North American Review* 124 (January 1877): 1 – 30.

Dawson, George Francis. *The Republican Campaign Text-Book for 1888.* New York: Brentano's, 1888.

Foner, Philip S., and George E. Walker, eds. *Proceedings of the Black National and State Conventions, 1865 – 1900.* Vol. 1. Philadelphia: Temple University Press, 1986.

Garfield, James A. "The Southern Question." *North American Review* 123 (October 1876): 248 – 81.

Hancock, John. *The Elective Franchise; or Who Has the Right to Vote?* Philadelphia: Merrihew & Son, 1865.

Kelley, William D., Wendell Phillips, and Frederick Douglass. *The Equality of All Men before the Law Claimed and Defended in Speeches by Hon. William D. Kelley, Wendell Phillips, and Frederick Douglass.* Boston: Rand and Avery, 1865.

Langston, John Mercer. *Freedom and Citizenship: Selected Lectures and Addresses*. Miami: Mnemosyne, 1969.

Leib, James R. *Thoughts on the Elective Franchise*. Philadelphia: John C. Clark, 1839.

Lieber, Francis. *Amendments of the Constitution, Submitted to the Consideration of the American People* . . . New York: Loyal Publication Society, 1865.

——. *Reflections on the Changes Which May Seem Necessary in the Present Constitution of the State of New York*. New York: New York Union League Club, 1867.

Morton, Oliver Perry. *Reconstruction and Negro Suffrage*. Indiana: Holloway, Douglass & Co., 1865.

[National Union Party]. *Campaign Documents of the National Union Party*. New York: New York Printing Co., 1866.

Nott, William E. *The Republican Campaign Text-Book for 1882*. Washington, D.C.: National Republican Printing and Publishing Co., 1882.

Owen, Robert. "The Political Results from the Varioloid." *Atlantic Monthly* 35 (June 1875): 660 – 70.

Proceedings of the American Anti-Slavery Society at Its Third Decade Held in the City of Philadelphia, December 3 – 4, 1863. Reported by Henry M. Parkhurst. 1864. Reprint, New York: Negro Universities Press, 1969.

Proceedings of the National Convention of Colored Men Held in Syracuse, New York, October 4 – 7, 1864; With the Bill of Wrongs and Rights and Address to the American People. 1864. Reprint, Wilmington, Del.: Scholarly Resources, 1974.

["A Republican"]. *Universal Suffrage, Female Suffrage*. Philadelphia: J. B. Lippincott, 1867.

Republican National Convention. *Official Proceedings of the Republican National Convention Held at Chicago, June 19, 20, 21, 22, 23 and 25, 1888* . . . Minneapolis: C. W. Johnson, 1903.

——. *Proceedings of the National Union Republican Convention. Held at Philadelphia. June 5 and 6, 1872* . . . *Reported by Francis H. Smith*. Washington, D.C.: Gibson Brothers, 1872.

Smalls, Robert. "Election Methods in the South." *North American Review* 151 (November 1890): 593 – 600.

Sumner, Charles. *No Compromise of Human Rights*. Washington, D.C.: Congressional Globe Office, 1866.

Trescot, William Henry. "The Southern Question." *North American Review* 123 (October 1876).

NEWSPAPERS AND PERIODICALS

Atlantic Monthly
Chicago Tribune
Douglass' Monthly (New York). Reprint, New York: Negro Universities Press, 1969
Forum
Harper's Weekly
Independent
Journal of Social Science
Nation
National Anti-Slavery Standard (New York)
New York Times
New York Tribune

New York World
North American Review
Public Opinion
Springfield (Massachusetts) Republican
Washington National Intelligencer
Washington National Republican
Washington New (National) Era

SECONDARY SOURCES

BOOKS AND MONOGRAPHS

Abbott, Richard H. *Cobbler in Congress: The Life of Henry Wilson, 1812–1875*. Lexington: University of Kentucky Press, 1972.

——. *The Republican Party and the South, 1855–1877: The First Southern Strategy*. Chapel Hill: University of North Carolina Press, 1986.

Anbinder, Tyler. *Nativism and Slavery: The Northern Know Nothings and the Politics of the 1850s*. New York: Oxford University Press, 1992.

Anderson, Eric, and Alfred A. Moss Jr., eds. *The Facts of Reconstruction: Essays in Honor of John Hope Franklin*. Baton Rouge: Louisiana State University Press, 1991.

Ayers, Edward L. *Southern Crossing: A History of the American South, 1877–1906*. New York: Oxford University Press, 1995.

Baker, Jean H. *The Politics of Continuity: Maryland Political Parties from 1858 to 1870*. Baltimore: Johns Hopkins University Press, 1973.

Barry, David. *Forty Years in Washington*. 1924. Reprint, New York: Beekman Publishers, 1974.

Beale, Howard K. *The Critical Year: A Study of Andrew Johnson and Reconstruction*. New York: Harcourt, Brace, 1930.

Belz, Herman. *Emancipation and Equal Rights: Politics and Constitutionalism in the Civil War Era*. New York: W. W. Norton, 1978.

——. *Reconstructing the Union: Theory and Policy during the Civil War*. Ithaca, N.Y.: Cornell University Press, 1969.

Benedict, Michael Les. *A Compromise of Principle: Congressional Republicans and Reconstruction, 1863–1869*. New York: W. W. Norton, 1974.

——. *The Fruits of Victory: Alternatives in Restoring the Union, 1865–1877*. Lanham, Md.: University Press of America, 1986.

Bernard, Bertram M. *Election Laws of the Forty-eight States: How to Register and Vote*. New York: Oceana, 1950.

Berry, Mary Frances. *Military Necessity and Civil Rights Policy: Black Citizenship and the Constitution, 1861–1868*. Port Washington, N.Y.: Kennikat, 1977.

Bishop, Cortlandt F. *History of Elections in the American Colonies*. New York: Columbia College, 1893.

Blue, Frederick, Jr. *Salmon P. Chase: A Life in Politics*. Kent, Ohio: Kent State University Press, 1987.

Bogue, Allan G. *The Earnest Men: Republicans of the Civil War Senate*. Ithaca, N.Y.: Cornell University Press, 1981.

Bowers, Claude G. *The Tragic Era: The Revolution after Lincoln*. Cambridge, Mass.: Riverside, 1929.

Braxton, A. Caperton. *The Fifteenth Amendment: An Account of Its Enactment*. 1903. Reprint, Lynchburg, Va.: J. P. Bell, 1934.

Brock, William R. *An American Crisis: Congress and Reconstruction, 1865–1867*. New York: St. Martin's, 1963.

Brown, Thomas H. *George Sewall Boutwell: Human Rights Advocate*. Groton, Mass.: Groton Historical Society, 1989.

Buck, Paul H. *The Road to Reunion: 1865–1900*. Boston: Little, Brown, 1937.

Burgess, John W. *The Administration of President Hayes*. New York: Charles Scribner's Sons, 1916.

———. *Reconstruction and the Constitution, 1866–1876*. New York: Charles Scribner's Sons, 1902.

Burnham, W. Dean. *Presidential Ballots, 1836–1892*. Baltimore: Johns Hopkins University Press, 1955.

Cain, Marvin R. *Lincoln's Attorney General: Edward Bates of Missouri*. Columbia: University of Missouri Press, 1965.

Caldwell, Robert G. *James A. Garfield, Party Chieftain*. New York: Dodd, Mead, & Co., 1931.

Chamber, William N., and Walter D. Burnham, eds. *The American Party Systems: Stages of Political Development*. 2d ed. New York: Oxford University Press, 1975.

Christopher, Maurine. *Black Americans in Congress*. New York: Thomas Y. Crowell, 1976.

Church, Charles A. *History of the Republican Party in Illinois, 1854–1912*. Rockford, Ill.: Press of Wilson Brothers Co., 1912.

Clapp, Margaret Antoinette. *Forgotten First Citizen: John Bigelow*. 1947. Reprint, New York: Greenwood, 1968.

Claude, Richard. *The Supreme Court and the Electoral Process*. Baltimore: Johns Hopkins University Press, 1970.

Clemenceau, George. *American Reconstruction, 1865–1870*. 1928. Reprint, New York: Dial Press, 1969.

Coakley, Robert W. *The Role of Federal Military Forces in Domestic Disorder, 1789–1878*. Washington, D.C.: Center of Military History, United States Army, 1988.

Coleman, Charles H. *The Election of 1868: The Democratic Effort to Regain Control*. New York: Columbia University Press, 1933.

Cox, LaWanda. *Lincoln and Black Freedom: A Study in Presidential Leadership*. Urbana: University of Illinois Press, 1985.

Cox, LaWanda, and John H. Cox. *Politics, Principle, and Prejudice, 1865–1866: Dilemma of Reconstruction America*. New York: Free Press of Glencoe, 1963.

———, eds. *Reconstruction, the Negro, and the New South*. Columbia: University of South Carolina Press, 1973.

Cresswell, Stephen. *Mormons and Cowboys, Moonshiners and Klansmen: Federal Law Enforcement in the South and West, 1870–1893*. Tuscaloosa: University of Alabama Press, 1991.

Cruden, Robert. *The Negro in Reconstruction.* Englewood Cliffs, N.J.: Prentice-Hall, 1969.

Cummings, Homer, and Carl McFarland. *Federal Justice: Chapters in the History of Justice and the Federal Executive.* New York: Macmillan, 1937.

Curry, Richard O., ed. *Radicalism, Racism, and Party Realignment: The Border States during Reconstruction.* Baltimore: Johns Hopkins University Press, 1969.

Daniels, Roger. *Asian America: Chinese and Japanese in the United States since 1850.* Seattle: University of Washington Press, 1988.

Davison, Kenneth E. *The Presidency of Rutherford B. Hayes.* Westport, Conn.: Greenwood, 1972.

Dawson, Joseph G., III. *Army Generals and Reconstruction.* Baton Rouge: Louisiana State University Press, 1982.

De Santis, Vincent P. *Republicans Face the Southern Question: The New Departure Years, 1877–1897.* Baltimore: Johns Hopkins University Press, 1959.

Dinkin, Robert J. *Voting in Revolutionary America: A Study of Elections in the Original Thirteen States, 1776–1789.* Westport, Conn.: Greenwood, 1982.

Doenecke, Justus D. *The Presidencies of James A. Garfield and Chester A. Arthur.* Lawrence: Regents Press of Kansas, 1981.

Donald, David H. *Charles Sumner and the Rights of Man.* New York: Alfred A. Knopf, 1970.

——. *Lincoln Reconsidered: Essays on the Civil War Era.* 1956. Reprint, New York: Vintage, 1989.

——. *The Politics of Reconstruction, 1863–1867.* Baton Rouge: Louisiana State University Press, 1965.

Drago, Edmund L. *Black Politicians and Reconstruction in Georgia: A Splendid Failure.* Baton Rouge: Louisiana State University Press, 1982.

Du Bois, W. E. Burghardt. *Black Reconstruction: An Essay toward a History of the Part Which Black Folk Played in the Attempt to Reconstruct Democracy in America, 1860–1880.* New York: Harcourt, Brace, 1935.

Dunham, Allison, and Philip B. Kurland, eds. *Mr. Justice.* Chicago: University of Chicago Press, 1964.

Dunn, Arthur Wallace. *From Harrison to Harding: A Personal Narrative, Covering a Third of a Century, 1888–1921.* 1921. Reprint, Port Washington, N.Y.: Kennikat, 1971.

Dunning, William Archibald. *Essays on the Civil War and Reconstruction and Related Topics.* 1897. Reprint, New York: Harper & Row, 1965.

——. *Reconstruction, Political and Economic, 1865–1877.* New York: Harper & Brothers, 1907.

Elliot, Ward E. Y. *The Rise of Guardian Democracy: The Supreme Court's Role in Voting Rights Disputes, 1845–1969.* Cambridge: Harvard University Press, 1974.

Elliott, Russell. *Servant of Power: A Political Biography of Senator William M. Stewart.* Reno: University of Nevada Press, 1983.

Ellis, Elmer. *Henry Moore Teller, Defender of the West.* Caldwell, Idaho: Caxton Printers, 1941.

Fairman, Charles. *Mr. Justice Miller and the Supreme Court, 1862–1890.* Cambridge: Harvard University Press, 1939.

——. *Reconstruction and Reunion: 1864–1888.* New York: Macmillan, 1971.

Fehrenbacher, Don E. *The Dred Scott Case: Its Significance in American Law and Politics.* New York: Oxford University Press, 1978.

Field, Phyllis F. *The Politics of Race in New York: The Struggle for Black Suffrage in the Civil War Era.* Ithaca, N.Y.: Cornell University Press, 1982.

Finkelman, Paul, ed. *Race, Law, and American History, 1700–1990.* Vol. 6, *African Americans and the Right to Vote.* New York: Garland, 1992.

Flack, Horace Edgar. *The Adoption of the Fourteenth Amendment.* Baltimore: Johns Hopkins Press, 1908.

Fleming, Walter L. *Sequel of Appomattox: A Chronicle of the Reunion of the States.* New Haven: Yale University Press, 1919.

Foner, Eric. *Freedom's Lawmakers: A Directory of Black Officeholders during Reconstruction.* New York: Oxford University Press, 1993.

——. *Free Soil, Free Labor, Free Men: The Ideology of the Republican Party before the Civil War.* New York: Oxford University Press, 1970.

——. *Nothing but Freedom: Emancipation and Its Legacy.* Baton Rouge: Louisiana State University Press, 1983.

——. *Reconstruction: America's Unfinished Revolution, 1863–1877.* New York: Harper & Row, 1988.

Foner, Eric, and John A. Garraty, eds. *The Reader's Companion to American History.* Boston: Houghton Mifflin, 1991.

Ford, Henry Jones. *The Cleveland Era: A Chronicle of the New Order in Politics.* New Haven: Yale University Press, 1919.

Fowler, Dorothy Ganfield. *John Coit Spooner: Defender of Presidents.* New York: University Publishers, 1961.

Franklin, Frank George. *The Legislative History of Naturalization in the United States.* Chicago: University of Chicago Press, 1906.

Franklin, John Hope. *Reconstruction: After the Civil War.* Chicago: University of Chicago Press, 1961.

Fredrickson, George M. *The Black Image in the White Mind: The Debate on Afro-American Character and Destiny, 1817–1914.* New York: Harper & Row, 1971.

Friedman, Lawrence M. *A History of American Law.* New York: Simon and Schuster, 1985.

Friedman, Leon, and Fred L. Israel, eds. *The Justices of the United States Supreme Court, 1789–1969: Their Lives and Major Opinions.* New York: R. R. Bowker, 1969.

Garner, James W., ed. *Studies in Southern History and Politics Inscribed to William Archibald Dunning . . . by His Former Pupils.* 1914. Reprint, Port Washington, N.Y.: Kennikat, 1964.

Garraty, John. *Henry Cabot Lodge: A Biography.* New York: Alfred A. Knopf, 1953.

Gettys, Luella. *The Law of Citizenship in the United States.* Chicago: University of Chicago Press, 1934.

Gienapp, William E. *The Origins of the Republican Party, 1852–1856.* New York: Oxford University Press, 1987.

Gillette, William. *Retreat from Reconstruction, 1869–1879.* Baton Rouge: Louisiana State University Press, 1979.

——. *The Right to Vote: Politics and the Passage of the Fifteenth Amendment.* Baltimore: Johns Hopkins University Press, 1965.

Goldman, Robert Michael. *"A Free Ballot and a Fair Count": The Department of Justice and the Enforcement of Voting Rights in the South, 1877–1893*. New York: Garland, 1990.

Gould, Lewis L. *The Presidency of Theodore Roosevelt*. Lawrence: University Press of Kansas, 1991.

———. *The Presidency of William McKinley*. Lawrence: Regents Press of Kansas, 1980.

Graff, Henry F., ed. *The Presidents: A Reference History*. New York: Charles Scribner's Sons, 1984.

Grimes, Alan P. *Democracy and the Amendments to the Constitution*. Lexington, Mass.: Lexington Books, 1978.

Grofman, Bernard, and Chandler Davidson, eds. *Controversies in Minority Voting: The Voting Rights Act in Perspective*. Washington, D.C.: Brookings Institution, 1992.

Hall, Kermit, William M. Wiecek, and Paul Finkelman. *American Legal History: Cases and Materials*. New York: Oxford University Press, 1991.

Hamilton, Charles V. *The Bench and the Ballot: Southern Federal Judges and Black Voters*. New York: Oxford University Press, 1973.

Hamilton, James Albert. *Negro Suffrage and Congressional Representation*. New York: Winthrop Press, 1910.

Haskins, James. *Pinckney Benton Stewart Pinchback*. New York: Macmillan, 1973.

Henig, Gerald S. *Henry Winter Davis: Antebellum and Civil War Congressman from Maryland*. New York: Twayne, 1973.

Hesseltine, William B. *Ulysses S. Grant, Politician*. New York: Dodd, Mead, & Co., 1935.

Hirshson, Stanley P. *Farewell to the Bloody Shirt: Northern Republicans and the Southern Negro, 1877–1893*. Bloomington: Indiana University Press, 1962.

Hoemann, George H. *What God Hath Wrought: The Embodiment of Freedom in the Thirteenth Amendment*. New York: Garland, 1987.

Hofstadter, Richard. *Social Darwinism in American Thought*. Boston: Beacon Press, 1955.

Holt, Michael F. *Forging a Majority: The Formation of the Republican Party in Pittsburgh, 1848–1860*. New Haven: Yale University Press, 1969.

Hoogenboom, Ari. *The Presidency of Rutherford B. Hayes*. Lawrence: University Press of Kansas, 1988.

Horn, Stanley F. *Invisible Empire: The Story of the Ku Klux Klan, 1866–1871*. Cos Cob, Conn.: John E. Edwards, 1969.

Howe, George Frederick. *Chester A. Arthur: A Quarter-Century of Machine Politics*. New York: Frederick Ungar, 1957.

Hutchinson, Edward P. *Legislative History of American Immigration Policy, 1789–1965*. Philadelphia: University of Pennsylvania Press, 1981.

Hyman, Harold M. *A More Perfect Union: The Impact of the Civil War and Reconstruction on the Constitution*. New York: Alfred A. Knopf, 1973.

———. *The Radical Republicans and Reconstruction, 1861–1870*. Indianapolis: Bobbs-Merrill, 1967.

Hyman, Harold M., and William M. Wiecek. *Equal Justice under Law: Constitutional Development, 1835–1875*. New York: Harper & Row, 1982.

Jackson, Carlton. *Presidential Vetoes, 1792–1945*. Athens: University of Georgia Press, 1967.

James, Joseph B. *The Framing of the Fourteenth Amendment.* Urbana: University of Illinois Press, 1956.

——. *The Ratification of the Fourteenth Amendment.* Macon, Ga.: Mercer University Press, 1984.

Jones, James Pickett. *John A. Logan, Stalwart Republican from Illinois.* Tallahassee: University Presses of Florida, 1982.

Jones, Stanley L. *The Presidential Election of 1896.* Madison: University of Wisconsin Press, 1964.

Jordan, David M. *Roscoe Conkling of New York: Voice in the Senate.* Ithaca, N.Y.: Cornell University Press, 1971.

Kaczorowski, Robert J. *The Nationalization of Civil Rights: Constitutional Theory and Practice in a Racist Society, 1866–1883.* New York: Garland, 1987.

——. *The Politics of Judicial Interpretation: The Federal Court, the Department of Justice, and Civil Rights, 1866–1876.* New York: Oceana, 1985.

Kehl, James A. *Boss Rule in the Gilded Age: Matt Quay of Pennsylvania.* Pittsburgh: University of Pittsburgh Press, 1981.

Kettner, James H. *The Development of American Citizenship, 1608–1870.* Chapel Hill: University of North Carolina Press, 1978.

Kleegberg, Gordon S. P. *The Formation of the Republican Party as a National Political Organization.* 1911. Reprint, New York: Lenox Hill, 1970.

Knoles, George Harmon. *The Presidential Campaign and Election of 1892.* Stanford: Stanford University Press, 1942.

Kousser, J. Morgan. *The Shaping of Southern Politics: Suffrage Restriction and the Establishment of the One-Party South, 1880–1910.* New Haven: Yale University Press, 1974.

Kousser, J. Morgan, and James McPherson, eds. *Region, Race, and Reconstruction.* New York: Oxford University Press, 1982.

Kutler, Stanley I. *Judicial Power and Reconstruction Politics.* Chicago: University of Chicago Press, 1967.

Lawson, Steven F. *Black Ballots: Voting Rights in the South, 1944–1969.* New York: Columbia University Press, 1976.

Leech, Margaret, and Harry J. Brown. *The Garfield Orbit.* New York: Harper & Row, 1978.

Lewinson, Paul. *Race, Class, and Party: A History of Negro Suffrage and White Politics in the South.* 1932. Reprint, New York: Russell & Russell, 1963.

Lewis, Frederick P. *The Dilemma in the Congressional Power to Enforce the Fourteenth Amendment.* Washington, D.C.: University Press of America, 1980.

Litwack, Leon F. *North of Slavery: The Negro in the Free States, 1790–1860.* Chicago: University of Chicago Press, 1961.

Logan, Rayford W. *The Betrayal of the Negro: From Rutherford B. Hayes to Woodrow Wilson.* 1954. Reprint, New York: Collier Books, 1968.

Lunde, Erik S. *Horace Greeley.* Boston: Twayne, 1981.

Lyman, Stanford M. *The Asian in the West.* Reno: Western Studies Center, Desert Research Institute, University of Nevada, 1970.

Magrath, Peter C. *Morrison R. Waite: The Triumph of Character.* New York: Macmillan, 1963.

Marcus, Robert D. *Grand Old Party: Politics Structure in the Gilded Age, 1880–1896.* New York: Oxford University Press, 1971.

Mason, Edward Campbell. *The Veto Power: Its Origin, Development, and Function in the Government of the United States (1789-1889).* Boston: Ginn & Co., 1891.

Mathews, John Mabry. *Legislative and Judicial History of the Fifteenth Amendment.* Baltimore: Johns Hopkins Press, 1909.

Maxson, Charles Hartshorn. *Citizenship.* New York: Oxford University Press, 1930.

Mayer, George H. *The Republican Party, 1854-1966.* 2d ed. New York: Oxford University Press, 1967.

McCall, Samuel W. *The Life of Thomas Brackett Reed.* Boston: Houghton Mifflin, 1914.

McCulloch, Albert J. *Suffrage and Its Problems.* Baltimore: Warwick and York, 1929.

McFeely, William S. *Grant: A Biography.* New York: W. W. Norton, 1981.

McGovney, Dudley O. *The American Suffrage Medley.* Chicago: University of Chicago Press, 1949.

McKay, Ernest. *Henry Wilson: Practical Radical: A Portrait of a Politician.* Port Washington, N.Y.: Kennikat, 1971.

McKinley, Albert E. *The Suffrage Franchise in the Thirteen Colonies in America.* Boston: Ginn and Com. Agents, 1905.

McKitrick, Eric L. *Andrew Johnson and Reconstruction.* Chicago: University of Chicago Press, 1960.

McMath, Robert C., Jr. *American Populism: A Social History, 1877-1898.* New York: Hill and Wang, 1993.

McPherson, James M. *The Abolitionist Legacy: From Reconstruction to the NAACP.* Princeton: Princeton University Press, 1975.

——. *Battle Cry of Freedom: The Civil War Era.* New York: Oxford University Press, 1988.

——. *The Negro's Civil War: How American Negroes Felt and Acted during the War for the Union.* New York: Pantheon Books, 1965.

——. *Ordeal by Fire: The Civil War and Reconstruction.* New York: Alfred A. Knopf, 1982.

——. *The Struggle for Equality: Abolitionists and the Negro in the Civil War and Reconstruction.* Princeton: Princeton University Press, 1964.

McWhiney, Grady, ed. *Reconstruction and the Freedmen.* Chicago: Rand McNally, 1963.

Mohr, James C. *The Radical Republicans and Reform in New York during Reconstruction.* Ithaca, N.Y.: Cornell University Press, 1973.

——, ed. *Radical Republicans in the North: State Politics during Reconstruction.* Baltimore: Johns Hopkins University Press, 1976.

Moos, Malcolm. *The Republicans: A History of Their Party.* New York: Random House, 1956.

Morgan, H. Wayne. *From Hayes to McKinley: National Party Politics, 1877-1896.* Syracuse: Syracuse University Press, 1969.

Muzzey, David Saville. *James G. Blaine: A Political Idol of Other Days.* New York: Dodd, Mead, & Co., 1934.

Naar, M. D. *The Law of Suffrage and Elections.* 1880. Reprint, Littleton, Colo.: Fred B. Rothman & Co., 1985.

Nelson, William E. *The Fourteenth Amendment: From Political Principle to Judicial Doctrine.* Cambridge: Harvard University Press, 1988.

Nevins, Allan. *Hamilton Fish: The Inner History of the Grant Administration.* New York: Dodd, Mead, & Co., 1936.

Olbrich, Emil. *The Development of Sentiment on Negro Suffrage to 1860.* 1912. Reprint, New York: Negro Universities Press, 1969.

Patterson, Samuel Charles, Roger H. Davidson, and Randall B. Ripley. *A More Perfect Union: Introduction to American Government.* 4th ed. Pacific Grove, Calif.: Brooks/Cole, 1989.

Perman, Michael. *Reunion without Compromise: The South and Reconstruction, 1865–1868.* Cambridge: Cambridge University Press, 1973.

——. *The Road to Redemption: Southern Politics, 1869–1879.* Chapel Hill: University of North Carolina Press, 1984.

Peskin, Allan. *Garfield: A Biography.* Kent, Ohio: Kent State University Press, 1978.

Polakoff, Keith Ian. *The Politics of Inertia: The Election of 1876 and the End of Reconstruction.* Baton Rouge: Louisiana State University Press, 1973.

Porter, Kirk H. *A History of Suffrage in the United States.* Chicago: University of Chicago Press, 1918.

Rable, George C. *But There Was No Peace: The Role of Violence in the Politics of Reconstruction.* Athens: University of Georgia Press, 1984.

Reeves, Thomas C. *Gentleman Boss: The Life of Chester Alan Arthur.* New York: Alfred A. Knopf, 1975.

Richardson, Leon Burr. *William E. Chandler, Republican.* New York: Dodd, Mead, & Co., 1940.

Riddleberger, Patrick W. *1866: The Critical Year Revisited.* Carbondale: Southern Illinois University Press, 1979.

——. *George Washington Julian Radical Republican: A Study in Nineteenth-Century Politics and Reform.* [Indianapolis:] Indiana Historical Bureau, 1966.

Rogers, Donald W., ed. *Voting, the Spirit of American Democracy: Essays on the History of Voting and Voting Rights in America.* Urbana: University of Illinois Press, 1992.

Ross, Earle Dudley. *The Liberal Republican Movement.* New York: Henry Holt, 1919.

Sage, Leland L. *William Boyd Allison: A Study in Practical Politics.* Iowa City: State Historical Society of Iowa, 1956.

Satcher, Buford. *Blacks in Mississippi Politics, 1865–1900.* Washington, D.C.: University Press of America, 1978.

Sefton, James E. *The United States Army and Reconstruction, 1865–1877.* Baton Rouge: Louisiana State University Press, 1967.

Sherman, Richard B. *The Republican Party and Black America: From McKinley to Hoover.* Charlottesville: University Press of Virginia, 1973.

Sievers, Harry J. *Benjamin Harrison, Hoosier Statesman: From the Civil War to the White House, 1865–1888.* New York: University Publishers, 1959.

Silbey, Joel H. *A Respectable Minority: The Democratic Party in the Civil War Era, 1860–1868.* New York: W. W. Norton, 1977.

Smith, Constance E. *Voting and Election Laws.* New York: Oceana, 1960.

Smith, Samuel Denny. *The Negro in Congress, 1870–1901.* 1940. Reprint, Port Washington, N.Y.: Kennikat, 1966.

Socolofsky, Homer E., and Allen B. Spetter. *The Presidency of Benjamin Harrison.* Lawrence: University Press of Kansas, 1987.

Sproat, John G. *"The Best Men": Liberal Reformers in the Gilded Age.* 1968. Reprint, Chicago: University of Chicago Press, 1982.

Stampp, Kenneth M. *The Era of Reconstruction, 1865–1877.* New York: Vintage, 1965.

Stanwood, James. *James Gillespie Blaine.* Boston: Houghton Mifflin, 1905.

Steiner, Bernard C. *Life of Reverdy Johnson.* Baltimore: Norman, Remington Co., 1914.

Stephenson, Gilbert Thomas. *Race Distinctions in American Law.* New York: D. Appleton and Co., 1910.

Summers, Mark W. *Railroads, Reconstruction, and the Gospel of Prosperity: Aid under the Radical Republicans, 1865–1877.* Princeton: Princeton University Press, 1984.

Swinney, Everette. *Suppressing the Ku Klux Klan: The Enforcement of the Reconstruction Amendments, 1870–1877.* New York: Garland, 1987.

Swisher, Carl Bent. *Stephen J. Field: Craftsman of the Law.* Washington, D.C.: Brookings Institution, 1930.

Taylor, Alrutheus A. *The Negro in South Carolina during the Reconstruction.* Washington, D.C.: Association for the Study of Negro Life and History, 1924.

Taylor, John M. *Garfield of Ohio: The Available Man.* New York: W. W. Norton, 1970.

Ten Broek, Jacobus. *The Antislavery Origins of the Fourteenth Amendment.* Berkeley and Los Angeles: University of California Press, 1951.

Trefousse, Hans L. *Carl Schurz, a Biography.* Knoxville: University of Tennessee Press, 1982.

——. *The Radical Republicans: Lincoln's Vanguard for Racial Justice.* New York: Alfred A. Knopf, 1969.

——. *Reconstruction: America's First Efforts at Racial Democracy.* New York: Van Nostrand Reinhold, 1971.

Trelease, Allen W. *White Terror: The Ku Klux Klan Conspiracy and Southern Reconstruction.* New York: Harper & Row, 1971.

Tutorow, Norman E. *James Gillespie Blaine and the Presidency: A Documentary Study and Source Book.* New York: Peter Lang, 1989.

Van Deusen, Glyndon G. *Thurlow Weed: Wizard of the Lobby.* Boston: Little, Brown, 1947.

Vincent, Charles. *Black Legislators in Louisiana during Reconstruction.* Baton Rouge: Louisiana State University Press, 1976.

Wallace, David Duncan. *The South Carolina Constitution of 1895.* Columbia: Bureau of Publications, University of South Carolina, 1927.

Ware, Edith Ellen. *Political Opinion in Massachusetts during Civil War and Reconstruction.* New York: Columbia University Press, 1916.

Welch, Richard E., Jr. *George Frisbie Hoar and the Half-Breed Republicans.* Cambridge: Harvard University Press, 1971.

——. *The Presidencies of Grover Cleveland.* Lawrence: University Press of Kansas, 1988.

Weymouth, Lally. *America in 1876: The Way We Were.* New York: Random House, 1976.

White, G. Edward. *The American Judicial Tradition: Profiles of Leading American Judges.* 1976. Reprint, New York: Oxford University Press, 1988.

White, Leonard D. *The Republican Era: 1869–1901: A Study in Administrative History.* New York: Macmillan, 1958.

Williamson, Chilton. *American Suffrage from Property to Democracy, 1760–1860.* Princeton: Princeton University Press, 1960.

Williamson, Joel. *After Slavery: The Negro in South Carolina during Reconstruction, 1861–1877.* Chapel Hill: University of North Carolina Press, 1965.

Woodward, C. Vann. *Origins of the New South, 1877–1913.* 1951. Reprint, Baton Rouge: Louisiana State University Press, 1971.

———. *Reunion and Reaction: The Compromise of 1877 and the End of Reconstruction.* Boston: Little, Brown, 1951.

ARTICLES

Beale, Howard K. "On Writing Reconstruction History." *American Historical Review* 45 (July 1940): 807–27.

Belz, Herman. "Origins of Negro Suffrage during the Civil War." *Southern Studies* 17 (Summer 1978): 115–30.

Benedict, Michael Les. "Equality and Expediency in the Reconstruction Era: A Review Essay." *Civil War History* 23 (December 1977): 322-25.

———. "Preserving Federalism: Reconstruction and the Waite Court." *Supreme Court Review* (1978): 39-79.

———. "Southern Democrats in the Crisis of 1876–1877: A Reconsideration of *Reunion and Reaction.*" *Journal of Southern History* 46 (1980): 429–524.

Blackburn, George M. "Radical Republican Motivation: A Case History." *Journal of Negro History* 54 (April 1969): 109–26.

Brown, Iro V. "Pennsylvania and the Rights of the Negro, 1865–1887." *Pennsylvania History* 28 (January 1961): 45-57.

Cox, LaWanda, and John H. Cox. "Negro Suffrage and Republican Politics: The Problem of Motivation in Reconstruction Historiography." *Journal of Southern History* 33 (August 1967): 303-30.

Cresswell, Stephen. "Enforcing the Enforcement Acts: The Department of Justice in Northern Mississippi, 1870–1890." *Journal of Southern History* 53 (August 1987): 421-40.

Currie, James T. "From Slavery to Freedom in Mississippi's Legal System." *Journal of Negro History* 65 (Spring 1980): 112–25.

Curry, Richard O. "The Civil War and Reconstruction, 1861–1877: A Critical Overview of Recent Trends and Interpretations." *Civil War History* 20 (September 1974): 215–38.

Davidson, Chandler. "The Voting Rights Act: A Brief History." In *Controversies in Minority Voting: The Voting Rights Act in Perspective*, ed. Bernard Grofman and Chandler Davidson, 7–51 (Washington, D.C.: Brookings Institution, 1992).

De Santis, Vincent P. "Negro Dissatisfaction with Republican Policy in the South, 1882–1884." *Journal of Negro History* 36 (April 1951): 148–59.

———. "President Hayes's Southern Policy." *Journal of Southern History* 21 (November 1955): 476–94.

———. "The Republican Party and the Southern Negro, 1877–1897." *Journal of Negro History* 45 (April 1960): 71–87.

Dunbar, Willis F., and William G. Shade. "The Black Man Gains the Vote: The Centennial of 'Impartial Suffrage' in Michigan." *Michigan History* 56 (Spring 1972): 42–57.

Dykstra, Robert R. "The Issue Squarely Met: Toward an Explanation of Iowans' Racial Attitudes, 1865–1868." *Annals of Iowa* 47 (1984): 430–50.

Eaton, Amasa M. "The Suffrage Clause of the New Constitution of Louisiana." *Harvard Law Review* 13 (1899): 3–17.

Field, Phyllis F. "Republicans and Black Suffrage in New York State: The Grass Roots Response." *Civil War History* 21 (June 1975): 136–47.

Fields, Barbara J. "Slavery, Race, and Ideology in the United States of America." *New Left Review* 181 (May/June 1990): 95–118.

Finkelman, Paul. "Prelude to the Fourteenth Amendment: Black Legal Rights in the Antebellum North." *Rutgers Law Journal* 17 (1986): 415–82.

Fishel, Leslie H., Jr. "Northern Prejudice and Negro Suffrage, 1865–1870." *Journal of Negro History* 39 (January 1954): 8–26.

Foner, Eric. "Reconstruction Revisited." *Reviews in American History* 10 (December 1982): 82–100.

Formisano, Ronald P. "The Edge of Caste: Colored Suffrage in Michigan, 1827–1861." *Michigan History* 56 (Spring 1972): 19–41.

Franklin, John Hope. "Legal Disfranchisement of the Negro." *Journal of Negro Education* 26 (Spring 1956): 241–68.

Frasure, Carl M. "Charles Sumner and the Rights of the Negro." *Journal of Negro History* 13 (April 1928): 126–49.

Fredrickson, George M. "A Man but Not a Brother: Abraham Lincoln and Racial Equality." *Journal of Southern History* 41 (February 1975): 39–58.

Hall, Kermit L. "Political Power and Constitutional Legitimacy: The South Carolina Ku Klux Klan Trials, 1871–1872." *Emory Law Journal* 32 (Fall 1984): 923–51.

Hiller, Amy M. "The Disfranchisement of Delaware Negroes in the Late Nineteenth Century." *Delaware History* 13 (October 1968): 124–53.

Kaczorowski, Robert J. "Revolutionary Constitutionalism in the Era of the Civil War and Reconstruction." *New York University Law Review* 61 (November 1986): 836–940.

———. "To Begin the Nation Anew: Congress, Citizenship, and Civil Rights after the Civil War." *American Historical Review* 92 (February 1987): 45–68.

Kousser, J. Morgan. "The Voting Rights Act and the Two Reconstructions." In *Controversies in Minority Voting: The Voting Rights Act in Perspective*, ed. Bernard Grofman and Chandler Davidson, 135–75 (Washington, D.C.: Brookings Institution, 1992).

Linden, Glenn M. "A Note on Negro Suffrage and Republican Politics." *Journal of Southern History* 36 (August 1970): 412–20.

Mabry, William Alexander. "Disfranchisement of the Negro in Mississippi." *Journal of Southern History* 4 (1938): 318–33.

Maltz, Earl M. "Slavery, Federalism, and the Structure of the Constitution." *American Journal of Legal History* 34 (October 1992): 466–98.

Meier, August. "Negroes in the First and Second Reconstructions of the South." *Civil War History* 13 (June 1967): 114–30.

Nieman, Donald G. "Andrew Johnson, the Freedmen's Bureau, and the Problem of Equal Rights, 1865–1866." *Journal of Southern History* 44 (August 1978): 399–420.

Price, Edward. "The Black Voting Rights Issue in Pennsylvania, 1700 – 1900." *Pennsylvania Magazine of History and Biography* 100 (July 1976): 356 – 73.

Quarles, Benjamin. "Frederick Douglass and the Woman's Rights Movement." *Journal of Negro History* 25 (January 1940): 35 – 44.

Rable, George. "Southern Interests and the Election of 1876: A Reappraisal." *Civil War History* 26 (1980): 347 – 61.

Riddleberger, Patrick. "Republican Abandonment of the Negro during the Reconstruction." *Journal of Negro History* 45 (April 1960): 88 – 102.

Shugg, Roger Wallace. "Negro Voting in the Ante-Bellum South." *Journal of Negro History* 21 (October 1936): 357 – 64.

Stone, James H. "A Note on Voter Registration under the Mississippi Understanding Clause, 1892." *Journal of Southern History* 38 (May 1972): 293 – 96.

Swinney, Everette. "Enforcing the Fifteenth Amendment, 1870 – 1877." *Journal of Southern History* 28 (May 1962): 202 – 18.

Tindall, George B. "The Campaign for the Disfranchisement of Negroes in South Carolina." *Journal of Southern History* 15 (May 1949): 213-34.

Weisberger, Bernard A. "The Dark and Bloody Ground of Reconstruction Historiography." *Journal of Southern History* 25 (November 1959): 427 – 47.

Welch, Richard E., Jr. "The Federal Election Bill of 1890: Postscripts and Prelude." *Journal of American History* 52 (December 1965): 511 – 26.

Wellborn, Fred A. "The Influence of the Silver-Republican Senators, 1889 – 1891." *Mississippi Valley Historical Review* 14 (1927 – 28): 462 – 80.

Wesley, Charles H. "Negro Suffrage in the Period of Constitution-Making, 1787 – 1865." *Journal of Negro History* 32 (April 1947): 143 – 68.

Wiecek, William. "The Reconstruction of Federal Judicial Power, 1863 – 1875." *American Journal of Legal History* 13 (1969): 333 – 59.

Williams, Frank B., Jr. "The Poll Tax as a Suffrage Requirement in the South, 1870 – 1901." *Journal of Southern History* 18 (November 1952): 469 – 96.

Wright, Marion Thompson. "Negro Suffrage in New Jersey, 1776 – 1875." *Journal of Negro History* 33 (April 1948): 168 – 224.

Wubben, Hubert H. "The Uncertain Trumpet: Iowa Republicans and Black Suffrage, 1860 – 1868." *Annals of Iowa* 47 (1984): 409 – 29.

DISSERTATIONS

Black, Ernest Patrick. "The Reconstruction Dilemma: Northern Theory and Southern Tragedy." Ph.D. diss., University of New York at Buffalo, 1983.

Brittain, Joseph Matt. "Negro Suffrage and Politics in Alabama since 1870." Ph.D. diss., Indiana University, 1958.

Burke, Albie. "Federal Regulation of Congressional Elections in Northern Cities, 1871 – 1894." Ph.D. diss., University of Chicago, 1968.

Christensen, Janice Evelyn. "The Constitutional Problems of National Control of the Suffrage in the United States." Ph.D. diss., University of Minnesota, 1952.

Cohen, Roger Alan. "The Lost Jubilee: New York Republicans and the Politics of Reconstruction and Reform, 1867 – 1878." Ph.D. diss., Columbia University, 1976.

Cook, Robert L. "Puritans, Pragmatists, and Progress: The Republican Coalition in Iowa, 1854 – 1878." D. Phil. diss., Oxford University, 1986.

Dotson, David Wendell. "Henry Cabot Lodge: A Political Biography, 1887 – 1901." Ph.D. diss., University of Oklahoma, 1980.

Dwight, Margaret L. "Black Suffrage in Missouri, 1865 – 1877." Ph.D. diss., University of Missouri, 1978.

Fishel, Leslie H. "The North and the Negro, 1865 – 1890." Ph.D. diss., Harvard University, 1954.

Hamilton, Howard Devon. "The Legislative and Judicial History of the Thirteenth Amendment." Ph.D. diss., University of Illinois, 1950.

Henry, George Selden, Jr. "Radical Republican Policy toward the Negro during Reconstruction (1862 – 1872)." Ph.D. diss., Yale University, 1963.

Horn, Robert A. "National Control of Congressional Elections." Ph.D. diss., Princeton University, 1942.

McBride, William Gillespie. "Blacks and the Race Issue in Tennessee Politics, 1865 – 1876." Ph.D. diss., Vanderbilt University, 1989.

McCarthy, John Lockhart. "Reconstruction Legislation and Voting Alignments in the House of Representatives, 1863 – 1869." Ph.D. diss., Yale University, 1971.

Miller, Clark Leonard. "'Let Us Die to Make Men Free': Political Terrorism in Post-Reconstruction Mississippi, 1877 – 1896." Ph.D. diss., University of Minnesota, 1983.

Mittrick, Robert. "A History of Negro Voting in Pennsylvania during the Nineteenth Century." Ph.D. diss., Rutgers University, 1985.

Nicklas, F. William. "William D. Kelley: The Congressional Years, 1861 – 1890." Ph.D. diss., Northern Illinois University, 1983.

Nolen, Claude Hunter. "Aftermath of Slavery, Southern Attitudes toward Negroes, 1865 – 1900." Ph.D. diss., University of Texas at Austin, 1963.

Otten, James T. "Grand Old Partyman: William A. Wheeler and the Republican Party, 1850 – 1880." Ph.D. diss., University of South Carolina, 1976.

Poole, William Joseph. "Race and the Chicago Press, 1850 – 1877." Ph.D. diss., University of Chicago, 1973.

Rusk, Jerrold Glenn. "The Effect of the Australian Ballot Reform on Split Ticket Voting: 1876 – 1908." Ph.D. diss., University of Michigan, 1968.

Salisbury, Robert Seward. "William Windom, the Republican Party, and the Gilded Age." Ph.D. diss., University of Minnesota, 1982.

Sanelli, Thomas A. "The Struggle for Black Suffrage in Pennsylvania, 1838 – 1870." Ph.D. diss., Temple University, 1977.

Swinney, Everette. "Suppressing the Ku Klux Klan: The Enforcement of the Reconstruction Amendments, 1870 – 1874." Ph.D. diss., University of Texas at Austin, 1966.

Tomlinson, Kenneth Larry. "Indiana Republicans and the Negro Suffrage Issue, 1865 – 1867." Ph.D. diss., Ball State University, 1971.

White, Edward A. "The Republican Party in National Politics, 1888 – 1891." Ph.D. diss., University of Minnesota, 1941.

Williams, Lou Falkner. "The Great South Carolina Ku Klux Klan Trials, 1871 – 1872." Ph.D. diss., University of Florida, 1991.

INDEX

Abolitionism, 1, 6–7, 156

Adams, Charles Francis, Jr., 103

African Americans. *See* Blacks

Akerman, Amos T., 96–97, 101, 107, 156, 340 (n. 16)

Alabama, 140, 181, 244, 249, 255; blacks and Reconstruction in, 40; Democrats' control of, 79, 111; black disfranchisement in, 260

Albright, Charles, 117

Aldrich, Nelson, 248–49

Allison, William B., 226

Amendments, constitutional, 21, 42, 312 (n. 45). *See also* Fifteenth Amendment; Fourteenth Amendment; Thirteenth Amendment

American Anti-Slavery Society, 13, 52

American party, 225

Ames, Adelbert, 113, 118–19

Anthony, Susan B., 7, 40, 231

Arkansas, 40, 115; Democrats' return to power in, 111

Arnold, Isaac N., 13

Arthur, Chester A., 198, 203, 206, 264; nominated as vice-president candidate, 186–87; background of, 199; and black suffrage, 199; southern policy of, 200–201

Ashley, James M., 2; and black suffrage legislation, 15–18, 27, 33, 36–37, 136, 249, 313 (n. 49), 323 (n. 169)

Atlantic Monthly: on Garfield, 186; on Arthur, 199; on the Republican party, 202–3

Ballard, Bland, 128

Ballot: freedom of, 187, 231; honest counting of, 200; purity of, 214; Australian system of, 230, 234–35; reform of, 234–35. *See also* Black suffrage; Chinese suffrage; Enforcement; Enforcement acts; Suffrage; Women's suffrage

Bancroft, George, 21

Banks, Nathaniel P., 12, 17, 27

Bates, Edward, 22; on the Republican party, 3–4; on U.S. citizenship, 8; on suffrage restrictions, 8, 14, 316 (n. 82)

Bayard, Thomas, 71–72, 77

Baylor, Charles, 154

Beckwith, James R., 125, 128

Beecher, Henry Ward, 160

Beecher, Thomas K., 160

Belknap, William W., 94, 136

Bertonneau, Arnold, 311 (n. 39); lobbies for black suffrage, 12; meets with Lincoln, 18–19

Beveridge, Albert J., 224

Bigelow, John, 8, 41, 107, 112

Bingham, John, 137; and black suffrage legislation, 25–26, 33, 36–37, 45, 323 (n. 170); and enforcement legislation, 58, 68, 80, 87, 137

Bird, Francis W., 315 (n. 69)

Black Codes, 24, 317 (n. 97)

Black conventions, 11–12, 108

Black disfranchisement, 222, 224, 230, 238; in the South, xviii, 259–60; condemned by Republicans, 194; statistics of, 259–61; ignored by Republican administrations, 261–62

Black enfranchisement. *See* Black suffrage

Black leaders: and Republican administrations, 154, 160, 360, 361 (nn. 67, 76); and federal appointments, 160; urge for enforcement, 241, 253; urge for reenforcement, 263, 265

Black male suffrage, 305 (n. 2)

397

CPSIA information can be obtained
at www.ICGtesting.com
Printed in the USA
LVHW030016200722
723869LV00003B/284